Research Methods for Business Students

Pearson
Education

Research Methods for Business Students

Third edition

Mark Saunders
Philip Lewis
Adrian Thornhill

An imprint of Pearson Education
Harlow, England • London • New York • Boston • San Francisco • Toronto • Sydney • Singapore • Hong Kong
Tokyo • Seoul • Taipei • New Delhi • Cape Town • Madrid • Mexico City • Amsterdam • Munich • Paris • Milan

Pearson Education Limited

Edinburgh Gate
Harlow
Essex CM20 2JE
England

and Associated Companies around the world

Visit us on the World Wide Web at
www.pearsoneduc.com

First published under the Pitman Publishing imprint in 1997
Second edition 2000
Third edition 2003

ISBN 0 273 65804 2

British Library Cataloguing-in-Publication Data
A catalogue record for this book is available from the British Library

Library of Congress Cataloging-in-Publication Data
Saunders, Mark, 1959-
Research methods for business students / Mark Saunders, Philip Lewis, Adrian Thornhill.-- 3rd ed.
p. cm.
Includes bibliographical references and index.
ISBN 0-273-65804-2
1. Business--Research--Methodology. 2. Business--Research--Data processing. 3. Management--Research--Methodology. 4. Management--Research--Data processing. I. Lewis, Philip, 1945- II. Thornhill, Adrian. III. Title.

HD30.4.S28 2003
650'.071--dc21 2002029313

10 9 8 7 6 5 4 3 2 1
06 05 04 03 02

Typeset in 10/12.5 pt Sabon by 3
Printed and bound by Rotolito Lombarda, Italy

The publisher's policy is to use paper manufactured from sustainable forests.

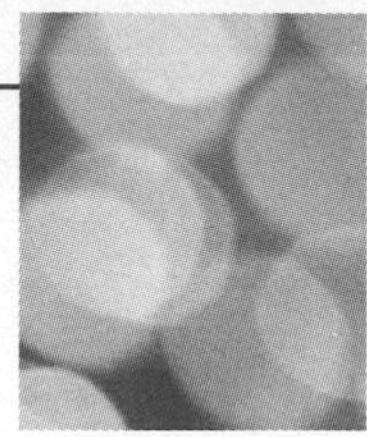

Contents

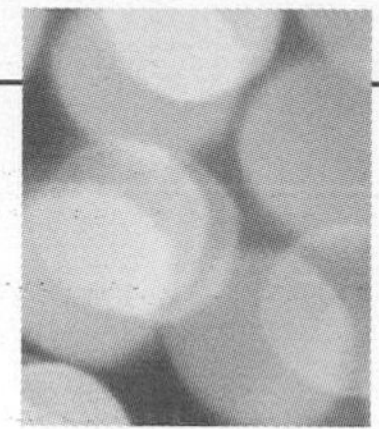

How to use this book

This book is written with a progressive logic, which means that terms and concepts are defined when they are first introduced. One implication of this is that it is sensible for you to start at the beginning and to work your way through the text and worked examples, self-check questions, case studies and case study questions. You can do this in a variety of ways depending on your reasons for using this book. However, this approach may not necessarily be suitable for your purposes, and you may wish to read the chapters in a different order or just dip into particular sections of the book. If this is true for you then you will probably need to use the glossary to check that you understand some of the terms and concepts used in the chapters you read. Suggestions for three of the more common ways in which you might wish to use this book are given below.

As part of a research methods course or for self-study for your research project

If you are using this book as part of a research methods course the order in which you read the chapters is likely to be prescribed by your tutors and dependent upon their perceptions of your needs. Conversely if you are pursuing a course of self-study for your research project or dissertation the order in which you read the chapters is your own choice. However, whichever of these you are, we would argue that the order in which you read the chapters is dependent upon your recent academic experience.

For many students, such as those taking an undergraduate degree in business or management, the research methods course and associated project or dissertation comes in either the second or the final year of study. In such situations it is probable that you will follow the chapter order quite closely (see Figure P.1). Groups of chapters within which we believe you can switch the order without affecting the logic of the flow too much are shown on the same level in this diagram and are:

- those chapters associated with data collection (Chapters 7, 8, 9 and 10);
- those associated with data analysis (Chapters 11 and 12).

In addition, you might wish to read the sections in Chapter 13 on writing prior to starting to draft your critical review of the literature (Chapter 3).

Alternatively, you may be returning to academic study after a gap of some years, to take a full-time or part-time course such as a Master of Business Administration. Many students in such situations need to refresh their study skills early in their programme, particularly those associated with critical reading of academic literature and academic writing. If you feel the need to do this, you may wish to start with those chapters that support you in developing and refining these skills (Chapters 3 and 13), followed by Chapter 7, which introduces you to the range of secondary data sources available that might be of use for other assignments (Fig P.2). Once again, groups of

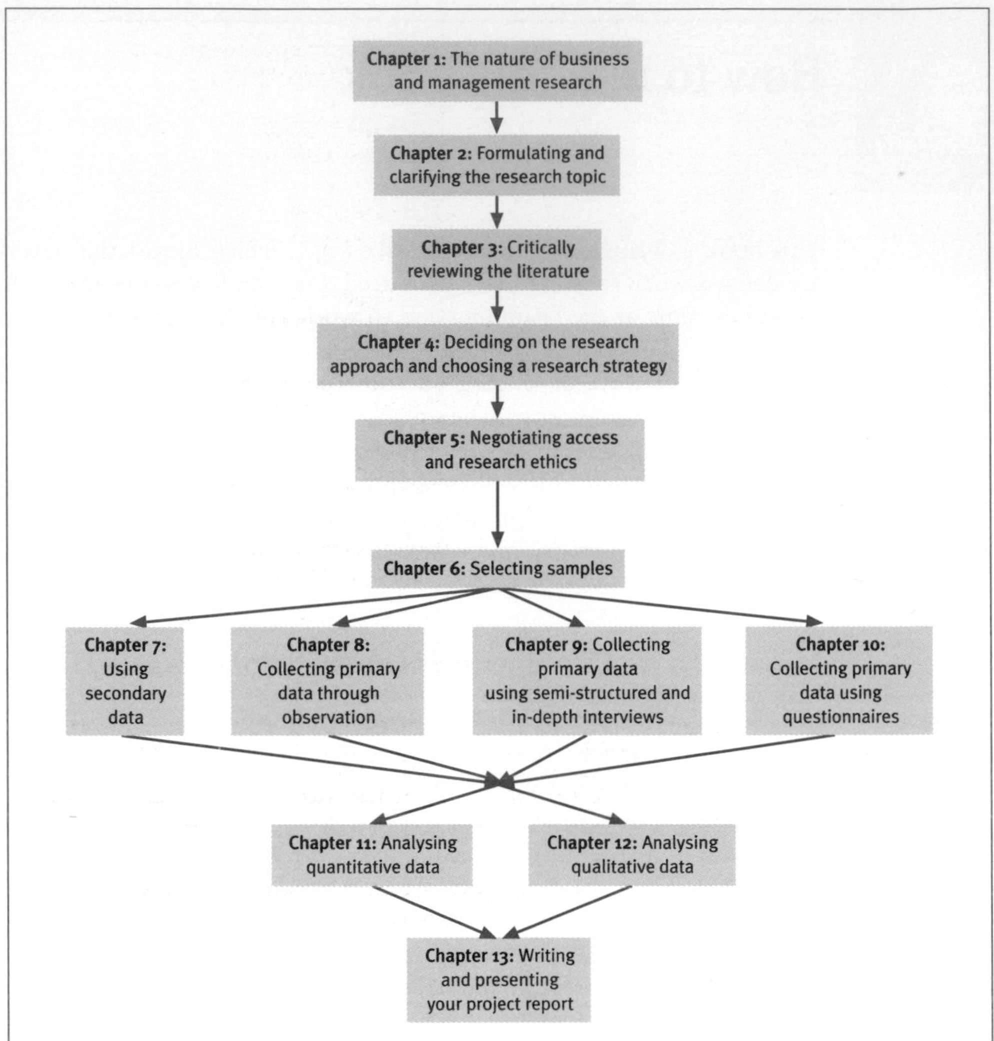

Figure P.1 Using this book in your second or final year of study

chapters within which we believe you can switch the order without affecting the logic of the flow too much are shown on the same level in the diagram and are:

- those chapters associated with primary data collection (Chapters 8, 9 and 10);
- those associated with data analysis (Chapters 11 and 12).

In addition, we would recommend you re-read Chapter 13 prior to starting to write your project report or dissertation.

Whichever order you choose to read the chapters in, we would recommend that you attempt all the self-check questions and those questions associated with the case studies. Your answers to the self-check questions can be self-assessed using the answers at the end of each chapter. However, we hope that you will actually have a go at the question prior to reading the answer! If you need further information on an idea or a technique then first look at the references in the further reading section.

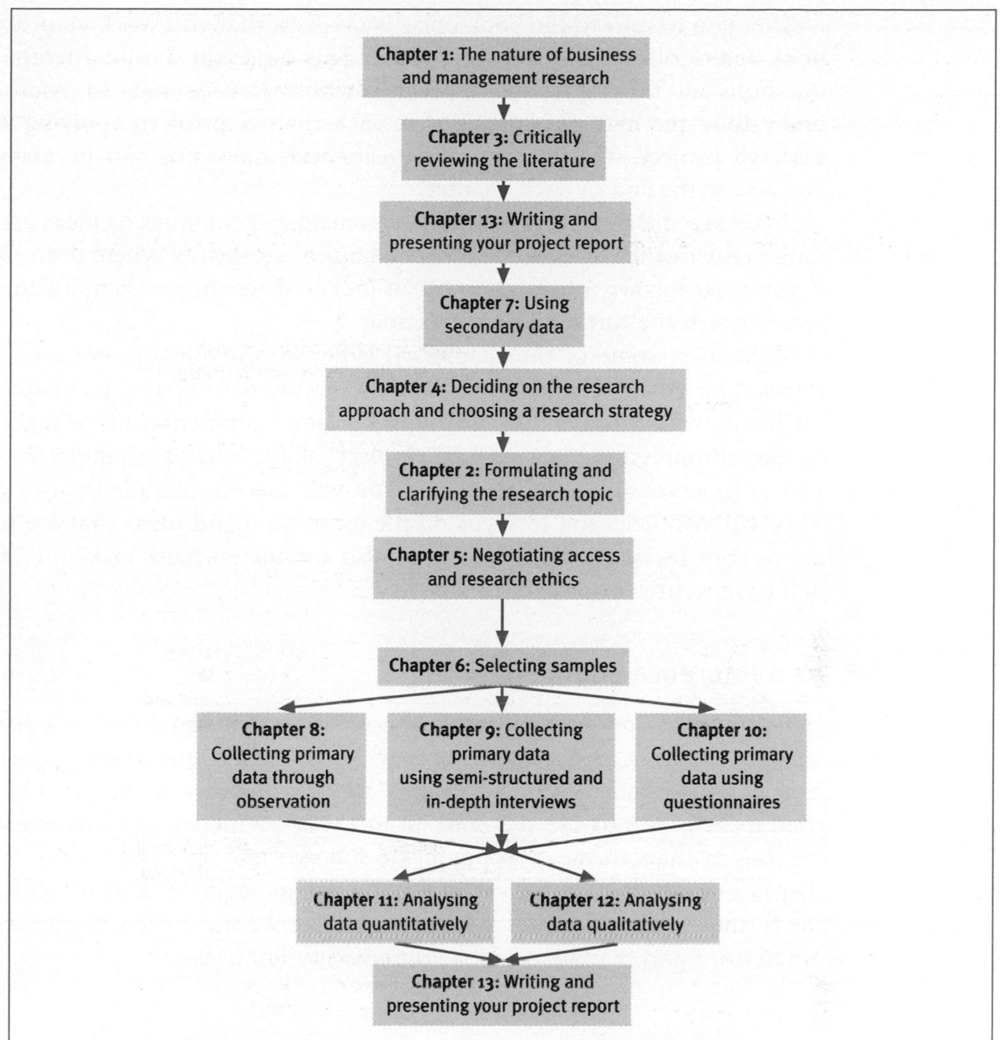

Figure P.2 **Using this book as a new returner to academic study**

At the end of Chapters 2–13 the section headed 'Progressing your research project' lists a number of tasks. Such tasks might involve you in just planning a research project or, alternatively, designing and administering a questionnaire of your own. When completed, these tasks will provide a useful *aide-mémoire* for assessed work and can be used as the basis for the first draft of your project report.

As a guide through the research process

If you are intending to use this book to guide you through the research process for a research project you are undertaking, such as your dissertation, we recommend that you read the entire book quickly before starting your research. In that way you will have a good overview of the entire process, including the range of techniques available, and will be better able to plan your work.

After you have read the book once, we suggest that you work your way through the book again following the chapter order. This time you should attempt the self-check questions and those questions associated with each case study to ensure that you have understood the material contained in each chapter prior to applying it to your own research project. Your responses to self-check questions can be assessed using the answers at the end of each chapter.

If you are still unsure as to whether particular techniques or ideas are relevant then look in the further reading for other examples of research where these have been used. If you need further information on an idea or a technique then, again, start with the references in the further reading section.

Material in some of the chapters is likely to prove less relevant to some research topics than others. However, you should beware of choosing techniques because you are happy with them, if they are inappropriate. Completion of the tasks in the section headed 'Progressing your research project' at the end of Chapters 2–12 will enable you to generate all the material that you will need to include in your project report. This will also help you to focus on the techniques and ideas that are most appropriate to your research. When you have also completed these tasks for Chapter 13 you will have written your project report.

As a reference source

It may be that you wish to use this book now or subsequently as a reference source. If this is the case, an extensive index will point you to the appropriate page or pages. You will also find the contents pages and the glossary useful. In addition, we have tried to help you to use the book in this way by including cross-references between sections in chapters as appropriate. Do follow these up as necessary. If you need further information on an idea or a technique then begin by consulting the references in the further reading section. Wherever possible we have tried to reference books that are in print and readily available in university libraries.

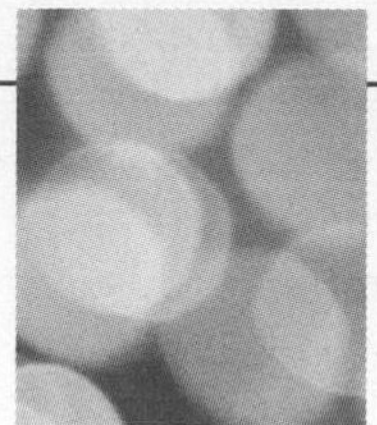

Preface to the third edition

The third edition of *Research Methods for Business Students* has been written as the role of the Internet as a means of accessing academic literature and research data sets has begun to mature. This, combined with the reality of relatively inexpensive and easily accessible computer processing power for almost all students, has had significant implications for business and management students' research. As in previous editions, we have taken a predominantly non-software-specific approach in our writing. By doing this, we have been able to focus on the general principles needed to utilise both analysis software and the Internet effectively for research. Inevitably, the rapid increase in the use of the Internet has necessitated substantial updating for Chapter 3, 'Critically reviewing the literature', and Chapter 7, 'Using secondary data'. We have also taken the opportunity to revise the tables of Internet addresses fully. As part of this we have included a selection of government web sites from around the world from which our students have downloaded useful data. In addition we have taken the opportunity to broaden our discussions regarding issues associated with the use of email, Internet chat rooms and on-line survey approaches.

In the preparation of the third edition we were fortunate to receive considerable feedback from colleagues in both UK and overseas universities. This was coordinated by Martin Sugden and Stuart Hay, and we are extremely grateful both to them and to all the anonymous reviewers who gave their time and shared their ideas. Particular responses to this feedback not outlined elsewhere have been the inclusion of a glossary, worked examples and advice on research in international settings, further discussion of the techniques and limitations of probability and non-probability sampling in Chapter 6, the development of a new section on presentations in Chapter 13, 'Writing and presenting your project report', and a discussion of Type I and Type II errors in Chapter 11, 'Analysing quantitative data'.

Inevitably the body of knowledge of research methods has developed since 1999, and we have revised the chapters accordingly. Once again we have taken the opportunity to update and refine existing worked examples and develop new ones where appropriate. New case studies at the end of each chapter have been developed with colleagues, providing up-to-date scenarios through which to illustrate issues associated with undertaking research.

Other minor changes and updating have been made throughout. Needless to say, any errors of omission and commission are our responsibility.

As with the second edition, much of our updating has been guided by comments from students and colleagues, to whom we are most grateful. We should like to thank our students at Oxford Brookes University and the University of Gloucestershire for their comments on all of the chapters. Colleagues and friends again deserve thanks for their assistance in providing examples of research across the spectrum of business and management, in writing case studies and in reviewing parts of this book, in particular Mike Blee (Bournemouth University), David Bowen (Oxford Brookes University),

Mick Church (Zarlink, Swindon, UK), Nigel Culkin (University of Hertfordshire), Ian Firns (Management Education, Australia), Andrew Guppy (University of Middlesex), Martin Jenkins (University of Gloucestershire), Jim Keane (University of Gloucestershire), Les Ozsdolay (Centrelink, Western Australia), Keith Randle (University of Hertfordshire), Judy Slinn (Oxford Brookes University), Teresa Smallbone (Oxford Brookes University), Laura Spira (Oxford Brookes University), Tony Travaglione (University of Adelaide), and Christine Williams (University of Gloucestershire). The contribution of Lynette Bailey to Chapter 3 in earlier editions of this book is gratefully acknowledged.

Geraldine Lyons, our commissioning editor, provided excellent support and enthusiasm throughout the process.

Once again our thanks are due to Jane, Jenny, Jan, Jemma, Ben, Andrew and Katie, who still allow us the evenings, weekends and 'holiday time' to be slaves to our computers. Next year we will take that holiday!

MNKS
PL
AT
September 2002

Publisher's acknowledgements

We are grateful to the following for permission to reproduce copyright material:

Table 8.1 from *Doing Research: A Handbook for Teachers* by Walker, R. (1985), published by Taylor & Francis; Figure 8.2 from *Management and Organisational Behaviour* (5th edition) by Mullins, L.J. (1999), published by Financial Times Pitman Publishing; Table 8.2 from *Real World Research* (2nd edition) by Robson, C. (2002) published by Blackwell; Figure 10.2 from *Construction Questions for Interviews and Questionnaires* by Foddy, W. (1994), published by Cambridge University Press; Table 10.7 from *Mail and Internet Surveys: The tailored design method* by Dillman, D.A. (2000), published by John Wiley, New York; Table 13.1 from *Real World Research* (2nd edition) by Robson, C. (2002), published by Blackwell; Appendix 4 from *Quantitative Approaches in Business Studies* (3rd edition) by Morris, C. (1993), published by Pitman publishing; Table A6.1 developed from the article 'Guidelines for the use of non-sexist language' in *The Psychologist*, February 1998 pp. 53–4, published by The British Psychological Society.

We are grateful to HMSO for permission to reproduce the Average Earning Index and the Retail Prices Index 1991–1999 published by the Office for National Statistics.

In some instances we have been unable to trace the owners of copyright material, and we would appreciate any information that would enable us to do so.

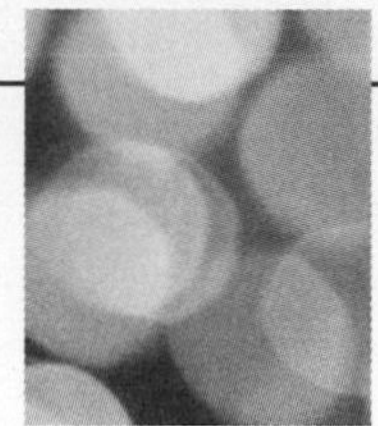

Contributors

Mark N.K. Saunders BA, MSc, PGCE, PhD, MCIPD, is Reader in Research Methods at Oxford Brookes University Business School. Prior to this he was head of the Human Resource Management Research Centre at Gloucestershire Business School. He currently teaches research methods to masters and doctoral students as well as supervising masters dissertations and research degrees. Mark has published a number of articles on research methods, service quality and downsizing and organisational justice perspectives on the management of change. He is co-author with Phil, Adrian and Mike Millmore of *Managing Change: A Human Resource Strategy Approach*, published by Financial Times Prentice Hall, and has also co-authored a book on business statistics. He has undertaken consultancy in public, private and not-for-profit sectors, prior to which he had a variety of research jobs in local government.

Philip Lewis BA, PhD, MSc, MCIPD, PGDipM, Cert Ed, is a Principal Lecturer in Human Resource Management (HRM) at Gloucestershire Business School, University of Gloucestershire. He teaches HRM and research methods to postgraduate, undergraduate and professional students, and is involved in research degree supervision. Phil's research interests are reward management and performance management, on which he has published several articles. He is co-author with Adrian, Mark and Mike Millmore of *Managing Change: A Human Resource Strategy Approach*, published by Financial Times Prentice Hall. He has undertaken consultancy in both public and private sectors. Prior to his career in higher education Phil was a training advisor with the Distributive Industry Training Board.

Adrian Thornhill BA, PhD, PGCE, FCIPD, is Head of the Department of Human Resource Management at Gloucestershire Business School, University of Gloucestershire. He teaches HRM and research methods to postgraduate, undergraduate and professional students, and is involved in research degree supervision. Adrian has published a number of articles principally associated with employee and justice perspectives related to managing change and the management of organisational downsizing and redundancy. He is co-author with Mark, Phil and Mike Millmore of *Managing Change: A Human Resource Strategy Approach*, published by Financial Times Prentice Hall, and has also co-authored a book on downsizing and redundancy. He has undertaken consultancy in both public and private sectors.

Mike Blee is a Senior Lecturer in Business Strategy at Bournemouth University Business School.

Dr David Bowen is the Field Chair for the Tourism Management degree and a Senior Lecturer at Oxford Brookes University Business School.

Mick Church is a Project Manager at Zarlink Semiconductor, Swindon.

Nigel Culkin is Associate Dean (Business Partnerships) and a member of the Film Industry Research Group at the University of Hertfordshire Business School.

Ian Firns is a Director of Management Education Australia, a private institution based in Perth, Western Australia.

Professor Andrew Guppy is Head of the Department of Psychology at the University of Middlesex.

Martin Jenkins is a Senior Learning Advisor with a special interest in business and management at the University of Gloucestershire.

Jim Keane is a Senior Lecturer in Financial Services at Gloucestershire Business School, University of Gloucestershire.

Dr Keith Randle is Head of Postgraduate Programmes and a member of the Film Industry Research Group at the University of Hertfordshire Business School.

Judy Slinn is a Senior Lecturer in Strategy and Business History at Oxford Brookes University Business School.

Teresa Smallbone is a Senior Lecturer in Marketing and Research Ethics Officer at Oxford Brookes University Business School.

Dr Laura Spira is Reader in Accounting at Oxford Brookes University Business School.

Professor Tony Travaglione is Dean of the Graduate School of Management at the University of Adelaide in South Australia.

Christine Williams is the Head of the Department of Marketing and Strategy at the University of Gloucestershire Business School, University of Gloucestershire.

Chapter 1

The nature of business and management research and structure of this book

By the end of this chapter you should:

- be able to outline the purpose and distinct focus of management research;
- be able to place your research project on a basic–applied research continuum according to its purpose and context;
- understand the stages you will need to complete (and revisit) as part of your research process;
- have an overview of this book's purpose and structure;
- be aware of some of the ways you can use this book.

1.1 The aims of this book

This book is designed to help you to undertake a research project, whether you are an undergraduate or postgraduate student of business and management or a manager. It provides a clear guide on how to undertake research as well as highlighting the realities of undertaking research, including the more common pitfalls. The book is written as an introductory text to provide you with a guide to the research process and with the necessary knowledge and skills to undertake a piece of research from thinking of a research topic to writing your project report. As such, you will find it useful as a manual or handbook on how to tackle your research project.

After reading the book you will have been introduced to and explored a range of approaches, strategies and methods with which you could tackle your research project. Of equal importance, you will know that there is no one best way for undertaking all research. Rather you will be aware of the choices you will have to make and how these choices will impact upon what you can find out. This means you will be able to make an informed choice about the approaches, strategies and methods that are most suitable to your own research project and be able to justify this choice. In reading the book you will have been introduced to the more frequently used techniques for analysing different types of data, have had a chance to practise them, and be able to make a reasoned choice regarding which to use. When selecting and using these techniques you will be aware of the contribution that the appropriate use of information technology can make to your research.

However, before you continue, a word of caution. In your study, you will inevitably read a wide range of books and articles. In many of these the terms 'research method' and 'research methodology' will be used interchangeably, perhaps just using methodology as a more verbose way of saying method. In this book we have been more precise in our use of these terms. Throughout the book we use the term *methods* to refer to tools and techniques used to obtain and analyse data. This therefore includes questionnaires, observation and interviews as well as both statistical and non-statistical analysis techniques and, as you have probably gathered from the title, is the main focus of this book. In contrast, the term *methodology* refers to the theory of how research should be undertaken. We believe that it is important that you have some understanding of this so that you can make an informed choice about your research. For this reason, we also discuss the theoretical and philosophical assumptions upon which research is based and the implications of these for the method or methods adopted.

1.2 The nature of research

When listening to the radio, watching the television or reading a daily newspaper it is difficult to avoid the term 'research'. The results of 'research' are all around us. A debate about the findings of a recent poll of people's opinions inevitably includes a discussion of 'research', normally referring to the way in which the data were collected. Politicians often justify their policy decisions on the basis of 'research'. Documentary programmes tell us about 'research findings', and advertisers may highlight the 'results of research' to encourage you to buy a particular product or brand. However, we believe that what these examples really emphasise is the wide range of meanings given to the term 'research' in everyday speech.

Walliman (2001) argues that many of these everyday uses of the term 'research' are not research in the true meaning of the word. As part of this, he highlights ways in which the term is used wrongly:

- just collecting facts or information with no clear purpose;
- reassembling and reordering facts or information without interpretation;
- as a term to get your product or idea noticed and respected.

The first of these highlights the fact that, although research often involves the collection of information, it is more than just reading a few books or articles, talking to a few people or asking people questions. While collecting data may be part of the research process, if it is not undertaken in a systematic way, on its own and in particular with a clear purpose, it will not be seen as research. The second of these is commonplace in many reports. Data are collected, perhaps from a variety of different sources, and then assembled in a single document with the sources of these data listed. However, there is no interpretation of the data collected. Again, while the assembly of data from a variety of sources may be part of the process of research, without interpretation it is not research. Finally, the term 'research' can be used to get an idea or product noticed by people and to suggest that people should have confidence in it.

In such instances, when you ask for details of the research process, these are either unclear or not forthcoming.

Based upon this brief discussion we can already see that research has a number of characteristics:

- Data are collected systematically.
- Data are interpreted systematically.
- There is a clear purpose: to find things out.

We can therefore define *research* as something that people undertake in order to find out things in a systematic way, thereby increasing their knowledge. Two phrases are important in this definition: 'systematic research' and 'to find out things'. 'Systematic' suggests that research is based on logical relationships and not just beliefs (Ghauri and Grønhaug, 2002). As part of this, your research will involve an explanation of the methods used to collect the data, will argue why the results obtained are meaningful, and will explain any limitations that are associated with them. 'To find out things' suggests there are a multiplicity of possible purposes for your research. These may include describing, explaining, understanding, criticising and analysing (Ghauri and Grønhaug, 2002). However, it also suggests that you have a clear purpose or set of 'things' that you want to find out, such as the answer to a question or number of questions.

1.3 The nature of business and management research

Using our earlier definition of research it would seem sensible to define business and management research as undertaking systematic research to find out things about business and management.

Easterby-Smith *et al.* (2002) argue that three things combine to make business and management a distinctive focus for research:

- the way in which managers (and researchers) draw on knowledge developed by other disciplines;
- the fact that managers tend to be powerful and busy people. Therefore, they are unlikely to allow research access unless they can see personal or commercial advantages;
- the requirement for the research to have some practical consequence. This means it either needs to contain the potential for taking some form of action or needs to take account of the practical consequences of the findings.

Recent discussion within the British Academy of Management has explored the status of management research. One feature, which has gained considerable support, is the *transdisciplinary* nature of such research. While this has similarities to Easterby-Smith *et al.*'s (2002) point regarding the use of knowledge from other disciplines, it also emphasises that the research 'cannot be reduced to any sum of parts framed in terms of contributions to associated disciplines' (Tranfield and Starkey, 1998:352). In other words, using knowledge from a range of disciplines enables management research to gain new insights that cannot be obtained through all of these disciplines separately. Another feature of management research highlighted by the debate is the belief that it should be able to develop ideas and to relate them to practice. In particular that research should complete a *virtuous circle* of theory and practice (Tranfield and Starkey, 1998) through which research on managerial practice informs practically derived theory. This in turn becomes a blueprint for managerial practice, thereby increasing the stock of relevant and practical management knowledge. Thus business and management research needs to engage with both the world of theory and the world of practice. Consequently, the problems addressed should grow out of interaction between these two worlds rather than either on their own.

In recent years debate about the nature of management research has focused on how it can meet the *double hurdle* of being both theoretically and methodologically rigorous, while at the same time embracing the world of practice and being of practical relevance (Hodgkinson *et al.*, 2001). Much of this debate has centred around Gibbons *et al.*'s (1994) work on the production of knowledge, and in particular the concepts of Mode 1 and Mode 2 knowledge creation. *Mode 1* knowledge creation emphasises research in which the questions are set and solved by academic interests, emphasising a fundamental rather than applied nature, where there is little if any focus on utilisation of the research by practitioners. In contrast, *Mode 2* emphasises a context for research governed by the world of practice, highlighting the importance of collaboration both with and between practitioners (Starkey and Madan, 2001) and the need for practical consequences. Based upon this Starkey and Madan (2001) argue that research within the Mode 2 approach offers a way of bringing the supply side of knowledge represented by universities together with the demand side represented by businesses and overcoming the double hurdle.

Drawing from these debates, we would argue that business and management research not only needs to provide findings that advance knowledge and understanding, it also needs to address business issues and practical managerial problems. This is not to say that the satisfaction of your intellectual curiosity, for its own sake, is out of the question. Rather, in this pursuit you should be considering the practical implications of your findings.

Within these boundaries of advancing knowledge, addressing business issues and solving managerial problems, the purpose and the context of your research project can differ considerably. For some research projects your purpose may be to understand and explain the impact of something, such as a particular policy. You may undertake this research within an individual organisation and suggest appropriate action on the basis of your findings. For other research projects you may wish to explore the ways in which various organisations do things differently. In such projects your purpose may be to discover and understand better the underlying processes in a wider context, thereby providing greater understanding for practitioners. For yet other research projects you may wish to place an in-depth investigation of an organisation within the context of a wider understanding of the processes that are operating.

Despite this variety, we believe that all business and management research projects can be placed on a continuum (Figure 1.1) according to their purpose and context. At one extreme of the continuum is research that is undertaken purely to understand the processes of business and management and their outcomes. Such research is undertaken largely in universities and largely as the result of an academic agenda. Its key consumer is the academic community, with relatively little attention being given to its practical applications. This is often termed *basic, fundamental* or *pure research*. Given

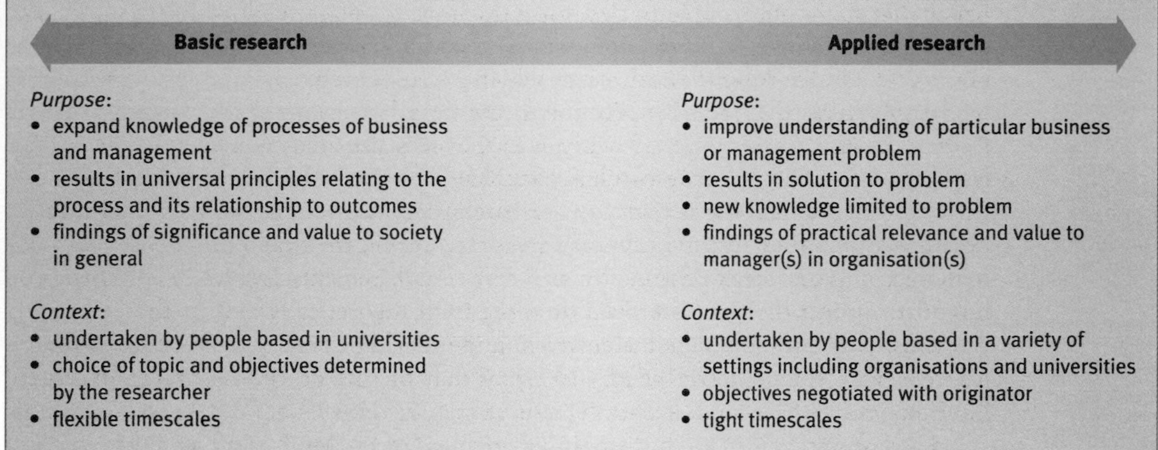

Basic research
Applied research
Purpose:
• expand knowledge of processes of business and management
• results in universal principles relating to the process and its relationship to outcomes
• findings of significance and value to society in general
Context:
• undertaken by people based in universities
• choice of topic and objectives determined by the researcher
• flexible timescales
Purpose:
• improve understanding of particular business or management problem
• results in solution to problem
• new knowledge limited to problem
• findings of practical relevance and value to manager(s) in organisation(s)
Context:
• undertaken by people based in a variety of settings including organisations and universities
• objectives negotiated with originator
• tight timescales

Figure 1.1 Basic and applied research

Sources: Author's experience; Easterby-Smith *et al.* (2002); Hedrick *et al.* (1993)

our earlier discussion it is unlikely that such research would fulfil our criteria for business and management research without some consideration being made of the practical consequences. Through doing this, the research would start to move towards the other end of the continuum (Figure 1.1). At this end is research that is of direct and immediate relevance to managers, addresses issues that they see as important, and is presented in ways that they understand and can act on. This is termed *applied research*.

Wherever your research project lies on this basic–applied continuum, we believe that you should undertake your research with rigour. To do this you will need to pay careful attention to the entire research process.

1.4 The research process

Most research textbooks represent research as a multi-stage process that you must follow in order to undertake and complete your research project. The precise number of stages varies, but they usually include formulating and clarifying a topic, reviewing the literature, choosing a strategy, collecting data, analysing data and writing up. In the majority of these the research process, although presented with rationalised examples, is described as a series of stages through which you must pass. Articles you have read may also suggest that the research process is rational and straightforward. Unfortunately this is very rarely true, and the reality is considerably messier, with what initially appear as great ideas sometimes having little or no relevance (Saunders and Lewis, 1997). While research is often depicted as moving through each of the stages outlined above, one after the other, this is unlikely to be the case. In reality you will probably revisit each stage more than once. Each time you revisit a stage you will need to reflect on the associated issues and refine your ideas. In addition, as highlighted by some textbooks, you will need to consider ethical and access issues during the process.

This textbook also presents the research process as a series of linked stages and gives the appearance of being organised in a linear manner. However, as you use the book you will see from the text, extensive use of cross-referencing, worked examples and case studies that we have recognised the iterative nature of the process you will follow. As part of this process, we believe that it is vital that you spend time formulating and clarifying your research topic. This we believe should be expressed as one or more research questions that your research must answer, accompanied by a set of objectives that your research must address. However, we would also stress the need to reflect on your ideas continually and revise both these and the way in which you intend to progress your research. Often this will involve revisiting stages (including your research question(s) and objectives) and working through them again. There is also a need to plan ahead, thereby ensuring that the necessary preliminary work for later stages has been undertaken. This is emphasised by Figure 1.2, which also provides a schematic index to the remaining chapters of the book. Within this flow chart (Figure 1.2) the stages you will need to complete as part of your research project are emphasised in the centre of the chart. However, be warned: the process is far messier than a brief glance at Figure 1.2 suggests!

1.5 The purpose and structure of this book

The purpose

As we stated earlier (Section 1.1), the overriding purpose of this book is to help you to undertake research. This means that early on in your research project you will need to be clear about what you are doing, why you are doing it, and the associated implications of what you are seeking to do. You will also need to ensure that you can show how your ideas relate to research that has already been undertaken in your topic area and that you have a clear approach and strategy for collecting and analysing your data. As part of this you will need to consider the validity and reliability of the data you intend to use, along with associated ethical and access issues. The appropriateness and suitability of the analytical techniques you choose to use will be of equal importance. Finally, you will need to write your research report as clearly and precisely as possible.

The structure of each chapter

Each of the subsequent chapters deals with part of the research process outlined in Figure 1.2. The ideas, techniques and methods are discussed using as little jargon as is possible. Where appropriate you will find summaries of these using tables, checklists or diagrams. When new terms are introduced for the first time they are shown in italics, and a definition or explanation follows shortly afterwards. They are also listed with a brief definition in the *glossary*. The application of appropriate information technology is considered, in most instances as an integral part of the text. Discussion of information technology is not software specific but is concerned with general principles. These will enable you to utilise whatever software you have available most effectively. Chapters have been cross-referenced as appropriate, and an index is provided to help you to find your way around the book.

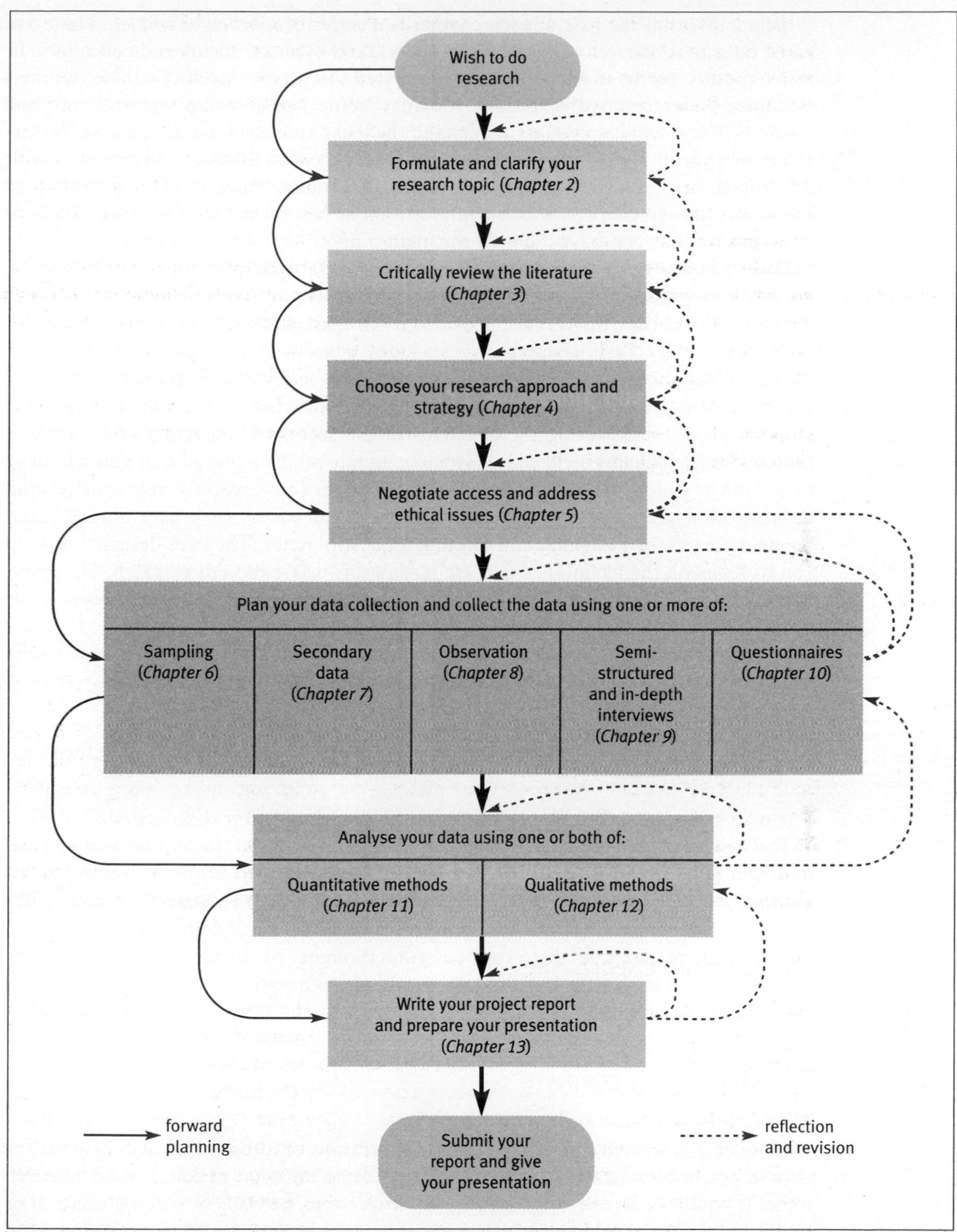

Figure 1.2 The research process

Included within the text of each chapter is a series of *worked examples*. These are based on actual research projects, often undertaken by our students and colleagues, in which points made in the text are illustrated. In many instances these worked examples illustrate possible pitfalls you may come across while undertaking your research. These will help you to understand the technique or idea and to assess its suitability or appropriateness to your research. Where a pitfall has been illustrated, it will, it is hoped, help you to avoid making the same mistake. There is also a summary of key points in each chapter, which you may look at before and after reading the chapter to ensure that you have digested the main points.

To enable you to check that you have understood the chapter a series of *self-check questions* is included at the end. These can be answered without recourse to other (external) resources. Answers are provided to all these self-check questions at the end of each chapter. Each chapter also includes a section towards the end headed 'Progressing your research project'. This contains a series of questions that will help you to consider the implications of the material covered by the chapter for your research project. Answering the questions in the section 'Progressing your research project' for each chapter will enable you to generate all the material that you will need to include in your project report. Each chapter's questions involve you in undertaking activities that are more complex than self-check questions, such as a library-based literature search or designing and piloting a questionnaire. They are designed to help you to focus on the techniques that are most appropriate to your research. However, as emphasised by Figure 1.2, you will almost certainly need to revisit and revise your answers as your research progresses.

Each chapter is also accompanied by references, further reading and a case study. *Further reading* is included for two distinct reasons:

- to direct you to other work on the ideas contained within the chapter;
- to direct you to further examples of research where the ideas contained in the chapter have been used.

The main reasons for our choice of further reading are therefore indicated.

The new *case studies* at the end of each chapter are drawn from a variety of business and management research scenarios and have been based on the case study's authors' or their students' experiences when undertaking a research project. They have been written to highlight real issues that occur when undertaking business and management research. To help to focus your thoughts or discussion on some of the pertinent issues each case is followed by evaluative questions. A case study follows every chapter other than Chapter 1.

An outline of the chapters

The book is organised in the following way.

Chapter 2 is written to assist you in the generation of ideas, which will help you to choose a suitable research topic, and offers advice on what makes a good research topic. If you have already been given a research topic, perhaps by an organisation or tutor, you will need to refine it into one that is feasible, and should still therefore read this chapter. After your idea has been generated and refined, the chapter discusses how to turn this idea into clear research question(s) and objectives. (Research questions and objectives are referred to throughout the book.) Finally, the chapter provides advice on how to write a research proposal.

The importance of the critical literature review to your research is discussed in Chapter 3. This chapter outlines what a critical review needs to include and the range of primary, secondary and tertiary literature sources available. The chapter explains the purpose of reviewing the literature, discusses a range of search strategies, and contains advice on how to plan and undertake your search and to write your review. The processes of identifying key words and searching using on-line databases and the Internet are outlined. It also offers advice on how to record items and to evaluate their relevance.

Chapter 4 examines different ways of approaching research. It considers different research philosophies including positivism, social constructionism and realism, inductive and deductive approaches to research, and a range of research strategies. The need for a clear research strategy is discussed and, crucially, the implications of this for the credibility of your research findings and conclusions.

Chapter 5 explores issues related to gaining access and to research ethics. It offers advice on how to gain access both to organisations and to individuals. Potential ethical issues are discussed in relation to each stage of the research process and different data collection methods. Issues of data protection are also introduced.

A range of the probability and non-probability sampling techniques available for use in your research is explained in Chapter 6. The chapter considers why sampling is necessary, and looks at issues of sample size and response rates. Advice on how to relate your choice of sampling techniques to your research topic is given, and techniques for assessing the representativeness of those who respond are discussed.

Chapters 7, 8, 9 and 10 are concerned with different methods of obtaining data. The use of secondary data is discussed in Chapter 7, which introduces the variety of data that are likely to be available and suggests ways in which they can be used. Advantages and disadvantages of secondary data are discussed, and a range of techniques for locating these data, including using the Internet, is suggested. Chapter 7 also offers advice on how to evaluate the suitability of secondary data for your research.

In contrast, Chapter 8 is concerned with collecting primary data through observation. The chapter examines two types of observation: participant observation and structured observation. Practical advice on using each is offered, and particular attention is given to ensuring that the data you obtain are both valid and reliable.

Chapter 9 is also concerned with collecting primary data, this time using semi-structured and in-depth interviews. The appropriateness of using these interviews in relation to your research strategy is discussed. Advice on how to undertake such interviews is offered, including the conduct of group interviews. Particular attention is given to ensuring that the data collected are both reliable and valid.

Chapter 10 is the final chapter concerned with collecting data. It introduces you to the use of both self-administered and interviewer-administered questionnaires, and explores their advantages and disadvantages. Practical advice is offered on the process of designing, piloting and administering questionnaires to enhance their response rates. Particular attention is again given to ensuring that the data collected are both reliable and valid.

Analysis of data is covered in Chapters 11 and 12. Chapter 11 outlines and illustrates the main issues that you need to consider when preparing data for quantitative analysis and when analysing these data by computer. Different types of data are defined, and advice is given on how to create a data matrix and to code data. Practical advice is also offered on the analysis of these data. The most appropriate diagrams to explore and illustrate data are discussed, and suggestions are made about which statistics to use to describe data, to explore relationships and to explore trends.

Chapter 12 outlines and discusses the main approaches available to you to analyse data qualitatively. The nature of qualitative data is discussed, and an overview of the analysis process is provided. The use of deductively based and inductively based analytical strategies and procedures is discussed. The chapter also considers the use of computer-assisted qualitative data analysis software, known as CAQDAS.

Chapter 13 helps you with the structure, content and style of your final project report and any associated oral presentations. Above all, it encourages you to see writing as an intrinsic part of the research process that should not be left until everything else is completed.

1.6 Summary

- This book is designed to help you to undertake a research project whether you are an undergraduate or postgraduate student of business and management or a manager. It is designed as an introductory text and will guide you through the entire research process.
- Business and management research involves undertaking systematic research to find out things. It is transdisciplinary, and should engage with both theory and practice.
- All business and management research projects can be placed on a basic–applied continuum according to their purpose and context.
- Wherever your research project lies on this continuum, you should undertake your research with rigour. To do this you will need to pay careful attention to the entire research process.
- In this book, research is represented as a multi-stage process; however, this process is rarely straightforward and will involve both reflecting on and revising stages already undertaken and forward planning.
- Each chapter contains advice with worked examples, self-check questions, an assignment and a case study with questions. Answers to all self-check questions are at the end of the appropriate chapter. Answering the questions in the section 'Progressing your research project' for Chapters 2–12 will enable you to generate all the material that you will need to include in your project report. When you have also answered the questions in this section for Chapter 13, you will have written your research report.

self-check Questions

1.1 Outline the features that make business and management research distinctive from research in other disciplines.

1.2 What are the key differences between basic and applied research?

1.3 Examine Figure 1.2. What does this suggest about the need to plan and to reflect on and revise your ideas?

References

Easterby-Smith, M., Thorpe, R. and Lowe, A. (2002) *Management Research: An Introduction* (2nd edn), London, Sage.

Ghauri, P., and Grønhaug, K. (2002) *Research Methods in Business Studies: A Practical Guide* (2nd edn), Harlow, Financial Times Prentice Hall.

Gibbons, M.L., Limoges, H., Nowotny, S., Schwartman, P., Scott, P. and Trow, M. (1994) *The New Production of Knowledge: The Dynamics of Science and Research in Contemporary Societies*, London, Sage.

Hedrick, T.E., Bickmann, L. and Rog, D.J. (1993) *Applied Research Design*, Newbury Park, CA, Sage.

Hodgkinson, G.P., Herriot, P. and Anderson, N. (2001) 'Re-aligning the stakeholders in management research: lessons from industrial, work and organizational psychology' *British Journal of Management*, 12, Special Edition, 41–8.

Saunders, M.N.K. and Lewis, P. (1997) 'Great ideas and blind alleys? A review of the literature on starting research', *Management Learning*, 28:3, 283–99.

Starkey, K. and Madan, P. (2001) 'Bridging the relevance gap: aligning stakeholders in the future of management research', *British Journal of Management*, 12, Special Issue, 3–26.

Tranfield, D. and Starkey, K. (1998) 'The nature, social organization and promotion of management research: towards policy', *British Journal of Management*, 9, 341–53.

Walliman, N. (2001) *Your Research Project: A Step by Step Guide for the First-Time Researcher*, London, Sage.

Further reading

Easterby-Smith, M., Thorpe, R. and Lowe, A. (2002) *Management Research: An Introduction* (2nd edn), London, Sage. Chapter 1 provides a very clear and readable introduction to management research and how it is distinct from other forms of research.

Starkey, K. and Madan, P. (2001) 'Bridging the relevance gap: aligning stakeholders in the future of management research', *British Journal of Management,* 12, Special Issue, 3–26. This paper argues the need for relevant management research within a Mode 2 framework, emphasising a need for research partnership.

self-check Answers

1.1 The features you outline are likely to include the:

- transdisciplinary nature of business and management research;
- development of ideas that are related to practice and in particular the requirement for the research to have some practical consequence;
- need for research to complete the virtuous circle of theory and practice;
- addressing of problems that grow out of the interaction between the worlds of theory and practice.

1.2 The key differences between basic and applied research relate to both the purpose and the context in which it is undertaken. They are summarised in Figure 1.1.

1.3 Figure 1.2 emphasises the importance of planning during your research project. Forward planning needs to occur at all stages up to submission. In addition, you will need to reflect on and to revise your work throughout the life of the research project. This reflection needs to have a wide focus. You should both consider the stage you have reached and revisit earlier stages and work through them again. Reflection may also lead you to amend your research plan. This should be expected, although large amendments in the later stages of your research project are unlikely.

Chapter 2

Formulating and clarifying the research topic

By the end of this chapter you should be able:

- to generate ideas that will help in the choice of a suitable research topic;
- to identify the attributes of a good research topic;
- to turn research ideas into a research project that has clear research question(s) and objectives;
- to draft a research proposal.

2.1 Introduction

Before you start your research you need to have at least some idea of what you want to do. This is probably the most difficult, and yet the most important, part of your research project. Up until now most of your studies have been concerned with answering questions that other people have set. This chapter is concerned with how to formulate and clarify your research topic and your research question. Without being clear about what you are going to research it is difficult to plan how you are going to research it. This reminds us of a favourite quote in *Alice's Adventures in Wonderland*. This is part of Alice's conversation with the Cheshire Cat. In this Alice asks the Cat (Carroll, 1989:63–4):

> 'Would you tell me, please, which way I ought to walk from here?'
> 'That depends a good deal on where you want to get to,' said the Cat.
> 'I don't much care where,' said Alice.
> 'Then it doesn't matter which way you walk,' said the Cat.

Formulating and clarifying the research topic is the starting point of your research project (Ghauri and Grønhaug, 2002; Smith and Dainty, 1991). Once you are clear about this you will be able to choose the most appropriate research strategy and data collection and analysis techniques. The formulating and clarifying process is time consuming and will probably take you up blind alleys (Saunders and Lewis, 1997). However, without spending time on this stage you are far less likely to achieve a successful project (Raimond, 1993).

In the initial stages of the formulating and clarifying process you will be generating and refining research ideas (Section 2.3). It may be that you have already been given a research idea, perhaps by an organisation or tutor. Even if this has happened you will still need to refine the idea into one that is feasible. Once you have done this you will need to turn the idea into research questions and objectives (Section 2.4) and to write the research proposal for your project (Section 2.5).

However, before you start the formulating and clarifying process we believe that you need to understand what makes a good research topic. For this reason we begin this chapter (Section 2.2) with a discussion of the attributes required for a good research topic.

2.2 Attributes of a good research topic

The attributes of a business and management research topic do not vary a great deal between universities (Raimond, 1993), although there will be differences in the emphasis placed on different attributes. If you are undertaking your research project as part of a course of study the most important attribute will be that it meets the examining body's requirements and, in particular, that it is at the correct level. This means that you must choose your topic with care. For example, some universities require students to collect their own data as part of their research project whereas others allow them to base their project on data that have already been collected. You therefore need to check the assessment criteria for your project and ensure that your choice of topic will enable you to meet these criteria. If you are unsure, you should discuss any uncertainties with your project tutor.

In addition, your research topic must be something you are capable of undertaking and one that excites your imagination. Capability can be considered in a variety of ways. At the personal level you need to feel comfortable that you have, or can develop, the skills that will be required to research the topic. We hope that you will develop your research skills as part of undertaking your project. However, some skills, for example foreign languages, may be impossible to acquire in the time you have available. As well as having the necessary skills we believe that you also need to have a genuine interest in the topic. Most research projects are undertaken over at least a six-month period. A topic in which you are only vaguely interested at the start is likely to become a topic in which you have no interest and with which you will fail to produce your best work.

Your ability to find the financial and time resources to undertake research on the topic will also affect your capability. Some topics are unlikely to be possible to complete in the time allowed by your course of study. This may be because they require you to measure the impact of an intervention over a long time period. Similarly, topics that are likely to require you to travel widely or need expensive equipment should also be disregarded unless financial resources permit.

Capability also means you must be reasonably certain of gaining access to any data you might need to collect. Gill and Johnson (1997) argue that this is usually relatively straightforward to assess. They point out that many people start with ideas where access to data will prove difficult. Certain, more sensitive topics, such as financial performance or decision-making by senior managers, are potentially fascinating.

However, they may present considerable access problems. You should therefore discuss this with your project tutor after reading Chapter 5.

For most topics it is important that the issues within the research are capable of being linked to theory (Raimond, 1993). Initially, theory may be based just on the reading you have undertaken as part of your study to date. However, as part of your assessment criteria you are almost certain to be asked to set your topic in context (Section 3.2). As a consequence you will need to have a knowledge of the literature and to undertake further reading as part of defining your research questions and objectives (Section 2.4).

Most project tutors will argue that one of the attributes of a good topic is clearly defined research questions and objectives (Section 2.4). These will, along with a good knowledge of the literature, enable you to assess the extent to which your research is likely to provide fresh insights into the topic. Many students believe this is going to be difficult. Fortunately, as pointed out by Phillips and Pugh (2000), there are many ways in which such insight can be defined as 'fresh' (Section 2.5).

If you have already been given a research idea (perhaps by an organisation) you will need to ensure that your questions and objectives relate clearly to the idea (Kervin, 1992). It is also important that your topic will have a *symmetry of potential outcomes*: that is, your results will be of similar value whatever you find out (Gill and Johnson, 1997). Without this symmetry you may spend a considerable amount of time researching your topic only to find an answer of little importance. Whatever the outcome, you need to ensure you have the scope to write an interesting project report.

worked example

Ensuring symmetry of potential outcomes

Karmen was a part-time student. Her initial research topic was concerned with finding out whether there was any relationship between the levels of stress experienced by social workers and the number of years they had been employed as social workers. If she established that there was a link between these factors this would be an interesting finding; if, however, she discovered no relationship the finding would be less interesting and would have no real practical relevance to her organisation.

She therefore decided to amend her topic to exploring and understanding the impact of a forthcoming stress management course on the relative levels of stress experienced by social workers before the course. The results of this research would be interesting and important whether or not the course had an impact.

Finally, it is important to consider your career goals (Creswell, 1994). If you wish to become an expert in a particular subject area or industry sector, it is sensible to use the opportunity to develop this expertise.

It is almost inevitable that the extent to which these attributes apply to your research topic will depend on your topic and the reasons for which you are undertaking the research. However, most of these attributes will apply. For this reason it is important that you check and continue to check any potential research topic against the summary checklist contained in Box 2.1.

Box 2.1 Checklist of attributes of a good research topic

- ✓ Does the topic fit the specifications and meet the standards set by the examining institution?
- ✓ Is the topic something with which you are really fascinated?
- ✓ Does your research topic contain issues that have a clear link to theory?
- ✓ Do you have, or can you develop within the project time frame, the necessary research skills to undertake the topic?
- ✓ Is the research topic achievable within the available time?
- ✓ Is the research topic achievable within the financial resources that are likely to be available?
- ✓ Are you reasonably certain of being able to gain access to data you are likely to require for this topic?
- ✓ Are you able to state your research question(s) and objectives clearly?
- ✓ Will your proposed research be able to provide fresh insights into this topic?
- ✓ Does your research topic relate clearly to the idea you have been given (perhaps by an organisation)?
- ✓ Are the findings for this research topic likely to be symmetrical: that is, of similar value whatever the outcome?
- ✓ Does the research topic match your career goals?

2.3 Generating and refining research ideas

Some business and management students are expected both to generate and to refine their own research ideas. Others, particularly those on professional and post-experience courses, are provided with a research idea by an organisation or their university. In the initial stages of their research they are expected to refine this to a clear and feasible idea that meets the requirements of the examining organisation. If you have already been given a research idea we believe you will still find it useful to read the next subsection, which deals with generating research ideas. Many of the techniques which can be used for generating research ideas can be used for the refining process.

Generating research ideas

If you have not been given an initial *research idea* there is a range of techniques that can be used to find and select a topic that you would like to research. They can be thought of as those that are predominantly *rational thinking* and those that involve more *creative thinking* (Box 2.2). The precise techniques that you choose to use and the order in which you use them are entirely up to you. However, like Raimond (1993), we believe you should use both rational and creative techniques, choosing those that you believe are going to be of most use to you and which you will enjoy using. By using one or more creative techniques you are more likely to ensure that your heart as well as your head is in your research project. In our experience, it is usually better to use a variety of techniques. In order to do this you will need to have some understanding of the techniques and the ways in which they work. We therefore outline the techniques in Box 2.2 and suggest possible ways they might be used to generate research ideas. These techniques will generate one of two outcomes:

- one or more possible project ideas that you might undertake;
- absolute panic because nothing in which you are interested or which seems suitable has come to mind (Jankowicz, 2000).

In either instance, but especially the latter, we suggest that you talk to your project tutor.

Box 2.2 More frequently used techniques for generating and refining research ideas

Rational thinking

- Examining your own strengths and interests
- Looking at past project titles
- Discussion
- Searching the literature

Creative thinking

- Keeping a notebook of ideas
- Exploring personal preferences using past projects
- Relevance trees
- Brainstorming

Examining own strengths and interests

It is important that you choose a topic in which you are likely to do well and, if possible, already have some academic knowledge. Jankowicz (2000) suggests that one way of doing this is to look at those assignments for which you have received good grades. For most of these assignments they are also likely to be the topics in which you were interested (Box 2.1). They will provide you with an area in which to search for and find a research idea. In addition you may, as part of your reading, be able to focus more precisely on the sort of ideas about which you wish to conduct your research.

As noted in Section 2.2, there is the need to think about your future. If you plan to work in financial management it would be sensible to choose a research project in the financial management field. One part of your course that will inevitably be discussed at any job interview is your research project. A project in the same field will provide you with the opportunity to display clearly your depth of knowledge and your enthusiasm.

Looking at past project titles

Many of our students have found looking at *past projects* a useful way of generating research ideas. For undergraduate and taught masters degrees these are often called *dissertations*. For research degrees they are termed *theses*. A common way of doing this is to scan a list of past project titles (such as those in Appendix 1) for anything that captures your imagination. Titles that look interesting or which grab your attention should be noted down, as should any thoughts you have about the title in relation to your own research idea. In this process the fact that the title is poorly worded or the project report received a low mark is immaterial. What matters is the fact that you have found a topic that interests you. Based on this you can think of new ideas in the same general area that will enable you to provide fresh insights.

Scanning actual research projects may also produce research ideas. However, you need to beware. The fact that a project is in your library is no guarantee of the quality of the arguments and observations it contains. In many universities all projects are placed in the library whether they are bare passes or distinctions.

Discussion

Colleagues, friends and university tutors are all good sources of possible project ideas. Often project tutors will have ideas for possible student projects, which they will be pleased to discuss with you. In addition, ideas can be obtained by talking to practitioners and professional groups (Gill and Johnson, 1997). It is important that as well as discussing possible ideas you also make a note of them. What seemed like a good idea in the coffee shop may not be remembered quite so clearly after the following lecture!

Searching the literature

As part of your discussions, relevant literature may also be suggested. Sharp and Howard (1996) discuss types of literature that are of particular use for generating research ideas. These include:

- articles in academic and professional journals;
- reports;
- books.

Of particular use are academic *review articles*. These articles contain both a considered review of the state of knowledge in that topic area and pointers towards areas where further research needs to be undertaken. In addition you can browse recent publications, in particular journals, for possible research ideas (Section 3.5). For many subject areas your project tutor will be able to suggest possible recent review articles, or articles that contain recommendations for further work. *Reports* may also be of use. The most recently published are usually up to date and, again, often contain recommendations that may form the basis of your research idea. *Books* by contrast are less up to date than other written sources. They do, however, often contain a good overview of research that has been undertaken, which may suggest ideas to you.

Searching for publications is only possible when you have at least some idea of the area in which you wish to undertake your research. One way of obtaining this is to re-examine your lecture notes and course textbooks and to note those subjects that appear most interesting (discussed earlier in this section) and the names of relevant authors. This will give you a basis on which to undertake a *preliminary search* (using techniques outlined in Sections 3.4 and 3.5). When the articles, reports and other items have been obtained it is often helpful to look for unfounded assertions and statements on the absence of research (Raimond, 1993), as these are likely to contain ideas that will enable you to provide fresh insights.

Keeping a notebook of ideas

One of the more creative techniques that we all use is to keep a *notebook of ideas*. All this involves is simply noting down any interesting research ideas as you think of them and, of equal importance, what sparked off your thought. You can then pursue the idea using more rational thinking techniques later. Mark keeps a notebook by his bed so he can jot down any flashes of inspiration that occur to him in the middle of the night!

Exploring personal preferences using past projects

Another way of generating possible project ideas is to explore your *personal preferences* using past project reports from your university. To do this Raimond (1993) suggests that you:

1 Select six projects that you like.
2 For each of these six projects note down your first thoughts in response to three questions (if responses for different projects are the same this does not matter):
   a What appeals to you about the project?
   b What is good about the project?
   c Why is the project good?
3 Select three projects that you do not like.
4 For each of these three projects note down your first thoughts in response to three questions (if responses for different projects are the same, or cannot be clearly expressed, this does not matter; note them down anyway):
   a What do you dislike about the project?
   b What is bad about the project?
   c Why is the project bad?

You now have a list of what you consider to be excellent and what you consider to be poor in projects. This will not be the same as a list generated by anyone else. It is also very unlikely to match the attributes of a good research project (Box 2.1). However, by examining this list you will begin to understand those project characteristics that are important to you and with which you feel comfortable. Of equal importance is that you will have identified those that you are uncomfortable with and should avoid. These can be used as the parameters against which to evaluate possible research ideas.

Relevance trees

Relevance trees may also prove useful in generating research topics. In this instance, their use is similar to that of mind mapping (Buzan with Buzan, 2000), in which you start with a broad concept from which you generate further (usually more specific) topics. Each of these topics forms a separate branch from which you can generate further more detailed sub-branches. As you proceed down the sub-branches more ideas are generated and recorded. These can then be examined and a number selected and combined to provide a research idea (Sharp and Howard, 1996).*

* This technique is discussed in more detail in Section 3.4, which also includes a worked example in which a relevance tree is used to help generate key words for a literature search.

Brainstorming

The technique of *brainstorming*, taught as a problem-solving technique on many business and management courses, can also be used to generate and refine research ideas. It is best undertaken with a group of people, although you can brainstorm on your own. To brainstorm, Moody (1983) suggests that you:

1 Define your problem – that is, the sorts of ideas you are interested in – as precisely as possible. In the early stages of formulating a topic this may be as vague as 'I am interested in marketing but don't know what to do for my research topic.'
2 Ask for suggestions relating to the problem.
3 Record all suggestions observing the following rules:
   - No suggestion should be criticised or evaluated in any way before all ideas have been considered.
   - All suggestions, however wild, should be recorded and considered.
   - As many suggestions as possible should be recorded.
4 Review all the suggestions and explore what is meant by each.
5 Analyse the list of suggestions and decide which appeal to you most as research ideas and why.

worked example

Brainstorming

George's main interest was football. When he finished university he wanted to work in marketing, preferably for a sports goods manufacturer. He had examined his own strengths and discovered that his best marks were in marketing. He wanted to do his research project on some aspect of marketing, preferably linked to football, but had no real research idea. He asked three friends, all taking business studies degrees, to help him brainstorm the problem.

George began by explaining the problem in some detail. At first the suggestions emerged slowly. He noted them down on the whiteboard. Soon the board was covered with suggestions. George counted these and discovered there were over 100.

Reviewing individual suggestions produced nothing that any of the group felt to be of sufficient merit for a research project. However, one of George's friends pointed out that combining the suggestions of Premier League football, television rights and sponsorship might provide an idea which satisfied the assessment requirements of the project.

They discussed the suggestion further, and George noted the research idea as 'something about how confining the rights to show live Premiership football to Sky TV would impact upon the sale of Premiership club-specific merchandise'.

George arranged to see his project tutor to discuss how to refine the idea they had just generated.

Refining research ideas

The Delphi technique

An additional approach that our students have found particularly useful in refining their research ideas is the *Delphi technique*. This involves using a group of people who are either involved or interested in the research idea to generate and choose a more specific research idea (Robson, 2002). To use this technique you need:

1 to brief the members of the group about the research idea (they can make notes if they wish);
2 at the end of the briefing to encourage group members to seek clarification and more information as appropriate;
3 to ask each member of the group, including the originator of the research idea, to generate independently up to three specific research ideas based on the idea that has been described (they can also be asked to provide a justification for their specific ideas);
4 to collect the research ideas in an unedited and non-attributable form and to distribute them to all members of the group;
5 a second cycle of the process (steps 2 to 4) in which individuals comment on the research ideas and revise their own contributions in the light of what others have said;
6 subsequent cycles of the process until a consensus is reached. These either follow a similar pattern (steps 2 to 4) or use discussion, voting or some other method.

This process works well, not least because people enjoy trying to help one another. In addition it is very useful in moulding groups into a cohesive whole.

worked example

Using a Delphi group

Tim explained to the group that his research idea was concerned with understanding the decision-making processes associated with mortgage applications and loan advances. His briefing to the three other group members, and the questions that they asked him, considered aspects such as:

- the influences on a potential first-time buyer to approach a specific financial institution;
- the influence of face-to-face contact between potential borrower and potential lender on decision-making.

The group then moved on to generate a number of more specific research ideas, among which were the following:

- the factors that influenced potential first-time house purchasers to deal with particular financial institutions;
- the effect of interpersonal contact on mortgage decisions;
- the qualities that potential applicants look for in mortgage advisers.

These were considered and commented on by all the group members. At the end of the second cycle Tim had, with the other students' agreement, refined his research idea to:

- the way in which a range of factors influenced potential first-time buyers' choice of lending institution.

He now needed to pursue these ideas by undertaking a preliminary search of the literature.

The preliminary study

Even if you have been given a research idea, it is still necessary to refine it in order to turn it into a research project. Some authors, for example Bennett (1991), refer to this process as a *preliminary study*. For some research ideas this will be no more than a review of some of the literature. This can be thought of as the first iteration of your critical literature review (Figure 3.1). For others it may include revisiting the techniques discussed earlier in this section as well as informal discussions with people who have personal experience of and knowledge about your research ideas. In some cases *shadowing* employees who are likely to be important in your research may also provide insights. If you are planning on undertaking your research within an organisation it is important to gain a good understanding of your host organisation (Kervin, 1992). However, whatever techniques you choose the underlying purpose is to gain a greater understanding so that your research question can be refined.

At this stage you need to be testing your research ideas against the checklist in Box 2.1 and where necessary changing them. It may be that after a preliminary study, or discussing your ideas with colleagues, you decide that the research idea is no longer feasible in the form in which you first envisaged it. If this is the case do not be too downhearted. It is far better to revise your research ideas at this stage than to have to do it later, when you have undertaken far more work.

Integrating ideas

The integration of ideas from these techniques is essential if your research is to have a clear direction and not contain a mismatch between objectives and your final research report. Jankowicz (2000:46–9) suggests an integrative process that our students have found most useful. This he terms 'working up and narrowing down'. It involves classifying each research idea first into its area, then its field, and finally the precise aspect in which you are interested. These represent an increasingly more detailed description of the research idea. Thus your initial area, based on examining your course work, might be accountancy. After browsing some recent journals and discussion with colleagues this becomes more focused on the field of financial accounting methods. With further reading, the use of the Delphi technique and discussion with your project tutor you decide to focus on the aspect of activity-based costing.

You will know when the process of generating and refining ideas is complete as you will be able to say 'I'd like to do some research on . . .'. Obviously there will still be a big gap between this and the point when you are ready to start serious work on your research. Sections 2.4 and 2.5 will ensure that you are ready to bridge that gap.

Refining topics given by your employing organisation

If, as a part-time student, your manager gives you a topic, this may present particular problems. It may be something in which you are not particularly interested. In this case you will have to weigh the advantage of doing something useful to the organisation against the disadvantage of a potential lack of personal motivation. You therefore need to achieve a balance. Often the project your manager wishes you to undertake is larger than that which is appropriate for your course project. In such cases, it may be possible to complete both by isolating an element of the larger organisational project that you find interesting and treating this as the project for your course.

One of our students was asked to do a preliminary investigation of the strengths and weaknesses of her organisation's pay system and then to recommend consultants to design and implement a new system. She was not particularly interested in this project. However, she was considering becoming a freelance personnel consultant. Therefore, for her course project she decided to study the decision-making process in relation to the appointment of personnel consultants. Her organisation's decision on which consultant to appoint, and why this decision was taken, proved to be a useful case study against which to compare management decision-making theory.

In this event you would write a larger report for your organisation and a part of it for your project report. Section 13.4 offers some guidance on writing two separate reports for different audiences.

2.4 Turning research ideas into research projects

Writing research questions

Much is made in this book of the importance of defining clear *research questions* at the beginning of the research process. The importance of this cannot be overemphasised. One of the key criteria of your research success will be whether you have a set of clear conclusions drawn from the data you have collected. The extent to which you can do that will be determined largely by the clarity with which you have posed your initial research questions.

worked example

Defining the research question

Imran was studying for a BA in Business Studies and doing his placement year in an advanced consumer electronics company. When he first joined the company he was surprised to note that the company's business strategy, which was announced in the company newsletter, seemed to be inconsistent with what Imran knew of the product market.

Imran had become particularly interested in corporate strategy in his degree. He was familiar with some of the literature that suggested that corporate strategy should be linked to the general external environment in which the organisation operated. He wanted to do some research on corporate strategy in his organisation for his degree dissertation.

After talking this over with his project tutor Imran decided on the following research question: 'Why does my organisation's corporate strategy not seem to reflect the major factors in the external operating environment?'

Defining research questions, rather like generating research ideas (Section 2.3), is not a straightforward matter. It is important that the question is sufficiently involved to generate the sort of project that is consistent with the standards expected of you (Box 2.1). A question that prompts a descriptive answer, for example 'What is the proportion of graduates entering the civil service who attended the old-established UK universities?' is far easier to answer than: 'Why are graduates from old-established UK universities more likely to enter the civil service than graduates from other universities?' More will be said about the importance of theory in defining the research question later in this section. However, beware of research questions that are too easy.

It is perhaps more likely that you fall into the trap of asking research questions that are too difficult. The question cited above, 'Why are graduates from old-established UK universities more likely to enter the civil service than graduates from other universities?' is a case in point. It would probably be very difficult to gain sufficient access to the inner portals of the civil service to get a good grasp of the subtle 'unofficial' processes that go on at staff selection which may favour one type of candidate over another. Over-reaching yourself in the definition of research questions is a danger.

The pitfall that you must avoid at all costs is asking research questions that will not generate new insights (Box 2.1). This raises the question of the extent to which you have consulted the relevant literature. It is perfectly legitimate to replicate research because you have a genuine concern about its applicability to your research setting (for example, your organisation). However, it certainly is not legitimate to display your ignorance of the literature.

It is often a useful starting point in the writing of research questions to begin with one *general focus research question* that flows from your research idea. This may lead to several more detailed questions or the definition of research objectives. Table 2.1 has some examples of general focus research questions.

Writing your research questions will be, in most cases, your individual concern but it is useful to get other people to help you. An obvious source of guidance is your project tutor. Consulting your project tutor will avoid the pitfalls of the questions that are too easy or too difficult or have been answered before. Discussing your area of interest with your project tutor will lead to your research questions becoming much clearer.

Prior to discussion with your project tutor you may wish to conduct a brainstorming session with your peers or use the Delphi technique (Section 2.3). Your research questions may flow from your initial examination of the relevant literature. As outlined in Section 2.3, journal articles reporting primary research will often end with a conclusion that includes the consideration of the author of the implications for future research of the work in the article. This may be phrased in the form of research questions. However, even if it is not, it may suggest pertinent research questions to you.

Writing research objectives

Your research may begin with a general focus research question that then generates more detailed research questions, or you may use your general focus research ques-

Table 2.1 Examples of research ideas and their derived focus research questions

Research idea	*General focus research question*
Job recruitment via the Internet	How effective is recruiting for new staff via the Internet in comparison with traditional methods?
Advertising and share prices	How does the running of a TV advertising campaign designed to boost the image of a company affect its share price?
The use of aromas as a marketing device	In what ways does the use of specific aromas in supermarkets affect buyer behaviour?
The future of trade unions	What are the strategies that trade unions should adopt to ensure their future viability?

tion as a base from which you write a set of *research objectives*. Objectives are more generally acceptable to the research community as evidence of the researcher's clear sense of purpose and direction. It may be that either is satisfactory. Do check whether your examining body has a preference.

We contend that research objectives are likely to lead to greater specificity than research or investigative questions. Table 2.2 illustrates this point. It summarises the objectives of some research conducted by one of our students. Expression of the first research question as an objective prompted a consideration of the objectives of the organisations. This was useful because it led to the finding that there often were no clear objectives. This in itself was an interesting theoretical discovery.

The second and third objectives operationalise the matching research questions by introducing the notion of explicit effectiveness criteria. In a similar way the fourth objective (parts a and b) and the fifth objective are specific about factors that lead to effectiveness in question 4. The biggest difference between the questions and objectives is illustrated by the way in which the fifth question becomes the sixth objective. They are similar but differ in the way that the objective makes clear that a theory will be developed that will make a causal link between two sets of variables: effectiveness factors and team briefing success.

This is not to say that the research questions could not have been written with a similar amount of specificity. They could. Indeed, you may find it easier to write specific research questions than objectives. However, we doubt whether the same level of precision could be achieved through the writing of research questions alone. Research objectives require more rigorous thinking, which derives from the use of more formal language.

The importance of theory in writing research questions and objectives

Section 4.1 outlines the role of theory in helping you to decide your approach to research design. However, your consideration of theory should begin earlier than this. It should inform your definition of research questions and objectives.

Table 2.2 Phrasing research questions as research objectives

Research question	*Research objective*
1 Why have organisations introduced team briefing?	1 To identify organisations' objectives for team briefing schemes.
2 How can the effectiveness of team briefing schemes be measured?	2 To establish suitable effectiveness criteria for team briefing schemes.
3 Has team briefing been effective?	3 To describe the extent to which the effectiveness criteria for team briefing have been met.
4 How can the effectiveness of team briefing be explained?	4a To determine the factors associated with the effectiveness criteria for team briefing being met. b To estimate whether some of those factors are more influential than other factors.
5 Can the explanation be generalised?	5 To develop an explanatory theory that associates certain factors with the effectiveness of team briefing schemes.

Theory is defined by Gill and Johnson (1997:178) as 'a formulation regarding the cause and effect relationships between two or more variables, which may or may not have been tested'.

There is probably no word that is more misused and misunderstood in education than the word 'theory'. It is thought that material included in textbooks is 'theory' whereas what is happening in the 'real world' is practice. The citing of references in students' written work is often referred to by them as 'theory'. Students who saw earlier drafts of this book remarked that they were pleased that the book was not too 'theoretical'. What they meant was that the book concentrated on giving lots of practical advice. Yet the book is full of theory. Advising you to carry out research in a particular way (variable A) is based on the theory that this will yield effective results (variable B). This is the cause and effect relationship referred to in the definition of theory cited above.

The definition demonstrates that 'theory' has a specific meaning. It refers to situations where if A is introduced B will be the consequence. Therefore the marketing manager may theorise that the introduction of loyalty cards by a supermarket will lead to customers being less likely to shop regularly at a competitor supermarket. That is a theory. Yet the marketing manager would probably not recognise it as such. He or she is still less likely to refer to it as a theory, particularly in the company of fellow managers. Many managers are very dismissive of any talk that smacks of 'theory'. It is thought of as something that is all very well to learn about at business school but bears little relation to what goes on in everyday organisational life. Yet the loyalty card example shows that it has everything to do with what goes on in everyday organisational life.

Section 4.1 notes that every purposive decision we take is based on theory: that certain consequences will flow from the decision. It follows from this that every managers' meeting that features a number of decisions will be a meeting that is highly *theory dependent* (Gill and Johnson, 1997). All that will be missing is a realisation of this fact. So, if theory is something that is so rooted in our everyday lives it certainly is something that we need not be apprehensive about. If it is implicit in all our decisions and actions then recognising its importance means making it explicit. In research the importance of theory must be recognised: therefore it must be made explicit.

Kerlinger and Lee (2000) reinforce Gill and Johnson's definition by noting that the purpose of examining relationships between two or more variables is to explain and predict these relationships. Gill and Johnson (1997:27) neatly tie these purposes of theory to their definition:

> ... it is also evident that if we have the expectation that by doing A, B will happen, then by manipulating the occurrence of A we can begin to predict and influence the occurrence of B. In other words, theory is clearly enmeshed in practice since explanation enables prediction which in turn enables control.

In our example, the marketing manager theorised that the introduction of loyalty cards by a supermarket would lead to customers being less likely to shop regularly at a competitor supermarket. Following Gill and Johnson's (1997:27) point that 'explanation enables prediction which in turn enables control', the supermarket would be well advised to conduct research that yielded an explanation of why loyalty cards encourage loyalty. Is it a purely economic rationale? Does it foster the 'collector' instinct in all of us? Does it appeal to a sense of thrift in us that helps us cope with an ever more wasteful world? These explanations are probably complex and interrelated. Reaching a better understanding of them would help the marketing manager to predict the outcome of any changes to the scheme. Increasing the amount of points per item would be effective if the economic explanation was valid. Increasing the range of products on which extra points were offered might appeal to the 'collector' instinct. More accurate prediction would offer the marketing manager increased opportunities for control.

Phillips and Pugh (2000) distinguish between research and what they call *intelligence gathering*. The latter is the gathering of facts. For example, what is the relative proportion of undergraduates to postgraduates reading this book? What is the current spend per employee on training in the UK? What provision do small businesses make for bad debts? This is often called descriptive research (Section 4.2) and may form part of your research project. Descriptive research would be the first step in our example of supermarket loyalty card marketing. Establishing that there had been a change in customer behaviour following the introduction of supermarket loyalty cards would be the first step prior to any attempt at explanation.

Phillips and Pugh contrast such 'what' questions with 'why' questions. Examples of these 'why' questions are as follows: Why do British organisations spend less per head on training than German organisations? Why are new car purchasers reluctant to take out extended warranties on their vehicles? Why do some travellers still prefer to use cross-channel ferries as opposed to the Channel Tunnel? Such questions go 'beyond description and require analysis'. They look for 'explanations, relationships, comparisons, predictions, generalisations and theories' (Phillips and Pugh, 2000:47–8).

It is a short step from the 'why' research question to the testing of an existing theory in a new situation or the development of your own theory. This may be expressed as a hypothesis that is to be tested (Section 4.1), or the eventual answer to your research question may be the development or amendment of a theory.

worked example

Writing a research question based on theory

David was a senior manager studying part time. He was worried that the many changes that had taken place in his organisation, including large-scale redundancies at all levels, meant that the nature of the relationship between the organisation and its employees was changing.

His reading led him to become fascinated by the idea of the psychological contract between the organisation and the employee: what each will give the other (e.g. security, loyalty, ambition, career progression) in return for work and employment over and above the normal terms and conditions that are part of the legal employment contract.

David's research question was: 'How are the structural changes in my organisation affecting the way in which employees think about the psychological contract they have with the organisation?'

David was asked to clarify the theory underpinning his research. He did so by explaining that redundancies created in employees feelings of insecurity such that they saw the employment relationship simply as a short-term 'wage–work bargain'. This meant that they were unprepared to put in the extra commitment normally associated with building a career.

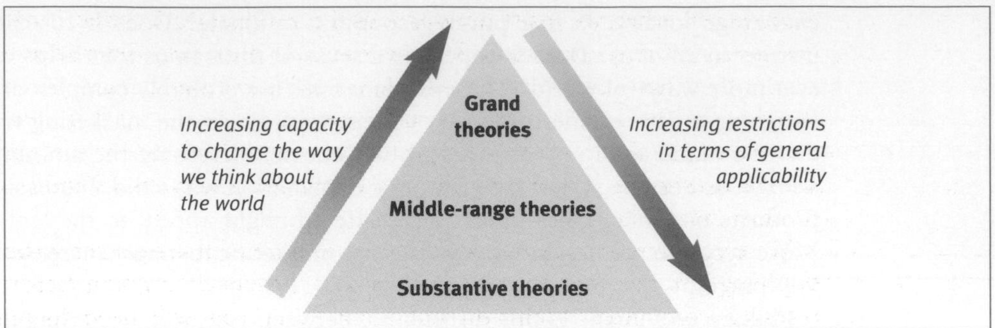

Figure 2.1 Grand, middle-range and substantive theories

Although intelligence gathering will play a part in your research, it is unlikely to be enough. You should be seeking to explain phenomena, to analyse relationships, to compare what is going on in different research settings, to predict outcomes and to generalise; then you will be working at the theoretical level. This is a necessary requirement for most assessed research projects.

You may still be concerned that the necessity to be theory dependent in your research project means that you will have to develop a ground-breaking theory that will lead to a whole new way of thinking about management. If this is the case you should take heart from the threefold typology of theories summarised by Creswell (1994) (see Figure 2.1). He talks of 'grand theories', usually thought to be the province of the natural scientists (e.g. Darwin and Newton). He contrasts these with 'middle-range theories', which lack the capacity to change the way in which we think about the world but are nonetheless of significance. Some of the theories of human motivation well known to managers would be in this category. However, most of us are concerned with 'substantive theories' that are 'restricted to a particular setting, group, time population or problem' (Creswell, 1994:83). For example, studying the reasons why a total quality initiative in a particular organisation failed would be an example of a substantive theory. Restricted they may be, but a host of 'substantive theories' that present similar propositions may lead to 'middle-range theories'. By developing 'substantive theories', however modest, we are doing our bit as researchers to enhance our understanding of the world about us. A grand claim, but a valid one!

This discussion of theory does assume that a clear theoretical position is developed prior to the collection of data (the *deductive* approach). This will not always be the case. It may be that your study is based on the principle of developing theory after the data have been collected (the *inductive* approach). This is a fundamental difference in research approach, and will be discussed in detail in Section 4.1.

2.5 Writing your research proposal

At the start of all courses or modules we give our students a plan of the work they will be doing. It includes the learning objectives, the content, the assessment strategy and the recommended reading. This is our statement of our side of the learning contract. Our students have a right to expect this.

However, when we insist on a proposal for a dissertation that is often the equivalent of at least two other modules, there is often a marked reluctance to produce anything other than what is strictly necessary. This is unsatisfactory. It is unfair to your project tutor because you are not making entirely clear what it is you intend to do in your research. You are also being unfair to yourself because you are not giving yourself the maximum opportunity to have your ideas and plans scrutinised and subjected to rigorous questioning.

Writing a research proposal is a crucial part of the research process. If you are applying for research funding, or if your proposal is going before an academic research committee, then you will know that you will need to put a great deal of time into the preparation of your proposal. However, even if the official need for a proposal is not so vital it is still a process that will repay very careful attention.

The purposes of the research proposal

Organising your ideas

Section 13.1 notes that writing can be the best way of clarifying our thoughts. This is a valuable purpose of the proposal. Not only will it clarify your thoughts but it will help you to organise your ideas into a coherent statement of your research intent. Your reader will be looking for this.

Convincing your audience

However coherent your ideas and exciting your research plan, it counts for little if the proposal reveals that what you are planning to do is simply not possible. As part of our research methods course for taught postgraduate students we have a three-stage assignment, the first stage of which is to write a proposal. This is then discussed with a project tutor. What usually happens is that this discussion is about how the plans can be amended so that something more modest in scope is attempted. Often work that is not achievable in the given timescale is proposed. If your proposal has not convinced your audience that the research you have proposed is achievable, then you will have saved yourself a great deal of time and frustration.

Contracting with your 'client'

If you were asked to carry out a research project for a commercial client or your own organisation it is unthinkable that you would go ahead without a clear proposal that you would submit for approval. Acceptance of your proposal by the client would be part of the contract that existed between you. So it is with your proposal to your project tutor or academic committee. Acceptance implies that your proposal is satisfactory. While this is obviously no guarantee of subsequent success, it is something of comfort to you to know that at least you started your research journey with an appropriate destination and journey plan. It is for you to ensure that you are not derailed!

The content of the research proposal

Title

This may be your first attempt at the title. It may change as your work progresses. At this stage it should closely mirror the content of your proposal.

Background

This is an important part of the proposal. It should tell the reader why you feel the research that you are planning is worth the effort. This may be expressed in the form of a problem that needs solving or something that you find exciting and has aroused your curiosity. The reader will be looking for evidence here that there is sufficient interest from you to sustain you over the long months (or years) ahead.

This is also the section where you will demonstrate your knowledge of the relevant literature. Moreover, it will clarify where your proposal fits into the debate in the literature. You will be expected to show a clear link between the previous work that has been done in your field of research interest and the content of your proposal. In short, the literature should be your point of departure. This is not the same as the critical literature review (Section 3.2) you will present in your final project report. It will just provide an overview of the key literature sources from which you intend to draw.

Research questions and objectives

The background section should lead smoothly into a statement of your research question(s) and objectives. These should leave the reader in no doubt as to precisely what it is that your research seeks to achieve. Be careful here to ensure that your objectives are precisely written and will lead to observable outcomes (look again at Table 2.2, e.g., 'to describe the extent to which the effectiveness criteria specified for the team briefing scheme have been met'). Do not fall into the trap of stating general research aims that are little more than statements of intent (e.g. 'to discover the level of effectiveness of the team briefing scheme').

Method

This and the background sections will be the longest sections of the proposal. It will detail precisely how you intend to go about achieving your research objectives. It will also justify your choice of method in the light of those objectives. These two aims may be met by dividing your method section into two parts: research design and data collection.

In the part on research design you will explain where you intend to carry out the research. If your earlier coverage has pointed out that your research is a single-organisation issue, then this will be self-evident. However, if your research topic is more generic you will wish to explain, for example, which sector(s) of the economy you have chosen to research and why you chose these sectors. You will also need to explain the identity of your research population (for example, managers or trade union officials) and why you chose this population.

This section should also include an explanation of the general way in which you intend to carry out the research. Will it be based on a survey, interviews, examination of secondary data or a combination of methods? Here again it is essential to explain why you have chosen your approach. Your explanation should be based on the most effective way of meeting your research objectives.

The research design section gives an overall view of the method chosen and the reason for that choice. The data collection section goes into much more detail about how specifically the data are to be collected. For example, if you are using a survey approach you should specify your population and sample size. You should also clarify how the questionnaires will be distributed and how they will be analysed. If you are using interviews you should explain how many interviews will be conducted, their intended duration, whether they will be tape recorded, and how they will be analysed. In short, you should demonstrate to your reader that you have thought carefully about all the issues regarding your method and their relationship to your research objectives. However, it is normally not necessary in the proposal to include precise detail of the method you will employ, for example the content of the observation schedule or questionnaire questions.

In addition, it may also be necessary to include a statement about how you are going to adhere to any ethical guidelines. This is particularly important in some research settings, e.g. the National Health Service.

Timescale

This will help you and your reader to decide on the viability of your research proposal. It will be helpful if you divide your research plan into stages. This will give you a clear idea as to what is possible in the given timescale. Experience has shown that however well the researcher's time is organised the whole process seems to take longer than anticipated.

worked example

A research timescale

As part of the final year of their undergraduate business studies degree all our students have to undertake an 8000–10 000-word research project. In order to assist them with their time management we discuss the following outline timescale with them.

Target date	*Month number*	*Task to be achieved*
Start October	1	Start thinking about research ideas (latest start date)
End November	2	Literature read Objectives clearly defined with reference to literature
End December	3	Literature review written Methodology literature read for dissertations involving secondary/primary date
End January	4	Secondary/primary data collected and analysed (analysis techniques linked to methodology/research literature) Literature review extended further
Mid-February	5	Further writing up and analysis
End March	6	Draft completed including formatting bibliography etc.
Mid-May	8	Draft revised as necessary
End May	8	Submission

As part of this section of their proposal, many researchers find it useful to produce a schedule for their research using a *Gannt chart*. Developed by Henry Gannt in 1917, this provides a simple visual representation of the tasks or activities that make up your research project, each being plotted against a time line. The time we estimate each task will take is represented by the length of an associated horizontal bar, whilst the task's start and finish times are represented by its position on the time line. Figure 2.2 shows a Gannt chart for a student's research project. As we can see from the first bar on this chart, the student has decided to schedule in two weeks of holiday. The first of these occurs over the Christmas and New Year period, and the second occurs while her tutor is reading a draft copy of the completed project in April. We can also see from the second and fourth bar that, like many of our students, she intends to begin to draft her literature review while she is still reading new articles and books. However, she has also recognised that some activities must be undertaken sequentially. For example, bars 9 and 10 highlight that before she can administer her questionnaire (bar 10) she must complete all the revisions highlighted as necessary by the pilot testing (bar 9).

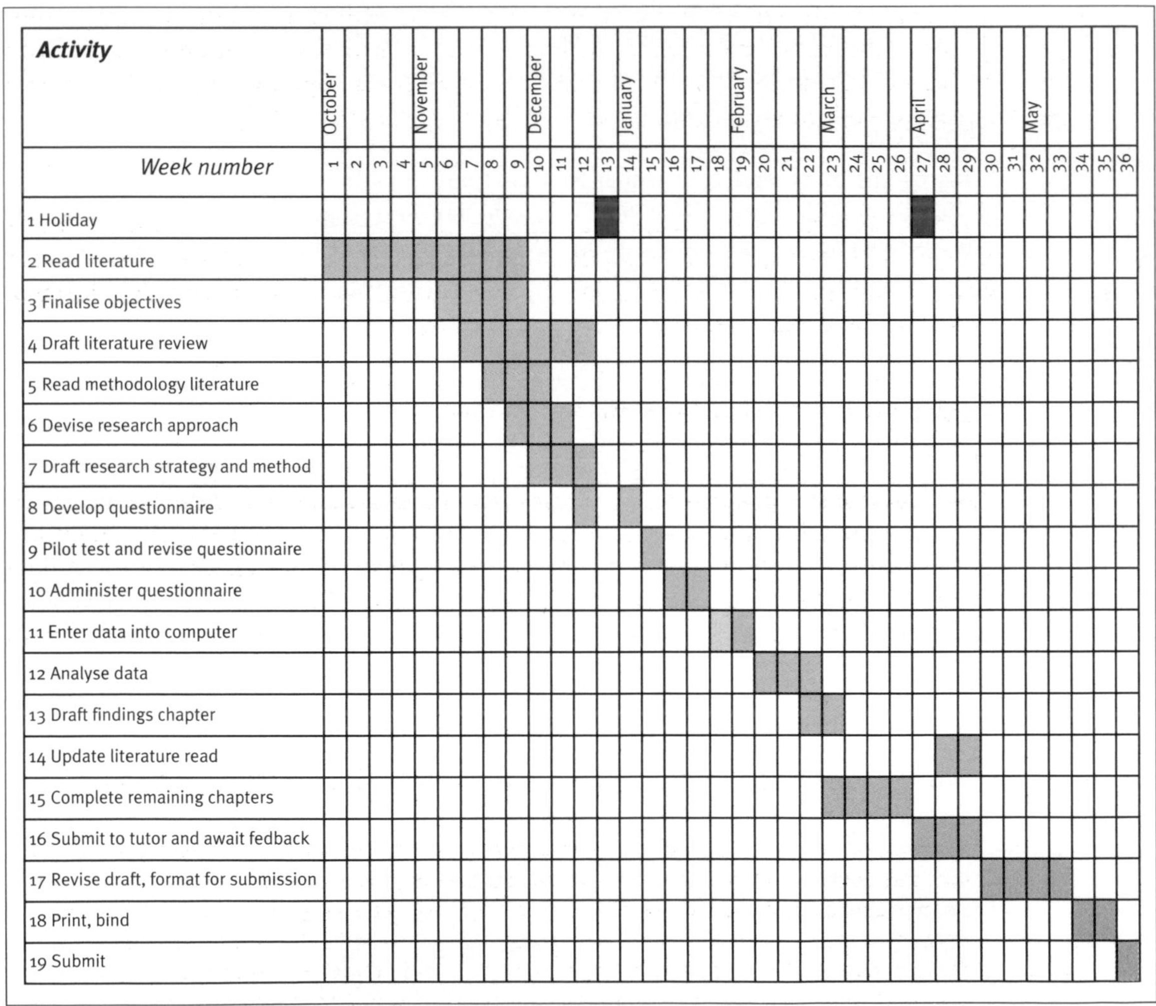

Activity
October
November
December
January
February
March
April
May
Week number
1 2 3 4 5 6 7 8 9 10 11 12 13 14 15 16 17 18 19 20 21 22 23 24 25 26 27 28 29 30 31 32 33 34 35 36
1 Holiday
2 Read literature
3 Finalise objectives
4 Draft literature review
5 Read methodology literature
6 Devise research approach
7 Draft research strategy and method
8 Develop questionnaire
9 Pilot test and revise questionnaire
10 Administer questionnaire
11 Enter data into computer
12 Analyse data
13 Draft findings chapter
14 Update literature read
15 Complete remaining chapters
16 Submit to tutor and await fedback
17 Revise draft, format for submission
18 Print, bind
19 Submit

Figure 2.2 Gantt chart for a student's research project

Resources

This is another facet of viability (Box 2.1). It will allow you and the reader to assess whether what you are proposing can be resourced. Resource considerations may be categorised as finance, data access and equipment.

Conducting research costs money. This may be for travel, subsistence, help with data analysis, or postage for questionnaires. Think through the expenses involved and ensure that you can meet these expenses.

Assessors of your proposal will need to be convinced that you have access to the data you need to conduct your research. This may be unproblematic if you are carrying out research in your own organisation. Many academic committees wish to see written approval from host organisations in which researchers are planning to conduct research. You will also need to convince your reader of the possibility of obtaining a reasonable response to any questionnaire that you send.

It is surprising how many research proposals have ambitious plans for large-scale surveys with no thought given to how the data will be analysed. It is important that you convince the reader of your proposal that you have access to the necessary computer hardware and software to analyse your data. Moreover, it is necessary for you to demonstrate that you have either the necessary skills to perform the analysis or can learn the skills in an appropriate time, or you have access to help.

References

It is not necessary to try and impress your proposal reader with an enormous list of references (Robson, 2002). A few literature sources to which you have referred in the background section and which relate to the previous work that is directly informing your own proposal should be all that is necessary.

Criteria for evaluating research proposals

The extent to which the components of the proposal fit together

Your rationale for conducting the research should include a study of the previous published research, including relevant theories in the topic area. This study should inform your research question(s) and objectives. Your proposed methodology should flow directly from these research question(s) and objectives. The time that you have allocated should be a direct reflection of the methods you employ, as should the resources that you need.

worked example

Fitting together the various components of the research proposal

Jenny was a middle manager in a large insurance company. She was very interested in the fact that electronic forms of communication meant that organisations could move information-based administrative work round different locations. Her company was scanning paper applications for insurance policies onto their computer system and delivering these into a central electronic bank of work. The company had employees in three different locations in the UK, and work was drawn from the bank on the basis of workload existing in each particular location. Recently senior management had been considering developing work locations in

South Asian cities, where it felt the standard of English meant that such functions could be fulfilled effectively. Jenny anticipated that this would pose certain logistical problems, for example staff training and communications. Knowledge of these problems would give her a clear picture of the limit of complexity of the work that could be done. This was particularly important since the complexity range went from the simple to the technically complex. Research into the literature on cross-cultural training justified Jenny's concern. As a consequence of her thought and reading she developed her research question as: 'What cross-cultural problems may be posed by international electronic work transfer in the insurance industry, and how may these problems limit the complexity of the work that may be transferred?'

Through her reading of the practitioner journals Jenny was aware that some other financial services organisations had been sending their work to Asia for some time. She decided that approaching these companies and interviewing their key personnel would be a fruitful approach. The main problem that Jenny would have with this research would be the time that the interview work would take, given that such companies were located all over the UK and North America. She was unsure how many interviews would be necessary. This would become clearer as she progressed in the research. However, it was unlikely that less than 10 companies would yield sufficient valuable data. She thought that she could collect the necessary data in a four-month period, which fitted in with her university deadline. There were no specific resources that Jenny needed other than finance and time. Since her research would be of immediate benefit to her employer she though that neither would pose a problem.

The viability of the proposal

This is the answer to the question: 'Can this research be carried out satisfactorily within the timescale and with available resources?'

The absence of preconceived ideas

Your research should be an exciting journey into the unknown. Do not be like the student who came to Phil to talk over a research proposal and said 'Of course, I know what the answer will be'. When asked to explain the purpose of doing the research if he already knew the answer he became rather defensive and eventually looked for another supervisor and, probably, another topic.

worked example

A written research proposal

Puvadol was a student from Thailand who returned home from the UK to complete his MA dissertation. His proposed dissertation concerned the applicability of Western methods of involving employees in decision-making in Thai organisations.

An abbreviated version of Puvadol's proposal follows:

Title

The influences of Thai culture on employee involvement.

Background

Involving employees in the decision-making of their employing organisations has been increasingly popular in Europe and North America in recent years. The influx of American organisations into Thailand has meant that similar approaches are being adopted. However, this assumes that Thai employees will respond to these techniques as readily as their European and American counterparts.

Doubts about the validity of these assumptions derive from studies of Thai national culture (Komin, 1990). Using Rokeach's (1979) conceptual framework, Komin characterised Thai culture in a number of ways. I have isolated those that relate to employee involvement. These are that Thais wish to:

a save face, to avoid criticism and to show consideration to others;
b exhibit gratitude to those who have shown kindness and consideration;
c promote smooth, conflict-free interpersonal relations;
d interpret 'rules' in a flexible way with little concern for principles;
e promote interdependent social relations;
f be seen to be achieving success through good social relations rather than individual success.

I intend to demonstrate in this section that these six cultural values contradict the values of employee involvement (e.g. employee involvement may involve employees in openly criticising managers, which directly contradicts **a** above).

Research objectives

1. To examine the assumptions behind the management technique of employee involvement.
2. To establish the characteristics of the Thai national culture.
3. To identify the opinions of Thai employees and their managers, working in American-owned organisations in Thailand, towards values underpinning employee involvement.
4. To draw conclusions about the applicability of employee involvement to Thai employees.

Method

1. Conduct a review of the literatures on employee involvement and Thai national culture in order to develop research hypotheses.
2. Carry out primary research in three American-owned petrochemical and manufacturing organisations in Thailand to assess the opinions of Thai employees and their managers towards values underpinning employee involvement. Informal approval has been gained from three organisations. American-owned organisations are relevant because it is in these that employee involvement is most likely to be found and values underpinning employee involvement exhibited. Petrochemical and manufacturing organisations are chosen because the occupations carried out in these organisations are likely to be similar, thus ensuring that any differences are a function of Thai national culture rather than of occupational culture.

A questionnaire will be developed with questions based on the Thai values a–f in the Background section above. Each value will lead to a hypothesis (e.g. employee involvement may not be appropriate to Thai culture because it may mean that employees openly criticise their managers). The questions in the questionnaire will seek to test these hypotheses. The questionnaire will be distributed to a sample (size to be agreed) of employees and of managers across all three organisations.

Data analysis will use the SPSS software. Statistical tests will be run to ensure that results are a function of Thai cultural values rather than of values that relate to the individual organisations.

Timescale

January–March 2002: review of literature
April 2002: draft literature review
May 2002: review research methods literature and agree research strategy
June 2002: agree formal access to three organisations for collection of primary data
July–August 2002: compile, pilot and revise questionnaire
September 2002: administer questionnaire
October–November 2002: final collection of questionnaires and analysis of data
November 2002–February 2003: completion of first draft of project report
March–May 2003: final writing of project report

Resources

I have access to computer hardware and software. Access to three organisations has been negotiated, subject to confirmation. My employer has agreed to pay all incidental costs as part of my course expenses.

References

Komin, S. (1990) *Psychology of the Thai People: Values and Behavioral Patterns*, Thailand, National Institute of Development Administration (in Thai).
Rokeach, M. (1979) *Understanding Human Values: Individual and Society*, New York, The Free Press.

If it is absolutely crucial that your proposal is of the highest quality then you may wish to use an *expert system* such as Peer Review Emulator. This software is available either on its own or as part of the Methodologist's Toolchest suite of programs. It asks you a series of questions about your proposed research. The program then critiques these answers to ensure that common research standards are achieved (Scolari Sage, 2002).

2.6 Summary

- The process of formulating and clarifying your research topic is the most important part of your research topic.
- Attributes of a research topic do not vary a great deal between universities. The most important of these is that your research topic will meet the requirements of the examining body.
- Generating and refining research ideas makes use of a variety of techniques. It is important that you use a variety of techniques including those that involve rational thinking and those that involve creative thinking.
- The ideas generated can be integrated subsequently using a technique such as working up and narrowing down.
- Clear research questions, based on the relevant literature, will act as a focus for the research that follows.
- Research can be distinguished from intelligence gathering. Research is theory dependent.
- Writing a research proposal helps you to organise your ideas, and can be thought of as a contract between you and the reader.

- The content of the research proposal should tell the reader what you want to do, why you want to do it, what you are trying to achieve, and how you to plan to achieve it.

self-check Questions

2.1 Why is it important to spend time formulating and clarifying your research topic?

2.2 You have decided to search the literature to 'try and come up with some research ideas in the area of Operations Management'. How will you go about this?

2.3 A colleague of yours wishes to generate a research idea in the area of accounting. He has examined his own strengths and interests on the basis of his assignments and has read some review articles, but has failed to find an idea about which he is excited. He comes and asks you for advice. Suggest two techniques that your colleague could use, and justify your choice.

2.4 You are interested in doing some research on the interface between business organisations and schools. Write three research questions that may be appropriate.

2.5 What may be the theory underpinning the decision by organisations sponsoring schools?

2.6 How would you demonstrate the influence of relevant theory in your research proposal?

progressing your research project

From research ideas to a research proposal

- ☐ If you have not been given a research idea consider the techniques available for generating and refining research ideas. Choose a selection of those with which you feel most comfortable, making sure to include both rational and creative thinking techniques. Use these to try to generate a research idea or ideas. Once you have got some research ideas, or if you have been unable to find an idea, talk to your project tutor.
- ☐ Evaluate your research ideas against the checklist of attributes of a good research project (Box 2.1).
- ☐ Refine your research ideas using a selection of the techniques available for generating and refining research ideas. Re-evaluate your research ideas against the checklist of attributes of a good research project (Box 2.1). Remember that it is better to revise (and in some situations to discard) ideas that do not appear to be feasible at this stage. Integrate your ideas using the process of working up and narrowing down to form one research idea.
- ☐ Use your research idea to write a general focus research question. Where possible this should be a 'why?' or a 'how?' rather than a 'what?' question.
- ☐ Use the general focus research question to write more detailed research questions and your research objectives.
- ☐ Write your research proposal making sure it includes a clear title and sections on:
  - ☐ the background to your research;

- ☐ your research questions and objectives;
- ☐ the method you intend to use;
- ☐ the timescale for your research;
- ☐ the resources you require;
- ☐ references to any literature to which you have referred.

References

Bennett, R. (1991) 'What is management research?', in Smith, N.C. and Dainty, P. (eds) *The Management Research Handbook*, London, Routledge, pp. 67–77.

Buzan, T. with Buzan, B. (2000) *The Mind Map Book* (Millennium edn), London, BBC Books.

Carroll, L. (1989) *Alice's Adventures in Wonderland*, London, Hutchinson.

Creswell, J. (1994) *Research Design: Quantitative and Qualitative Approaches*, Thousand Oaks, CA, Sage.

Ghauri. P. and Grønhaug, K. (2002) *Research Methods in Business Studies: A Practical Guide* (2nd edn), Harlow, Financial Times Prentice Hall.

Gill, J. and Johnson, P. (1997) *Research Methods for Managers* (2nd edn), London, Paul Chapman.

Jankowicz, A.D. (2000) *Business Research Projects* (3rd edn), London, Thomson Learning.

Kerlinger, F. and Lee, H. (2000) *Foundations of Behavioral Research* (4th edn), Fort Worth, Harcourt College Publishers.

Kervin, J.B. (1992) *Methods for Business Research*, New York, HarperCollins.

Moody, P.E. (1983) *Decision Making: Proven Methods for Better Decisions*, Maidenhead, McGraw-Hill.

Phillips, E.M. and Pugh, D.S. (2000) *How to get a PhD* (3rd edn), Buckingham, Open University Press.

Raimond, P. (1993) *Management Projects*, London, Chapman & Hall.

Robson, C. (2002) *Real World Research* (2nd edn), Oxford, Blackwell.

Saunders, M.N.K. and Lewis, P. (1997) 'Great ideas and blind alleys? A review of the literature on starting research', *Management Learning*, 28:3, 283–99.

Scolari Sage (2002) Methodologist's Toolchest (online) (cited 24th February 2002). Available from <URL:http://www.scolari.co.uk>.

Sharp, J. and Howard, K. (1996) *The Management of a Student Research Project* (2nd edn), Aldershot, Gower.

Smith, N.C. and Dainty, P. (1991) *The Management Research Handbook*, London, Routledge.

Further reading

Gill, J. and Johnson, P. (1997) *Research Methods for Managers* (2nd edn), London, Paul Chapman. Chapter 3 is a particularly clear account of the role of theory in research methods and is worth reading to gain a better understanding of this often-misunderstood area.

Raimond, P. (1993) *Management Projects*, London, Chapman & Hall. Chapter 4 contains a useful discussion of techniques for helping to identify project ideas. It is particularly good for those techniques that we have classified as creative rather than rational.

Robson, C. (2002) *Real World Research* (2nd edn), Oxford, Blackwell. Appendix A is devoted to the writing of research proposals and is a very useful source of further information.

CASE 2 Strategic issues in the UK brewing industry

Steve was thinking about how to write his research proposal. A few weeks earlier he had been allocated a project tutor on the basis of his wanting to do something in the area of strategic management. Now his project tutor had emailed him and suggested they meet early next week to discuss Steve's ideas for the research topic. He asked Steve to bring along his research proposal. Steve started to look through his lecture notes from the Strategic Management module, and the following extract caught his eye:

> As companies reach maturity in their product's life cycle a number of occurrences tend to become commonplace. Competition increases, international competitors achieve market entry, overcapacity within the industry increases, profit margins in gross profit terms generally begin to fall, and acquisitions and mergers take place. Certainly within the UK marketplace these trends have recently occurred in a number of industries: banking and brewing would be two good examples.

Steve decided that he would look at these ideas by undertaking 'in-depth' research on the UK brewing industry. Steve used the *Financial Times* CD-ROMs available in his university library to produce a time line of what had happened in the industry since 1989 and added a few notes regarding what he intended to do for his research project. This was what he produced:

Changes in the United Kingdom brewing industry
A research proposal by Steve Smith

There have been numerous changes to the UK brewing industry since the Monopolies and Mergers Commission Report of 1989:

Year	*What happened*
1989	Monopolies & Mergers Commission restricted brewers to 2000 public houses plus 50% of their original holdings. This ruling was modified in 1997; however, the commencement of dismantling of vertical integration within the industry had commenced by that date. This dramatically changed the distribution system, brewers having sold off many of their public houses.
1995	Scottish & Newcastle purchases Courage; now known as Scottish Courage it becomes the largest brewer in the UK.
1996	Allied Domecq decides to sell its 50% share of Carlsberg-Tetley to Bass; merger not allowed by Monopolies & Mergers Commission as it is considered to be anti-competitive. This decision appears to be instrumental to a change of strategy at Bass plc. It sells its brewing interests in 1999 unconditionally to Belgian brewer Interbrew. Bass plc is renamed Six Continents and refocuses its operations in the hotel business.
1999–2002	Interbrew grows further by the acquisition of Whitbread's brewing division and Becks lager. The UK Monopolies & Mergers Commission orders Interbrew to sell Bass brewing. After appeal this is reduced, allowing Interbrew to retain some of the Bass brands including Tennents Scottish Lager. However, it is ordered to reduce its monopoly in the lager market, resulting in the Carling division of Bass brewers being sold to the American brewers Coors, with completion in February 2002.

Notes

The major growth trends within the industry are:

- increased sales of brewery products by supermarkets;
- growth of personal imports;
- traditional town and country style public houses closing rapidly;
- a massive growth in dining out, with town centre theme pub chains growing in popularity.

However, this is no more than a change of buying and lifestyle habits. The brewing production part of the industry currently reflects overcapacity, is experiencing low profit margins, and is in the mature part of its life cycle.

There is a wealth of material on UK brewing, particularly on the Web.

Approach

I am thinking of using the Competitive Advantage model developed by M. E. Porter (*Competitive Strategy*, Free Press, 1980) to help explain the competitive situation.

Convinced he had a solid proposal, Steve attended the appointment with his project tutor. The project tutor was obviously interested in Steve's ideas but was concerned about Steve's lack of clear thought and the fact that he had still to develop a project proposal. The project tutor suggested that Steve's perspective of the industry appeared to be extremely vague, and asked him to define his intended project area more clearly, thinking not only in terms of the industry but also in relation to academic theories and research in the area of company consolidation. He also said that Steve must think carefully about the research strategy and data collection techniques he was going to use, keeping in mind that it was a course requirement to collect some primary data for the project. They then spent 15 minutes discussing what Steve's research proposal should look like. At the end of the meeting Steve's project tutor asked him to produce a clearly thought proposal prior to their next tutorial, arguing that, until this was done, there was little point in their meeting again.

Questions

1 From the information collected by Steve on the brewing industry, suggest at least two possible research questions.

2 What criteria would you use to assess whether or not these research questions form the basis of a good research topic?

3 How do you think Steve should address the requirement for collecting at least some primary data?

4 Outline the structure that Steve's research proposal should take, indicating:
  a those areas where Steve will need to do more work;
  b how the content will be formulated to address one of the titles you have chosen at question 1.

5 Outline a possible research timescale for Steve's project, taking into account your answers to question 4.

6 What lessons can you learn from Steve's first meeting with his project tutor?

self-check Answers

2.1 There are numerous reasons you could include in your answer. Some of the more important include:

- without being clear what you are going to do it is difficult to plan your research;
- to enable you to choose the most appropriate research strategy and data collection and analysis techniques;
- to ensure that your topic meets the examining body's requirements;
- to ensure that your topic is one that you are capable of doing and excites your imagination;
- to ensure that you will have sufficient time and money resources to undertake your topic;
- to ensure that you will be able to gain access to the data you require;
- to ensure that the issues in your topic are capable of being linked to theory.

2.2 One starting point would be to ask your project tutor for suggestions of possible recent review articles or articles containing recommendations for further work that he or she has read. Another would be to browse recent editions of operations management journals such as the *International Journal of Operations & Production Management* for possible research ideas. These would include both statements of the absence of research and unfounded assertions. Recent reports held in your library may also be of use here. You could also scan one or two recently published operations management textbooks for overviews of research that has been undertaken.

2.3 From the description given it would appear that your colleague has considered only rational thinking techniques. It would therefore seem sensible to suggest two creative thinking techniques, as these would hopefully generate an idea that would appeal to his heart. One technique that you could suggest is brainstorming, perhaps emphasising the need to do it with other colleagues. Exploring past projects in the accountancy area would be another possibility. You might also suggest that he keeps a notebook of ideas.

2.4 Your answer will probably differ from that below. However, the sorts of things you could be considering include:

1 How do business organisations benefit from their liaison with schools?
2 Why do business organisations undertake school liaison activities?
3 To what degree do business organisations receive value for money in their schools liaison activities?

2.5 Undoubtedly organisations would be looking for a 'pay-off'. This may be left undefined: that it is bound to be a 'good thing' or it may be linked to a specific theory that it will create an image of the organisation as one that is community minded. This is a particularly important concept if the product or service is one that has community values, for example water or electricity.

2.6 Try including a subsection in the background section that is headed 'how the previous published research has informed my research questions and objectives'. Then show how, say, a gap in the previous research that is there because nobody has pursued a particular approach before has led to you filling that gap.

Chapter 3

Critically reviewing the literature

By the end of this chapter you should:

- understand the importance and purpose of the critical literature review to your research project;
- know what you need to include when writing your critical review;
- be aware of the range of primary, secondary and tertiary literature sources available;
- be able to identify key words and to undertake a literature search using a range of paper-based and electronic methods including the Internet;
- be able to evaluate the relevance and sufficiency of the literature found;
- be able to reference the literature found accurately;
- be able to apply the knowledge, skills and understanding gained to your own research project.

3.1 Introduction

Two major reasons exist for reviewing the literature (Sharp and Howard, 1996). The first, the preliminary search that helps you to generate and refine your research ideas, has already been discussed in Section 2.3. The second, often referred to as the *critical review*, is part of your research project proper. Most research textbooks, as well as your project tutor, will argue that this critical review of the literature is necessary. Although you may feel that you already have a good knowledge of your research area, we believe that reviewing the literature is essential. Project assessment criteria usually require you to demonstrate awareness of the current state of knowledge in your subject, its limitations, and how your research fits in this wider context (Gill and Johnson, 1997). In Jankowicz's (2000:159) words:

> Knowledge doesn't exist in a vacuum, and your work only has value in relation to other people's. Your work and your findings will be significant only to the extent that they're the same as, or different from, other people's work and findings.

You therefore need to establish what research has been published in your chosen area and try to identify any other research that might currently be in progress. The items you read and write about will enhance your subject knowledge and help you to clarify your research question(s) further. This process is called *critically reviewing the literature*.

For most research projects, your literature search will be an early activity. Despite this early start, it is usually necessary to continue searching throughout your project's life. The process can be likened to an upward spiral, culminating in the final draft of a written critical literature review (Figure 3.1). In the initial stage of your literature review, you will start to define the parameters to your research question(s) and objectives (Section 3.4). After generating key words and conducting your first search (Section 3.5), you will have a list of references to authors who have published on these subjects. Once these have been obtained, you can read and evaluate them (Section 3.6), record the ideas (Section 3.7), and start drafting your review. After the initial search, you will be able to redefine your parameters more precisely and undertake further searches, keeping in mind your research question(s) and objectives. As your thoughts develop, each subsequent search will be focused more precisely on material that is likely to be relevant. At the same time, you will probably be refining your research question(s) and objectives in the light of your reading (Section 2.4).

Unlike some academic disciplines, business and management research makes use of a wide range of literature. While your review is likely to include specific business disciplines such as finance, marketing and human resource management, it is also likely to include other disciplines. Those most frequently consulted by our students include economics, psychology, sociology and geography. Given this, and the importance of the review to your research, it is vital for you to be aware of what a critical literature review is and the full range of literature available before you start the reviewing process. For these reasons, we start this chapter by outlining what your critical review of the literature needs to include (Section 3.2) and the literature resources available (Section 3.3).

3.2 The critical review

The purpose of the critical review

Your critical literature review will form the foundation on which your research is built. As you will have gathered from the introduction, its main purpose is to help you to develop a good understanding and insight into relevant previous research and the trends that have emerged. You would not expect a scientific researcher inquiring into the causes of cot death to start his or her research without first reading about the findings of other cot death research. Likewise you should not expect to start your research without first reading what other researchers in your area have already found out.

The precise purpose of your reading of the literature will depend on the approach you are intending to use in your research. For some research projects you will use the literature to help you to identify theories and ideas that you will test using data. This is known as a *deductive approach* (Section 4.1) in which you develop a theoretical or conceptual framework, which you subsequently test using data. For other research

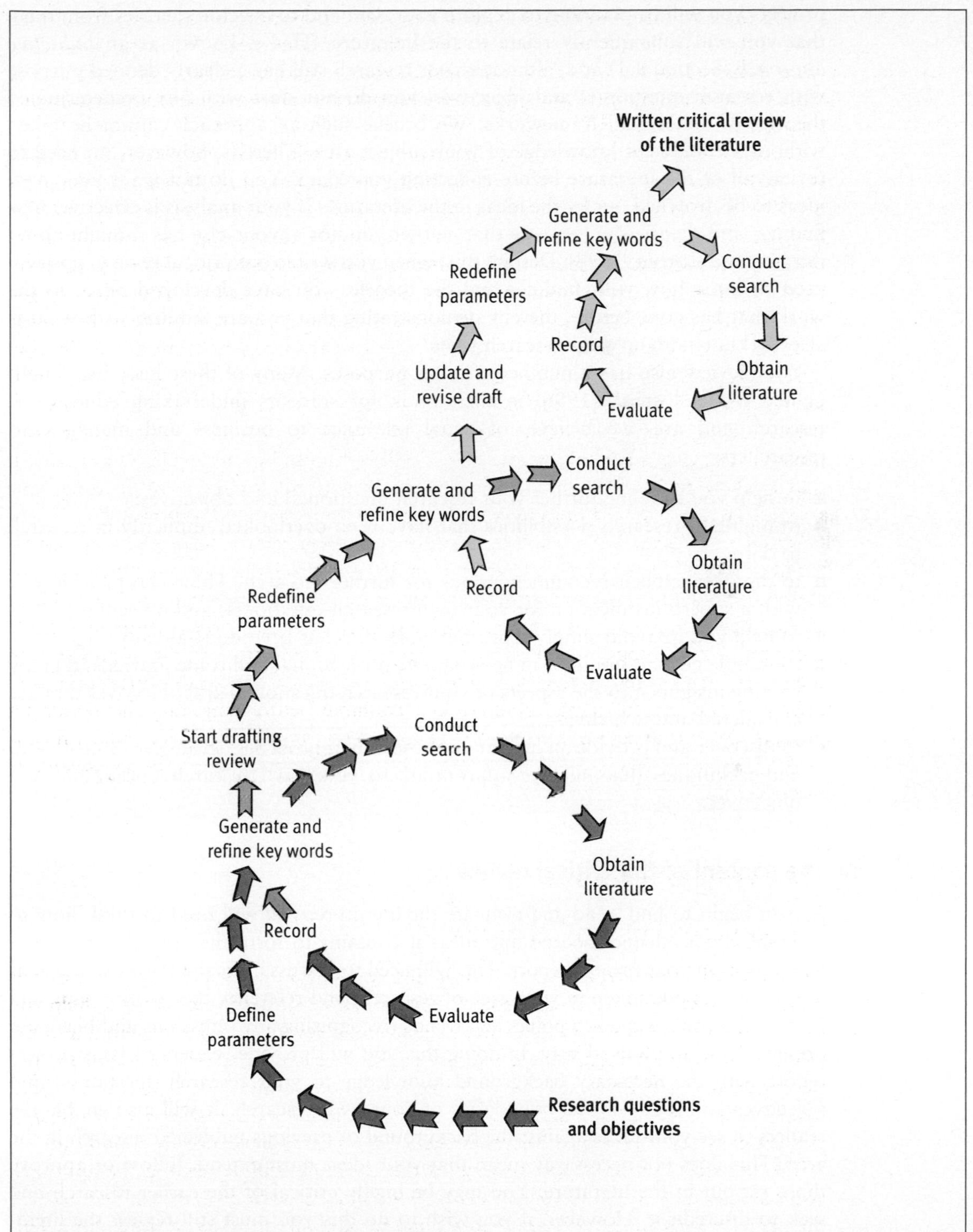

Figure 3.1 The literature review process

projects you will be planning to explore your data and to develop theories from them that you will subsequently relate to the literature. This is known as an *inductive approach* (Section 4.1) and, although your research still has a clearly defined purpose with research question(s) and objectives, you do not start with any predetermined theories or conceptual frameworks. We believe such an approach cannot be taken without a competent knowledge of your subject area. There is, however, no need to review all of the literature before collecting your data. You do not want your own ideas to be drowned out by the ideas in the literature. If your analysis is effective, new findings and theories will emerge that neither you nor anyone else has thought about (Strauss and Corbin, 1998). Despite this, when you write your critical review, you will need to show how your findings and the theories you have developed relate to the work that has gone before, thereby demonstrating that you are familiar with what is already known about your research topic.

Your review also has a number of other purposes. Many of these have been highlighted by Gall *et al.* (1996) in their book for students undertaking educational research and are, we believe, of equal relevance to business and management researchers:

- to help you to refine further your research question(s) and objectives;
- to highlight research possibilities that have been overlooked implicitly in research to date;
- to discover explicit recommendations for further research. These can provide you with a superb justification for your own research question(s) and objectives;
- to help you to avoid simply repeating work that has been done already;
- to sample current opinions in newspapers, professional and trade journals, thereby gaining insights into the aspects of your research question(s) and objectives that are considered newsworthy;
- to discover and provide an insight into research approaches, strategies (Section 4.2) and techniques that may be appropriate to your own research question(s) and objectives.

The content of the critical review

As you begin to find, read and evaluate the literature, you will need to think how to combine the academic theories and ideas it contains to form the critical review that will appear in your project report. This will need to discuss critically the work that has already been undertaken in your area of research, and reference that work (Appendix 2). It will draw out the key points and trends (recognising any omissions and bias) and present them in a logical way. In doing this you will provide readers of your project report with the necessary background knowledge to your research question(s) and objectives and establish the boundaries of your own research. It will also enable the readers to see your ideas against the background of previous published research in the area. This does not necessarily mean that your ideas must extend, follow or approve those set out in the literature. You may be highly critical of the earlier research and seek to discredit it. However, if you wish to do this you must still review the literature, argue clearly why it is problematic, and then justify your own ideas.

In writing your critical review you will therefore need:

- to include the key academic theories within your chosen area;
- to demonstrate that your knowledge of your chosen area is up to date;
- to show how your research relates to previous published research;
- to assess the strengths and weaknesses of previous work, including omissions or bias, and take these into account in your arguments;
- to justify your arguments by referencing previous research;
- through clear referencing, to enable those reading your project report to find the original work you cite.

In addition, by fully acknowledging the work of others you will avoid charges of *plagiarism* and the associated penalties.

What is meant by 'critical'

Within the context of reviewing the literature, the term 'critical' refers to the judgement you exercise. It therefore describes the process of providing a detailed and justified analysis of and commentary on the merits and faults of the key literature within your chosen area. This means that, for your review to be critical, you will need to develop critical judgement. Dees (2000) suggests that this means you should:

- refer to work by recognised experts in your chosen area;
- consider and discuss work that supports and work that opposes your ideas;
- make reasoned judgements regarding the value of others' work to your research;
- support your arguments with valid evidence in a logical manner;
- distinguish clearly between fact and opinion.

The structure of the critical review

The literature review that you write for your project report should therefore be a description and critical analysis of what other authors have written (Jankowicz, 2000). When drafting your review you therefore need to focus on your research question(s) and objectives. One way of helping you to focus is to think of your literature review as discussing how far the literature goes in answering your research question(s). The shortfall in the literature will be addressed, at least partially, in the remainder of your project report. Another way of helping you to focus is to ask yourself how your review relates to your objectives. If it does not, or does only partially, there is a need for a clearer focus on your objectives. The precise structure of the critical review is usually your choice, although you should check, as your examining body may specify it. Three common structures are:

- a single chapter;
- a series of chapters;
- throughout the project report as you tackle various issues.

In all project reports, you should return to the key issues from the literature in your conclusions (Section 13.3).

Within your critical review, you will need to juxtapose different authors' ideas and form your own opinions and conclusions based on these. Although you will not be able to start writing until you have undertaken some reading, we recommend that you start drafting your review early (Figure 3.1). What you write can then be updated and revised as you read more.

A common mistake with critical literature reviews is that they become uncritical listings of previous research, often being little more than annotated bibliographies (Hart, 1998). Haywood and Wragg (1982:2, cited by Bell 1999:92) describe this adeptly as:

> . . . the furniture sale catalogue, in which everything merits a one paragraph entry no matter how skilfully it has been conducted: Bloggs (1975) found this, Smith (1976) found that, Jones (1977) found the other, Bloggs, Smith and Jones (1978) found happiness in heaven.

Although there is no single structure that your critical review should take, our students have found it useful to think of the review as a funnel in which you:

1. start at a more general level before narrowing down to your specific research question(s) and objectives;
2. provide a brief overview of key ideas;
3. summarise, compare and contrast the work of the key writers;
4. narrow down to highlight the work most relevant to your research;
5. provide a detailed account of the findings of this work;
6. highlight those issues where your research will provide fresh insights;
7. lead the reader into subsequent sections of your project report, which explore these issues.

Whichever way you structure your review you must demonstrate that you have read, understood and evaluated the items you have located. The key to writing a critical literature review is therefore to link together the different ideas you find in the literature to form a coherent and cohesive argument, which set in context and justify your research. Obviously, it should relate to your research question and objectives. It should show a clear link from these as well as a clear link to the empirical work that will follow. Box 3.1 provides a checklist to help you do this. Subsequent parts of your project report (Section 13.3) must follow on from this 'seamlessly as a continuation of the argument' (Jankowicz, 2000:161).

Box 3.1 Checklist for evaluating your literature review

- ✓ Does your review start at a more general level before narrowing down?
- ✓ Does the literature covered relate clearly to your research question and objectives?
- ✓ Have you covered the key theories of recognised experts in the area?
- ✓ Have you covered the key literature or at least a representative sample?
- ✓ Are those issues highlighted where your research will provide fresh insights?
- ✓ Is the literature you have included up to date?
- ✓ Have you been objective in your discussion and assessment of other people's work?
- ✓ Have you included references that are counter to your own opinion?
- ✓ Have you distinguished clearly between facts and opinions?

- ✓ Have you made reasoned judgements about the value of others' work to your own?
- ✓ Have you justified clearly your own ideas?
- ✓ Is your argument coherent and cohesive – do the ideas link together?
- ✓ Does your review lead the reader into subsequent sections of your project report?

Sources: Authors' experience; Higgins (1996); Dees (2000)

worked example

A critical review of the literature

An article published by Mark and Christine in the *Journal of European Industrial Training* (Saunders and Williams, 2000:220–21) includes a short review of the literature on measures of service quality. The following extract from this review illustrates:

- the overall structure of starting at a more general level before narrowing down;
- the provision of a brief overview of the key ideas;
- narrowing down to highlight that work which is most relevant to the research reported in the paper;
- providing more detail about the findings of that work which is most relevant.

Traditional measures of service quality (for example Parasuraman *et al.*, 1985) focus on measurement of the gap between service users' perceptions and expectations across a series of dimensions that characterise the service. Notwithstanding shortcomings of conceptualising service quality in this manner, recognised in the SERVQUAL debates (for example Carmen, 1990; Cronin and Taylor, 1992; Van Dyke *et al.*, 1997), the use of such a disconfirmation approach is widely reported in the literature (for example: Robinson, 1999).

The number and nature of constructs, which represent the service encounter, are a function of a service relationship in a particular industry or situation. Each of these relationships differs and is, in reality, unique. Gummesson (1994) identifies a series of general qualities characterising relationships such as collaboration, dependency, trust, power, longevity, frequency, closeness, content, as well as personal and social properties. In so doing, he emphasises the breadth of properties that may be deemed relevant by the parties involved in a particular service relationship. However, it is unlikely that all of these properties are of similar relevance to every relationship. Consequently it has been argued that a series of generic dimensions against which to measure service quality is inappropriate (Carmen, 1990). In a review of quality, as one of the primary outcome measures of service relationships, Rosen and Supernant (1998) support this view. They conclude that global measures of service quality (such as SERVQUAL) may not provide the details necessary to assess the strengths and weaknesses of a relationship. In particular, they may fail to take account of the uniqueness and the realities of specific relationships and how they are interpreted and expressed by the parties involved.

Research has also highlighted that interdependencies between organisations are established and maintained through the encounters and interactions of individuals within each organisation (de Burca, 1995). The measurement of the quality of such encounters therefore needs to reflect the perspectives of all these individuals. Rosen and Supernant (1998) suggest that traditional measures fail to reflect fully the dyadic nature of service encounters as they generally assess the quality construct from only one partner's point of view. They call for the evaluation of service relationships to accommodate this by including the perspectives of both parties. Although they suggest that this may result in the need to reconcile different views, they also highlight the need for awareness and understanding of the views of all parties involved in a service encounter. We would contend that these processes could result in both parties involved in the service questioning the relevance of the norms against which they evaluate the encounter. This, we believe,

▶

supports our contention that approaches which have the ability to capture a diversity of service users' and providers' experiences of such concepts, are likely to be of more value. Furthermore, we have argued that where measures focus only on specific transactions, they may fail to take account of the ongoing nature of service relationships that are based upon repeated encounters (Williams *et al.*, 1999).

Rosen and Supernant (1998) support Smith's (1995) arguments when they point to the shortcomings of the global nature of the quality construct as a diagnostic tool for remedial action. This implies that the assessment of the relationship's quality should lead to action to enhance the benefits obtained by both parties from it. Data collected to assess quality should therefore be useful. In this context, usefulness can be viewed from two key perspectives...

3.3 Literature sources available

An overview

The literature sources available to help you to develop a good understanding of and insight into previous research can be divided into three categories: primary (published and unpublished), secondary, and tertiary (Figure 3.2). In reality these categories often overlap: for example, primary literature sources including conference proceedings can appear in journals, and some books contain indexes to primary and secondary literature.

The different categories of literature resources represent the flow of information from the original source. Often as information flows from primary to secondary to tertiary sources it becomes less detailed and authoritative but more easily accessible. It is because primary sources can be difficult to trace that they are sometimes referred

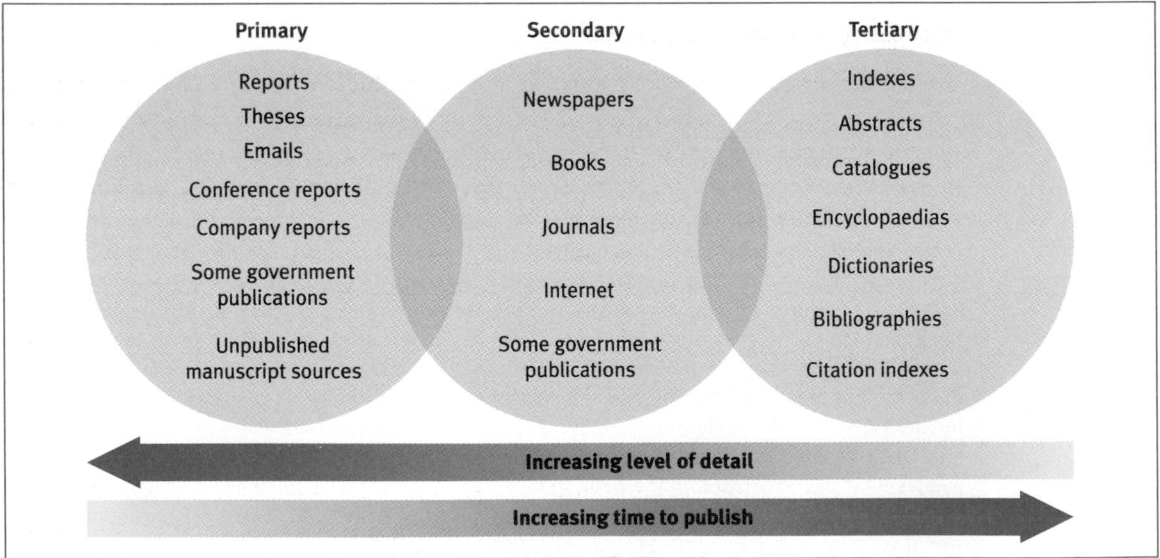

Figure 3.2 Literature sources available

to as *grey literature*. Recognising this information flow helps you to identify the most appropriate sources of information for your needs. Some research projects may access only secondary information sources whereas others will necessitate the use of primary sources.

Figure 3.2 also illustrates the reduced currency of secondary sources, which are utilising information already published in primary sources. Because of the time taken to publish, the information in these sources can be dated. Your literature review should reflect current thinking as far as possible, so the limitations of such sources must be recognised.

Primary literature sources (also known as grey literature) are the first occurrence of a piece of work. They include published sources such as reports and some central and local government publications such as White Papers and planning documents. They also include unpublished manuscript sources such as letters, memos and committee minutes that may be analysed as data in their own right (Section 7.2).

Secondary literature sources such as books and journals are the subsequent publication of primary literature. These publications are aimed at a wider audience. They are easier to locate than primary literature as they are better covered by the tertiary literature.

Tertiary literature sources, also called *search tools*, are designed either to help to locate primary and secondary literature or to introduce a topic. They therefore include indexes and abstracts as well as encyclopaedias and bibliographies.

Your use of these literature sources will depend on your research question(s) and objectives, the need for secondary data to answer them (Section 7.3), and the time available. For some research projects you may use only tertiary and secondary literature; for others you may need to locate primary literature as well. Most research projects will make the greatest use of secondary literature, and so it is this we consider first, followed by the primary literature. Tertiary literature sources are not discussed until Section 3.5, as their major use is in conducting a literature search.

Secondary literature sources

The number of secondary literature sources available to you is expanding rapidly, especially as new resources are developed or made available via the Internet. Your university's librarians are likely to be aware of a wide range of secondary literature in business and management that can be accessed from your library, and will keep themselves up to date with new resources.

The main secondary literature sources that you are likely to use, along with those primary sources most frequently used for a literature review, are outlined in Table 3.1. The most important when placing your ideas in the context of earlier research are refereed academic journals. Books are, however, likely to be more important than professional and trade journals in this context.

Journals

Journals are also known as *periodicals*, *serials* and *magazines*, and are published on a regular basis. At present, although most are printed, they are appearing increasingly in electronic form as well via the Internet. Journals are a vital literature source for any research. The articles in them are easily accessible as they are well covered by tertiary literature, and a good selection is kept for reference in most university libraries (Table 3.1). However, trade and some professional journals may be covered only partially by the tertiary literature (see Table 3.2). You therefore need to browse these journals regularly to be sure of finding useful items. Increasingly, journals' content pages can also be browsed via the Internet (Section 3.5).

Articles in *refereed academic journals* (such as the *Journal of Management Studies*) are evaluated by academic peers prior to publication to assess their quality and suitability. These are usually the most useful for research projects as they will contain detailed reports of relevant earlier research. Not all academic journals are refereed. Most *other academic journals* will have an editor and possibly an editorial board with subject knowledge to select articles. The relevance and usefulness of such journals varies considerably, and occasionally you may need to be wary of possible bias (Section 3.6).

Professional journals (such as *People Management*) are produced for their members by organisations such as the Chartered Institute of Personnel and Development, The Institute of Chartered Accountants and the American Marketing Association. They contain a mix of news-related items and articles that are more detailed. However, you need to exercise caution, as articles can be biased towards their author's or the organisation's views. Articles are often of a more practical nature and more closely related to professional needs than those in academic journals. Some organisations will also produce newsletters or current awareness publications that you may find useful for up-to-date information. Some professional organisations now give access to selected articles in their journals via their web pages (see Table 7.2 and Section 3.5). *Trade journals* fulfil a similar function to professional journals. They are published by trade organisations or aimed at particular industries or trades such as catering or mining. Often they focus on new products or services and news items. They rarely contain articles based on empirical research although some provide summaries of research.

Books

Books or *monographs* are written for a specific audience. Some are aimed at the academic market, with a theoretical slant. Others, aimed at practising professionals, may be more applied in their content. The material in books is usually presented in a more ordered and accessible manner than in journals, pulling together a wider range of topics. They are therefore particularly useful as introductory sources to help clarify your research question(s) and objectives or the research methods you intend to use. Beware: books may contain out-of-date material even by the time they are published. Some academic textbooks, such as this one, are now supported by web pages providing additional information.

Newspapers

Newspapers are a good source of topical events, developments within business and government, and recent statistical information such as share prices. They also produce special reports such as the *Financial Times* industrial sector reports. The main broadsheet newspapers have web sites carrying the main stories and supporting information. Back copies starting in the early 1990s are available on CD-ROM or on line

Table 3.1 **Main secondary and primary literature sources**

Source	*Frequency of publication*	*Format of publication*	*Coverage by abstracts and indexes (tertiary sources)*	*Likely availability*
Refereed academic journal **Other academic journal**	Mainly monthly or quarterly	Mainly printed but many now available on the Internet. Can be also available on CD-ROM and microfiche	Well covered	Kept as reference in most university libraries. Those not available locally can usually be obtained using inter-library loans or, increasingly, via the Internet. Professional organisations may also provide access to their journals via their own web pages
Professional journal	Mainly weekly or monthly		Not as good as academic and refereed journals, will probably need to browse actual copies of journal	
Trade journal				Not as widely available in university libraries as academic and refereed journals. Can be obtained using inter-library loans
Books	Once; subsequent editions may be published	As for refereed academic journals	Well covered by abstracts and indexes. Searches can be undertaken on remote university OPACs* via the Internet	Widely available. Those not available locally can be obtained using inter-library loans
Newspapers	Mainly daily or weekly	All UK broadsheets now available on the Internet or through subscription on-line databases. Also available on CD-ROM and microfilm. Many international broadsheets are available via the Internet	Specialised indexes available. CD-ROM and Internet format easy to search using key words	Home nation broadsheets kept as reference in most university libraries. Internet access to stories, often with additional information on the web sites with most national and international broadsheets
Conference proceedings	Dependent on the conference, sometimes as part of a journal	As for refereed academic journals. May be published in book form. Some conference proceedings or abstracts are published on the Internet.	Depends on conference although often limited. Specialist indexes sometimes available	Not widely held by university libraries. May be possible to obtain using inter-library loans
Reports	Once	As for refereed academic journals	Poor compared with most secondary sources although some specialised indexes exist	
Theses	On the awarding of the research degree	Mainly printed but increasingly available on microfiche	Good for PhD and MPhil research degrees, otherwise poor	Usually obtained using inter-library loans. Often only one copy

*OPAC, Online Public Access Catalogue

in most university libraries (Table 3.1). Consequently finding items in these newspapers is quick and easy. Items in earlier issues are more difficult to access, as they are usually stored on microfilm and need to be located using printed indexes. However, you need to be careful, as newspapers may contain bias in their coverage, be it political, geographical or personal. Reporting can also be inaccurate, and you may not pick up any subsequent amendments. In addition the news presented is filtered depending on events at the time, with priority given to more headline-grabbing stories (Stewart and Kamins, 1993).

Primary literature sources

Primary literature sources are more difficult to locate (Table 3.1). The most accessible, and those most likely to be of use in showing how your research relates to that of other people, are reports, conference proceedings and theses.

Reports

Reports include market research reports such as those produced by Mintel and Keynote, government reports and academic reports. Even if you are able to locate these, you may find it difficult to gain access to them as they are not as widely available as books (Section 7.4). Reports are not well indexed in the tertiary literature, and you will need to rely on specific search tools such *British National Bibliography for Report Literature* and the British Library Public Catalogue (see Table 3.2).

Individual academics are also increasingly publishing reports and their research on the Internet. These can be a useful source of information. However, they may not have gone through the same review and evaluation process as journal articles and books. It is therefore important to try to assess the authority of the author, and to beware of personal bias.

Conference proceedings

Conference proceedings, sometimes referred to as *symposia,* are often published as unique titles within journals or as books. Most conferences will have a theme that is very specific, but some have a wide-ranging overview. Proceedings are not well indexed by tertiary literature so, as with reports, you may have to rely on specific search tools such as *Index to Conference Proceedings* and the British Library Public Catalogue (see Table 3.2). If you do locate and are able to obtain the proceedings for a conference on the theme of your research, you will have a wealth of relevant information. Many conferences have associated web pages providing abstracts and occasionally the full papers presented at the conference.

Theses

Theses are unique and so for a major research project can be a good source of detailed information; they will also be a good source of further references. Unfortunately, they can be difficult to locate and, when found, difficult to access as there may be only one copy at the awarding institution. Specific search tools are available such as *Index to Theses* and *British National Bibliography for Report Literature* (see Table 3.2). Only research degrees such as PhD and MPhil are covered well by these tertiary resources. Research undertaken as part of a taught masters degree is not covered as systematically.

3.4 Planning the literature search

It is important that you plan this search carefully to ensure that you locate relevant and up-to-date literature. This will enable you to establish what research has been previously published in your area and to relate your own research to it. All our students have found their literature search a time-consuming process, which takes far longer than expected. Fortunately, time spent planning will be repaid in time saved when searching the literature. As you start to plan your search, you need to beware of information overload! One of the easiest ways to achieve this is to start the main search for your critical review without a clearly defined research question(s), objectives and outline proposal (Sections 2.4 and 2.5). Before commencing your literature search, we suggest that you undertake further planning by:

- defining the parameters of your search;
- generating key words and search terms;
- discussing your ideas as widely as possible.

Defining parameters

For most research questions and objectives you will have a good idea of which subject matter is going to be relevant. You will, however, be less clear about the parameters within which you need to search. In particular you need to be clear about the (Bell, 1999):

- language of publication (for example English);
- subject area (for example accountancy);
- business sector (for example manufacturing);
- geographical area (for example Europe);
- publication period (for example the last 10 years);
- literature type (for example refereed journals and books).

One way of starting to firm up these parameters is to re-examine your lecture notes and course textbooks in the area of your research question. While re-examining these, we suggest you make a note of subjects that appear most relevant to your research question and the names of relevant authors. These will be helpful when generating possible key words later.

For example, if your research was on the marketing benefits of arts sponsorship to UK banking organisations you might identify the subject area as marketing and sponsorship. Implicit in this is the need to think broadly. A common comment we hear from students who have attempted a literature search is 'there's nothing written on my research topic'. This is usually because they have identified one or more of their parameters too narrowly (or chosen key words that do not match the control language, Section 3.5). We therefore recommend that if you encounter this problem you broaden one or more of your parameters to include material that your narrower search would not have located.

worked example

Defining parameters for a research question

Simon's research question was 'How have green issues influenced the way in which manufacturers advertise cars?' To be certain of finding material he defined each parameter in narrow and, in most instances, broader terms:

Parameter	*Narrow*	*Broader*
Language	UK (e.g. car)	UK and USA (e.g. car and automobile)
Subject area	Green issues Motor industry Advertising	Environmental issues Manufacturing Marketing
Business sector	Motor industry	Manufacturing
Geographical area	UK	Europe and North America
Publication period	Last 5 years	Last 15 years
Literature type	Academic journals and books	Journals and books

Generating key words

Undertaking reading of articles by key authors and recent review articles in your research area is also important at this stage. It will help you to define your subject matter and to suggest appropriate key words. Recent *review articles* are often helpful here. Their discussion of the current state of research for a particular topic will help you to refine your key words. In addition, they will probably contain references to other work that is pertinent to your research question(s) and objectives. If you are unsure about review articles, your project tutor should be able to point you in the right direction. Another potentially useful source of references is dissertations and theses in your university's library.

After rereading your lecture notes and textbooks and undertaking the limited reading you will have a list of subjects that appear relevant to your research project. You now need to define precisely what is relevant to your research in terms of key words.

The identification of *key words* or *search terms* is the most important part of planning your search for relevant literature (Bell, 1999). Key words are the basic terms that describe your research question(s) and objectives, and will be used to search the tertiary literature. Key words (which can include authors' surnames identified in the examination of your lecture notes and course textbooks) can be identified using one or a number of different techniques in combination. Those found most useful by our students include:

- discussion with colleagues, your project tutor and librarians;
- initial reading;
- dictionaries, thesauruses, encyclopaedias and handbooks;
- brainstorming;
- relevance trees.

Discussion

We believe you should be taking every opportunity to discuss your research. In discussing your work with others, whether face to face, by email or by letter, you will be sharing your ideas, getting feedback and obtaining new ideas and approaches.

Initial reading, dictionaries, encyclopaedias, handbooks and thesauruses

To produce the most relevant key words you may need to build on your brainstorming session with support materials such as *dictionaries*, *encyclopaedias*, *handbooks* and *thesauruses*, both general and subject specific. These are also good starting points for new topics with which you may be unfamiliar and for related subject areas. Initial reading, particularly of recent review articles, may also be of help here. Project tutors, colleagues and librarians can also be useful sources of ideas.

Brainstorming

Brainstorming has already been outlined as a technique for helping you to develop your research question (Section 2.3). However, it is also helpful for generating key words. Either individually or as part of a group, you write down all the words and short phrases that come to mind on your research topic. These are then evaluated and key words (and phrases) selected.

worked example

Generating key words

Han's research question was 'How do the actual management requirements of a school pupil record administration system differ from those suggested by the literature?' She brainstormed this question with her peer group, all of whom were teachers in Hong Kong. The resulting list included the following key words and phrases:

> *schools, pupil records, administration, user requirements, computer, management information system, access, legislation, information, database, security, UK, Hong Kong, theories*

The group evaluated these and others. As a result, the following key words (and phrases) were selected:

> *pupil records, management information system, computer, database, user requirement*

Dictionaries and encyclopaedias were used subsequently to add to the choice of key words:

> *student record, MIS, security*

These were then used in combination to search the tertiary literature sources.

Relevance trees

Relevance trees provide a useful method of bringing some form of structure to your literature search and of guiding your search process (Sharp and Howard, 1996). They look similar to an organisation chart and are a hierarchical 'graph-like' arrangement of headings and subheadings. These headings and subheadings describe your research question(s) and objectives and may be key words (including authors' names) with which you can search. Relevance trees are often constructed after brainstorming. They enable you to decide either with help or on your own (Jankowicz, 2000):

- which key words are directly relevant to your research question(s) and objectives;
- which areas you will search first and which your search will use later;
- which areas are more important – these tend to have more branches.

To construct a relevance tree you:

1. Start with your research question or objective at the top level.
2. Identify two or more subject areas that you think are important.
3. Further subdivide each major subject area into subareas that you think are of relevance.
4. Further divide the subareas into more precise subareas that you think are of relevance.
5. Identify those areas that you need to search immediately and those that you particularly need to focus on. Your project tutor will be of particular help here.
6. As your reading and reviewing progress, add new areas to your relevance tree.

worked example

Using a relevance tree

Jemma's research question asked 'Is there a link between benchmarking and Total Quality Management?' After brainstorming her question, she decided to construct a relevance tree using the key words and phrases that had been generated:

Using her relevance tree Jemma identified those areas that she needed to search immediately (underlined) and those that she particularly needed to focus on (starred*).

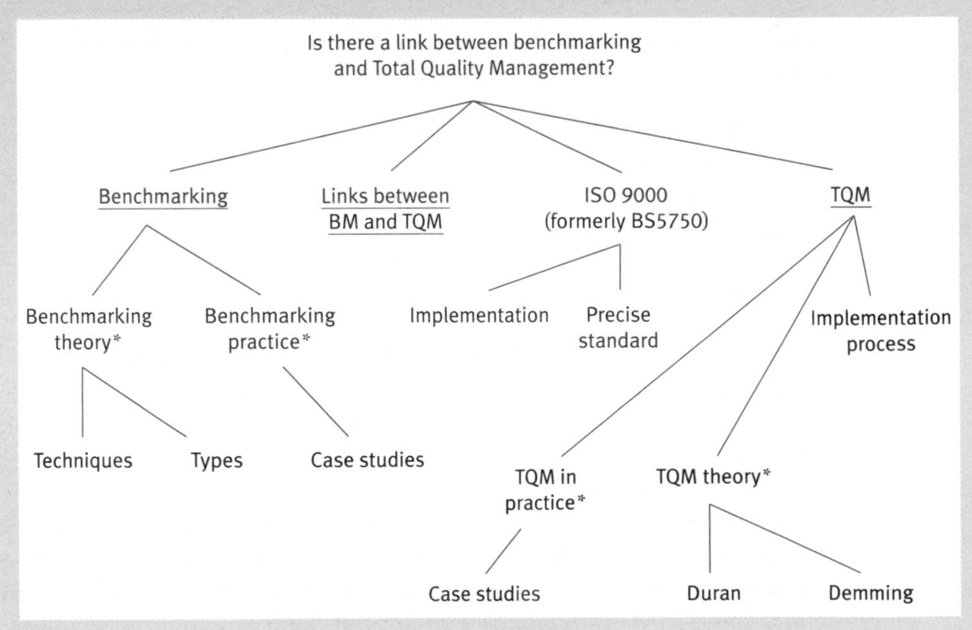

3.5 Conducting the literature search

Your literature search will probably be conducted using a variety of approaches:

- searching using tertiary literature sources;
- obtaining relevant literature (Section 3.6) referenced in books and journal articles you have already read;
- scanning and browsing secondary literature in your library;
- searching using the Internet.

Eventually you will be using a variety of these in combination. However, we suggest that you start your search by obtaining relevant literature that has been referenced in books and articles you have already read. Although books are unlikely to give adequate up-to-date coverage of your research question they provide a useful starting point and usually contain some references to further reading. Reading these will enable you to refine your research question(s), objectives and the associated key words prior to searching using tertiary literature sources. It will also help you to see more clearly how your research relates to previous research, and will provide fresh insights.

Tertiary literature sources

A variety of tertiary literature is available to help you in your search. Most of these publications are called indexes and abstracts, and a selection will be accessible via the Internet or held by your university library. An *index* will, as its name suggests, index articles from a range of journals and sometimes books, chapters from books, reports, theses, conferences and research. The information provided will be sufficient to locate the item – for example, for journal articles:

- author or authors of the article;
- date of publication;
- title of the article;
- title of the journal;
- volume and part number of the journal issue;
- page numbers of the article.

Most index searches will be undertaken to find articles using key words, including the author's name. Occasionally you may wish to search by finding those authors who have referenced (cited) a key article after it has been published. A *citation index* enables you to do this as it lists by author the other authors who have cited that author's publications subsequent to their publication.

An *abstract* provides the same information as an index but also includes a summary of the article, hence the term abstract. This abstract can be useful in helping you to assess the content and relevance of an article to your research before obtaining a copy. You should beware of using abstracts, as a substitute for the full article, as a source of information for your research. They contain only a summary of the article and are likely to exclude much of relevance.

Indexes and abstracts are produced in printed and electronic (computerised) formats, the latter often being referred to as *databases*. This is the term we shall use to refer to all electronic information sources. With the increasing amount of information available electronically, printed indexes and abstracts may be overlooked. Yet they are still a valuable resource, providing a varied and sometimes more specific range of information. Searching printed sources and databases is normally free, although some libraries may charge for printing from electronic databases. One way round this is to take a computer disk on which to save the results of your search. This can subsequently be read into your word-processing software. Increasingly you may also be able to email the results of your search to your chosen email account to be accessed later.

Access to the majority of external databases that you will use via the Internet will be paid for by a subscription from your university. There are though some pay-as-you-use databases, where the costs of the search may be passed on to the user. *On-line databases* provide a wealth of information. They may be updated daily or even several times during one day, an advantage over CD-ROM databases that are usually updated quarterly. It is advisable to obtain a librarian's help or to attend a training session prior to using on-line databases because of the variety of software and the volume of information. It is also vital to have planned and prepared your search in advance so your time is not wasted. With the development of the Internet, many databases can now be accessed using this technology. For some databases, access may be possible from remote sites such as home or work as well as from your university. Some use a generic username and password specific to your university, although an increasing number use the ATHENS service. To gain access via the Internet you will need either your university's specific username and password or to set up an ATHENS account. Your librarian should have more information on this. An additional source of information via the Internet, which our students have found useful, is publishers' web pages. These often include journals' content pages (see Table 3.4).

Most university OPACs (library catalogues) are now accessible via the Internet (see Table 3.5). These provide a very useful means of locating resources. If you identify useful collections of books and journals, it is possible to make use of other university libraries in the vacations. The SCONUL Vacation Access Scheme gives details of access policies of the libraries in UK higher-education institutions. Details of these can be found on the Internet at http://www.sconul.ac.uk/vacation.html. In addition your university may be part of the UK Libraries Plus scheme, a cooperative venture allowing part-time, distance and placement students to borrow resources from their local university libraries and full-time students access rights for reference. Your librarian should have more information on this. Alternatively, look on the Internet at http://www.roehampton.ac.uk/uklibrariesplus/index.html.

To ensure maximum coverage in your search you need to use all appropriate abstracts and indexes. One mistake many people make is to restrict their searches to one or two business and management tertiary sources rather than to use a variety. The coverage of each abstract and index differs both in geographical coverage and type of journals (Section 3.3). In addition an abstract or index may state that it indexes a particular journal yet may do so only selectively. This emphasises the importance of using a range of databases to ensure a wide coverage of available literature. Some of those more frequently used are outlined in Table 3.2. However, new databases are being developed all the time so it is worth asking a librarian for advice.

Table 3.2 **Tertiary literature sources and their coverage**

Name	*Format*	*Coverage*
ABI Inform	Internet, CD-ROM	Indexes approximately 1000 international business and management journals. Also covers subjects such as engineering, law and medicine. Full text of selected articles from 500 journals may be available depending on subscription (CD-ROM updated monthly)
BIDS	Internet	Includes access to a wide range of services including journals contents pages
British National Bibliography (BNB)	CD-ROM, print	Bibliographic information for books and serials (journals) deposited at the British Library by UK and Irish publishers since 1950
British National Bibliography for Report Literature (formerly British Reports, Translations and Theses)	Microfiche, print	Detailed listings of research and practice reports produced by non-commercial publishers, local and national government, industry, research institutions and charities. Includes UK doctoral theses since 1970
British Library Public Catalogue	Internet	Gives access to British Library catalogues including reference collections and document supply collections (books, journals, reports, conferences, theses)
Business Periodicals Index	Internet, CD-ROM, print	Indexes English language business periodicals (articles and book reviews). North American focus. Selection for indexing is by subscriber preference and has altered over time (since 1959)
EBSCO Business Source Premier	Internet	Full-text articles from over 2000 management, business and economics journals, over 600 of which are refereed
EMERALD Fulltext	Internet	80+ full-text journals from MCB University Press
Emerald Management Reviews	Internet, CD-ROM	Abstracts of articles selected from more than 400 English language publications on the basis of a significant contribution to knowledge
European Business ASAP	Internet, CD-ROM	100 journals, mostly full text. Includes a mix of academic journals and business press
Global Books in Print	Internet	English language bibliographic information for books in print from most of the world!
Helecon	Internet, CD-ROM	Combined indexes from seven European databases on business and management. European focus (updated three times a year)
Index to Conference Proceedings	CD-ROM, on line, print	Indexes all conference publications, regardless of subject or language, held by British Library Document Supply Centre (updated monthly – print, quarterly – CD-ROM)
Index to Theses	Internet, print	Indexes theses accepted for higher degrees by universities in Great Britain and Ireland and by the CNAA
Ingenta	Internet	Journals contents page service, updated daily
ISI Web of Science	Internet	Includes access to a wide range of services including citation indexes
HMSO Monthly Catalogue	Print	Lists all publications published and distributed through HMSO (includes parliamentary, government department and European)
Key Note Reports	Internet	Key Note market information reports
Lexis Nexis Executive	Internet	Worldwide business media database, includes national and regional newspapers, trade journals and company annual reports
MINTEL	Internet, CD-ROM	Mintel reports plus short business press articles used in the compilation of the reports

▶

Table 3.2 Continued

Name	*Format*	*Coverage*
Research Index	Internet, print	Indexes articles and news items of financial interest that appear in the UK national newspapers, professional and trade journals (updated frequently)
Sage Publications/SRM Database of Social Research Methodology	CD-ROM	Abstracts of methodological literature published in English, German, French and Dutch since 1970
Social Science Citation Index	Internet, on line	Indexes 130 000 articles each year from over 1400 journals in behavioural and social sciences and selected articles from 3100 journals from physical and natural sciences

Searching using tertiary literature

Once your key words have been identified, searching using tertiary literature is a relatively straightforward process.

You need:

1 to ensure your key words match the controlled index language (unless you can use free text searching);
2 to search appropriate printed and database sources;
3 to note the full reference of relevant items found.

Printed sources

Searching printed indexes and abstracts requires a different technique from electronic databases. The coverage of printed indexes tends to be smaller and possibly more specialised than that of databases. Unlike databases, it is normally only possible to search by author or one broad subject heading, although some cross-references may be included. Because they are paper based each issue or annual accumulation must be searched individually, which can be time consuming.

Databases

Most databases, in contrast, allow more precise searches using combinations of key words. These key words need to match the database's *controlled index language* of preselected terms and phrases or *descriptors*. If your key words do not match this vocabulary your search will be unsuccessful. Your first stage should therefore be to check your key words with the *index* or *browse* option. This is especially useful for checking how an author is indexed or whether hyphens should be used when entering terms. Some databases will also have a *thesaurus* which links words in the controlled index language to other terms. Some thesauruses will provide a definition of the term used as well as indicating other broader subject areas, more specific subject areas or subjects related to the original term. Despite using these your searches may still be unsuccessful. The most frequent causes of failure are summarised in Box 3.2 as a checklist.

Box 3.2 Checklist for key words

- ✓ Is the spelling incorrect? Behaviour is spelt with a 'u' in the UK but without in the USA
- ✓ Is the language incorrect? Chemists in the UK but drug stores in the USA
- ✓ Are you using incorrect terminology? In recent years some terms have been replaced by others, such as 'redundancy' being replaced by 'downsizing'
- ✓ Are you using acronyms and abbreviations? For example, UK for United Kingdom or ICI instead of Imperial Chemical Industries
- ✓ Are you using jargon rather than accepted terminology? For example, de-recruitment rather than redundancy
- ✓ Are you using a word that is not in the controlled index language?

Once individual key words have been checked, subsequent searches normally use a combination of key words linked using *Boolean logic*. This enables you to combine, limit or widen the variety of items found using *link terms* (Table 3.3). Boolean logic can also be used to construct searches using dates, journal titles and names of organisations or people. Initially it may be useful to limit your search to journal titles held by your library or accessible via the Internet. It may also be valuable to narrow your search to specific years, especially if you are finding a wealth of items and need to concentrate on the most up to date. By contrast, searching by author allows you to broaden your search to find other work by known researchers in your area.

You can also search just one or more specified fields in the database such as the author, title or abstract. This may be useful if you wish to find articles by a key author in your subject area. Alternatively, many databases allow you to search the entire database rather than just the controlled vocabulary using *free text searching*. Free text searching is increasingly common for electronic publications both on CD-ROM and accessed via the Internet, in particular broadsheet newspapers and journals. These

Table 3.3 Common link terms that use Boolean logic

Link term	*Purpose*	*Example*	*Outcome*
AND	Narrows search	Recruitment AND interviewing AND skills	Only articles containing all three key words selected
OR	Widens search	Recruitment OR selection	Articles with at least one key word selected
NOT	Excludes terms from search	Recruitment NOT selection	Selects articles containing the key word 'recruitment' that do not contain the key word 'selection'
*** (truncation)**	Uses word stems to pick up different words	Motivat*	Selects articles with: Motivate Motivation Motivating
? (wild card)	Picks up different spellings	behavio?r	Selects articles with: Behavior Behaviour

may not have a controlled index language. There are, however, problems with using a free text search. The context of a key word may be inappropriate, leading to retrieval of irrelevant articles and information overload.

worked example

Searching printed and electronic indexes and abstracts

Matthew described his research project using the key words 'performance related pay' and 'organisational change'. As a technophobe, he decided to use printed indexes rather than electronic databases. He chose the printed versions of *Emerald Management Reviews* and *Business Periodicals Index*. He checked his key words against each of these tertiary sources, and found they matched with *Emerald Management Reviews*. However, for *Business Periodicals Index* he needed to use 'Pay for Performance'. 'Organizational change' used the American spelling, but this did not matter with the printed index. Unfortunately, he encountered problems when carrying out the search:

- there were large numbers of references under each index heading;
- many of the references were not relevant to his research;
- the search terms could not be combined to make his search more specific.

After discussing the problem, the librarian showed Matthew how to use the electronic versions of these printed tertiary sources. Using the databases' indexes, he checked his key words again. It was now crucial that he got the appropriate spelling, such as for 'organizational change'. The link term AND enabled him to combine his key words and to obtain a manageable list of references. Furthermore, he was able to print out the results of the search rather than noting them by hand.

Scanning and browsing

Any search will find only some of the relevant literature. You will therefore also need to scan and browse the literature. New publications such as journals are unlikely to be indexed immediately in tertiary literature, so you will need to *browse* these publications to gain an idea of their content. In contrast, *scanning* will involve you going through individual items such as a journal article to pick out points that relate to your own research. It is particularly important that you browse and scan trade and professional journals, as these are less likely to be covered by the tertiary literature.

To make browsing and scanning easier you should:

- identify when those journals that are the most relevant are published and regularly browse them;
- browse new book displays in libraries;
- scan new book reviews in journals and newspapers;
- scan publishers' new book catalogues where available;
- discuss your research with your project tutor and librarians, who may be aware of other relevant literature.

Internet access to resources now allows you to browse journals that may not be held in or accessible from your university library. Some publishers make the contents pages of their journals available without charge on the web (Table 3.4) and may offer an *article alert* service where they will provide a regular email update of articles in your area of interest. Alternatively, databases such as Ingenta provide access to thousands of journals' contents pages (Table 3.2). Professional journals may also be accessible through the web page of the professional organisation (Table 7.2). Many publishers make their current book catalogues available on the Internet, and these can be accessed either directly (Table 3.4) or through the publishers' catalogues home page information gateway (see Table 3.5). In addition, web sites of bookshops such as Amazon, Blackwell and the Internet Book Shop provide access to catalogues of books in print. These can usually be searched, at least by author, title and subject (Table 3.4).

Table 3.4 **Selected publishers' and bookshops' Internet addresses**

Name	*Internet address*	*Contents*
Publishers		
Blackwell Publishers	http://www.blackwellpublishers.co.uk	Books and journals
Cambridge University Press	http://www.cup.cam.ac.uk	Books and journals; links to other university presses and publishing-related services
Pearson Education Limited	http://www.pearsoneduc.com	Business and management books for practitioners and students. Links to book-specific web pages
The Stationery Office	http://www.hmso.gov.uk	TSO publications including full text of Statutory Instruments and Public Acts
MCB University Press	http://www.mcb.co.uk	Over 100 professional and academic management journals
Open University Press	http://www.openup.co.uk	Books and journals
Oxford University Press	http://www.oup.co.uk	Books and journals including full-text on-line journals, a database of abstracts
Prentice Hall	http://www.prenhall.com	Books and other study information
Routledge	http://www.routledge.com	Books
Sage	http://www.sagepub.co.uk	Books, journals, software, CD-ROMs
Bookshops		
Amazon	http://www.amazon.co.uk	Searchable database principally of books (UK site)
	http://www.amazon.com	Searchable database principally of books (USA site)
Blackwell	http://bookshop.blackwell.co.uk/	Searchable database principally of books
Internet Book Shop	http://www.bookshop.co.uk	Searchable database principally of books
The Book Place	http://www.thebookplace.com	Searchable database principally of books

NB. All services in this table were free at the time of writing.

Searching the Internet

The *Internet* is a worldwide network of computers that can provide access to a vast range of literature and other resources stored on computers around the world. The most widely used part of the Internet is the *World Wide Web* (WWW). Its popularity is due largely to *hypertext links* whereby pointing and clicking on the screen takes you to a new document and to colour graphics. Searching these will uncover further material, with which you can compare and contrast your ideas. Some of the resources may be of use either for your literature review or as secondary data (Chapter 7). However, you should beware as these resources may be difficult to locate and the quality of the material is highly variable. This is emphasised by Clausen (1996:4), who likens the Internet to:

> ... a huge vandalized library where someone has destroyed the catalogue and removed the front matter and indexes from most of the books. In addition thousands of unorganized fragments are added daily by a myriad of cranks, sages and persons with time on their hands who launch their unfiltered messages into cyberspace.

As a student, you are likely to have access to the Internet through your university's or another organisation's computer network. Alternatively, you can connect to the Internet through a service provider using a microcomputer, modem and telephone. Once you have decided to search the Internet, there are a variety of approaches. These are summarised in Figure 3.3. Printed guides, such as Branscomb (1998) and Dochartaigh (2002), can be a useful starting point for information. However, because of the rate at which the Internet is growing and the fact that material can literally disappear overnight, these guidebooks are likely to become out of date extremely quickly.

Home pages

Addresses of Internet sites or *home pages* (such as http://www.brookes.ac.uk) can be the quickest and most direct method of accessing these resources. Addresses can be obtained from many sources, the most frequently used of which are guidebooks (for example: Hahn, 2002), newspaper reviews, articles in journals, librarians and lecturers. These home pages, which can have multiple linked pages and hypertext links to other web sites, are similar to a title or contents page. Although home pages often contain publicity for a company or institution, they are an excellent way of navigating around the Internet, as they bring a selection of Internet site addresses and search tools together (Table 3.5). A problem with going directly to one address is that your search is constrained by other people's ideas. Similarly, hypertext links are limited by other people's ideas and the way they have linked pages.

Search tools

Search tools, often referred to as *search engines*, are probably the most important method of Internet searching for your literature review as they will enable you to locate most current and up-to-date items. Although normally accessed through home pages, each search tool will have its own address (Table 3.5).

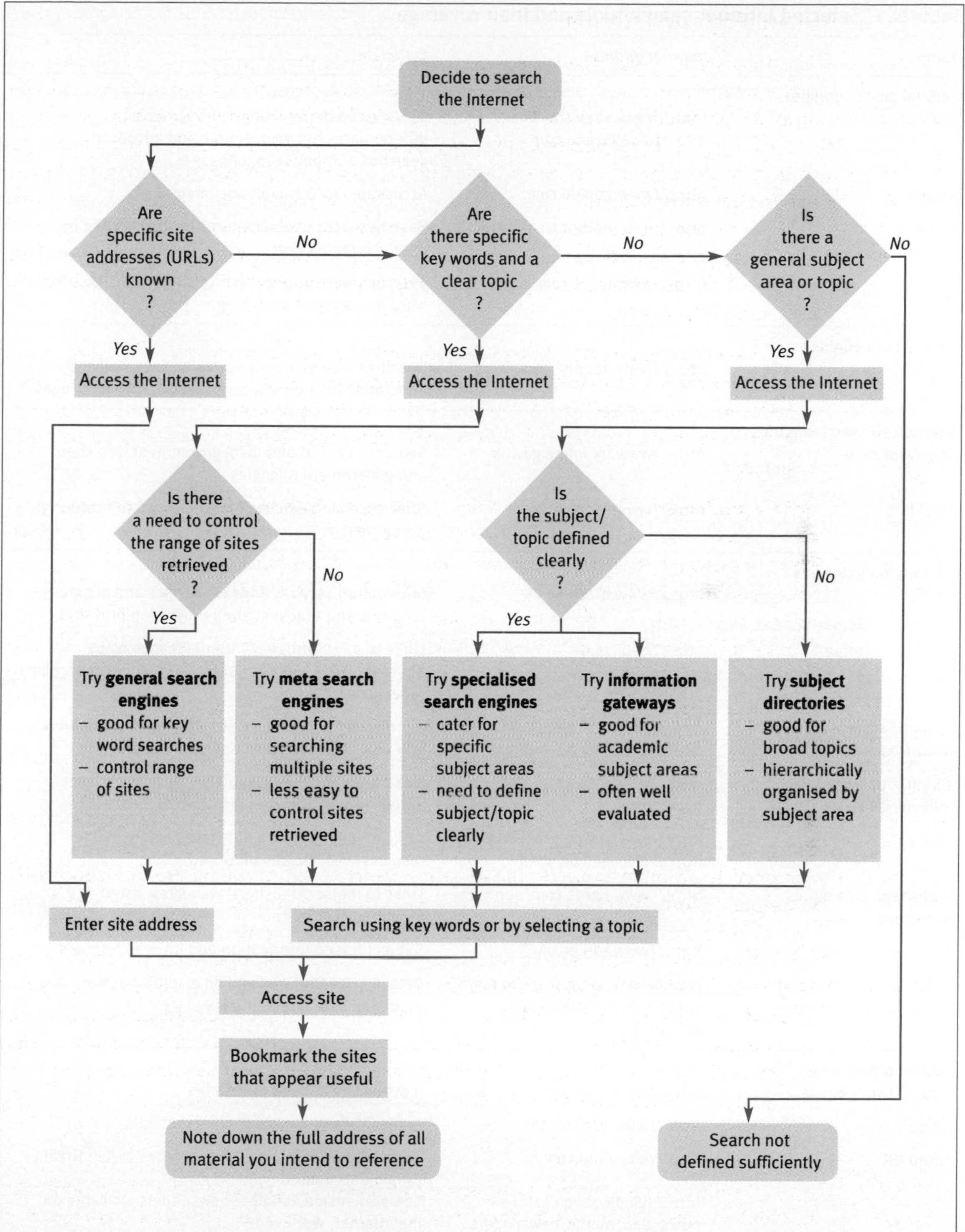

Figure 3.3 Searching the Internet

Table 3.5 Selected Internet search tools and their coverage

Name	*Internet address*	*Comment*
General search engines		
Alta Vista Search	http://www.altavista.com http://uk.altavista.com	Searches web and Usenet newsgroups; differentiates between simple and advanced searches and between languages
Google	http://www.google.com	Access to over 3 billion documents
HotBot	http://www.hotbot.lycos.co.uk	Searches web; useful features include sorting by date and media type
Lycos	http://www.lycos.com	Searches web, gopher and ftp sites; offers both key word and subject searching
Meta search engines		
Dogpile	http://www.dogpile.com	Searches a selection of search engines and subject directories including Yahoo, Lycos and Yellow Pages.
Specialised search engines		
UK government	http://www.ukonline.gov.uk	Searches central and local government web sites and government agencies
Hotel Net	http://www.hotelnet.co.uk	Specialises in searches for hotels and self-catering properties
Information gateways		
Biz/Ed	http://www.bized.ac.uk	Information service, links economics and business students and teachers and information providers
BUBL subject tree	http://bubl.ac.uk	Links to a vast range of Internet resources by alphabetical subject list or by class (subject) number order
Human Resource Management Resources on the Internet	http://www.nbs.ntu.ac.uk/depts/hrm/hrm_link.html	Annotated list of links. List split into subcategories, and provides short description of content
NISS (UK Universities and Colleges OPACs)	http://www.niss.ac.uk/lis/opacs.html	Links to UK university and college online public access (library) catalogues (OPACs)
Pinakes	http://www.hw.ac.uk/libWWW/irn/pinakes/pinakes.html	Links to major information gateways to Internet resources (especially UK based)
Publishers' catalogues homepage	http://www.lights.com/publisher	Links to major publishers' web sites, listed alphabetically by country
Resource Discovery Network	http://www.rdn.ac.uk/	Subject-based information and Internet tutorials
SOSIG UK Business and Industrial Management Resources	http://www.sosig.ac.uk/roads/subject-listing/World-cat/busgen.html	Detailed descriptions and links to UK business and industrial management sites
Subject directories		
Argus Clearinghouse	http://www.clearinghouse.net	Indexes specialised directories
Yahoo	http://www.yahoo.com	Subject-based directory
Yahoo UK	http://uk.yahoo.com	Brings the option of limiting searches to just Great Britain and Ireland
	http://uk.dir.yahoo.com/news_and_media/newspapers	Comprehensive listing of newspapers available on the Internet, worldwide
Yellow Pages UK	http://www.yell.co.uk	Telephone yellow pages with useful links to UK companies' home pages

Most search tools search by key words or subject trees. A *subject tree* is similar to a contents page or index. Some are in the form of alphabetical subject lists, whereas others are in hierarchical groups of subjects that are then further subdivided with links to more narrowly focused subject groups. It is vital that you do not rely on one search tool but use a variety, evaluating each as you use them. Each search tool will have different interfaces, ways of searching and methods of displaying information. They will search different areas of the Internet and are likely to display different results.

Search tools can be divided into four distinct categories (Figure 3.3, Table 3.5):

- general search engines;
- meta search engines;
- specialised search engines and information gateways;
- subject directories.

Most search engines index every separate document. In contrast, subject directories index only the 'most important' Internet documents. Therefore, if you are using a clear term to search for an unknown vaguely described document, use a search engine. If you are looking for a document about a particular topic, use a subject directory (Schmitz, 2002).

General search engines normally search parts of the Internet using key words and Boolean logic (Table 3.3) or a phrase. Each search engine uses an automated computer process to index and search, often resulting in a very large number of sites being found. As these sites have not been evaluated by people, many are usually inappropriate or unreliable. As no two general search engines search in precisely the same way it is advisable (and often necessary) to use more than one. In contrast, *meta search engines* allow you to search using a selection of search engines at the same time, using the same interface. This makes searching easier, and the search can be faster. Unfortunately, it is less easy to control the sites that are retrieved. Consequently, meta search engines often generate more inappropriate or unreliable sites than general search engines.

Specialised search engines cater for specific subject areas. To use these it is necessary to define your general subject area prior to your search. *Information gateways* also require you to define your subject area. Information gateways are often compiled by staff from departments in academic institutions. Although the number of web sites obtained is fewer, they can be far more relevant, as each site is evaluated prior to being added to the gateway.

Subject directories are hierarchically organised indexes categorised into subject areas, and are useful for searching for broad topics. As people normally compile them, their content has been partly censored and evaluated. Consequently, the number of sites retrieved is fewer but they usually provide material that is more appropriate. Most of the subject directories now offer some form of key word search and links to other search tools.

Search tools are becoming more prolific and sophisticated all the time. Be careful: their use can be extremely time consuming. Your search will probably locate a mass of resources, many of which will be irrelevant to you. It is also easy to become sidetracked to more interesting and glossy web sites not relevant to your research needs! There are an increasing number of web-based tutorials to help you learn to search the web. One, which our students have found useful and informative, is hosted by Tilburg

University in the Netherlands. This offers interactive tutorials on searching as well as a brief history of the Internet and a glossary of terms. It is available at: http://www.tilbrguniversity.nl/services/library/instruction/www/onlinecourse/.

Bookmarking

Once you have found a useful Internet site, you need to note its address electronically. This process is termed *bookmarking* or *add to favourites* depending on your Internet software. It uses the software to note the Internet address, and means that you will be able to access it again directly. The vast amount of resources available, and the fact that resources, home pages and sites can be added and deleted by their producers, means it is vital to keep a record of the addresses (Section 3.7). These will be needed to reference your sources when you write your critical review (Section 3.2). When sufficient sites have been bookmarked, it is possible to arrange them in whatever hierarchical way you wish.

3.6 Obtaining and evaluating the literature

Obtaining the literature

After your initial search of books and journal articles, tertiary literature will provide you with details of what literature is available and where to locate it. The next stage (Figure 3.1) is to obtain these items. To do this you need:

1 to check your library catalogue to find out whether your library holds the appropriate publication. Remember many libraries now hold publications such as journals and newspapers in electronic form on CD-ROM or provide access via the Internet;
2 (for those publications that are held by your library or available via the Internet) to note their location:
  a locate the publication and scan it to discover whether it is likely to be worth reading thoroughly;
  b browse other books and journals with similar class marks to see whether they may also be of use;
3 (for those items that are not held by your library or available via the Internet) to order the item from another library on *inter-library loan*. As Bell (1999) points out, this is not a free service so make sure you really need it first. Our students have found that, in general, it is only worthwhile to use inter-library loan for articles from refereed journals and books.

Evaluating the literature

Two questions frequently asked by our students are 'How do I know what I'm reading is relevant?' and 'How do I know when I've read enough?' Both of these are concerned with the process of evaluation. They involve defining the scope of your review and assessing the value of the items that you have obtained in helping you to answer your research question(s). Although there are no set ways of approaching these questions our students have found the following advice helpful.

You should, of course, read all the literature that is closely related to your research question(s) and objectives. The literature that is most likely to cause problems is that which is less closely related (Gall *et al.*, 1996). For some research questions, particularly for new research areas, there is unlikely to be much closely related literature and so you will have to review more broadly. For research questions where research has been going on for some years you may be able to focus on more closely related literature.

Assessing relevance

Assessing the relevance of the literature you have collected to your research depends on your research question(s) and objectives. Remember that you are looking for relevance, not critically assessing the ideas contained within. Box 3.3 provides a checklist to help you in this process.

Remember to make notes about the relevance of each item as you read it and the reasons why you came to your conclusion. You may need to include your evaluation as part of your critical review.

Assessing sufficiency

Your assessment of whether you have read a sufficient amount is even more complex. It is impossible to read everything, as you would never start to write your critical review, let alone your project report. Yet you need to be sure that your critical review discusses what research has already been undertaken and that you have positioned your research project in the wider context, citing the main writers in the field (Section 3.2). One clue that you have achieved this is when further searching provides mainly references to items you have already read. You also need to check what constitutes an acceptable amount of reading, in terms of both quality and quantity, with your project tutor.

Box 3.3 Checklist for evaluating the relevance of literature

- ✓ How recent is the item?
- ✓ Is the item likely to have been superseded?
- ✓ Is the context sufficiently different to make it marginal to your research question(s) and objectives?
- ✓ Have you seen references to this item (or its author) in other items that were useful?
- ✓ Does the item support or contradict your arguments? For either it will probably be worth reading!
- ✓ Does the item appear to be biased? Even if it is it may still be relevant to your critical review!
- ✓ What are the methodological omissions within the work? Even if there are many it still may be of relevance!
- ✓ Is the precision sufficient? Even if it is imprecise it may be the only item you can find and so still of relevance!

Sources: Authors' experience; Bell (1999); Jankowicz (2000); McNeill (1990)

worked example

Undertaking an Internet search

Eline's research question was reasonably defined, if somewhat broad. She wanted to assess the impact of the euro on small to medium-sized organisations. She decided to search the Internet using a general search engine. Her first key word 'euro' revealed that there were over 300 000 sites and displayed the first 10, ranked in order of relevance. Of these, none had anything to do with European Monetary Union. She decided to refine her search using the key word 'European Monetary Union'. Although the search engine found fewer than 20 000 sites, the content of the first 10 appeared slightly more relevant to her research question.

Among these was:

European Union Politics
Available Electronically! European Union Politics. Executive Editor Gerald Schneider University of Konstanz, Germany. Associated Editors Simon Hix London School of Economics and Political… http://www.sagepub.co.u/journals/details/j0296.html

Eline looked at this site and found that it was a publisher's site for a new refereed journal on the processes of government, politics and policy in the European Union. She decided to use the link to the journal's table of contents later to see if there were any refereed articles relevant to her research.

At the end of the first 10 sites, the search engine also offered Eline the facility to extend her search using another search engine. She did this, and a new search engine suggested six further web sites. These included:

European Monetary Union and the Euro
Homepage of the European Monetary Union and the Euro NOTES ON EUROPE, EMU and EURO Recent articles from the Economist Click here to get the Economist articles Recent artic…
From **www.stern.nyu.edu**

The Association for the Monetary Union of Europe
The Association for the Monetary Union of Europe is an organization which promotes the Euro as a Single Currency for Europe. The Website contains extensive reports, guides for…
From amue.lf.net

The Euro-Europe's Single Common Currency
What are the prospects for European monetary union? A page of links to official EU information sources and to other sources expressing a variety of viewpoints.
From **www.ex.ac.uk**

Eline noted that the first of these appeared to provide a link to recent articles from *The Economist*. As she had already browsed this journal in her university's library, she decided not to go to this web site. The text associated with the second web site indicated it was for an organisation that promoted the euro as a single currency. Eline noted that, although this might be relevant, it was likely to be biased in favour of the euro.

However, the web addresses for one of these sites had the suffix '.ac.uk'. This told Eline that it was a UK academic institution and suggested that the information might be more balanced. She therefore clicked on the address to view the site. This resulted in a four-page list of links to official EU information sources and other sources, which the collator of the links stressed contained a variety of viewpoints. One of these, 'The Official Treasury SME Euro Resource', appeared to be directly relevant to her research and would provide information about the UK government's viewpoint. Unfortunately, clicking on the entry merely told her that the web page no longer existed and redirected her to the UK government's Treasury web page. By using the 'Search' facility on this web page she was able to find details regarding the UK government's policy on economic and monetary union and a statement of implications for small and medium-sized companies.

Eline returned to the results from the first search engine she had used and visited the next 40 sites that had been listed by the search engine. After this, she noted that the sites were becoming, at best, marginally relevant. She therefore decided to ignore the remaining sites and to narrow her search using the refine feature of the search engine.

3.7 Recording the literature

The literature search, as you will now be aware, is a vital part of your research project, in which you will invest a great deal of time and effort. As you read each item, you need to ask yourself how it contributes to your research question(s) and objectives and to make *notes* with this focus (Bell, 1999). When doing this many students photocopy articles and pages from books to ensure that they have all the material. We believe that, even if you photocopy, you still need to make notes. The process of note making will help you to think through the ideas in the literature in relation to your research.

In addition to making notes Sharp and Howard (1996) identify three sets of information you need to record. These are:

- bibliographic details;
- brief summary of content;
- supplementary information.

Until the advent of inexpensive microcomputers it was usual to write this information on *index cards*. Database software such as Access or specialist bibliographic software such as Reference Manager for Windows provide a powerful and flexible alternative method for recording the literature, although they will probably mean noting it down and transferring it to your database later. Recording can seem very tedious, but it must be done. We have seen many students frantically repeating searches for items that are crucial to their research because they failed to record all the necessary details, either in their database of references or on index cards.

Bibliographic details

For some project reports you will be required to include a *bibliography*. Convention dictates that this should include all the relevant items you consulted for your project, including those not referred to directly in the text. For others, you will be asked only to include a list of *references* for those items referred to directly in the text. The *bibliographic details* contained in both need to be sufficient to enable readers to find the original items. These details are summarised in Table 3.6.

If an item has been taken from an electronic source you need to record as much of the information in Table 3.6 as is available along with details of format (e.g. CD-ROM). If you located the item via the Internet, you need to record the full address of the resource and the date you accessed the information as well (Appendix 2). This address is often referred to as the *URL* or *unique resource location*.

Table 3.6 Bibliographic details required

Journal	*Book*	*Chapter in an edited book*
■ Author(s) – surname, first name initials ■ Year of publication (in parentheses) ■ Title of article ■ Title of journal (underlined) ■ Volume ■ Part/issue ■ Page numbers (preceded by 'p.' for page or 'pp.' for pages)	■ Author(s) – surname, first name initials ■ Year of publication (in parentheses) ■ Title and subtitle of book (underlined) ■ Edition ■ Place of publication ■ Publisher	■ Author(s) – surname, first name initials ■ Year of publication (in parentheses) ■ Title of chapter ■ Author(s) of book – surname, first name initials ■ Title and subtitle of book (underlined) ■ Edition ■ Place of publication ■ Publisher ■ Page numbers of chapter

Most universities have a preferred *referencing style* that you must use in your project report. This will normally be prescribed in your assessment criteria. Three of the most common styles are the *Harvard system* (a version of which we have used in this book), the *American Psychological Association (APA) System* and the *Vancouver* or *footnotes system*. Guidelines on using these are given in Appendix 2.

Brief summary

A brief summary of the content of each item on your index card or in your reference database will help you to locate the relevant items and facilitate reference to your notes and photocopies. This can be done by annotating each record with the key words used to locate the item and the abstract. It will also help you to maintain consistency in your searches.

Table 3.7 Supplementary information

Information	*Reason*
ISBN	The identifier for any book, and useful if the book has to be requested on inter-library loan
Class (Dewey decimal) number	Useful to locate books in your university's library and as a pointer to finding other books on the same subject
Quotations	Always note useful quotations in full and with the page number of the quote; if possible also take a photocopy
Where it was found	Noting where you found the item is useful, especially if it is not in your university library and you could only take notes
The tertiary resource used	Useful to help identify resources for follow-up searches
Evaluative comments	Your personal notes on the value of the item to your research (Box 3.3 will help here)
When the item was consulted	Especially important for items found via the Internet as these may disappear without trace

Supplementary information

As well as recording the details discussed earlier, other information may also be worth recording. These items can be anything you feel will be of value. In Table 3.7 we outline those that we have found most useful.

3.8 Summary

- A critical review of the literature is necessary to help you to develop a thorough understanding of and insight into previous research that relates to your research question(s) and objectives. Your review will set your research in context by critically discussing and referencing work that has already been undertaken, drawing out key points and presenting them in a logically argued way, and highlighting those areas where you will provide fresh insights. It will lead the reader into subsequent sections of your project report.
- There is no one correct structure for a critical review, although it is helpful to think of it as a funnel in which you start at a more general level prior to narrowing down to your specific research question(s) and objectives.
- Literature sources can be divided into three categories: primary, secondary and tertiary. In reality, these categories often overlap. Your use of these resources will depend on your research question(s) and objectives. Some may use only tertiary and secondary literature. For others, you may need to locate primary literature as well.
- When planning your literature search you need:
  - to have clearly defined research question(s) and objectives;
  - to define the parameters of your search;
  - to generate key words and search terms;
  - to discuss your ideas as widely as possible.

  Techniques to help you in this include brainstorming and relevance trees.
- Your literature search will be undertaken using a variety of approaches in tandem. These will include:
  - searching using tertiary sources and the Internet;
  - following up references in articles you have already read;
  - scanning and browsing secondary literature in your library.
- Once obtained, the literature must be evaluated for its relevance to your research question(s) and objectives. This must include a consideration of each item's currency. Each item must be read and noted. Bibliographic details, a brief description of the content and appropriate supplementary information should also be recorded.

self-check Questions

3.1 The following extract and associated references are taken from the first draft of a critical literature review. The research project was concerned with the impact of direct insurers on the traditional motor insurer.

List the problems with this extract in terms of its:
a content;
b structure.

Jackson (1995) suggests that businesses must be developed from a customer rather than a product perspective. Lindesfarne (1995) demonstrates that direct selling gives the consumer increased control as it is up to them when and if they wish to respond to adverts or direct mail. MacKenzie (1995) comments that free gifts are useful for getting responses to adverts, which is ultimately what all direct insurers need. Bowen (1995) suggests that this type of company can be split into three equally important parts: marketing, insurance and information technology. Motor insurance is particularly price sensitive because of its compulsory nature and its perception by many to have no real 'value' to themselves.

Bowen I (1994) Short Cut To Success *Post Magazine* 2 July 26
Jackson DR (1995) Prudential's Prudent Parochialism *Direct Marketing* April 26–29
Lindisfarne I (1995) Death Of A Salesman *Post Magazine* 15 June 30–31
MacKenzie G (1995) Rise Of The Freebie *Post Magazine* 2 February 56

3.2 Outline the advice you would give a colleague on:
a how to plan her search
b which literature to search first.

3.3 Brainstorm at least one of the following research questions, either on your own or with a colleague, and list the key words that you have generated.
a How effective is profit-related pay as a motivator?
b How do the opportunities available to a first-time house buyer through interpersonal discussion influence the process of selecting a financial institution for the purposes of applying for a house purchase loan?
c To what extent do new methods of direct selling of financial services pose a threat to existing providers?

3.4 You are having considerable problems with finding relevant material for your research when searching databases. Suggest possible reasons why this might be so.

3.5 Rewrite the following passage as part of a critical literature review using the Harvard system of referencing:

> Most of the writers[1] I've read on the European Union's future employment needs reckon that there's going to be an increase in the need for highly qualified employees. Yet the European Commission[2] have worked out that there's going to be fewer of these people about due to technological and economic changes and because there are fewer people are entering the labour market. Now that we're all in one 'single European market' these problems are likely to get even worse as some countries have a far higher demand for such people than they can supply internally.[3]

[1] for example: Atkinson J (1989) Corporate Employment Policies for the Single European Market *IMS Report No 179* Sussex, Institute of Manpower Studies; Pearson R & Pike G (1989) The Graduate Labour Market in the 1990s *IMS Report No. 167* Sussex, Institute of Manpower Studies; Werner H (1990) Free movement of labour in the Single European Market *Intereconomics* 25.2 77–81
[2] Commission of the European Communities (1991) *Employment in Europe* COM (89)339
[3] Walwei U and Werner H (1993) Europeanising the Labour Market: Employee Mobility and Company Recruiting Methods *Intereconomics* Feb. 3–10

progressing your research project

Critically reviewing the literature

- ☐ Consider your research questions and objectives. Use your lecture notes, course textbooks and relevant review articles to define both narrow and broader parameters of your literature search considering language, subject area, business sector, geographical area, publication period and literature type.
- ☐ Generate key words and search terms using one or a variety of techniques such as reading, brainstorming and relevance trees. Discuss your ideas widely, including with your project tutor and colleagues.
- ☐ Start your search using both database and printed tertiary sources to identify relevant secondary literature. Begin with those tertiary sources that abstract and index academic journal articles and books. At the same time, obtain relevant literature that has been referenced in articles you have already read.
- ☐ Expand your search via other sources such as the Internet and by browsing and scanning.
- ☐ Obtain copies of relevant items, read them and make notes. Remember also to record bibliographic details, a brief description of the content and supplementary information on an index card or in your reference database.
- ☐ Start drafting your critical review as early as possible keeping in mind its purpose.
- ☐ Continue to search the literature throughout your research project to ensure that your review remains up to date.

References

Bell, J. (1999) *Doing Your Research Project* (3rd edn), Buckingham, Open University Press.

Branscomb, H.E. (1998) *Casting Your Net: A Student's Guide to Research on the Internet*, Boston, MA, Allyn and Bacon.

Clausen, H. (1996) 'Web information quality as seen from libraries', *New Library World* 97: 1130, 4–8.

Dees, R. (2000) *Writing the Modern Research Paper* (3rd edn), Boston, MA, Allyn and Bacon.

Dochartaigh, N.O. (2002) *The Internet Research Handbook*, London, Sage

Gall, M.D., Borg, W.R. and Gall, J.P. (1996) *Educational Research: An Introduction* (6th edn), New York, Longman.

Gill, J. and Johnson, P. (1997) *Research Methods for Managers* (2nd edn), London, Paul Chapman.

Hahn, H. (2002) *Harley Hahn's Internet Yellow Pages*, New York, McGraw-Hill.

Hart, C. (1998) *Doing a Literature Review*, London, Sage.

Haywood, P. and Wragg, E.C. (1982) *Evaluating the Literature: Rediguide 2*, University of Nottingham School of Education, Nottingham.

Higgins, R. (1996) *Approaches to Research: A Handbook for Those Writing a Dissertation*, London, Jessica Kingsley.

Jankowicz, A.D. (2000) *Business Research Projects* (3rd edn), London, Thompson Learning.

McNeill, P. (1990) *Research Methods* (2nd edn), London, Routledge.

Saunders, M.N.K. and Williams C.S. (2000) 'Towards a new approach to understanding service encounters: establishing, learning about and reconciling different views', *Journal of European Industrial Training* 24: 2/3/4, 220–7.

Schmitz, R. (2002) 'Searching the World Wide Web: a basic tutorial' [online](cited 18 February 2002). Available from <URL:http://www.tilbrguniversity.nl/services/library/instruction/www/onlinecourse/>.

Sharp, J.A. and Howard, K. (1996) *The Management of a Student Research Project* (2nd edn), Aldershot, Gower.

Stewart, D.W. and Kamins, M.A. (1993) *Secondary Research: Information Sources and Methods* (2nd edn), Newbury Park, CA, Sage.

Strauss, A. and Corbin, J. (1998) *Basics of Qualitative Research* (2nd edn), Newbury Park, CA, Sage.

Further reading

Bell, J. (1999) *Doing Your Research Project* (3rd edn), Buckingham, Open University Press. Chapter 6 provides a good introduction to the process of reviewing the literature. The section on the critical review of the literature is especially helpful.

Jankowicz, A.D. (2000) *Business Research Projects* (2nd edn), London, Chapman & Hall. Chapter 8 provides a good discussion of reviewing and using the literature for business research projects.

Schmitz, R. (2002) 'Searching the World Wide Web: a basic tutorial' [online](cited 18 February 2002). Available from <URL:http://www.tilbrguniversity.nl/services/library/instruction/www/onlinecourse/>. This web site provides an introduction to and history of the Internet and WWW along with an interactive tutorial. The tutorial offers an explanation of different types of information that you can find on the Internet and how to access them. It also contains a common sense guide to searching for particular web sites.

Sharp, J.A. and Howard, K. (1996) *The Management of a Student Research Project* (2nd edn), Aldershot, Gower. Chapter 4 contains a useful in-depth discussion of the use of relevance trees in your literature search.

CASE 3 The problems of valuing intellectual capital

Geoff had decided to research how companies valued intellectual capital, and was very keen to get started. He began by contacting several big accountancy firms asking if they had any publications on this topic, and was pleased when they responded by sending material very quickly. He spent two full days in the university library, where he searched the library's on-line catalogue and the *Financial Times* archive on line. He also tried using the Internet search engine Google, but he found over 700 000 hits relating to intellectual capital and realised that it would take years to read them all.

He arrived for his tutorial with the file of material that he had collected as the foundation for his literature review. This comprised photocopied extracts from some textbooks on financial reporting, the reports he had received from professional accountancy firms, and copies of articles from the *Financial Times*. Geoff showed his tutor how he had started writing his literature review. This summarised everything he had read so far in chronological order of publication, including extensive quotations from each source.

Geoff was disappointed that his tutor did not seem more enthusiastic about his progress. As they discussed the purpose of a literature review, Geoff commented 'I've done a really thorough search, there's nothing else about intellectual capital in the library – I think I've read nearly everything written on the topic now!'

The tutor pointed out that, although Geoff had collected some relevant and up-to-date material, he had not looked into the academic literature. He therefore suggested two refereed journal articles that he should read. Geoff began to realise that the reading he needed to do was going to be very time consuming. His tutor gave him some advice on learning to skim texts to speed up the process and how to organise information efficiently, keeping careful notes on sources.

Geoff returned to the library and searched for the two refereed journal articles. One journal was in the library, but he had to request the second article through the inter-library loan service. He sat down to read the first article and discovered that some of the points that the author made had also appeared in the professional reports. He made some notes on these connecting ideas and began to think about the reasons why companies might want to put a value on intellectual capital, as well as the ways in which they might perform the calculations. The article contained references to books and other articles that dealt with this. Geoff noted their references in full so that he could obtain copies.

Over the next few weeks, Geoff concentrated on reading the academic literature. Many of the articles that he read contained references to the work of two particular researchers, so he looked for other published works by these people, who were clearly authorities in the area. The library staff helped him to use several electronic resources, including ABI-Inform and EBSCO, which provided speedy access to the articles he needed. Soon he was able to read quickly through a list of titles to pick out those relevant to his work, although the amount of material previously written on the subject seemed daunting. Talking to other students on his course, he found that they had similar concerns. One student said that she had collected so many references that she had decided to record everything she had read in a simple database. She showed Geoff how she had set this up, and he decided to copy the idea. He also began to organise his notes around themes that seemed to be repeated in the articles he was reading. Over time he began to realise that the practical issues, which had first attracted him to the topic, could be explained more clearly when they were placed in the theoretical context discussed in the academic literature.

Geoff was still worried that he hadn't located all the relevant literature. However, he was reassured by his tutor's comments after reading the first draft of his literature review. These emphasised that there was no need to read everything that had been written and that, although the structure of the review still needed further work, it provided a reasonable overview of current thinking. They discussed ways in which he could take a more critical approach to the literature and use this evaluation to support his arguments in a logical way. As part of the discussion Geoff's tutor asked him to select the article that he considered the most authoritative on the problems of valuing intellectual capital and then to explain why. This exercise helped Geoff to reorganise his material in a more focused way.

▶

When he had completed the second draft of his review Geoff felt really pleased with it, and his tutor congratulated him on making excellent progress. He was even more enthusiastic about his project now that he could be confident about his basic understanding of the area and had identified specific issues to focus on.

Questions

1. How do you think Geoff's view of the purpose of undertaking a literature review changed?
2. What specific skills did Geoff develop in the course of preparing the review?
3. Why do you think Geoff's friend recorded everything she had read in a database rather than just those articles she felt would definitely be of use to her dissertation?
4. How could Geoff have made better use of Internet search engines in researching his topic?

self-check Answers

3.1 There are numerous problems with the content and structure of this extract. Some of the more obvious include:

a The content consists of predominantly trade magazines, in particular *Post Magazine*, and there are no references of academic substance. Some of the references to individual authors have discrepancies: for example, was the article by Lindisfarne (or is it Lindesfarne?) published in 1994 or 1995?

b The items referenced are from 1994 and 1995. It is likely that more recent items are available.

c There is no real structure or argument in the extract. The extract is a list of what people have written with no attempt to critically evaluate or juxtapose the ideas.

3.2 This is a difficult one without knowing her research question! However, you could still advise her on the general principles. Your advice will probably include:

a Define the parameters of the research, considering language, subject area, business sector, geographical area, publication period and literature type. Generate key words and search terms using one or a variety of techniques such as reading, brainstorming or relevance trees. Discuss her ideas as widely as possible including with tutor, librarians and you.

b Start the search using tertiary sources to identify relevant secondary literature. She should commence with those tertiary sources that abstract and index academic journal articles and books. At the same time she should obtain relevant literature that has been referenced in articles that she has already read.

3.3 There are no incorrect answers with brainstorming! However, you might like to check your key words for suitability prior to using them to search an appropriate database. We suggest that you follow the approach outlined in Section 3.5 under 'searching using the tertiary literature'.

3.4 There are a variety of possible reasons, including:

- One or more of the parameters of your search are defined too narrowly.
- The key words you have chosen do not appear in the controlled index language.
- Your spelling of the key word is incorrect.
- The terminology you are using is incorrect.
- The acronyms you have chosen are not used by databases.
- You are using jargon rather than accepted terminology.

3.5 There are two parts to this answer: rewriting the text and using the Harvard system of referencing. Your text will inevitably differ from the answer given below owing to your personal writing style. Don't worry about this too much as it is discussed in far more detail in Section 13.5. The references should follow the same format.

> The vast majority of writers on the European Union's (EU) future employment needs emphasise a growth in the requirements for highly qualified, specialist employees (Atkinson, 1989; Pearson and Pike, 1989; Werner, 1990). Such employees are forecast to become a scarce resource within the EU, owing to technological change, the decline in young people entering the labour market, and predictions that the economic climate will improve in the latter half of the 1990s (Commission of the European Communities, 1991). The completion of the Single European Market has magnified these problems. Demand for highly qualified labour in some states is forecast to be greater than supply, whereas in others the converse will be true (Walwei and Werner, 1993).

Atkinson, J. (1989) *Corporate Employment Policies for the Single European Market*, IMS Report No. 179, Sussex, Institute of Manpower Studies.

Commission of the European Communities (1991) *Employment in Europe* COM (89)339.

Pearson, R. and Pike, G. (1989) *The Graduate Labour Market in the 1990s*, IMS Report No. 167, Sussex, Institute of Manpower Studies.

Walwei, U. and Werner, H. (1993) 'Europeanising the labour market: employee mobility and company recruiting methods', *Intereconomics* Feb. pp. 3–10.

Werner, H. (1990) 'Free movement of labour in the Single European Market', *Intereconomics*, 25.2 pp. 77–81.

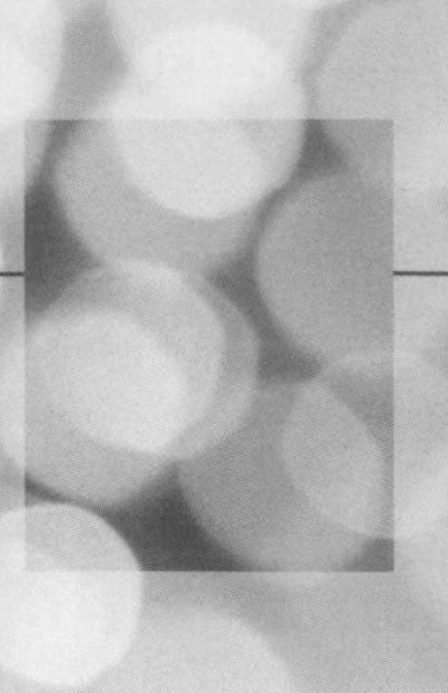

Chapter 4

Deciding on the research approach and choosing a research strategy

By the end of this chapter you should be able:

- to outline the key assumptions of the positivist, interpretivist and realist research philosophies;
- to distinguish between two main approaches to research: deductive and inductive;
- to identify the main research strategies and explain why these should not be thought of as mutually exclusive;
- to explain the benefits of adopting a multi-method approach to the conduct of research;
- to explain the concepts of validity and reliability and identify the main threats to validity and reliability;
- to understand some of the main ethical issues implied by the choice of research strategy.

4.1 Differing approaches to research

Much of this book is concerned with the way in which you collect data to answer your research question. You are not unusual if you begin thinking about your research by considering whether you should, for example, administer a questionnaire or conduct interviews. However, thoughts on this question belong in the centre of the research 'onion', by which means we have chosen to depict the issues underlying the choice of data collection methods in Figure 4.1. Before coming to this central point we argue that there are important layers of the onion that need to be peeled away.

The first of these layers raises the question of the research philosophy you adopt. The second considers the subject of your research approach that flows from that research philosophy. Third, we examine what we call the research strategy, and the fourth layer refers to the time horizons you apply to your research. The fifth layer, data collection methods, is dealt with in Chapters 6–10.

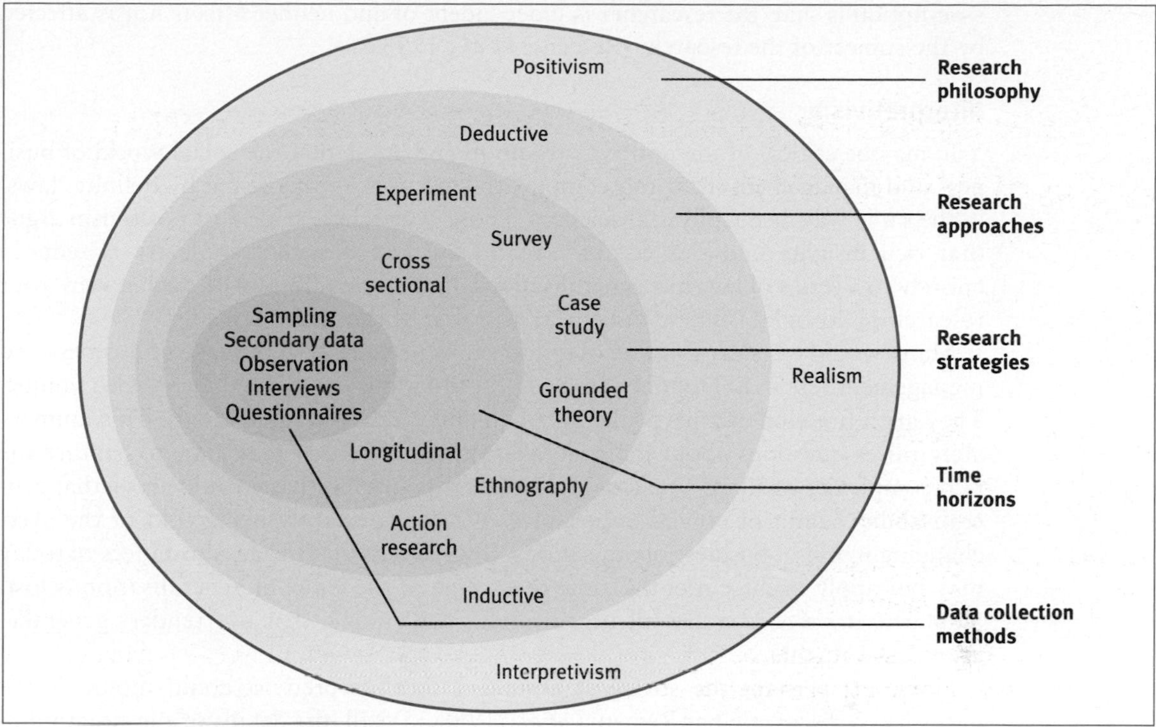

Figure 4.1 The research process 'onion'

Research philosophy

Your research philosophy depends on the way that you think about the development of knowledge. This seems rather profound, and not something to which you would normally give much thought. Yet the way we think about the development of knowledge affects, albeit unwittingly, the way we go about doing research. Three views about the research process dominate the literature: positivism, interpretivism and realism. They are different, if not mutually exclusive, views about the way in which knowledge is developed and judged as being acceptable. All three have an important part to play in business and management research.

Positivism

If your research philosophy reflects the principles of *positivism* then you will probably adopt the philosophical stance of the natural scientist. You will prefer 'working with an observable social reality and that the end product of such research can be law-like generalisations similar to those produced by the physical and natural scientists' (Remenyi *et al.*, 1998:32). The researcher in this tradition assumes the role of an objective analyst, coolly making detached interpretations about those data that have been collected in an apparently value-free manner. There will be an emphasis on a highly structured methodology to facilitate replication (Gill and Johnson, 1997) and on quantifiable observations that lend themselves to statistical analysis. The assumption is that 'the researcher is independent of and neither affects nor is affected by the subject of the research' (Remenyi *et al.*, 1998:33).

Interpretivism

You may be critical of the positivist tradition and argue that the social world of business and management is far too complex to lend itself to theorising by definite 'laws' in the same way as the physical sciences. Those researchers critical of positivism argue that rich insights into this complex world are lost if such complexity is reduced entirely to a series of law-like generalisations. If you sympathise with such a view your research philosophy is likely to be nearer to that of the *interpretivist*.

Many would consider this line of argument as persuasive in the case of business and management research. Not only are business situations complex, they are also unique. They are a function of a particular set of circumstances and individuals. This immediately raises questions about the generalisability of research that aims to capture the rich complexity of social situations. However, the interpretivist would argue that generalisability is not of crucial importance. We are constantly being told of the ever-changing world of business organisations. If we accept that the circumstances of today may not apply in three months' time then some of the value of generalisation is lost. Similarly, if we accept that all organisations are unique, that too renders generalisation less valuable.

However, perhaps the strongest argument the interpretivist could mount is the necessity to discover what Remenyi *et al.* (1998:35) call 'the details of the situation to understand the reality or perhaps a reality working behind them'. This is often associated with the term *constructionism*, or *social constructionism*. This follows from the interpretivist position that it is necessary to explore the subjective meanings motivating people's actions in order to be able to understand these. Social constructionism views reality as being socially constructed. People may place many different interpretations on the situations in which they find themselves. These different interpretations are likely to affect their actions and the nature of their social interaction with others. In this sense, people not only interact with their environment, they also seek to make sense of it through their interpretation of events and the meanings that they draw from these. In turn their own actions may be seen as being meaningful in the context of these socially constructed interpretations and meanings. It is therefore the role of the interpretivist to seek to understand the subjective reality of those that they study in order to be able to make sense of and understand their motives, actions and intentions in a way that is meaningful for these research participants.

Realism

Social constructionism also recognises that people are likely to share interpretations of their socially constructed environment. This may point to the existence of commonly experienced stimuli in terms of generating a shared interpretation. Such stimuli may or may not be explicitly evident to those in a given situation or environment. These stimuli will nevertheless exert an influence on the way in which those affected socially construct their world.

Realism is based on the belief that a reality exists that is independent of human thoughts and beliefs. In the social sciences and in the study of business and management this can be seen as indicating that there are large-scale social forces and processes that affect people without their necessarily being aware of the existence of such influences on their interpretations and behaviours. Social objects or phenomena that are external to, or independent of, individuals will therefore affect the way in which these people perceive their world, whether they are aware of these forces or not. However, while realism therefore shares some philosophical aspects with positivism, for example related to the external, objective nature of some macro aspects of society, it also recognises that people themselves are not objects to be studied in the style of natural science. In this way, realism, as applied to the study of human subjects, recognises the importance of understanding people's socially constructed interpretations and meanings, or subjective reality, within the context of seeking to understand broader social forces, structures or processes that influence, and perhaps constrain, the nature of people's views and behaviours.

It would be easy to fall into the trap of thinking that one research approach is 'better' than another. This would miss the point. They are 'better' at doing different things. As always, which is 'better' depends on the research question(s) you are seeking to answer. Of course, the practical reality is that research rarely falls neatly into only one philosophical domain as suggested in the 'onion' (Figure 4.1). Business and management research is often a mixture between positivist and interpretivist, perhaps reflecting the stance of realism. Indeed, later in this chapter we shall also be encouraging you to think in a more flexible way about the research approach and methods you adopt.

You may ask what practical use is an understanding of your philosophical position. Is it as much use as the outer layer on a real onion, which is cast aside, with only the inner layers retained? We think that it is of practical benefit to understand the taken-for-granted assumptions that we all have about the way the world works. Only if we have such an understanding can we examine these assumptions, challenge them if we think it appropriate, and behave in a different way.

Choosing a research approach

Section 2.4 notes that your research project will involve the use of theory. That theory may or may not be made explicit in the design of the research, although it will usually be made explicit in your presentation of the findings and conclusions. The extent to which you are clear about the theory at the beginning of your research raises an important question concerning the design of your research project. This is whether your research should use the *deductive* approach, in which you develop a theory and hypothesis (or hypotheses) and design a research strategy to test the hypothesis, or the *inductive* approach, in which you would collect data and develop theory as a result of your data analysis. Insofar as it is useful to attach these approaches to the different research philosophies, the deductive approach owes more to positivism and the inductive approach to interpretivism, although we believe that such labelling is potentially misleading and of no practical value.

The next two sections of this chapter explain the differences between these two approaches and the implications of these differences.

Deduction: testing theory

As noted earlier, this approach to research owes much to what we would think of as *scientific* research. It involves the development of a theory that is subjected to a rigorous test. As such, it is the dominant research approach in the natural sciences, where 'laws provide the basis of explanation, permit the anticipation of phenomena, predict their occurrence and therefore allow them to be controlled' (Hussey and Hussey, 1997:52).

Robson (1993:19) lists five sequential stages through which deductive research will progress:

1 deducing a *hypothesis* (a testable proposition about the relationship between two or more events or concepts) from the theory;
2 expressing the hypothesis in operational terms (that is, ones indicating exactly how the variables are to be measured), which propose a relationship between two specific variables;
3 testing this operational hypothesis (this will involve an experiment or some other form of empirical inquiry);
4 examining the specific outcome of the inquiry (it will either tend to confirm the theory or indicate the need for its modification);
5 if necessary, modifying the theory in the light of the findings.

An attempt is then made to verify the revised theory by going back to the first step and repeating the whole cycle.

There are several important characteristics of the deductive approach. First, there is the search to explain causal relationships between variables. It may be that you wish to establish the reasons for high employee absenteeism in a retail store. After studying absence patterns it occurs to you that there seems to be a relationship between absence, the age of workers and length of service. Consequently you develop a hypothesis that states that absenteeism is more likely to be prevalent among younger workers who have worked for the organisation for a relatively short period of time. To test this hypothesis you utilise another characteristic, the collection of quantitative data. (This is not to say that deductive research may not use qualitative data.) It may be that there are important differences in the way work is arranged in different stores: therefore you would need to employ a further important characteristic of the deductive approach, *controls to allow the testing of hypotheses*. These controls would help to ensure that any change in absenteeism was a function of worker age and length of service rather than any other aspect of the store, for example the way in which people were managed. Your research would use a *highly structured methodology* to facilitate replication (Gill and Johnson, 1997), an important issue to ensure reliability, as we shall emphasise in Section 4.4.

In order to pursue the principle of scientific rigour, the deductive approach dictates that the researcher should be independent of what is being observed. This is easy in our example because it only involves the collection of absence data. It is also unproblematic if a postal survey is being conducted, although the high level of objectivity this suggests appears less convincing when one considers the element of subjectivity in the choice of questions and the way these are phrased.

An additional important characteristic of deduction is that concepts need to be *operationalised* in a way that enables facts to be measured quantitatively. In our example above the obvious one is absenteeism. Just what constitutes absenteeism would have to be strictly defined: an absence for a complete day would probably count, but what about absence for two hours? In addition, what would constitute a 'short period of employment' and 'younger' employees? What is happening here is that the principle of *reductionism* is being followed. This holds that problems as a whole are better understood if they are reduced to the simplest possible elements.

The final characteristic of the deductive approach is *generalisation*. In order to be able to generalise about regularities in human social behaviour it is necessary to select samples of sufficient numerical size. In our example above, research at a particular store would allow us only to make inferences about that store; it would be dangerous to predict that worker youth and short length of service lead to absenteeism in all cases.

Induction: building theory

An alternative approach to conducting research on DIY store employee absenteeism would be to go on to the shopfloor and interview a sample of the employees and their supervisors about the experience of working at the store. The purpose here would be to get a feel of what was going on, so as to understand better the nature of the problem. Your task then would be to make sense of the interview data you had collected by analysing those data. The result of this analysis would be the formulation of a theory. This may be that there is a relationship between absence and relatively short periods of employment. Alternatively, you may discover that there are other competing reasons for absence that may or may not be related to worker age or length of service. You may end up with the same theory, but you would have gone about the production of that theory in an *inductive* way: theory would follow data rather than vice versa as in the deductive approach.

We noted earlier that the deductive approach has its origins in research in the natural sciences. However, the emergence of the social sciences in the 20th century led social science researchers to be wary of the deductive approach. They were critical of an approach that enabled a cause–effect link to be made between particular variables without an understanding of the way in which humans interpreted their social world. Developing such an understanding is, of course, a strength of inductive research. In our absenteeism example we would argue that it is more realistic to treat workers as humans whose attendance behaviour is a consequence of the way in which they perceive their work experience, rather than as if they were unthinking research objects who respond in a mechanistic way to certain circumstances.

Followers of the inductive approach would also criticise the deductive approach because of its tendency to construct a rigid methodology that does not permit alternative explanations of what is going on. In that sense, there is an air of finality about the choice of theory and definition of the hypothesis. Alternative theories may be suggested by the deductive approach. However, these would be within the limits set by the highly structured research design. In this respect, a significant characteristic of the absenteeism research design noted above is that of the operationalisation of concepts. As we saw in the absenteeism example, age was precisely defined. However, a less structured approach might reveal alternative explanations of the absenteeism–age relationship denied by a stricter definition of age.

Research using the inductive approach would be particularly concerned with the context in which such events were taking place. Therefore the study of a small sample of subjects might be more appropriate than a large number as with the deductive approach. As can be seen in Chapter 9, researchers in this tradition are more likely to work with qualitative data and to use a variety of methods to collect these data in order to establish different views of phenomena (Easterby-Smith *et al.*, 2002).

At this stage you may be asking yourself: So what? Why is the approach that I take to my research project important? Easterby-Smith *et al.* (2002) suggest three reasons. First, it enables you to take a more informed decision about your research design, which is

> . . . more than simply the methods by which data are collected and analysed. It is the overall configuration of a piece of research: what kind of evidence is gathered and from where, and how such evidence is interpreted in order to provide good answers to the basic research question.

Second, it will help you to think about those research approaches that will work for you and, crucially, those that will not. For example, if you are particularly interested in understanding why something is happening, rather than being able to describe what is happening, it may be more appropriate to adopt the inductive approach rather than the deductive.

Third, Easterby-Smith *et al.* (2002) argue that a knowledge of the different research traditions enables you to adapt your research design to cater for constraints. These may be practical, involving, say, limited access to data, or they may arise from a lack of prior knowledge of the subject. You simply may not be in a position to frame a hypothesis because you have insufficient understanding of the topic to do this.

Combining approaches to research

So far we have conveyed the impression that there are rigid divisions between the two approaches to research. This would be misleading. Not only is it perfectly possible to combine approaches within the same piece of research, but in our experience it is often advantageous to do so.

worked example

Deductive and inductive research

Sadie decided to conduct a research project on violence at work and its effects on the stress levels of staff. She considered the different ways she would approach the work were she to adopt:

- the deductive approach;
- the inductive approach.

If she decided to adopt a deductive approach to her work she would have:

1 to start with the hypothesis that staff working with the public are more likely to experience the threat or reality of violence and resultant stress;

2 to decide to research a population in which she would have expected to find evidence of violence, for example a sizeable social security office;

3 to administer a questionnaire to a large sample of staff in order to establish the extent of violence (either actually experienced or threatened) and the levels of stress experienced by them;

4 to be particularly careful about how she defined violence;

5 to standardise the stress responses of the staff, for example days off sick or sessions with a counsellor.

On the other hand, if she decided to adopt an inductive approach she might have decided to interview some staff who had been subjected to violence at work. She might have been interested in their feelings about the events that they had experienced, how they coped with the problems they experienced, and their views about the possible causes of the violence.

Either approach would have yielded valuable data about this problem (indeed, both may be used in this project, at different stages). Neither approach should be thought of as better than the other. They are better at different things. It depends where her research emphasis lies.

We return to the topic of using multiple method in Section 4.3. At this point we summarise some of the major differences between deductive and inductive approaches to research. This is done in Box 4.1.

Box 4.1 Major differences between deductive and inductive approaches to research

Deduction emphasises

- scientific principles
- moving from theory to data
- the need to explain causal relationships between variables
- the collection of quantitative data
- the application of controls to ensure validity of data
- the operationalisation of concepts to ensure clarity of definition
- a highly structured approach
- researcher independence of what is being researched
- the necessity to select samples of sufficient size in order to generalise conclusions

Induction emphasises

- gaining an understanding of the meanings humans attach to events
- a close understanding of the research context
- the collection of qualitative data
- a more flexible structure to permit changes of research emphasis as the research progresses
- a realisation that the researcher is part of the research process
- less concern with the need to generalise

At this point you may be wondering about which research approach you should adopt. Creswell (1994) suggests a number of practical criteria. Perhaps the most important of these is the nature of the research topic. A topic on which there is a wealth of literature from which you can define a theoretical framework and a hypothesis lends itself more readily to the deductive approach. With research into a topic that is new, is exciting much debate, and on which there is little existing literature, it may be more appropriate to generate data and analyse and reflect on what theoretical themes the data are suggesting.

The time you have available will be an issue. Deductive research can be quicker to complete, albeit that time must be devoted to setting up the study prior to data collection and analysis. Data collection is often based on 'one take'. It is normally possible to predict the time schedules accurately. On the other hand, inductive research can be much more protracted. Often the ideas, based on a much longer period of data collection and analysis, have to emerge gradually. This leads to another important consideration, the extent to which you are prepared to indulge in risk. The deductive approach can be a lower-risk strategy, albeit that there are risks, such as the non-return of questionnaires. With induction you have constantly to live with the fear that no useful data patterns and theory will emerge. Finally, there is the question of audience. In our experience, most managers are familiar with the deductive approach and much more likely to put faith in the conclusions emanating from this approach. You may also wish to consider the preferences of the person marking your research report. We all have our preferences about the approach to adopt. You may be wise to establish these before nailing your colours too firmly to one mast.

This last point suggests that not all the decisions about the research approach that you make should always be so practical. Hakim (1987) uses an architectural metaphor to illustrate the approach choice process. She introduces the notion of the researcher's preferred style, which, rather like the architect's, may reflect '... the architect's own preferences and ideas ... and the stylistic preferences of those who pay for the work and have to live with the finished result' (Hakim, 1987:1). This echoes the feelings of Buchanan *et al.* (1988:59), who argue that 'needs, interests and preferences (of the researcher) ... are typically overlooked but are central to the progress of fieldwork'. However, a note of caution: it is important that your preferences do not lead to your changing the essence of the research question.

4.2 The need for a clear research strategy

Your *research strategy* will be a general plan of how you will go about answering the research question(s) you have set (the importance of clearly defining the research question cannot be overemphasised). It will contain clear objectives, derived from your research question(s), specify the sources from which you intend to collect data, and consider the constraints that you will inevitably have (for example access to data, time, location and money, ethical issues). Crucially, it should reflect the fact that you have thought carefully about why you are employing your particular strategy. It would be perfectly legitimate for your assessor to ask you why you chose to conduct your research in a particular organisation, why you chose the particular department, why you chose to talk to one group of staff rather than another. You must have valid reasons for all your research strategy decisions. The justification should always be based on your research question(s) and objectives.

At this point we should make a clear distinction between strategy and *tactics*. The former is concerned with the overall approach you adopt; the latter is about the finer detail of data collection and analysis methods. Decisions about tactics will involve your being clear about the different data collection methods (for example questionnaires, interviews, focus groups, published data) and subsequent analysis, which will be dealt with in detail in subsequent chapters. At this point we are concerned with general questions of strategy.

The different research strategies

In this section we turn our attention to the research strategies you may employ. Some of these clearly belong to the deductive tradition, others to the inductive approach. However, often allocating strategies to one tradition or the other is unduly simplistic. What matters is not the label that is attached to a particular strategy, but whether it is appropriate for your particular research question(s) and objectives. We must also emphasise that these strategies should not be thought of as being mutually exclusive. The strategies that we consider here are:

- experiment;
- survey;
- case study;
- grounded theory;
- ethnography;
- action research;
- cross-sectional and longitudinal studies;
- exploratory, descriptive and explanatory studies.

Experiment

Experiment is a classical form of research that owes much to the natural sciences, although it features strongly in much social science research, particularly psychology. It will involve typically:

- definition of a theoretical hypothesis;
- selection of samples of individuals from known populations;
- allocation of samples to different experimental conditions;
- introduction of planned change on one or more of the variables;
- measurement on a small number of the variables;
- control of other variables.

worked example

Using the experimental strategy

Deci (1972) studied the effect of external rewards and controls on the intrinsic motivation of individuals. He set up a laboratory study in which each subject participated in three one-hour sessions of puzzle solving. It had been established by an earlier experiment that the puzzles were intrinsically interesting. There were two participant groups: the experimental group and the control group. Both groups were asked to solve four puzzles during each of the three sessions. The only difference between the two groups was that the experimental group was paid one dollar per puzzle solved during the second session.

During each of the three sessions each group was left alone for an eight-minute 'free-choice period'. Deci reasoned that if the subjects continued puzzle solving in the 'free-choice period' (there were other activities to pursue, such as reading magazines) then they must be intrinsically motivated to do so. In the event, the experimental group that had been given the external incentive spent less of their 'free' time puzzle solving. The result of this led to Deci theorising that the introduction of external incentives to intrinsically interesting tasks will lead to a decrease in intrinsic motivation, a theory that has interesting implications for those introducing pay incentive schemes for employees who do jobs that they find intrinsically interesting!

Survey

The survey strategy is usually associated with the deductive approach. It is a popular and common strategy in business and management research. Surveys are popular for some of the reasons mentioned earlier. They allow the collection of a large amount of data from a sizeable population in a highly economical way. Often obtained by using a questionnaire, these data are standardised, allowing easy comparison. In addition, the survey strategy is perceived as authoritative by people in general. This is because it is easily understood. Every day a news bulletin or a newspaper reports the results of a new survey that indicates, for example, that a certain percentage of the population thinks or behaves in a particular way.

Using a survey strategy should give you more control over the research process. However, much time will be spent in designing and piloting the questionnaire. Analysing the results, even with the aid of an appropriate computer package, will also be time consuming. However, it will be your time – you will be independent. Many researchers complain that their progress is delayed by their dependence on others for information.

However, the data collected by the survey strategy may not be as wide-ranging as those collected by other research strategies. There is a limit to the number of questions that any questionnaire can contain if the goodwill of the respondent is not to be presumed on too much. However, perhaps the biggest drawback with the questionnaire method is, as emphasised in Section 10.2, the capacity to do it badly!

The questionnaire, however, is not the only data collection method that belongs to the survey strategy. Structured observation, of the type most frequently associated with organisation and methods (O & M) research, and structured interviews, where standardised questions are asked of all interviewees, also often fall into this strategy. Observation methods are dealt with in detail in Section 8.4 and structured interviews in Section 10.5.

Case study

Robson (2002:178) defines *case study* as 'a strategy for doing research which involves an empirical investigation of a particular contemporary phenomenon within its real life context using multiple sources of evidence'. This strategy will be of particular interest to you if you wish to gain a rich understanding of the context of the research and the processes being enacted (Morris and Wood, 1991). The case study strategy also has considerable ability to generate answers to the question 'why?' as well as the 'what?' and 'how?' questions, although 'what?' and 'how?' questions tend to be more the concern of the survey strategy. The data collection methods employed may be various. They may include questionnaires, interviews, observation, documentary analysis and (as if to emphasise the dangers of constructing neat boxes in which to categorise the approaches, strategies and methods) questionnaires.

You may be suspicious of conducting case study research because of the 'unscientific' feel it has. We would argue that case study can be a very worthwhile way of exploring existing theory. In addition, a simple, well-constructed case study can enable you to challenge an existing theory and also provide a source of new hypotheses.

Grounded theory

Grounded theory (Glaser and Strauss, 1967) is often thought of as the best example of the inductive approach, although this conclusion would be too simplistic. It is better to think of it as 'theory building' through a combination of induction and deduction. Sections 12.4 and 12.6 go into detail about grounded theory. Here all we shall do is explain what this strategy involves.

In grounded theory, data collection starts without the formation of an initial theoretical framework. Theory is developed from data generated by a series of observations (Section 12.6 explains in some detail how data analysis is conducted to develop such theory deductively). These data lead to the generation of predictions that are then tested in further observations which may confirm, or otherwise, the predictions. Constant reference to the data to develop and test theory leads Hussey and Hussey (1997) to call grounded theory an inductive/deductive approach, theory being grounded in such continual reference to the data.

Ethnography

Ethnography is also firmly rooted in the inductive approach. It emanates from the field of anthropology. The purpose is to interpret the social world the research subjects inhabit in the way in which they interpret it. This is obviously a research strategy that is very time consuming and takes place over an extended time period. The research process needs to be flexible and responsive to change since the researcher will constantly be developing new patterns of thought about what is being observed.

Although not a dominant research strategy in business, ethnography may be very appropriate, as we demonstrate in Section 8.2. This deals in some detail with participant observation, the research method that dominates ethnography.

Action research

Lewin first used the term '*action research*' in 1946. It has been interpreted subsequently by management researchers in a variety of ways, but there are three common themes within the literature. The first focuses on and emphasises the purpose of the research: the management of a change (Cunningham, 1995). The second relates to the involvement of practitioners in the research and in particular to a close collaboration between practitioners and researchers, for example academics or external consultants. Eden and Huxham (1996:75) argue that the findings of action research result from 'involvement with members of an organisation over a matter which is of genuine concern to them'. Therefore the researcher is part of the organisation within which the research and change process are taking place (Zuber-Skerritt, 1996).

The final theme suggests that action research should have implications beyond the immediate project; in other words it must be clear that the results could inform other contexts. For academics undertaking action research, Eden and Huxham (1996) link this to an explicit concern for the development of theory. However, they emphasise that for consultants this is more likely to focus on the subsequent transfer of knowledge gained from one specific context to another. Such use of knowledge to inform other contexts we believe also applies to others undertaking action research, such as practitioners.

Thus action research differs from other forms of applied research because of its explicit focus on action, in particular promoting change within the organisation (Marsick and Watkins, 1997). As Coghlan and Brannick (2001) note: 'the purpose of (action) research and discourse is not just to describe, understand and explain the world but also to change it'. In addition the person undertaking the research is involved in this action for change and subsequently application of the knowledge gained elsewhere.

The action research strategy, as illustrated in Figure 4.2, commences with an initial idea for a change intervention. This is likely to be expressed as an objective. Reconnaissance (fact finding and analysis) about the change intervention is undertaken in order to generate an overall plan and a decision about the first steps to be taken. The remainder of the first cycle is concerned with carrying out this plan, monitoring and evaluating. Subsequent cycles involve revising the change intervention to ensure it meets the needs of the organisation using information gathered through the monitoring and evaluation process. Planned action steps are amended and implemented to take account of unforeseen changes. Their effects are monitored and evaluated and further amendments made.

The strengths of an action research strategy are a focus upon change, the recognition that time needs to be devoted to reconnaissance, monitoring and evaluation and the involvement of employees (practitioners) throughout the process.

Schein (1995) emphasises the importance of employee involvement throughout the process, as employees are more likely to implement change they have helped to create. Once employees have identified a need for change and have widely shared this need it becomes difficult to ignore, and the pressure for change comes from within the organisation. Action research therefore combines both information gathering and facilitation of change.

Action research can have two distinct foci (Schein, 1995). The first of these aims to fulfil the agenda of those undertaking the research rather than that of the sponsor. This does not, however, preclude the sponsor from also benefiting from the changes brought about by the research process. The second focus starts with the needs of the sponsor and involves those undertaking the research in the sponsor's issues, rather than the

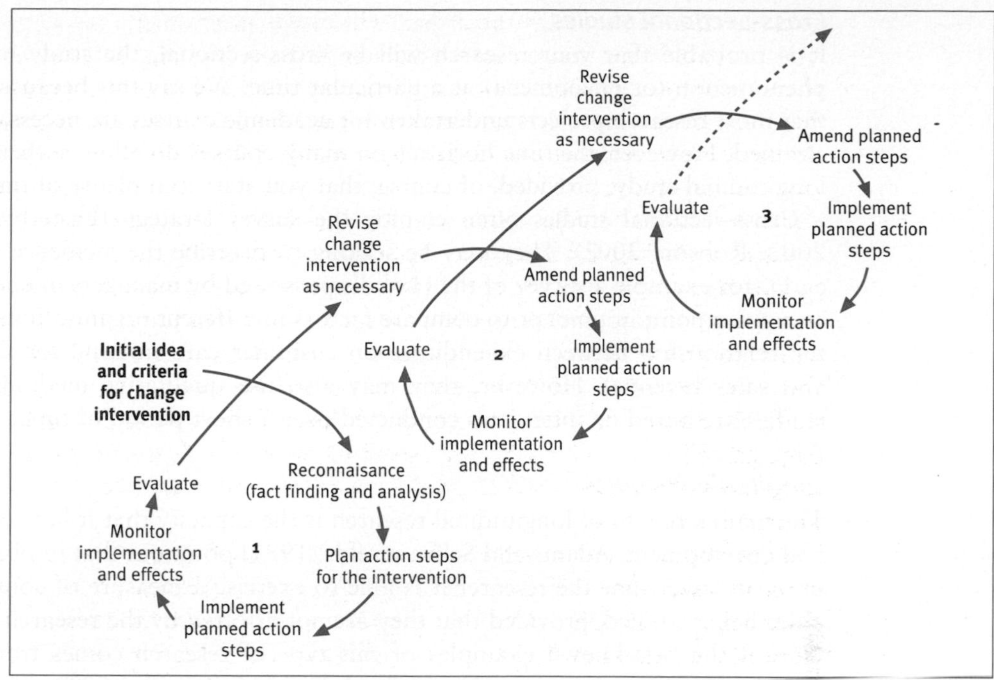

Figure 4.2 The action research spiral

Source: Thornhill *et al.* (2000); reproduced by permission

sponsor in their issues. These consultant activities are termed 'process consultation' by Schein (1999). The consultant, he argues, assists the client to perceive, understand and act upon the process events that occur within their environment in order to improve the situation as the client sees it. (Within this definition the term 'client' refers to the persons or person, often senior managers, who sponsor the research.) Using Schein's analogy of a clinician and clinical enquiry, the consultant (researcher) is involved by the sponsor in the diagnosis (action research), which is driven by the sponsor's needs. It therefore follows that subsequent interventions are jointly owned by the consultant and the sponsor, who is involved at all stages. The process consultant therefore helps the sponsor to gain the skills of diagnosis and fixing organisational problems so that she or he can develop autonomy in improving the organisation.

Time horizons

An important question to be asked in planning your research is 'Do I want my research to be a "snapshot" taken at a particular time or do I want it to be more akin to a "diary" and be a representation of events over a given period?' (As always, of course, the answer should be 'It depends on the research question'.) The 'snapshot' approach is what we call here *cross-sectional* while the 'diary' perspective we call *longitudinal*.

We should emphasise here that these time perspectives to research design are independent of which research strategy you are pursuing. So, for example, you may be studying the change in manufacturing processes in one company over a period of a year. This would be a longitudinal case study.

Cross-sectional studies

It is probable that your research will be cross-sectional, the study of a particular phenomenon (or phenomena) at a particular time. We say this because we recognise that most research projects undertaken for academic courses are necessarily time constrained. However, the time horizons on many courses do allow sufficient time for a longitudinal study, provided, of course, that you start it in plenty of time!

Cross-sectional studies often employ the survey strategy (Easterby-Smith *et al.*, 2002; Robson, 2002). They may be seeking to describe the incidence of a phenomenon (for example a survey of the IT skills possessed by managers in one organisation at a given point in time) or to compare factors in different organisations (for example the relationship between expenditure on customer care training for sales assistants and sales revenue). However, they may also use qualitative methods. Many case studies are based on interviews conducted over a short period of time.

Longitudinal studies

The main strength of longitudinal research is the capacity that it has to study change and development. Adams and Schvaneveldt (1991) point out that in observing people or events over time the researcher is able to exercise a measure of control over variables being studied, provided that they are not affected by the research process itself. One of the best-known examples of this type of research comes from outside the world of business. It is the long-running television series *Seven Up*. This has charted the progress of a cohort of people every seven years of their life. Not only is this fascinating television, it has also provided the social scientist with a rich source of data on which to test and develop theories of human development.

Even with time constraints it is possible to introduce a longitudinal element to your research. As Section 7.2 indicates, there is a massive amount of published data collected over time just waiting to be analysed! An example is the Workplace Industrial Relations Survey, which was conducted in 1980, 1984, 1990 (Millward *et al.*, 1992) and 1998 (Cully *et al.*, 1999). From these surveys you would be able to gain valuable data, which would give you a powerful insight into developments in personnel management and industrial relations over a period of wide-ranging change. In longitudinal studies the basic question is 'Has there been any change over a period of time?' (Bouma and Atkinson, 1995:114).

Exploratory, descriptive and explanatory studies

Enquiries can be classified in terms of their purpose as well as by the research strategy used (Robson, 2002). The classification most often used is the threefold one of exploratory, descriptive and explanatory. In the same way as you may employ more than one strategy in your research project, so you may have more than one purpose. Indeed, as Robson (2002) points out, the purpose of your enquiry may change over time.

Exploratory studies

Exploratory studies are a valuable means of finding out 'what is happening; to seek new insights; to ask questions and to assess phenomena in a new light' (Robson, 2002:59). It is particularly useful if you wish to clarify your understanding of a problem. It may well be that time is well spent on exploratory research, as it may show that the research is not worth pursuing!

There are three principal ways of conducting exploratory research:

- a search of the literature;
- talking to experts in the subject;
- conducting focus group interviews.

Exploratory research can be likened to the activities of the traveller or explorer (Adams and Schvaneveldt, 1991). Its great advantage is that it is flexible and adaptable to change. If you are conducting exploratory research you must be willing to change your direction as a result of new data that appears and new insights that occur to you. A quotation from the travel writer V.S. Naipaul (1989:222) illustrates this point beautifully:

> I had been concerned, at the start of my own journey, to establish some lines of enquiry, to define a theme. The approach had its difficulties. At the back of my mind was always a worry that I would come to a place and all contacts would break down ... If you travel on a theme the theme has to develop with the travel. At the beginning your interests can be broad and scattered. But then they must be more focused; the different stages of a journey cannot simply be versions of one another. And ... this kind of travel depended on luck. It depended on the people you met, the little illuminations you had. As with the next day's issue of fast-moving daily newspaper, the shape of the character in hand was continually being changed by accidents along the way.

Adams and Schvaneveldt (1991) reinforce this point by arguing that the flexibility inherent in exploratory research does not mean absence of direction to the enquiry. What it does mean is that the focus is initially broad and becomes progressively narrower as the research progresses.

Descriptive studies

The object of *descriptive research* is 'to portray an accurate profile of persons, events or situations' (Robson, 2002:59).This may be an extension of, or a forerunner to, a piece of exploratory research. It is necessary to have a clear picture of the phenomena on which you wish to collect data prior to the collection of the data. One of the earliest well-known examples of a descriptive survey is the Domesday Book, which described the population of England in 1085.

Often project tutors are rather wary of work that is too descriptive. There is a danger of their saying 'That's very interesting ... but so what?' They will want you to go further and draw conclusions from your data. They will encourage you to develop the skills of evaluating data and synthesising ideas. These are higher-order skills than those of accurate description. Description in management and business research has a very clear place. However, it should be thought of as a means to an end rather than an end in itself.

Explanatory studies

Studies that establish causal relationships between variables may be termed *explanatory studies*. The emphasis here is on studying a situation or a problem in order to explain the relationships between variables. You may find, for example, that a cursory analysis of quantitative data on manufacturing scrap rates shows a relationship between scrap rates and the age of the machine being operated. You could go ahead and subject the data to statistical tests such as correlation (discussed in Section 11.5) in order to get a clearer view of the relationship.

worked example

An explanatory study

Phil studied individual performance-related pay systems for managers. He was interested in explaining the relationship between success (a concept that needed to be given a working definition) of such systems and the factors that seemed to lead to such success. This research adopted a case study approach in examining three organisations in some detail. The data collected were mainly qualitative, although some secondary quantitative data were used. What emerged was that the way in which implementing managers conducted the processes of assessing the performance of their managers and translating these assessments into rewards was more important than the design of such systems.

Practitioner–researcher

All of the above strategies may involve you in pursuing research in your own organisation, thus adopting the role of the *practitioner–researcher*. If you are a part-time student, or if you are undertaking research as part of your job, you will be surrounded by exciting opportunities to pursue business and management research. You are unlikely to encounter one of the most difficult hurdles that the participant observer has to overcome: that of negotiating research access. Indeed, like many people in such a position, you may be asked to research a particular problem by your employer that lends itself to this methodological approach.

Another advantage is your knowledge of the organisation and all this implies about understanding the complexity of what goes on in that organisation. It just is not necessary to spend a good deal of valuable time in 'learning the context' in the same way as the outsider does. However, that advantage carries with it a significant disadvantage. You must be very conscious of the assumptions and preconceptions that you carry around with you. This is an inevitable consequence of knowing the organisation well. It can prevent you from exploring issues that would enrich the research.

Familiarity has other problems. When we were doing case study work in a manufacturing company, we found it very useful to ask 'basic' questions revealing our ignorance about the industry and the organisation. These 'basic' questions are ones that as the practitioner–researcher you would be less likely to ask because you would feel that you should know the answers already.

There is also the problem of status. As a junior employee you may feel that working with more senior colleagues inhibits your interactions as researcher–practitioner. The same may be true if you are more senior than your colleagues.

A more practical problem is that of time. Combining two roles at work is obviously very demanding, particularly as it may involve you in much data recording 'after hours'. This activity is hidden from those who determine your workload. They may not appreciate the demands that your researcher role is making on you. For this reason, Robson (2002) makes much of practitioner–researchers negotiating a proportion of their 'work time' to devote to their research. There are no easy answers to these problems. All you can do is be aware of the threats to the quality of your data by being too close to your research setting. As will now be obvious to you, all methods have their strengths and weaknesses.

4.3 Using multi-methods

These approaches and strategies obviously do not exist in isolation and therefore can be 'mixed and matched'. Not only can they, but it is often beneficial to do so. It is quite usual for a single study to combine quantitative and qualitative methods and to use primary and secondary data.

There are two major advantages to employing *multi-methods* in the same study. First, different methods can be used for different purposes in a study. You may wish to employ, for example, interviews, in order to get a feel for the key issues before embarking on a questionnaire. This would give you confidence that you were addressing the most important issues.

worked example

Combining survey and case study methods

We conducted an employee attitude survey in a small insurance company, which used three different types of method. Two of these were qualitative and one was quantitative. The research consisted of four stages:

1. In-depth interviews with senior managers in order to get a picture of the important issues we were likely to encounter in the research. These were essential contextual data.
2. Discussion groups with six to ten employees representing different grades and occupations in the company. This was to establish the types of issues that were important to staff. This would inform the content of the questionnaire.
3. A questionnaire that was administered to 100 of the 200 head office employees. We wanted to get the sort of data that would allow us to compare the attitudes of different employee groups: by age, gender, length of service, occupation and grade. This was particularly important to the company.
4. Semi-structured group interviews with further representative employee groups to clarify the content of some of the questionnaire results. This was essential to get at the meaning behind some of the data.

The second advantage of using multi-methods is that it enables *triangulation* to take place. Triangulation refers to the use of different data collection methods within one study in order to ensure that the data are telling you what you think they are telling you. For example, semi-structured group interviews may be a valuable way of triangulating data collected by other means such as a questionnaire.

Each method, tool or technique has its unique strengths and weaknesses (Smith, 1975). There is an inevitable relationship between the data collection method you employ and the results you obtain. In short, the results will be affected by the method used. The problem here is that it is impossible to ascertain the nature of that effect. Since all different methods will have different effects, it makes sense to use different methods to cancel out the 'method effect'. That will lead to greater confidence being placed in your conclusions.

The question that may occur to you at this stage is: 'How do I know which method to use in which situation?' There is no simple answer. We encourage you to use your imagination and to think of research as a highly creative process. However, above all it is vital to have clear objectives for your study. It is a great temptation to think about the methods to be employed before the objectives are clarified.

worked example

Using a multi-method approach

Darren wanted to establish how new supervisors learned to do the job. In order to do this he thought it essential that he should have the clearest possible grasp of what the supervisor's job entailed.

This involved him in shadowing a new supervisor for a week, talking to night shift supervisors to establish any differences in approach, sending a questionnaire to supervisors in different locations in the company and interviewing the managers to whom those supervisors reported.

This gave Darren a much better grasp of the content of the supervisor's job. It also did much to enhance his credibility in the eyes of the supervisors. He was then able to draw on the valuable data he had collected to complete his main research task: to find out how new supervisors learned to do the job.

4.4 The credibility of research findings

Underpinning the above discussion on multi-method usage has been the issue of the credibility of research findings. This is neatly expressed by Raimond (1993:55) when he subjects findings to the 'how do I know?' test: '. . . will the evidence and my conclusions stand up to the closest scrutiny?' How do you know that new supervisors learn their jobs by largely informal methods? How did we know that manual employees in our electronics factory had more negative feelings towards their employer than their clerical counterparts? The answer, of course, is that, in the literal sense of the question, you cannot know. All you can do is to reduce the possibility of getting the answer wrong. This is where sound research design is important. This is aptly summarised by Rogers (1961, cited by Raimond 1993:55): 'scientific methodology needs to be seen for what it truly is, a way of preventing me from deceiving myself in regard to my creatively formed subjective hunches which have developed out of the relationship between me and my material'.

Reducing the possibility of getting the answer wrong means that attention has to be paid to two particular emphases on research design: reliability and validity.

Reliability

Reliability can be assessed by posing the following three questions (Easterby-Smith *et al.*, 2002:53):

1 Will the measures yield the same results on other occasions?
2 Will similar observations be reached by other observers?
3 Is there transparency in how sense was made from the raw data?

Threats to reliability

Robson (2002) asserts that there may be four threats to reliability. The first of these is *subject or participant error*. If you are studying the degree of enthusiasm employees have for their work and their employer it may be that you will find that a questionnaire completed at different times of the week may generate different results. Friday afternoons may show a different picture from Monday mornings! This should be easy to control. You should choose a more 'neutral' time when employees may be expected to be neither on a 'high', looking forward to the weekend, nor on a 'low' with the working week in front of them.

Similarly, there may be *subject or participant bias*. Interviewees may have been saying what they thought their bosses wanted them to say. This is a particular problem in organisations that are characterised by an authoritarian management style or when there is a threat of employment insecurity. Researchers should be aware of this potential problem when designing research. For example, elaborate steps can be taken to ensure the anonymity of respondents to questionnaires, as Section 10.4 indicates. Care should also be taken when analysing the data to ensure that your data are telling you what you think they are telling you.

Third, there may have been *observer error*. In one piece of research we undertook, there were three of us conducting interviews with potential for at least three different approaches to eliciting answers. Introducing a high degree of structure to the interview schedule (Section 9.2) will lessen this threat to reliability.

Finally, there may have been *observer bias*. Here, of course, there may have been three different approaches to interpreting the replies!

There is more detail on how these threats to reliability may be reduced later in the book in the chapters dealing with specific data collection methods.

Validity

Validity is concerned with whether the findings are really about what they appear to be about. Is the relationship between two variables a *causal relationship*? For example, in a study of an electronics factory we found that employees' failure to look at new product displays was caused not by employee apathy but by lack of opportunity (the displays were located in a part of the factory that employees rarely visited). This potential lack of validity in the conclusions was minimised by a research design that built in the opportunity for focus groups after the questionnaire results had been analysed.

Robson (2002) has also charted the threats to validity, which provides a useful way of thinking about this important topic.

Threats to validity

History

You may decide to study the opinions that employees have about job security in a particular organisation. However, if the research is conducted shortly after a major redundancy programme this may well have a dramatic, and quite misleading, effect on the findings (unless, of course, the specific objective of the research was to find out about post-redundancy opinions).

Testing

Your research may include measuring how long it takes telesales operators to deal with customer enquiries. If the operators believe that the results of the research may disadvantage them in some way, then this is likely to affect the results.

Instrumentation

In the above example, the telesales operators may have received an instruction that they are to take every opportunity to sell new policies between the times you tested the first batch and the second batch of operators. Consequently, the calls are likely to last longer.

Mortality

This refers to participants dropping out of studies. This was a major problem for one of our students, who was studying the effects on the management styles of managers exposed to a year-long management development programme.

Maturation

In the earlier management development example above it could be that other events happening during the year have an effect on their management style.

Ambiguity about causal direction

This is a particularly difficult issue. One of our part-time students was studying the effectiveness of performance appraisal in her organisation. One of her findings was that poor performance ratings of employees were associated with a negative attitude about appraisal among those same employees. What she was not clear about was whether the poor performance ratings were causing the negative attitude to appraisal or whether the negative attitude to appraisal was causing the poor performance ratings.

Generalisability

This is sometimes referred to as *external validity*. A concern you may have in the design of your research is the extent to which your research results are generalisable: that is, whether your findings may be equally applicable to other research settings, such as other organisations. This is a particular worry if you are conducting case study research in one organisation, or a small number of organisations. It may also be important if the organisation is markedly 'different' in some way.

In such cases the purpose of your research will not be to produce a theory that is generalisable to all populations. Your task will be simply to try to explain what is going on in your particular research setting. It may be that you want to test the robustness of your conclusions by exposing them to other research settings in a follow-up study. In short, as long as you do not claim that your results, conclusions or theory can be generalised, then there is no problem.

Logic leaps and false assumptions

So far in this chapter we have shown that there are a host of decisions that need to be made in order that your research project can yield sufficient data of the sort that will result in valid conclusions being drawn. Those decisions necessitate careful thought from you. However, more than just the quantity of thought is involved. It is vital that your thought processes are of high quality. Your research design will be based on a flow of logic and a number of assumptions, all of which must stand up to the closest scrutiny.

These points have been illustrated skilfully by Raimond (1993). Raimond takes the research of Peters and Waterman on 'excellent' US companies and subjects it to just such scrutiny. The ideas of Peters and Waterman (1982) have been enormously influential in the last two decades. Their book is a management 'cookbook' that gives managers eight principles to which they must adhere if their organisations are to be successful. As such, it is fairly typical of a prescriptive type of writing in management books and journals that suggests that 'this is the way it should be done'.

Raimond's (1993) analysis of Peters and Waterman can be categorised into four 'logic steps'.

Identification of the research population

This is similar to the point made about generalisability above. If the intention is to be able to generalise the conclusions across the whole population (in the Peters and Waterman case, all organisations), is the choice of population logical? If your research project is in the National Health Service, for example, it would be fanciful to assume that the findings were valid for software houses or advertising agencies.

Data collection

Is it logical to assume that the way you are collecting your data is going to yield valid data? If you interview top bosses you are likely to encounter the 'good news' syndrome. If you collect press cuttings from newspapers how can you assume there has been no political bias put on them?

Data interpretation

It is here that there is probably the greatest danger of logic leaps and false assumptions. You will need to move from a position where you have a mountain of data to one where you write a set of conclusions that are presented coherently. This is at the same time an intellectually challenging and highly creative and exciting process.

You are likely to be using a theoretical framework against which you will analyse your data. If you are working deductively (from theory to data), this framework may have given rise to the hypothesis that you are testing in your research. One of our students studied the introduction of pay bonuses assessed by performance appraisal in the police service. Her hypothesis was based on the Meyer *et al.* (1965) hypothesis that the non-pay benefits of appraisal (such as improvement of job performance) will be prejudiced by the introduction of pay considerations to the process, rendering the appraisal interview little more than a salary discussion.

It is less likely that you will be working completely inductively where you collect your data and then analyse it to what theory emerges.

You may employ a hybrid approach. This could involve using an established theoretical construct to help you to make sense of your findings. For example, you may be studying the way in which different companies within the group in which you work formulate their business strategies. In order to structure your analysis you could use the categorisation of different types of organisational strategy suggested by Mintzberg and Waters (1989). This may lead you to conclude that the dominant strategy employed is a mixture of those suggested by Mintzberg and Waters.

The important point here is that in both the deductive and the hybrid cases you are making assumptions about the appropriateness of the theory that you are using. In both cases it is clear that the theory with which you are working will shape your conclusions. Therefore it is essential that you choose an appropriate theoretical framework. It is essential that you ask yourself 'Why am I using this theory and not another which may be equally, or more, appropriate?'

We are making the assumption here that you will use a theory to analyse your data. For most undergraduate and postgraduate courses this is likely to be a requirement of your project tutor. Some professional courses may be more concerned with practical management reports that emphasise the importance of the report making viable recommendations, which are the result of clear conclusions based on a set of findings. It is important that you clarify this point with the project tutor prior to commencing the research.

Development of conclusions

The question to ask yourself here is 'Do my conclusions (or does my theory) stand up to the closest scrutiny?' If the declared theory in the police appraisal study is that the introduction of pay to appraisal will lead to the appraisal process being useful for pay purposes only, does this apply to all police appraisals? Will it be true for younger as well as older police and for all grades and locations? In other words, are you asking your readers to make logic leaps?

4.5 The ethics of research design

Section 5.4 deals in more detail with the subject of research ethics. This has important implications for the negotiation of access to people and organisations and the collection of data. Here we shall address only the ethical issues that you should consider when designing your research strategy.

Your choice of topic will be governed by ethical considerations. You may be particularly interested to study the consumer decision to buy flower bouquets. Although this may provide some interesting data collection challenges (who buys, for whom and why?), there are not the same ethical difficulties as will be involved in studying, say, the funeral purchasing decision. Your research design in this case may have to concentrate on data collection from the undertaker and, possibly, the purchaser at a time as distant from the death as delicacy permits. The ideal population, of course, may be the purchaser at a time as near as possible to the death. It is a matter of judgement as to whether the strategy and data collection method(s) suggested by ethical considerations will yield data that are valid. The general ethical issue here is that the research design should not subject the research population to embarrassment or any other material disadvantage.

Your research design needs to consider the extent to which you should collect data from a research population that is unaware of the fact they are the subject of research and so have not consented. There was a dispute between solicitors and the Consumers' Association (CA). Telephone enquiries were conducted by the CA with a sample of solicitors for the purpose of assessing the accuracy of legal advice given and the cost of specified work. The calls were, allegedly, made without the CA's identity, or the purpose of the research, being disclosed (Gibb, 1995). It is for you to decide whether a similar research design adopted in your project would be ethical.

It may be quite a different matter if you are collecting data from individuals, rather than from organisations as in the above example. This may be the case if you are conducting your research while working as an employee in an organisation. It may also be so if you are working on a student placement. In this case you would be researching as a *participant observer*. If the topic you were researching was one where it might be beneficial for your research that the fact that you were collecting data on individuals was not disclosed, then this would pose a similar ethical dilemma. This will be discussed in more detail when we deal with observation as a data collection method in Chapter 8.

4.6 Summary

- Three main philosophical positions in relation to research have been discussed in the chapter: positivism, interpretivism and realism. They are different, if not mutually exclusive views about the way in which knowledge is developed and judged as being acceptable. All three have an important part to play in business and management research.
- The two main approaches to research are deductive and inductive. These should not be thought of as mutually exclusive. You can use both in combination on the same research project. The main influence on your choice of research approach should be your research questions and objectives.
- The main research strategies are experiment, survey, case study, grounded theory, ethnography and action research. Again, you should not think of these as discrete entities. There may be a combination of some of these in the same research project.
- Research projects may be cross-sectional or longitudinal. In addition, they may be classed as exploratory, descriptive or explanatory.
- Using multi-methods to research means that different purposes may be served and that triangulation of results is facilitated.

- You should take care to ensure that your results are valid and reliable.
- You should always think carefully about the ethical issues implied by the choice of your research strategy.

self-check Questions

4.1 You have decided to undertake a project and have defined the main research question as 'What are the opinions of consumers to a 10% reduction in weight, with the price remaining the same, of "Snackers" chocolate bars?' Write a hypothesis that you could test in your project.

4.2 You are about to embark on a year-long study of customer service training for sales assistants in two supermarket companies. The purpose of the research is to compare the way in which the training develops and its effectiveness. What measures would you need to take in the research design stage to ensure that the results were valid?

4.3 You are working in an organisation that has branches throughout the UK. The managing director is mindful of the fact that managers of the branches need to talk over common problems on a regular basis. That is why there have always been monthly meetings.

However, she is becoming increasingly concerned that these meetings are not cost-effective. Too many managers see them as an unwelcome intrusion. They feel that their time would be better spent pursuing their principal job objectives. Other managers see it as a 'day off': an opportunity to recharge the batteries.

She has asked you to carry out some research on the cost-effectiveness of the monthly meetings. You have defined the research question you are seeking to answer as 'What are the managers' opinions of the value of their monthly meetings?'

Your principal data collection method will be a questionnaire to all managers who attend the monthly meetings. However, you are keen to triangulate your findings. How might you do this?

4.4 You have started conducting interviews in a university with the university's hourly paid staff (such as porters, gardeners and caterers). The research objective is to establish the extent to which those employees feel a sense of 'belonging' to the university. You have negotiated access to your interviewees through the head of each of the appropriate departments. In each case you have been presented with a list of interviewees.

It soon becomes apparent to you that you are getting a rather rosier picture than you expected. The interviewees are all very positive about their jobs, their managers and the university. This makes you suspicious. Are all the hourly paid staff as positive as this? Are you being given only the employees who can be relied on to tell the 'good news'? Have they been 'got at' by their manager?

There is a great risk that your results will not be valid. What can you do?

4.5 You wish to study the way in which the job of the bank manager has changed over the past 10 years. Your chosen research design is to have unstructured discussions with some bank managers who have been in banking for at least that 10-year period. You are asked by a small audience of peers and supervisors to explain why your chosen research design is as valid as a questionnaire-based survey. What would be your answer?

progressing your research project

Deciding on your research design

- ☐ Return to your research question(s) and objectives. Decide on whether you intend to pursue a deductive (your theory will be tested by observation) or an inductive (the collection of your data will be followed by the development of theory) approach. Explain clearly why you have decided on the approach chosen.
- ☐ Decide which of the research strategies is most appropriate for your research question(s) and objectives. Look at studies in the literature that are similar to your own. Which strategies have been used? What explanations do the researchers give for their choice of strategy?
- ☐ Prepare notes on the constraints under which your research is being conducted. Do they, for example, preclude the pursuit of longitudinal research?
- ☐ How may you combine different research methods in your study? Make notes on the advantages such a multi-method approach would bring.
- ☐ List all the threats to reliability and validity contained in your research design.

References

Adams, G. and Schvaneveldt, J. (1991) *Understanding Research Methods* (2nd edn), New York, Longman.

Bouma, G. and Atkinson, G. (1995) *A Handbook of Social Science Research: A Comprehensive and Practical Guide for Students* (2nd edn), Oxford, Oxford University Press.

Buchanan, D., Boddy, D. and McAlman, J. (1988) 'Getting in, getting on, getting out and getting back', *in* Bryman, A. (ed.), *Doing Research in Organisations*, London, Routledge, pp. 53–67.

Coghlan, D. and Brannick, T. (2001) *Doing Action Research in Your Own Organisation*, London, Sage.

Creswell, J. (1994) *Research Design: Quantitative and Qualitative Approaches*, Thousand Oaks, CA, Sage.

Cully, M., O'Reilly, A., Millward, N., Forth, J., Woodlands, S., Dix, G. and Bryson, A. (1999) *The 1998 Workplace Employment Relations Survey: First Findings* [on-line] [cited 28 July], available from <url:http://www.dti.gov.uk/emar>.

Cunningham, J.B. (1995) 'Strategic considerations in using action research for improving personnel practices', *Public Personnel Management*, 24:2, 515–29.

Deci, E.L. (1972) 'The effects of contingent and non-contingent rewards and controls on intrinsic motivation', *Organisational Behaviour and Human Performance*, 8: 217–19.

Easterby-Smith, M., Thorpe, R. and Lowe, A. (2002) *Management Research: An Introduction* (2nd edn), London, Sage.

Eden, C. and Huxham, C. (1996) 'Action research for management research', *British Journal of Management*, 7:1, 75–86.

Gibb, F. (1995) 'Consumer group accuses lawyers of shoddy service', *The Times*, 5 October.

Gill, J. and Johnson, P. (1997) *Research Methods for Managers*, London, Paul Chapman.

Glaser, B. and Strauss, A. (1967) *The Discovery of Grounded Theory*, Chicago, IL, Aldine.

Hakim, C. (1987) *Research Design: Strategies and Choices in the Design of Social Research*, London, Allen & Unwin.

Hussey, J. and Hussey, R. (1997) *Business Research: A Practical Guide for Undergraduate and Postgraduate Students*, Basingstoke, Macmillan Business.

Marsick, V.J. and Watkins, K.E. (1997) 'Case study research methods', *in* Swanson, R.A. and Holton, E.F. (eds), *Human Resource Development Research Handbook*, San Francisco, CA, Berrett-Koehler, pp. 138–57.

Meyer, H., Kay, E. and French, J. (1965) 'Split roles in performance appraisal', *Harvard Business Review*, 43:1, 123–9.

Millward, N., Stevens, M., Smart, D. and Hawes, W.R. (1992) *Workplace Industrial Relations in Transition*, Aldershot, Dartmouth.

Mintzberg, H. and Waters, J. (1989) 'Of strategies, deliberate and emergent', *in* Asch, D. and Bowman, C. (eds) *Readings in Strategic Management*, Basingstoke, Macmillan Education, pp. 4–19.

Morris, T. and Wood, S. (1991) 'Testing the survey method: continuity and change in British industrial relations', *Work Employment and Society*, 5:2, 259–82.

Naipaul, V.S. (1989) *A Turn in the South*, London, Penguin.

Oja, S.N. and Smulyan, L. (1989) *Collaborative Action Research: A Developmental Approach*, London, Falmer Press.

Peters, T. and Waterman, R. (1982) *In Search of Excellence*, New York, Harper & Row.

Raimond, P. (1993) *Management Projects*, London, Chapman & Hall.

Remenyi, D., Williams, B., Money, A. and Swartz, E. (1998) *Doing Research in Business and Management: An Introduction to Process and Method*, London, Sage.

Robson, C. (1993) *Real World Research: A Resource for Social Scientists and Practitioner–researchers*, Oxford, Blackwell.

Robson, C. (2002) *Real World Research* (2nd edn), Oxford, Blackwell.

Rogers, C.R. (1961) *On Becoming a Person*, Constable, London.

Schein, E. (1992) 'Coming to a new awareness of organisational culture', *in* Salaman, G., *Human Resource Strategies*, London, Sage, pp. 237–9.

Schein, E. (1995), 'Process consultation, action research and clinical enquiry: are they the same?', *Journal of Managerial Psychology*, 10:6, 14–19.

Schein, E. (1999) *Process Consultation Revisited: Building the Helping Relationship*, Reading, MA, Addison-Wesley.

Smith, H. (1975) *Strategies of Social Research: The Methodological Imagination*, Englewood Cliffs, NJ, Prentice-Hall.

Thornhill, A., Lewis, P., Millmore, M. and Saunders, M.N.K. (2000) *Managing Change: A Human Resource Strategy Approach*, Harlow, Financial Times Prentice Hall.

Zuber-Skerritt, O. (1996) 'Emancipatory action research for organisational change and management development, *in* Zuber-Skerritt, O. (ed.) *New Directions in Action Research*, London, Falmer, pp. 83–105.

Further reading

Coghlan, D. and Brannick, T. (2001), *Doing Action Research in Your Own Organisation*, London, Sage. A valuable guide for those wishing to conduct research in their own organisation.

Easterby-Smith, M., Thorpe, R. and Lowe, A. (2002) *Management Research: an Introduction* (2nd edn), London, Sage. Chapter 3 gives a comprehensive and highly readable introduction to different research approaches.

Gill, J. and Johnson, P. (1997) *Research Methods for Managers*, London, Paul Chapman. Chapters 3, 9 and 10 provide a detailed discussion on the choice of approach and strategy and the philosophical and theoretical assumptions underlying that choice.

Raimond, P. (1993) *Management Projects*, London, Chapman & Hall. Chapters 5 and 6 provide an excellent insight into the issue of validity and reliability.

Robson, C. (2002) *Real World Research* (2nd edn), Oxford, Blackwell. Chapters 4–7 give an excellent account of all the topics covered in this chapter. It is very readable, not least for the attractive and accessible way it is laid out. The examples are not drawn principally from management and business. However, do not let that put you off.

CASE 4 Embedded quality at Zarlink Semiconductor

Mick is a project manager at Zarlink, a multinational manufacturer of semiconductors for a variety of high-technology military, medical and consumer applications. Mick is also a part-time MBA student at his local university. As part of his MBA Mick has to complete a dissertation on a management topic of his choice. Since Mick had recently been selected to embed a new quality management system called TS 16949 into his manufacturing site at Swindon in the West of England it seemed sensible that he chose to study quality for his dissertation. Mick's particular fascination was his firm belief that the route to high-quality process in organisations was not through introducing specific techniques but through ensuring that quality was embedded in everything done at Zarlink: part of the lifeblood of the organisation. 'Quality is even about more than people's attitudes' said Mick; 'it's about their beliefs. Quality must be a way of life and dominate the thoughts of everyone in the organisation, irrespective of their job.' Mick wanted to use his dissertation as a way not only of obtaining his MBA but also of learning how he could be more effective in introducing embedded quality at Swindon.

Mick started off his research by searching the quality literature. There was no shortage of this. But soon Mick realised that he was concerned with that branch of the quality literature that dealt with the 'soft' issues of organisational culture change. He became rather disenchanted with much of the literature because it was largely prescriptive. 'I was dubious about a lot of what the gurus were saying,' said Mick. 'They seemed to be saying that if you get your employees to believe this and do that then everything will be fine. I was sceptical of this because I knew through my MBA studies that the success of certain techniques is usually contingent upon the individual circumstances of the organisation.' Nonetheless Mick became attracted to the idea that embedding certain core values in the organisation was a good way of achieving quality goals. The problem was that he did not know which core values were appropriate for his site. Therefore his research question became: 'What are the core values that need to be adopted in Zarlink, Swindon, if embedded quality is to become a success?'

More specifically, Mick's research objectives were:

1. to identify general constructs that constitute 'embedding quality' within an organisation;
2. to compare these beliefs with those espoused by a sample from the senior Zarlink management team;
3. to establish the behaviours and attitudes of the current workforce towards the quality management system at the Zarlink foundry, Swindon;

4 to propose a framework of core values to facilitate the embedding of quality into Zarlink, Swindon.

Having used the literature to refine his research question and objectives Mick then turned his attention to collecting primary data within Zarlink. Initially he thought of using a positivist approach based on a questionnaire using qualitative data, but discussions with Philippa, his tutor, convinced him that there were other ways of collecting data. Mick began to think more deeply about his research strategy, and thought that the advantage of triangulating his data by using multi-method would convince not only his examiners that his data were valid but also the managers at Zarlink who he was hoping would give him the go-ahead to introduce his ideas.

Mick's first research objective had been met by his coverage of the literature. This had been useful in concentrating his mind on embedded quality, but it only took him a limited way. The second and third objectives would lead to a much more meaningful management dissertation.

The second objective involved conducting interviews with key managers in order to 'test' the ideas that Mick had developed about core values as a result of the literature review. The managerial sample he chose comprised managers from other Zarlink sites in the world who had an excellent reputation for embedding quality. At the same time Mick thought it important to include those managers who were concerned with implementing quality at Swindon. Mick conducted six interviews across three sites: one in Canada and one in southern England in addition to the third in Swindon. In each site he interviewed the foundry director and the quality manager. These were the key managers concerned with quality. The non-Swindon managers were interviewed by telephone, and the Swindon managers were interviewed face to face by Mick. He hoped this phase of data collection would give him a very clear idea of Zarlink's view of quality.

In order to meet the third objective he decided to collect data in two ways. The first was to conduct what he called a 'gap analysis'. The purpose of this was to establish the current behaviours concerned with quality – that is, what people actually did in their working lives. This would tell Mick what was being done well and what was being done badly, or not at all, and therefore identify what needed to be done to embed quality. In order to do this Mick designed an audit form based on a purpose-made audit that had been used before in similar organisations. This was administered in all departments of Zarlink, Swindon. Ten of Mick's colleagues were responsible for carrying out the audit. This involved Mick in training them in its use in order to achieve reliability. Mick was opportunistic in the second way he collected data in respect of the third objective. He was fortunate that a general employee attitude survey was imminent. He decided to insert a subsection in this survey that consisted of questions to establish employees' attitudes to quality. This went to each of the 130 employees at Swindon.

Mick was confident that his research strategy would yield rich, valid and reliable data on management beliefs and employee attitudes and practice, which would enable him to propose a framework of core values to facilitate the embedding of quality into Zarlink, Swindon. This would enable him to make a valuable contribution to the well-being of Zarlink and pass his MBA!

Questions

1 Which type(s) of research strategy is Mick employing?

2 In what other ways could Mick have used the literature to refine his research question?

3 In what other ways might Mick have achieved his research aim?

4 What are the benefits of using multiple methods of data collection?

5 What threats to validity are inherent in the research design, and how may these be overcome?

self-check Answers

4.1 Probably the most realistic hypothesis here would be 'consumers of "Snackers" chocolate bars did not notice the difference between the current bar and its reduced weight successor'. Doubtless that is what the Snackers' manufacturers would want confirmed!

4.2 This would be a longitudinal study. Therefore, the potential of some of the threats to validity explained in Section 4.4 is greater simply because they have longer to develop. You would need to make sure that most of these threats were controlled as much as possible. For example, you would need:

- to account for the possibility of a major event during the period of the research (wide-scale redundancies, which might affect employee attitudes) in one of the companies but not the other;
- to ensure that you used the same data collection devices in both companies;
- to be aware of the 'mortality' problem. Some of the sales assistants will leave. You would be advised to replace them with assistants with similar characteristics, as far as possible.

4.3 The questionnaire will undoubtedly perform a valuable function in obtaining a comprehensive amount of data that can be compared easily, say by district or age and gender. However, you would add to the understanding of the problem if you observed managers' meetings. Who does most of the talking? What are the non-verbal behaviour patterns displayed by managers? Who turns up late, or does not turn up at all?

You could also consider talking to managers in groups or individually. Your decision here would be whether to talk to them before or after the questionnaire, or both.

In addition, you could study the minutes of the meetings to discover who contributed the most. Who initiated the most discussions? What were the attendance patterns?

4.4 There is no easy answer to this question! You have to remember that access to organisations to research is an act of goodwill on the part of managers, and they do like to retain a certain amount of control. Selecting whom researchers may interview is a classic way of managers doing this. If this is the motive of the managers concerned then they are unlikely to let you have free access to their employees.

What you could do is ask to see all the employees in a particular department rather than a sample of employees. Alternatively, you could explain that your research was still uncovering new patterns of information and more interviews were necessary. This way you would penetrate deeper into the core of the employee group and might start seeing those who were rather less positive. All this assumes that you have the time to do this!

You could also be perfectly honest with the managers and confess your concern. If you did a sound job at the start of the research in convincing them that you are purely interested in academic research, and that all data will be anonymous, then you may have less of a problem.

Of course, there is always the possibility that the employees generally are positive and feel as if they really do 'belong'!

4.5 You would need to stress here that your principal interest would be in getting a deep understanding of the changes in the manager's job and the reasons why the job had changed. You would discover what the managers thought of the changes and the ways in which they had responded to the changes. In other words, you would establish what you set out to establish and, no doubt, a good deal besides.

You will remember from Section 4.4 that validity is concerned with whether the findings are really about what they appear to be about. There is no reason why your discussions with managers should not be as valid as a questionnaire survey. However, you should ensure that you talk to managers (and others) who are in a position to speak with authority on the subject. Your questioning should be skilful enough to elicit rich responses from your interviewees (see Chapter 9). You should be sensitive to the direction in which the discussion is moving. This will mean not being too directive, while still moving the interview in the direction you as the interviewer want.

Of course, you may alleviate any fears about validity by administering a questionnaire and conducting interviews so that your findings may be triangulated!

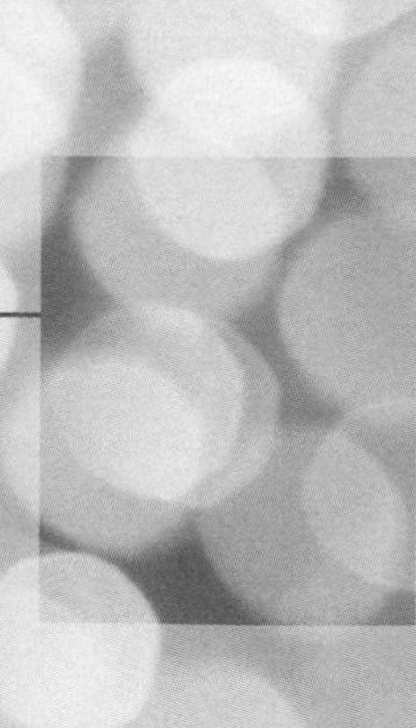

Chapter 5

Negotiating access and research ethics

By the end of this chapter you should be:

- aware of issues related to gaining access and research ethics;
- able to evaluate a range of strategies to help you to gain access to organisations and to individual participants;
- able to anticipate ethical issues at each stage of your research process, to help you to deal with these;
- able to evaluate the ethical issues associated with particular data collection methods, so that you can consider these in relation to your proposed research methods.

5.1 Introduction

Access and ethics are critical aspects for the conduct of research. Many newcomers to research want to 'get on with it' once they have identified a topic area. Insufficient attention may therefore be paid to gaining access and even less to the likelihood of ethical concerns arising in relation to the conduct of the research project. These are aspects that require careful attention at the outset of any research project. Without this, what seem like good ideas for research may flounder and prove impractical or problematic once you attempt to carry them out.

The next section (5.2) of this chapter defines the types and levels of access and the issues associated with these. It discusses the key issues of feasibility and sufficiency in relation to gaining access and the effect of these on the nature and content of your research question and objectives. The following section (5.3) presents a number of proven strategies to help you to gain access to organisations and to intended participants within them. The next section (5.4) is devoted to a discussion of research ethics and the types of issues that are likely to occur at the various stages of your research project and also in relation to the use of particular research methods.

Two summary checklists are included in this chapter: one in relation to gaining access and the other to help you to anticipate and deal with ethical concerns. These are designed to help you during the development of your research proposal and when you conduct your research project.

5.2 Problems associated with access

Your ability to collect data will depend on gaining access to their source or to appropriate sources where there is a choice. The appropriateness of a source will of course depend on your research question, related objectives and strategy. The first level of access is *physical access* or entry (Gummesson, 2000). Gaining physical access can be difficult for a number of reasons. First, organisations or individuals may not be prepared to engage in additional, voluntary activities because of the time and resources required. Many organisations receive frequent requests for access and cooperation and would find it impossible to agree to all or even some of these. Second, the request for access and cooperation may fail to interest the person who receives it. This may be for a number of reasons, related to:

- a lack of perceived value in relation to the work of the organisation or the individual;
- the nature of the topic because of its potential sensitivity, or because of concerns about the confidentiality of the information that would be required;
- perceptions about your credibility and doubts about your competence.

Third, the organisation may find itself in a difficult situation owing to external events totally unrelated to any perceptions about the nature of the request or the person making it, so that they have no choice but to refuse access. Even where a particular organisational participant is prepared to offer access this may be overruled at a higher level in the organisation. This may result in a 'false start' and an associated feeling of disappointment (Johnson, 1975). Where you are unable to gain this type of access, you will therefore need to adopt a different case study organisation, or even to modify your research question and objectives.

However, even where you are able to negotiate entry into an organisation there are other levels of access that you will need to consider and plan for if your research strategy is to be realised. Many writers see access as a *continuing* process and not just an initial or single event (Gummesson, 2000; Marshall and Rossman, 1999). This may take two forms. First, access may be an iterative process, so that you gain entry to carry out part of your research and then seek further access in order to conduct another part. You may also seek to repeat your collection of data in different parts of the organisation and therefore engage in the negotiation of access in each part (Marshall and Rossman, 1999). Second, those from whom you wish to collect data may be a different set of people from those who considered and agreed to your request for access. Physical access to an organisation will be formally granted through its management. However, it will also be necessary for you to gain informal acceptance from intended participants within the organisation in order to gain access to the data that they are able to provide (Robson, 2002).

Access may also refer to your ability to select a representative sample of organisational participants (or secondary data) in order to attempt to answer your research question and meet your objectives in an unbiased way and to produce reliable and valid data (Chapters 4 and 6). For example, we recall a well-known current affairs programme that broadcast a feature including short extracts of interviews conducted with employees of a case study organisation. All of the interviewees' responses were very positive about the organisation. However, the reporter had prefixed the showing of these extracts saying that it was the organisation that had selected all of the employees to be interviewed. The viewer was therefore left to wonder whether these very positive employees were typical of all those employed in the organisation, or whether they were providing an unreliable and untypical view of employee attitudes in this business.

We might refer to this broader meaning of access as *cognitive* access. Where you achieve this you will have gained access to the data that you need your intended participants to share with you in order to understand their social reality and to be able to address your research question and objectives. Simply obtaining physical access into an organisation will be inadequate unless you are also able to negotiate yourself into a position where you can reveal the reality of what is occurring in relation to your research question and objectives. This fundamental point requires you to consider material included throughout this book. However, there are two specific issues that we shall consider now. The first of these relates to whether you have sufficiently considered, and therefore fully realised, the extent and nature of the access that you will require in order to be able to answer your research question and meet your objectives. The second point relates to whether you are able to gain sufficient access in practice to answer your research question and meet your objectives. These two points may be linked in some instances. Your clarity of thought, which should result from sufficiently considering the nature of the access that you require, may be helpful in persuading organisations to grant entry since they are more likely to be convinced about your credibility and competence.

Access is therefore likely to be a problematic area, in terms of gaining permission for physical access, maintaining that access, and being able to create sufficient scope to address fully the research question and objectives that guide your work. This suggests that the *feasibility* of your research will also be an important guiding principle alongside the recognised hallmarks of good research outlined in a number of sources (Cooper and Schindler, 1998; Marshall and Rossman, 1999; Sekaran, 2000). The issue of feasibility will determine the construction or refinement of your research question and objectives, and may sometimes lead to a clash with these hallmarks of good research. This has been recognised by Buchanan *et al.* (1988:53–4):

> Fieldwork is permeated with the conflict between what is theoretically desirable on the one hand and what is practically possible on the other. It is desirable to ensure representativeness in the sample, uniformity of interview procedures, adequate data collection across the range of topics to be explored, and so on. But the members of organisations block access to information, constrain the time allowed for interviews, lose your questionnaires, go on holiday, and join other organisations in the middle of your unfinished study. In the conflict between the desirable and the possible, the possible always wins.

The extent to which feasibility will affect the nature of your research, or at least the approach that you adopt, is made clear by Johnson (1975). He recognises that the reality of undertaking a research project may be to consider where you are likely to be able to gain access and to develop a topic to fit the nature of that access.

A request to undertake research may involve you seeking access to a range of participants based on an organisational sample. In order to select such a sample you will require access to organisational data, either directly or indirectly through a request that outlines precisely how you require the sample to be selected (Chapter 6). Where you wish to undertake a longitudinal study, you will require access to the organisation and your research participants on more than one occasion. The difficulty of obtaining access in relation to these more *intrusive* methods and approaches has been recognised many times in the literature (for example: Buchanan *et al.*, 1988; Johnson, 1975; Raimond, 1993).

The nature of these problems of access will vary in relation to your status as either a full-time or a part-time student. As a full-time student, approaching an organisation where you have no prior contact, you will be seeking to operate in the role of an *external researcher*. You will need to negotiate access at each level discussed above (physical, continuing and cognitive). Operating as an external researcher is likely to pose problems, although it may have some benefits. Your lack of status in relation to an organisation in which you wish to conduct research will mean not only that gaining physical access is a major issue to overcome but also that this concern will remain in relation to negotiating continued and cognitive access. Goodwill on the part of the organisation and its participants is something that external researchers need to rely on at each level of access. In this role, you need to remain sensitive to the issue of goodwill and seek to foster it at each level. The demonstration of competence and integrity will also be critical at each level of access. These are key issues of access faced by all external researchers. Where you are able to demonstrate competence (see Chapters 8–10 in particular) and integrity, your role as an external researcher may prove to be beneficial. This is because participants are willing to accept you as being objective and without a covert organisational agenda, where they see your questions as being worthwhile and meaningful. Many organisations are also well disposed to reasonable research approaches for a number of reasons, some of which are discussed in the following section.

worked example

Researcher's organisational status

Dave recalls an amusing tale of being a research student several years ago. The project involved gaining access to several employers' and trade union organisations. Having gained access to the regional office of one such organisation, Dave used various types of organisational documentation situated there over a period of a few days. During the first day Dave was located in a very nice room and frequently brought refreshments by the janitor of the building. This appeared to Dave to be very kind treatment. However, Dave did not know that a rumour had spread among some staff that he was from 'head office' and was there to 'monitor' in some way the work of the office. On attending the second day, Dave was met by the janitor and taken to a small, plain room, and no more refreshments appeared for the duration of the research visit. The rumour had been corrected!

Of course, this example of the effect of the researcher's (lack of) organisational status is most unfair on the very considerable proportion of participants who treat very well those who undertake research within their organisation in full knowledge of their status. However, it illustrates the way in which some participants may react to perceptions about status.

As a part-time student or an organisational employee operating in the role of an *internal* or *participant researcher* you are still likely to face problems of access to data, although these will vary in relation to those faced by external researchers. As an internal researcher you will not face the problem associated with negotiating physical or continuing access, at least where you undertake research in your 'own part' of the organisation. However, your status in the organisation may pose particular problems in relation to cognitive access. This may be related to suspicions about why you are undertaking your research project and the use that will be made of the data, perceptions about the part of the organisation for which you work, and your grade status in relation to those whom you wish to be your research participants. Any such problem may be exacerbated if you are given a project to research where others are aware that this is an issue about which management would like to implement change. This is particularly likely to be the case where resulting change would be perceived as being harmful to those whom you would wish to be your research participants. This will not only provide a problem for you in terms of gaining cognitive access but may also suggest ethical concerns as well (which are discussed in Section 5.4). As an internal researcher, you will need to consider these issues and, where appropriate, discuss them with those who wish to provide you with a project to research.

5.3 Strategies to gain access

The preceding section has outlined problems associated with gaining access and the sufficiency of any access obtained. It has stressed the need to identify a feasible research question and objectives, from the perspective of gaining access. This section will outline and discuss a number of strategies that may help you to obtain physical and cognitive access to appropriate data. The discussion in this section will be applicable to you where you wish to gain *personal entry* to an organisation. It will be less applicable where you send a self-administered, postal questionnaire to organisational participants, in situations where you do not need to gain physical access in order to identify participants. As Raimond (1993:67) recognises, 'provided that people reply to the questionnaires, the problem of access to data is solved'. Even in this case, however, some of the points that follow will still apply to the way in which you construct the pre-survey contact and the written request to complete the questionnaire (see also Chapter 10). The applicability of these strategies will also vary in relation to your status as either an internal or an external researcher. Self-check question 5.3 is specifically designed to allow you to explore this aspect, and Box 5.5 offers suggestions about the use of these strategies in relation to the respective roles of internal and external researcher.

The strategies to help you to gain access are summarised in Box 5.1. These strategies will be developed in the remainder of this section of the chapter.

Box 5.1 Summary of strategies to gain access

- Allowing yourself sufficient time
- Using existing contacts and developing new ones
- Providing a clear account of purpose and type of access required
- Overcoming organisational concerns about the granting of access
- Identifying possible benefits to the organisation in granting you access
- Using suitable language
- Facilitating ease of reply when requesting access
- Developing your access on an incremental basis
- Establishing your credibility with intended participants

Allowing yourself sufficient time

Physical access may take weeks or even months to arrange, and in many cases the time invested will not result in access being granted (Buchanan *et al.*, 1988). An approach to an organisation will result in either a reply or no response at all. A politely worded but clearly reasoned refusal at least informs you that access will not be granted. The non-reply situation means that, if you wish to pursue the possibility of gaining access to a particular organisation, you will need to allow sufficient time before sending further correspondence or making a follow-up telephone call. Easterby-Smith *et al.* (1991) report the need to make up to four telephone calls in order to gain access. Great care must be taken in relation to this type of activity so that no grounds for offence are given. Seeking access into a large, complex organisation, where you do not have existing contacts, may also necessitate several telephone calls simply to make contact with the appropriate person, in order to ensure that your request for access will be considered by the right individual. In our experience this can take days or even a couple of weeks to achieve. You may also consider using email where you have access to this as a way of obtaining a reply.

If you are able to contact a participant directly, such as a manager, an exchange of correspondence may be sufficient to gain access. Here you should clearly set out what you require from this person and persuade him or her of the value of your work and your credibility. Even so, you will still need to allow time for your request to be received and considered and an interview meeting to be arranged at a convenient time for your research participant. This may take a number of weeks, and you may have to wait for longer to schedule the actual interview.

Where you are seeking access to a range of organisational participants to conduct a number of interviews, to undertake a survey, to engage in observation or to use secondary data, your request may be passed 'up' the organisation for clearance and may be considered by a number of people. Where you are able to use a known contact in the organisation this may help, since you can probably feel assured that your request is being attended to, but you will still need to allow for this process to take weeks rather than days. Where the organisation is prepared to consider granting access it is likely that you will be asked to attend a meeting to discuss this. There may also be a period of delay after this stage while the case that you have made for access is evaluated in terms of its implications for the organisation, and it may be necessary to make a number of telephone calls to pursue your request politely.

In the situation where your intended participants are not the same people who grant you physical access, you will need to allow further time to gain their acceptance. This may involve you making *pre-survey contact* by telephone calls to these intended participants, or engaging in correspondence or holding an explanatory meeting with them (discussed later). You may well need to allow a couple of weeks or more to establish contact with your intended participants and to secure their cooperation, especially given any operational constraints that restrict their availability.

Once you have gained physical access to the organisation and to your participants, you will be concerned with gaining 'cognitive access'. Whichever method you are using to gather data will involve you in a time-consuming process, although some methods will require that more of your time be spent within the organisation to understand what is happening. The use of a questionnaire will mean less time spent in the organisation compared with the use of non-standardised interviews, whereas the use of observation techniques may result in even more time being spent to gather data (Bryman, 1988). Where you are involved in a situation of 'continuing access', as outlined in the section above, there will also be an issue related to the time that is required to negotiate, or re-negotiate, access at each stage. You will need to consider how careful planning may help to minimise the possibility of any 'stop–go' approach to your research activity.

Using existing contacts and developing new ones

Other management and organisational researchers suggest that you are more likely to gain access where you are able to use *existing contacts* (Buchanan *et al.*, 1988; Easterby-Smith *et al.*, 2002; Johnson, 1975). Buchanan *et al.* (1988:56) say that 'we have been most successful where we have a friend, relative or student working in the organisation'. We have also found this to be the case. In order to request access we have approached those whom we would consider to be professional colleagues, who may also be present or past students, course advisers, external examiners, or otherwise known to us through local, regional or national networks. Their knowledge of us means that they should be able to trust our stated intentions and the assurances given about the use of any data provided. It can also be useful to start a research project by utilising these existing contacts in order to establish a track record that you can refer to in approaches that you make to other organisations where you do not have such contacts. This should help your credibility with these new contacts.

The use of known contacts will depend largely on your choice of research strategy and approach to selecting a sample, as suggested by your research question and objectives. It will undoubtedly be easier to use this approach where you are using a case-study-based research strategy and non-probability sampling (Section 6.3). This will certainly be the case where you undertake an in-depth study that focuses on a small, purposively selected sample. There will clearly be a high level of *convenience* in terms of gaining access through contacts who are familiar; however, these contacts may also be used as part of a quota sample, or in relation to purposive or snowball sampling (Section 6.3).

Jankowicz (2000) refers to the possibility of using your work placement organisation as a context for your research project, where this applies to your situation as a full-time undergraduate or postgraduate student. Where you have enjoyed a successful work placement, you will undoubtedly have made a number of contacts who may be able to be very helpful in terms of cooperating with you and granting access to data. You may have become interested in a particular topic because of the time that you spent in your placement organisation. Where this applies to your situation, you can spend time reading theoretical work that may be relevant to this topic, then identify a research question and objectives and plan a research project to pursue your interest within the context of your placement organisation. The combination of genuine interest in the topic and relatively easy access to organisational participants should help towards the production of a good-quality and useful piece of work.

Where you need to develop *new contacts*, consideration of the points discussed throughout this section will help you to cultivate these. In addition, you will need to be able to identify the most appropriate person to contact for help, either directly or indirectly. There may be a number of ways to seek to do this, depending on your research topic. You may consider contacting the local branch of an appropriate professional association for the names and business addresses of key employees to contact in organisations where it would be suitable for you to conduct research. You could also contact this professional association at national level, where this is more appropriate to your research question and objectives. It might also be appropriate to contact either an employers' association for a particular industry, or a trade union, at local or national level. Alternatively, it might be appropriate for you to contact one or more chambers of commerce, learning skills councils or other employers' networks (Jankowicz, 2000).

You may also consider making a direct approach to an organisation in an attempt to identify the appropriate person to contact in relation to a particular research project. This has the advantage of potentially providing access to organisations that you would like to include in your research project; however, great care needs to be exercised at each stage of this exercise.

worked example

Identifying the appropriate person through whom to request access

Adrian and another colleague identified a number of specific organisations that matched the criteria established for the types of business that they wished to include in a research project. Many of these were organisations where they did not have an appropriate contact, or indeed any contact at all. The different types of organisational structure in these organisations added to their difficulties in tracking down the most appropriate employee to contact in order to request access.

National directories that were available were used to identify the corporate headquarters of each organisation. This part of the organisation was contacted by telephone. In each case the name of the researcher was given and that of the institution through which they were conducting the research. A very brief explanation was provided in order to identify the name and location of that part of the organisation that dealt with the area of their research interest. This resulted in the researchers being provided with a telephone number or connected to that part of the organisation that the receptionist to whom they spoke thought was appropriate for the enquiry (see next paragraph). This initial telephone call was always ended by thanking the person for the help that had been provided.

At the next stage, the researchers again provided their name and that of the institution through which they were conducting the research. At this stage, the purpose of the research was also briefly explained to the secretary who inevitably answered the telephone. The researchers asked for the name and business address of the person whom the secretary thought would be the most appropriate person to write to. In most cases the people to whom the researchers spoke at this stage were most helpful and provided some excellent leads.

Sometimes, particularly in relation to complex organisations, the researchers found that they were not talking to someone in the appropriate part of the organisation. They therefore asked the person to help by transferring the call. Sometimes this led to a series of calls to identify the right person. They always maintained politeness and thanked the person whom they spoke to for their help. They always gave their names and organisational affiliation to reduce the risk of appearing to be threatening in any way. It was most important to create a positive attitude in what could be perceived as a tiresome enquiry.

The researchers chose to ask for the name and business address of a hoped-for organisational 'lead'. Using this they could send a written request to this person, which could be considered when it was convenient, rather than attempt to talk to them at that point in time, when it might well have not been a good time to make to such a request. This process resulted in many successes, and Adrian and his colleague have added a number of good contacts to their previous list. However, the key point to note is that great care needs to be exercised when using this approach.

Using the approach outlined in this worked example may also allow you to obtain the business email addresses of possible organisational 'leads'. In this case you may consider using the Internet to send a written request to such a person. Where you consider this to be appropriate you will of course still need to follow the standards of care that you should use in drafting and sending a letter. The ease of using email may tempt some to use a lower level of care about the way their written communication is constructed. It may also lead to a temptation to send repeated messages. The use of email is considered below in the discussion about 'netiquette'; however, from a practical point of view it is also a possibility that using this means to make contact may result in a greater danger that the recipient of your request simply deletes the message! Those people who receive large numbers of email every day may cope with these by deleting any that aren't essential. It is possible that sending a letter to a potential 'lead' may result in that person considering your request more carefully!

Making the type of contact outlined in the worked example above may result in identifying the person whom you wish to participate in your research. Alternatively, your reason for making contact with this person may be to ask them to grant you access to others in the organisation whom you wish to be your participants, or to secondary data. This second type of contact is sometimes referred to as a *broker* or a *gatekeeper* (Easterby-Smith *et al.*, 2002; Gummesson, 2000). Easterby-Smith *et al.* (1991) suggest approaching an organisation's personnel manager because this person will have contacts across the organisation and can therefore be very helpful in terms of facilitating access. This type of contact may also be the functional manager or director of those staff to whom you would like access. Having identified an organisational broker or gatekeeper you will have to persuade them about your credibility, to overcome any issues they have about the sensitivity of your research project and to demonstrate the potential value of this for them.

Providing a clear account of purpose and type of access required

Providing a clear account of your requirements will allow your intended participants to be aware of what will be required from them (Robson, 2002). Asking for access and cooperation without being specific about your requirements will probably lead to a cautious attitude on their part since the amount of time that could be required might prove to be disruptive. Even where the initial contact or request for access involves a telephone call, it is still probably advisable to send a letter that outlines your proposed research and requirements. Your *introductory letter* requesting access should outline in brief the purpose of your research, how the person being contacted might be able to help, and what would be required (see the example in the next worked example). Healey (1991) suggests that the success of this letter will be helped by the use of short and clear sentences. Its tone should be polite, and it should seek to generate interest on the part of intended respondents.

Establishing your credibility will be vital in order to gain access. The use of known contacts will mean that you can seek to trade on your existing level of credibility. However, when you are making contact with a potential participant for the first time, the nature of your approach will be highly significant in terms of beginning to establish credibility – or not doing so! Any telephone call or introductory letter will need to demonstrate your clarity of thought and purpose. Any lack of preparation at this stage will be apparent and is likely to reduce the possibility of gaining access (see Section 9.4 for further consideration of these issues).

The presentation of the introductory letter will also serve to establish credibility. Healey (1991:210) says 'a well-designed and presented letter, typed on headed note paper, which is personally addressed with a hand-written signature, would seem to be a sensible way of trying to persuade ... managers of businesses to cooperate'.

Overcoming organisational concerns about the granting of access

Organisational concerns may be placed into one of three categories. First, concerns about the amount of *time* or *resources* that will be involved in the request for access. Easterby-Smith *et al.* (2002) suggest that your request for access is more likely to be accepted if the amounts of time and resources you ask for are kept to a minimum. As a complementary point to this, Healey (1991) reports earlier work that found that introductory letters containing multiple requests are also less likely to be successful. However, while the achievement of access may be more likely to be realised where your demands are kept to a minimum, there will still be a need to maintain honesty. For example, where you wish to conduct an interview you may be more likely to gain access if the time requested is kept within reason. However, falsely stating that it will last for only a short time and then deliberately exceeding this is very likely to upset your participant and may prevent your gaining further access.

The second area of concern is related to *sensitivity* about the topic. We have found that organisations are less likely to cooperate where the topic of the research has a negative implication. Organisations do not normally wish to present themselves in a bad light. If this is likely to be the case you will need to consider carefully the way in which your proposed research topic may be perceived by those whom you ask to grant access. In such cases you may be able to highlight a positive approach to the issue by, for example, emphasising that your work will be designed to identify individual and organisational learning in relation to the topic (a positive inference). You should avoid sending any request that appears to concentrate on aspects associated with non-achievement or failure if you are to gain access. Your request for access is therefore more likely to be favourably considered where you are able to outline a research topic that does not appear to be sensitive to the organisation (Easterby-Smith *et al.*, 2002).

The third area of concern is related to the *confidentiality* of the data that would have to be provided and the *anonymity* of the organisation or individual participants. To overcome this concern, you will need to provide clear assurances about these aspects. One advantage of using an introductory letter is to give this guarantee in writing at the time of making the request for access, when this issue may be uppermost in the minds of those who will consider your approach. Once initial access has been granted you will need to repeat the assurance about anonymity to those who act as your participants. You will also need to consider how to maintain this when you write up your work in situations where particular participants could be indirectly identified (Bell, 1999) (Section 13.5). Illustrations of this are provided in the worked example in Section 5.4 titled 'Inadvertently revealing participants' identities'.

Possible benefits to the organisation of granting you access

Apart from any general interest that is generated by the subject of your proposed research, you may find that it will have some level of *applicability* to the jobs of those whom you approach for access. Practitioners often wrestle with the same subject issues as researchers and may therefore welcome the opportunity to discuss their own analysis and course of action related to such an issue, in a non-threatening, non-judgemental environment. A discussion may allow them to think through an issue and to reflect on the action that they have adopted to manage it. In our own interviews with practitioners we are pleased when told that the discussion has been of value to the interviewee, because of this reason.

For those who work in organisations where they are perhaps the only subject practitioner, this may be the first time they have had this type of opportunity. You therefore need to consider whether your proposed research topic may provide some advantage to those from whom you wish to gain access, although this does not mean that you should attempt to 'buy' your way in based on some promise about the potential value of your work. Where it is unlikely that your proposed research will suggest any advantage to those whose cooperation you seek, you will need to consider what alternative course of action to take. This may involve redesigning your research question and objectives before seeking any access.

It may also help to offer a report of your findings to those who grant access. The intention would be to provide each of your participants with something of value and to fulfil any expectations about exchange between the provider and receiver of the research data, thereby prompting some of those whom you approach to grant access (Johnson, 1975). Buchanan *et al.* (1988) suggest that this type of report should be specially designed to be of use to those who participated rather than, say, a copy of the document you need to submit for academic examination. They also suggest that feedback about this report may help you further with your research.

Where access is granted in return for supplying a report of your findings it may be important to devise a simple 'contract' to make clear what has been agreed. This should make clear the broad form of the report and the nature and depth of the analysis that you agree to include in it. This may vary from a summary report of key findings to a much more in-depth analysis. For this reason it will be important to determine what will be realistic to supply to those who grant you access.

Using suitable language

Some researchers advise against referring to certain terms used in relation to research activity when making an approach to an organisation for access, because these may be perceived as threatening or not interesting to the potential participant (e.g. Buchanan *et al.*, 1988, Easterby-Smith *et al.*, 2002). Buchanan *et al.* (1988:57) suggest using 'learn from your experience' in place of research, 'conversation' instead of interview and 'write an account' rather than publish. Easterby-Smith *et al.* (2002:91) suggest that the term 'researcher' will have greater credibility than that of 'student'.

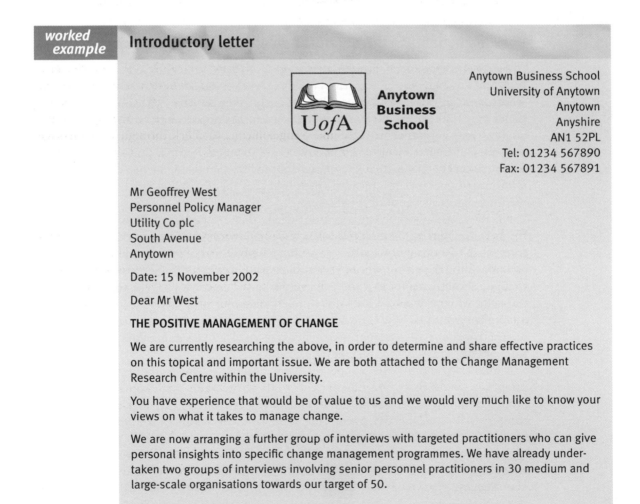

worked example

Introductory letter

Anytown Business School

Anytown Business School
University of Anytown
Anytown
Anyshire
AN1 52PL
Tel: 01234 567890
Fax: 01234 567891

Mr Geoffrey West
Personnel Policy Manager
Utility Co plc
South Avenue
Anytown

Date: 15 November 2002

Dear Mr West

THE POSITIVE MANAGEMENT OF CHANGE

We are currently researching the above, in order to determine and share effective practices on this topical and important issue. We are both attached to the Change Management Research Centre within the University.

You have experience that would be of value to us and we would very much like to know your views on what it takes to manage change.

We are now arranging a further group of interviews with targeted practitioners who can give personal insights into specific change management programmes. We have already undertaken two groups of interviews involving senior personnel practitioners in 30 medium and large-scale organisations towards our target of 50.

An outline of the interview structure is attached, although it is not our intention to follow this slavishly. We will conduct interviews during January and February 2003 and envisage that these will take up to two hours.

We are aware of the need to treat our findings with the utmost confidentiality. No source, individual or organisational, will be identified or comment attributed without the express permission of the originator.

One of our intended outputs will be a report summarising our findings and we will be sending a copy of this to each of the participants in the study.

We hope you are able to help us and should be grateful if you would return the attached pro forma. We will contact you on receipt to confirm arrangements where you are able to participate. If you prefer to talk with us to agree a suitable time and venue please call us on the following numbers:

If you require any further information please do not hesitate to get in touch.

Yours sincerely

Adrian Thornhill *Andrew Gibbons*

Dr Adrian Thornhill and Andrew Gibbons

Use of language will depend largely on the nature of the people you are contacting. Your language should be appropriate to the type of person being contacted, without any hint of being patronising, threatening or just boring. Given the vital role of initial telephone conversations or introductory letters, we would suggest allowing adequate time to consider and draft these and using someone to check through your message. You are intending to engender interest in your research project, and the initial point of contact needs to convey this.

Facilitating ease of reply when requesting access

We have found that the inclusion of a simple pro forma for recipients of our written requests for access to use generally ensures a reply. It may not be suitable in all cases, and should be designed to fit the research method being used. Nevertheless, its use is worth considering in cases where it would be necessary for your recipient to draft their own letter to reply. Inclusion of a stamped or freepost addressed envelope, or a fax number or email address, may also facilitate a reply.

Developing your access on an incremental basis

Reference has been made above to the strategy of achieving access by stages, as a means of overcoming organisational concerns about time-consuming, multiple requests. Johnson (1975) provides an example of developing access on an incremental basis. He used a three-stage strategy to achieve his desired depth of access. The first stage involved a request to conduct interviews. This was the minimum requirement in order to commence his research. The next stage involved negotiating access to undertake observation. The final stage was in effect an extension to the second stage and involved gaining permission to tape-record the interactions being observed.

There are potentially a number of advantages related to the use of this strategy. As suggested above, a request to an organisation for multiple access may be sufficient to cause them to decline entry. Using an incremental strategy at least gains you access to a certain level of data. This strategy will also allow you the opportunity to develop a positive relationship with those who are prepared to grant initial access of a restricted nature. As you establish your credibility, you can develop the possibility of achieving a fuller level of access. A further advantage may follow from the opportunity that you have to design your request for further access specifically to the situation and in relation to opportunities that may become apparent from your initial level of access. On the other hand, this incremental process will be time consuming, and you need to consider the amount of time that you will have for your research project before embarking on such a strategy.

worked example

Pro forma to facilitate replies

Variations of the following pro forma have been used successfully to facilitate replies from organisations whom we have requested to participate in research activity.

For the attention of K Thornhill, The Business School

Dear Katie and Andrew

Managing change

☐ I am able to talk to you about managing change. I can be available to meet you at the following times, date and locations . . .

Date/s	Time	Location/s

☐ Please contact me to arrange a suitable date, time and venue.

☐ I also recommend that you speak with . . .

____

☐ I am unable to talk to you about managing change.

☐ I do recommend that you speak with . . .

____

Yours sincerely,

Position:

Organisation:

Telephone:
Fax:
Email:

Establishing your credibility with intended participants

In Section 5.2 we differentiated between physical and cognitive access. Just because you have been granted entry into an organisation, you will not be able to assume that those whom you wish to interview, survey or observe will be prepared to provide their cooperation. Indeed, assuming that this is going to happen raises an ethical issue that is considered in the next section. Robson (2002) says that gaining cooperation from these intended participants is a matter of developing relationships. This will mean repeating much of the process that you will have used to gain entry into the organisation. You will need to share with them the purpose of your research project, state how you believe that they will be able to help your study, and provide assurances about confidentiality and anonymity. This may involve writing to your intended participants or talking to them individually or in a group. Which of these means you use will depend on the intended research method, your opportunity to make contact with them, the numbers of participants involved, and the nature of the setting. Where your intended method may be considered intrusive, you may need to exercise even greater care and take longer to gain acceptance. This might be the case, for example, where you wish to undertake observation. The extent to which you succeed in gaining cognitive access will depend on this effort.

worked example

A request to participate in a discussion group

20 March 2003

Dear (*staff name*)

Edcoll is holding a communications audit that we have been asked to undertake. In order to explore attitudes held by members of staff we will be holding a series of discussion groups. As a member of staff randomly selected by us to be invited to one of these discussion groups, your views will be important in order for us to be able to build up a clear picture of staff attitudes about internal communication. The attitudes revealed at these discussion groups will then be used by us to inform the design of a questionnaire to be sent to all members of staff.

Each discussion group should last no longer than one hour. Comments made during the discussion group will not be attributed to any individual or to the group and will only be used by us to inform the design of the questionnaire. On completion of the audit, key results will be communicated to all members of staff.

The discussion group which you have been invited to take part in will be held on:

(*time; day; date; room; location*)

If you will not be able to attend please can you contact one of us by (*date*), so that an appropriate alternative person can be invited in your place. Our telephone number is:

We very much hope that you can attend and look forward to seeing you.

(*Signed in ink by the members of the research team*)

Key points from the strategies that we have outlined to help you to gain access to organisations and to those whom you wish to participate in your research project have been summarised as a checklist for you to use in Box 5.2.

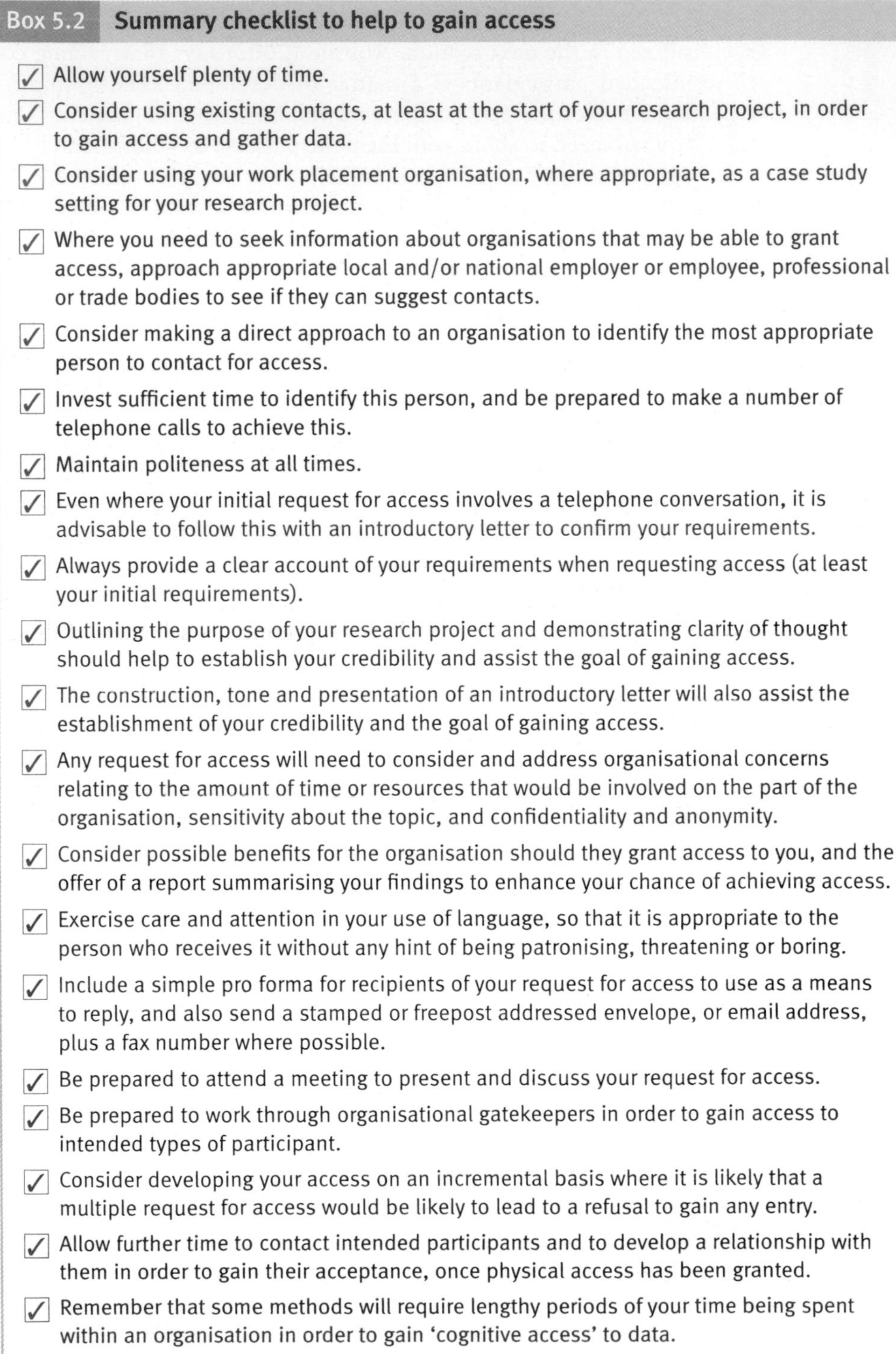

Box 5.2 Summary checklist to help to gain access

- ✓ Allow yourself plenty of time.
- ✓ Consider using existing contacts, at least at the start of your research project, in order to gain access and gather data.
- ✓ Consider using your work placement organisation, where appropriate, as a case study setting for your research project.
- ✓ Where you need to seek information about organisations that may be able to grant access, approach appropriate local and/or national employer or employee, professional or trade bodies to see if they can suggest contacts.
- ✓ Consider making a direct approach to an organisation to identify the most appropriate person to contact for access.
- ✓ Invest sufficient time to identify this person, and be prepared to make a number of telephone calls to achieve this.
- ✓ Maintain politeness at all times.
- ✓ Even where your initial request for access involves a telephone conversation, it is advisable to follow this with an introductory letter to confirm your requirements.
- ✓ Always provide a clear account of your requirements when requesting access (at least your initial requirements).
- ✓ Outlining the purpose of your research project and demonstrating clarity of thought should help to establish your credibility and assist the goal of gaining access.
- ✓ The construction, tone and presentation of an introductory letter will also assist the establishment of your credibility and the goal of gaining access.
- ✓ Any request for access will need to consider and address organisational concerns relating to the amount of time or resources that would be involved on the part of the organisation, sensitivity about the topic, and confidentiality and anonymity.
- ✓ Consider possible benefits for the organisation should they grant access to you, and the offer of a report summarising your findings to enhance your chance of achieving access.
- ✓ Exercise care and attention in your use of language, so that it is appropriate to the person who receives it without any hint of being patronising, threatening or boring.
- ✓ Include a simple pro forma for recipients of your request for access to use as a means to reply, and also send a stamped or freepost addressed envelope, or email address, plus a fax number where possible.
- ✓ Be prepared to attend a meeting to present and discuss your request for access.
- ✓ Be prepared to work through organisational gatekeepers in order to gain access to intended types of participant.
- ✓ Consider developing your access on an incremental basis where it is likely that a multiple request for access would be likely to lead to a refusal to gain any entry.
- ✓ Allow further time to contact intended participants and to develop a relationship with them in order to gain their acceptance, once physical access has been granted.
- ✓ Remember that some methods will require lengthy periods of your time being spent within an organisation in order to gain 'cognitive access' to data.

5.4 Research ethics

Defining research ethics

Ethical concerns will emerge as you plan your research, seek access to organisations and to individuals, collect, analyse and report your data. In the context of research, *ethics* refers to the appropriateness of your behaviour in relation to the rights of those who become the subject of your work, or are affected by it. Wells (1994:284) defines 'ethics in terms of a code of behaviour appropriate to academics and the conduct of research'. The appropriateness or acceptability of our behaviour as researchers will be affected by broader social norms of behaviour (Wells, 1994; Zikmund, 2000). A *social norm* indicates the type of behaviour that a person ought to adopt in a particular situation (Robson, 2002; Zikmund, 2000). However, as Wells (1994) recognises, the norms of behaviour that prevail will in reality allow for a range of ethical positions. You will therefore need to consider ethical issues throughout the period of your research and to remain sensitive to the impact of your work on those whom you approach to help, those who provide access and cooperation, and those affected by your results.

The conduct of your research may be guided by a code of ethics. A *code of ethics* will provide you with a statement of principles and procedures for the conduct of your research. This will be helpful and, where followed, should ensure that you do not transgress the behavioural norms established by your institution or association. Where you are a member of an educational institution or a professional association you should seek out the existence of such guidelines. Use of the Internet will provide access to a number of very useful codes of ethics. A selection of these is contained in Table 5.1.

You may also be required to submit your research proposal to a faculty or institutional research ethics committee. *Research ethics committees* may fulfil a number of objectives. One of these may be a proactive or educational role, which would include constructing an ethical code and disseminating advice about aspects of research. An ethics committee may also adopt a reactive role in relation to the consideration of

Table 5.1 A selection of Internet locations for codes of ethics

Name	*Internet address*	*Comment*
The Social Research Association's Ethical Guidelines (2002)	http://www.the-sra.org.uk/index2.htm	This also provides an extensive bibliography and a range of further Internet locations.
British Psychological Society's Code of Conduct	http://www.bps.org.uk/about/rules5.cfm	The full version of its Code of Conduct, Ethical Principles and Guidelines can also be located through this address.
American Psychological Association's Ethical Principles of Psychologists and Code of Conduct	http://www.apa.org/ethics/code.html	
The British Sociological Association's Statement of Ethical Practice	http://www.britsoc.org.uk/about/ethic.htm	

research proposals and calls for advice arising from dilemmas that confront researchers. A research ethics committee is likely to be composed of experienced researchers from a range of backgrounds, who are able to draw on their range of experience and knowledge of different ethical perspectives to provide advice. A committee may also be used in particular cases to form a judgement about the publication of work that is associated with ethical problems. In some cases you may also have to satisfy the requirements of an ethics committee established in your host organisation. This is likely to apply where your research is based in the health service. For example, our part-time students undertaking research within the UK's National Health Service have had to meet the requirements established by their local NHS Trust's ethics committee. Such a requirement is often time consuming to meet.

However, even where you use a code of ethics in the design of your research and perhaps submit your proposal to a research ethics committee for approval, this is unlikely to indicate the end of your consideration of ethical concerns, as we now discuss. The nature of business and management research means that you will be dependent on other people for access, as we have seen above. This will inevitably lead to a range of ethical issues. As Wells (1994:290) puts it: 'In general, the closer the research is to actual individuals in real-world settings, the more likely are ethical questions to be raised.' Related to this, the nature of *power relationships* in business and management research will raise ethical issues that also need to be considered. Managers will be in a very powerful position in relation to researchers who request organisational access. They will remain in a powerful position in terms of the nature and extent of the access that they allow in an organisational setting. However, researchers need to be sensitive to the way in which the granting of access affects this type of relationship. Face-to-face interviews, even with managers, will place researchers in a position of some 'power', albeit for a short time, because they are able to formulate questions, including probing ones, which may cause levels of discomfort. In addition, as a researcher in an organisational setting you will need to remain sensitive to the fact that your presence is a temporary one, whereas the people from whom you collect data will need to work together after you depart. We shall consider these ethical issues related to business and management research in the discussion that follows.

Nature and scope of ethical issues in business and management

This discussion of ethical issues is divided into four subsections. In the first subsection we outline the range of ethical issues that affect the research process across its various stages. In the second subsection we discuss ethical issues that arise in particular during the design stage and when seeking initial access. In the third subsection we discuss ethical issues that are prominent during the data collection stage and examine particular issues related to the use of different methods. In the fourth subsection we discuss ethical issues related to the analysis and reporting stages. A fifth subsection at the end of the chapter introduces a discussion about the related issue of data protection and research.

Ethical issues that affect the research process generally

A number of key ethical issues arise across the stages and duration of a research project. Before we embark on a discussion of these in relation to the particular stages outlined, it is worth summarising these key ethical issues. They relate to ethical issues around the:

- privacy of possible and actual participants;
- voluntary nature of participation and the right to withdraw partially or completely from the process;
- consent and possible deception of participants;
- maintenance of the confidentiality of data provided by individuals or identifiable participants and their anonymity;
- reactions of participants to the way in which you seek to collect data;
- effects on participants of the way in which you use, analyse and report your data;
- behaviour and objectivity of the researcher.

Privacy may be seen as the cornerstone of the ethical issues that confront those who undertake research. For example, consent, confidentiality, participant reactions and the effects of the way in which you use, analyse and report your data all have the capacity to affect, or are related to, the privacy of participants. Box 5.3 summarises the implications of seeking to respect privacy within the context of business and management research.

Box 5.3 The implications of respecting privacy in business and management research

Respecting privacy in business and management research means the right:

- not to participate;
- not to be harassed or offered inducements to participate or to extend the scope of participation beyond that freely given;
- not to be contacted at unreasonable times or at home (where the scope of the research is related to an organisational setting);
- of participants to determine, within reason, when they will participate in the data collection process;
- of participants to expect the researcher to abide by the extent of the consent given and not to find that the researcher wishes to widen the scope of the research without first seeking and obtaining permission;
- of participants not to be subject to any attempt to prolong the duration of an interview or observation beyond that previously agreed unless the participant freely proposes this as an option;
- of participants not to answer any question, or set of questions, or provide any related data where requested;
- of participants not to be subjected to questions that create stress or discomfort;
- to expect agreed anonymity and confidentiality to be observed strictly both in relation to discussions with other research or organisational participants and during the reporting of findings (including from those who gain subsequent access to data).

There may well be additional points to the ones that we list in Box 5.3, particularly in relation to specific settings or data collection methods. Indeed, this key ethical issue of privacy is explored further in the discussion of informed consent later in this section. Consideration of the points included in Box 5.3 provides sufficient evidence that this is an area that should be treated with great concern and which is likely to require continuous evaluation to help you to take appropriate action at each stage of your research.

Where you have access you may find it useful to use the ETHX module of the Methodologist's Toolchest (Scolari Sage, 2002). This includes a range of features that for example allow you to consider ethical issues involving human subjects, and to develop an appropriate consent form.

You may also consider using the Internet in relation to your research project. This possibility will undoubtedly continue to generate a debate and evaluation about the ethical use of this particular means to collect data. The expression *netiquette* has been developed to provide a heading for a number of 'rules' or guidelines about how to act ethically when using the Internet. As such it allows us to identify a range of potential ethical issues that arise from using the Internet. The Internet may allow you to contact possible participants more easily and even to do this repeatedly – a possibility that may be an invasion of their privacy in a number of ways. Forms of covert observation may also be possible that impinge on the rights of 'participants' (Cooper and Schindler, 1998). In general terms, you should apply the ethical principles that are discussed in this chapter and elsewhere in this book when considering using the Internet as a means to collect data. We return to other aspects of research netiquette below and offer particular advice about on-line surveys in Section 10.5.

Ethical issues during the design and initial access stages

A number of management researchers state that ethical problems should be anticipated and dealt with during the design stage of any research project. This should be attempted by planning to conduct the research project in line with the ethical principles outlined above and by altering the research strategy or choice of methods where this is appropriate. Evidence that these issues have been considered and evaluated at this stage, through a discussion in your research proposal, should be one of the criteria against which your research proposal is judged (Cooper and Schindler, 1998; Marshall and Rossman, 1999).

One of the key stages at which you need to consider the potential for ethical problems to arise is when you seek initial access. As referred to above, you should not attempt to apply any pressure on intended participants to grant access (Robson, 2002; Sekaran, 2000). This is unlikely to be the case where you are approaching a member of an organisation's management to request access. However, where you are undertaking a research project as an internal researcher within your employing organisation (Section 5.3), in relation to a part-time qualification, there may be a temptation to apply pressure on others (colleagues or subordinates) to cooperate. Individuals have a right to privacy (Box 5.3), which means that you will have to accept any refusal to take part (Cooper and Schindler, 1998; Robson, 2002). Privacy may also be affected by the nature and timing of any approach that you make to intended participants – say by telephoning at 'unsociable' times, or, where possible, by 'confronting' intended participants. Access to secondary data may also raise ethical problems in relation to privacy. Where you happen to obtain access to personal data about individuals who have not consented to let you have this (through personnel or client records) you will be obliged to treat this in the strictest confidence and not to abuse it in any way.

Consent to participate in a research project is not a straightforward matter. In general terms, an approach to a potential participant is an attempt to gain consent. However, this raises a question about the scope of any consent given. Where someone agrees to participate in a particular data collection method, this does not necessarily *imply* consent about the way in which the data provided are subsequently used. Clearly, any assurances that you provide about anonymity and confidentiality will help to develop an understanding of the nature of the consent being entered into, but even this may be inadequate in terms of clarifying the nature of that consent. This suggests a continuum that ranges across a lack of consent, involving some form of deception, a lack of clarity about the nature of consent so that the researcher *implies consent* from taking part, and consent that is fully informed as well as freely given (known as *informed consent*). This is shown in Figure 5.1.

Three points are described in Figure 5.1, although in reality this is likely to operate as a continuum in the proper sense that a multitude of positions are possible around the key points described. For example, research that is conducted with those who have agreed to participate can still involve an attempt to *deceive* them in some way. This may be related to deceit over the real purpose of the research (Sekaran, 2000), or in relation to some undeclared sponsorship (Zikmund, 2000), or related to an association with another organisation that will use any data gained for commercial advantage. Where this is the case, it will cause embarrassment to those who promote your request for access within their employing organisation, as well as to yourself.

There are a number of aspects to the concept of informed consent. These are detailed in Box 5.4. The extent of the detail of informed consent that you will require will depend on the nature of your research project. The nature of establishing informed consent will also vary. Correspondence may be exchanged, such as that shown in Section 5.3, to establish informed consent. This may be supplemented by a more detailed written agreement and signed by both parties. Informed consent may also be entered into through a verbal agreement. You will also need to operate on the basis that informed consent is a continuing requirement. This, of course, will be particularly significant where you seek to gain access on an incremental basis (Section 5.3). Although you may have established informed consent through prior written correspondence, it will still be worthwhile to reinforce this at the point of collecting data.

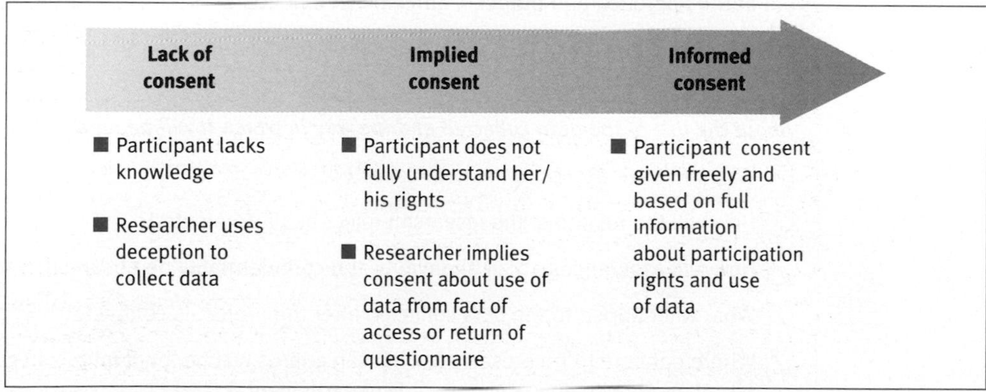

Figure 5.1 The nature of participant consent

Box 5.4 Checklist of requirements for informed consent

Organisational 'gatekeepers' (discussed earlier in Section 5.3) and intended participants need to be informed about the following aspects of the research.

About the nature of the research

- ✓ What is its purpose?
- ✓ Who is or will be undertaking it?
- ✓ Is it being funded or sponsored – if so, by whom and why?
- ✓ Who is being asked to participate – i.e. broad details about the sampling frame, sample determination and size?
- ✓ How far has the research project progressed?

About the requirements of taking part

- ✓ What type of data will be required from those who agree to take part?
- ✓ How will these data be collected (e.g. interview, observation or questionnaire)?
- ✓ How much time will be required, and on how many occasions?
- ✓ What are the target dates to undertake the research and for participation?

About the implications of taking part and participants' rights

- ✓ Recognition that participation is voluntary.
- ✓ Recognition that participants have the right to decline to answer a question or set of questions, or to be observed in particular circumstances.
- ✓ Recognition that participants have control over the right to record any of their responses where use of a tape recorder is contemplated.
- ✓ Recognition that participants may withdraw at any time.
- ✓ What are the consequences of participating – possible risks, depending on the nature of the approach and purpose, and expected benefits?
- ✓ What assurances will be provided about participant anonymity and data confidentiality?

About the use of the data collected and the way in which it will be reported

- ✓ Who will have access to the data collected?
- ✓ How will the results of the research project be disseminated?
- ✓ How will assurances about anonymity and confidentiality be observed at this stage?
- ✓ What will happen to the data collected after the project is completed?
- ✓ Where data are to be preserved, what safeguards will be 'built in' to safeguard the future anonymity and confidentiality of participants?

An example of this is provided in Section 9.4 in the worked example about opening a semi-structured interview. You will also need to gain informed consent from those whom you wish to be your intended participants as well as those who act as organisational gatekeepers, granting you access.

In the preceding section we discussed possible strategies to help you to gain access. One of these was related to possible benefits to an organisation of granting you access. You should be realistic about this. Where you are anxious to gain access, you may be tempted to offer more than is feasible. Alternatively, you may offer to supply information arising from your work without intending to do this. Such behaviour would clearly be unethical, and to compound this the effect of such action (or inaction) may result in a refusal to grant access to others who come after you.

Ethical issues during the data collection stage

The data collection stage is associated with a range of ethical issues. Some of these are general issues that will apply to whichever method is being used to collect data. Other issues are more specifically related to a particular method of collecting data. We shall consider the issues related to all methods first and then examine issues related to particular methods of data collection.

Irrespective of method, there are a number of ethical principles to which you need to adhere. In the previous subsection we referred to the importance of not intruding on an intended participant's privacy. This was in relation to the participant's right not to take part. Once participants have agreed to take part in your research, they still maintain their right to privacy. This means that they have the right to withdraw as participants, and that they may decline to take part in a particular aspect of your research. You should not ask them to participate in anything that will intrude on their privacy where this goes beyond the scope of the access agreed. We also referred to rights in relation to deceit in the previous subsection. Once access has been granted you should remain within the aims of your research project that you shared and agreed with your intended participant(s) (Zikmund, 2000). To do otherwise, without raising this with your participant(s) and renegotiating access, would be, in effect, another type of deceit. This would be likely to cause upset, and could result in the premature termination of your data collection. There are perhaps some situations where deception may be accepted in relation to 'covert' research, and we shall discuss this later in this subsection.

Another general ethical principle is related to the maintenance of your *objectivity*. During the data collection stage this means making sure that you collect your data accurately and fully – that you avoid exercising subjective selectivity in what you record. The importance of this action also relates to the validity and reliability of your work, which is discussed in Chapters 4 and 6–10. Without objectively collected data, your ability to analyse and report your work accurately will also be impaired. We return to this as an ethical issue in the next subsection. Obviously any invention of data is also a totally unacceptable and unethical course of action.

worked example

The ethical dilemma of dubious data

One of the most famous debates about whether research data were invented concerns some of the work of one of the most famous British psychologists, Cyril Burt. His research concerned the relationship between IQ and genetic factors. He believed that 'individual differences in IQ are caused in part by genetic factors' (Morgan, 1995).

Claims about such a relationship are politically contentious, and in the mid-1970s, after Burt's death, doubts were raised about the statistical reliability of some of Burt's data and about whether two of his research assistants had really existed. Because of the significance of the implications of Burt's work a debate has continued to exist over two decades among those in his academic discipline about some of the data that he produced to justify his conclusions (see Mackintosh, 1995).

Confidentiality and *anonymity* have also been shown to be important in terms of gaining access to organisations and individuals (Section 5.3). Once promises about confidentiality and anonymity have been given it is of great importance to make sure that these are maintained. Easterby-Smith *et al.* (2002) raise the important point that, in a qualitatively based approach to primary data collection, points of significance will emerge as the research progresses, and this will probably lead you to wish to explore these with other participants. However, Easterby-Smith *et al.* recognise that where you do this within an organisation it may lead to participants indirectly identifying which person was responsible for making the point that you wish to explore with them. This may result in harmful repercussions for the person whose openness allowed you to identify this point for exploration. Great care therefore needs to be exercised in maintaining each participant's right to anonymity. You will need to consider where the use of any data gained may have harmful consequences for the disclosing participant. Where you wish to get others to discuss such a potentially sensitive point you may attempt to steer the discussion to see if they will raise it without in any way making clear that one of the other participants has already referred to it.

Use of the Internet and email during data collection will lead to the possibility of serious ethical, or netiquette, issues related to confidentiality and anonymity. For example, it would be technically possible to forward the email (or interview notes) of one research participant to another such participant in order to ask this second person to comment on the issues being raised. Such an action would infringe the right to confidentiality and anonymity and should definitely be avoided. Moreover, it is also likely to lead to a data protection issue related to the use of personal data (discussed below). While the use of the Internet may allow you to correspond with participants in distant locations, this approach may also be seen as intrusive and demanding for any participant where they are expected to supply written answers via this medium. Alternatively, the use of this means to collect data may adversely affect the reliability of the data where participants are not able to devote the time required to supply extensive written answers via their computer. Any consideration of the use of Internet discussion groups or 'chat rooms' to collect data is also likely to suggest ethical and data protection issues related to confidentiality and anonymity, as well as potential issues related to the reliability of any data. At the time of writing there is relatively little research about the use of Internet discussion groups or 'chat rooms' to collect data. However, the use of these will clearly be constrained by the nature of research questions in business and management research and by ethical concerns and doubts about data validity and reliability that would be raised by their use.

The ability to explore data or to seek explanations through qualitatively based methods means that there will be greater scope for ethical and other issues to arise in relation to this approach to research (Easterby-Smith *et al.*, 2002). The general ethical issues that we considered above (see also Zikmund, 2000) may arise in relation to the use of quantitative research. However, in qualitatively based research the resulting personal contact, scope to use non-standardised questions or to observe on a 'face-to-face' basis, and capacity to develop your knowledge on an incremental basis mean that you will be able to exercise a greater level of control (Chapter 9). This contrasts with the use of a quantitative approach based on structured interviews or self-administered questionnaires (Chapter 10).

The relatively greater level of control associated with qualitatively based research methods should be exercised with care so that your behaviour remains within appropriate and acceptable parameters. In face-to-face *interviews*, you should avoid overzealous questioning and pressing your participant for a response. Doing so may make the situation stressful for your participant (Sekaran, 2000). You should also make clear to your interview participant that they have the right to decline to respond to any question (Cooper and Schindler, 1998). The nature of questions to be asked also requires consideration. Sekaran (2000) states that you should avoid asking questions that are in any way demeaning to your participant (Sections 9.4, 9.5 and 9.7 provide a fuller consideration of related issues). In face-to-face interviews it will clearly be necessary to arrange a time that is convenient for your participant; however, where you seek to conduct an interview by telephone (Sections 10.2 and 10.5) you should not attempt to do this at an unreasonable time of the day. In the interview situation, whether face to face or using a telephone, it would also be unethical to attempt to prolong the discussion when it is apparent that your participant needs to attend to the next part of their day's schedule (Zikmund, 2000).

The use of *observation* techniques raises its own ethical concerns (Section 8.3). The boundaries of what is permissible to observe need to be clearly drawn. Without this type of agreement the principal participants may find that their actions are being constrained (Bryman, 1988). You should also avoid attempting to observe behaviour related to your participant's private life, such as personal telephone calls and so forth. Without this, the relationship between observer and observed will break down, with the latter finding the process to be an intrusion on their right to privacy. There is, however, a second problem related to the use of this method. This is the issue of '"*reactivity*" – the reaction on the part of those being investigated to the investigator and his or her research instruments' (Bryman, 1988:112). This issue applies to a number of strategies and methods (Bryman, 1988) but is clearly a particular problem in observation.

A solution to this problem might be to undertake a *covert* study so that those being observed are not aware of this fact. In a situation of likely 'reactivity' to the presence of an observer you might use this approach in a deceitful yet benign way, since to declare your purpose at the outset of your work might lead to non-participation or to problems related to validity and reliability if those being observed altered their behaviour (Bryman, 1988; Gummesson, 2000; Wells, 1994). The rationale for this choice of approach would thus be related to a question of whether 'the ends justify the means' provided that other ethical aspects are considered (Wells, 1994:284). However, the ethical concern with deceiving those being observed may prevail over any pragmatic view (Bryman, 1988; Cooper and Schindler, 1998). Indeed the problem of reactivity may be a diminishing one where those being observed adapt to your presence as declared observer (Bryman, 1988). This adaptation is known as *habituation* (Section 8.6).

Where access is denied after being requested you may have no other choice but to carry out covert observation – where this is practical (Gummesson, 2000). However, this course of action may prove to be a considerable source of irritation when revealed, and you will need to evaluate this possibility very carefully. Irrespective of the reason why a deception occurred, it is widely accepted that after the observation has taken place you should inform those affected about what has occurred and why. This process is known as *debriefing*.

One group who may consider using a covert approach are those of you whom we refer to as internal or practitioner–researchers (see Sections 5.3 and 8.3). There are recognised advantages and disadvantages associated with being an internal researcher (Sections 5.3 and 8.3). One of the possible disadvantages is related to your relationship with those from whom you will need to gain cooperation in order to gain cognitive access to their data. This may be related to the fact that your status is relatively junior to these colleagues, or that you are more senior to them. Any status difference may act to inhibit your intended data collection. One solution would therefore be to adopt a covert approach in order to seek to gain data. Thus you may decide to interview subordinate colleagues, organise focus groups through your managerial status, or observe interactions during meetings without declaring your research interest. The key question to consider is: Will this approach be more likely to yield trustworthy data than declaring your real purpose and acting overtly? The answer will depend on a number of factors:

- the existing nature of your relationships with those whom you wish to be your participants;
- the prevailing managerial style within the organisation or that part of it where these people work;
- the time and opportunity that you have to attempt to develop the trust and confidence of these intended participants in order to gain their cooperation.

Absolute assurances about the use of the data collected may also be critical to gain trust, and the time you invest in achieving this may be very worthwhile.

In comparison with the issues discussed in the preceding paragraphs, Dale *et al.* (1988:57) believe that the 'ethical problems of survey research may be rather less difficult than those of qualitative research'. This is due to the nature of structured survey questions that are clearly not designed to explore responses and the avoidance of the in-depth interview situation, where the ability to use probing questions leads to more revealing information (Dale *et al.*, 1988). Zikmund (2000) believes that the ethical issues linked with survey research are those associated with more general issues discussed earlier: privacy, deception, openness, confidentiality and objectivity. Dale *et al.* (1988) point to particular ethical issues that arise in relation to the analysis of secondary data derived from survey research, and it is to the issues associated with the analysis and reporting stages of research that we now turn.

Ethical issues related to the analysis and reporting stages

The maintenance of your objectivity will be vital during the analysis stage to make sure that you do not misrepresent the data collected. This will include not being selective about which data to report or, where appropriate, misrepresenting its statistical accuracy (Zikmund, 2000). A great deal of trust is placed in each researcher's integrity, and it would clearly be a major ethical issue were this to be open to question. This duty to represent your data honestly extends to the analysis and reporting stage of your research. Lack of objectivity at this stage will clearly distort your conclusions and any course of action that appears to stem from your work.

The ethical issues of confidentiality and anonymity also come to the fore during the reporting stage of your research. Wells (1994) recognises that it may be difficult to maintain the assurances that have been given. However, it is vital to attempt to ensure that these are maintained. Allowing a participating organisation to be identified by those who can 'piece together' the characteristics that you reveal may result in embarrassment and also in access being refused to those who seek this after you. Great care therefore needs to be exercised to avoid this situation. You also have the option of requesting permission from the organisation to use their name. To gain this permission you will undoubtedly need to let them read your work to understand the context within which they will be named.

This level of care also needs to be exercised in making sure that the anonymity of individuals is maintained. Embarrassment and even harm could result from reporting data that are clearly attributable to a particular individual (Cooper and Schindler, 1998; Robson, 2002). Care therefore needs to be taken to protect those who participated in your research.

worked example

Inadvertently revealing participants' identities

The following examples demonstrate how the identities of research participants can be inadvertently revealed because of a lack of thought on the part of researchers presenting their findings:

- reporting a comment made by a female accounts manager when in fact there is only one such person;
- referring to a comment made by a member of the sales team, when in fact the data being reported could only have come from one person;
- reporting data and comments related to a small section of staff, where it was possible to attribute the particular opinions being reported to specific individuals, or where there was a tendency on the part of other participants to seek to attribute these opinions because of the small numbers to whom these comments related.

A further ethical concern stems from the use made by others of the conclusions that you reach and any course of action that is explicitly referred to or implicitly suggested, based on your research data. How ethical will it be to use the data collected from a group of participants effectively to disadvantage them because of the decisions that are then made in the light of your research? On the other hand, there is a view that says that while the identity of your participants should not be revealed, they cannot be exempt from the way in which research conclusions are then used to make decisions (Dale *et al.*, 1988). This is clearly a very tricky ethical issue!

Where you are aware that your findings may be used to make a decision that could adversely affect the collective interests of those who were your participants, it may be ethical to refer to this possibility even though it reduces the level of access that you achieve. An alternative position is to construct your research question and objectives to avoid this possibility, or so that decisions taken as a result of your research should have only positive consequences for the collective interests of those who participate. You may find that this alternative is not open to you, perhaps because you are a part-time student in employment and your employing organisation directs your choice of research topic. If so, it will be more honest to concede to your participants that you are in effect acting as an internal consultant rather than in a (dispassionate) researcher's role.

This discussion about the impact of research on the collective interests of those who participate brings us back to the reference made above to the particular ethical issues that arise in relation to the analysis of secondary data derived from survey research. Dale *et al.* (1988) point out that where survey results are subsequently used as secondary data the original assurances provided to those who participated in the research may be set aside, with the result that the collective interests of participants may be disadvantaged through this use of data. The use of data for secondary purposes therefore also leads to ethical concerns of potentially significant proportions, and you will need to consider these in the way in which you make use of this type of data.

Data protection and research: an introduction

Since the publication of the second edition of this book, issues of data protection have assumed an even greater importance through the transposition and implementation of legislation within the European Economic Area (EEA). This arose from Directive 95/46/EC of the European Union, which provides protection for individuals in relation to the processing of personal data and the movement of such data. Data protection legislation is likely to exist in countries outside the EEA, and you will need to be familiar with legislative requirements where you wish to undertake your research project.

Article 1 of Directive 95/46/EC requires Member States to protect individuals' rights and freedoms, including their right to privacy, with regard to the processing of personal data. Article 2 provides a number of definitions related to the purpose of the Directive. *Personal data* is defined as any information relating to identified or identifiable persons. Where you process and control this type of data your work will become subject to the provisions of the data protection legislation of the country in which you live. In the context of UK legislation, this refers to the provisions of the Data Protection Act 1998. This Act, in following the Articles of the Directive, outlines the principles with which anyone processing personal data must comply. The following list provides a summary of these principles, although you are strongly advised to familiarise yourself with the definitive legal version and to determine its implications for your proposed research project and the nature of data collection.

Personal data must be:

- processed fairly and lawfully;
- obtained for specified, explicit and lawful purposes and not processed further in a manner incompatible with those purposes;
- adequate, relevant and not excessive in relation to the purpose for which they are processed;
- accurate and, where necessary, kept up to date;
- kept (in a form that allows identification of data subjects) for no longer than is necessary;
- processed in accordance with the rights granted to data subjects by the Act;
- kept securely;
- not transferred to a country outside the European Economic Area unless it ensures an adequate level of protection in relation to the rights of data subjects.

These principles will have implications for all research projects that involve the processing of personal data. There are certain, limited exemptions to the second, fifth and seventh data principles (and to Section 7 of the 1998 Act) related to the processing and use of personal data for research purposes. These are contained in Section 33 of the Data Protection Act 1998. Where data are not processed to support measures or decisions with respect to particular individuals and are not processed in a way that will cause substantial damage or distress to a data subject:

- personal data may be processed further for a research purpose, although it may be necessary to inform data subjects about this new purpose and who controls these data;
- personal data, where processed only for research purposes, may be kept indefinitely;
- personal data that are processed only for research will be exempt from Section 7, which provides data subjects with rights to request information, where the results of the research including any statistics are not made available in a form that identifies any data subject (Data Protection Act 1998 and Data Protection web site, whose copyright owner is the Information Controller).

However, this brief summary of the legislation should be treated as providing a general guideline only and not as providing advice. You should instead seek advice that is appropriate to the particular circumstances of your research project where this involves the collection and processing of personal data. In addition, there is a further category of personal data, known as *sensitive personal data*, which covers information held about a data subject's racial or ethnic origin, political opinions, religious or other similar beliefs, trade union membership etc. This type of data may be processed only if at least one of the conditions in Schedule 3 of the 1998 Act is met. The first of these conditions refers to the data subject providing his or her explicit consent to the processing of such data. Effective explicit consent is likely to mean clear and unambiguous written consent in this context.

These legally based data protection concerns will be likely to focus all researchers' minds on the question of keeping personal data and also on whether the use of their data allows any participant to be identified. Unless there is a clear reason for processing these types of data, the best course of action is likely to be the adoption of a research approach that leads to data that are completely and genuinely anonymised and where any 'key' to identify data subjects is not retained by those who control these data.

A summary checklist on ethical issues is given in Box 5.5.

Box 5.5 Summary checklist to anticipate and deal with ethical issues

- ✓ Attempt to recognise potential ethical issues that will affect your proposed research.
- ✓ Utilise your university's code on research ethics to guide the design and conduct of your research.
- ✓ Anticipate ethical issues at the design stage of your research and discuss how you will seek to control these in your research proposal.
- ✓ Seek informed consent through the use of openness and honesty, rather than using deception.
- ✓ Do not exaggerate the likely benefits of your research for participating organisations or individuals.
- ✓ Respect others' rights to privacy at all stages of your research project.
- ✓ Maintain objectivity and quality in relation to the processes you use to collect data.
- ✓ Recognise that the nature of a qualitatively based approach to research will mean that there is greater scope for ethical issues to arise, and seek to avoid the particular problems related to interviews and observation.
- ✓ Avoid referring to data gained from a particular participant when talking to others, where this would allow the individual to be identified with potentially harmful consequences to that person.
- ✓ Covert research should be considered only where reactivity is likely to be a significant issue or where access is denied (and a covert presence is practical). However, other ethical aspects of your research should still be respected when using this approach.
- ✓ Maintain your objectivity during the stages of analysing and reporting your research.
- ✓ Maintain the assurances that you gave to participating organisations with regard to confidentiality of the data obtained and their organisational anonymity.
- ✓ Consider the implications of using the Internet and email carefully in relation to the maintenance of confidentiality and anonymity of your research participants and their data, before using this means to collect any data. Avoid using this technology to share any data with other participants.
- ✓ Protect individual participants by taking great care to ensure their anonymity in relation to anything that you refer to in your research project report, dissertation or thesis.
- ✓ Consider how the collective interests of your research participants may be adversely affected by the nature of the data that you are proposing to collect, and alter the nature of your research question and objectives where this possibility is likely. Alternatively, declare this possibility to those who you wish to participate in your proposed research.
- ✓ Consider how you will use secondary data in order to protect the identities of those who contributed to its collection or who are named within it.
- ✓ Unless necessary, base your research on genuinely anonymised data. Where it is necessary to process personal data, comply with all of the data protection legal requirements carefully.

5.5 Summary

- Access and ethics are critical aspects for the conduct of research.
- Different types and levels of access have been identified that help us to understand the problem of gaining entry: physical access to an organisation; access to intended participants; continuing access in order to carry out further parts of your research or to be able to repeat the collection of data in another part of the organisation; cognitive access in order to get sufficiently close to find out valid and reliable data.
- Feasibility has been recognised to be an important determinant of what you choose to research and how you undertake the research.
- Strategies to help you to gain access to organisations and to intended participants within them have been described and discussed.
- Research ethics refer to the appropriateness of your behaviour in relation to the rights of those who become the subject of your work or are affected by the work.
- Potential ethical issues should be recognised and considered from the outset of your research and be one of the criteria against which your research proposal is judged.
- Ethical concerns are likely to occur at all stages of your research project: when seeking access, during data collection, as you analyse data and when you report them.
- Qualitative research is likely to lead to a greater range of ethical concerns in comparison with quantitative research, although all research methods have specific ethical issues associated with them.
- Ethical concerns are also associated with the 'power relationship' between the researcher and those who grant access, and the researcher's role (as external researcher, internal researcher or internal consultant).
- The use of the Internet and email to collect data may also generate ethical concerns.
- The introduction of data protection legislation has led to this aspect of research assuming a greater importance and to a need for researchers to comply carefully with a set of legal requirements to protect the privacy and interests of their data subjects.

self-check Questions

5.1 How can you differentiate between types of access, and why is it important to do this?

5.2 What do you understand by the use of the terms 'feasibility' and 'sufficiency' when applied to the question of access?

5.3 Which strategies to help to gain access are likely to apply to the following scenarios:

a an 'external' researcher seeking direct access to managers who will be the research participants;

b an 'external' researcher seeking access through an organisational gatekeeper/broker to her/his intended participants;

c an internal researcher planning to undertake a research project within her/his employing organisation?

5.4 What are the principal ethical issues you will need to consider irrespective of the particular research methods that you use?

5.5 What problems might you encounter in attempting to protect the interests of participating organisations and individuals despite the assurances that you provide?

progressing your research project

Negotiating access and addressing ethical issues

- ☐ Consider the following aspects:
  - ☐ Which types of data will you require in order to be able to answer sufficiently your proposed research question and objectives?
  - ☐ Which research methods will you attempt to use to yield this data?
  - ☐ What type(s) of access will you require in order to be able to collect data?
  - ☐ What problems are you likely to encounter in gaining access?
  - ☐ Which strategies to gain access will be useful to help you to overcome these problems?
- ☐ Depending on the type of access envisaged and your research status (i.e. as external researcher or practitioner–researcher), produce appropriate requests for organisational access, together with a return pro forma, and/or requests to intended participants for their cooperation.
- ☐ Describe the ethical issues that are likely to affect your proposed research project. Discuss how you might seek to overcome or control these. This should be undertaken in relation to the various stages of your research project.
- ☐ Note down your answers.

References

Bell, J. (1999) *Doing your Research Project* (3rd edn), Buckingham, Open University Press.

Bryman, A. (1988) *Quantity and Quality in Social Research*, London, Unwin Hyman.

Buchanan, D., Boddy, D. and McCalman, J. (1988) 'Getting in, getting on, getting out and getting back', *in* Bryman, A. (ed.), *Doing Research in Organisations*, London, Routledge, pp. 53–67.

Cooper, D.R. and Schindler, P.S. (1998) *Business Research Methods* (6th edn), Boston, MA, Irwin McGraw-Hill.

Dale, A., Arber, S. and Procter, M. (1988) *Doing Secondary Research*, London, Unwin Hyman.

Easterby-Smith, M., Thorpe, R. and Lowe, A. (1991) *Management Research: An Introduction*, London, Sage.

Easterby-Smith, M., Thorpe, R. and Lowe, A. (2002) *Management Research: An Introduction* (2nd edn), London, Sage.

Gummesson, E. (2000) *Qualitative Methods in Management Research* (2nd edn), Thousand Oaks, CA, Sage.

Healey, M.J. (1991) 'Obtaining information from businesses', in Healey, M.J. (ed.), *Economic Activity and Land Use*, Harlow, Longman, pp. 193–251.

Jankowicz, A.D. (2000) *Business Research Projects* (3rd edn), London, Business Press Thomson Learning.

Johnson, J.M. (1975) *Doing Field Research*, New York, Free Press.

Mackintosh, N. (ed.) (1995) *Cyril Burt: Fraud or Framed?*, Oxford, Oxford University Press.

Marshall, C. and Rossman, G.B. (1999) *Designing Qualitative Research* (3rd edn), Thousand Oaks, CA, Sage.

Morgan, M. (1995) 'The case of the dubious data', *The Guardian*, 4 August, second section, pp. 10–11.

Raimond, P. (1993) *Management Projects*, London, Chapman & Hall.

Robson, C. (2002) *Real World Research* (2nd edn), Oxford, Blackwell.

Scolari Sage (2002) 'Research methodology and CD-ROMS' (online)(cited 16 June 2002). Available from <URL:http://www.scolari.co.uk>.

Sekaran, U. (2000) *Research Methods for Business: A Skill-Building Approach* (3rd edn), New York, Wiley.

Wells, P. (1994) 'Ethics in business and management research', in Wass, V.J. and Wells, P.E. (eds), *Principles and Practice in Business and Management Research*, Aldershot, Dartmouth, pp. 277–97.

Zikmund, W.G. (2000) *Business Research Methods* (6th edn), Fort Worth, TX, Dryden Press.

Further reading

Buchanan, D., Boddy, D. and McCalman, J. (1988) 'Getting in, getting on, getting out and getting back', *in* Bryman, A. (ed.) *Doing Research in Organisations*, London, Routledge, 53–67. This provides a highly readable and very useful account of the negotiation of access. Other chapters in Bryman's book also consider issues related to access and research ethics.

Gummesson, E. (2002) *Qualitative Methods in Management Research* (2nd edn), Thousand Oaks, CA, Sage. Chapter 2 provides a very useful examination of access and researcher roles and some highly valuable means of differentiating types of access.

Miles, M.B. and Huberman, A.M. (1994) *Qualitative Data Analysis*, Thousand Oaks, CA, Sage. Chapter 11 provides a very useful examination of a range of ethical issues principally from the perspective of their implications for data analysis.

Wells, P. (1994) 'Ethics in business and management research', *in* Wass, V.J. and Wells, P.E. (eds), *Principles and Practice in Business and Management Research*, Aldershot, Dartmouth, pp. 277–97. This provides a very useful exploration of ethics in a range of subject areas as well as a discussion of a number of key issues related to business research.

Zikmund, W.G. (2000) *Business Research Methods* (6th edn), Fort Worth, TX, Dryden Press. Chapter 5 very usefully examines ethical issues associated with business research from the perspective of the rights and obligations of participants, researchers and clients.

CASE 5 Getting in, getting on...? Misreading issues related to access and ethics in a small-scale enterprise

Lefteris was a Greek student studying for a one-year Master's degree in International Management at a United Kingdom university. Now halfway through his course he was thinking about possible dissertation topics. In his hometown in Greece, Lefteris' uncle had a factory that made patio doors and window frames for both the domestic and export markets. Lefteris was very friendly with his uncle and had worked in the accounts and marketing sections at the factory during holidays from university. Through this work he had got to know some of the managers, who had always been very supportive and kind to him. Aware of the problems associated with gaining access to organisations to collect primary data, Lefteris decided to base his dissertation on a case study of his uncle's company.

On the basis of the modules he had studied, Lefteris had become particularly interested in the future enlargement of the European Union and the challenges this was likely to create for Greek companies, and he wondered whether he could link this to a dissertation on his uncle's company. Since commencing his studies, he had come to realise that his uncle's company was faced with major competitive challenges, which had to be overcome if it were to survive. He wondered whether this might be possible by better marketing or by entering into some form of strategic alliance with either a Greek or foreign company. Eventually he thought of a working title for his dissertation, which he could refine later: 'Can the use of marketing or strategic alliances help SMEs survive the competitive challenges of greater European Union (EU) integration and enlargement? A case study of a Greek SME.'

Lefteris realised that he had to start his case study research with clear research questions. After discussion with his tutor he felt that the main issue he was trying to clarify at this stage was the extent to which his uncle's company was planning its marketing strategies, and how these were integrated into the company's corporate plan. These findings could subsequently be linked to EU enlargement.

Fired up by his research methods course, Lefteris was keen to use some of the new research techniques he had learnt about. He had enjoyed the class on participant observation and felt, as he had excellent access, it would be a good idea to use this technique alongside a survey of the employees, and some depth interviews with the managers he knew. Lefteris decided to return to Greece for the Easter vacation to start his primary research with his employee survey and the first of his observations, completing the rest of his data collection at the start of the summer vacation.

On arrival in Greece, Lefteris found that his uncle was happy to grant him access to the company, and instructed all his managers to cooperate with him. To Lefteris' surprise, although his uncle asked him detailed questions about what he had learned about business and marketing planning, he did not appear particularly interested in the research topic. However, his uncle did insist that he was told the results of the research before it was written up, arguing that he did not want his company to appear foolish in the eyes of the UK academic and business community. Lefteris promised to do this.

Lefteris decided to start with his employee survey, as he thought it would take a long time to analyse and write up. He knew from his research methods course that being interviewed by the owner's nephew could cause the employees psychological stress. He therefore decided to give out 'anonymous' self-completion questionnaires to all the employees and ask them to put answered questionnaires in an empty box, which he would collect later. However, in order to ensure that he could send a follow-up letter and questionnaire to those who did not respond, Lefteris decided to number each questionnaire discreetly.

The questionnaire asked employees for personal details such as age, sex, and length of service with the company, and then explored the respondents' attitudes to greater competition and the extent to which in their view it could be a threat. Finally, it asked questions about a range of measures that might help improve the company's ability to meet competition. Lefteris had drawn on his reading of the academic literature for these. They ranged from quality circles and team working to better internal communications and increased expenditure on advertising.

While waiting for the completed questionnaires to be returned, Lefteris started his first observation in the marketing section. Although he had worked there before, people no longer seemed particularly friendly, and tended to stop talking when he walked into a room. This made observation of meetings and work conversations extremely difficult.

A few days later, Lefteris' uncle called him into his office. He told his nephew that, although he fully supported his research efforts, in the real world business school theories are a waste of time and never got him anywhere. He went on to say that the production manager had warned him that the survey was upsetting some of the employees, who saw it as evidence that the company was in difficulties. Some of them were now asking difficult questions and requesting consultation about the future. His uncle hoped that the survey might reveal who these agitators were, and he was looking forward to seeing the results as promised.

Unfortunately, the employees were right. The accounts for the first quarter of the year released a few days later confirmed the trend of a dramatic fall in sales. In a subsequent meeting, Lefteris' uncle blamed this on the marketing section. He told Lefteris that he 'owed it to the rest of the family' to find out what was really going on in the marketing section and to report to him as soon as possible on the results of his research there.

Questions

1. What are the key ethical issues raised in this case study?
2. Should Lefteris continue with his research?
3. With hindsight, how could Lefteris have designed his research to avoid some of the ethical issues outlined above?

self-check Answers

5.1 The types of access that we have referred to in this chapter are: physical entry or initial access to an organisational setting; continuing access, which recognises that researchers often need to develop their access on an incremental basis; and cognitive access, where you will be concerned to gain the cooperation of individual participants once you have achieved access to the organisation in which they work. We also referred to personal access, which allows you to consider whether you actually need to meet with participants in order to carry out an aspect of your research as opposed to corresponding with them or sending them a self-administered, postal questionnaire. Access is strategically related to the success of your research project and needs to be carefully planned. In relation to many research designs, it will need to be thought of as a multifaceted aspect and not a single event.

Table 5.2 **Considering access**

	Scenario A	Scenario B	Scenario C
Allowing yourself sufficient time to gain access	Universally true in all cases. The practitioner–researcher will be going through a very similar process to those who wish to gain access from the outside in terms of contacting intended participants, meeting with them to explain the research, providing assurances etc. The only exception will be related to a covert approach, although sufficient time for planning etc. will of course still be required		
Using any existing contacts	Where possible		Yes
Developing new ones	Probably necessary		This may still apply within large, complex organisations, depending on the nature of the research
Providing a clear account of the purpose of your research and what type of access you require, with the intention of establishing your credibility	Definitely necessary		Still necessary although easier to achieve (verbally or internal memo) with familiar colleagues. Less easy with unfamiliar colleagues, which suggests just as much care as for external researchers
Overcoming organisational concerns in relation to the granting of access	Definitely necessary	Absolutely necessary. This may be *the* major problem to overcome since you are asking for access to a range of employees	Should not be a problem unless you propose to undertake a topic that is highly sensitive to the organisation! We know of students whose proposal has been refused *within* their organisation
Outlining possible benefits of granting access to you and any tangible outcome from doing so	Probably useful		Work-based research projects contain material of value to the organisation although they may largely be theoretically based
Using suitable language	Definitely necessary		Still necessary at the level of participants in the organisation
Facilitating ease of reply when requesting access	Definitely useful		Might be useful to consider in relation to certain internal participants
Developing your access on an incremental basis	Should not be necessary, although you may wish to undertake subsequent work	Definitely worth considering	Might be a useful strategy depending on the nature of the research and the work setting
Establishing your credibility in the eyes of your Intended participants	Access is not being sought at 'lower' levels within the organisation; however, there is still a need to achieve credibility in relation to those to whom you are applying directly	Definitely necessary	May still be necessary with unfamiliar participants in the organisation

5.2 Gaining access can be problematic for researchers for a number of reasons. The concept of feasibility recognises this and suggests that in order to be able to conduct your research it will be necessary to design it with access clearly in mind. You may care to look again at the references to the work of Buchanan *et al.* (1988) and Johnson (1975) in Section 5.2, which demonstrate the relationship between research design and feasibility.

Sufficiency refers to another issue related to access. In Section 5.2 we stated that there are two aspects to the issue of sufficiency. The first of these relates to whether you have sufficiently considered and therefore fully realised the extent and nature of the access that you will require in order to be able to answer your research question and objectives. The second aspect relates to whether you are able to gain sufficient access in practice in order to be able to answer your research question and objectives.

5.3 We may consider the three particular scenarios outlined in the question through Table 5.2.

5.4 The principal ethical issues you will need to consider irrespective of which research methods you use are:

- to respect intended and actual participants' rights to privacy;
- to avoid deceiving participants about why you are undertaking the research, its purpose and how the data collected will be used;
- maintaining your objectivity during the data collection, analysis and reporting stages;
- respecting assurances provided to organisations about the confidentiality of (certain types of) data;
- respecting assurances given to organisations and individuals about their anonymity;
- considering the collective interests of participants in the way you use the data which they provide.

5.5 A number of ethical problems might emerge. These are considered in turn. You may wish to explore a point made by one of your participants but to do so might lead to harmful consequences for this person where the point was attributed to them.

It may be possible for some people who read your work to identify a participating organisation, although you do not actually name it. This may cause embarrassment to the organisation.

Individual participants may also be identified by the nature of the comments that you report, again leading to harmful consequences for them.

Your report may also lead to action being taken within an organisation that adversely affects those who were kind enough to act as participants in your research.

Finally, others may seek to reuse any survey data that you collect, and this might be used to disadvantage those who provided the data by responding to your questionnaire.

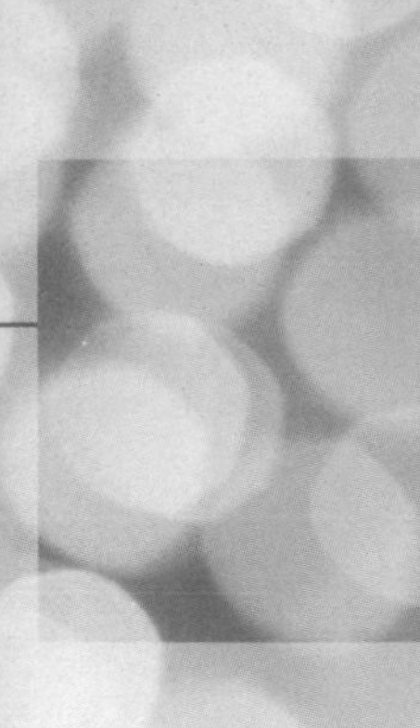

Chapter 6

Selecting samples

By the end of this chapter you should:

- understand the need for sampling in business and management research;
- be aware of a range of probability and non-probability sampling techniques and the possible need to combine techniques within a research project;
- be able to select appropriate sampling techniques for a variety of research scenarios and be able to justify their selection;
- be able to use a range of sampling techniques;
- be able to assess the representativeness of respondents;
- be able to apply the knowledge, skills and understanding gained to your own research project.

6.1 Introduction

Whatever your research question(s) and objectives you will need to collect data to answer them. If you collect and analyse data from every possible case or group member this is termed a *census*. However, for many research questions and objectives it will be impossible for you either to collect or to analyse all the data available to you owing to restrictions of time, money and often access. *Sampling* techniques provide a range of methods that enable you to reduce the amount of data you need to collect by considering only data from a subgroup rather than all possible *cases* or *elements* (Figure 6.1). Some research questions will require sample data to generalise about all the cases from which your sample has been selected. For example, if you asked a sample of consumers what they thought of a new chocolate bar and 75 per cent said that they thought it was too expensive you might infer that 75 per cent of all consumers felt that way. Other research questions may not involve such generalisations. However, even if you are undertaking case study research within a large organisation using in-depth interviews, you will still need to select your case study (sample) organisation and a group (sample) of employees and managers to interview. Techniques for selecting samples will therefore still be important.

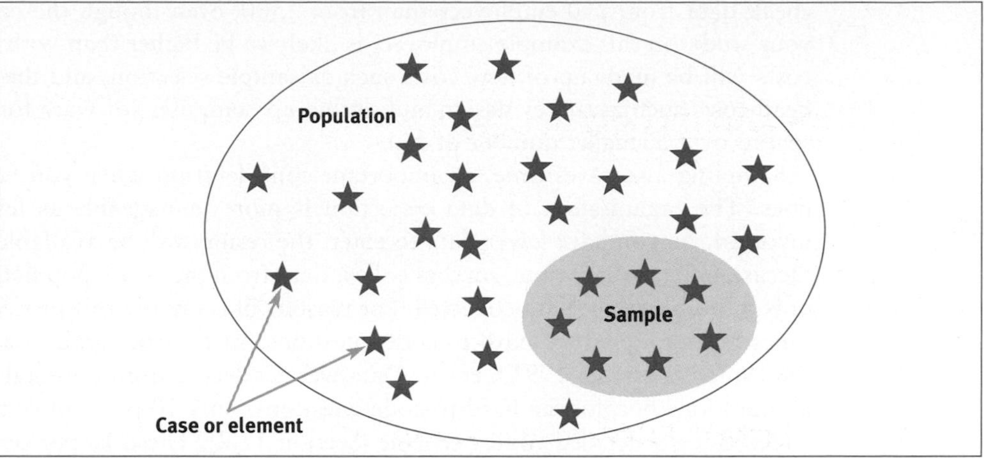

Figure 6.1 Population, sample and individual cases

The full set of cases from which a sample is taken is called the *population*. In sampling, the term 'population' is not used in its normal sense, as the full set of cases need not necessarily be people. For research to discover relative levels of service at burger bars throughout the country, the population from which you would select your sample would be all burger bars in the country. Alternatively, you might need to establish the normal 'life' of a long-life battery produced over the past month by a particular manufacturer. Here the population would be all the long-life batteries produced over the past month by that manufacturer.

The need to sample

For some research questions it is possible to survey an entire population as it is of a manageable size. However, you should not assume that a census survey would necessarily provide more useful results than a well-planned sample survey. Sampling provides a valid alternative to a census when:

- it would be impracticable for you to survey the entire population;
- your budget constraints prevent you from surveying the entire population;
- your time constraints prevent you from surveying the entire population;
- you have collected all the data but need the results quickly.

For all research questions where it would be impracticable for you to survey the whole population you need to select a sample. This will be important whether you are planning to use a predominantly qualitative or quantitative research strategy. You might be able to obtain permission to collect data from only two or three organisations. Alternatively, testing an entire population of products to destruction, such as to establish the crash protection provided by cars, would be impractical for any manufacturer.

With other research questions it might be theoretically possible for you to be able to survey the whole population but the overall cost would prevent it. It is obviously cheaper for you to collect, enter (if you are analysing the data using a computer) and check data from 250 employees than from 2500, even though the cost per case for your study (in this example employee) is likely to be higher than with a census. Your costs will be made up of new costs such as sample selection, and the fact that overhead costs such as survey design and setting up computer software for data entry are spread over a smaller number of cases.

Sampling also saves time, an important consideration when you have tight deadlines. The organisation of data collection is more manageable as fewer people are involved. As you have fewer data to enter, the results will be available more quickly. Occasionally, to save time, surveys collect data from the entire population but analyse only a sample of the data collected. For reasons of economy this procedure has sometimes been adopted for hard-to-code questions, such as occupation and industry, in the United Kingdom 1991 Census. Data were collected from the total population for all questions but, for the hard-to-code questions, only 10 per cent of these data were coded using a detailed coding scheme (Section 11.2). These 10 per cent were entered into the computer and subsequently analysed, although it should be noted that, for the 2001 Census, advances in automated and computer assisted coding software meant all these data were coded (Teague, 2000).

Many researchers, for example Henry (1990), argue that using sampling makes possible a higher overall accuracy than a census. The smaller number of cases for which you need to collect data means that more time can be spent designing and piloting the means of collecting these data. Collecting data from fewer cases also means that you can collect information that is more detailed. In addition, if you are employing people to collect the data (perhaps as interviewers) you can use higher-quality staff. You also can devote more time to trying to obtain data from the more difficult cases. Once your data have been collected, proportionally more time can be devoted to checking and testing the data for accuracy prior to analysis.

An overview of sampling techniques

The sampling techniques available to you can be divided into two types:

- probability or representative sampling;
- non-probability or judgemental sampling.

Those discussed in this chapter are highlighted in Figure 6.2. With *probability samples* the chance, or probability, of each case being selected from the population is known and is usually equal for all cases. This means that it is possible to answer research questions and to achieve objectives that require you to estimate statistically the characteristics of the population from the sample. Consequently, probability sampling is often associated with survey and to a lesser extent experiment research (Section 4.2). For *non-probability samples*, the probability of each case being selected from the total population is not known and it is impossible to answer research questions or to address objectives that require you to make statistical inferences about the characteristics of the population. You may still be able to generalise from non-probability samples about the population, but not on statistical grounds. For this reason non-probability sampling (other than quota sampling) is more frequently used for case study research (Section 4.2). However, with both types of sample you can answer other forms of research questions such as 'What attributes attract people to jobs?' or

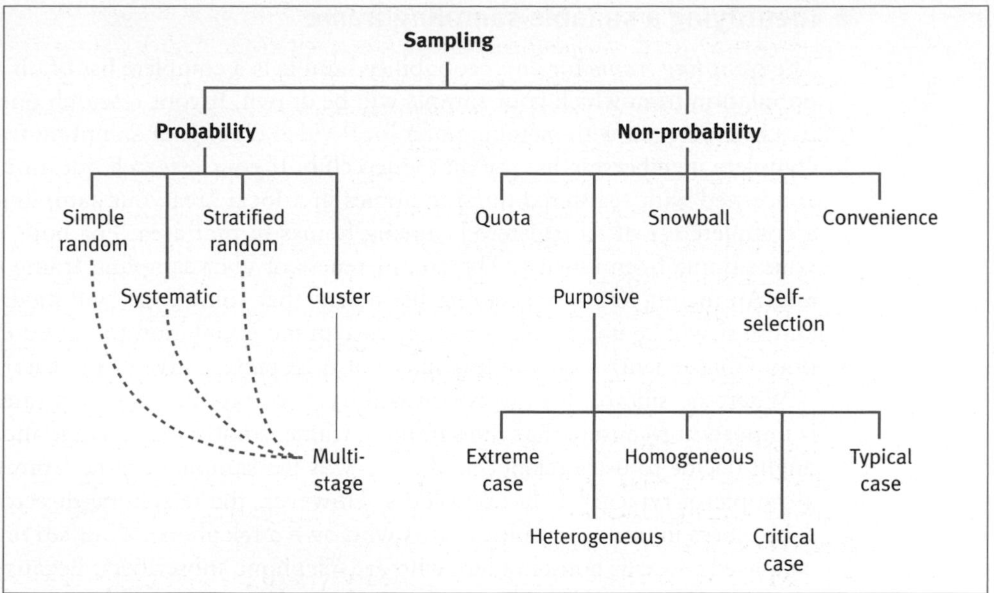

Figure 6.2 **Sampling techniques**

'How are financial institutions adapting the services they provide to meet recent legislation?'

Subsequent sections of this chapter outline a variety of probability (Section 6.2) and non-probability (Section 6.3) sampling techniques, discuss their advantages and disadvantages, and give examples of when you might use them. Although each technique is discussed separately, for many research projects you will need to use a variety of sampling techniques at different stages. This is illustrated by the case study.

6.2 Probability sampling

Probability sampling is most commonly associated with survey-based research where you need to make inferences from your sample about a population to answer your research question(s) or to meet your objectives. The process of probability sampling can be divided into four stages:

1 Identify a suitable sampling frame based on your research question(s) or objectives.
2 Decide on a suitable sample size.
3 Select the most appropriate sampling technique and select the sample.
4 Check that the sample is representative of the population.

Each of these stages will be considered in turn. However, for populations of less than 50 cases Henry (1990) advises against probability sampling. He argues that you should collect data on the entire population as the influence of a single extreme case on subsequent statistical analyses is more pronounced than for larger samples.

Identifying a suitable sampling frame

The *sampling frame* for any probability sample is a complete list of all the cases in the population from which your sample will be drawn. If your research question or objective is concerned with members of a local video club, your sampling frame will be the complete membership list for that video club. If your research question or objective is concerned with registered nursing homes in a local area your sampling frame will be a complete list of all registered nursing homes in that area. For both you then select your sample from this list. The completeness of your sampling frame is very important. An incomplete or inaccurate list means that some cases will have been excluded and so it will be impossible for every case in the population to have a chance of selection. Consequently your sample may not be representative of the total population.

Where no suitable list exists you will have to compile your own sampling frame. It is important to ensure that the sampling frame is unbiased, current and accurate. You might decide to use a telephone directory as the sampling frame from which to select a sample of typical UK householders. However, the telephone directory covers only subscribers in one geographical area who own a telephone. Your survey will therefore be biased towards householders who are telephone subscribers. Because the telephone directory is only published annually, the sampling frame will be out of date (*non-current*). As some householders choose to be ex-directory, it will be inaccurate as it does not include all those who own telephones. This means that you will be selecting a sample of telephone subscribers at the date the directory was compiled who chose not to be ex-directory!

In recent years a number of organisations have been established that specialise in selling lists of names and addresses for surveys. These lists include a wide range of people such as company directors, chief executives, marketing managers, production managers and human resource managers, for public, private and non-profit-making organisations. They are usually in a format suitable for being read by word-processing and database computer software and can easily be merged into standard letters such as those included with questionnaires (Section 10.4). Because you pay for such lists by the case (individual address), the organisations that provide them usually select your sample. It is therefore important to establish precisely how they will select your sample as well as how the list was compiled and when it was last revised. From this, you will be able to assess the currency and accuracy of your sample and whether or not any bias is likely to exist. Box 6.1 provides a checklist against which to check your sampling frame.

Box 6.1 Checklist for selecting a sampling frame

- ✓ Are cases listed in the sampling frame relevant to your research topic, for example are they current?
- ✓ Does the sampling frame include all cases, in other words is it complete?
- ✓ Does the sampling frame exclude irrelevant cases, in other words is it precise?
- ✓ (For purchased lists) Can you establish and control precisely how the sample will be selected?

Deciding on a suitable sample size

Generalisations about populations from data collected using any probability sample are based on probability. The larger your sample's size the lower the likely error in generalising to the population. Probability sampling is therefore a compromise between the accuracy of your findings and the amount of time and money you invest in collecting, checking and analysing the data. Your choice of sample size within this compromise is governed by:

- the confidence you need to have in your data – that is, the level of certainty that the characteristics of the data collected will represent the characteristics of the total population;
- the margin of error that you can tolerate – that is, the accuracy you require for any estimates made from your sample;
- the types of analyses you are going to undertake – in particular the number of categories into which you wish to subdivide your data, as many statistical techniques have a minimum threshold of data cases for each cell (for example chi square, Section 11.5);

and to a lesser extent:

- the size of the total population from which your sample is being drawn.

Given these competing influences it is not surprising that the final sample size is almost always a matter of judgement as well as of calculation. For many research questions and objectives, your need to undertake particular statistical analyses (Section 11.5) will determine the threshold sample size for individual categories. These will affect the overall sample size. In such instances, *The Economist*'s (1997) advice of a minimum number of 30 for statistical analyses provides a useful rule of thumb for the smallest number in each category within your overall sample. Where the population in the category is less than 30, and you wish to undertake your analysis at this level of detail, you should normally collect data from all cases in that category. Alternatively you may have access to an *expert system* such as Ex-Sample. This software uses artificial intelligence to calculate the minimum sample size required for statistical analyses along with the maximum possible sample size, given resources such as time, money and response rates. In addition, it automatically provides a brief justification for the sample size calculated. It is available both on its own and as part of the Methodologist's Toolchest suite of programs (Scolari Sage, 2002).

Researchers normally work to a 95 per cent level of certainty. This means that if your sample was selected 100 times at least 95 of these samples would be certain to represent the characteristics of the population. The *margin of error* describes the precision of your estimates of the population. Table 6.1 provides a rough guide to the different *minimum sample sizes* required from different sizes of population at the 95 per cent level of certainty. It assumes that data are collected from all cases in the sample (full details of the calculation for minimum sample size and adjusted minimum sample size are given in Appendix 3). For most business and management research, researchers are content to estimate the population's characteristics to within plus or minus 3–5 per cent of its true values. This means that if 45 per cent of your sample are in a certain category then your estimate for the total population within the same category will be 45 per cent plus or minus the margin of error – somewhere between 42 and 48 per cent for a 3 per cent margin of error.

As you can see from Table 6.1, the smaller the sample and, to a far lesser extent, the smaller the proportion of the total population sampled, the greater the margin of error. Within this, the relative impact of sample size on the margin of error decreases for larger sample sizes. deVaus (2002) argues that it is for this reason that many market research companies limit their samples' sizes to approximately 2000. Unfortunately, for many sample surveys, a 100 per cent response rate is unlikely and so your sample will need to be larger to ensure sufficient responses for the margin of error you require.

The importance of a high response rate

The most important aspect of a probability sample is that it represents the population. A perfect *representative sample* is one that exactly represents the population from which it is taken. If 60 per cent of your sample were small service sector companies then, provided that the sample was representative, you would expect 60 per cent of the population to be small service sector companies. You therefore need to obtain as high a response rate as possible to ensure that your sample is representative.

In reality, you are likely to have non-responses. Non-respondents are different from the rest of the population because they have refused to be involved in your research for whatever reason. Consequently, your respondents will not be representative of the total population, and the data you collect may be biased. In addition, any non-responses will necessitate extra respondents being found to reach the required sample size, thereby increasing the cost of your survey.

Table 6.1 **Sample sizes for different sizes of population at a 95 per cent level of certainty (assuming data are collected from all cases in the sample)**

	Margin of error			
Population	*5%*	*3%*	*2%*	*1%*
50	44	48	49	50
100	79	91	96	99
150	108	132	141	148
200	132	168	185	196
250	151	203	226	244
300	168	234	267	291
400	196	291	434	384
500	217	340	414	475
750	254	440	571	696
1 000	278	516	706	906
2 000	322	696	1091	1655
5 000	357	879	1622	3288
10 000	370	964	1936	4899
100 000	383	1056	2345	8762
1 000 000	384	1066	2395	9513
10 000 000	384	1067	2400	9595

You should therefore analyse the refusals to respond to both individual questions and entire surveys to check for bias (Section 11.2). Non-response is due to four interrelated problems:

- refusal to respond;
- ineligibility to respond;
- inability to locate respondent;
- respondent located but unable to make contact.

The most common reason for non-response is that your respondent refuses to answer all the questions or be involved in your research, but does not give a reason. Such non-response can be minimised by paying careful attention to the methods used to collect your data (Chapters 8, 9 and 10). Alternatively, some of your selected respondents may not meet your research requirements and so will be *ineligible* to respond. Non-location and non-contact create further problems; the fact that these respondents are *unreachable* means they will not be represented in the data you collect.

As part of your research report, you will need to include your *response rate.* Neumann (2000) suggests that when you calculate this you should include all eligible respondents:

$$\text{total response rate} = \frac{\text{total number of responses}}{\text{total number in sample} - \text{ineligible}}$$

This he calls the *total response rate.* A more common way of doing this excludes ineligible respondents and those who, despite repeated attempts (Sections 9.3 and 10.5), were unreachable. This is known as the *active response rate*:

$$\text{active response rate} = \frac{\text{total number of responses}}{\text{total number in sample} - (\text{ineligible} + \text{unreachable})}$$

Even after ineligible and unreachable respondents have been excluded, it is probable that you will still have some non-responses. You therefore need to be able to assess how representative your data are and to allow for the impact of non-response in your calculations of sample size. These issues are explored in subsequent sections.

worked example

Calculation of total and actual response rates

Hans had decided to undertake a telephone survey of people who had left his company's employment over the past five years. He obtained a list of the 1034 people who had left over this period (the total population) and selected a 50% sample. Unfortunately he could obtain current telephone numbers for only 311 of the 517 ex employees who made up his total sample. Of these 311 people who were potentially reachable, he obtained a response from 147. In addition, his list of people who had left his company was inaccurate, and 9 of those he contacted were ineligible to respond having left the company over 5 years earlier.

$$\text{His total response rate} = \frac{147}{517 - 9} = \frac{147}{508} = 28.9\%$$

$$\text{His active response rate} = \frac{147}{311 - 9} = \frac{147}{302} = 48.7\%$$

Estimating response rates and actual sample size required

With all probability samples, it is important that your sample size is large enough to provide you with the necessary confidence in your data. The margin of error must therefore be within acceptable limits, and you must ensure that you will be able to undertake your analysis at the level of detail required. You therefore need to estimate the likely response rate – that is, the proportion of cases from your sample who will respond or from which data will be collected – and increase the sample size accordingly. Once you have an estimate of the likely response rate and the minimum or the adjusted minimum sample size, the *actual sample size* you require can be calculated using the following formula:

$$n^a = \frac{n \times 100}{re\%}$$

where n^a is the actual sample size required, n is the minimum (or adjusted minimum) sample size (see Table 6.1 or Appendix 3) and $re\%$ is the estimated response rate expressed as a percentage.

worked example

Calculation of actual sample size

Jan was a part-time student employed by a large manufacturing company. He had decided to undertake a survey of customers and calculated that an adjusted minimum sample size of 439 was required. Jan estimated the response rate would be 30 per cent. From this, he could calculate his actual sample size:

$$n^a = \frac{439 \times 100}{30}$$

$$= \frac{43\,900}{30}$$

$$= 1463$$

Jan's actual sample therefore needed to be 1463 customers. Because of time and financial constraints this was rounded down to 1400 customers. The likelihood of 70 per cent non-response meant that Jan needed to include a check that his sample was representative when he designed his data collection method.

If you are collecting your sample data from a secondary source (Section 7.2) within an organisation that has already granted you access, your response rate should be virtually 100 per cent. In research Mark recently undertook he established that all the data he required were available from employees' personnel files. Once access had been granted to these files by the organisation he was ensured of virtually a 100 per cent response rate. His actual sample size was therefore the same as his minimum sample size.

In contrast, estimating the likely response rate from a sample to which you will be sending a questionnaire or interviewing is more difficult. One way of obtaining this estimate is to consider the response rates achieved for similar surveys that have already been undertaken and base your estimate on these. Alternatively, you can err on the side of caution. For postal surveys a response rate of approximately 30 per cent is reasonable (Owen and Jones, 1994). For interviews you should expect a response rate of approximately 50 per cent (Kervin, 1992).

However, beware: response rates can vary considerably when collecting primary data. Willimack *et al.* (2002) report response rates for North American university-based questionnaire surveys of business ranging from 50 per cent to 65 per cent, with even higher non-response for individual questions. Work by Healey (1991) also records a wide variation in response rates. He suggests average response rates of about 50 per cent for postal surveys and 75 per cent for face-to-face interviews, principally in the UK. More recently, Neuman (2000) suggests response rates of between 10 per cent and 50 per cent for postal surveys and up to 90 per cent for face-to-face interviews. The former rate concurs with a recent questionnaire survey we undertook for a multinational organisation that had an overall response rate of 52 per cent. In our survey response rates for individual sites varied from 41 to 100 per cent, again emphasising variability. Our examination of response rates to recent business surveys reveals rates as low as 10–20 per cent for postal surveys, an implication being that respondents' questionnaire fatigue was a contributory factor! Fortunately a number of different techniques, depending on your data collection method, can be used to enhance your response rate. These are discussed with the data collection method in the appropriate sections (Sections 9.3 and 10.5).

Selecting the most appropriate sampling technique and the sample

Once you have chosen a suitable sampling frame and established the actual sample size required, you need to select the most appropriate sampling technique to obtain a representative sample. Five main techniques can be used to select a probability sample (Figure 6.2):

- simple random;
- systematic;
- stratified random;
- cluster;
- multi-stage.

Your choice of probability sampling depends on your research question(s) and your objectives and whether you will need to make statistical inferences from your sample. Subsequently, your need for face-to-face contact with respondents, the geographical area over which the population is spread, and the nature of your sampling frame will affect your choice of probability sampling technique (Figure 6.3). The structure of the sampling frame, the size of sample you need and, if you are using support workers, the ease with which the technique may be explained will also influence your decision. The impact of each of these is summarised in Table 6.2.

Table 6.2 Impact of various factors on choice of probability sampling techniques

Sample technique	*Sampling frame required*	*Size of sample needed*	*Geographical area to which suited*	*Relative cost*	*Easy to explain to support workers?*	*Advantages compared with simple random*
Simple random	Accurate and easily accessible	Better with over a few hundred	Concentrated if face-to-face contact required, otherwise does not matter	High if large sample size or sampling frame not computerised	Relatively difficult to explain	–
Systematic	Accurate, easily accessible and not containing periodic patterns. Actual list not always needed	Suitable for all sizes	Concentrated if face-to face contact required, otherwise does not matter	Low	Relatively easy to explain	Normally no difference
Stratified random	Accurate, easily accessible, divisible into relevant strata (see comments for simple random and systematic as appropriate)	See comments for simple random and systematic as appropriate	Concentrated if face-to-face contact required, otherwise does not matter	Low, provided that lists of relevant strata available	Relatively difficult to explain (once strata decided see comments for simple random and systematic as appropriate)	Better comparison across strata. Differential response rates may necessitate re-weighting
Cluster	Accurate, easily accessible, relates to relevant clusters not individual population members	As large as practicable	Dispersed if face-to-face contact required and geographically based clusters used	Low, provided that lists of relevant clusters available	Relatively difficult to explain until clusters selected	Quick but reduced precision
Multi-stage	Initial stages: geographical. Final stage: needed only for geographical areas selected, see comments for simple random and systematic as appropriate	Initial stages: as large as practicable. Final stage: see comments for simple random and systematic as appropriate	Dispersed if face-to-face contact required, otherwise no need to use this technique!	Low as sampling frame for actual survey population required only for final stage	Initial stages: relatively difficult to explain. Final stage: see comments for simple random and systemtic as appropriate	Difficult to adjust for differential response rates. Substantial errors possible!

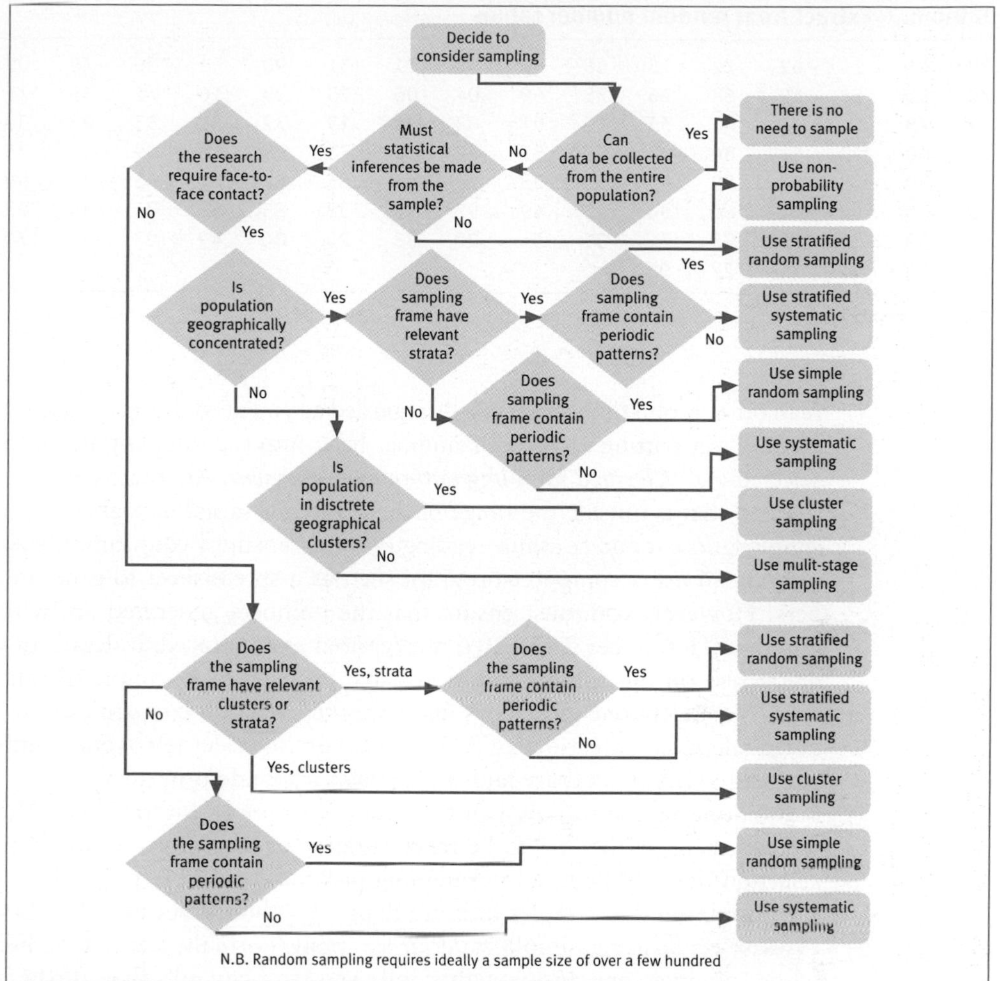

Figure 6.3 **Selecting a probability sampling technique**

Simple random sampling

Simple random sampling involves you selecting the sample at random from the sampling frame using either random number tables (Appendix 4) or a computer. To do this you:

1. Number each of the cases in your sampling frame with a unique number. The first case is numbered 0, the second 1 and so on.
2. Select cases using random numbers (Table 6.3, Appendix 4) until your actual sample size is reached.

It is usual to select your first random number at random (closing your eyes and pointing with your finger is a good way!) as this ensures that the set of random numbers obtained for different samples is unlikely to be the same. If you do not you will obtain sets of numbers that are random but identical.

Starting with this number you read off the random numbers (and select the cases) in a regular and systematic manner until your sample size is reached. If the same number is

Table 6.3 Extract from random number tables

78	41	11	62	72	18	66	69	58	71	31	90	51	36	78	09	41	00
70	50	58	19	68	26	75	69	04	00	25	29	16	72	35	73	55	85
32	78	14	47	01	***55***	10	91	83	21	13	32	59	53	03	38	79	32
71	60	20	53	86	78	50	57	42	30	73	48	68	09	16	35	21	87
35	30	15	57	99	96	33	25	56	43	65	67	51	45	37	99	54	89
09	08	05	41	66	54	01	49	97	34	38	85	85	23	34	62	60	58
02	59	34	51	98	71	31	54	28	85	23	84	49	07	33	71	17	88
20	13	44	15	22	95												

Source: Appendix 4

read off a second time it must be disregarded as you need different cases. This means that you are not putting each case's number back into the sampling frame after it has been selected and is termed *sampling without replacement*. Alternatively, a number might be selected that is outside the range of those in your sampling frame. If this happens you simply ignore it and continue reading off numbers until your sample size is reached.

You can use a computer program such as a spreadsheet to generate random numbers. However, you must ensure that the numbers generated are within your range and that if a number is repeated it is ignored and replaced. If details of the population are stored on the computer it is possible to generate a sample of randomly selected cases. For telephone interviews many market research companies now use computer-aided telephone interviewing (CATI) software to select telephone numbers at random from an existing database and to dial each respondent in turn.

Random numbers allow you to select your sample without bias. The sample selected can therefore be said to be representative of the whole population. However, the selection that simple random sampling provides is more evenly dispersed throughout the population for samples of more than a few hundred cases. The first few hundred cases selected using simple random sampling normally consist of bunches of cases whose numbers are close together followed by a gap and then further bunching. For over a few hundred cases this pattern occurs far less frequently. Because of the technique's random nature it is therefore possible that the chance occurrence of such patterns will result in certain parts of a population being over- or under-represented.

Simple random sampling is best used when you have an accurate and easily accessible sampling frame that lists the entire population, preferably stored on a computer. While you can often obtain these for employees within organisations or members of clubs or societies, adequate lists are often not available for types of organisation. If your population covers a large geographical area random selection means that selected cases are likely to be dispersed throughout the area. Consequently, this form of sampling is not suitable if you are undertaking a survey that covers a large geographical area and requires face-to-face contact, owing to the associated high travel costs. Simple random sampling would still be suitable for a geographically dispersed area if you used an alternative technique of collecting data such as postal questionnaires or telephone interviewing (Chapter 10).

Sampling frames used for telephone interviewing are being replaced increasingly by *random digital dialling*. This provides a chance to reach any household within an area that has a telephone line, regardless of whether or not the number is ex-directory (Lavrakas, 1993). However, care must be taken as, increasingly, households have more than one telephone number. Consequently there is a higher probability of these households being selected as part of the sample.

worked example

Simple random sampling

You have a population of 5011 supermarket customers, all of whom use the supermarket's charge card for their weekly purchases. You wish to find out why they use the charge card. There is insufficient time to interview all of them and so you decide to interview a sample. Your calculations reveal that to obtain acceptable levels of confidence and accuracy you need an actual sample size of approximately 360 customers. You decide to select them using simple random sampling.

First you give each of the cases (customers) in the sampling frame a unique number. In order that each number is made up in exactly the same way you use 5011 four-digit numbers starting with 0000 through to 5010. So customer 677 is given the number 0676.

The first random number you select is 55 (shown in bold and italics in Table 6.3). Starting with this number you read off the random numbers in a regular and systematic manner (in this example continuing along the line):

5510 9183 2113 3259 5303 3879 3271 6020

until 360 different cases have been selected. These form your random sample. Numbers selected that are outside the range of those in your sampling frame (such as 5510, 9183, 5303 and 6020) are simply ignored.

Systematic sampling

Systematic sampling involves you selecting the sample at regular intervals from the sampling frame. To do this you:

1 Number each of the cases in your sampling frame with a unique number. The first case is numbered 0, the second 1 and so on.
2 Select the first case using a random number.
3 Calculate the sampling fraction.
4 Select subsequent cases systematically using the sampling fraction to determine the frequency of selection.

To calculate the *sampling fraction* – that is, the proportion of the total population that you need to select – you use the formula

$$\text{sampling fraction} = \frac{\text{actual sample size}}{\text{total population}}$$

If your sampling fraction is ⅓ you need to select one in every three cases – that is, every third case from the sampling frame. Unfortunately your calculation will usually result in a more complicated fraction. In these instances it is normally acceptable to round your population down to the nearest 10 (or 100) and to increase your minimum sample size until a simpler sampling fraction can be calculated.

On its own, selecting one in every three would not be random as every third case would be bound to be selected, whereas those between would have no chance of selection. To overcome this a random number is used to decide where to start on the sampling frame. If your sampling fraction is ⅓ the starting point must be one of the first three cases. You therefore select a random number (in this example a one-digit random number between 0 and 2) as described earlier and use this as the starting point.

Once you have selected your first case at random you then select, in this example, every third case until you have gone right through your sampling frame. As with simple random sampling you can use a computer to generate the first random and subsequent numbers that are in the sample.

In some instances it is not necessary to construct a list for your sampling frame. Research Mark undertook for a local authority required data to be collected about every tenth client of a social services department. Although these data were not held on computer they were available from each client's manual file. The files were stored in alphabetical order and, once the first file (client) was selected at random, it was easy to extract every tenth file (client) thereafter. This process had the additional advantage that it was easy to explain to social services' employees, although Mark still had to explain to inquisitive employees that he needed a representative sample and so their 'interesting' clients might not be selected!

worked example

Systematic sampling

You have a population of approximately 1500 patients and wish to find out their attitudes to a new voucher scheme. There is insufficient time and money to collect data from all of them using a questionnaire and so you decide to send the questionnaire to a sample. Your calculation of sample size reveals that to obtain acceptable levels of confidence and accuracy you need an actual sample size of approximately 300 patients to whom you will send the questionnaire. You decide to select them using systematic sampling.

First you need to work out the sampling fraction:

$$\frac{300}{1500} = \frac{1}{5}$$

Your sampling fraction is therefore ⅕. This means that you need to select every fifth patient from the sampling frame.

You use a random number to decide where to start on the sampling frame. As your sampling fraction is ⅕ the starting point must be one of the first five patients. You therefore select a one-digit random number between 0 and 4.

Once you have selected your first patient at random you select every fifth patient until you have gone right through your sampling frame. If the random number you selected was 2, then you would select the following patient numbers:

2 7 12 17 22 27 32 37

and so on until 300 patients had been selected.

Despite the advantages you must be careful when using existing lists as sampling frames. You need to ensure that the lists do not contain periodic patterns.

A high street bank needs you to undertake a sample survey of individual customers with joint bank accounts. A sampling fraction of ¼ means that you will need to select

Table 6.4 The impact of periodic patterns on systematic sampling

Number	*Customer*	*Sample*	*Number*	*Customer*	*Sample*
000	Mr L. Baker	***M***	006	Mr E. Saunders	
001	Mrs B. Baker		007	Mrs M. Saunders	***F***
002	Mr S. Davies		008	Mr J. Smith	***M***
003	Mrs P. Davids	***F***	009	Mrs K. Smith	
004	Mr J. Lewis	***M***	010	Mr J. Thornhill	
005	Mrs P. Lewis		011	Mrs A. Thornhill	***F***

M all male sample selected if start with 000, ***F*** all female sample selected if start with 003

every fourth customer on the list. The names on the customer lists, which you intend to use as the sampling frame, are arranged alphabetically by account with males followed by females (Table 6.4). If you start with a male customer all those in your sample will be male. Conversely, if you start with a female customer all those in your sample will be female. Consequently your sample will be biased (Table 6.4). This sampling frame is therefore not suitable without reordering or stratifying (discussed later).

Unlike simple random sampling, systematic sampling works equally well with a small or large number of cases. However, if your population covers a large geographical area, the random selection means that the sample cases are likely to be dispersed throughout the area. Consequently systematic sampling is suitable for geographically dispersed cases only if you do not require face-to-face contact when collecting your data.

Stratified random sampling

Stratified random sampling is a modification of random sampling in which you divide the population into two or more relevant and significant strata based on one or a number of attributes. In effect your sampling frame is divided into a number of subsets. A random sample (simple or systematic) is then drawn from each of the strata. Consequently stratified sampling shares many of the advantages and disadvantages of simple random and systematic sampling.

Dividing the population into a series of relevant strata means that the sample is more likely to be representative, as you can ensure that each of the strata is represented proportionally within your sample. However, it is only possible to do this if you are aware of, and can easily distinguish, significant strata in your sampling frame. In addition the extra stage in the sampling procedure means that it is likely to take longer, to be more expensive, and to be more difficult to explain than simple random or systematic sampling.

In some instances, as pointed out by deVaus (2002), your sampling frame will already be divided into strata. A sampling frame of employee names that is in alphabetical order will automatically ensure that, if systematic sampling is used (discussed earlier), employees will be sampled in the correct proportion to the letter with which their name begins. Similarly, membership lists that are ordered by date of joining will automatically result in stratification by length of membership if systematic sampling is used. Therefore if you are using simple random sampling or your sampling frame contains periodic patterns you will need to stratify it. To do this you:

1 Choose the stratification variable or variables.
2 Divide the sampling frame into the discrete strata.
3 Number each of the cases within each stratum with a unique number, as discussed earlier.
4 Select your sample using either simple random or systematic sampling, as discussed earlier.

The stratification variable (or variables) chosen should represent the discrete characteristic (or characteristics) for which you want to ensure correct representation within the sample.

Samples can be stratified using more than one characteristic. You may wish to stratify a sample of an organisation's employees by both department and salary grade. To do this you would:

1 Divide the sampling frame into the discrete departments.
2 Within each department divide the sampling frame into discrete salary grades.
3 Number each of the cases within each salary grade within each department with a unique number, as discussed earlier.
4 Select your sample using either simple random or systematic sampling, as discussed earlier.

In some instances the relative sizes of different strata mean that, in order to have sufficient data for analysis, you need to select larger samples from the strata with smaller populations. Here the different sample sizes must be taken into account when aggregating data from each of the strata to obtain an overall picture. The more sophisticated statistical analysis software packages enable you to do this by differentially weighting the responses for each stratum (Section 11.2).

worked example

Stratified random sampling

In the survey of joint bank account holders we discussed earlier an important stratum would be each account customer's gender, and so the sampling frame is divided into two discrete strata: females and males. Within each stratum the individual cases are numbered:

Female stratum			*Male stratum*		
Number	*Customer*	*Selected*	*Number*	*Customer*	*Selected*
000	Mrs B. Baker		000	Mr L. Baker	
001	Mrs P. Davis	✓	001	Mr S. Davis	
002	Mrs P. Lewis		002	Mr J. Lewis	
003	Mrs M. Saunders		003	Mr E. Saunders	✓
004	Mrs K. Smith		004	Mr J. Smith	
005	Mrs A. Thornhill	✓	005	Mr J. Thornhill	
005	Mrs D. Woollons		006	Mr J. Woollons	
007	Mrs P. Wordden		007	Mr F. Wordden	✓

You decide to select a systematic sample. A sampling fraction of ¼ means that you will need to select every fourth customer on the list. As indicated by the ticks (✓) random numbers select the first case in the female (1) and male (3) strata. Subsequently every fourth customer in each stratum is selected.

Cluster sampling

Cluster sampling is, on the surface, similar to stratified sampling as you need to divide the population into discrete groups prior to sampling (Henry, 1990). The groups are termed *clusters* in this form of sampling and can be based on any naturally occurring grouping. For example, you could group your data by type of manufacturing firm or geographical area.

For cluster sampling your sampling frame is the complete list of clusters rather than a complete list of individual cases within the population. You then select a few clusters, normally using simple random sampling. Data are then collected from every case within the selected clusters. The technique has three main stages:

1 Choose the cluster grouping for your sampling frame.
2 Number each of the clusters with a unique number. The first cluster is numbered 0, the second 1 and so on.
3 Select your sample using some form of random sampling as discussed earlier.

Selecting clusters randomly makes cluster sampling a probability sampling technique. However, the technique normally results in a sample that represents the total population less accurately than stratified random sampling. Restricting the sample to a few relatively compact geographical subareas (clusters) maximises the number of interviews you can undertake within the resources available. However, it may also reduce the representativeness of your sample. For this reason you need to maximise the number of subareas to allow for variations in the population within the available resources. Your choice is between a large sample from a few discrete subgroups and a smaller sample distributed over the whole group. It is a trade-off between the amount of precision lost by using a few subgroups and the amount gained from a larger sample size.

worked example

Cluster sampling

Ceri needed to select a sample of firms to undertake an interview-based survey about the use of photocopiers. As she had limited resources with which to pay for travel and other associated data collection costs she decide to interview firms in four geographical areas selected from a cluster grouping of local administrative areas. A list of all local administrative areas formed her sampling frame. Each of the local administrative areas (clusters) was given a unique number, the first being 0, the second 1 and so on. The four sample clusters were selected from this sampling frame of local administrative areas using simple random sampling.

Ceri's sample was all firms within the selected clusters. She decided that the appropriate telephone directories would probably provide a suitable list of all firms in each cluster.

Multi-stage sampling

Multi-stage sampling, sometimes called *multi-stage cluster sampling*, is a development of cluster sampling. It is normally used to overcome problems associated with a geographically dispersed population when face-to-face contact is needed or where it is expensive and time consuming to construct a sampling frame for a large geographical area. However, like cluster sampling you can use it for any discrete groups including those that are not geographically based. The technique involves taking a series of cluster samples, each involving some form of random sampling. This aspect is represented by the dotted lines in Figure 6.2. It can be divided into four phases. These are outlined in Figure 6.4.

Because multi-stage sampling relies on a series of different sampling frames you need to ensure that they are all appropriate and available. In order to minimise the impact of selecting smaller and smaller subgroups on the representativeness of your sample you can apply stratified sampling techniques (discussed earlier). This technique can be further refined to take account of the relative size of the subgroups by adjusting the sample size for each subgroup. As you have selected your subareas using different sampling frames you only need a sampling frame that lists all the members of the population for those subgroups you finally select. This provides considerable savings in time and money.

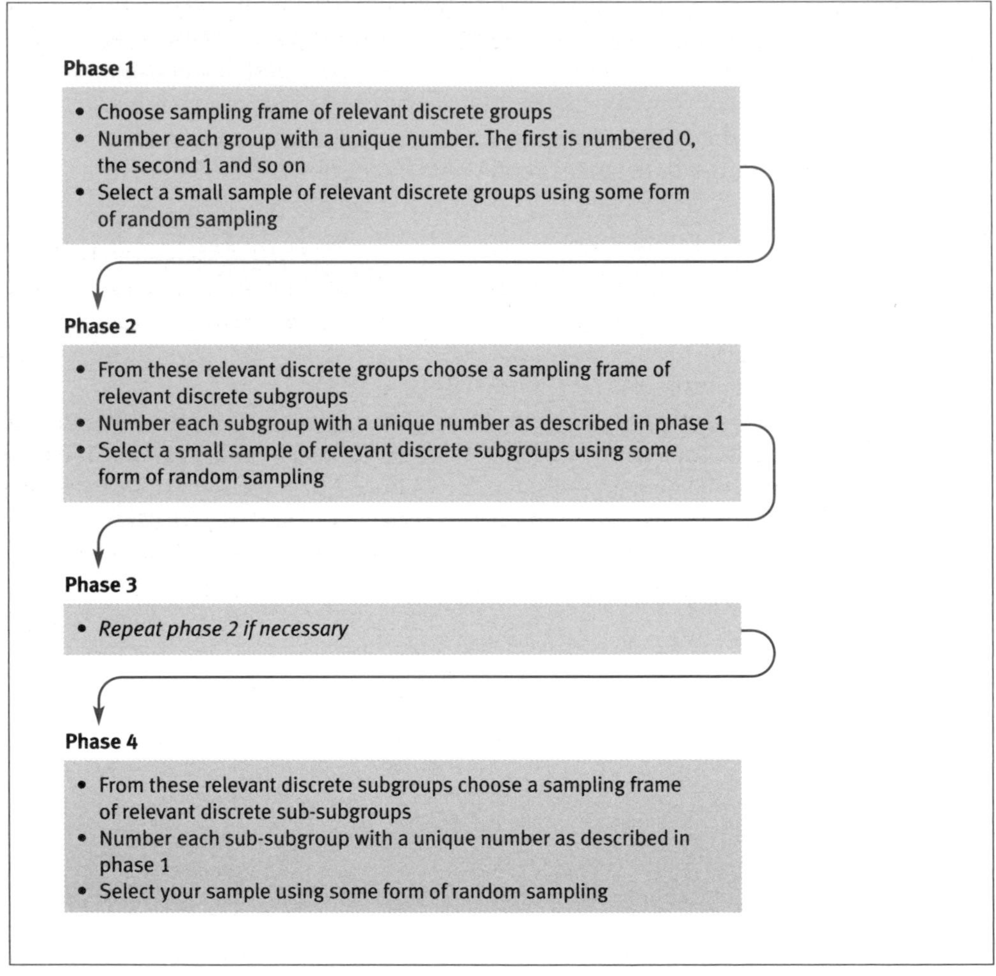

Phase 1
• Choose sampling frame of relevant discrete groups
• Number each group with a unique number. The first is numbered 0, the second 1 and so on
• Select a small sample of relevant discrete groups using some form of random sampling
Phase 2
• From these relevant discrete groups choose a sampling frame of relevant discrete subgroups
• Number each subgroup with a unique number as described in phase 1
• Select a small sample of relevant discrete subgroups using some form of random sampling
Phase 3
• Repeat phase 2 if necessary
Phase 4
• From these relevant discrete subgroups choose a sampling frame of relevant discrete sub-subgroups
• Number each sub-subgroup with a unique number as described in phase 1
• Select your sample using some form of random sampling

Figure 6.4 **Phases of multi-stage sampling**

worked example

Multi-stage sampling

A market research organisation needs you to interview a sample of 400 households in England and Wales. The electoral register provides a possible sampling frame. Selecting 400 households using either systematic or simple random sampling would probably result in these 400 households being dispersed throughout England and Wales. The time and cost of travelling to and interviewing your sample would be enormous. By using multi-stage sampling these problems can be overcome.

In the first stage the geographical area (England and Wales) is split into discrete subareas (counties). These form the sampling frame. After numbering, a small number of counties are selected using simple random sampling. Since each case (household) is located in a county each has an equal chance of being selected for the final sample.

As the counties selected are still too large the selected counties are subdivided into smaller geographically discrete areas (electoral wards), which form the next sampling frame (stage 2). Another simple random sample is selected. A larger number of wards are selected to allow for likely important variations in households between wards.

A sampling frame is generated for each ward using a combination of the electoral register and the UK Royal Mail's postcode address file. The cases (households) that will be interviewed are then selected using either simple random or systematic techniques.

Checking the sample is representative

Often it is possible to compare data you collect from your sample with data from another source for the population. For example, you can compare data on the age and socioeconomic characteristics of respondents in a marketing survey with these characteristics for the population in that country as recorded by the latest national census of population. If there is no statistically significant difference then the sample is representative with respect to these characteristics.

When working within an organisation comparisons can also be made. In a recent survey we undertook of all types of employees in a multinational organisation we asked closed questions about salary grade, gender, length of service and place of work. Possible responses to each question were designed to provide sufficient detail to compare the characteristics of our sample with the characteristics of the entire population of employees as recorded by the organisation's computerised personnel system. At the same time we kept the categories sufficiently broad to preserve, and to be seen to preserve, the confidentiality of individual respondents. The two questions on length of service and salary grade from a recent questionnaire we developed illustrate this:

58 How long have you worked for *organisation's name*?

up to 3 years ☐ over 3 years to 10 years ☐ over 10 years ☐

59 Which one of the following best describes your job?

Technical/clerical (grades 1–3)	☐	Senior management (grades 12–14)	☐
Supervisor (grades 4–5)	☐	Directorate (grades 15–17)	☐
Professional (grades 6–8)	☐	Other (please say)	☐
Management (grades 9–11)	☐	....	

Using the Kolmogorov–Smirnov one-sample test (Section 11.5) we found there was no statistically significant difference between the proportions of respondents in each of the length of service groups and the data obtained from the computerised personnel database. This meant that our sample was representative of all employees with respect to length of service. However, those responding were (statistically) significantly more likely to be in professional and managerial grades than in technical, clerical or supervisory grades. We therefore added a note of caution about the representativeness of our findings.

You can also assess the representativeness of samples for longitudinal studies. Obviously it is still possible to compare respondent characteristics with data from another source. In addition the characteristics of those who responded can be compared for different data collection periods. For example, you could compare the characteristics of those in your sample who responded to a survey at the start of a research project with those who responded to a survey six months later. We should like to add a note of caution here. Such a comparison will enable you to discuss the extent to which the groups of respondents differed for these characteristics over time. However, depending on your choice of characteristics, these differences might be expected owing to some form of managerial intervention or change between the data collection periods.

6.3 Non-probability sampling

The techniques for selecting samples discussed earlier have all been based on the assumption that your sample will be statistically chosen at random. Consequently, it is possible to specify the probability that any case will be included in the sample. However, within business research, such as market surveys and case study research, this is often not possible and so your sample must be selected some other way. Non-probability sampling provides a range of alternative techniques based on your subjective judgement. In the exploratory stages of some research projects, such as a pilot survey, a non-probability sample may be the most practical although it will not allow the extent of the problem to be determined. Subsequent to this, probability sampling techniques may be used. For other business and management research projects your research question(s), objectives and choice of research strategy (Sections 4.1–4.3) may dictate non-probability sampling. To answer your research question(s) and to meet your objectives you may need to undertake an in-depth study that focuses on a small, perhaps one, case selected purposively. This sample would provide you with an information-rich case study in which you explore your research question. Alternatively, limited resources or the inability to specify a sampling frame may dictate the use of one or a number of non-probability sampling techniques.

Selecting the most appropriate sampling technique and the sample

A range of non-probability sampling techniques is available that should not be discounted as they can provide sensible alternatives to select cases to answer your research question(s) and to address your objectives (Figure 6.2). At one end of this range is quota sampling, which, like probability samples, tries to represent the total population. Quota sampling has similar requirements for sample size as probabilistic sampling techniques.

At the other end of this range are techniques based on the need to obtain a sample as quickly as possible where you have little control over the content and there is no attempt to obtain a representative sample. These include convenience and self-selection sampling techniques. Purposive sampling and snowball sampling techniques lie between these extremes (Table 6.5). For these techniques the issue of sample size is ambiguous. Unlike quota and probability samples there are no rules. Rather it depends on your research question(s) and objectives – in particular what you need to find out, what will be useful, what will have credibility and what can be done within your available resources (Patton, 2002). This is particularly so where you are intending to collect qualitative data. The validity and understanding that you will gain from your data will be more to do with your data collection and analysis skills than with

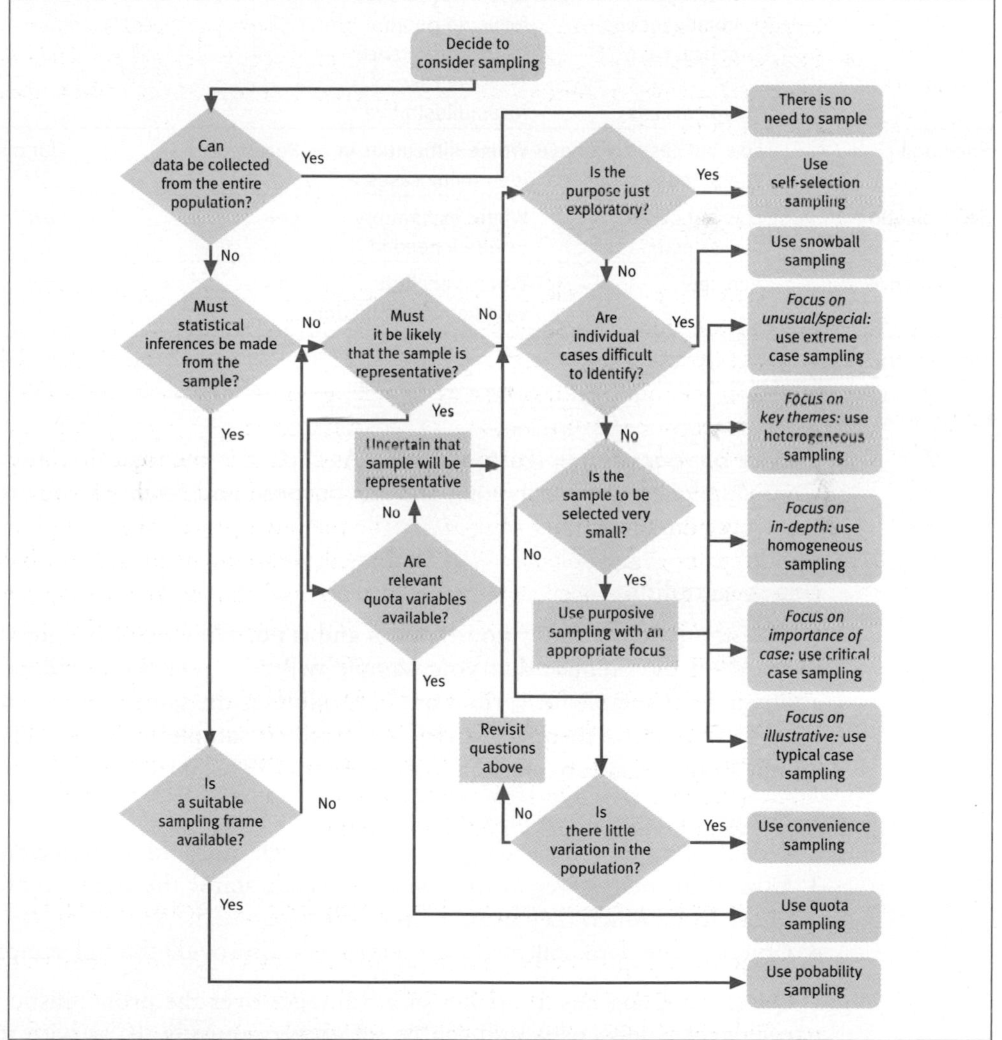

Figure 6.5 Selecting a non-probability sampling technique

Table 6.5 **Impact of various factors on choice of non-probability sample techniques**

Sample type	*Likelihood of sample being representative*	*Types of research in which useful*	*Relative costs*	*Control over sample contents*
Quota	Reasonable to high although dependent on selection of quota variables	Where costs constrained/data needed very quickly so an alternative to probability sampling needed	Moderately high to reasonable	Relatively high
Purposive	Low although dependent on researcher's choices: extreme case heterogeneous homogeneous critical case typical case	Where working with very small samples focus: unusual or special focus: key themes focus: in-depth focus: importance of case focus: illustrative	Reasonable	Reasonable
Snowball	Low but cases will have characteristics desired	Where difficulties in identifying cases	Reasonable	Quite low
Self-selection	Low but cases self-selected	Where exploratory research needed	Low	Low
Convenience	Very low	Where very little variation in population	Low	Low

Developed from: Kervin (1992); Patton (2002).

the size of your sample (Patton, 2002). As such it is the logical relationship between your sample selection technique and the purpose and focus of your research that is important (Figure 6.5).

Quota sampling

Quota sampling is entirely non-random and is normally used for interview surveys. It is based on the premise that your sample will represent the population as the variability in your sample for various quota variables is the same as that in the population. Quota sampling is therefore a type of stratified sample in which selection of cases within strata is entirely non-random (Barnett, 1991). To select a quota sample you:

1 Divide the population into specific groups.
2 Calculate a quota for each group based on relevant and available data.
3 Give each interviewer an *assignment*, which states the number of cases in each quota from which they must collect data.
4 Combine the data collected by interviewers to provide the full sample.

Quota sampling has a number of advantages over the probabilistic techniques. In particular it is less costly and can be set up very quickly. If, as with television audience research surveys, your data collection needs to be undertaken very quickly then quota sampling may be the only possibility. In addition it does not require a sampling frame and may therefore be the only technique you can use if one is not available.

Quota sampling is normally used for large populations. For small populations it is usually possible to obtain a sampling frame. Decisions on sample size are governed by the need to have sufficient responses in each quota to enable subsequent statistical analyses to be undertaken. This normally necessitates a sample size of between 2000 and 5000.

Calculations of quotas are based on relevant and available data and are usually relative to the proportions in which they occur in the population. Without sensible and relevant quotas data collected may be biased. For many market research projects quotas are derived from census data. Your choice of quota is dependent on two main factors:

- usefulness as a means of stratifying the data;
- ability to overcome likely variations between groups in their availability for interview.

Where pensioners are likely to have different opinions from working couples a quota that does not ensure that these differences are captured may result in the data being biased as it would probably be easier to collect the data from pensioners. Quotas used in market research surveys usually include measures of age, gender and socioeconomic status or social class. These may be supplemented by additional quotas dictated by the research question(s) and objectives.

Once you have given each interviewer their particular assignment they decide whom to interview until they have completed their quota. You then combine the data from this assignment with those collected by other interviewers to provide the full sample. Because the interviewer can choose within quota boundaries whom he or she interviews your quota sample may be subject to bias. Interviewers tend to choose respondents who are easily accessible and who appear willing to answer the survey. Clear

worked example

Devising a quota sample

A market research survey requires you to interview a sample of people representing those aged 20–64 who are in employment. No sampling frame is available. You wish to disaggregate your findings into groups dependent on respondents' age and type of employment. Previous research suggests that gender will also have an impact on responses and so you need to make sure that those interviewed in each group also reflect the proportions of males and females in the population. Fortunately the national census of population contains a breakdown of the number of people in employment by gender, age and socioeconomic status. These form the basis of the categories for your quotas:

gender ×	**age group** ×	**socioeconomic status**
male	20–29	professional
female	30–34	managers/employers
45–64		intermediate and junior non-manual
		skilled manual
		semi-skilled manual
		unskilled manual

▶

As you wish to analyse the data for individual age and socioeconomic status groups it is important that each of these categories has sufficient respondents (at least 30) to enable meaningful statistical analyses. You calculate that a 5 per cent quota for each of the groups will provide sufficient numbers for all groups, provided your analyses are not also disaggregated by gender. This gives you the following quotas:

Gender	*Age group*	*Socioeconomic status*	*Population*	*Quota*
Male	20–29	Professional	1121	56
		Managers/employers	798	40
		Intermediate and junior non-manual	910	43
		Skilled manual	1611	79
		Semi-skilled manual	1260	63
		Unskilled manual	503	25
	30–44	Professional	2143	107
		Managers/employers	2327	116
		Intermediate and junior non-manual	799	40
		Skilled manual	2141	107
		Semi-skilled manual	1924	96
		Unskilled manual	498	25
	45–64	Professional	1661	83
		Managers/employers	2397	120
		Intermediate and junior non-manual	999	49
		Skilled manual	2001	100
		Semi-skilled manual	1761	88
		Unskilled manual	576	29
Female	20–29	Professional	881	44
		Managers/employers	678	34
		Intermediate and junior non-manual	2158	108
		Skilled manual	175	9
		Semi-skilled manual	963	48
		Unskilled manual	357	18
	30–44	Professional	1638	82
		Managers/employers	976	49
		Intermediate and junior non-manual	2842	142
		Skilled manual	221	11
		Semi-skilled manual	1180	59
		Unskilled manual	879	41
	45–64	Professional	882	44
		Managers/employers	784	39
		Intermediate and junior non-manual	2197	110
		Skilled manual	157	8
		Semi-skilled manual	942	47
		Unskilled manual	816	41
Total sample			44156	2200

These are then divided into assignments of 50 people for each interviewer.

controls may therefore be needed. In addition it has been known for interviewers to fill in quotas incorrectly. This is not to say that your quota sample will not produce good results; they can and often do! However, you cannot measure the level of certainty or margins of error as the sample is not probability based.

Purposive sampling

Purposive or *judgemental sampling* enables you to use your judgement to select cases that will best enable you to answer your research question(s) and to meet your objectives. This form of sample is often used when working with very small samples such as in case study research and when you wish to select cases that are particularly informative (Neuman, 2000). Purposive sampling may also be used by researchers following the grounded theory approach. For such research, findings from data collected from your initial sample inform the way you extend your sample into subsequent cases (Section 12.6). Such samples cannot, however, be considered to be statistically representative of the total population. The logic on which you base your strategy for selecting cases for a purposive sample should be dependent on your research question(s) and objectives. Patton (2002) emphasises this point by contrasting the need to select information-rich cases in purposive sampling with the need to be statistically representative in probability sampling. The more common purposive sampling strategies were outlined in Figure 6.2 and are discussed below:

- *Extreme case* or *deviant* sampling focuses on unusual or special cases on the basis that the data collected about these unusual or extreme outcomes will enable you to learn the most and to answer your research question(s) and to meet your objectives most effectively. This is often based on the premise that findings from extreme cases will be relevant in understanding or explaining more typical cases (Patton, 2002). Peters and Waterman's (1982) research on excellent companies was based on a purposive sample of extreme (excellent) companies.
- *Heterogeneous* or *maximum variation* sampling enables you to collect data to describe and explain the key themes that can be observed. Although this might appear a contradiction, as a small sample may contain cases that are completely different, Patton (2002) argues that this is in fact a strength. Any patterns that do emerge are likely to be of particular interest and value and represent the key themes. In addition the data collected should enable you to document uniqueness. To ensure maximum variation within a sample Patton (2002) suggests you identify your diverse characteristics (sample selection criteria) prior to selecting your sample.
- In direct contrast to heterogeneous sampling, *homogeneous* sampling focuses on one particular subgroup in which all the sample members are similar. This enables you to study the group in great depth.
- *Critical case* sampling selects critical cases on the basis that they can make a point dramatically or because they are important. The focus of data collection is to understand what is happening in each critical case so that logical generalisations can be made. Patton (2002) outlines a number of clues that suggest critical cases. These can be summarised by the questions:
  - If it happens there, will it happen everywhere?
  - If they are having problems, can you be sure that everyone will have problems?
  - If they cannot understand the process, is it likely that no one will be able to understand the process?
- In contrast *typical case* sampling is usually used as part of a research project to provide an illustrative profile using a representative case. Such a sample enables you to provide an illustration of what is 'typical' to those who will be reading your research report and may be unfamiliar with the subject matter. It is not intended to be definitive.

worked example

Purposive sampling

Phil was undertaking case study research in three organisations in the financial sector. He needed to interview managers to discover their organisations' objectives for a particular pay system and the extent to which the system seemed to be successful. He decided to talk to three homogeneous samples of managers:

- senior general managers and personnel directors (the policy designers), to establish pay objectives and the extent to which they felt these had been achieved;
- line managers (the policy operators), to establish their views on the pay system's objectives and the level of success being achieved;
- middle and junior managers reporting directly to these line managers (the policy recipients), to test their perceptions of the pay system's objectives and the extent to which they considered it successful. Where appropriate Phil also interviewed trade union officials.

Snowball sampling

Snowball sampling is commonly used when it is difficult to identify members of the desired population, for example people who are working while claiming unemployment benefit. You therefore need to:

1 Make contact with one or two cases in the population.
2 Ask these cases to identify further cases.
3 Ask these new cases to identify further new cases (and so on).
4 Stop when either no new cases are given or the sample is as large as is manageable.

The main problem is making initial contact. Once you have done this, these cases identify further members of the population, who then identify further members, and so the sample snowballs. For such samples the problems of representativeness are huge, as respondents are most likely to identify other potential respondents who are similar to themselves. The next problem is to find these new cases. However, for populations that are difficult to identify snowball sampling may provide the only possibility.

worked example

Snowball sampling

Steve was a part-time student. His project was concerned with the career paths of managing directors of large companies. As part of this Steve needed to interview managing directors. He arranged his first interview with the managing director of his own company. Towards the end of the interview the managing director asked Steve whether he could be of further assistance. Two other managing directors that Steve could interview were suggested. Steve's managing director offered to 'introduce' Steve to them and provided him with contact telephone numbers and the names of their personal assistants. Steve's sample had started to snowball!

Self-selection sampling

Self-selection sampling occurs when you allow a case, usually an individual, to identify their desire to take part in the research. You therefore:

1 Publicise your need for cases, either by advertising through appropriate media or by asking them to take part.
2 Collect data from those who respond.

Cases that self-select often do so because of their feelings or opinions about the research question(s) or stated objectives. In some instances, as in research undertaken by Adrian and colleagues on the positive management of redundancy, this is exactly what the researcher wants. In this research a letter in the personnel trade press generated a list of self-selected organisations that were interested in the research topic, considered it important and were willing to devote time to being interviewed.

worked example

Self-selection sampling

Siân's research was concerned with teleworking. She had decided to administer her questionnaire using the Internet. She publicised her research on a range of bulletin boards and through the teleworkers' association asking for volunteers to fill in a questionnaire. Those who responded were sent a short questionnaire by email.

Convenience sampling

Convenience or *haphazard sampling* involves selecting haphazardly those cases that are easiest to obtain for your sample, such as the person interviewed at random in a shopping centre for a television programme. The sample selection process is continued until your required sample size has been reached. Although this technique of sampling is widely used it is prone to bias and influences that are beyond your control, as the cases only appear in the sample because of the ease of obtaining them. Often the sample is intended to represent the total population, for example managers taking an MBA course as a surrogate for all managers! In such instances the choice of sample is likely to have biased the sample, meaning that subsequent generalisations are likely to be at best flawed. These problems are less important where there is little variation in the population, and such samples often serve as pilots to studies using more structured samples.

6.4 Summary

- Your choice of sampling techniques is dependent on the feasibility and sensibility of collecting data to answer your research question(s) and to address your objectives from the entire population. For populations of under 50 it is usually more sensible to collect data from the entire population where you are considering using probability sampling.

- Choice of sampling technique or techniques is dependent on your research question(s) and objectives:
  - Research question(s) and objectives that need you to estimate statistically the characteristics of the population from a sample require probability samples.
  - Research question(s) and objectives that do not require such generalisations can make use of non-probability sampling techniques.
- Factors such as the confidence that is needed in the findings, accuracy required and likely categories for analyses will affect the size of the sample that needs to be collected:
  - Statistical analyses usually require a minimum sample size of 30.
  - Research question(s) and objectives that do not require statistical estimation may need far smaller samples.
- Sample size and the technique used are also influenced by the availability of resources, in particular financial support and time available to select the sample and to collect, enter into a computer and analyse the data.
- Probability sampling techniques all necessitate some form of sampling frame, so they are often more time consuming than non-probability techniques.
- Where it is not possible to construct a sampling frame you will need to use non-probability sampling techniques.
- Non-probability sampling techniques also provide you with the opportunity to select your sample purposively and to reach difficult-to-identify members of the population.
- For many research projects you will need to use a combination of different sampling techniques.
- All your choices will be dependent on your ability to gain access to organisations. The considerations summarised earlier must therefore be tempered with an understanding of what is practically possible.

self-check Questions

6.1 Identify a suitable sampling frame for each of the following research questions:

a How do company directors of manufacturing firms of over 500 employees think a specified piece of legislation will affect their companies?

b Which factors are important in accountants' decisions regarding working in mainland Europe?

c How do employees at Cheltenham Gardens Ltd think the proposed introduction of compulsory Saturday working will affect their working lives?

6.2 You have been asked to select a sample of manufacturing firms using the sampling frame below. This also lists the value of their annual output in tens of thousands of pounds over the past year. To help you in selecting your sample the firms have been numbered from 0 to 99.

	Output		Output		Output		Output		Output
0	1163	*20*	1072	*40*	1257	*60*	1300	*80*	1034
1	10	*21*	7	*41*	29	*61*	39	*81*	55
2	57	*22*	92	*42*	84	*62*	73	*82*	66
3	149	*23*	105	*43*	97	*63*	161	*83*	165
4	205	*24*	157	*44*	265	*64*	275	*84*	301
5	163	*25*	214	*45*	187	*65*	170	*85*	161
6	1359	*26*	1440	*46*	1872	*66*	1598	*86*	1341
7	330	*27*	390	*47*	454	*67*	378	*87*	431
8	2097	*28*	1935	*48*	1822	*68*	1634	*88*	1756
9	1059	*29*	998	*49*	1091	*69*	1101	*89*	907
10	1037	*30*	1298	*50*	1251	*70*	1070	*90*	1158
11	59	*31*	10	*51*	9	*71*	37	*91*	27
12	68	*32*	70	*52*	93	*72*	88	*92*	66
13	166	*33*	159	*53*	103	*73*	102	*93*	147
14	302	*34*	276	*54*	264	*74*	157	*94*	203
15	161	*35*	215	*55*	189	*75*	168	*95*	163
16	1298	*36*	1450	*56*	1862	*76*	1602	*96*	1339
17	329	*37*	387	*57*	449	*77*	381	*97*	429
18	2103	*38*	1934	*58*	1799	*78*	1598	*98*	1760
19	1061	*39*	1000	*59*	1089	*79*	1099	*99*	898

a Select two simple random samples, each of 20 firms, and mark those firms selected for each sample on the sampling frame.

b Describe and compare the pattern on the sampling frame of each of the samples selected.

c Calculate the average (mean) annual output in tens of thousands of pounds over the past year for each of the samples selected.

d Given that the true average annual output is £6 608 900 is there any bias in either of the samples selected?

6.3 You have been asked to select a 10 per cent sample of firms from the sampling frame used for self-check question 6.2.

a Select a 10 per cent systematic sample and mark those firms selected for the sample on the sampling frame.

b Calculate the average (mean) annual output in tens of thousands of pounds over the past year for your sample.

c Given that the true average annual output is £6 608 900 why does systematic sampling provide such a poor estimate of the annual output in this case?

6.4 You need to undertake a face-to-face interview survey of managing directors of small to medium-sized organisations. From the data you collect you need to be able to generalise about the attitude of such managing directors to recent changes in government policy towards these firms. Your generalisations need to be accurate to within plus or minus 5 per cent. Unfortunately you have limited resources to pay for interviewers, travelling and other associated costs.

a How many managing directors will you need to interview?

b You have been given the choice between cluster and multi-stage sampling. Which technique would you choose for this research? You should give reasons for your choice.

6.5 You have been asked to undertake a survey of residents' opinions regarding the siting of a new supermarket in an inner city suburb (estimated catchment population 111 376 at the last census). The age and gender distribution of the catchment population at the last census is listed below:

Gender	*Age group*							
	0–4	*5–15*	*16–19*	*20–29*	*30–44*	*45–59/64**	*60/65•–74*	*75+*
Males	3498	7106	4884	7656	9812	12892	4972	2684
Females	3461	6923	6952	9460	8152	9152	9284	4488

*59 females, 64 males, •60 females, 65 males

a Devise a quota for a quota sample using these data.
b What other data would you like to include to overcome likely variations between groups in their availability for interview and replicate the total population more precisely? Give reasons for your answer.
c What problems might you encounter in using interviewers?

6.6 For each of the following research questions it has not been possible for you to obtain a sampling frame. Suggest the most suitable non-probability sampling technique to obtain the necessary data, giving reasons for your choice.
a What support do people sleeping rough believe they require from social services?
b Which television advertisements do people remember watching last weekend?
c How do employers' opinions vary regarding the impact of European Union legislation on employee recruitment?
d How are manufacturing companies planning to respond to the introduction of road tolls?
e Would users of the squash club be prepared to pay a 10 per cent increase in subscriptions to help fund two extra courts (answer needed by tomorrow morning!)?

progressing your research project

Using sampling as part of your research

- ☐ Consider your research question(s) and objectives. You need to decide whether you will be able to collect data on the entire population or will need to collect data from a sample.
- ☐ If you decide that you need to sample you must establish whether your research question(s) and objectives require probability sampling. If they do, make sure that a suitable sampling frame is available or can be devised, and calculate the actual sample size required taking into account likely response rates. If your research question(s) and objectives do not require probability sampling, or you are unable to obtain a suitable sampling frame, you will need to use non-probability sampling.
- ☐ Select the most appropriate sampling technique or techniques after considering the advantages and disadvantages of all suitable techniques and undertaking further reading as necessary.
- ☐ Select your sample or samples following the technique or techniques as outlined in this chapter.
- ☐ Remember to note down the reasons for your choices when you make them as you will need to justify your choices when you write about your research method.

References

Barnett, V. (1991) *Sample Survey Principles and Method*, London, Edward Arnold.

Economist, The (1997) *The Economist Numbers Guide: The Essentials of Business Numeracy* (3rd edn), London, Profile Books.

Healey, M.J. (1991) 'Obtaining information from businesses', *in* Healey, M.J. (ed.), *Economic Activity and Land Use: The Changing Information Base for Local and Regional Studies*, Harlow, Longman, pp. 193–250.

Henry, G.T. (1990) *Practical Sampling*, Newbury Park, CA, Sage.

Kervin, J.B. (1992) *Methods for Business Research*, New York, HarperCollins.

Lavrakas, P.J. (1993) *Telephone Survey Methods: Sampling, Selection and Supervision* (2nd edn), Newbury Park, CA, Sage.

Neuman, W.L. (2000) *Social Research Methods* (2nd edn), London, Allyn and Bacon.

Owen, F. and Jones, R. (1994) *Statistics* (4th edn), London, Pitman Publishing.

Patton, M.Q. (2002) *Qualitative Research and Evaluation Methods* (3rd edn), Thousand Oaks, CA, Sage.

Peters, T. and Waterman, R. (1982) *In Search of Excellence*, New York, Harper & Row.

Scolari Sage (2002) Methodologist's Toochest (online)(cited 1 January 2002). Available from <URL:http://www.scolari.co.uk>.

Teague, A. (2000) 'New methodologies for the 2001 Census in England and Wales' (online) (cited 11 February 2002). Available from <URL:http://www.statistics.gov.uk/nsbase/census2001/pdfs/NewMethodologies.pdf>.

deVaus, D.A. (2002) *Surveys in Social Research* (5th edn), London, Routledge.

Willimack, D.K., Nichols, E. and Sudman, S. (2002) 'Understanding unit and item nonresponse in business surveys' *in* Dillman, D.A., Eltringe, J.L., Groves, J.L. and Little, R.J.A. (eds) (2002) *Survey Nonresponse*, New York, Wiley Interscience, pp. 213–27.

Further reading

Barnett, V. (1991) *Sample Survey Principles and Method*, London, Edward Arnold. Chapters 2, 5 and 6 provide an explanation of statistics behind probability sampling and quota sampling as well as the techniques.

Diamantopoulos, A. and Schlegelmilch, B.B. (1997) *Taking the Fear Out of Data Analysis*, London, Dryden Press. Chapter 2 contains a clear, humorous discussion of both probability and non-probability sampling.

Dillman, D.A., Eltringe, J.L., Groves, J.L. and Little, R.J.A. (eds) (2002) *Survey Nonresponse*, New York, Wiley Interscience. This book contains a wealth of information on survey non-response. Chapter 1 provides a useful overview in relation to the impact of survey design on non-response. This is discussed in more detail in Chapters 7 to 17, Chapter 14 referring specifically to business surveys and Chapter 15 to Internet-based surveys.

Patton, M.Q. (2002) *Qualitative Research and Evaluation Methods* (3rd edn), Thousand Oaks, CA, Sage. Chapter 5, 'Designing qualitative studies', contains a useful discussion of non-probability sampling techniques, with examples.

deVaus, D.A. (2002) *Surveys in Social Research* (5th edn), London, Routledge. Chapter 6 provides a useful overview of both probability and non-probability sampling techniques.

Wass, V.J. (1994) 'Minimizing and managing bias in a mail survey: a study of redundant miners', *in* Wass, V.J. and Wells, P.E. (eds), *Principles and Practice in Business and Management Research*, Aldershot, Dartmouth, pp. 91–121. This includes a useful account of the realities of sample selection for a postal questionnaire survey.

CASE 6 Employment networking in the Hollywood film industry

In May 1998 the United Kingdom's (UK) Film Review Group announced a radical agenda for a new kind of partnership between the film industry and government to achieve a step change in the industry's performance over the next decade (Film Review Policy Group, 1998). Part of the government's interest in the industry appeared to stem from the belief that the loss of manufacturing jobs in the UK could be compensated for by the growth of employment in knowledge industries such as the media. The UK film industry has been described as a 'cottage industry' (Blair, Culkin and Randle, 2002 forthcoming) employing an estimated 33 000 people, while in Los Angeles, centre of the American industry, independent productions alone directly employ about 131 000 people . The latter represents approximately one third of total film production, major film studios accounting for much of the rest.

From the perspective of employment generation and the development of the UK film industry, the location decisions of major American film studios are of considerable interest. Canada, Australia and Mexico already benefit from the tendency for film-making traditionally carried out in Los Angeles to be located elsewhere, and a small proportion of American film production also takes place in the UK (Randle and Culkin, 2000). For example, Warner Brothers' children's blockbuster *Harry Potter and the Philosopher's Stone* was shot at Leavesden Studios in Watford and on location.

Prior to the demise of the American studio system in the 1950s, work in the movies was characterised by direct, permanent employment by one of the major film studios in an oligopolistic industry (Christopherson, 1996). However, since this time the majority of film crew have worked freelance on a project basis, the average length of employment on a single project being between six and eight weeks. There is no longer a formal apprenticeship scheme; yet entrants might start in a low-level role such as production assistant and move on, in time, to become a director. Training is a mixture of film school attendance and informal on-the-job training. Many jobs are never advertised.

There has been widespread concern among those working in the American film industry, and the unions representing them, regarding the impact of relocating production elsewhere on future employment prospects. Against this background of uncertainty, Keith Randle and Nigel Culkin of the University of Hertfordshire's Film Industry Research Group were keen to explore film-related employment in the United States and, in particular, to examine the way in which crew entered the industry, found second and subsequent jobs, and developed their careers. In particular they were interested to find out what an industry that epitomised freelance work could tell them about the nature of work and management in such an environment.

Keith and Nigel chose to adopt a qualitative approach to explore the mechanisms that technical crew used to find both their first and subsequent jobs in the film industry. Being located in a UK university they foresaw considerable problems in negotiating access to these people. The film unions could potentially provide access only to the specific group that each represented (for example wardrobe, grips, camera, hair and make-up). Any refusal to cooperate could therefore exclude a key group from the research. In addition, union membership reflected a degree of prior success in securing ongoing work in the industry, as evidence of achieving a threshold of paid work was a prerequisite for membership.

Surfing the Internet, the researchers discovered several databases of film crew. These were promoted as being of mutual benefit to both employers and potential employees. For a fee individuals could advertise themselves on a database, which those wishing to employ crew could search. The amount of information available on these databases was considerable. Film crew provided details of their education and training, previous experience and, what seemed especially surprising for a publicly accessible database, extensive contact details including email addresses, telephone numbers, fax numbers and pager numbers.

The research team decided to use a database that held details of some 3800 crew in around 80 film-related occupations in the Los Angeles area as their sampling frame. Selecting a range of occupations to the film industry they sent 180 email messages, inviting randomly selected individuals in Los Angeles to take part in the research project. The response rate was surprisingly high, with around 25 per cent of those contacted agreeing to take part in the study. The researchers were able to plot the home addresses of the respondents on a street directory of Los Angeles and gain a visual impression of the spread. This in turn allowed them to choose a central location to which they could invite respondents for interview. They then sent out a blank interview timetable and asked prospective interviewees to choose a convenient slot.

Subsequently Keith and Nigel travelled to Los Angeles to carry out the first phase of a planned longitudinal panel study, which would track individuals over a period of their working lives. Following each interview the researchers asked whether respondents would be prepared to recommend other crew members they had worked with to take part in the study, as some occupations had proved more resistant to responding than others. Interviewees would first telephone these contacts before calling back to give the researchers permission to ring and arrange an interview. Interviewees represented a wide variety of occupations and backgrounds. Some worked in feature films, others in the independent sector, documentaries, music video, advertising and television; others were still trying to find their first 'paid' film work in Los Angeles.

The research team planned to further the research with an on-line questionnaire to gather data from a wider sample, which could be triangulated against the qualitative data gained from the series of interviews they carried out over a three-year period. Although on-line research has some inherent problems, the researchers believe that their experiences in accessing a difficult-to-study population justify the use of the Web as an innovative research tool.

References

Blair, H., Culkin, N. and Randle, K. (forthcoming 2002) 'From London to Los Angeles: a comparison of local labour market processes in the US and UK film industries', *International Journal of Human Resource Management*.

Christopherson, S. (1996) 'Flexibility and adaptation in industrial relations: the exceptional case of the US media entertainment industries', *in* Gray, L.S. and Seeber, R.L. (eds), *Under The Stars: Essays on Labor Relations in Arts and Entertainment*, Ithaca and London: Cornell University Press, pp. 82–112.

▶

Film Policy Review Group (1998) *A Bigger Picture*, London, Department of Culture Media and Sport.

Randle, K. and Culkin, N. (2000) '*Fleeting stardom for Hatfield*' *The Guardian* , 15 May, p. 20.

Questions

1 What are the major benefits and drawbacks of using the Internet as part of an international research study?

2 How valid are the results of the research likely to be?

3 Outline the advantages and disadvantages of 'snowballing'.

4 What do you consider are the ethical issues raised by this research?

5 What sampling techniques are being used in this research?

self-check Answers

6.1 a A complete list of all directors of large manufacturing firms could be purchased from an organisation that specialised in selling such lists to use as the sampling frame. Alternatively a list that contained only those selected for the sample could be purchased to reduce costs. These data are usually in a format suitable for being read by word-processing and database computer software, and so they could easily be merged into standard letters such as those included with questionnaires.

b A complete list of accountants, or one that contained only those selected for the sample, could be purchased from an organisation that specialised in selling such lists. Care would need to be taken regarding the precise composition of the list to ensure that it included those in private practice as well as those working for organisations. Alternatively if the research was interested only in qualified accountants then the professional accountancy bodies' yearbooks, which list all their members and their addresses, could be used as the sampling frame.

c The personnel records or payroll of Cheltenham Gardens Ltd could be used. Either would provide an up-to-date list of all employees with their addresses.

6.2 a Your answer will depend on the random numbers you selected. However, the process you follow to select the samples is likely to be similar to that outlined. Starting at randomly selected points two sets of 20 two-digit random numbers are read from the random number tables (Appendix 4). If a number is selected twice it is disregarded. Two possible sets are:

Sample 1: 38 41 14 59 53 03 52 86 21 88 55 87 85 90 74 18 89 40 84 71

Sample 2: 28 00 06 70 81 76 36 65 30 27 92 73 20 87 58 15 69 22 77 31

These are then marked on the sampling frame (sample 1 is enclosed by a box, sample 2 is shaded) as shown opposite:

0	1163	20	1072	40	1257	60	1300	80	1034
1	10	21	7	41	29	61	39	81	55
2	57	22	92	42	84	62	73	82	66
3	149	23	105	43	97	63	161	83	165
4	205	24	157	44	265	64	275	84	301
5	163	25	214	45	187	65	170	85	161
6	1359	26	1440	46	1872	66	1598	86	1341
7	330	27	390	47	454	67	378	87	431
8	2097	28	1935	48	1822	68	1634	88	1756
9	1059	29	998	49	1091	69	1101	89	907
10	1037	30	1298	50	1251	70	1070	90	1158
11	59	31	10	51	9	71	37	91	27
12	68	32	70	52	93	72	88	92	66
13	166	33	159	53	103	73	102	93	147
14	302	34	276	54	264	74	157	94	203
15	161	35	215	55	189	75	168	95	163
16	1298	36	1450	56	1862	76	1602	96	1339
17	329	37	387	57	449	77	381	97	429
18	2103	38	1934	58	1799	78	1598	98	1760
19	1061	39	1000	59	1089	79	1099	99	898

b Your samples will probably produce patterns that cluster around certain numbers in the sampling frame, although the amount of clustering may differ, as illustrated by samples 1 and 2 above.

c The average (mean) annual output in tens of thousands of pounds will depend entirely upon your sample. For the two samples selected the averages are:

Sample 1 (boxed): £6 752 000
Sample 2 (shaded): £7 853 500

d There is no bias in either of the samples, as both have been selected at random. However, the average annual output calculated from sample 1 represents the total population more closely than that calculated from sample 2, although this has occurred entirely at random.

6.3 a Your answer will depend on the random number you select as the starting point for your systematic sample. However, the process you followed to select your sample is likely to be similar to that outlined. As a 10 per cent sample has been requested the sampling fraction is 1/10. Your starting point is selected using a random number between 0 and 9, in this case 2. Once the firm numbered 2 has been selected, every tenth firm is selected:

2 12 22 32 42 52 62 72 82 92

These are marked with a box on the sampling frame and will result in a regular pattern whatever the starting point:

0	1163	*20*	1072	*40*	1257	*60*	1300	*80*	1034
1	10	*21*	7	*41*	29	*61*	39	*81*	55
2	57	*22*	92	*42*	84	*62*	73	*82*	66
3	149	*23*	105	*43*	97	*63*	161	*83*	165
4	205	*24*	157	*44*	265	*64*	275	*84*	301
5	163	*25*	214	*45*	187	*65*	170	*85*	161
6	1359	*26*	1440	*46*	1872	*66*	1598	*86*	1341
7	330	*27*	390	*47*	454	*67*	378	*87*	431
8	2097	*28*	1935	*48*	1822	*68*	1634	*88*	1756
9	1059	*29*	998	*49*	1091	*69*	1101	*89*	907
10	1037	*30*	1298	*50*	1251	*70*	1070	*90*	1158
11	59	*31*	10	*51*	9	*71*	37	*91*	27
12	68	*32*	70	*52*	93	*72*	88	*92*	66
13	166	*33*	159	*53*	103	*73*	102	*93*	147
14	302	*34*	276	*54*	264	*74*	157	*94*	203
15	161	*35*	215	*55*	189	*75*	168	*95*	163
16	1298	*36*	1450	*56*	1862	*76*	1602	*96*	1339
17	329	*37*	387	*57*	449	*77*	381	*97*	429
18	2103	*38*	1934	*58*	1799	*78*	1598	*98*	1760
19	1061	*39*	1000	*59*	1089	*79*	1099	*99*	898

b The average (mean) annual output of firms for your sample will depend upon where you started your systematic sample. For the sample selected above it is £757 000.

c Systematic sampling has provided a poor estimate of the annual output because there is an underlying pattern in the data, which has resulted in firms with similar levels of output being selected.

6.4 **a** If you assume that there are at least 100 000 managing directors of small to medium-sized organisations from which to select your sample you will need to interview approximately 380 to make generalisations that are accurate to within plus or minus 5 per cent (Table 6.1).

b Either cluster or multi-stage sampling could be suitable; what is important is the reasoning behind your choice. This choice between cluster and multi-stage sampling is dependent on the amount of limited resources and time you have available. Using multi-stage sampling will take longer than cluster sampling as more sampling stages will need to be undertaken. However, the results are more likely to be representative of the total population owing to the possibility of stratifying the samples from the subareas.

6.5 **a** Prior to deciding on your quota you will need to consider the possible inclusion of residents who are aged less than 16 in your quota. Often in such research projects residents aged under 5 (and those aged 5–15) are excluded. You would need a quota of between 2000 and 5000 residents to obtain a reasonable accuracy. These should be divided proportionally between the groupings as illustrated in the possible quota below:

Gender	*Age group*					
	16–19	*20–29*	*30–44*	*45–59/64*	*60/65–74*	*75+*
Males	108	169	217	285	110	59
Females	154	209	180	203	205	99

b Data on social class, employment status, socioeconomic status or car ownership could also be used as further quotas. These data are available from the Census and are likely to affect shopping habits.

c Interviewers might choose respondents who were easily accessible or appeared willing to answer the questions. In addition they might fill in their quota incorrectly or make up the data.

6.6 **a** Either snowball sampling as it would be difficult to identify members of the desired population or, possibly, convenience sampling because of initial difficulties in finding members of the desired population.

b Quota sampling to ensure that the variability in the population as a whole was represented.

c Purposive sampling to ensure that the full variety of responses are obtained from a range of respondents from the population.

d Self-selection sampling as it requires people who are interested in the topic.

e Convenience sampling owing to the very short timescales available and the need to have at least some idea of members' opinions.

Chapter 7

Using secondary data

By the end of this chapter you should be able:

- to identify the full variety of secondary data that are available;
- to appreciate ways in which secondary data can be utilised to help to answer research question(s) and to meet objectives;
- to understand the advantages and disadvantages of using secondary data in research projects;
- to use a range of techniques, including published guides and the Internet, to locate secondary data;
- to evaluate the suitability of secondary data for answering research question(s) and meeting objectives in terms of coverage, validity, reliability and measurement bias;
- to apply the knowledge, skills and understanding gained to your own research project.

7.1 Introduction

When first considering how to answer their research question(s) or meet their objectives, few of our students consider initially the possibility of reanalysing data that have already been collected for some other purpose. Such data are known as *secondary data*. Most automatically think in terms of collecting new (*primary*) *data* specifically for that purpose. Yet, despite this, such secondary data can provide a useful source from which to answer, or to begin to answer, your research question(s).

Secondary data include both raw data and published summaries. Most organisations collect and store a variety of data to support their operations: for example, payroll details, copies of letters, minutes of meetings and accounts of sales of goods or services. Broadsheet daily newspapers contain a wealth of data including reports about takeover bids and companies' share prices. Government departments undertake surveys and publish official statistics covering social, demographic and economic topics. Consumer research organisations collect data that are used subsequently by different clients. Trade organisations survey their members on topics such as sales that are subsequently aggregated and published.

Some of these data, in particular documents such as company minutes, are available only from the organisations that produce them, and so access will need to be negotiated (Section 5.3). Others, including government surveys such as the population census, are widely available in published form as well as on CD-ROM in university libraries and increasingly via the Internet. A growing variety have been deposited in and are available from data archives (Dale *et al.*, 1988). In addition, the vast majority of companies and professional organisations have their own Internet sites from which data may be obtained. On-line computer databases containing company information can be accessed via the Internet through information gateways such as Biz/Ed (Table 3.5).

For certain types of research project, such as those requiring national or international comparisons, secondary data will probably provide the main source to answer your research question(s) and to address your objectives. However, if you are undertaking your research project as part of a course of study, we recommend that you check the examination regulations before deciding to rely entirely on secondary data. You may be required to collect primary data for your research project. Most research questions are answered using some combination of secondary and primary data. Where limited appropriate secondary data are available you will have to rely mainly on data you collect yourself.

In this chapter we examine the different types of secondary data that are likely to be available to help you to answer your research question(s) and meet your objectives, how you might use them (Section 7.2), and a range of methods, including published guides, for locating these data (Section 7.3). We then consider the advantages and disadvantages of using secondary data (Section 7.4) and discuss ways of evaluating their validity and reliability (Section 7.5). We do not attempt to provide a comprehensive list of secondary data sources, as this would be an impossible task within the space available.

7.2 Types of secondary data and uses in research

Secondary data include both quantitative and qualitative data, and they can be used in both descriptive and explanatory research. The data you use may be *raw data*, where there has been little if any processing, or *compiled data* that have received some form of selection or summarising (Kervin, 1999). Within business and management research such data are used mostly in case study and survey-type research. However, there is no reason not to include secondary data in experimental research.

Different researchers (for example Bryman, 1989; Dale *et al.*, 1988; Hakim, 1982, 2000; Robson, 2002) have generated a variety of classifications for secondary data. These classifications do not, however, capture the full variety of data. We have therefore built on their ideas to create three main subgroups of secondary data: documentary data, survey-based data, and those compiled from multiple sources (Figure 7.1).

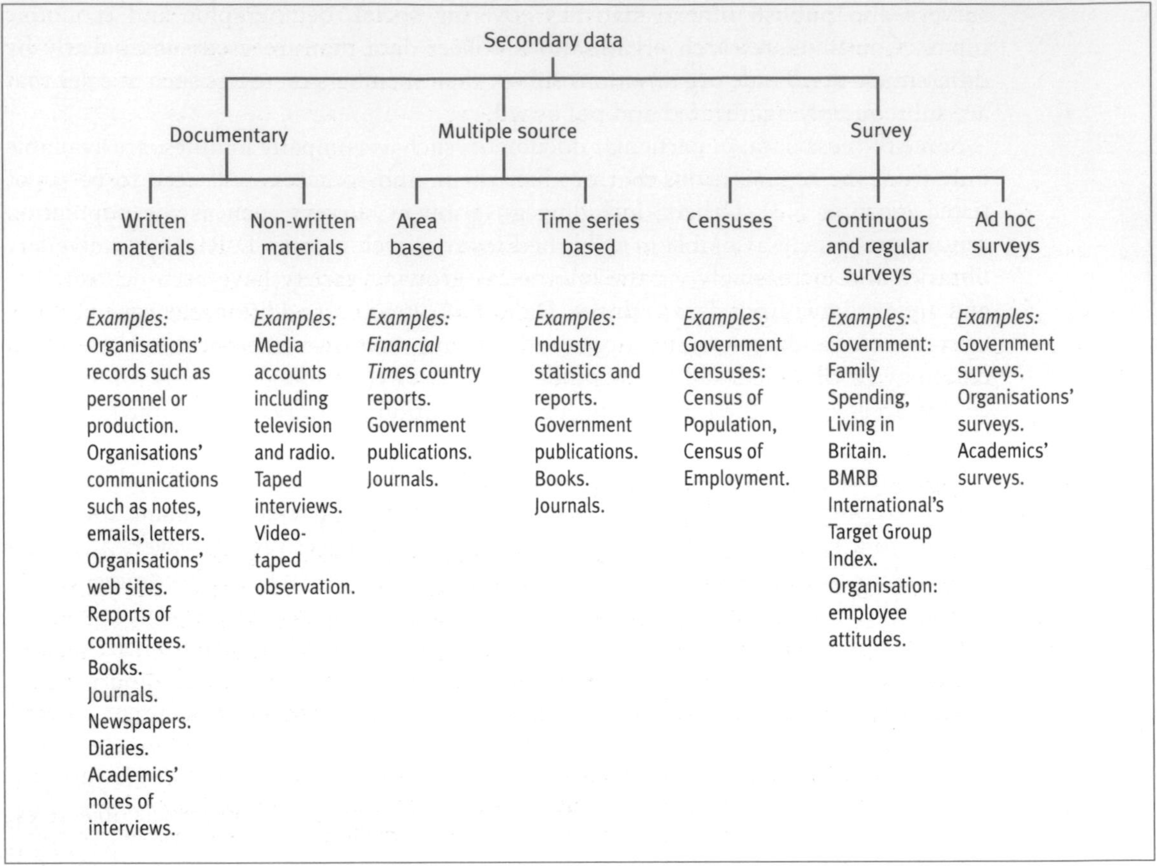

Figure 7.1 Types of secondary data

Documentary secondary data

Documentary secondary data are often used in research projects that also use primary data collection methods. However, you can also use them on their own or with other sources of secondary data, in particular for historical research. Research based almost exclusively on documentary secondary data is termed *archival research* and, although this term has historical connotations, it can refer to recent as well as historical documents (Bryman, 1989).

Documentary secondary data include *written documents* such as notices, correspondence, minutes of meetings, reports to shareholders, diaries, transcripts of speeches and administrative and public records. Written documents can also include books, journal and magazine articles and newspapers. These can be important raw data sources in their own right, as well as a storage medium for compiled data. You could use written documents to provide qualitative data such as managers' espoused reasons for decisions. They could also be used to generate statistical measures such as data on absenteeism and profitability derived from company records (Bryman, 1989).

Documentary secondary data also include *non-written documents* (Figure 7.1) such as tape and video recordings, pictures, drawings, films and television programmes

(Robson, 2002), digital versatile disks (DVDs) and CD-ROMs. These data can be analysed both quantitatively and qualitatively. In addition, they can be used to help to triangulate findings based on other data such as written documents and primary data collected through observation, interviews or questionnaires (Chapters 8, 9 and 10).

For your research project the documentary sources you have available will depend on whether you have been granted access to an organisation's records as well as on your success in locating library, data archive and commercial sources (Section 7.4). Access to an organisation's data will be dependent on gatekeepers within that organisation (Section 5.3). In our experience, those research projects that make use of documentary secondary data often do so as part of a within-company research project or a case study of a particular organisation.

worked example

Using documentary secondary data

You are interested in the impact of private sector values on the organisational culture of United Kingdom (UK) local authorities. As part of this research you wish to discover whether there has been a shift from recruiting people with only public sector experience to recruiting those with at least some private sector experience. To provide quantitative data about changes you have gained access to individual employees' personnel records (documentary secondary data) over a 15-year period in the local authority where you undertook your work placement. Fortunately, this authority has not been affected by local government reorganisation. The records contain the date when each vacancy was filled, how it was notified, and the age, gender, qualifications and previous occupation of the successful applicant.

Your next stage will be to abstract data for each externally notified vacancy and to match these with data from vacancy advertisement invoice instructions (also documentary secondary data). The latter will enable you to obtain a complete list of all notification outlets used for each vacancy. Once your data have been combined you will be able to analyse these data quantitatively.

Survey-based secondary data

Survey-based secondary data refers usually to data collected by questionnaires (Chapter 10) that have already been analysed for their original purpose. Such data can refer to organisations, people or households (Hakim, 1982). They are made available as compiled data tables or as a computer-readable matrix of raw data (Section 11.2) for secondary analysis.

Survey-based secondary data will have been collected through one of three distinct types of survey: censuses, continuous/regular surveys or ad hoc surveys (Figure 7.1). *Censuses* are usually carried out by governments and are unique because, unlike surveys, participation is obligatory (Hakim, 2000). Consequently, they provide very good coverage of the population surveyed. They include population censuses, which have been carried out every 10 years in the UK since 1801 with the exception of 1941 (Teague, 2001) and other surveys such as the UK New Earnings Survey. Published tabulations are available via the Internet for more recent UK censuses, but it is now also possible to obtain the raw data 100 years after census via the Internet (see Table

7.3). In contrast, the UK New Earnings Survey has been carried out only since 1970 and provides information on the levels, make-up and distribution of earnings as well as details of hours worked (Jenkins and Bird, 2001). The data from censuses conducted by many governments are intended to meet the needs of government departments as well as of local government. As a consequence they are usually clearly defined, well documented and of a high quality. Such data are easily accessible in compiled form, and are widely used by other organisations and individual researchers.

Continuous and regular surveys are those surveys, excluding censuses, that are repeated over time (Hakim, 1982). They include surveys where data are collected throughout the year, such as the UK's General Household Survey (Walker, 2002), and those repeated at regular intervals. The latter include the Labour Force Survey, which since 1998 has been undertaken quarterly by member states throughout the European Union with a core set of questions. This means that some comparative data are available for member states, although access to these data is limited by European and individual countries' legislation (Jones and Smith, 2001). Non-governmental bodies also carry out regular surveys. These include general-purpose market research surveys such as BMRB International's Target Group Index. Because of the Target Group Index's commercial nature, the data are very expensive. However, BMRB International has provided copies of reports (usually over three years old) to between 20 and 30 UK university libraries. Many large organisations undertake regular surveys, a common example being the employee attitude survey. However, because of the sensitive nature of such information it is often difficult to gain access to such survey data, especially in its raw form.

Census and continuous and regular survey data provide a useful resource with which to compare or set in context your own research findings. Aggregate data are often available on CD-ROMs, in published form in libraries or via the Internet (Section 7.3), in particular for government surveys. When using these data you need to check when they were collected, as it often takes at least two years for publication to occur! If you are undertaking research in one UK organisation you could use these data to place your case study organisation within the context of its industry group or division using the Census of Employment. Aggregated results of the Census of Employment can be found in *Labour Market Trends* as well as via the UK government's information gateway *UKonline*. Alternatively, you might explore issues already highlighted by data from an organisation survey through in-depth interviews.

Survey secondary data may be available in sufficient detail to provide the main data set from which to answer your research question(s) and to meet your objectives. Alternatively, they may be the only way in which you can obtain the required data. If your research question is concerned with national variations in consumer spending it is unlikely that you will be able to collect sufficient data. You will therefore need to rely on secondary data such as those contained in *Family Spending* (formerly the Family Expenditure Survey; Dennis, 2000). This reports findings from the Expenditure and Foods Survey. For some research questions and objectives suitable data will be available in published form. For others, you may need more disaggregated data. This may be available on CD-ROM, via the Internet (Section 3.4), or from archives (Section 7.3). We have found that for most business and management research involving secondary data you are unlikely to find all the data you require from one survey. Rather, your research project is likely to involve detective work in which you build your own multiple-source data set using different data items from a variety of surveys and other secondary data sources. Like all detective work, finding data that help to answer a research question or meet an objective is immensely satisfying.

Ad hoc surveys are usually one-off surveys and are far more specific in their subject matter. They include data from questionnaires that have been undertaken by independent researchers as well as surveys undertaken by organisations and governments. Because of their ad hoc nature, you will probably find it more difficult to discover relevant surveys. However, it may be that an organisation in which you are undertaking research has conducted its own questionnaire, on an issue related to your research. Some organisations will provide you with a report containing aggregated data; others may be willing to let you reanalyse the raw data from this ad hoc survey. Alternatively, you may be able to gain access to and use raw data from an ad hoc survey that has been deposited in an archive (Section 7.3).

worked example

Integrating secondary and primary data

Sue's research was on the impact of European Union legislation on employee mobility between member states. In particular she was interested in how legislation relating to the mutual recognition of qualifications had affected those working in the accountancy profession. This legislation should mean that an accountant who has qualified in any European Union state can, after an aptitude test and a period of adaptation, apply to have that qualification recognised by another member state.

As part of her research, Sue undertook a series of in-depth interviews with UK accountants at different stages of their careers. These explored their attitudes to working elsewhere in the European Union. Within the interviews, Sue concentrated on the importance of mutual recognition of qualifications relative to other factors such as the accountants' need to move their families and their foreign language ability.

Sue's own data were set in context by analysing a variety of published secondary data. Published tables from the International Passenger Survey were reanalysed to ascertain the level of professional migration out of and into the UK. These aggregate data were also used to ascertain the proportion of professional migrants whose families move with them when they migrate. Secondary data were used to explore the frequency of applications for mutual recognition of qualifications in the UK. Unpublished tables, obtained from the Department of Trade and Industry, provided details regarding how many accountants and other professionals have applied to have their qualifications recognised by UK professions (see Davis and Saunders, 1997).

Multiple-source secondary data

Multiple-source secondary data can be based entirely on documentary or on survey data, or can be an amalgam of the two. The key factor is that different data sets have been combined to form another data set prior to your accessing the data. One of the more common types of multiple-source data that you are likely to come across in document form is various compilations of company information such as *Europe's 15,000 Largest Companies* (ELC International, 2001). This contains comparable data on the top 15 000 European companies ranked by sales, profits and number of employees as well as alphabetical listings. Others multiple-source secondary data include the various shares price listings for different stock markets in the financial pages of broadsheet newspapers. These are available in most university libraries, including back copies on microfilm or CD-ROM. However, you need to beware of relying on CD-ROM copies for tabular data or diagrams as some still contain only the text of articles.

The way in which a multiple-source data set has been compiled will dictate the sorts of research question(s) or objectives with which you can use it. One method of compilation is to extract and combine selected comparable variables from a number of surveys or from the same survey that has been repeated a number of times to provide a *time-series* of data. For many undergraduate and taught masters courses' research projects, this is one of the few ways in which you will be able to get data over a long period to undertake a *longitudinal* study. Other ways of obtaining time-series data are to use a series of company documents such as appointment letters or public and administrative records to create your own longitudinal secondary data set. Examples include the UK Employment Department's stoppages at work data held by the Data Archive based at the University of Essex and those derived by researchers from 19th century population census returns, which, in the UK, are accessible to the public after 100 years.

Data can also be compiled for the same population over time using a series of 'snapshots' to form *cohort studies*. Such studies are relatively rare, owing to the difficulty of maintaining contact with members of the cohort from year to year. An example is the television series *Seven Up* (already mentioned in Section 4.2), which has followed a cohort since they were schoolchildren at seven-year intervals for over 40 years.

Secondary data from different sources can also be combined, if they have the same geographical basis, to form *area-based* data sets (Hakim, 2000). Such data sets usually draw together quantifiable information and statistics, and are commonly produced by governments for their country. Area-based multiple-source data sets are usually available in published form for the countries and their component standard economic planning regions. The more widely used by our students include the UK's *Annual Abstract of Statistics* (Tyrrell, 2001), *Regional Trends* (Office for National Statistics, 1996; McGinty and Williams, 2001) and the journal *Labour Market Trends*. Area-based multiple-source data sets are also available from data archives. These include data such as the Labour Force Survey (UK Data Archive, 2002).

7.3 Locating secondary data

Unless you are approaching your research project with the intention of analysing one specific secondary data set that you already know well, your first step will be to ascertain whether the data you need are available. Your research question(s), objectives and the literature you have reviewed will guide this. For many research projects you are likely to be unsure as to whether the data you require are available as secondary data. Fortunately, there are a number of pointers to the sorts of data that are likely to be available.

The breadth of data discussed in the previous sections serves only to emphasise the variety of possible locations in which such data may be found. Finding relevant secondary data requires detective work, which has two interlinked stages:

1 establishing that the sort of data you require are likely to be available as secondary data;
2 locating the precise data you require.

The availability of secondary data

There are a number of clues to whether the secondary data you require are likely to be available. As part of your literature review you will have already read books and journal articles on your chosen topic. Where these have made use of secondary data, they will provide you with an idea of the sort of data that are available. In addition, these books and articles should contain full references to the sources of the data. Where these refer to published secondary data such as multiple-source or survey reports it is usually relatively easy to track down the original source.

References for unpublished and documentary secondary data are often less specific, referring to 'unpublished survey results' or an 'in-house company survey'. Although these may be insufficient to locate or access the actual secondary data they still provide useful clues about the sort of data that might be found within organisations and which might prove useful. Textbooks that discuss data likely to be held on organisations' management information systems, such as Kingsbury's (1997) *IT Answers to HR Questions*, can provide you with valuable clues about the sort of documentary secondary data that are likely to exist within organisations.

Tertiary literature such as indexes and catalogues can also help you to locate secondary data (Sections 3.2–3.4). Data archive catalogues, such as for the UK Data Archive at the University of Essex, may prove a useful source of the sorts of secondary data available.* This archive holds the UK's largest collection of qualitative and quantitative digital social science and humanities data sets for use by the research community (UK Data Archive, 2002). These data have been acquired from academic, commercial and government sources, and relate mainly to post-war Britain. The complete catalogue of these can be accessed and searched via the Internet (Section 3.5) through the Archive's home page (see Table 7.2). However, it should be remembered that the supply of data and documentation for all of the UK Data Archive's data sets is charged at cost, and there may be additional administrative and royalty charges.

More recently, on-line indexes and catalogues have become available with direct linkages to downloadable files, often in spreadsheet format. Government web sites such as the UK Government's *UKonline* and the European Union's *Europa* provide useful gateways to a wide range of statistical data, reports and legislative documents. However, although data from such government sources are usually of good quality, those from other sources may be neither valid nor reliable. It is therefore important that you evaluate the suitability of such secondary data for your research (Section 7.5).

Informal discussions are also often a useful source. Acknowledged experts, colleagues, librarians or your project advisor may well have knowledge of the sorts of

---

* There are numerous other data archives in Europe and the USA. The UK Data Archive can provide access to international data through cooperative agreements and memberships of data archives throughout the world. It also provides a useful gateway to other data archives' web sites such as the Danish Data Archive, DDA, and the Dutch Data Archive, Steinmetz (UK Data Archive, 2002).

data that might be available (Stewart and Kamins, 1993). In addition, there is a range of published guides to secondary data sources. Those business and management guides that we, and our students, have found most useful are outlined in Table 7.1. However, there are also guides that provide more detail on sources for specific subject areas such as marketing and finance.

Finding secondary data

Once you have ascertained that secondary data are likely to exist, you need to find their precise location. For secondary data published by governments this will be quite easy. Precise references are often given in published guides (Table 7.1) and, where other researchers have made use of them, a full reference should exist. Locating published secondary data that are likely to be held by libraries or secondary data held in archives is relatively straightforward. Specialist libraries with specific subject collections such as market research reports can usually be located using the Library Association's (1997)

Table 7.1 Published guides to possible secondary data sources

Guide	*Coverage*
Corris, A., Yin, B. and Ricketts, C. (2000) *Guide to Official Statistics*, London, Stationery Office Books	Official statistics produced by UK government
Croner (no date) *A–Z of Business Information Sources*, Kingston, Croner Publications	Loose-leaf regularly updated. Alphabetical list of subjects showing relevant sources including trade associations and institutional sources; UK focus (see also http://www.croner.co.uk)
Mort, D. (2000) *Business Information Handbook*, Headland, Headland Press	Company and market information, on-line business information and a who's who in business information
Mort, D. and Wilkins, W. (2000) *Sources of Unofficial United Kingdom Statistics* (4th edn), Aldershot, Gower	Unofficial UK statistics collected by major survey organisations; lists of who produces these data
Library Association (1997) *Libraries in the United Kingdom and Republic of Ireland*, London, Library Association	Lists of 2500 libraries in the UK and Eire
Dale, P. (1998) *Guide to Libraries and Information Units in Government Departments and Other Organisations*, London, British Library	Lists libraries and information services in UK Government departments and related agencies
Dale, P. (1993) *Guide to Libraries in Key UK Companies*, London, British Library	Lists libraries in UK companies that are prepared to accept serious enquiries from outside
Patzer, G.L. (1996) *Using Secondary Data in Marketing Research: United States and World-wide*, Westport, CT, Quorum Books	Includes lists of sources specific to marketing, global information sources, US Census data, and more general business-related sources
McGuinness, K. and Short, T. (1998) *Research on the Net*, London, Old Bailey Press	Lists over 4000 Internet sites that offer information of research value. Chapters include accounting and finance, business, industry and labour as well as country-by-country information

publication or guides by Dale (1993, 1998) (Table 7.1). If you are unsure where to start, confess your ignorance and ask a librarian. This will usually result in a great deal of helpful advice, as well as saving you time. Once the appropriate abstracting tool or catalogue has been located and its use demonstrated, it can be searched using similar techniques to those employed in your literature search (Section 3.5).

Data that are held by organisations are more difficult to locate. For within-organisation data we have found that the information or data manager within the appropriate department is most likely to know the precise secondary data that are held. This is the person who will also help or hinder your eventual access to the data and can be thought of as the *gatekeeper* to the information (Section 5.3).

Data on the Internet can be located using site guides such as McGuinness and Short (1998, see Table 7.1), information gateways such as the University of Michigan's Documents Center (2002, see Table 7.2), and *search tools* where you search for all possible locations that match key words associated with your research question(s) or objectives (Section 3.5). In some cases data will be located at sites hosted by companies and professional organisations such as those listed in Table 7.3. A good way of finding an organisation's home page is to use a general search engine (Table 3.5) or, in the case of UK-based companies, the links provided by the Yellow Pages UK subject directory (Table 3.5). However, although the amount of data on the Internet is increasing rapidly, much of it is, in our experience, of dubious quality. In addition, searching for relevant data is often very time consuming.

Once you have located a possible secondary data set, you need to be certain that it will meet your needs. For documentary data or data in a published form the easiest way is to obtain and evaluate a sample copy of the data and a detailed description of

Table 7.2 Selected information gateways to secondary data on the Internet

Name	*Internet address*	*Comment*
Business Zone	http://www.businesszone.co.uk	Up-to-date resource. Browsable libraryof research findings in condensedformat. UK focus.
Europa	http://europa.eu.int	Information (including press releases,legislation, fact sheets) published byEuropean Union. Links include Eurostat statistics gateway.
UK Data Archive	http://www.data-archive.ac.uk	Links to Data Archives worldwide.
UK online	http://www.ukonline.gov.uk	UK government information service with links to government departments,official statistics etc.
University of Michigan	http://www.lib.umich.edu/govdocs/statsnew.html	Although predominantly American in focus has excellent annotated links to non-American governments' statistical agencies.
SOSIG	http://www.sosig.ac.uk	Evaluates and describes social science sites including those with statistical data. UK focus.

Table 7.3 **Selected secondary data sites on the Internet**

Name	*Internet address*	*Comment*
FT Info	http://www.news.ft.com	Company information on 11 000 companies including financial performance.
FT Interactive Data	http://www.ftinteractivedata.com	Global securities pricing, dividend, corporate action and descriptive information from around the world.
Hoover's Online	http://www.hoovers.com	Company information on 12 000 US and international companies with links to CNN and *Washington Post*.
MIMAS	http://www.mimas.ac.uk	National data centre for UK higher education institutions providing access to key data and information sources such as e-journals and the UK census. N.B. for some data sets you will need to register through your university.
UK Equities Direct	http://www.hemscott.net	Hemmington Scott's guide to companies and investment trusts, report service and market activity analysis.
Countries		
European Union	http://www.eurostat.eu.int	Site of European Union's statistical information service. This site is available in English as well as other languages.
France	http://www.insee.fr	Site of France's National Institute for Statistics including both statistics and government publications. Much of this web site is available in English.
Germany	http://www.destatis.de	Site of Germany's Federal Statistical Office with a number of useful links. Much of this web site is available in English.
Ireland (Eire)	http://www.cso.ie	Site of the Irish Central Statistical Office (CSO), the government body responsible for compiling Irish official statistics.
Netherlands	http://www.cbs.nl	Site of Holland's Central Bureau of Statistics (CBS). Much of this web site is available in English. Provides access to *StatLine*, which contains statistical data that can be downloaded free of charge.

Table 7.3 **Continued**

Name	*Internet address*	*Comment*
Norway	http://www.ssb.no	Site of Statistics Norway, providing the official Norwegian government statistics. Much of this web site is available in English.
United Kingdom	http://www.statistics.gov.uk	The official UK statistics site containing official UK statistics and information about statistics, which can be accessed and download free of charge. Has direct link to *StatBase* – the UK statistics information gateway.
Organisations		
Advertising Association	http://www.adassoc.org.uk	
Advertising Standards Authority	http://www.asa.org.uk	
Advisory Conciliation and Arbitration Service	http://www.acas.org.uk	
American Marketing Association	http://www.marketingpower.com	
Association of Chartered Certified Accountants	http://www.accaglobal.com	
Confederation of British Industry (CBI)	http://www.cbi.org.uk	
Chartered Institute of Management Accountants	http://www.cima.org.uk	
Chartered Institute of Marketing (CIM)	http://www.cim.co.uk	
Chartered Institute of Personnel and Development	http://www.cipd.co.uk	
UK Department of Trade and Industry	http://www.dti.gov.uk	
Industrial Society	http://www.indsoc.co.uk	
Institute of Directors	http://www.iod.com	
Institute of Financial Services	http://www.cib.org.uk	
Institute of Management	http://www.inst-mgt.org.uk	
Institute of Practitioners in Advertising (IPA)	http://www.ipa.co.uk	
KPMG UK	http://www.kpmg.co.uk	
London Stock Exchange	http://www.londonstockexchange.com	
Public Record Office (UK)	http://www.pro.gov.uk	
Trade Union Congress (TUC)	http://www.tuc.org.uk	
United Nations (UN)	http://www.un.org	

how it was collected. For survey data that are available in computer-readable form, this is likely to involve some cost. One alternative is to obtain and evaluate detailed variable definitions for the data set (which include how they are coded; Section 11.2) and the documentation that describes how the data were collected. This evaluation process is discussed in Section 7.5.

worked example: Establishing that the secondary data you require are available

Dunkerley (1988) undertook a three-year historical research project on the naval dockyard in the Devonport area of the city of Plymouth, UK. The proposed research strategy used interviews with dockyard workers as well as secondary data sources including:

- enumerators' books for population censuses from 1851;
- records relating to dockyard employment, labour relations and skills;
- Admiralty and Treasury papers;
- Poor Law records;
- a sample of local newspapers.

Initially it had been assumed that these secondary data would be readily available. Unfortunately, much of the secondary data that it had been assumed were available locally had been destroyed during enemy action in the Second World War. In addition, data that still existed had been obscurely catalogued in the Public Records Office at Kew, London. This made these data difficult to find.

Although copies of enumerators' books for the population censuses were available locally the use of census material 'proved more difficult than had been imagined' (Dunkerley, 1988:86). Data collected differed between successive censuses. In addition, the 100-year confidentiality rule meant that the enumerators' books were not available for more recent censuses.

Because of these and other problems, a rethink of the aims and methods of the research was undertaken prior to proceeding further.

7.4 Advantages and disadvantages of secondary data

Advantages

May have fewer resource requirements

For many research questions and objectives the main advantage of using secondary data is the enormous saving in resources, in particular your time and money (Ghauri and Grønhaugh, 2002). In general, it is much less expensive to use secondary data than to collect the data yourself. Consequently, you may be able to analyse far larger data sets such as those collected by government surveys. You will also have more time to think about theoretical aims and substantive issues, as your data will already be collected, and subsequently you will be able to spend more time and effort analysing and interpreting the data.

Unobtrusive

If you need your data quickly, secondary data may be the only viable alternative. In addition, they are likely to be higher-quality data than could be obtained by collecting your own (Stewart and Kamins, 1993). Using secondary data within organisations may also have the advantage that, because they have already been collected, they provide an unobtrusive measure. Cowton (1998) refers to this advantage as *eavesdropping*, emphasising its benefits for sensitive situations.

Longitudinal studies may be feasible

For many research projects time constraints mean that secondary data provide the only possibility of undertaking longitudinal studies. This is possible either by creating your own or by using an existing multiple-source data set (Section 7.2). Comparative research may also be possible if comparable data are available. You may find this to be of particular use for research questions and objectives that require regional or international comparisons. However, you need to ensure that the data you are comparing were collected and recorded using methods that are comparable. Comparisons relying on unpublished data or data that are currently unavailable in that format such as the creation of new tables from existing census data are likely to be expensive, as such tabulations will have to be specially prepared. In addition, your research is dependent on access being granted by the owners of the data, principally governments (Dale *et al.*, 1988), and upon your request not being contrary to relevant data protection legislation or agreements (Chapter 5.4).

Can provide comparative and contextual data

Often it can be useful to compare data that you have collected with secondary data. This means that you can place your own findings within a more general context or, alternatively, triangulate your findings (Section 4.3). If you have undertaken a sample survey, perhaps of potential customers, secondary data such as the census can be used to assess the generalisability of findings, in other words how representative these data are of the total population (Section 6.2).

Can result in unforeseen discoveries

Reanalysing secondary data can also lead to unforeseen or unexpected new discoveries. Dale *et al.* (1988) cite establishing the link between smoking and lung cancer as an example of such a serendipitous discovery. In this example the link was established through secondary analysis of medical records that had not been collected with the intention of exploring any such relationship.

Permanence of data

Unlike data that you collect yourself, secondary data generally provide a source of data that is both permanent and available in a form that may be checked relatively easily by others (Denscombe, 1998). This means that the data and your research findings are more open to public scrutiny.

Disadvantages

May be collected for a purpose that does not match your need

Data that you collect yourself will be collected with a specific purpose in mind: to answer your research question(s) and to meet your objectives. Unfortunately, secondary data will have been collected for a specific purpose that differs from your research question(s) or objectives (Denscombe, 1998). Consequently, the data you are considering may be inappropriate to your research question. If this is the case then you need to find an alternative source, or collect the data yourself! More probably, you will be able to answer your research question or address your objective only partially. A common reason for this is that the data were collected a few years earlier and so are not current. Where this is the case, such as in a research project that is examining an issue within an organisation, you are likely to have to combine secondary and primary data.

Access may be difficult or costly

Where data have been collected for commercial reasons, gaining access may be difficult or costly. Market research reports, such as those produced by Mintel or Keynote, may cost hundreds of pounds. If the report(s) that you require are not available in your library they can rarely be borrowed on inter-library loan and you will need to identify (Section 7.3) and visit the library that holds that collection.

worked example

Making international comparisons

An article in *Labour Market Trends* (Davies, 2001) outlines the differences in definitions and coverage of labour dispute statistics for the 23 Organisation for Economic Cooperation and Development (OECD) countries. In this article, Davies argues that international comparisons need to be made with care and that apparent differences between countries may not be significant when the method of data collection and the coverage of the data is taken into account. The differences she highlights in her article's technical note are outlined for selected countries in the table below:

Country	*How data collected*	*Threshold for inclusion*	*Sectors/types of dispute excluded*
Australia	From Industrial Relations Department, employers, trades unions and newspapers	10 workdays not worked	None mentioned
Belgium	Questionnaires to employers following police or media coverage	None	Public sector stoppages, indirectly affected workers
France	From labour inspectors' reports	1 workday not worked	None mentioned
Germany	Compulsory notification by employers to local employment offices. Pre-1993 data represents West Germany only	10 workers involved and of 1 day duration unless 100 workdays not worked	Public administration, indirectly affected workers
Italy	Not known	None	Indirectly affected workers
Japan	Legal requirement to report to Labour Commission	½ day duration	Unofficial disputes, indirectly affected workers

Netherlands	Questionnaires to employers following a strike report news item	None	None mentioned
United Kingdom	Initially from press reports, then contacts with employers and trades unions directly	10 workers involved and of 1 day duration unless 100 workdays not worked	Political stoppages
United States	Reports from newspapers, employers, trades unions and agencies	1 day or 1 shift duration and 1000 workers involved	Political stoppages

Based upon such differences, direct comparisons are in some instances not possible. For example, although some countries including Germany, Italy and Japan exclude workers indirectly affected by stoppages (that is, those who are unable to work because others at their workplace are on strike), others such as the UK, France, Belgium and the Netherlands include these workers in their statistics. Consequently, even though a country such as Germany has a similar threshold for inclusion, the recorded number of workers involved in any one stoppage is likely to be lower than in the UK.

Davies highlights the fact that, although the article covers data for a 10-year period, there have been changes in the way the statistics have been collected and calculated and in their coverage over time. For example, prior to 1993, data for Germany covered only West Germany as opposed to the Federal Republic. In addition she warns readers to be careful when comparing data in her article with that reported in earlier articles, as data on 'working days lost' or 'employment' are often revised, resulting in significant changes.

Aggregations and definitions may be unsuitable

The fact that secondary data were collected for a particular purpose may result in other, including ethical (Section 5.4), problems. Much of the secondary data you use are likely to be in published reports. As part of the compilation, process data will have been aggregated in some way. These aggregations, while meeting the requirements of the original research, may not be quite so suitable for your research. The definitions of data variables may not be the most appropriate for your research question(s) or objectives. In addition, where you are intending to combine data sets, definitions may differ markedly or have been revised over time. Alternatively, the documents you are using may represent the interpretations of those who produced them, rather than offer an objective picture of reality.

No real control over data quality

Although many of the secondary data sets available from governments and data archives are of higher quality than you could ever collect yourself, this is not always the case. For this reason care must be taken and data sources must be evaluated carefully, as outlined in section 7.5.

Initial purpose may affect how data are presented

When using data that are presented as part of a report you also need to be aware of the purpose of that report and the impact that this will have on the way the data are presented. This is especially so for internal organisational documents and external documents such as published company reports and newspaper reports. Reichman (1962; cited by Stewart and Kamins, 1993) emphasises this point referring to newspapers, although the sentiments apply to many documents. He argues that newspapers select what they consider to be the most significant points and emphasise these at the expense of supporting data. This, Reichman states, is not a criticism as the purpose of the reporting is to bring these points to the attention of readers rather than to provide a full and detailed account. However, if we generalise from these ideas, we can see that the culture, predispositions and ideals of those who originally collected and collated your secondary data will have influenced the nature of these data at least to some extent. For these reasons you must evaluate carefully any secondary data you intend to use. Possible ways of doing this are discussed in the next section.

7.5 Evaluating secondary data sources

Secondary data must be viewed with the same caution as any primary data that you collect. You need to be sure that:

- they will enable you to answer your research question(s) and to meet your objectives;
- the benefits associated with their use will be greater than the costs;
- you will be allowed access to the data (Section 5.3).

Secondary sources that appear relevant at first may not on closer examination be appropriate to your research question(s) or objectives. It is therefore important to evaluate the suitability of secondary data sources for your research.

Stewart and Kamins (1993) argue that, if you are using secondary data, you are at an advantage compared with researchers using primary data. Because the data already exist you can evaluate them prior to use. The time you spend evaluating any potential secondary data source is time well spent, as rejecting unsuitable data earlier can save much wasted time later! Such investigations are even more important when you have a number of possible secondary data sources you could use. Most authors suggest a range of validity and reliability (Section 4.4) criteria against which you can evaluate potential secondary data. These, we believe, can be incorporated into a three-stage process (Figure 7.2).

Alongside this process you also need to consider the accessibility of the secondary data. For some secondary data sources, in particular those available via the Internet or in your library, this will not be a problem. It may, however, still necessitate long hours working in the library if the sources are 'for reference only'. For other data sources, such as those within organisations, you need to obtain permission prior to gaining access. This will be necessary even if you are working for the organisation. These issues are discussed in Section 5.3, so we can now consider the evaluation process in more detail.

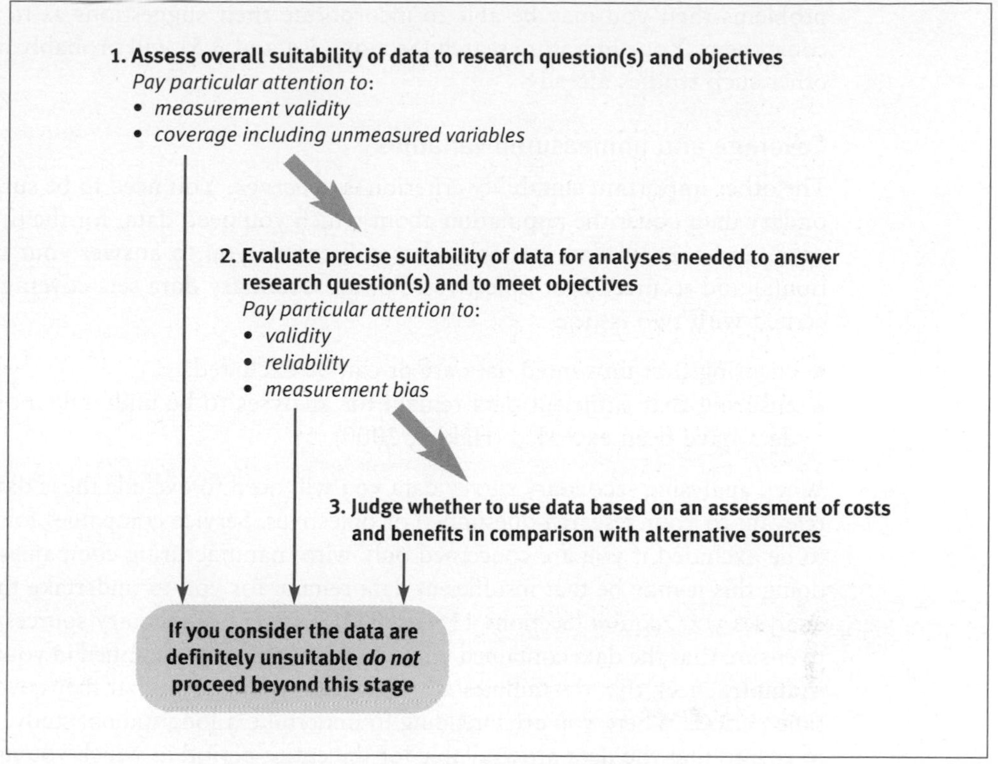

1. Assess overall suitability of data to research question(s) and objectives
Pay particular attention to:
• measurement validity
• coverage including unmeasured variables
2. Evaluate precise suitability of data for analyses needed to answer research question(s) and to meet objectives
Pay particular attention to:
• validity
• reliability
• measurement bias
3. Judge whether to use data based on an assessment of costs and benefits in comparison with alternative sources
If you consider the data are definitely unsuitable do not proceed beyond this stage

Figure 7.2 Evaluating potential secondary data sources

Overall suitability

Measurement validity

One of the most important criteria for the suitability of any data set is *measurement validity*. Secondary data that fail to provide you with the information that you need to answer your research question(s) or meet your objectives will result in invalid answers (Kervin, 1999). Often when you are using secondary survey data you will find that the measures used do not quite match those that you need (Jacob, 1994). For example, a manufacturing organisation may record monthly sales whereas you are interested in monthly orders. This may cause you a problem when you undertake your analyses believing that you have found a relationship with sales whereas in fact your relationship is with the number of orders. Alternatively, you may be using minutes of company meetings as a proxy for what actually happened in those meetings. These are likely to reflect a particular interpretation of what happened, the events being recorded from a particular viewpoint, often the chairperson's. You therefore need to be cautious before accepting such records at face value (Denscombe, 1998).

Unfortunately, there are no clear solutions to problems of measurement invalidity. All you can do is try to evaluate the extent of the data's validity and make your own decision. A common way of doing this is to examine how other researchers have coped with this problem for a similar secondary data set in a similar context. If they found that the measures, while not exact, were suitable then you can be more certain that they will be suitable for your research question(s) and objectives. If they had problems then you may be able to incorporate their suggestions as to how to overcome them. Your literature search (Sections 3.4 and 3.5) will probably have identified other such studies already.

Coverage and unmeasured variables

The other important suitability criterion is *coverage*. You need to be sure that the secondary data cover the population about which you need data, for the time period you need, and contain data variables that will enable you to answer your research question(s) and to meet your objectives. For all secondary data sets coverage will be concerned with two issues:

- ensuring that unwanted data are or can be excluded;
- ensuring that sufficient data remain for analyses to be undertaken once unwanted data have been excluded (Hakim, 2000).

When analysing secondary survey data you will need to exclude those data that are not relevant to your research question(s) or objectives. Service companies for example need to be excluded if you are concerned only with manufacturing companies. However, in doing this it may be that insufficient data remain for you to undertake the quantitative analyses you require (Sections 11.4 and 11.5). For documentary sources you will need to ensure that the data contained relate to the population identified in your research. For example, check that the minutes are of board meetings and that they cover the required time period. Where you are intending to undertake a longitudinal study, you also need to ensure that the data are available for the entire period in which you are interested.

Some secondary data sets, in particular for survey data, may not include variables you have identified as necessary for your analysis. These are termed *unmeasured variables*. Their absence may not be particularly important if you are undertaking descriptive research. However, it could drastically affect the outcome of explanatory research as a potentially important variable has been excluded.

Precise suitability

Reliability and validity

The *reliability* and *validity* (Section 4.4) you ascribe to secondary data are functions of the method by which the data were collected and the source. You can make a quick assessment of these by looking at the source of the data. Dochartaigh (2002) and others refer to this as assessing the *authority* or reputation of the source. Survey data from large, well-known organisations such as those found in Mintel and Keynote market research reports are likely to be reliable and trustworthy. The continued existence of such organisations is dependent on the credibility of their data. Consequently, their procedures for collecting and compiling the data are likely to be well thought through and accurate. Survey data from government organisations are also likely to be reliable. However, you will probably find the validity of documentary data such as organisations' records more difficult to assess. While organisations may argue that their records are reliable, there are often inconsistencies and inaccuracies. You therefore need also to examine the method by which the data were collected and try to ascertain the precision needed by the original (primary) user.

Dochartaigh (2002) suggests a number of areas for initial assessment of the authority of documents available via the Internet. These, we believe, can be adapted to assess the authority of all types of secondary data. First, as suggested in the previous paragraph, it is important to discover the person or organisation responsible for the data and to be able to obtain additional information through which you can assess the reliability of the source. For data in printed publications this is usually reasonably straightforward (Section 3.6). However, for secondary data obtained via the Internet it may be more difficult. Although organisation names such as the 'Center for Research into. . .' or 'Institute for the Study of . . .' may appear initially to be credible, publication via the Internet is not controlled, and such names are sometimes used to suggest pseudo-academic credibility. Dochartaigh (2002) therefore suggests that you look also for a copyright statement and the existence of published documents relating to the data to help validation. The former of these, when it exists, can provide an indication of who is responsible for the data. The latter, he argues, reinforces the data's authority, as printed publications are regarded as more reliable. In addition, Internet sources often contain an email address or other means of contacting the author for comments and questions about the Internet site and its contents (Dees, 2000). However, beware of applying these criteria too rigidly as sometimes the most authoritative web pages do not include the information outlined above. Dochartaigh (2002) suggests that this is because those with most authority often feel the least need to proclaim it!

For all secondary data a detailed assessment of the validity and reliability will involve you in an assessment of the method or methods used to collect the data (Dale *et al.*, 1988). These may be provided by hyperlinks for Internet-based data sets. Alternatively, they may be discussed in the methodology section of an associated report. Your assessment will involve looking at who were responsible for collecting or recording the information and examining the context in which the data were collected. From this you should gain some feeling regarding the likelihood of potential errors or biases. In addition, you need to look at the process by which the data were selected and collected or recorded. Where sampling has been used to select cases (usually for surveys) the sampling procedure adopted and the associated sampling error and response rates (Section 6.2) will give clues to validity. Secondary data collected through a survey with a high response rate are also likely to be more reliable than from that with a low response rate. However, commercial providers of high-quality, reliable data sets may be unwilling to disclose details about how data were collected. This is particularly the case where these organisations see the methodology as important to their competitive advantage.

For some documentary sources, such as diaries, transcripts of interviews or meetings, it is unlikely that there will be a formal methodology describing how the data were collected. The reliability of these data will therefore be difficult to assess, although you may be able to discover the context in which the data were collected. For example, letters and memos contain no formal obligation for the writer to give a full and accurate portrayal of events. Rather they are written from a personal point of view and expect the recipient to be aware of the context (Denscombe, 1998). This means that these data are more likely to be useful as a source of the writer's perceptions and views than as an objective account of reality. The fact that you did not collect and were not present when these data were collected will also affect your analyses. Dale *et al.* (1988) argue that full analyses of in-depth interview data require an understanding derived from participating in social interactions that cannot be fully recorded on tape or by transcript.

The validity and reliability of collection methods for survey data will be easier to assess where you have a clear explanation of the methodology used to collect the data. This needs to include a clear explanation of any sampling techniques used and response rates (discussed earlier) as well as a copy of the survey instrument, which will usually be a questionnaire. By examining the questions by which data were collected, you will gain a further indication of the validity.

Where data have been compiled, as in a report, you need to pay careful attention to how these data were analysed and how the results are reported. Where percentages (or proportions) are used without actually giving the totals on which these figures are based you need to examine the data very carefully. For example, a 50 per cent increase in the number of clients from two to three for a small company may be of less relevance than the 20 per cent increase in the number of clients from 1000 to 1200 for a larger company in the same market! Similarly, where quotations appear to be used selectively without other supporting evidence you should beware, as the data may be unreliable. Remember, the further away you are from the original data, the more difficult it will be to judge their quality (Patzer, 1996).

worked example

Graphical distortion of data

Pamela examined the use of diagrams and tables in company reports as part of her dissertation. Based on a sample of 47 companies' reports she found that 68 per cent of companies used at least one form of graph, and all companies used tables.

Of considerable interest was the finding that 47 per cent of diagrams used to present key financial information had distorted the data. This was done by either overstating or understating the size of the bar or graphic that represented each value in some way. One of the more frequently used techniques – not starting the value axis at zero – is illustrated below:

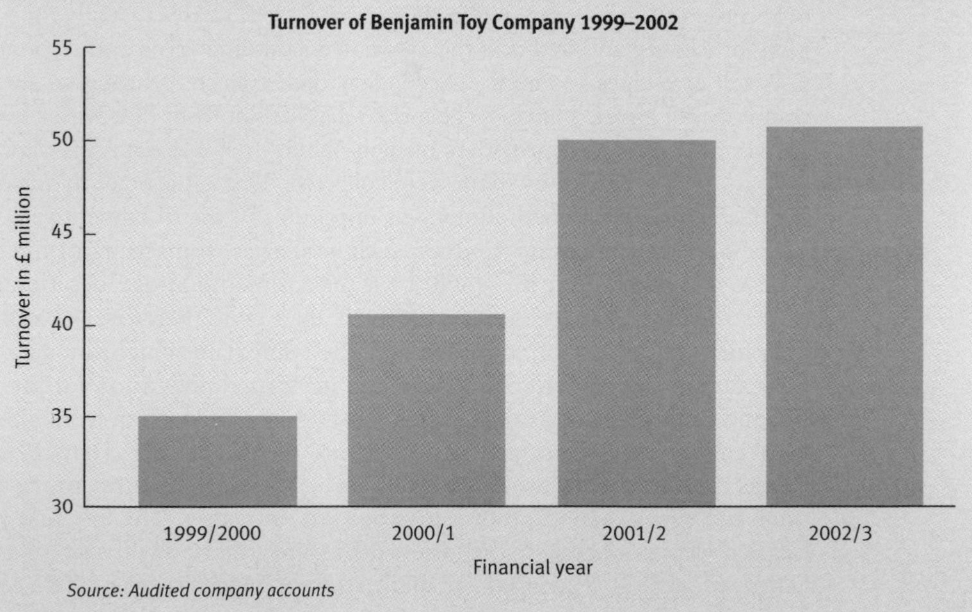

Source: Audited company accounts

Measurement bias

Measurement bias can occur for two reasons (Kervin, 1999):

- deliberate or intentional distortion of data;
- changes in the way data are collected.

Deliberate distortion occurs when data are recorded inaccurately on purpose, and is most common for secondary data sources such as organisational records. Managers may deliberately fail to record minor accidents to improve safety reports for their departments. Data that have been collected to further a particular cause or the interests of a particular group are more likely to be suspect as the purpose of the study may be to reach a predetermined conclusion (Jacob, 1994). Reports of consumer satisfaction surveys may deliberately play down negative comments to make the service appear better to their target audience of senior managers and shareholders.

Other distortion may be deliberate but not intended for any advantage. Employees keeping time diaries may record only the approximate time spent on their main duties rather than accounting precisely for every minute. People responding to a structured interview (questionnaire) may adjust their responses to please the interviewer (Section 10.2).

Unfortunately, measurement bias resulting from deliberate distortion is difficult to detect. While we believe that you should adopt a neutral stance about the possibility of bias you still need to look for pressures on the original source that might have biased the data. For written documents such as minutes, reports and memos the intended target audience may suggest possible bias, as indicated earlier in this section. Therefore, where possible you will need to triangulate the findings with other independent data sources. This is sometimes referred to as a *cross-check verification* (Patzer, 1996). Where data from two or more independent sources suggest similar conclusions, you can have more confidence that the data on which they are based are not distorted. Conversely, where data suggest different conclusions you need to be more wary of the results.

Changes in the way in which data were collected can also introduce changes in measurement bias. Provided that the method of collecting data remains constant in terms of the people collecting it and the procedures used, the measurement biases should remain constant. Once the method is altered, perhaps through a new procedure of taking minutes or a new data collection form, then the bias also changes. This is very important for longitudinal data sets such as the UK's Retail Price Index where you are interested in trends rather than actual numbers. Your detection of biases is dependent on discovering that the way data are recorded has changed. Within-company sources are less likely to have documented these changes than government-sponsored sources.

Costs and benefits

Kervin (1999) argues that the final criterion for assessing secondary data is a comparison of the costs of acquiring them with the benefits they will bring. Costs include both time and financial resources that you will need to devote to obtaining the data. Some data will be available in your local library and so will be free, although you will have to pay for any photocopying you need. Other data will require lengthy negotiations before access is granted (Section 5.3). Even then, the granting of access may not be certain (Stewart and Kamins, 1993). Data from market research companies or special tabulations from government surveys will have to be ordered specially and will normally be charged for: consequently, these will be relatively costly.

worked example

Assessing the suitability of data available via the Internet

As part of a research project on changing consumer spending patterns, Jemma wished to establish how the cost of living had altered year on year over the last five years within Britain. Other research that she had read as part of her literature review had utilised the UK Office for National Statistics' Retail Price Index. She therefore decided to see whether this information was available via the Internet from the UK government's statistics web site http://www.statistics.gov.uk using the *StatBase* information gateway. Within five minutes of starting to use StatBase's 'Use Datasets to Search for Data' hyperlink she found a data set titled 'Average earning index and retail prices index, 1991–1999: Social Trends'. She decided to assess the suitability of these data using the information provided on the web page:

Extract from web page

Data set name:	ST30507
Type of dataset:	Cross-sectional
Title:	Average earning index and retail prices index, 1991–1999: Social Trends Dataset
Last updated:	5/4/00
Description:	*(Although not included in this extract, this provides only limited information about the Retail Price Index)*
Associated web links:	There are no web links stored for this product
For linked contacts and documents:	See product details
Source:	Office for National Statistics
Time frame:	1991–1999
Geographic coverage:	United Kingdom and Great Britain
Universe:	Earnings and prices
Measure:	Average earnings and retail prices
Units:	Percentage change over 12 months
Availability:	This dataset may be viewed on screen or downloaded to your own PC

Source: Office for National Statistics (2000)

Initial examination of this information to assess the data's overall suitability revealed that the source was credible, having been compiled by the UK government's Office for National Statistics. However, it also highlighted one immediate problem: the data are not as up to date as she would have liked, 1999 being the most recent year. Despite this she decided to download the retail prices data to her PC as a spreadsheet-compatible file. The resulting file contained two footnotes. The second of these stated that the 'Data are for United Kingdom', highlighting a second possible problem, that the data did not refer to the precise geographical area required as Great Britain, unlike the United Kingdom, excludes Northern Ireland. She decided that this would not present too great a problem as she was only going to use these data to contextualise her research.

However, in order to be certain about the suitability of the RPI, she also needed to find out precisely how it had been calculated and how the data on which it was based had been collected. Twenty minutes' searching within StatBase failed to provide sufficient information. She therefore decided to return to the National Statistics web site home page and use those search facilities to find out more. Her search revealed a series of articles on the RPI. One (Office for National Statistics, 2001) explained how and why the items that make up the 'basket' of goods and services used in the RPI were chosen, and in particular how they had been revised recently to take account of changing consumer spending patterns, including the increasing use of the Internet.

The article also described clearly the methodology for calculating the index, suggesting that RPI would be suitable for her research. The one issue she had was that the article stated that the data measured changes in prices rather than being a cost of living index. However, because other researchers had shown that the RPI provides a reasonable surrogate for cost of living Jemma decided to use the data she had downloaded from StatBase.

Benefits from data can be assessed in terms of the extent to which they will enable you to answer your research question(s) and meet your objectives. You will be able to form a judgement on the benefits from your assessment of the data set's overall and precise suitability (discussed earlier in this section). This assessment is summarised as a checklist of questions in Box 7.1. An important additional benefit is the form in which you receive the data. If the data are already in computer-readable form this will save you considerable time as you will not need to re-enter the data prior to analysis (Sections 11.2 and 12.8). However, when assessing the costs and benefits you must remember that data that are not completely reliable and contain some bias are better than no data at all, if they enable you to start to answer your research question(s) and achieve your objectives.

Box 7.1 Checklist to evaluate secondary data sources

Overall suitability

- ✓ Does the data set contain the information you require to answer your research question(s) and meet your objectives?
- ✓ Do the measures used match those you require?
- ✓ Is the data set a proxy for the data you really need?
- ✓ Does the data set cover the population that is the subject of your research?
- ✓ Can data about the population that is the subject of your research be separated from unwanted data?
- ✓ Are the data sufficiently up to date?

▶

- ☑ Are data available for all the variables you require to answer your research question(s) and meet your objectives?

Precise suitability

- ☑ How reliable is the data set you are thinking of using?
- ☑ How credible is the data source?
  - ☑ Is it clear what the source of the data is?
  - ☑ Is the source of the data likely to be reliable?
  - ☑ Do the data have an associated copyright statement?
  - ☑ Do associated published documents exist?
- ☑ Is the methodology clearly described?
  - ☑ If sampling was used what was the procedure and what were the associated sampling errors and response rates?
  - ☑ Who were responsible for collecting or recording the data?
  - ☑ (For surveys) Is a copy of the questionnaire or interview checklist included?
  - ☑ (For compiled data) Are you clear how the data were analysed and compiled?
- ☑ Are the data likely to contain measurement bias?
  - ☑ What was the original purpose for which the data were collected?
  - ☑ Who was the target audience and what was their relationship to the data collector or compiler (were there any vested interests)?
  - ☑ Have there been any documented changes in the way the data are measured or recorded including definition changes?
  - ☑ How consistent are the data obtained from this source when compared with data from other sources?
- ☑ Are you happy that the data have been recorded accurately?

Costs and benefits

- ☑ What are the financial and time costs of obtaining these data?
- ☑ Have the data already been entered into a computer?
- ☑ Do the overall benefits of using these secondary data sources outweigh the associated costs?

Sources: Authors' experience; Dale *et al.* (1988); Dochartaigh (2002); Jacob (1994); Kervin (1999); Stewart and Kamins (1993)

7.6 Summary

- Data that have already been collected for some other purpose, perhaps processed and subsequently stored, are termed secondary data. There are three main types of secondary data: documentary, survey and those from multiple sources.
- Most research projects require some combination of secondary and primary data to answer your research question(s) and to meet your objectives. You can use secondary data in a variety of ways. These include:

  - to provide your main data set;
  - to provide longitudinal (time-series data);
  - to provide area-based data;
  - to compare with, or set in context, your own research findings.
- Any secondary data you use will have been collected for a specific purpose. This purpose may not match that of your research. In addition, the secondary data are likely to be less current than any data you collect yourself.
- Finding the secondary data you require is a matter of detective work. This will involve you in:
  - establishing whether the sort of data that you require are likely to be available;
  - locating the precise data.
- Once located you must assess secondary data sources to ensure their overall suitability for your research question(s) and objectives. In particular you need to pay attention to the measurement validity and coverage of the data.
- You must also evaluate the precise suitability of the secondary data. Your evaluation should include both reliability and any likely measurement bias. You can then make a judgement on the basis of the costs and benefits of using the data in comparison with alternative sources.
- When assessing costs and benefits you need to be mindful that secondary data that are not completely reliable and contain some bias are better than no data at all if they enable you partially to answer your research question(s) and to meet your objectives.

self-check Questions

7.1 Give three examples of different situations where you might use secondary data as part of your research.

7.2 You are undertaking a research project as part of your course. Your initial research question is 'How has the UK's import and export trade with other countries altered since its entry into the European Union?'

List the arguments that you would use to convince someone of the suitability of using secondary data to answer this research question.

7.3 Suggest possible secondary data that would help you answer the following research questions. How would you locate these secondary data?

a To what extent do organisations' employee relocation policies meet the needs of employees?

b How have consumer-spending patterns in the UK altered in the last 10 years?

c How have governments' attitudes to the public sector altered since 1979?

7.4 As part of case study research based in a manufacturing company with over 500 customers you have been given access to an internal market research report. This was undertaken by the company's marketing department. The report presents the results of a recent customer survey as percentages. The section in the report that describes how the data were collected and analysed Is reproduced below:

Data were collected from a sample of current customers selected from our customer database. The data were collected using a telephone questionnaire administered by marketing department staff. 25 customers responded, resulting in a 12.5 per cent response rate. These data were analysed using the SNAP computer software. Additional qualitative data based on in-depth interviews with customers were also included.

a Do you consider these data are likely to be reliable?
b Give reasons for your answer.

progressing your research project

Assessing the suitability of secondary data for your research

- ☐ Consider your research question(s) and objectives. Decide whether you need to use secondary data or a combination of primary and secondary data to answer your research question. (If you decide that you need only use secondary data and you are undertaking this research as part of a course of study check your course's examination regulations to ensure that this is permissible.)
- ☐ If you decide that you need to use secondary data make sure that you are clear why and how you intend to use these data.
- ☐ Locate the secondary data that you require and make sure that permission for them to be used for your research is likely to be granted. Evaluate the suitability of the data for answering your research question and make your judgement based on assessment of its suitability, other benefits and the associated costs.
- ☐ Note down the reasons for your choices, including the possibilities and limitations of the data. You will need to justify your choices when you write your research methodology.

References

Bryman, A. (1989) *Research Methods and Organisation Studies*, London, Unwin Hyman.

Cowton, C.J. (1998) 'The use of secondary data in business ethics research', *Journal of Business Ethics*, 17:4, 423–34.

Dale, P. (1993) *Guide to Libraries in Key UK Companies*, London, British Library.

Dale, P. (1998) *Guide to Libraries and Information Units in Goverment Departments and Other Organisations*, Westport, CT, Quorum Books.

Dale, A., Arber, S. and Proctor, M. (1988) *Doing Secondary Analysis*, London, Unwin Hyman.

Davies, J. (2001) 'International comparisons of labour disputes in 1999', *Labour Market Trends*, 109:4, 195–201.

Davis, S.M. and Saunders, M.N.K. (1997) 'Freedom of movement for professionals: an assessment of the European Union policy and the barriers that remain', *Journal of Applied Management Studies*, 6:2, 199–218.

Dees, R. (2000) *Writing the Modern Research Paper*, Boston, Allyn and Bacon.

Dennis, D. (ed.) (2000) *Family Spending: A Report on the 1999–2000 Family Expenditure Survey*, London, Stationery Office.

Denscombe, M. (1998) *The Good Research Guide*, Buckingham, Open University Press.

Dochartaigh, N.O. (2002) *The Internet Research Handbook: A Practical Guide for Students and Researchers in the Social Sciences*, London, Sage.

Dunkerley, D. (1988) 'Historical methods and organizational analysis', *in* Bryman, A. (ed.), *Doing Research in Organisations*, London, Routledge, pp. 82–95.

ELC International (2001) *Europe's 15,000 Largest Companies* (27th edn), Oxford, ELC International.

Ghauri, P. and Grønhaugh, K. (2002) *Research Methods in Business Studies: A Practical Guide* (2nd edn), Harlow, Financial Times Prentice Hall.

Hakim, C. (1982) *Secondary Analysis in Social Research*, London, Allen & Unwin.

Hakim, C. (2000) *Research Design: Successful Designs for Social and Economic Research*, London, Routledge.

Jacob, H. (1994) 'Using published data: errors and remedies', *in* Lewis-Beck, M.S. (ed.) *Research Practice*, London, Sage and Toppan Publishing, pp. 339–89.

Jenkins, J. and Bird, D. (2001) 'Patterns of pay: results of the new earnings survey', *Labour Market Trends*, 109:3, 145–57.

Jones, A. and Smith, A. (eds) (2001) 'What exactly is the Labour Force Survey?' [online] (cited 20 December 2001). Available from: <URL:http://www.statistics.gov.uk/nsbase/down loads.theme_labour/what_exactly_is_LFS1.pdf>

Kervin, J.B. (1999) *Methods for Business Research* (2nd edn), New York, HarperCollins.

Kingsbury, P. (1997) *IT Answers to HR Questions*, London, Institute of Personnel and Development.

Library Association (1997) *Libraries in the United Kingdom and Republic of Ireland*, London, Library Assocation.

McGinty, J. and Williams, T. (eds.) (2001) *Regional Trends 36* (2001 edn), London, Stationery Office.

McGuinness, K. and Short, T. (1998) *Research on the Net*, London, Old Bailey Press.

Office for National Statistics (1996) *30 Years of Regional Trends*, London, Stationery Office.

Office for National Statistics (2000) 'Dataset: average earning index and retail prices index, 1991–1999: social trends'. [online] (cited 19 December 2001). Available from: <URL:http://www.statistics.gov.uk/statbase/xsdataset.asp?vlnk=202&More=Y>.

Office for National Statistics (2001) 'Retail Price Index: price indicators used in 2000'. [online](cited 19 December 2001). Available from: <URL:http://www.statistics.gov.uk/ themes/economy/articles/pricesandinflation/rpiitart.pdf>.

Patzer, G.L. (1996) *Using Secondary Data in Market Research: United States and World-wide*, Westport, CT, Quorum Books.

Reichman, C.S. (1962) *Use and Abuse of Statistics*, New York, Oxford University Press.

Robson, C. (2002) *Real World Research* (2nd edn), Oxford, Blackwell.

Stewart, D.W. and Kamins, M.A. (1993) *Secondary Research: Information Sources and Methods* (2nd edn), Newbury Park, CA, Sage.

Teague, A. (2001) 'New methodologies for the 2001 Census in England and Wales'. [online] (cited 11 February 2002). Available from: <URL:http://www.statistics.gov.uk/nsbase/ census2001/pdfs/NewMethodologies.pdf>.

Tyrrell, K. (ed.) (2001) *Annual Abstract of Statistics 2001*, London, Stationery Office.

UK Data Archive (2002) 'UK Data Archive' [online] [cited 3 January] available from <URL: http://www.data-archive.ac.uk>.

Walker, A. (2002) *Living in Britain: Results from the 2000 General Household Survey*, London, Stationery Office.

Further reading

Bryman, A. (1989) *Research Methods and Organisation Studies*, London, Unwin Hyman. Chapter 9 contains a good discussion with a series of examples of how archival research and secondary analysis of survey data have been used in management and business research.

Dunkerley, D. (1988) 'Historical methods and organizational analysis', *in* Bryman, A. (ed.), *Doing Research in Organisations*, London, Routledge, pp. 82–95. This chapter provides an open and honest account of the realities of doing historical research on an organisation using secondary data.

Levitas, R. and Guy, W. (eds) (1996) *Interpreting Official Statistics*, London, Routledge. This book provides a fascinating insight into UK published statistics. Of particular interest are Chapter 1, which outlines the changes in UK statistics since the 1980 Raynor review, Chapter 3, which looks at the measurement of unemployment, the discussion in Chapter 6 of the measurement of industrial injuries and their limitations, and Chapter 7, which examines gender segregation in the labour force, utilising data from the Labour Force Survey.

Stewart, D.W. and Kamins, M.A. (1993) *Secondary Research: Information Sources and Methods* (2nd edn), Newbury Park, CA, Sage. This provides a good discussion on the evaluation of secondary data (Chapter 2). It also provides a wealth of information on American government and non-government data sets and their acquisition.

CASE 7 Research and development in the UK pharmaceutical industry in the 1960s

Clare's thesis was concerned with exploring and answering the question 'How innovative was the UK pharmaceutical industry in the 1960s?' At that time there was a considerable debate among those with an interest in the industry, including government, business journalists, City analysts and academics as to whether companies with larger research establishments were likely to be more innovative than companies with smaller R&D (research and development) departments. The debate came to a head in 1972 when the Beecham Group, arguing that the UK industry needed a larger company to compete with the then more successful US, German and Swiss corporations, made a takeover bid for Glaxo. The bid was fiercely opposed by Glaxo, which produced its own scheme for a merger with Boots. Both bids were referred to the Monopolies Commission, which after four months of investigation and deliberation recommended that neither merger should take place, on the grounds that there was no evidence that one larger organisation would be more innovative. The debate about the relationship between size and innovation has resurfaced from time to time since, particularly through the 1980s and 1990s as the industry went through a spate of mergers creating much larger transnational corporations.

Clare's literature survey had found a great deal written on certain aspects of innovation, on the process and its management, and on the drugs launched in the period, but relatively little on the relationship between size and research productivity in the 1960s. It therefore seemed to be an area worth exploring. The usual way of measuring a company's research productivity was through the number of patents taken out by that company and the number of scientific papers published by its scientists. Clare decided to link this information on companies' research productivity where it was available with that on the drugs they launched on the market between 1960 and 1969, the companies' R&D expenditure and the number of scientists employed in R&D departments.

Clare therefore gathered information on the six companies she hypothesised were the most innovative in the UK at that time: Glaxo, ICI, Wellcome, Boots, Beechams, and May & Baker. By trawling various publications by the Department of Trade, Department of Health, the Patent Office and other semi-government bodies such as the National Economic Development Office she began to build up a picture of these companies' research productivity. This picture was further informed by reports from stockbrokers and the Association of the British Pharmaceutical Industry (ABPI) as well as by publications and good quality journalist reports on the industry. However, there was a problem in finding out the numbers of people employed in R&D and the amounts spent on R&D. Today the obvious source might seem to be the companies, which now include such information in their annual reports and accounts. However, they did not always do so. Approaching the companies for the information posed a new set of problems, as much has changed over the last decade. Glaxo took over Wellcome in 1995 and then in 2001 merged with SmithKline Beecham (itself the product of an Anglo-US merger in the late 1980s) to form GlaxoSmithKline. ICI spun off its pharmaceuticals division in 1990 to form Zeneca, which subsequently merged with the Swedish pharmaceutical company Astra. Boots sold off its pharmaceutical operations in 1995 to the German company Knoll, already owned by BASF, and in 2001 BASF sold its pharmaceutical interests to the US company Abbott Laboratories. May & Baker, although owned by the French chemical company Rhone-Poulenc since the 1920s, became more integrated in the 1990s with its parent, which in the late 1990s merged its pharmaceutical interests with those of the German company Hoechst to form a new company called Aventis. In the wake of this restructuring sites have been closed down, archives boxed up and moved around, and it is not always easy to find or gain access to the archives.

Fortunately, however, Clare had been using the Ministry of Health records in the Public Record Office at Kew (London), and these include the papers of several government committees established to examine the industry in the 1950s and the 1960s. Papers from the Guillebaud and Hinchcliffe committees of the 1950s contained some figures of expenditure on research in the 1950s, which provided useful background. The papers of the Sainsbury Committee, which investigated the industry in the mid-1960s, provided a rich treasure trove of information. A memorandum to the committee from the industry association, the ABPI, listed each of the companies in which she was interested along with the numbers employed in their R&D departments. Given that the committee had been established in part because of the rising cost of pharmaceuticals supplied to the National Health Service, it was perhaps not surprising that submissions to the committee had been written to present the best possible image of the industry. Despite this, these submissions provided further detailed information of the kind she needed. In the ABPI (1965) memorandum the

▶

figures for employees engaged in pharmaceutical research for the six companies mentioned above were listed as follows:

Beecham Group	380
Glaxo Group	756
ICI	1100
Boots	516
May & Baker	598
Wellcome	844

The memorandum also highlighted that two United States subsidiaries had larger R&D establishments than Clare had anticipated (ABPI, 1965). Pfizer employed 372 such people and Smith, Kline and French Laboratories employed 216. Only one other UK company had more than 100 employees in R&D, namely British Drug Houses Ltd (BDH) with 142. Glaxo acquired this company early in 1968.

With these and other data Clare felt she could argue with certainty that the size of an R&D establishment in the 1960s was a significant factor in R&D productivity. In addition, she was aware that the 30-year closure rule for public documents meant that the files of the Monopolies Commission 1972 investigation of Glaxo, Beechams and Boots were likely to become available to researchers early in 2003. As she was due to submit her research project in June 2003 she hoped that this source would enable her to add some extra information and evidence to her argument prior to submitting her work.

Reference

Association of the British Pharmaceutical Industry (1965) *Memo to the Sainsbury Committee*. PRO.MH 104/45, 12 October.

Questions

1 a List the data sources used by Clare in this research.
  b Which are secondary data and which are primary data?
  c Give reasons for your answers.

2 a What other methods (if any) might Clare have used to find the information she needed?
  b Give reasons for your answer.

3 Outline the problems that Clare faced in using these data.

4 What lessons can you draw from Clare's research experience?

self-check Answers

7.1 Although it would be impossible to list all possible situations, the key features that should appear in your examples are listed below:

- to compare findings from your primary data;
- to place findings from your primary data in a wider context;
- to triangulate findings from other data sources;
- to provide the main data set where you wish to undertake research over a long period, to undertake historical research or to undertake comparative research on a national or international scale with limited resources.

7.2 The arguments you have listed should focus on the following issues:

- The study suggested by the research question requires historical data so that changes that have already happened can be explored. These data will, by definition, have already been collected.
- The timescale of the research (if part of a course) will be relatively short term. One solution for longitudinal studies in a short time frame is to use secondary data.
- The research question suggests an international comparative study. Given your likely limited resources secondary data will provide the only feasible data sources.

7.3 **a** The secondary data required for this research question relate to organisations' employee relocation policies. The research question assumes that these sorts of data are likely to be available from organisations. Textbooks, research papers and informal discussions would enable you to confirm that these data were likely to be available. Informal discussions with individuals responsible for the personnel function in organisations would also confirm the existence and availability for research of such data.

b The secondary data required for this research question relate to consumer spending patterns in the UK. As these appear to be the sort of data in which the government would be interested they may well be available in published form. Examination of various published guides (both governmental and non-governmental sources) would reveal that these were collected by the annual Family Expenditure Survey, summary results of which are published (for example Dennis, 2000). These reports could then be borrowed either from your library or by using inter-library loan. In addition, the UK Government's StatBase information gateway could be searched via the Internet. This would reveal that summary data from the survey were available for downloading.

c The secondary data required for this research question are less clear. What you require is some source from which you can infer past and present government attitudes. Transcripts of ministers' speeches (such as in Hansard) and newspaper reports might prove useful. However, to establish suitable secondary sources for this research question you would need to pay careful attention to those used by other researchers. These would be outlined in research papers and textbooks. Informal discussions could also prove useful.

7.4 **a** The data are unlikely to be reliable.

b Your judgement should be based on a combination of the following reasons:

- Initial examination of the report reveals that it is an internally conducted survey. As this has been undertaken by the marketing department of a large manufacturing company, you might assume that those undertaking the research had considerable expertise. Consequently, you might conclude the report contains credible data. However:
- The methodology is not clearly described. In particular:
  - The sampling procedure and associated sampling errors are not given.
  - It does not appear to contain a copy of the questionnaire. This means that it is impossible to check for bias in the way that questions were worded.
  - The methodology for the qualitative in-depth interviews is not described.
- In addition, the information provided in the methodology suggests that the data may be unreliable:
  - The reported response rate of 12.5 per cent is very low for a telephone survey (Chapter 6, Section 6.2).
  - Responses from 25 people means that all tables and statistical analyses in the report are based on a maximum of 25 people. This may be too few for reliable results (Chapters 6 and 11, Sections 6.2 and 11.5).

Chapter 8

Collecting primary data through observation

By the end of this chapter you should be able:

- to understand the role that observation may play as a data collection method in your research design;
- to identify two types of observation, participant observation and structured observation, and their differing origins and applications;
- to adopt particular approaches to data collection and analysis for both participant observation and structured observation;
- to identify threats to validity and reliability faced by the two types of observation.

8.1 Introduction

If your research question(s) and objectives are concerned with what people do, an obvious way in which to discover this is to watch them do it. This is essentially what *observation* involves: the systematic observation, recording, description, analysis and interpretation of people's behaviour.

The two types of observation examined in this chapter are very different. *Participant observation* is qualitative and derives from the work of social anthropology earlier in the twentieth century. Its emphasis is on discovering the meanings that people attach to their actions. By contrast, *structured observation* is quantitative and is more concerned with the frequency of those actions.

A common theme in this book is our effort to discourage you from thinking of the various research methods as the sole means that you should employ in your study. This is also true of observation methods. It may meet the demands of your research question(s) and objectives to use both participant and structured observation in your study, either as the main methods of data collection or to supplement other methods.

8.2 Participant observation: an introduction

What is participant observation?

If you have studied sociology or anthropology in the past you are certain to be familiar with *participant observation*. This is where 'the researcher attempts to participate fully in the lives and activities of subjects and thus becomes a member of their group, organisation or community. This enables the researcher to share their experiences by not merely observing what is happening but also feeling it' (Gill and Johnson, 1997:113). It has been used extensively in these disciplines to attempt to get to the root of 'what is going on' in a wide range of social settings.

Participant observation has its roots in social anthropology, but it was the Chicago school of social research that encouraged its students to study by observation the constantly changing social phenomena of Chicago in the 1920s and 1930s.

Participant observation has been used much less in management and business research. However, this does not mean to say that it has limited value for management and business researchers. Indeed, it can be a very valuable tool, usually as the principal research method, but possibly in combination with other methods.

Delbridge and Kirkpatrick (1994:37) note that participant observation implies a research strategy of 'immersion [by the researcher] in the research setting, with the objective of sharing in peoples' lives while attempting to learn their symbolic world'. It is worth dwelling on this explanation. Whichever role you adopt as the participant observer (the choices open to you will be discussed later), there will be a high level of immersion. This is quite different from data collection by means of questionnaire, where you probably will know little of the context in which the respondents' comments are set or the delicate nuances of meaning with which the respondents garnish their responses. In participant observation the purpose is to discover those delicate nuances of meaning. As Delbridge and Kirkpatrick (1994:39) state: 'in the social sciences we cannot hope to adequately explain the behaviour of social actors unless we at least try to understand their meanings'.

This last comment gives a clue to the point that Delbridge and Kirkpatrick make about 'attempting to learn the [respondents'] symbolic world'. Some understanding of this point is vital if you are to convince yourself and others of the value of using participant observation.

The symbolic frame of reference is located within the school of sociology known as *symbolic interactionism*. In symbolic interactionism the individual derives a sense of identity from interaction and communication with others. Through this process of interaction and communication the individual responds to others and adjusts his or her understandings and behaviour as a shared sense of order and reality is 'negotiated' with others. Central to this process is the notion that people continually change in the light of the social circumstances in which they find themselves. The transition from full-time student to career employee is one example of this. (How often have you heard people say 'she's so different since she's worked at that new place'?) The individual's sense of identity is constantly being constructed and reconstructed as he or she moves through differing social contexts and encounters different situations and different people.

This is a necessarily brief explanation of symbolic interactionism. However, we hope that you can see why Delbridge and Kirkpatrick (1994:37) think that participant observation is about 'attempting to learn the [respondents'] symbolic world'. It is a quest for understanding the identity of the individual, but, more importantly, it is about trying to get to the bottom of the processes by which the individual constantly constructs and reconstructs his or her identity.

worked example

Discovering the meanings respondents convey in their responses

The head office of a large company operating in a town with a world-famous horse-racing festival was plagued annually by some of the more junior staff going sick at the time of the festival. Over the years there had been attempts to cure the problem by 'making examples' of particular employees. However, nothing had succeeded. It seemed that the absentees always had a valid reason for their absence. Yet managers were convinced that many absentees attended the horse-racing festival.

Sarah was intrigued to discover why this phenomenon was occurring. Discovering the answer to this research question would heighten considerably Sarah's knowledge and understanding of employee absenteeism.

Answering the research question entailed Sarah working in the sections that were staffed mainly by junior employees. Sarah needed to 'become one of them' (as far as it was possible to do this). She needed to immerse herself in the social context of the junior employees' work.

A period of immersion as the participant observer enabled Sarah to unravel the complicated social processes by which junior staff 'negotiated' with one another to cover the work of absentees. Sarah also learned that staff consider taking time off work as a 'legitimate perk'. Often in their past, schools, colleges and employers 'turned a blind eye' to this practice.

NB: It may have occurred to you that this example may be thought of as ethically rather dubious research. The ethical implications of participant observation are discussed in Section 8.3.

Situations in which participant observation has been used

One of the most famous examples of participant observation is that of Whyte (1955), who lived among a poor American–Italian community in order to understand 'street corner society'. A celebrated business example is the work of Roy (1952). Roy worked in a machine shop for 10 months as an employee. He wanted to understand how and why his 'fellow workers' operated the piecework bonus system. Rather more colourfully, Rosen (1991) worked as a participant observer in a Philadelphia advertising agency. Rosen was working within the theoretical domain of dramaturgy. He wanted to understand how organisations used social drama to create and sustain power relationships and social structures.

These may strike you as rather elaborate examples that suggest little relevance to you as you contemplate your own research project. Yet this would be a disappointing conclusion. You may already be a member of an organisation that promises a fertile territory for research. This may be your employing organisation or a social body of which you are a member. One of Phil's students undertook research in his church community. He was a member of the church council and conducted observational research on the way in which decisions were reached in council meetings. A more specific focus was adopted by another of our students. She was a member of a school governing body. Her specific hypothesis was that the focus of decision-making power was the head teacher. Her study confirmed this hypothesis. All the significant decisions were in effect taken prior to governors' meetings as a consequence of the head teacher canvassing the support of those committee members whom he defined as 'influential'.

So, adopting the participant observer role as an existing member of an organisation does present opportunities to you. However, it also has its dangers. We shall deal with these later.

8.3 Participant observation: researcher roles

We have explained what participant observation is, but we have not explained clearly what participant observers do. A number of questions may have occurred to you. For example, should the participant observer keep his or her purpose concealed? Does the participant observer need to be an employee or an organisational member, albeit temporary? Can the participant observer just observe? The answers here are not straightforward. The role you play as participant observer will be determined by a number of factors. However, before examining those factors, we need to look at the different roles in which the participant observer may be cast.

Gill and Johnson (1997) develop a fourfold categorisation (Figure 8.1) of the role the participant observer can adopt. The roles are:

- complete participant;
- complete observer;
- observer as participant;
- participant as observer.

The first two of these roles, the complete participant and the complete observer, involve you as the researcher in concealing your identity. This has the significant advantage of your not conditioning the behaviour of the research subjects you are

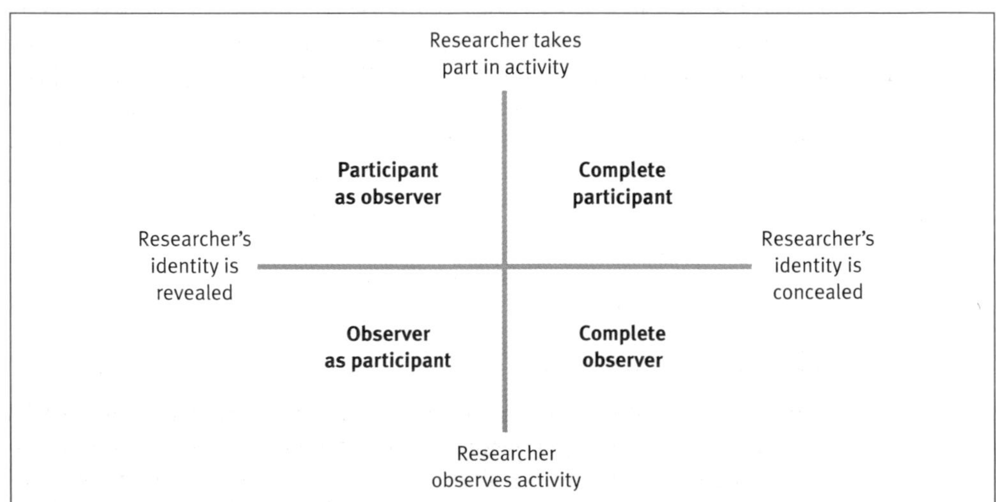

Figure 8.1 Typology of participant observation researcher roles

studying. The second two, observer as participant and participant as observer, entail your revealing your purpose to those with whom you are mixing in the research setting. Ethically, the latter two roles are less problematic.

Complete participant

The *complete participant* role sees you as the researcher attempting to become a member of the group in which you are performing research. You do not reveal your true purpose to the group members. You may be able to justify this role on pure research grounds in the light of your research questions and objectives. For example, you may be interested to know the extent of lunchtime drinking in a particular work setting. You would probably be keen to discover which particular employees drink at lunchtimes, what they drink, how much they drink, and how they explain their drinking. Were you to explain your research objectives to the group you wished to study it is rather unlikely that they would cooperate since employers would usually discourage lunchtime drinking. In addition, they might see your research activity as prying.

This example raises questions of ethics. You are in a position where you are 'spying' on people who have probably become your friends as well as colleagues. They may have learned to trust you with information that they would not share were they to know your true purpose. On these grounds alone you may agree with us that this is a role that the researcher should not adopt.

There are also objections on pure research grounds. You may work so hard at gaining the trust of your 'colleagues', and value that trust when it is gained, that you lose sight of your research purpose. The objective, detached perspective all researchers need will be lost.

Complete observer

Here too you would not reveal the purpose of your activity to those you were observing. However, unlike the complete participant role, you do not take part in the activities of the group. For example, the *complete observer* role may be used in studying consumer behaviour in supermarkets. Your research question may concern your wish to observe consumers at the checkout. Which checkouts do they choose? How much interaction is there with fellow shoppers and the cashier? How do they appear to be influenced by the attitude of the cashier? What level of impatience is displayed when delays are experienced? This behaviour may be observed by the researcher being located near the checkout in an unobtrusive way. The patterns of behaviour displayed may be the precursor to research by structured observation (Section 8.5). This would be the exploratory stage of this research.

Observer as participant

You might adopt the role of *observer as participant* in an outward-bound course to assist team building if you were attending to observe without taking part in the activities in the same way as the 'real' candidates. In other words, you would be a 'spectator'. However, your identity as a researcher would be clear to all concerned. They would know your purpose, as would the trainers running the course. This would present the advantage of your being able to focus on your researcher role. For example, you would be able to jot down insights as they occurred to you. You would be able to concentrate on your discussions with the participants. What you would lose, of course, would be the emotional involvement: really knowing what it feels like to be on the receiving end of the experience.

Participant as observer

In the role of *participant as observer* you reveal your purpose as a researcher. Both you and the subjects are aware of the fact that it is a fieldwork relationship (Ackroyd and Hughes, 1992). You are particularly interested to gain the trust of the group. This was the role adopted by the sociologist Punch (1993) in his study of police work in Amsterdam. Because of the trust developed by Punch with police officers whom he was researching he was able to gain admission to activities that otherwise would have been 'out of bounds' to him. Because his identity as researcher was clear he could ask questions of his subjects to enhance his understanding. Robson (2002:317) argues that this leads to another advantage of this role. This is that key informants are likely to adopt a perspective of *analytic reflection* on the processes in which they are involved.

worked example

Adopting the participant as observer role

Your research project is concerned with your wishing to understand what the experience of a one-day assessment centre is like for the graduates who attend these as prospective employees.

You decide that there is no better way of doing this than 'getting in on the action' and being a guinea-pig. You negotiate access with the company managers who are running the assessment centre. You also explain your research to the graduates who are there 'for real'. You become involved in all the activities and speak to as many of your fellow graduates as possible in order to discover their feelings about the experience. At the end of the day you are utterly exhausted!

Factors that will determine the choice of participant observer role

The purpose of your research

You should always be guided by the appropriateness of the method for the research question(s) and objectives. A research question about developing an understanding of a phenomenon about which the research subjects would be naturally defensive is one that lends itself to the complete participant role. Discovering what it is like to be a participant on a particular training course is more appropriate to the participant as observer role.

The time you have to devote to your research

Some of the roles covered above may be very time consuming. If you are really to develop a rich and deep understanding of an organisational phenomenon it will need much careful study. A period of attachment to the organisation will often be necessary. However, many full-time courses have placement opportunities that may be used for this purpose. In addition, most full-time students now have part-time jobs, which provide wonderful opportunities to understand the 'meanings' that their fellow employees, for whom the work is their main occupation, attach to a variety of organisational processes. What is needed is a creative perspective on what constitutes research and research opportunities. The possibilities are endless.

The degree to which you feel suited to participant observation

Delbridge and Kirkpatrick (1994) note that not everybody is suited to this type of research. Much of it relies on the building of relationships with others. A certain amount of personal flexibility is also needed. As the participant observer you have to be 'all things to all people'. Your own personality must be suppressed to a greater extent. This is not something with which you may feel comfortable.

Organisational access

This may present a problem for some researchers. It is obviously a key issue. More is said about gaining access to organisations for research in Section 5.3.

Ethical considerations

The degree to which you reveal your identity as the researcher will be dictated by ethical considerations. The topic of ethics in research is dealt with in detail in Section 5.4.

8.4 Participant observation: data collection and analysis

Delbridge and Kirkpatrick (1994) categorise the types of data generated by participant observation as 'primary', 'secondary' and 'experiential'.

Primary observations are those where you would note what happened or what was said at the time. Keeping a diary is a good way of doing this.

Secondary observations are statements by observers of what happened or was said. This necessarily involves those observers' interpretations.

Experiential data are those data on your perceptions and feelings as you experience the process you are researching. Keeping a diary of these perceptions proves a valuable source of data when the time comes to write up your research. This may also include notes on how you feel that your values have intervened, or changed, over the research process.

Finally, you will also collect data on factors material to the research setting: for example, roles played by key participants and how these may have changed; organisational structures and communication patterns.

Data collection

What will be clear from the types of data you will collect as the participant observer is that formal set-piece interviewing is unlikely to take place. Such 'interviewing' that does take place is likely to be informal discussion. It will be part of the overall approach of asking questions that should be adopted in this research method. These questions are of two types (Robson, 2002): first, to informants to clarify the situations you have observed and, second, to yourself to clarify the situation and the accounts given of the situation.

worked example

A diary account

For a period of ten months between 1944 and 1945 Donald Roy worked on the factory floor as a production operative in order to study how workers restricted production. He kept a diary, an extract of which is reproduced below as an example of a narrative account. The 'technical' content of the piece is irrelevant. What is important is to get a feel for narrative account.

> On April 7 I was able to enjoy four hours of 'free time'.
>
> I turned out 43 pieces in the four hours from 3 to 7, averaging nearly 11 an hour (or $2.085 per hour). At 7 o'clock there were only 23 pieces left in the lot, and I knew there would be no point in building up a kitty for Monday if Joe punched off the job before I got to work. I could not go ahead with the next order . . . because the new ruling made presentation of a work order to the stock-chaser necessary before material could be brought up. So I was stymied and could do nothing for the rest of the day. I had 43 pieces plus 11 from yesterday's kitty to turn in for a total of 54.

Source: Roy (1952:432)

Of course, the data that you collect depend on your research question(s) and objectives which have given a particular focus to your observation. Robson (2002:320) suggests that your data may well be classed as '*descriptive observation*' and '*narrative account*'. In descriptive observation you may concentrate on observing the physical setting, the key participants and their activities, particular events and their sequence and the attendant processes and emotions involved. This description may be the basis for your writing of a narrative account, in much the same way as an investigative journalist would write one. However, Robson (2002) makes the point forcefully that the researcher must go much further than the journalist. Your job as the researcher is to go on and develop a framework of theory that will help you to understand, and to explain to others, what is going on in the research setting you are studying.

How you record your data will depend to a great extent on the role you play as the participant observer. The more 'open' you are the more possible it will be for you to make notes at the time the event is being observed or reported. In any event, there is one golden rule: recording must take place on the same day as the fieldwork in order that you do not forget valuable data. The importance placed on this by one complete participant observer, working in a bakery, is evident from the following quotation:

> Right from the start I found it impossible to keep everything I wanted in my head until the end of the day . . . and had to take rough notes as I was going along. But I was 'stuck on the line', and had nowhere to retire to privately to note things down. Eventually, the wheeze of using innocently provided lavatory cubicles occurred to me. Looking back, all my notes for that third summer were on Bronco toilet paper! Apart from the awkward tendency for pencilled notes to be self-erasing from hard

> toilet paper ... my frequent requests for 'time out' after interesting happenings or conversations in the bakehouse and the amount of time that I was spending in the lavatory began to get noticed ...
>
> Ditton (1977), cited in Bryman (1989:145)

Data analysis

We deal with this in more depth in Chapters 11 and 12. However, you should bear in mind that in participant observation research your data collection and analysis activity may be part of the same process. That is, you will be carrying out analysis and collection of data simultaneously. Let us say you were acting as the complete participant observer in attempting to establish 'what is going on' in terms of sex discrimination at the workplace in which you were researching. You would observe informal banter, hear conversations of a discriminatory nature, talk to those who 'approved' and 'disapproved' of the activity. All this would be part of your everyday work. You might mix socially with colleagues in situations where discriminatory attitudes and behaviour might be evident. All these events would yield data that you would record, as far as possible, on the spot, or at least write up soon afterwards. You would turn these rough notes into something rather more systematic along the lines of the procedures suggested in Section 12.4. What would be emerging is what the investigative journalist might call 'promising lines of enquiry' that you might wish to follow up in your continued observation. However, remember that the journalist is interested in the story, while you are interested in generating a theory to help you understand 'what is going on'. This will lead you to adopt the researcher's equivalent of 'promising lines of enquiry'. A common approach to this is what is called *analytic induction*.

Threats to reliability and validity

Participant observation is very high on *ecological validity* because it involves studying social phenomena in their natural contexts. Nonetheless, participant observation is subject to the same threats to validity as noted in Section 4.4 (e.g. history and maturation), although the fact that your study is likely to be over an extended time period will overcome most of these.

worked example

Using analytic induction

As a result of data already collected you form an initial hypothesis that pilfering at the workplace at which you were researching was restricted to a group of employees who mixed socially outside work, and they defined this as an extension of their social activities. You search for further evidence to support this hypothesis.

You find that the pilfering group included colleagues who do not mix socially, although these 'new' pilferers do define this as an extension of their own individual social activities.

You redefine your hypothesis to state that pilferers at your workplace define their workplace pilfering as an extension of their social activities: that is, they make no distinction in this respect between work and non-work situations.

Further data collection supports this refined hypothesis.

▶

NB: This worked example is a simplified version of analytic induction. It involves only *one* redefinition of the hypothesis whereas several may be involved. Moreover, an alternative to the redefining of the hypothesis is redefining the phenomenon to be explained so that the particular instance that casts doubt on the hypothesis is excluded (Denzin, 1989).

The greatest threat to the reliability of your research conclusions produced as a result of a participant observation study is that of *observer bias*. As Delbridge and Kirkpatrick (1994:43) note, 'because we are part of the social world we are studying we cannot detach ourselves from it, or for that matter avoid relying on our common sense knowledge and life experiences when we try to interpret it'.

The propensity that we all have for our own perceptions to colour our interpretation of what we believe to be 'true' is well known. What we advocate here is that we cannot avoid observer bias. All we can do is to be aware of the threat to reliability it poses and seek to control it.

The first way this may be done is to revert to the process of asking yourself questions about your conclusions: Did she really mean that? What other interpretations could I have put on this? The second way is that adopted by our student who was researching decision-making power in a school governing body. Her approach was to use *informant verification*. After each of her informal discussions with fellow PTA members she wrote these up, including her own conclusions as to the meanings of the discussions in the light of her research hypothesis. She then presented the written accounts to her informants for them to verify the content. Not only is this a form of *triangulation*, but it can be a source of new interpretations that have not occurred to the researcher. This method of triangulation is also one that can be used with more formal interview results.

Advantages and disadvantages of participant observation

Before leaving the subject of participant observation, we summarise some of the advantages and disadvantages of this method.

Advantages of participant observation

- It is good at explaining 'what is going on' in particular social situations.
- It heightens the researcher's awareness of significant social processes.
- It is particularly useful for researchers working within their own organisations.
- Some participant observation affords the opportunity for the researcher to experience 'for real' the emotions of those who are being researched.
- Virtually all data collected are useful.

Disadvantages of participant observation

- It can be very time consuming.

- It can pose difficult ethical dilemmas for the researcher.
- There can be high levels of role conflict for the researcher (e.g. 'colleague' versus researcher).
- The closeness of the researcher to the situation being observed can lead to significant observer bias.
- The participant observer role is a very demanding one, to which not all researchers will be suited.
- Access to organisations may be difficult.
- Data recording is often very difficult for the researcher.

8.5 Structured observation: an introduction

So far this chapter might have given you the impression that research using observational techniques is unsystematic and unstructured. This need not be the case. A sound research design based on clear research questions and objectives using participant observation should be highly systematic. However, it would be true to say that the degree of predetermined structure in participant observation may not be that high. After all, one of the strengths of this method is its responsiveness.

In contrast, structured observation is systematic and has a high level of predetermined structure. If you use this method in your data collection strategy you will be adopting a more detached stance. Your concern would be in quantifying behaviour. As such, structured observation may form only a part of your data collection approach because its function is to tell you how often things happen rather than why they happen. Once again we see that all research methods have their place in an overall research strategy. What is important is choosing the method that meets the research questions and objectives.

worked example

Using self-completion diaries

As part of a review of staffing levels in residential homes for elderly people Mark needed to establish:

- how much time care assistants actually spent on various caring activities;
- how the pattern of caring activities varied throughout a 24-hour day;
- how much time care assistants felt that they needed to undertake their caring activities adequately.

Ideally this would have involved structured observation of each care assistant throughout their working day. Unfortunately there were insufficient resources and so, in consultation with care assistants and their managers, a self-completion diary form was devised. In the extract below 'act.' refers to actual time spent on each activity; 'adeq.' refers to the amount of time that care assistants felt they needed to undertake their caring activities adequately.

Care Assistant's name:

Residential home:

Date: Time started work: a.m. / p.m.

hour ▶	1		2		3		4	
minutes taken ▶	act.	adeq.	act.	adeq.	act.	adeq.	act.	adeq.
activity ▼								
washing / bathing								
dressing / undressing								
eating / drinking								
continence / toileting								
personal hygiene								
mobility / lifting								
medication								
counselling								
social interaction								

After pilot testing of the diary form, care assistants received training on its completion. This focused on the importance of being honest, on precise definitions of activities, and on how to fill in the form. A definition of each activity was also provided. Data were subsequently collected from 10 residential homes over a two-week period.

Situations in which structured observation may be used

The most powerful image that occurs to many people when they think of structured observation is that of the 'time-and-motion' study expert. This inscrutable figure stalked the factory floor, complete with clipboard and pencil, making notes on what tasks machine operators were performing and how long these tasks took. This may seem to you a long way from the definition of 'research' that we have assumed in this book. Is it not simply fact-finding? Yes it is, but establishing straightforward facts may play an important role in answering your research questions and meeting your objectives. This is straightforward descriptive research, as we noted in Section 4.2.

One of the best-known examples of managerial research that used structured observation as part of its data collection approach was the study of the work of senior managers by Mintzberg (1973). This led to Mintzberg casting doubt on the long-held theory that managerial work was a rational process of planning, controlling and directing. Mintzberg studied what five chief executives actually did during one of each of the executives' working weeks. He did this by direct observation and the recording of events on three predetermined coding schedules. This followed a period of 'unstructured' observation in which the categories of activity that formed the basis of the coding schedules he used were developed. So Mintzberg 'grounded' (see Section 12.6 for an explanation of grounded theory) his structured observation on data collected in the period of participant observation.

Of course, studying what job-holders of the type not normally 'observed' actually do in their everyday lives lends itself to approaches other than observation. Self-completion of diaries is one approach that is often used. However, involvement of the researcher in the process is one that lends a degree of impartiality and thoroughness. This has benefits for reliability and validity that may not be evident when the job-holder is the 'observer'.

Advantages and disadvantages of structured observation

As with other research methods, structured observation has its advantages and disadvantages.

Advantages of structured observation

- It can be used by anyone after suitable training in the use of the measuring instrument. Therefore you could delegate this extremely time-consuming task. In addition, structured observation may be carried out simultaneously in different locations. This would present the opportunity of comparison between locations.
- It should yield highly *reliable* results by virtue of its replicability. We shall deal with threats to reliability in Section 8.6 but suffice it to say here that the easier the observation instrument to use and understand, the more reliable the results will be.
- Structured observation is capable of more than simply observing the frequency of events. It is also possible to record the relationship between events. For example, is the visit to the retail chemist's counter to present a prescription preceded by an examination of merchandise unrelated to the prescription transaction?
- The method allows the collection of data at the time they occur in their natural setting. Therefore there is no need to depend on 'second-hand' accounts of phenomena from respondents who put their own interpretation on events.
- Structured observation secures information that most participants would ignore because to them it was too mundane or irrelevant.

Disadvantages of structured observation

- The observer must be in the research setting when the phenomena under study are taking place.
- Research results are limited to overt action or surface indicators from which the observer must make inferences.
- Data are slow and expensive to collect.

8.6 Structured observation: data collection and analysis

Using coding schedules to collect data

One of the key decisions you will need to make before undertaking structured observation is whether you use an 'off-the-shelf' coding schedule or design your own. You will hardly be surprised to hear us say that this should depend on your research questions and objectives. What follows are two sets of guidelines for assessing the suitability of existing tailor-made coding schedules.

Choosing an 'off-the-shelf ' coding schedule

There are a number of questions you should ask yourself when choosing an 'off-the-shelf' coding schedule. These are detailed in Box 8.1.

One of the most frequent uses of established coding schedules in management and business is for recording interpersonal interactions in social situations such as meetings or negotiations. This lends itself to structured observation particularly well. Figure 8.2 is an example of just such an 'off-the-shelf' coding schedule that may be used for this purpose.

We would encourage you to use an 'off-the-shelf' coding schedule if you can find one that is suitable. Not only will it save you a lot of time, but it will be tried and tested. Therefore it should make your results and conclusions more reliable and valid.

Box 8.1 Checklist of questions to ask when choosing an 'off-the-shelf' coding schedule

- ✓ For what purpose was the coding schedule developed? Is it consistent with your research question(s) and objectives? (It should be.)
- ✓ Is there overlap between the behaviours to be observed? (There should not be.)
- ✓ Are all behaviours in which you are interested covered by the schedule? (They should be.)
- ✓ Are the behaviours sufficiently clearly specified so that all observers will place behaviours in the same category? (They should be.)
- ✓ Is any observer interpretation necessary? (It should not be.)
- ✓ Are codes to be used indicated on the recording form to avoid the necessity for memorisation by the observer? (They should be.)
- ✓ Will the behaviours to be observed be relevant to the inferences you make? (They should be.)
- ✓ Have all sources of observer bias been eliminated? (They should have been.)

Source: Developed from Walker (1985)

However, you may decide that no 'off-the-shelf' coding schedule is suitable for your purposes. In this case you will need to develop your own schedule. Table 8.1 contains useful guidelines for this activity. The observation categories in your schedule should be devised to be consistent with your research question(s) and objectives. To ensure

Nature of group:

Nature of activity:

Date Name of observer:

Initial arrangement of group:

C D
B E
A F

Name of group members (or reference letters)	A	B	C	D	E	F
Taking initiative – e.g. attempted leadership, seeking suggestions, offering directions.						
Brainstorming – e.g. offering ideas or suggestions, however valid						
Offering positive ideas – e.g. making helpful suggestions, attempting to problem-solve						
Drawing in others – e.g. encouraging contributions, seeking ideas and opinions						
Being responsive to others – e.g. giving encouragement and support, building on ideas						
Harmonising – e.g. acting as peacemaker, calming things down, compromising						
Challenging – e.g. seeking justification, showing disagreement in a constructive way						
Being obstructive – e.g. criticising, putting others down, blocking contributions						
Clarifying/summarising – e.g. linking ideas, checking progress, clarifying objectives/proposals						
Performing group roles – e.g. spokesperson, recorder, time-keeper, humorist						

Other comments

Figure 8.2 Recording sheet for observing behaviour in groups

Source: Mullins, L.J. (2002) *Management and Organisational Behaviour*, 6th edn, Financial Times Prentice Hall. © L.J. Mullins 2002. Reprinted with permission.

Table 8.1 Guidelines for developing your own coding schedule

Attribute	*Comment*
Focused	Do not observe and record all that is going on. Concern yourself only with what is strictly relevant
Unambiguous	Therefore requiring the absolute minimum of observer interpretation
Non-context dependent	The observer's job is more difficult if the coding of behaviours is dependent on the context in which the behaviour occurs. It may be essential for your research question(s) and objectives to record contextual data, but this should be kept to a minimum
Explicitly defined	Provide examples for the observer (even if this is you) of behaviours that fall into each category and those that do not
Exhaustive	Ensure that it is always possible to make a coding for those behaviours you wish to observe
Mutually exclusive	Ensure that there is no overlap between behaviour categories
Easy to record	The observer must be able to tick the correct box quickly without having to memorise appropriate categories

Source: Developed from Robson (2002)

ease of use and reliability the categories should reflect the attributes shown in Table 8.1.

An alternative to the use of an 'off-the-shelf' coding schedule or the development of your own may be a combination of the two. If this is the option that seems most appropriate in the light of your research question(s) and objectives, we recommend that you still use the checklist in Box 8.1 and the guidelines in Table 8.1 to ensure that your schedule is as valid and reliable as possible.

Data analysis

The complexity of your analysis will depend on your research question(s) and objectives. It may be that you are using Figure 8.2 to establish the amount of interactions by category in order to relate the result to the output of the meeting. This may enable you to conclude that 'positive' behaviours (e.g. brainstorming) may be more strongly associated with meetings that make clear decisions than 'negative' behaviours (e.g. being obstructive). Simple manual analysis may be sufficient for this purpose.

Alternatively, you may be using Figure 8.2 to see what patterns emerge. It may be that the amount of interactions varies by the nature of the group or its activity, or that seating position is associated with the amount of contributions. Patterns reflecting relationships between amounts of interaction categories may become evident (for example, when 'drawing in others' was high 'clarifying/summarising' was also high). This level of analysis is obviously more complex and will need computer software to calculate the cross-classifications. Chapter 11, Section 11.2 contains guidance on preparing data for quantitative analysis by computer.

Threats to validity and reliability

The main threats here are ones of reliability. This section deals with three of these: subject error, time error and observer effects.

Subject error

Subject error may cause your data to be unreliable. You may be concerned with observing the output of sales administrators as measured by the amount of orders they process in a day. Subject error may be evident if you chose administrators in a section that was short-staffed owing to illness. This may mean that they were having to spend more time answering telephones, and less time processing orders, as there were fewer people available to handle telephone calls. The message here is clear: choose subjects who in as many respects as possible are 'normal' examples of the population under study.

Time error

Closely related to the issue of subject error is that of *time error*. It is essential that the time at which you conduct the observation does not provide data that are untypical of the total time period in which you are interested. So the output of the sales administrators may be less in the immediate hour before lunch as their energy levels are lower. If you were interested in the amount of customers using a retail store you would need to conduct observations at different times of the day and week to provide a valid picture of total customer flow.

Observer effect

One of the most powerful threats to the validity and reliability of data collected through observation is that of *observer effect*. This is quite simply that the process of the observer's observation of behaviour changes the nature of that behaviour owing to the fact that the subject is conscious of being observed. The simplest way to overcome this effect is for the observation to take place in secret. However, this is often not possible, even if it were ethically sound to do so.

Robson (2002) notes two strategies for overcoming observer effect. The first, *minimal interaction*, means that the observer tries as much as possible to 'melt into the background' – having as little interaction as possible with the subjects of the observation. This may involve sitting in an unobtrusive position in the room and avoiding eye contact with those being observed. The second strategy is *habituation*, where the subjects being observed become familiar with the process of observation so that they take it for granted. Those of you who use a tape-recorder to record discussions may notice that initially the respondent is very wary of the machine, but after a short period this apprehension wears off and the machine is not noticed.

Adopting a strategy of habituation to reduce observer effect may mean that several observation sessions are necessary in the same research setting with the same subjects. As the observer effect diminishes, so the pattern of interaction will settle down into a predictable pattern.

8.7 Summary

- Participant observation is a method in which the researcher participates in the lives and activities of those whom they are studying. It is used to attempt to get to the root of 'what is going on' in a wide range of social settings.
- You may use the participant observation method in a student placement or you may already be a member of an organisation that will enable you to adopt the role of the practitioner–researcher.
- Participant observation means that you adopt a number of potential roles differentiated by the degree to which your identity is concealed from the subjects of the research and the degree to which you participate in the events you are studying.
- Participant observation must avoid the trap of mere storytelling. The purpose is to develop theory.
- A prevalent form of data analysis used in participant observation is analytic induction. This may lead to an initial hypothesis being redeveloped more than once.
- Structured observation is concerned with the frequency of events. It is characterised by a high level of predetermined structure and quantitative analysis.
- A choice may be made between 'off-the-shelf' coding schedules and a schedule that you design for your own purpose. Alternatively you may decide to use a 'hybrid'.
- The main threats to reliability and validity inherent in structured observation are subject error, time error and observer effects.

self-check Questions

8.1 You have been asked to give a presentation to a group of managers at the accountancy firm in which you are hoping to negotiate access for research. You wish to pursue the research question, 'What are the informal rules that govern the way in which trainee accountants work, and how do they learn these rules?'

You realise that talk of 'attempting to learn the trainee accountants' symbolic world' would do little to help your cause with this group of non-research-minded business people. However, you wish to point out some of the benefits to the organisation that your research may yield. Outline what you believe these would be.

8.2 You are a building society branch manager. You feel your staff are too reluctant to generate sales 'leads' from ordinary investors and borrowers, which may be passed on to the society's consultants in order that they can attempt to sell life insurance policies, pensions and unit trusts. You would like to understand the reasons for their reluctance. As the participant observer, how would you go about this?

8.3 You are conducting your research project on the extent to which staff become involved in the decision-making processes conducted by a newly privatised regional electricity supplier. Staff 'involvement' is a new thing in the company, and senior managers want to get some idea of 'how it is working'.

A main part of the involvement strategy is to have regular team meetings where staff can have their 'say'. You have been given access to these meetings. You decide that you will observe the meetings to get some feel for how they are working.

How would you record your observations?

8.4 Look again at Figure 8.2 and Box 8.1. Ask the questions contained in Box 8.1 of the coding schedule in Figure 8.2. How well does it match?

progressing your research project

Deciding on the appropriateness of observation

- ☐ Return to your research question(s) and objectives. Decide on how appropriate it would be to use observation as part of your research strategy.
- ☐ If you decide that this is appropriate, explain the relationship between your research question(s) and objectives and observation. If you decide that using observation is not appropriate, justify your decision.
- ☐ Look again at the previous paragraph and ensure that you have responded for both participant observation and structured observation *separately*.
- ☐ If you decide that participant observation is appropriate, what practical problems do you foresee? Are you likely to be faced with any moral dilemmas? How might you overcome both sets of problems?
- ☐ If you decide that participant observation is appropriate, what threats to validity and reliability are you likely to encounter? How might you overcome these?
- ☐ If you decide that structured observation is appropriate, what practical problems do you foresee? How might you overcome these?
- ☐ If you decide that structured observation is appropriate, what threats to validity and reliability are you likely to encounter? How might you overcome these?
- ☐ If you decide that structured observation is appropriate, design your own research instrument.

References

Ackroyd, S. and Hughes, J. (1992) *Data Collection in Context* (2nd edn), London, Longman.

Bryman, A. (1989) *Research Methods and Organisation Studies*, London, Unwin Hyman.

Delbridge, R. and Kirkpatrick, I. (1994) 'Theory and practice of participant observation', *in* Wass, V. and Wells, P. (eds), *Principles and Practice in Business and Management Research*, Aldershot, Dartmouth, pp. 35–62.

Denzin, N. (1989) *The Research Act: A Theoretical Introduction to Sociological Methods* (3rd edn), Englewood Cliffs, NJ, Prentice-Hall.

Ditton, J. (1977) *Part-Time Crime: An Ethnography of Fiddling and Pilferage*, London, Macmillan.

Gill, J. and Johnson, P. (1997) *Research Methods for Managers* (2nd edn), London, Paul Chapman.

Mintzberg, H. (1973) *The Nature of Managerial Work*, New York, Harper & Row.

Mullins, L. (2002) *Management and Organisational Behaviour* (6th edn), Harlow, Financial Times Prentice Hall.

Punch, M. (1993) 'Observation and the police: the research experience', *in* Hammersley, M., *Social Research: Philosophy, Politics and Practice*, London, Sage, pp. 181–99.

Robson, C. (2002) *Real World Research* (2nd edn), Oxford, Blackwell.

Rosen, M. (1991) 'Breakfast at Spiro's dramaturgy and dominance', *in* Frost, P., Moore, L., Louis, M., Lundberg, C. and Martin, J. (eds), *Reframing Organisational Culture*, Newbury Park, CA, Sage, pp. 77–89.

Roy, D. (1952) 'Quota restriction and goldbricking in a machine shop', *American Journal of Sociology*, 57:427–42.

Walker, R. (1985) *Doing Research: A Handbook for Teachers*, London, Methuen.

Whyte, W. (1955) *Street Corner Society* (2nd edn), Chicago, IL, University of Chicago Press.

Further reading

Ackroyd, S. and Hughes, J. (1992) *Data Collection in Context* (2nd edn), London, Longman. Chapter 6 contains a helpful analysis of the origins of and problems with participant observation. It also has a full analysis of symbolic interactionism.

Hammersley, M. and Atkinson, P. (1995) *Ethnography Principles in Practice* (2nd edn), London, Routledge. Chapters 4 and 8 on field relations and data analysis in participant observation are well worth reading.

Mintzberg, H. (1973) *The Nature of Managerial Work*, New York, Harper & Row. Appendix C has a full account of the methodology that Mintzberg employed. You will be struck by how such a seemingly simple methodology can lead to such important conclusions.

Punch, M. (1993) 'Observation and the police: the research experience', *in* Hammersley, M. (ed.), *Social Research: Philosophy, Politics and Practice*, London, Sage, pp. 181–99. An absorbing account of fieldwork experience with the Amsterdam police that makes riveting reading; particularly good at the process of negotiating relationships with fellow participants.

Robson, C. (2002) *Real World Research* (2nd edn), Oxford, Blackwell. Chapter 11 is a most thorough and practical guide to observational methods. There is an interesting section at the end of the chapter on inter-observer reliability that you should look at if you intend to use a number of observers.

Taylor, S. and Bogdan, R. (1984) *Introduction to Qualitative Research Methods: A Guidebook and Resource*, New York, Wiley. Chapters 2 and 3 are very practical accounts of how to approach and conduct participant observation.

CASE 8 Customer satisfaction on a long-haul tour holiday

Expeditions is a successful, specialist, long-haul tour operator based in London. Set up in the early 1980s it offers a portfolio of worldwide, small group, long-haul, activity-based holidays. As a result of end-of-tour questionnaires the three senior managers of Expeditions considered that they had a good knowledge of their clients and their satisfaction with various aspects of the long-haul tour holidays they had taken with the company.

Sometimes the company's senior managers attended trade association meetings and also presentations attended by academics. In such a meeting Ric Melody, one of the senior managers, was intrigued by, although highly sceptical of, an academic presentation by a Dr Suzanne Martin. In this she argued that observation provided a powerful research tool, especially for research that sought to understand and explain customer satisfaction (see Bowen, 2001).

Ric arranged a meeting with Suzanne, urged on by the knowledge that a key competitor had just started to consider an ad hoc programme of tourist observation. After the meeting, Ric began to wonder whether he might have only a superficial knowledge of his customers' behaviours and, in particular, of what satisfied them. He began to think about what role the tour leader, other employees, tourists and other factors played in his customers' satisfaction. Over a few hours he developed two questions to which he wanted to know the answers:

1 What factors contribute to Expeditions' customers' satisfaction?

2 Through what processes do these factors become evident during the customers' holiday experiences?

A study of the Expeditions client base suggested that Suzanne matched the profile of the company's clients. This meant she could be a suitable observer of one or more chosen tours. Suzanne insisted that, although she would tell other people on the tour she was a university lecturer, the actual observing itself would be covert. After negotiating ethical approval from her university, she was booked as a tour member onto a 12-day tour of Malaysia.

On the first day, Suzanne approached her observations from a wide focus. Subsequently she narrowed down to the two research questions. Her initial observations allowed her to become familiar with the workings of the tour group; the emergent patterns of everyday life in terms of activities, transport and accommodation; characteristics of individuals within the group and the initial relationships between them. It also allowed her to become familiar with Malaysia. Suzanne's informal conversations and casual questioning resembled those of ordinary everyday life. From the first day, there were many listening opportunities. Of course, little could be accomplished without trusting relationships between Suzanne and the other tour members. This required her to act fully as one of the tour party and become fully engaged in events and conversations across the range of subgroups. Despite introducing herself as a lecturer, Suzanne had anticipated that the covert nature of her research would be both physically and psychologically demanding. In reality, the physical burden of recording observations was heavier than expected, and on many occasions this process lasted late into the night. However, the psychological burden was less than expected, probably because Suzanne's actual and assumed identities were very similar.

The main method of recording was through field notes compiled either during the day when opportunities arose or at the end of each day. These were recorded in a field notebook or on other unobtrusive materials such as writing paper or postcard letters. Photographs were also taken providing some documentary evidence and as an *aide-mémoire*. These activities, along with the collecting of tourist documents such as guides, brochures and maps, were seen by the other members of the party as perfectly normal tourist behaviour.

Suzanne used her notes, in the first instance, to write a narrative account of her experiences in the form of a chronological story. An extract from this follows – it describes part of an afternoon in a local market:

> . . . Asif (the tour leader) suggested a rearrangement of the taxi groups. . . and six group members. . . continued on with the taxis a short distance across country roads to where there were reputed to be numerous good local traders selling batik, silverware workers and a renowned kite-maker called Ismail (a craft particular to the East Coast and especially Kota Bahru). Although contact with locals, even buyer–seller contact, was not pronounced on the EM tour, this was an exception. Jane, Susi and Sinead, stirred on by the stories told by Robbi, attempted some elementary haggling over prices in a number of batik places, and Donald also attempted to do the same at Ismail the kite-maker's place. This was perhaps inappropriate . . . Ismail's pride in his handicraft was such that he spent close on 30 minutes sewing up two kites. . . in cardboard outer containers. The taxi drivers also entered into the spirit of the visit and bought miniature kites for themselves – Donald noticed this and believed that it rather suggested the specialness of their trip. So, a part of the pleasure from the afternoon was derived not only from the familiarity with the people within the EM group but also from the tentative, transient relationships with the local seller-people and taxi drivers.

Based on the narrative account, Suzanne drew out generalisations and attempted to identify and evaluate the role of factors either highlighted by the academic literature or suggested by interviews with tour managers as influencing customer satisfaction. The extract above illustrates one of her findings, namely the importance of others, including the host population, in creating customer satisfaction. This generalisation was supported by over 30 similar incidents in her narrative. Based upon her participation and observation Suzanne was therefore able to describe, analyse and interpret tour group experience and relate this to customer satisfaction.

After Suzanne presented her report, Ric and the other senior managers were convinced that she had discovered what their clients really thought, felt and did rather than what they said they thought, felt and did. Although Ric was not prepared to abandon the existing tourist questionnaires, he was keen to ensure that future customer research incorporated other approaches such as observation.

Reference

Bowen, D. (2001) Research of tourist satisfaction and dissatisfaction: overcoming the limitations of a positivist and quantitative approach, *Journal of Vacation Marketing*, 7:1, 31–40.

Questions

1. Why do you think Suzanne used participant observation to answer the research questions suggested by Ric?
2. How do you think Suzanne would have justified adopting the role of complete participant and undertaking covert observation to her university's ethic committee?
3. Why are businesses often reluctant to use a research method such as participant observation?

self-check Answers

8.1 The research question is very broad. It allows you plenty of scope to discover a host of interesting things about the world of the trainee accountant. Without doubt, one of the things you will emerge with a clear understanding of is what they like about their work and what they do not like. This has practical implications for the sort of people that the firm ought to recruit, how they should be trained and rewarded. You may learn about some of the short cuts practised by all occupations that may not be in the interest of the client. By the same token you will probably discover aspects of good practice that managers can disseminate to other accountants. The list of practical implications is endless.

All this assumes, of course, that you will supply the managers with some post-research feedback. This does raise issues of confidentiality, which you must have thought through beforehand.

8.2 This is a difficult one. The question of status may be a factor. However, this would depend on your relationship with the staff. If you are, say, of similar age and have an open, friendly, 'one of the team' relationship with them, then it may not be too difficult. The element of threat that would attend a less open relationship would not be present.

You could set aside a time each day to work on the counter in order really to get to know what life is like for them. Even if you have done their job, you may have forgotten what it is like! It may have changed since your day. Direct conversations about lead generation would probably not feature in your research times. However, you would need to have a period of reflection after each 'research session' to think about the implications for your research question of what you have just experienced.

8.3 You may start your meetings' attendance with an unstructured approach where you simply get the 'feel' of what is happening. Analysis of the data you have collected will allow you to develop an observational instrument that can be used in further meetings you attend. This instrument would be based on a coding schedule that allowed you to record, among other things, the amount of contribution by each person at the meeting and the content of that contribution.

You would need to make sure that all those attending the meetings understood fully the purpose of your research. You would also be well advised to ensure that your findings were communicated to them.

8.4 Clearly there are some question marks about the coding schedule in Figure 8.2. There does appear to be some overlap in the behavioural categories covered in the schedule. For example, it could be difficult to distinguish between what is 'offering directions' (taking initiative) and 'offering ideas' (brainstorming). It might be even more difficult to draw a distinction between 'offering suggestions' (brainstorming) and 'making helpful suggestions' (offering positive ideas). Similarly, there does not appear to be much difference between the behaviours in 'drawing in others' and 'being responsive to others'. You may argue that the first is defined by *invitation*, the second by *response*. But making the distinction when the interactions are coming thick and fast in the research setting will be much less easy.

The point about all these potential confusions is that different observers may make different estimations. This obviously has potentially harmful implications for the reliability of the coding schedule.

A much smaller point is: How does the observer indicate on the schedule the occurrence of a particular interaction?

Chapter 9

Collecting primary data using semi-structured and in-depth interviews

By the end of this chapter you should be:

- able to classify research interviews in order to help you to understand the purpose of each type;
- aware of research situations favouring the use of semi-structured and in-depth interviews, and their limitations;
- able to analyse potential data quality issues and evaluate how to overcome these;
- able to consider the development of your competence to undertake semi-structured and in-depth interviews, and the logistical and resource issues that affect their use;
- aware of particular issues and advantages associated with the use of group interviews and those conducted by telephone.

9.1 Introduction

An interview is a purposeful discussion between two or more people (Kahn and Cannell, 1957). The use of interviews can help you to gather valid and reliable data that are relevant to your research question(s) and objectives. Where you have not yet formulated such a research question and objectives, an interview or interviews may help you to achieve this. In reality, the research interview is a general term for several types of interview. This fact is significant since the nature of any interview should be consistent with your research question(s) and objectives, the purpose of your research and the research strategy that you have adopted. We define types of interview in the next section of this chapter (Section 9.2) and show how these are related to particular research purposes. In order to provide a typology of research interviews we briefly outline all types in the next section, although the chapter will be concerned with those that we refer to as semi-structured and in-depth interviews.

Section 9.3 considers situations favouring the use of semi-structured and in-depth interviews. The following three sections examine issues associated with the use of these types of interview. Section 9.4 identifies data quality issues associated with their use and discusses how to overcome them. Section 9.5 considers the areas of competence that you will need to develop. Section 9.6 discusses logistical and resource issues and how to manage these. Throughout the discussion of issues related to the use of semi-structured and in-depth interviews the focus is centred on what you will need to consider in order to be able to conduct these interviews. To draw this consideration together, a checklist is presented in Section 9.7 that offers you advice about how to conduct these types of research interview. Finally, Section 9.8 considers the particular advantages and issues associated with the use of group interviews and those conducted by telephone.

9.2 Types of interview and their link to the purposes of research and research strategy

Types of interview

Interviews may be highly formalised and structured, using standardised questions for each respondent (Section 10.2), or they may be informal and unstructured conversations. In between there are intermediate positions. One typology that is commonly used is thus related to the level of formality and structure, whereby interviews may be categorised as one of:

- structured interviews (Section 10.2);
- semi-structured interviews;
- unstructured interviews.

Another typology (Healey, 1991; Healey and Rawlinson, 1993, 1994) differentiates between:

- standardised interviews;
- non-standardised interviews.

Robson (2002), based on the work of Powney and Watts (1987), refers to a different typology:

- respondent interviews;
- informant interviews.

There is overlap between these different typologies, although consideration of each typology adds to our overall understanding of the nature of research interviews.

Structured interviews use questionnaires based on a predetermined and *standardised* or identical set of questions (Section 10.2). You read out each question and then record the response on a standardised schedule, usually with pre-coded answers (Sections 10.4 and 11.2). While there is social interaction between you and the respondent, such as explanations that you will need to provide, you should read out the questions in the same tone of voice so that you do not indicate any bias.

By comparison, semi-structured and unstructured interviews are *non-standardised*. In *semi-structured interviews* the researcher will have a list of themes and questions to be covered, although these may vary from interview to interview. This means that you may omit some questions in particular interviews, given the specific organisational context that is encountered in relation to the research topic. The order of questions may also be varied depending on the flow of the conversation. On the other hand, additional questions may be required to explore your research question and objectives given the nature of events within particular organisations. The nature of the questions and the ensuing discussion mean that data will be recorded by note-taking, or perhaps by tape-recording the conversation (Section 9.5).

Unstructured interviews are informal. You would use these to explore in depth a general area in which you are interested. We therefore refer to these as *in-depth interviews* in this chapter and elsewhere in the book. There is no predetermined list of questions to work through in this situation, although you need to have a clear idea about the aspect or aspects that you want to explore. The interviewee is given the opportunity to talk freely about events, behaviour and beliefs in relation to the topic area, so that this type of interaction is sometimes called *non-directive*. It has been labelled as an *informant interview* since it is the interviewee's perceptions that guide the conduct of the interview. In comparison, a *respondent interview* is one where the interviewer directs the interview and the interviewee responds to the questions of the researcher (Easterby-Smith *et al.*, 2002; Ghauri and Grønhaug, 2002; Healey and Rawlinson, 1994; Robson, 2002).

We may also differentiate between types of interview related to the form of interaction that is established between the researcher and those who participate in this process. Interviews may be conducted on a one-to-one basis, between you and a single participant. Such interviews are most commonly conducted by meeting your participant 'face to face', but there may be some situations where you conduct an interview by telephone. There may be other situations where you conduct a semi-structured or in-depth interview on a group basis, where you meet with a small number of participants to explore an aspect of your research through a group discussion that you facilitate. These forms of interview are summarised in Figure 9.1. The discussion throughout most of this chapter applies to each of these forms. However, the final section (Section 9.8) includes specific consideration of the issues and advantages related to the use of a telephone interview as a substitute for a 'face-to-face' meeting and to the use of group interviews.

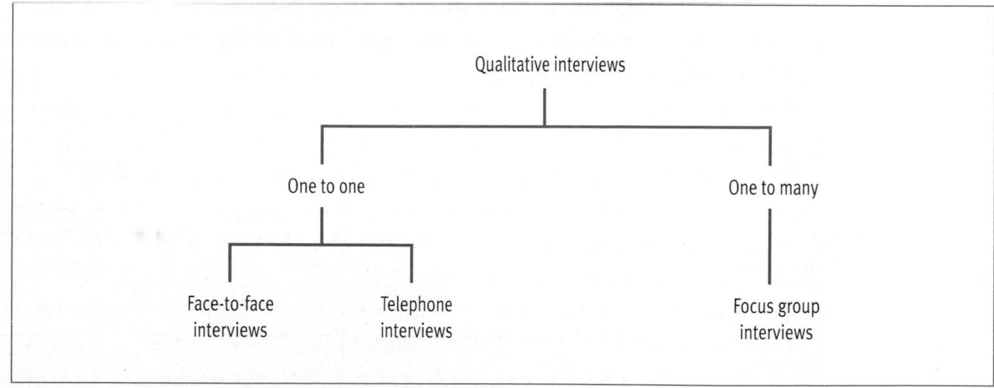

Figure 9.1 Forms of qualitative interview

Links to the purpose of research and research strategy

Each type of interview outlined above has a different purpose. Structured or standardised interviews can be used in survey research to gather data, which will then be the subject of quantitative analysis (Sections 11.3–11.5). Semi-structured and in-depth, or non-standardised, interviews are used in qualitative research in order to conduct discussions not only to reveal and understand the 'what' and the 'how' but also to place more emphasis on exploring the 'why'.

In Chapter 4 we outlined various ways in which your research can be classified. One classification is related to exploratory, descriptive and explanatory studies (Section 4.2). By examining the categories within this classification, we can see how the various types of interview may be used to gather information for, and assist the progress of, each kind of study:

- In an exploratory study, in-depth interviews can be very helpful to 'find out what is happening [and] to seek new insights' (Robson, 2002:59). Semi-structured interviews may also be used in relation to an exploratory study.
- In descriptive studies, structured interviews can be used as a means to identify general patterns.
- In an explanatory study, semi-structured interviews may be used in order to understand the relationships between variables, such as those revealed from a descriptive study (Section 4.2). Structured interviews may also be used in relation to an explanatory study, in a statistical sense (Section 11.5).

This is summarised in Table 9.1.

Your research may incorporate more than one type of interview. In a quantitative approach to research, for example, you may decide to use in-depth or non-standardised interviews initially to identify variables. The data that you gather from such exploratory interviews will be used in the design of your questionnaire or structured interview (Section 4.2). Semi-structured interviews may be used to explore and explain themes that have emerged from the use of your questionnaire (Wass and Wells, 1994). In addition to this staged approach, Healey and Rawlinson (1994:130) state that a combination of styles may be used within one interview: 'one section of an interview may ask a common set of factual questions . . . while in another section a semi-structured qualitative approach may be used to explore [responses]'. Wass and Wells (1994) make the point that interviews, presumably semi-structured or in-depth ones, may also be used as a means to validate findings from the use of questionnaires.

Table 9.1 Uses of different types of interview in each of the main research categories

	Exploratory	*Descriptive*	*Explanatory*
Structured		✓✓	✓
Semi-structured	✓		✓✓
In depth	✓✓		

✓✓ = more frequent, ✓ = less frequent

We can therefore see that the various types of interview have a number of potentially valuable uses in terms of undertaking your research project. The key point for you to consider is the need for consistency between the research question and objectives, the strategy to be employed and the methods of data collection used – their fitness for purpose.

worked example

Using interviews in a research project

During a research project to survey employee attitudes in a public sector organisation, the use of interviews was considered for each stage of this undertaking. The first stage of data collection consisted of a series of in-depth interviews, which were undertaken with a representative cross-section of employees, to reveal variables to be tested empirically at the second stage of the research project. A number of decisions were made about these in-depth interviews during the initial planning phase:

- to obtain personnel data relating to job categories and grades, gender, age and length of service in order to select a representative sample;
- to combine similar employee categories and to use group interviews in order to overcome time constraints and assist the researcher's capacity to handle the data to be collected. As a result six group interviews were arranged, consisting of about 10 participants in each group, in order to cover all employee categories;
- not to mix managerial and non-managerial participants within a group because this could have meant that non-managerial employees would be reluctant to take part.

At the next stage of the research project a decision had to be taken about whether to use a questionnaire or structured and standardised interviews. Because the number of employees in the organisational sample to be surveyed exceeded 30, it was decided that it would be more efficient to use a questionnaire rather than interviews (Wass and Wells, 1994).

After the analysis of the questionnaire data a further stage used a series of semi-structured interviews in order to explore and explain the findings obtained through the survey. These were also conducted as group interviews. Care was again taken in relation to the representativeness, size and composition of each group as well as in relation to choosing the setting for the discussion to occur.

9.3 Situations favouring qualitative research interviews

There are many situations in which the use of qualitative research interviews as a method of data collection may be advantageous, taking into account the points made in the previous section. These situations may be grouped into four categories:

- the nature of the approach to research;
- the significance of establishing personal contact;
- the nature of the data collection questions;
- length of time required and completeness of the process.

These are examined in turn.

The nature of the approach to research

We have discussed the way in which research can be classified according to its purpose. Where you are undertaking an exploratory study, or a study that includes an exploratory element, it is likely that you will include qualitative research interviews in your approach (Cooper and Schindler, 1998). Similarly, an explanatory study is also likely to include interviews in order for the researcher to be able to infer causal relationships between variables (Sections 4.2 and 10.4). Essentially, where it is necessary for you to understand the reasons for the decisions that your research participants have taken, or to understand the reasons for their attitudes and opinions, it will be necessary for you to conduct a qualitative interview.

Semi-structured and in-depth interviews also provide you with the opportunity to 'probe' answers, where you want your interviewees to explain, or build on, their responses. This is important if you are adopting a phenomenological approach, where you will be concerned to understand the meanings that respondents ascribe to various phenomena (Section 4.1). Interviewees may use words or ideas in a particular way, and the opportunity to probe these meanings will add significance and depth to the data obtained. It may also lead the discussion into areas that you had not previously considered but which are significant for your understanding, and which help you to address your research question and objectives, or indeed to help you formulate such a question. It also affords the interviewee an opportunity to hear herself or himself 'thinking aloud' about things she or he may not have previously thought about. The result should be that you are able to collect a rich and detailed set of data.

The significance of establishing personal contact

We have found that managers are more likely to agree to be interviewed, rather than complete a questionnaire, especially where the interview topic is seen to be interesting and relevant to their current work. An interview provides them with an opportunity to reflect on events without needing to write anything down. Other researchers report similar conclusions, where participants prefer to be interviewed rather than fill in a questionnaire (North *et al.*, 1983, cited in Healey, 1991). This situation also provides the opportunity for interviewees to receive feedback and personal assurance about the way in which information will be used.

Potential research participants who receive a questionnaire through the post may be reluctant to complete it for a number of reasons. They may feel that it is not appropriate to provide sensitive and confidential information to someone they have never met. They may also not completely trust the way in which the information provided is to be used. They may be reluctant to spend time providing written explanatory answers, where these are requested, especially if the meaning of any question is not entirely clear. The use of personal interviews, where appropriate, may therefore achieve a higher response rate than using questionnaires. Healey (1991:206) also makes the point that 'the interviewer . . . has more control over who answers the questions' in comparison with a questionnaire, which may be passed from one person to another.

The nature of the questions

An interview will undoubtedly be the most advantageous approach to attempt to obtain data in the following circumstances (Easterby-Smith *et al.*, 2002; Healey, 1991; Jankowicz, 2000):

- where there are a large number of questions to be answered;
- where the questions are either complex or open-ended;
- where the order and logic of questioning may need to be varied.

A semi-structured or in-depth interview will be most appropriate for the latter two types of situation.

worked example

The need to vary the order and logic of questioning

Adrian undertook a series of interviews, along with another colleague, into the management of redundancy in 40 organisations. It soon became evident that it would not be meaningful to ask exactly the same questions in each organisation. For example, some organisations made employees redundant only through a compulsory approach, whereas some other organisations relied on obtaining volunteers for redundancy. Another significant variable was associated with whether the organisation recognised trade unions in respect of any category of employees or whether it was non-unionised.

The impact of these and other variables meant that it was meaningless to ask exactly the same questions at each interview, even though many questions remained applicable in all cases and the underlying intention was to ensure consistency between interviews. It was not until each interview had started that they were able to learn which of these different variables operated within the particular organisation. This illustrates that a semi-structured or in-depth interview can allow for the flexibility that may well be required.

Length of time required and completeness of the process

Apart from the difficulty of trying to design a viable questionnaire schedule to cope with questions that are complex, or open ended, or large in number, the time needed to obtain the required data may mean that an interview is in any case the best or only alternative. In our experience, where expectations have been clearly established about the length of time required, and participants understand and agree with the objectives of the research interview, they have generally been willing to agree to be interviewed. Some negotiation is, in any case, possible and the interview can be arranged at a time when the interviewee will be under least pressure. We have found that our respondents tend to be generous with their time, and sometimes when interviews have been arranged to start at mid-morning they often arrange for lunch, which can allow the discussion and exploration of issues to continue. However, for those of you who fancy a free lunch, we do not want to raise your expectations falsely, and the start time for an interview should not be set with this in mind!

Your aim will be to obtain answers to all of the questions that you ask, allowing for the right of participants to decline to respond to any question, and where you conduct the event skilfully an interview is more likely to achieve this than the use of a self-administered or telephone questionnaire. Where your respondent does not provide an answer to a particular question or questions in an interview, you should be able to form some indication of why a response could not be provided. This may even lead you to modify the question or to compose another where this would be appropriate. Section 5.4 provides a consideration of the ethical issues associated with seeking to obtain answers.

While there are a number of situations favouring the use of qualitative research interviews, there are also a number of issues associated with them. The next three sections will describe issues associated with semi-structured and in-depth interviews, and discuss how you can manage them, under the following headings:

- data quality issues;
- the researcher's interviewing competence;
- logistical and resource issues.

9.4 Data quality issues and how to overcome them

Data quality issues

A number of data quality issues can be identified in relation to the use of semi-structured and in-depth interviews, related to:

- reliability;
- forms of bias;
- validity and generalisability.

These are discussed in turn.

The lack of standardisation in these interviews may lead to concerns about *reliability*. In relation to qualitative research, reliability is concerned with whether alternative researchers would reveal similar information (Easterby-Smith *et al.*, 2002; Healey and Rawlinson, 1994). The concern about reliability in these types of interview is also related to issues of bias. There are various types of bias to consider. The first of these is related to *interviewer bias*. This is where the comments, tone or non-verbal behaviour of the interviewer create bias in the way that interviewees respond to the questions being asked. This may be where you attempt to impose your own beliefs and frame of reference through the questions that you ask. It is also possible that you will demonstrate bias in the way you interpret responses (Easterby-Smith *et al.*, 2002). Where you are unable to develop the trust of the interviewee, or perhaps where your credibility is seen to be lacking, the value of the information given may also be limited, raising doubts about its validity and reliability.

Related to this is *interviewee* or *response bias*. This type of bias may be caused by perceptions about the interviewer, as referred to above, or in relation to perceived interviewer bias. However, the cause of this type of bias is not necessarily linked to any perception related to the interviewer. Taking part in an interview is an intrusive process. This is especially true in the case of in-depth or semi-structured interviews, where your aim will be to explore events or to seek explanations. The interviewee may, in principle, be willing to participate but may nevertheless be sensitive to the in-depth exploration of certain themes. Interviewees may therefore choose not to reveal and discuss an aspect of the topic that you wish to explore, because this would lead to probing questions that would intrude on sensitive information that they do not wish, or are not empowered, to discuss with you. The outcome of this may be that the interviewee provides a partial 'picture' of the situation that casts himself or herself in a 'socially desirable' role, or the organisation for which they work in a positive or even negative fashion.

Bias may also result from the nature of the individuals or organisational participants who agree to be interviewed. The time-consuming requirements of the interview process may result in a reduction in willingness to take part on behalf of some of those to whom you would like to talk. This may bias your sample from whom data are collected (Robson, 2002). This is an issue that you will need to consider carefully and attempt to overcome through the approach taken to sampling (Sections 6.2 and 6.3).

There is also likely to be an issue about the generalisability of the findings from qualitatively based interview studies, although the validity of such studies is not raised as an issue. If we consider *validity* first, this refers to the extent to which the researcher gains access to their participants' knowledge and experience, and is able to infer a meaning that the participant intended from the language that was used by this person. The high level of validity that is possible in relation to qualitative interviews that are conducted carefully is made clear by the following quotation:

> The main reason for the potential superiority of qualitative approaches for obtaining information is that the flexible and responsive interaction which is possible between interviewer and respondent(s) allows meanings to be probed, topics to be covered from a variety of angles and questions made clear to respondents.
>
> (Sykes, 1991:8, cited in Healey and Rawlinson, 1994:132)

However, qualitative research using semi-structured or in-depth interviews will not be able to be used to make *generalisations* about the entire population (whatever this may relate to in the context of the research topic) where this is based on a small and unrepresentative number of cases. This will be the situation in a case study approach (Yin, 1994).

Overcoming data quality issues

Reliability

One response to the issue of reliability is that the findings derived from using non-standardised research methods are not necessarily intended to be repeatable since they reflect reality at the time they were collected, in a situation which may be subject to change (Marshall and Rossman, 1999). The assumption behind this type of research is that the circumstances to be explored are complex and dynamic. The value of using this non-standardised approach is derived from the flexibility that you may use to explore the complexity of the topic. Therefore an attempt to ensure that qualitative, non-standardised research could be replicated by other researchers would not be realistic or feasible without undermining the strength of this type of research. Marshall and Rossman (1999) suggest that researchers using a qualitative, non-standardised approach need to make this clear – perhaps to transform an aspect perceived to be a weakness by some into a strength based on realistic assumptions about the ability to replicate research findings.

However, they suggest that where you use this approach you should make and retain notes relating to the design of the research, the reasons underpinning the choice of strategy and methods, and the data obtained. Justification of the choice of your research strategy and methods should initially be discussed in your research proposal. These records can be referred to by other researchers in order to understand the processes that you used and to enable them to reuse the data that you collected. The use of a qualitative approach should not lead to a lack of rigour in relation to the research process – if anything, greater rigour is required to overcome the views of those who may be wedded to the value of quantitative research to the exclusion of any other approach.

Interviewer and interviewee bias

Overcoming these forms of bias is related to the way in which qualitative research interviews should be conducted. In order to attempt to avoid the sources of bias discussed earlier, you will need to consider the points in Box 9.1.

Box 9.1 Key measures to overcome bias in qualitative interviews

You will need to consider the following points in order to attempt to avoid sources of bias in qualitative interviews:

- Your own preparation and readiness for the interview
- The level of information supplied to the interviewee
- The appropriateness of your appearance at the interview
- The nature of the opening comments to be made when the interview commences
- Your approach to questioning
- The impact of your behaviour during the course of the interview
- Your ability to demonstrate attentive listening skills
- Your scope to test understanding
- Your approach to recording information

The relationship between the points in Box 9.1 and the management of interviewer and interviewee bias will be explored in the discussion that follows. The aim in relation to each of these points will be to demonstrate your credibility and to obtain the confidence of the interviewee.

Preparation and readiness for the interview

You need to be knowledgeable about the organisational or situational context in which the interview is to take place. A prior search in your university library (Sections 3.4 and 3.5) may reveal journal articles written by senior employees of the organisation that is participating in your research. There may also be other material about the organisation, and this is particularly likely to be found in the 'trade' press and the quality newspapers. It may also be appropriate to look at company reports and other publications, or financial data relating to the organisation. The ability to draw on this type of information in the interview should help to demonstrate your credibility and thereby encourage the interviewee to offer a more detailed account of the topic under discussion. A further benefit of this is made clear by Healey and Rawlinson (1994:136): 'A well informed interviewer has a basis for assessing the accuracy of some of the information offered.'

Your level of knowledge about your research topic should also help to establish your credibility in the view of your research participant. This knowledge may be gleaned through the review of the literature that you undertake. As you undertake a number of interviews, you will also be able to draw on the initial analysis that you make of data previously collected.

Level of information supplied to the interviewee

Credibility may also be promoted through the supply of relevant information to participants before the interview. Providing participants with a list of the interview themes before the event, where this is appropriate, should help this aim. This provision should also promote validity and reliability by enabling the interviewee to consider the information being requested and allowing them the opportunity to assemble supporting organisational documentation from their files. We can testify to this approach and the value of allowing participants to prepare themselves for the discussion in which they are to engage. Access to organisational documentation also allows for triangulation of the data provided (Sections 7.2 and 7.3). Our experience is that participants are generally willing to supply a photocopy of such material, although of course it will be necessary to conceal any confidential or personal details that this contains.

worked example

Interview themes

You have been asked to undertake semi-structured interviews with a number of employees to ascertain their views about the nature and efficiency of internal communication within an organisation. This subject is felt to be significant in relation to both customer service and employee commitment perspectives. You have been requested to provide a list of themes that you wish to explore with interviewees. After some deliberation and reading you come up with the following list of themes that you wish to explore during the course of these interviews:

- what interviewees understand by the term 'internal communication';
- the nature and sources of internal communications received;
- perceptions about the channels used for internal communication and their impact on its intended purpose;
- the value of internal communication in providing information about performance (of the organisation and more locally) and strategic direction;
- the use of internal communication and its impact on the work of the interviewee's department;
- the effect of internal communication on the work of the interviewee;
- the scope for upward communication;

▶

- the impact of upward communication on organisational procedures and practices;
- perceptions about improving the processes, content and efficiency of internal communication in relation to the twin foci of the research.

These can be used as your guide through the substantive part of the interview.

Interview themes may be derived from the literature that you read, the theories that you consider, your experience of a particular topic, common sense, discussions with co-workers, fellow students, tutors and research participants, or some combination of these approaches. You will need to have some notion of the theme or themes that you wish to discuss with your participants even if you intend to commence with exploratory, in-depth interviews and adopt a grounded theory approach to your research project (Section 12.6). Without at least some focus, your work will clearly lack a sense of direction and purpose. It will be necessary for you to formulate a focus if your work is to make progress. You should therefore start with a set of themes that reflect the variables being studied, or at least one or more general questions related to your research topic that you could use where you intend to commence by using in-depth, unstructured interviews. Using this approach, you will be able to develop and/or explore research themes through the qualitative interviews that you conduct to see whether you can identify and test relationships between them (Chapter 12).

Appropriateness of the researcher's appearance at the interview

Your appearance may affect the perception of the interviewee. Where this has an adverse affect on your credibility in the view of the interviewee, or results in a failure to gain their confidence, the resulting bias may affect the reliability of the information provided. Robson (2002) advises researchers to adopt a similar style of dress to those to be interviewed. Essentially, you will need to wear clothing that will be generally acceptable for the setting within which the interview is to occur.

worked example

Checking out the dress code

Phil and Adrian arranged to visit the administration centre of a large financial services organisation on a Friday to conduct a group interview with staff drawn from one of its operating divisions and two one-to-one interviews with senior managers. They felt that it was appropriate to wear fairly 'formal' clothes to match what they thought would be the dress code of the organisation. Indeed, for four days of the working week this assumption would have been appropriate. However, the organisation had recently introduced the practice of not wearing such formal work clothes on Fridays. Thus they found themselves the only ones to be dressed formally in the organisation on the day of their visit. Taking lunch proved to be a memorable experience, as they intermingled with everyone else dressed in jeans and tee shirts etc. Their 'mistake' proved to be an amusing opening at the start of each interview rather than a barrier to gaining access to participants' data. Indeed it might not have been appropriate for visitors such as Phil and Adrian to match too closely the 'dress-down' style of participants. Nevertheless, it does provide a useful example of the way in which expectations about appearance are likely to be noticed.

Nature of the opening comments to be made when the interview commences

Where the interviewee has not met you before, the first few minutes of conversation may have a significant impact on the outcome of the interview – again related to the issue of your credibility and the level of the interviewee's confidence. The interview is likely to occur in a setting that is unfamiliar to you, but it will nevertheless be your responsibility to shape the start of the discussion. You will need to establish your credibility and gain the interviewee's confidence. The interviewee may have some uncertainties about sharing information, and about the manner in which these data may be used. Alternatively, they may still need clarification about the exact nature of the data that you wish to obtain. There may also be a degree of curiosity on the part of the interviewee and probably a genuine level of interest in the research, related to the reason why the request to participate was accepted. This curiosity and interest will offer an opening for both parties to start a conversation, probably before the 'intended discussion' commences. You may find it appropriate to follow up by demonstrating interest in the interviewee by asking about their role within the host organisation (Ghauri and Grønhaug, 2002). However, you need to make sure that these opening moves to demonstrate credibility and friendliness, and to relax and develop a positive relationship, are not overstated, so that too much time is used and the interviewee starts to become bored or restive.

The commencement of the intended discussion needs to be shaped by you. This will be your opportunity to allay, wherever possible, the interviewee's uncertainties about providing information. The following example provides a structure that might be appropriate to commence an interview and to fulfil this purpose.

worked example

Opening a semi-structured interview

As part of a research project a series of semi-structured interviews was undertaken with participants from a range of organisations. The interviewer introduced the following points at the start of each interview:

- The participant was thanked for considering the request for access and for agreeing to the meeting.
- The purpose of the research, its funding and progress to date were briefly outlined.
- The previously agreed right to confidentiality and anonymity was reiterated by stating that nothing said by the participant would be attributed to her or him or their employing organisation without first seeking and obtaining permission.
- The participant's right not to answer any question was carefully emphasised and that the interview would be stopped if they wished.
- The participant was told about the nature of the outputs to which the research was intended to lead and what would happen to the data collected during and after the project.
- The offer of any written documentation to the interviewee was also restated and when this was intended to occur.
- Before the substantive discussion got under way the final points were to ask permission about the way in which the interviewer wished to conduct the meeting, to state the themes to be covered and to confirm the amount of time available.

All of these points were generally dealt with in a couple of minutes.

Healey and Rawlinson (1994) say that an assurance from you that confidential information is not being sought should make interviewees more relaxed and open about the information that they are willing to discuss. Combined with assurances about anonymity, this should increase the level of confidence in your trustworthiness and reduce the possibility of interviewee or response bias. You may also demonstrate your commitment to confidentiality by not naming other organisations that have participated in your research, or by talking about the data you obtained from them.

Approach to questioning

When conducted appropriately, your approach to questioning should reduce the scope for bias during the interview and increase the reliability of the information obtained. Your questions need to be phrased clearly, so that the interviewee can understand them, and you should ask them in a neutral tone of voice. Easterby-Smith *et al.* (2002) point out that the use of open questions (Section 9.5) should help to avoid bias. These can then be followed up by the use of appropriately worded probing questions (Section 9.5). The use of these types of question will help you to explore the topic and to produce a fuller account. Conversely, questions that seek to lead the interviewee or which indicate bias on your part should be avoided. Perceived interviewer bias may well lead to interviewee or response bias. Long questions or those that are really made up of two or more questions should also be avoided if you are to obtain a response to each aspect that you are interested to explore (Robson, 2002).

Questions should also avoid too many theoretical concepts or jargon since your understanding of such terms may vary from that of your interviewees. Where theoretical concepts or specific terminology need to be used, you will have to ensure that the interviewee understands your intended meaning (Easterby-Smith *et al.*, 2002; Ghauri and Grønhaug, 2002).

worked example

(Mis)understanding terminology

When Adrian and Andrew conducted interviews about the 'survivors' of redundancies, one participant initially thought that this referred to those made redundant but who had managed to overcome and 'survive' the experience – which is a very understandable interpretation. In fact, the meaning was intended to relate to employees who remained in the organisation! The term 'survivor syndrome' has now become accepted jargon by those interested in this area. However, many people would not specifically relate it to those who stay in employment. You will therefore need to exercise great care in the way that you use similar bits of jargon that you take for granted but which others do not.

Healey and Rawlinson (1994:138) suggest that 'it is usually best to leave sensitive questions until near the end of an interview because this allows a greater time for the respondent to build up trust and confidence in the researchers.' They report cases where the first part of an interview is used by participants to assess the level of trust that can be placed in the researcher. Others have witnessed this experience, as the following example illustrates, affecting the nature of the questions that may be asked during the early part of an interview.

worked example

Establishing trust and asking sensitive questions

Sam recalls an occasion when this type of treatment was particularly noticeable: for the first hour of a two-hour interview it appeared to her that the participants were convinced that she was really there to offer them a consultancy service. When they accepted that she was not going to try to sell them something, the mood of the meeting changed and they became much more relaxed and responsive to the questions that Sam wished to ask. It was at this point that she was able to ask and pursue more sensitive questions that could have led to the interview being terminated during the period when the participants mistrusted her motives.

Once this position of trust has been reached and you wish to seek responses to potentially sensitive questions, Ghauri and Grønhaug (2002) point out that the wording of these deserve very particular attention in order to avoid any negative inferences related to, for example, responsibility for failure or error. Care taken over the exploration of sensitive questions should help towards the compilation of a fuller and more reliable account.

Nature and impact of the interviewer's behaviour during the course of the interview

Appropriate behaviour by the researcher should also reduce the scope for bias during the interview. Comments or non-verbal behaviour, such as gestures, which indicate any bias in your thinking should be avoided. A neutral (but not an uninterested) response should be projected in relation to the interviewee's answers in order not to provide any lead that may result in bias. Robson (2002) says that you should enjoy the interview opportunity, or at least appear to do so. An appearance of boredom on your part is hardly likely to encourage your interviewee!

Your posture and tone of voice may also encourage or inhibit the flow of the discussion. You should sit slightly inclined towards the interviewee and adopt an open posture, avoiding folded arms. This should provide a signal of attentiveness to your interviewee (Torrington, 1991). Tone of voice can also provide a signal to the interviewee. You need to project interest and enthusiasm through your voice, avoiding any impression of anxiety, disbelief, astonishment or any other negative signal.

Demonstration of attentive listening skills

The purpose of a semi-structured or in-depth interview will be to understand the participant's explanations and meanings. This type of interaction will not be typical of many of the conversations that you normally engage in, where those involved often compete to speak rather than concentrate on listening. You therefore need to recognise that different skills will be emphasised in this kind of interaction. Torrington (1991:43) says that listening involves people being 'on the look-out for signals and willing to spend the time needed to listen and build understanding, deliberately holding back our own thoughts, which would divert or compete with the other's.'

It will be necessary for you to explore and probe explanations and meanings, but you must also provide the interviewee with reasonable time to develop their responses, and you must avoid projecting your own views (Easterby-Smith *et al.*, 2002; Ghauri and Grønhaug, 2002; Robson, 2002). Careful listening should allow you to identify comments that are significant to the research topic and to explore these with the interviewee (Torrington, 1991).

Scope to test understanding

You may test your understanding by summarising an explanation provided by the interviewee. This will allow the interviewee to 'evaluate the adequacy of the interpretation and correct where necessary' (Healey and Rawlinson, 1994:138). This can be a powerful tool for avoiding a biased or incomplete interpretation. It may also act as a means to explore and probe the interviewee's responses further.

In addition to this opportunity to test understanding at the interview, you may also ask the interviewee to read through the factual account that you produce of the interview. Where the interviewee is prepared to undertake this, it will provide a further opportunity for you to test your understanding and for the interviewee to add any further points of relevance that may occur to them.

Approach to recording data

A full record of the interview should be compiled as soon as possible after it has taken place (Healey, 1991; Healey and Rawlinson, 1994; Robson, 2002). Where you do not do this, the exact nature of explanations provided may be lost as well as general points of value. There is also the possibility that you may mix up data from different interviews, where you carry out several of these within a short period of time and you do not complete a record of each one at the time it takes place (Ghauri and Grønhaug, 2002). Either situation will clearly lead to an issue about the trustworthiness of any data. You therefore need to allocate time to write up a full set of notes soon after the event. Recording information is considered further in Section 9.5.

Cultural differences and bias

As a final note to this particular discussion, we need to recognise that it is often difficult to attempt to control bias in all cases. Other factors may become significant. For example, there may be misinterpretation of responses because of cultural differences between the interviewee and the interviewer (Marshall and Rossman, 1999). This issue is not exclusively related to interviews and can be associated with a number of data collection methods. For example, we encountered it in relation to the interpretation of the data produced from a cross-national survey. An in-depth interview at least offers the opportunity to explore meanings, including those that may be culturally specific, but you will need to be aware of cultural differences and their implications (see, for example, Hofstede, 2001).

Generalisability

In the previous section, which described data quality issues relating to semi-structured and in-depth interviews, we stated that there is likely to be a concern surrounding the generalisability of findings from qualitative research, based on the use of a small and unrepresentative number of cases. However, two arguments have been advanced that seek to clarify and modify the approach often adopted to the generalisability or transferability of qualitative research. The first of these relates to the situation where a single case study is used because of the in-depth nature of the research. Bryman

(1988:90) states that 'within a case study a wide range of different people and activities are invariably examined so that the contrast with survey samples is not as acute as it appears at first glance'. The single case may in fact encompass a number of settings, where for example it involves a study in a large organisation with sites across the country, or even around the world. By contrast, Bryman (1988) points out that many survey samples may be restricted to one particular locality. A well-completed and rigorous case study is thus more likely to be useful in other contexts than one that lacks such rigour.

The second argument with the approach that questions the generalisability of qualitative research or a case study is related to the significance of this type of research to theoretical propositions (Bryman, 1988; Yin, 1994). Where you are able to relate your research project to existing theory you will be in a position to demonstrate that your findings will have a broader significance than the case or cases that form the basis of your work (Marshall and Rossman, 1999). It will clearly be up to you to establish this relationship to existing theory in order to be able to demonstrate the broader significance of your particular case study findings.

This relationship will allow your study to test the applicability of existing theory to the setting(s) that you are examining and where this is found wanting to suggest why. It will also allow theoretical propositions to be advanced that can then be tested in another context. However, as Bryman (1988) points out, this also has implications for the relationship between theory and research, since the identification of existing theory and its application will be necessary before the researcher embarks on the collection of data (Section 12.4).

9.5 The researcher's interviewing competence

There are several areas where you need to develop and demonstrate competence in relation to the conduct of semi-structured and in-depth research interviews. These areas are:

- opening the interview;
- using appropriate language;
- questioning;
- listening;
- testing and summarising understanding;
- behavioural cues;
- recording data.

Most of these competence areas have been discussed in relation to overcoming interviewer and interviewee bias in Section 9.4. A list of competences is also contained in Box 9.3. However, there is scope to discuss further approaches to questioning and recording information in order to be able to develop your competence.

Questioning

Even in an in-depth interview, as well as in a semi-structured one, you will need to consider your approach to questioning. Allowing the interviewee to talk freely throughout an in-depth interview is unlikely to lead to a clearly focused discussion on issues relevant to the research topic (Easterby-Smith *et al.*, 2002; Robson, 2002) unless the purpose is simply to discover important concerns relating to the topic at a given time. It will therefore be necessary to devise relevant interview themes (Section 9.4), even though you can adopt a flexible approach about the way these are dealt with during the interview. The use of this approach demands a significant level of competence on your part. Formulating appropriate questions to explore areas in which you are interested will be critical to achieving success in this type of interviewing. We shall now discuss the types of question that you will use during semi-structured and in-depth interviews.

Open questions

The use of *open questions* will allow participants to define and describe a situation or event. An open question is designed to encourage the interviewee to provide an extensive and developmental answer, and may be used to reveal attitudes or obtain facts (Grummitt, 1980). It encourages the interviewee to reply as they wish. An open question is likely to start with, or include, one of the following words: 'what', 'how' or 'why'. Examples of open questions include:

'Why did the organisation introduce its marketing strategy?'

'What methods have been used to make employees redundant?'

'How has corporate strategy changed over the past five years?'

Probing questions

Probing questions can be used to explore responses that are of significance to the research topic. They may be worded like open questions but request a particular *focus* or direction. Examples of this type of question include:

'How would you evaluate the success of this new marketing strategy?'

'Why did you choose a compulsory method to make redundancies?'

'What external factors caused the corporate strategy to change?'

These questions may be prefaced with, for example, 'That's interesting . . .' or 'Tell me more about . . .'.

Probing questions may also be used to seek an *explanation* where you do not understand the interviewee's meaning or where the response does not reveal the reasoning involved. Examples of this type of question include:

'What do you mean by "bumping" as a means to help to secure volunteers for redundancy?'

'What is the relationship between the new statutory requirements that you referred to and the organisation's decision to set up its corporate affairs department?'

The use of *reflection* may also help you to probe a theme. This is where you will 'reflect' a statement made by the interviewee by paraphrasing their words. An example of this might be:

'Why don't you think that the employees understand the organisation's mission statement?'

The intention will be to encourage exploration of the point made without offering a view or judgement on your part.

Where an open question does not reveal a relevant response, you may also probe the area of interest by using a *supplementary* question that finds a way of rephrasing the original question (Torrington, 1991).

Specific and closed questions

These types of question may be used to obtain specific information or to confirm a fact or opinion, and are more generally used in questionnaires (Section 10.4). Examples of these types of question include:

'How many people responded to the customer survey?'

This question is designed to obtain a specific piece of data.

'Did I hear you say that the new warehouse opened on 25 March?'

This is a closed question seeking a yes or no answer.

In phrasing questions, remember that you should avoid using leading or proposing types of question in order to control any bias that may result from their use (Section 9.4).

Recording information

The need to create a full record of the interview soon after its occurrence was identified in Section 9.4 as one of the means to control bias and to produce reliable data for analysis. This particular discussion looks briefly at the need to develop the skill of making notes during the interview and evaluates the use of tape recorders. Most people have their own means of making notes, which may range from an attempt to create a verbatim account to a diagrammatic style that records key words and phrases, or perhaps some combination of these styles. The task of note making in this situation will be a demanding one. As you seek to test your understanding of what your interviewee has told you, this will allow some time to complete your notes concurrently in relation to the particular aspect being discussed. Most interviewees recognise the demands of the task and act accordingly. However, the interview will not be the occasion to perfect your style, and you may be advised to practise in a simulated situation: for example by watching an interview on television and attempting to produce a set of notes.

One option is to tape-record the interview. However, the disadvantages of doing so may outweigh the advantages. These are considered in Box 9.2.

Box 9.2 Advantages and disadvantages of tape-recording the interview

Advantages

- Allows interviewer to concentrate on questioning and listening
- Allows questions formulated at an interview to be accurately recorded for use in later interviews where appropriate
- Can re-listen to the interview
- Accurate and unbiased record provided
- Allows direct quotes to be used
- Permanent record for others to use

Disadvantages

- May adversely affect the relationship between interviewee and interviewer (possibility of 'focusing' on the recorder)
- May inhibit some interviewee responses and reduce reliability
- Possibility of a technical problem
- Disruption to discussion when changing tapes
- Time required to transcribe the tape

Sources: Authors' experience; Easterby-Smith *et al.* (2002); Ghauri and Grønhaug (2002); Healey and Rawlinson (1994)

Permission should always be sought to tape-record an interview. Healey and Rawlinson (1994) report an earlier study that advises that you should explain why you would prefer to use a recorder rather than simply requesting permission. Where it is likely to have a detrimental effect, it is better not to use a recorder. However, some interviewees may adapt quickly to the use of the recorder.

Where a recorder is used, it will still be necessary for you to continue to listen attentively. You are advised to make notes even when using a tape recorder in order to maintain your concentration and focus (Ghauri and Grønhaug, 2002). It is more ethical to allow your interviewee to maintain control over the tape recorder so that if you ask a question that they are prepared to respond to, but only if their words are not tape-recorded, they have the option to switch it off (see the discussion of ethical issues in Section 5.4). It will therefore be necessary to make notes in this situation.

9.6 Logistical and resource issues and how to manage these

Logistical and resource issues

Interviewing is a time-consuming process. Where the purpose of the interview is to explore themes or to explain findings, the process may call for a fairly lengthy discussion. In such cases the time required to obtain data is unlikely to be less than one hour and could easily exceed this, perhaps taking two hours or longer. This may have an adverse impact on the number and representativeness of those who are willing to be interview participants, as we discussed above. Where managers or other potential participants receive frequent requests to participate in research projects, they will clearly need to consider how much of their time they may be willing to devote to such activities. This issue may arise in relation to either the completion of a questionnaire or participation in an interview. However, there will be more flexibility about when and where to fill in a questionnaire. It is therefore incumbent on you to establish credibility with, and to engender the interest of, potential interviewees.

Your choice of an approach that involves data collection through interviewing will have particular resource issues. Conducting interviews may become a costly process where it is necessary to travel to the location of participants, although this can be kept to a minimum by cluster sampling (Section 6.2). Interviews are almost certainly likely to be more expensive than using self-administered or telephone questionnaires to collect data. Choice of method should be determined by the nature of the research question and objectives and not by cost considerations. This highlights the need to examine the feasibility of the proposed question and research strategy in relation to resource constraints, including time available and expense, before proceeding to the collection of data. Where your research question and objectives require you to undertake semi-structured or in-depth interviews, you need to consider the logistics of scheduling interviews. Thought needs to be given to the number of interviews to be arranged within a given period, and to the time required to compose notes and/or transcribe tape recordings of each one, and undertake an initial analysis of the data collected (Section 12.3).

Managing logistical and resource issues

In the preceding subsection, the issue of time required to collect data through interviewing was raised. You need to consider very carefully the amount of time that will be required to conduct an interview. In our experience, the time required to undertake qualitative research interviews is usually underestimated. The likely time required should be clearly referred to in any initial contact, and it may be better to suggest that interviews are envisaged to last up to, say, one, one and a half, or two hours, so that a willing participant sets aside sufficient time. They may then be in a position to recoup time not required from a shorter interview should this be the case. Some negotiation is in any case possible with an interested participant who feels unable to agree to a request for say two hours but who is prepared to agree to a briefer meeting. The interview can also be arranged at a time when the interviewee will be under least pressure.

Another possible strategy is to arrange two or more shorter interviews in order to explore a topic thoroughly. This might have the added advantage of allowing participants to reflect on the themes raised and questions being asked, and therefore to provide a fuller account and more accurate set of data. In order to establish this option it may be beneficial to arrange an initial meeting with a potential participant to discuss this request, where you will be able to establish your credibility. A series of exploratory interviews may then be agreed.

Consideration also needs to be given to the number of interviews that may be undertaken in a given period. It is easy to overestimate what is practically possible, as the worked example on p. 266 demonstrates.

These are all factors that need to be considered in the scheduling of semi-structured and in-depth interviews. Where you are involved in a study at one establishment, it may be more practical to undertake a number of interviews in one day, although there is still a need to maintain concentration, to make notes and write up information and to conduct your initial analysis. Phil found that undertaking three interviews per day in this type of study was enough.

worked example

Calculating the number of qualitative interviews to be undertaken in one day

Feroz arranged two interviews in London during the course of a day, which involved travelling some miles across the city during the lunch hour. Two interviews appeared to be a reasonable target. However, a number of logistical issues were experienced even in relation to the plan to undertake two such interviews in one day. These issues included the following: the total travelling time to and from London; the time to find the appropriate buildings; the transfer time during a busy period; the time to conduct the interviews; the need to maintain concentration, to probe responses, to make initial notes and then to write these up without too much time elapsing. Because of his experience, Feroz took a decision not to conduct more than one interview per day where significant travel was involved, even though this necessitated more journeys and greater expense.

The nature of semi-structured or in-depth interviews also has implications for the management of the time available during the meeting. The use of open-ended questions and reliance on informant responses means that, while you must remain responsive to the objectives of the interview and the time constraint, interviewees need the opportunity to provide developmental answers. You should avoid making frequent interruptions but will need to cover the themes and questions indicated and probe responses in the time available (Ghauri and Grønhaug, 2002). The intensive nature of the discussion and the need to optimise one's understanding of what has been revealed means that time must be found to write up notes as soon as possible after an interview. Where a tape recorder has been used, time will be required to produce a transcription, and Robson (2002) states that a one-hour recording may take up to ten hours to transcribe.

9.7 A checklist for using semi-structured and in-depth interviews

Following the discussion about types of research interview (Section 9.2), this chapter has considered situations favouring their use (Section 9.3) and issues relating to data quality (Section 9.4), the level of competence required by the researcher (Section 9.5) and resources (Section 9.6). Throughout this discussion the focus has been centred on what you will need to consider in order to be able to conduct semi-structured or in-depth interviews. The checklist contained in Box 9.3 brings together the key points from the discussion above in order to help you to think about when and how to conduct these types of research interview. You may use the checklist as a means to test your understanding of the points included in it, to indicate where you need to return to a section of the text above to reinforce this.

Box 9.3 Checklist for the use of semi-structured and in-depth interviews

Deciding whether to use these types of interview

- ✓ Does the purpose of your research suggest using semi-structured and/or in-depth interviews?
- ✓ Will it help to seek personal contact in terms of gaining access to participants and their data?
- ✓ Are your data collection questions large in number, complex or open ended, or will there be a need to vary the order and logic of questioning?
- ✓ Will it help to be able to probe interviewees' responses to build on or seek explanation of their answers?
- ✓ Will the data collection process with each individual involve a relatively lengthy period?

Aspects to consider before conducting a semi-structured or in-depth interview

- ✓ What will be the aim of your research interview? How can you prepare yourself to gain access to the data that you hope your participants will be able to share with you?
- ✓ What will be the broad focus of your in-depth interview, or what are the themes that you wish to explore or seek explanations for during a semi-structured interview?
- ✓ How will you seek to overcome potential issues related to the reliability of the data you collect, including forms of interviewer bias (related to your role and conduct), interviewee bias (the level of access that you gain to the data of those whom you interview) and sampling bias?
- ✓ What type of information, if any, will it be useful to send to your interviewee prior to the interview?
- ✓ What did you agree to supply to your interviewee when you arranged the interview? Has this been supplied?
- ✓ How might your level of preparation and knowledge (in relation to the research context and your research question) affect the willingness of the interviewee to share data?
- ✓ How would you like to record the data that are revealed to you during the interview? Where this involves using a tape recorder have you raised this as a request and provided a reason why it would help you to use this technique?
- ✓ How will your appearance during the interview affect the willingness of the interviewee to share data?

Opening the interview

- ✓ How will you prepare yourself to be able to commence the interview with confidence and purpose?
- ✓ What will you tell your interviewee about yourself, the purpose of your research, its funding and your progress?
- ✓ What concerns, or need for clarification, may your interviewee have?
- ✓ How will you seek to overcome these concerns or provide this clarification?
- ✓ In particular, how do you intend to use the data to which you are given access, ensuring, where appropriate, its confidentiality and your interviewee's anonymity?
- ✓ What will you tell your interviewee about their right not to answer particular questions and to end the interview should they wish?

▶

- ✓ How do you intend to record the data that are shared with you? What rights will your interviewee have in relation to the use of a tape recorder where they have agreed in principle to let you use one?
- ✓ What reference do you need to make about sending your interviewee an output from your data analysis and when this is due to occur?
- ✓ How long will you have to conduct the interview?
- ✓ How do you wish to conduct (or structure) the interview?

Conducting the interview

How will you prepare yourself to be able:

- ✓ to use appropriate language and tone of voice, and avoid jargon when asking questions or discussing themes?
- ✓ to ask appropriately worded open questions to obtain relevant data?
- ✓ to ask appropriately worded probing questions to build on, clarify or explain your interviewee's responses?
- ✓ to avoid asking leading questions that may introduce forms of bias?
- ✓ to devise an appropriate order for your questions, where the early introduction of sensitive issues may introduce interviewee bias?
- ✓ to avoid over-zealously asking questions and pressing your interviewee for a response where it should be clear that they do not wish to provide one?
- ✓ to listen attentively and to demonstrate this to your interviewee?
- ✓ to summarise and test your understanding of the data that are shared with you in order to ensure accuracy in your interpretation?
- ✓ to allow your interviewee to maintain control over the use of a tape recorder, where used, where they may wish to exercise this?
- ✓ to carry out a number of tasks at the same time, including listening, note taking and the identification of probes?
- ✓ to identify actions and comments made by your interviewee that indicate an aspect of the discussion that should be explored in order to reveal the reason for the response?
- ✓ to avoid projecting your own views or feelings through your actions or comments?
- ✓ to maintain a check on the interview that you intend to cover and to steer the discussion where appropriate to raise and explore these aspects?
- ✓ to draw the interview to a close within the agreed time limit and to thank the interviewee for their time and the data they have shared with you?

Recording the information

- ✓ How will you prepare your approach to note making so that you may recall the interviewee's responses for long enough to make an accurate and more permanent record?
- ✓ Has your schedule of work been formulated to permit you to find sufficient time in order to write up your notes and to analyse them before undertaking further data collection?
- ✓ How will you organise your material so that you retain a copy of your original notes, an extended version of your notes after writing them up or a transcript of relevant material, and a set of additional notes or memos relating to the interview and your learning from that particular experience? (See Chapter 12 for further discussion.)

9.8 A final word about telephone and group interviews

Most qualitative interviews occur on a one-to-one, face-to-face basis. However, one-to-one interviews may also be conducted by telephone in particular circumstances. Qualitative interviews may also be conducted on a group basis, where the interviewer facilitates a group discussion involving a small number of participants. Figure 9.1 summarised these variations earlier in this chapter. While the discussion in this chapter relates to both one-to-one and group interviews, the use of telephone and group interviews poses particular problems as well as providing advantages in certain circumstances. We shall consider each category in turn and provide a brief evaluation of their effectiveness.

Telephone interviews

Attempting to conduct qualitative interviews by telephone may lead to advantages associated with access, speed and lower cost. This method may allow you to make contact with participants with whom it would be impractical to conduct an interview on a face-to-face basis because of the distance and prohibitive costs involved and time required. Even where 'long-distance' access is not an issue, conducting interviews by telephone may still offer advantages associated with speed of data collection and lower cost. In other words, this approach may be seen as more convenient.

However, there are a number of significant issues that militate against attempting to collect qualitative data by telephone contact. We have already discussed the importance of establishing personal contact in this type of interviewing. The intention of qualitative interviewing is to be able to explore the participant's responses. This is likely to become more feasible once a position of trust has been established, as discussed earlier. This situation, of establishing trust, will become particularly important where you wish to ask sensitive questions. For these reasons, seeking to conduct qualitative interviews by telephone may lead to issues of (reduced) reliability, where your participants are less willing to engage in an exploratory discussion, or even a refusal to take part.

There are also some other practical issues that would need to be managed. These relate to your ability to control the pace of a telephone interview and to record any data that were forthcoming. Conducting an interview by telephone and recording data is a difficult process. The normal visual cues that allow your participant to control the flow of the data that they share with you would be absent. Indeed, you would lose the opportunity to witness the non-verbal behaviour of your participant, which may adversely affect your interpretation of how far to pursue a particular line of questioning. Your participant may be less willing to provide you with as much time to talk to them in comparison with a face-to-face interview. You may also encounter difficulties in developing more complex questions in comparison with a face-to-face interview situation. Finally, attempting to gain access through a telephone call may lead to ethical issues, as we discussed in Section 5.4.

For these reasons, we believe that qualitative interviewing by telephone is likely to be appropriate only in particular circumstances. It may be appropriate to conduct a short, follow-up telephone interview to clarify the meaning of some data, where you have already undertaken a face-to-face interview with a participant, with whom you have been able to establish your integrity and to demonstrate your competence. It may also be appropriate where access would otherwise be prohibited because of long distance, where you have already been able to establish your credibility through prior contact, perhaps through correspondence, and have made clear that your requirements are reasonable and guided by ethical principles. Where this situation involves a request to undertake a telephone interview with a participant from another country, you will need to be aware of any cultural norms related to the conduct and duration of telephone conversations.

Group interviews

In a *group interview* you will act as a facilitator or *moderator* of the discussion that occurs. This type of interview is likely to be relatively unstructured and fairly free-flowing (Zikmund, 2000), although of course where you use this method you will have a particular theme or themes that you wish to explore. The onus will be placed firmly on you to explain its purpose, to encourage participants to relax, and to initiate the discussion. The use of this method is likely to necessitate a balance between encouraging participants to discuss the particular question or questions that you introduce and allowing them to range more freely in their discussion where this may reveal data that provide you with important insights. Thus once the discussion is established it will need to be managed carefully. Group interaction may lead to a highly productive discussion as interviewees respond to your questions and evaluate points as a group. This type of interaction is likely to lead to a rich flow of data that you will seek to record. However, as your opportunity to develop an individual level of rapport with each participant will not be present (compared with a one-to-one interview), there may also emerge a group effect where certain participants effectively try to dominate the discussion. This situation will leave you with the task of trying to encourage involvement by all group members and of maintaining the interview's exploratory purpose. A high level of skill will therefore be required in order for you to be able to conduct this type of discussion successfully, as well as to try to record its outcomes.

Despite this reference to the potential difficulties of using group interviews, there are distinct advantages arising from their use. Because of the presence of several participants, this type of situation allows a variety of points of view to emerge and for the group to respond to and to discuss these views. A dynamic group can generate or respond to a number of ideas and evaluate them, thus helping you to explain or explore concepts. You are also likely to benefit from the opportunity that this method provides in terms of allowing your participants to discuss points between themselves and to challenge one another's views. In one-to-one interviews, discussion is of course limited to the interviewer and interviewee. The use of group interviews may also provide an efficient way to interview a larger number of individuals than would be possible through the use of one-to-one interviews. Linked to this point, their use may allow you to adopt an interview-based strategy that can more easily be related to a representative sample, particularly where the research project is being conducted within a specific organisation or in relation to a clearly defined population. This may help to establish the credibility of this research where an attempt is made to overcome issues of bias associated with interviews in general and this type in particular.

Group interviews can also be used to identify key themes that will be used to develop items that are included in a survey questionnaire. This particular use of group interviews may suggest that this part of your data collection commences with a reasonably clear focus. For example, in an attitude survey the initial use of group interviews can lead to a 'bottom-up' generation of concerns and issues, which helps to establish the survey. This approach to the use of group interviews is often associated with the label *focus groups*. Their purpose is thus more specific, or focused, and linked to the exploration of a known theme or topic. Focus groups are well known because of the way they have been used by political parties to test voter reactions to particular policies and election strategies, and through their use in market research to test reactions to products.

Where group interviews are being used for a specific purpose, as in the use of focus groups, this is likely to be associated with a higher level of interviewer-led structure and intervention. By comparison, where group interviews are being used without such a specific purpose in mind, this is likely to be associated with a lower level of structure and less intervention by the facilitator. The size of groups may also be related to factors such as these. Thus a focus group designed to obtain views about a product range is likely to be larger than a group interview that explores a topic related to a more emotionally involved construct, such as attitudes to performance-related pay or the way in which employees rate their treatment by management. You may also choose to design smaller groups as you seek to develop your competence in relation to the use of this means to collect qualitative data. Typically a group interview may range from about four to eight participants, or perhaps even 10, depending on the factors referred to above and the envisaged level of complexity that is likely to arise from the use of this means to collect and record data.

If you are thinking about using group interviews, consideration of the following specific issues may help.

- Where your research project (or part of it) occurs within an organisation the request to participate in a group interview may be received by individuals as an instruction rather than allowing them a choice about whether to take part. This may be the case where an organisation is acting as a host for your research and the request is sent out on official notepaper or in the name of a manager, or where you work in the organisation. Where this is the case it is likely to lead to some level of non-attendance, or to unreliable data. In our experience participants often welcome the chance to 'have their say'. However, where any request may be perceived as indicating lack of choice, to gain their confidence and participation you will need to exercise care over the wording to be used in the request that is sent to them to take part. You will also need to exercise similar care in your introduction to the group when the interview occurs in order to provide a clear assurance about confidentiality.
- The effect of gathering people together may be to inhibit possible contributions. This may be related to lack of trust, to perceptions about status differences, or because of the dominance of certain individuals. The nature and selection of each group will affect the first two elements. We would advise using a *horizontal slice* through an organisation to select a sample of people who have a similar status and similar work experiences to construct each group. (Using a *vertical slice* would

introduce perceptions about status differences and variations in work experience.) In this way, group interviews can be conducted at a number of levels within an organisation. A reference may be made about the nature of the group to provide reassurance, and you may consider asking people to introduce themselves by their first name only without referring to their exact job.

- Where one or two people dominate the discussion, you should seek to reduce their contributions carefully and to bring others in. Torrington (1991) suggests that this may be attempted in a general way:

  'What do you think, Barry?'

  'What do other people think about this?'

  Alternatively, more specifically:

  'How does Sally's point relate to the one that you raised, Sheila?'

  A question posed to other group members should also have the effect of inhibiting the contribution of a dominant member:

  'What do you think about John's suggestion?'

- You will need to ensure that participants understand each other's contributions and that you develop an accurate understanding of the points being made. Asking a participant to clarify the meaning of a particular contribution, where it has not been understood, and testing understanding through summarising should help to ensure this.
- You will need to consider the location and setting for a group interview. It is advisable to conduct the interview in a neutral setting rather than, say, in a manager's office, where participants may not feel relaxed. There should be no likelihood of interruption or being overheard. You should consider the layout of the seating in the room where the interview is to be held. Where possible, arrange the seating in a circular fashion so that everyone will be facing inward and so that they will be an equal distance from the central point of this circle.
- The demands of conducting this type of interview and the potential wealth of ideas that may flow from it mean that it is likely to be difficult to manage the process and note key points at the same time. We have managed to overcome this by using two interviewers, where one person facilitates the discussion and the other person makes notes. Where you cannot use this approach, you need to write up notes almost immediately after undertaking this type of interview so as not to lose data. Your research may also benefit from the making of notes about the nature of the interactions that occur in the group interviews that you conduct. We would not advise one person to undertake interviews like this 'back to back' because of the danger of losing or confusing data.

9.9 Summary

- The use of qualitative research interviews should allow you to collect a rich and detailed set of data, although you will need to develop a sufficient level of competence to conduct these and to be able to gain access to the type of data associated with their use.
- Interviews can be differentiated according to the level of structure and standardis-

ation adopted. Different types of interviews are useful for different research purposes.

- Qualitative interviews include two broad types that are generally referred to as unstructured or in-depth interviews and semi-structured interviews. You can use qualitative interviews to explore topics and explain other findings.
- Your research design may incorporate more than one type of interview.
- In-depth and semi-structured interviews can be used in quantitative as well as qualitative research.
- There are situations favouring qualitative interviews that will lead you to use this method to collect data. Apart from the nature of your research strategy, these are related to the significance of establishing personal contact, the nature of your data collection questions, and the length of time required from those who provide data.
- Data quality issues, your level of competence and logistical and resource matters will all need to be considered when you use in-depth and semi-structured interviews.
- Apart from one-to-one interviews conducted on a face-to-face basis, you may consider conducting such an interview by telephone in particular circumstances. In addition, you may consider using group interviews. There may be particular advantages associated with group interviews, but these are considerably more difficult to manage than one-to-one interviews.

self-check Questions

9.1 What type of interview would you use in each of the following situations:

a a market research project?

b a research project seeking to understand whether trade union attitudes have changed?

c following the analysis of a questionnaire?

9.2 What are the advantages of using semi-structured and in-depth interviews?

9.3 During a presentation of your proposal to undertake a research project, which will be qualitatively based using semi-structured or in-depth interviews, you feel that you have dealt well with the relationship between the purpose of the research and the proposed methodology when one of the panel leans forward and asks you to discuss the trustworthiness and usefulness of your work for other researchers. This is clearly a challenge to see whether you can defend such a qualitative approach. How do you respond?

9.4 Having quizzed you about the trustworthiness and usefulness of your work for other researchers, the panel member decides that one more testing question is in order. He explains that qualitatively based work isn't an easy option. 'It is not an easier alternative for those who want to avoid quantitative work,' he says. 'How can we be sure that you're competent to get involved in interview work, especially where the external credibility of this organisation may be affected by the impression that you create in the field?' How will you respond to this concern?

▶

9.5 What are the key issues to consider when planning to use semi-structured or in-depth interviews?

9.6 What are the key areas of competence that you need to develop in order to conduct an interview successfully?

progressing your research project

Using semi-structured or in-depth interviews in your research

- ☐ Review your research question(s) and objectives. How appropriate would it be to use qualitative interviews to collect data? Where it is appropriate, explain the relationship between your research question(s) and objectives, and the use of such interviews. Where this type of interviewing is not appropriate, justify your decision.
- ☐ If you decide that semi-structured or in-depth interviews are appropriate, what practical problems do you foresee? How might you attempt to overcome these practical problems?
- ☐ What threats to the trustworthiness of the data collected are you likely to encounter? How might you overcome these?
- ☐ Draft a list of interview themes to be explored and compare these thoroughly with your research question(s) and objectives.
- ☐ Ask your project tutor to comment on your judgement about the use of qualitative interviews, the issues and threats that you have identified, your suggestions to overcome these, and the fit between your interview themes and the research question(s) and objectives.

References

Bryman, A. (1988) *Quantity and Quality in Social Research*, London, Unwin Hyman.

Cooper, D.R. and Schindler, P.S. (1998) *Business Research Methods* (6th edn), Boston, MA, Irwin McGraw-Hill.

Easterby-Smith, M., Thorpe, R. and Lowe, A. (2002) *Management Research: An Introduction* (2nd edn), London, Sage.

Ghauri, P. and Grønhaug, K. (2002) *Research Methods in Business Studies: A Practical Guide* (2nd edn), London, Financial Times Prentice Hall.

Grummitt, J. (1980) *Interviewing Skills*, London, Industrial Society.

Healey, M.J. (1991) 'Obtaining information from businesses', *in* Healey, M.J. (ed.), *Economic Activity and Land Use*, Harlow, Longman, pp. 193–251.

Healey, M.J. and Rawlinson, M.B. (1993) 'Interviewing business owners and managers: a review of methods and techniques', *Geoforum*, 24:3, 339–55.

Healey, M.J. and Rawlinson, M.B. (1994) 'Interviewing techniques in business and management research', *in* Wass, V.J. and Wells, P.E. (eds), *Principles and Practice in Business and Management Research*, Aldershot, Dartmouth, pp. 123–46.

Hofstede, G. (2001) *Culture's Consequences: Comparing Values, Behaviours, Institutions and Organisations Across Nations*, London, Sage.

Jankowicz, A.D. (2000) *Business Research Projects* (3rd edn), London, Business Press Thomson Learning.

Kahn, R. and Cannell, C. (1957) *The Dynamics of Interviewing*, New York and Chichester, Wiley.

Marshall, C. and Rossman, G.B. (1999) *Designing Qualitative Research* (3rd edn), Thousand Oaks, CA, Sage.

North, D.J., Leigh, R. and Gough, J. (1983) 'Monitoring industrial change at the local level: some comments on methods and data sources', *in* Healey, M.J. (ed.), *Urban and Regional Industrial Research: The Changing UK Data Base*, Norwich, Geo Books, pp. 111–29.

Powney, J. and Watts, M. (1987) *Interviewing in Educational Research*, London, Routledge and Kegan Paul.

Robson, C. (2002) *Real World Research* (2nd edn), Oxford, Blackwell.

Sykes, W. (1991) 'Taking stock: issues from the literature in validity and reliability in qualitative research', *Journal of Market Research Society*, 33:1, 3–12.

Torrington, D. (1991) *Management Face to Face*, London, Prentice Hall.

Wass, V. and Wells, P. (1994) 'Research methods in action: an introduction', *in* Wass, V.J. and Wells, P.E. (eds), *Principles and Practice in Business and Management Research*, Aldershot, Dartmouth, pp. 1–34.

Yin, R.K. (1994) *Case Study Research: Design and Methods* (2nd edn), Beverly Hills, CA, Sage.

Zikmund, W.G. (2000) *Business Research Methods* (6th edn), Fort Worth, TX, Dryden Press.

Further reading

Easterby-Smith, M., Thorpe, R. and Lowe, A. (2002) *Management Research: an Introduction* (2nd edn), London, Sage. Chapter 5 provides a useful and highly readable overview of qualitative methods. This includes in-depth interviews and other methods to supplement them.

Healey, M.J. and Rawlinson, M.B. (1994) 'Interviewing techniques in business and management research', *in* Wass, V.J. and Wells, P.E. (eds), *Principles and Practice in Business and Management Research*, Aldershot, Dartmouth, pp. 123–46. This is an excellent contribution and a 'must' for those of you intending to use qualitative research and interviews.

Krueger, R.A. and Casey, M.A. (2000) *Focus Groups: A Practical Guide for Applied Research* (3rd edn), Thousand Oaks, CA, Sage. A very useful work for those considering the use of this method of interviewing.

Marshall, C. and Rossman, G.B. (1999) *Designing Qualitative Research* (3rd edn), Thousand Oaks, CA, Sage. This provides many excellent insights into the design of qualitative research and the methods associated with it.

CASE 9 Students' use of work-based learning in their studies

Work-based learning (WBL) refers to the learning that people achieve through undertaking work. It is recognized as a legitimate form of learning that can be used to enhance what higher education students do in class. For 50 000 UK students in higher education, WBL is achieved through undertaking a placement in industry of either six months or a year (Bowes and Harvey, 2000). These students are normally referred to as *sandwich* students because their placements and the associated work experience are 'sandwiched' between their time at university.

Jim was an experienced lecturer at a new university who was interested in exploring how sandwich students at his business school used WBL from placement when they returned to his university to complete their undergraduate studies. His review of the academic literature in this area revealed that there was a great deal of research to support the argument that WBL offered potential benefits to students, but little about how this learning was actually used in the classroom. Evidence from two survey-based studies suggested that students, in general, did not appear to be using WBL in the classroom. Jim therefore decided that he could contribute something to the understanding of this topic by exploring the extent to which students at his business school used WBL from their placement in their final year of study.

From his reading of the literature, Jim felt that the use of survey data had certain limitations as a means of understanding how students used WBL. The topic is highly complex, making the construction of a valid questionnaire problematic, and the resources Jim had for the study were limited. Jim felt that there might be other equally valid ways of understanding how students were using WBL in the classroom. In his reading Jim had discovered Kolb's (1984) research on the use of reflection in understanding and learning. This argued that reflection was an important stage in learning, enabling theory and concepts to be learnt at a deep level, using the context of specific experiences. Jim reasoned that, if WBL from the placement was being utilised by students in the final year, it would reveal itself in any reflective work they might be producing for assessment. Demonstrating their learning through reflection would involve the students applying theoretical knowledge to their experiences, including those they had on placement. Analysing such work by the students should therefore offer a good indication of whether the students were using WBL from placement in the final year.

Jim identified one final-year module in the business school in which students were asked to reflect on theoretical aspects of business practice such as company culture, use of technology, strategy, operations and logistics, and present these reflections in the form of learning logs. The module tutor required the students to demonstrate through the logs that they had understood these topics and could apply them in some way to their experiences. Jim realised that the logs for sandwich students, if they were using their WBL, should contain specific references to their placement. With the module tutor's and the students' permission, Jim analysed a sample of learning logs chosen at random by the module tutor. Half were by students who had been on placement and half by students who had not. His analysis of the logs was guided by the work of Moon (1999), who is an acknowledged expert on the use of reflection in learning.

Jim completed his analysis of the learning logs and came to four main conclusions that he wished to explore with the students. He therefore wrote to the students asking them whether they were willing to be interviewed as a group about their learning logs, and the letter outlined what, in broad terms, the interview would be about and how long it was likely to last. After students responded positively, Jim then found a date for the interview that was convenient for all of them.

The management of the interview with the students was divided into three stages. In stage 1, Jim outlined the purpose of the meeting and why it was needed for his study. In particular, he stressed that the discussion would be treated as confidential. He also asked for permission to tape the interview, and stated that at any point any of the students could ask for the tape to be switched off, or for a piece of the interview to be deleted from the tape. After making sure the students were ready to begin Jim formally started the interview. This was the second stage. The interview took just over one hour, during which Jim tried at all times to make sure the students, rather than he himself, were the ones talking. He encouraged dialogue across the group to try and broaden the discussion, and only interrupted on occasions when the direction of the debate had wandered well beyond the topic. Jim found that the students became increasingly motivated to make their views known, and he made copious notes as the interview progressed. The third and final stage of the interview was to close the discussion, ensuring that everybody had had a final opportunity to raise any points that had not been mentioned during the interview. Jim then formally closed the interview, thanked the students for their time, and reiterated the fact that everything that they had said would be treated as confidential. The students responded by saying that they had enjoyed the meeting.

The results from the interview left Jim with a number of questions relating to the comments made by the students about their final-year tutors. These comments had highlighted that students perceived that lecturers did not encourage them to use their placement experience in the final year. Jim therefore decided to explore some of the detail behind these comments with three experienced tutors of final-year students. The subsequent interviews with these tutors revealed a very different perception from that of the students. Tutors were resolute that students' WBL from their placement was used in the classroom, and they offered a range of examples as to how this was done. However, the interview revealed that lecturers' encouragement might be implicit rather than explicit much of the time.

The research had confirmed that students at the business school were not on the whole using WBL from placement in their final year. It also suggested that this was because of their perception that tutors were not encouraging them to do this. A key recommendation was that sandwich students needed to have explicit encouragement from lecturers if they were to make use of WBL in their final year.

References

Bowes, L. and Harvey, L. (2000) *The Impact of Sandwich Education on the Activities of Graduates Six Months Post-Graduation*, London, National Council for Work Experience and the Centre for Research into Quality.

Kolb, D.A. (1984) *Experiential Learning: Experience as the Source of Learning and Development*, New Jersey, Prentice Hall.

Moon, J. (1999) *Learning Journals: A Handbook for Academics, Students and Professional Development*, London, Kogan Page.

Questions

1 Why did Jim feel it necessary to analyse reflective material produced by students rather than just interview final-year students in his research?

2 Why was it important to plan and manage the interviews in the way described?

3 How did Jim deal with the ethical issues in his research?

4 Why was it valid for Jim to decide to interview tutors when originally he had not intended to?

5 Jim used literature from three distinct areas.
   a What were they?
   b Why did he need to use each of them?

6 What were the main strengths and weaknesses of this research?

self-check Answers

9.1 The type of interview that is likely to be used in each of these situations is as follows:

a A standardised and structured interview where the aim is to develop response patterns from the views of people. The interview schedule might be designed to combine styles so that comments made by interviewees in relation to specific questions could also be recorded.

b The situation outlined suggests an exploratory approach to research, and therefore an in-depth interview would be most appropriate.

c The situation outlined here suggests that an explanatory approach is required in relation to the data collected, and in this case a semi-structured interview is likely to be appropriate.

9.2 Reasons that suggest the use of interviews include:

- the exploratory or explanatory nature of your research;
- situations where it will be significant to establish personal contact, in relation to interviewee sensitivity about the nature of the information to be provided and the use to be made of this;
- situations where the researcher needs to exercise control over the nature of those who will supply data;
- situations where there are a large number of questions to be answered;
- situations where questions are complex or open ended;
- situations where the order and logic of questioning may need to be varied.

9.3 Certainly politely! Your response needs to show that you are aware of the issues relating to reliability, bias and generalisability that might arise. It would be useful to discuss how these might be overcome through the following: the design of the research; the keeping of records or a diary in relation to the processes and key incidents of the research project as well as the recording of data collected; attempts to control bias through the process of collecting data; the relationship of the research to theory.

9.4 Perhaps it will be wise to say that you understand his position. You realise that any approach to research calls for particular types of competence. Your previous answer touching on interviewee bias has highlighted the need to establish credibility and to gain the interviewee's confidence. While competence will need to be developed over a period of time, allowing for any classroom simulations and dry runs with colleagues, probably the best approach will be your level of preparation before embarking on interview work. This relates first to the nature of the approach made to those whom you would like to participate in the research project and the information supplied to them, second to your intellectual preparation related to the topic to be explored and the particular context of the organisations participating in the research, and third to your ability to conduct an interview. You also recognise that piloting the interview themes will be a crucial element in building your competence.

9.5 Key issues to consider include the following:

- planning to minimise the occurrence of forms of bias where these are within your control, related to interviewer bias, interviewee bias and sampling bias;
- considering your aim in requesting the research interview and how you can seek to prepare yourself in order to gain access to the data that you hope your participants will be able to share with you;
- devising interview themes that you wish to explore or seek explanations for during the interview;
- sending a list of your interview themes to your interviewee prior to the interview, where this is considered appropriate;
- requesting permission and providing a reason where you would like to use a tape recorder during the interview;
- making sure that your level of preparation and knowledge (in relation to the research context and your research question and objectives) is satisfactory in order to establish your credibility when you meet your interviewee;
- considering how your intended appearance during the interview will affect the willingness of the interviewee to share data.

9.6 There are several areas where you need to develop and demonstrate competence in relation to the conduct of semi-structured and in-depth research interviews. These areas are:

- opening the interview;
- using appropriate language;
- questioning;
- listening;
- testing and summarising understanding;
- behavioural cues;
- recording data.

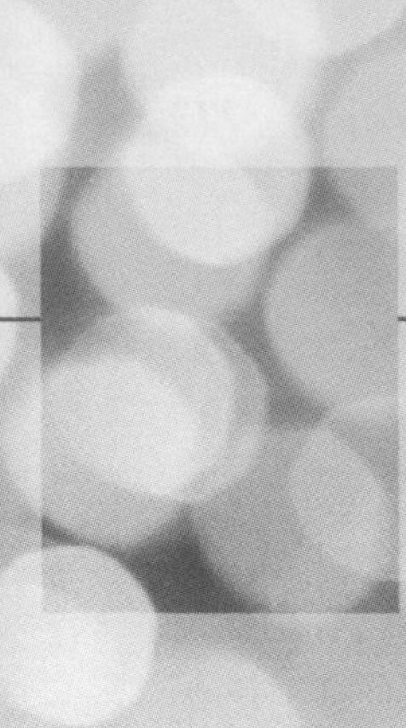

Chapter 10

Collecting primary data using questionnaires

By the end of this chapter you should:

- understand the advantages and disadvantages of questionnaires as a data collection method;
- be aware of a range of self-administered and interviewer-administered questionnaires;
- be aware of the possible need to combine techniques within a research project;
- be able to select and justify the use of appropriate questionnaire techniques for a variety of research scenarios;
- be able to design, pilot and administer a questionnaire to answer research questions and to meet objectives;
- be able to take appropriate action to enhance response rates and to ensure the validity and reliability of the data collected;
- be able to apply the knowledge, skills and understanding gained to your own research project.

10.1 Introduction

The greatest use of questionnaires is made by the survey strategy (Section 4.2). However, both experiment and case study research strategies can make use of these techniques. There are various definitions of the term 'questionnaire' (Oppenheim, 2000). Some authors (for example Kervin, 1999) reserve it exclusively for surveys where the person answering the question actually records their own answers. Others (for example Bell, 1999) use it as a more general term to include interviews that are administered either face to face or by telephone.

In this book we use *questionnaire* as a general term to include all techniques of data collection in which each person is asked to respond to the same set of questions in a predetermined order (deVaus, 2002). It therefore includes both structured interviews and telephone questionnaires as well as those in which the questions are answered without an interviewer being present. The range of techniques that fall under this broad heading are outlined in the next section (10.2), along with their relative advantages and disadvantages.

The use of questionnaires is discussed in many research methods texts. These range from those that devote a few pages to those that specify precisely how you should construct and use them, such as Dillman's (2000) *tailored design method*. Perhaps not surprisingly, the questionnaire is one of the most widely used survey data collection techniques. Because each person (*respondent*) is asked to respond to the same set of questions, it provides an efficient way of collecting responses from a large sample prior to quantitative analysis (Chapter 11). However, before you decide to use a questionnaire we should like to include a note of caution. Many authors (for example Bell, 1999; Oppenheim, 2000) argue that it is far harder to produce a good questionnaire than you might think. You need to ensure that it will collect the precise data that you require to answer your research question(s) and achieve your objectives. This is of paramount importance, as you are unlikely to be able to go back to people and collect additional data using another questionnaire. These issues are discussed in Section 10.3.

The design of your questionnaire will affect the response rate and the reliability and validity of the data you collect. Response rates, validity and reliability can be maximised by:

- careful design of individual questions;
- clear layout of the questionnaire form;
- lucid explanation of the purpose of the questionnaire;
- pilot testing;
- carefully planned and executed administration.

Together these form Sections 10.4 and 10.5. In section 10.4 we discuss designing your questionnaire. Administering the actual questionnaire is considered in Section 10.5 along with actions to help ensure high response rates.

10.2 An overview of questionnaire techniques

When to use questionnaires

We have found that many people use a questionnaire to collect data without considering other methods such as examination of secondary sources (Chapter 7), observation (Chapter 8), and semi-structured or in-depth interviews (Chapter 9). Our advice is to evaluate all possible data collection methods and to choose those most appropriate to your research question(s) and objectives. Questionnaires are usually not particularly good for exploratory or other research that requires large numbers of open-ended questions (Sections 9.2 and 9.3). They work best with standardised questions that you can be confident will be interpreted the same way by all respondents (Robson, 2002).

Questionnaires can therefore be used for descriptive or explanatory research. *Descriptive research*, such as that undertaken using attitude and opinion questionnaires and questionnaires of organisational practices, will enable you to identify and describe the variability in different phenomena. In contrast, *explanatory* or *analytical research* will enable you to examine and explain relationships between variables, in particular cause-and-effect relationships. These two purposes have different research design requirements (Gill and Johnson, 1997), which we shall discuss later (Section 10.3).

Although questionnaires may be used as the only data collection method, it is usually better to link them with other methods in a *multi-method* approach (Section 4.3). For example, a questionnaire to discover customers' attitudes can be complemented by in-depth interviews to explore and understand these attitudes (Section 9.3). In addition questionnaires, if worded correctly, normally require less skill and sensitivity to administer than semi-structured or in-depth interviews (Jankowicz, 2000).

Types of questionnaire

The design of a questionnaire differs according to how it is administered, and in particular the amount of contact you have with the respondents (Figure 10.1). *Self-administered questionnaires* are usually completed by the respondents. Such questionnaires are delivered and returned electronically using either email or the Internet (*on-line questionnaires*), posted to respondents who return them by post after completion (*postal* or *mail questionnaires*), or delivered by hand to each respondent and collected later (*delivery and collection questionnaires*). Responses to *interviewer-administered questionnaires* are recorded by the interviewer on the basis of each respondent's answers. A growing number of surveys, particularly in the area of market research, contact respondents and administer questionnaires using the telephone. These are known as *telephone questionnaires.* The final category, *structured interviews* (sometimes known as *interview schedules*), refers to those questionnaires where interviewers physically meet respondents and ask the questions face to face. These differ from semi-structured and in-depth interviews (Section 9.2), as there is a defined schedule of questions, from which interviewers should not deviate.

The choice of questionnaire

Your choice of questionnaire will be influenced by a variety of factors related to your research question(s) and objectives (Table 10.1), and in particular the:

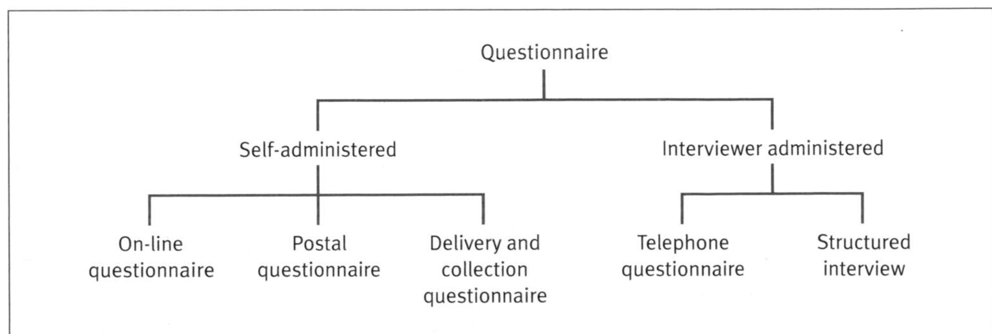

Figure 10.1 Types of questionnaire

- characteristics of the respondents from whom you wish to collect data;
- importance of reaching a particular person as respondent;
- importance of respondents' answers not being contaminated or distorted;
- size of sample you require for your analysis, taking into account the likely response rate;
- types of question you need to ask to collect your data;
- number of questions you need to ask to collect your data.

These factors will not apply equally to your choice of questionnaire, and for some research questions or objectives may not apply at all. The type of questionnaire you choose will dictate how sure you can be that the respondent is the person whom you wish to answer the questions and thus the reliability of responses (Table 10.1). Even if you address a postal questionnaire to a company manager by name, you have no way of ensuring that she or he will be the respondent. Her or his assistant or someone else could complete it! Email offers greater control because most users read and respond to their own mail at their personal computer (Witmer *et al.*, 1999). With delivery and collection questionnaires, you can sometimes check who has answered the questions at collection. By contrast, interviewer-administered questionnaires enable you to ensure that the respondent is whom you want. This improves the reliability of your data. In addition you can record who were non-respondents, thereby avoiding unknown bias caused by refusals.

Any *contamination* of respondents' answers will reduce your data's reliability (Table 10.1). Sometimes, if they have insufficient knowledge or experience they may deliberately guess at the answer, a tendency known as *uninformed response*. This is particularly likely when the questionnaire has been incentivised (Section 10.5). Respondents to self-administered questionnaires are relatively unlikely to answer to please you or because they believe certain responses are more *socially desirable* (Dillman, 2000). They may, however, discuss their answers with others, thereby contaminating their response. Respondents to telephone questionnaires and structured interviews are more likely to answer to please owing to contact with you, although the impact of this can be minimised by good interviewing technique (Section 9.5). Responses can also be contaminated or distorted when recorded. In extreme instances, interviewers may invent responses. For this reason, random checks of interviewers are often made by survey organisations.

The type of questionnaire you choose will affect the number of people who respond (Section 6.2). Interviewer-administered questionnaires will usually have a higher response rate than self-administered questionnaires (Table 10.1). The size of your sample and the way in which it is selected will have implications for the confidence you can have in your data and the extent to which you can generalise (Section 6.2).

Longer questionnaires are best presented as a structured interview. In addition, they can include more complicated questions than telephone questionnaires or self-administered questionnaires (Oppenheim, 2000). The presence of an interviewer means that it is also easier to route different subgroups of respondents to answer different questions using a filter question (Section 10.4). The suitability of different types of question also differs between techniques.

Your choice of questionnaire will also be affected by the resources you have available (Table 10.1), and in particular the:

Table 10.1 **Main attributes of questionnaires**

Attribute	*On line*	*Postal*	*Delivery and collection*	*Telephone*	*Structured interview*
Population's characteristics for which suitable	Computer-literate individuals who can be contacted by email or Internet	Literate individuals who can be contacted by post; selected by name, household, organisation etc.		Individuals who can be telephoned; selected by name, household, organisation etc.	Any; selected by name, household, organisation, in the street etc.
Confidence that right person has responded	High if using email	Low	Low but can be checked at collection	High	
Likelihood of contamination or distortion of respondent's answer	Low	May be contaminated by consultation with others		Occasionally distorted or invented by interviewer	Occasionally contaminated by consultation or distorted/invented by interviewer
Size of sample	Large, can be geographically dispersed		Dependent on number of field workers	Dependent on number of interviewers	
Likely response rate[a]	Variable, 30% reasonable within organisations, Internet 10% or lower	Variable, 30% reasonable	Moderately high, 30–50% reasonable	High, 50–70% reasonable	
Feasible length of questionnaire	Conflicting advice; however, fewer 'screens' probably better	6–8 A4 pages		Up to half an hour	Variable depending on location
Suitable types of question	Closed questions but not too complex, complicated sequencing fine if uses IT, must be of interest to respondent	Closed questions but not too complex, simple sequencing only, must be of interest to respondent		Open and closed questions, but only simple questions, complicated sequencing fine	Open and closed questions, including complicated questions, complicated sequencing fine
Time taken to complete collection	2–6 weeks from distribution (dependent on number of follow-ups)	4–8 weeks from posting (dependent on number of follow-ups)	Dependent on sample size, number of field workers etc.	Dependent on sample size, number of interviewers etc. but slower than self-administered for same sample size	
Main financial resource implications	World Wide Web page design	Outward and return postage, photocopying, clerical support, data entry	Field workers, travel, photocopying, clerical support, data entry	Interviewers, telephone calls, clerical support. Photocopying and data entry if not using CATI[c]. Programming, software and computers if using CATI	Interviewers, travel, clerical support. Photocopying and data entry if not using CAPI[d]. Programming, software and computers if using CAPI
Role of the interviewer/ field worker	None		Delivery and collection of questionnaires, enhancing respondent participation	Enhancing respondent participation, guiding the respondent through the questionnaire, answering respondents' questions	
Data input[b]	May be automated	Closed questions can be designed so that responses may be entered using optical mark readers after questionnaire has been returned		Response to all questions entered at time of collection using CATI[c]	Response to all questions can be entered at time of collection using CAPI[d]

[a]Discussed in Chapter 6 [b]Discussed in Section 11.2 [c]Computer-aided telephone interviewing [d]Computer-aided personal interviewing
Sources: Authors' experience; Dillman (2000); Oppenheim (2000); deVaus (2002); Witmer *et al.* (1999)

- time available to complete the data collection;
- financial implications of data collection and entry;
- availability of interviewers and field workers to assist;
- ease of automating data entry.

The time needed for data collection increases markedly for delivery and collection questionnaires and structured interviews where the samples are geographically dispersed (Table 10.1). One way you can overcome this constraint is to select your sample using cluster sampling (Section 6.2). Unless your questionnaire is administered on-line, or *computer-aided personal interviewing (CAPI)* or *computer-aided telephone interviewing (CATI)* are used, you will need to consider the costs of reproducing the questionnaire, clerical support and entering the data for computer analysis. For postal and telephone questionnaires, cost estimates for postage and telephone calls will need to be included. If you are working for an organisation postage costs may be reduced by using *Freepost* for questionnaire return. This means that you pay only postage and a small handling charge for those questionnaires that are returned by post. However, the use of Freepost rather than a stamp may adversely affect your response rates (see Table 10.4).

Virtually all data collected by questionnaires will be analysed by computer. Some packages (for example Snap and SphinxSurvey) allow you both to design your questionnaire and to enter and analyse the data within the same software. Once your data have been coded and entered into the computer you will be able to explore and analyse them far more quickly and thoroughly than by hand (Section 11.2). As a rough rule, you should analyse questionnaire data by computer if they have been collected from 30 or more respondents. For larger surveys, you may wish to automate the input of data. For self-administered questionnaires, this can be done for closed questions where respondents select and mark their answer from a prescribed list.

worked example

Closed question designed for an optical mark reader

The following question is typical of those used for large-scale market research. Similar questions can be found in many postal questionnaires. Respondents are given clear instructions on how to mark their responses on the questionnaire:

Please use a pencil to mark your answer as a solid box like this: [▬]

If you make a mistake use an eraser to rub out your answer.

1 Please mark all the types of music that you regularly listen to:	Pop/Rock	[ ]
	Reggae	[ ]
	New Age	[ ]
	Jazz	[ ]
	Classical	[ ]
	Easy listening	[ ]
	Other	[ ]
	(please describe):	
	....	

The mark is read using an *optical mark reader*, which recognises and converts marks into data at rates often exceeding 200 pages a minute. Data for interviewer-administered questionnaires can be entered directly into the computer at the time of interview using CATI or CAPI software. With both types of software you read the questions to the respondent from the screen and enter their answers directly into the computer. Because of the costs of high-speed and high-capacity scanning equipment, software and pre-survey programming, CATI and CAPI are financially viable only for very large surveys or where repeated use of the computers and software will be made.

In reality, you are almost certain to have to make compromises in your choice of questionnaire. These will be unique to your research as the decision about which questionnaire is most suitable cannot be answered in isolation from your research question(s) and objectives and the population that you are surveying.

10.3 Deciding what data need to be collected

Research design requirements

Unlike in-depth and semi-structured interviews (Chapter 9), the questions you ask in questionnaires need to be defined precisely prior to data collection. Whereas you can prompt and explore issues further with in-depth and semi-structured interviews, this will not be possible for questionnaires. In addition, the questionnaire offers only one chance to collect the data, as it is often difficult to identify respondents or to return to collect additional information. This means that the time you spend planning precisely what data you need to collect, how you intend to analyse them (Chapter 11) and designing your questionnaire to meet these requirements is crucial if you are to answer your research question(s) and meet your objectives.

For most management and business research the data you collect using questionnaires will be used for either descriptive or explanatory purposes. For questions where the main purpose is to describe the population's characteristics either at a fixed time or at a series of points over time to enable comparisons, you will normally need to administer your questionnaire to a sample. The sample needs to be as representative and accurate as possible where it will be used to generalise about the total population (Sections 6.1–6.3). You will also probably need to relate your findings to earlier research. It is therefore important that you select the appropriate characteristics to answer your research question(s) and to address your objectives. You therefore need to have:

- reviewed the literature carefully;
- discussed your ideas with colleagues, your project tutor and other interested parties.

For research involving organisations, we have found it essential to understand the organisations in which we are undertaking the research. Similarly, for international or cross-cultural research it is important to have an understanding of the countries or cultures in which you are undertaking the research. Without this it is easy to make mistakes, such as using the wrong terminology or language, and to collect useless data. For many research projects an understanding of relevant organisations can be achieved through browsing company publications or their Internet sites (Section 7.3), observation (Chapter 8) and in-depth and semi-structured interviews (Chapter 9).

Explanatory research requires data to test a theory or theories. This means that, in addition to those issues raised for descriptive research, you need to define the theories you wish to test as relationships between variables prior to designing your questionnaire. You therefore need to have reviewed the literature carefully, discussed your ideas widely, and conceptualised your own research clearly prior to designing your questionnaire (Ghauri and Grønhaugh, 2002). In particular you need to be clear about which relationships you think are likely to exist between variables:

- variables are *dependent* – that is, change in response to changes in other variables;
- variables are *independent* – that is, cause changes in dependent variables;
- variables are *extraneous* – that is, might also cause changes in dependent variables, thereby providing an alternative explanation to your independent variables.

worked example

Defining theories in terms of relationships between variables

As part of her research Han wished to test the theory that the incidence of repetitive strain injury (RSI) was linked to the number of rest periods that keyboard operators took each working day.

The relationship that was thought to exist between the variables was that the incidence of RSI was higher when fewer or no rest periods were taken each day. The dependent variable was the incidence of RSI and the independent variable was the number of rest periods taken each day. Han thought that extraneous variables such as the use of proper seating and wrist rests might also influence the incidence of RSI. Data were therefore collected on these variables as well.

As these relationships are likely to be tested through statistical analysis (Section 11.5) of the data collected by your questionnaire you need to be clear about the way they will be measured at the design stage. Where possible you should ensure that measures are compatible with those used in other relevant research so that comparisons can be made (Section 11.2).

Types of variable

Dillman (2000) distinguishes between three types of data variable that can be collected through questionnaires:

- opinion;
- behaviour;
- attribute.

These distinctions are important, as they will influence the way your questions are worded. *Opinion* variables record how respondents feel about something or what they think or believe is true or false. In contrast, data on behaviours and attributes record what respondents do and are. When recording what respondents do, you are recording their *behaviour*. This differs from respondents' opinions because you are recording a concrete experience. Behavioural variables contain data on what people (or their organisations) did in the past, do now or will do in the future. By contrast, *attribute* variables contain data about the respondents' characteristics. Attributes are best thought of as things a respondent possesses, rather than things a respondent does (Dillman, 2000). They are used to explore how opinions and behaviour differ between respondents as well as to check that the data collected are representative of the total population (Section 6.2). Attributes include characteristics such as age, gender, marital status, education, occupation and income.

worked example

Opinion, behaviour and attribute questions

You have been asked to undertake an anonymous survey of financial advisors' ethical values. In particular your sponsors are interested in the advice given to clients. After some deliberation you come up with three questions that address the issue of putting clients' interests before their own:

2 How do you feel about the following statement? 'Financial advisors should place their clients' interest before their own.'

	strongly agree	☐
	mildly agree	☐
(please tick the appropriate box)	neither agree or disagree	☐
	mildly disagree	☐
	strongly disagree	☐

3 In general, do financial advisors place their clients' interests before their own?

	always yes	☐
	usually yes	☐
(please tick the appropriate box)	sometimes yes	☐
	seldom yes	☐
	never yes	☐

4 How often do you place your clients' interests before your own?

	80–100% of my time	☐
	60–79% of my time	☐
(please tick the appropriate box)	40–59% of my time	☐
	20–39% of my time	☐
	0–19% of my time	☐

Your choice of question or questions to include in your questionnaire will depend on whether you need to collect data on financial advisors' opinions or behaviours. Question 2 is designed to collect data on respondents' opinions about financial advisors placing their clients' interest before their own. This question asks respondents how they feel. In contrast, question 3 asks respondents whether financial advisors in general place their clients' interests before their own. It is therefore concerned with their opinions in terms of their individual beliefs. Question 4 focuses on how often the respondents actually places their clients' interests before their own. Unlike the previous questions it is concerned with their actual behaviour rather than their opinion.

To answer your research questions and to meet your objectives you also need to collect data to explore how ethical values differ between subgroupings of financial advisors. One theory you have is that ethical values are related to age. To test this you need to collect data on the attribute age. After further deliberation you come up with question 5:

5 How old are you?

	less than 30 years	☐
	30 to less than 40 years	☐
(please tick the appropriate box)	40 to less than 50 years	☐
	50 to less than 60 years	☐
	60 years or over	☐

Ensuring that essential data are collected

A problem experienced by many students and organisations we work with is how to ensure that the data collected will enable the research question(s) to be answered and the objectives achieved. Although no method is infallible, one way is to create a data requirements table (Table 10.2). This summarises the outcome of a process:

1 Decide whether the main outcome of your research is descriptive or explanatory.
2 Subdivide each research question or objective into more specific investigative questions about which you need to gather data.
3 Repeat the second stage if you feel that the investigative questions are not sufficiently precise.
4 Identify the variables about which you will need to collect data to answer each investigative question.
5 Establish how to measure the data for each variable.

Investigative questions are the questions that you need to answer in order to address satisfactorily each research question and to meet each objective (Cooper and Schindler, 2001). They need to be generated with regard to your research question(s) and objectives. For some investigative questions you will need to subdivide your first attempt into more detailed investigative questions. For each you need to be clear whether you are interested in respondents' opinions, behaviours or attributes (discussed earlier) as what appears to be a need to collect one sort of variable frequently turns out to be a need for another. We have found the literature review, discussions with interested parties and pilot studies to be of help here.

You then need to identify the variables about which you need to collect data to answer each investigative question and to decide the detail at which these are

Table 10.2 Data requirements table

Research question/objective:			
Type of research:			
Investigative questions	Variable(s) required	Detail in which data measured	Check included in questionnaire ✓

measured. Again, the review of the literature and associated research can suggest possibilities. However, if you are unsure about the detail needed you should measure at the more precise level. Although this is more time consuming, it will give you flexibility in your analyses. In these you will be able to use computer software to group or combine data (Section 11.2).

Once your table is complete, it must be checked to make sure that all data necessary to answer your investigative questions are included. When checking you need to be disciplined and to ensure that only data that are essential to answering your research question(s) and meeting your objectives are included. We added the final column to remind us to check that our questionnaire actually includes a question that collects the data!

worked example

Data requirements table

Sarah was asked to discover staff attitudes to the possible introduction of a no smoking policy at her workplace. Discussion with senior management and colleagues and reading relevant literature helped her to firm up her objective and investigative questions. A selection of these is included in the extract from her table of data requirements:

Research question/objective: *To establish employees' attitudes to the possible introduction of a no-smoking policy at their workplace*			
Type of research: *Predominantly descriptive, although wish to examine differences between employees*			
Investigative questions	**Variable(s) required**	**Detail in which data measured**	**Check included in questionnaire ✓**
Do employees feel that they should be able to smoke in their office if they want to as a right? (opinion)	*Opinion of employee to smoking in their office as a right*	*Feel... should be allowed, should not be allowed, no strong feelings*	
Do employees feel that the employer should provide a smoking room for smokers if smoking in offices is banned? (opinion)	*Opinion of employee to the provision of a smoking room for smokers*	*Feel... very strongly that it should, quite strongly that it should, no strong opinions, quite strongly that it should not, very strongly that it should not*	
Would employees accept a smoking ban at work if the majority of people agreed toit? (behaviour)	*Likely behaviour of employee regarding the acceptance of a ban*	*Would... accept with no preconditions, accept if a smoking room was provided, not accept without additional conditions (specify conditions), would not accept whatever the conditions*	
Do employee opinions differ depending on	*(Opinion of employee – outlined above)*	*(Included above)*	

■ age? (attribute) ■ whether or not a smoker? (behaviour)	■ Age of employee ■ Smoker	■ To nearest 5-year band (youngest 16, oldest 65) ■ Non-smoker, smokes but not in office, smokes in office	
How representative are the responses? (attributes)	Age of employee Gender of employee Job	(Included above) Male, female Senior management, management, supervisory, other	

10.4 Designing the questionnaire

The validity and reliability of the data you collect and the response rate you achieve depend, to a large extent, on the design of your questions, the structure of your questionnaire, and the rigour of your pilot testing (all discussed in this section). A valid question will enable accurate data to be collected, and one that is reliable will mean that these data are collected consistently. Foddy (1994:17) discusses this in terms of the questions and answers making sense. In particular he emphasises that 'the question must be understood by the respondent in the way intended by the researcher and the answer given by the respondent must be understood by the researcher in the way intended by the respondent'. This means that there are at least four stages that must occur if the question is to be valid and reliable (Figure 10.2). It also means that the design stage is likely to involve you in substantial rewriting in order to ensure that the respondent decodes the question in the way you intended. We therefore recommend that you use a word processor or survey design software such as Snap or SphinxSurvey.

Designing individual questions

The design of each question should be determined by the data you need to collect (Section 10.3). When designing individual questions researchers do one of three things (Bourque and Clark, 1994):

- adopt questions used in other questionnaires;
- adapt questions used in other questionnaires;
- develop their own questions.

Adopting or adapting questions may be necessary if you wish to replicate, or to compare your findings with, another study. This can allow reliability to be assessed. It is also more efficient than developing your own questions provided that you can still collect the data you need to answer your research question(s) and to meet your objectives. Some survey design software includes questions that you may use. Alternatively, you may find questions and coding schemes that you feel will meet your needs in existing surveys or in *question banks* such as the ESRC's Question Bank.* However, before you adopt questions, beware! There are a vast number of poor questions in

* The Internet address for the ESRC Question Bank is http://qb.soc.surrey.ac.uk

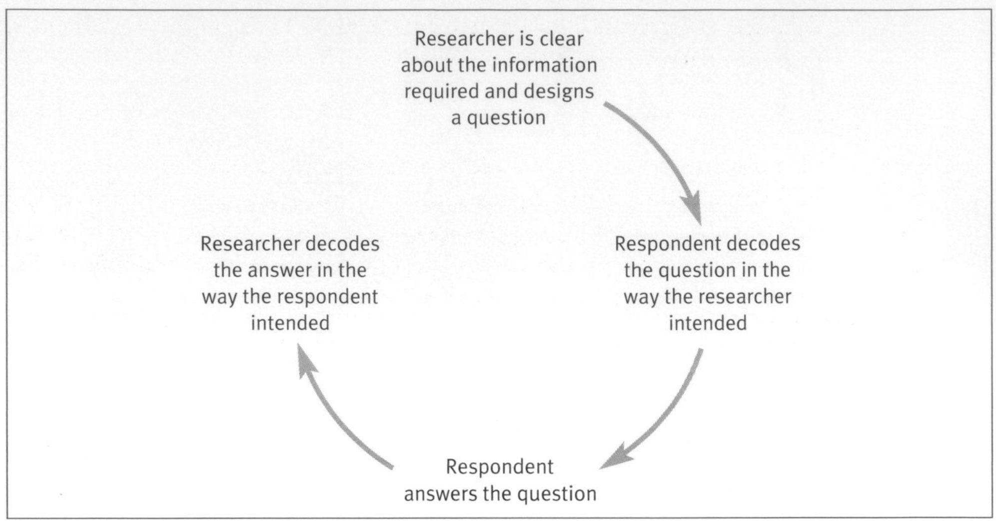

Figure 10.2 Stages that must occur if a question is to be valid and reliable
Source: Developed from Foddy (1994)

circulation, so always assess each question carefully. In addition, you need to check whether they are under copyright. If they are, you need to obtain the author's permission to use them. Even where there is no formal copyright you should note where you obtained the questions and give credit to their author.

Initially you need only consider the type and wording of individual questions rather than the order in which they will appear on the form. Clear wording of questions using terms that are likely to be familiar to, and understood by, respondents can improve the validity of the questionnaire. Most types of questionnaire include a combination of open and closed questions. *Open questions*, sometimes referred to as *open-ended questions* (Dillman, 2000), allow respondents to give answers in their own way (Fink, 1995a). *Closed questions*, sometimes referred to as *closed-ended questions* (Dillman, 2000) or *forced-choice questions* (deVaus, 2002), provide a number of alternative answers from which the respondent is instructed to choose. The latter type of question is usually quicker and easier to answer, as they require minimal writing. Responses is also easier to compare as they have been predetermined. However, if these responses cannot be easily interpreted then these benefits are, to say the least, marginal (Foddy, 1994). Youngman (1986; cited in Bell, 1999) identifies six types of closed question that we discuss later:

- *list*, where the respondent is offered a list of items, any of which may be selected;
- *category*, where only one response can be selected from a given set of categories;
- *ranking*, where the respondent is asked to place something in order;
- *scale or rating*, in which a rating device is used to record responses;
- *quantity*, to which the response is a number giving the amount;
- *grid*, where responses to two or more questions can be recorded using the same matrix.

Prior to data analysis, you will need to group and code responses to each question.

Detailed coding guidance is given in Section 11.2. You are strongly advised to read the entire chapter prior to designing your questions.

Open questions

Open questions are used widely in in-depth and semi-structured interviews (Section 9.5). In questionnaires they are useful if you are unsure of the response, such as in exploratory research, when you require a detailed answer or when you want to find out what is uppermost in the respondent's mind. An example of an open question (from a self-administered questionnaire) is:

6 Please list up to three things you like about your job:

1...

2...

3...

With open questions, the precise wording of the question and the amount of space partially determine the length and fullness of response. However, if you leave too much space the question becomes off-putting. Question 6 collects data about what each respondent believes they like about their job. Thus if salary had been the reason uppermost in their mind this would probably have been recorded first. Unfortunately, for large-scale questionnaire surveys responses to open questions are extremely time consuming to code (Section 11.2). For this reason, it is usually advisable keep their use to a minimum.

List questions

List questions offer the respondent a list of responses, any of which they can choose. Such questions are useful when you need to be sure that the respondent has considered all possible responses. However, the list of responses must be defined clearly and meaningfully to the respondent. For structured interviews, it is often helpful to present the respondent with a *prompt card* listing all responses. The response categories you can use vary widely and include 'yes/no', 'agree/disagree' and 'applies/does not apply' along with 'don't know' or 'not sure'. If you intend to use what you hope is a complete list you may wish to add a catch-all category of 'other'. This has been included in question 7 to illustrate this point although, in reality, the question does not contain a complete list of services.

7 Please tick ✓ the box in the provided column for services you provided as a home care assistant for this client in the past month.

If you have not provided a particular service, please leave the box blank.

service	**provided**
cleaning rooms	☐
shopping	☐
bed making	☐
laundry	☐
other	☐
(please describe:)..	

Question 7 collects data on the behaviour of the home care assistant, in this instance the services he or she provided for a particular client. In this list question, the common practice of omitting negative response boxes has been adopted. Consequently, negative responses are inferred from each unmarked response. If you choose to do this, beware: non-response could also indicate uncertainty or, for some questions, that an item does not apply!

Category questions

In contrast, *category questions* are designed so that each respondent's answer can fit only one category. Such questions are particularly useful if you need to collect data about behaviour or attributes. The number of categories that you can include without affecting the accuracy of responses is dependent on the type of questionnaire. Self-administered questionnaires and telephone questionnaires should usually have no more than five response categories (Fink, 1995a). Structured interviews can have more categories provided that a *prompt card* is used or, as in question 8, the interviewer categorises the responses.

8 How often do you visit this shopping centre?

Interviewer: listen to the respondent's answer and tick ✓ as appropriate.

☐ first visit	2 or more times a week ☐
☐ once a week	less than once a week to fortnightly ☐
☐ less than fortnightly to once a month	less often ☐

You should arrange responses in a logical order so that it is easy to locate the response category that corresponds to each respondent's answer. Your categories should be *mutually exclusive* (should not overlap), and should cover all possible responses. The

worked example

Use of a prompt card as part of a structured interview

As part of a market research questionnaire, interviewers asked the following question:

Which of the following daily newspapers have you read during the past month?

Show respondent card 3 with the names of the newspapers. Read out names of the newspapers one at a time. Record their response with a ✓ in the appropriate box.

	read	not read	don't know
The Daily Telegraph	☐	☐	☐
The Times	☐	☐	☐
Daily Express	☐	☐	☐
The Sun	☐	☐	☐
The Daily Mirror	☐	☐	☐
The Guardian	☐	☐	☐

Daily Mail	☐	☐	☐
Financial Times	☐	☐	☐
Daily Star	☐	☐	☐

Card 3 was given to the respondent prior to reading out newspaper names and collected back after the question had been completed:

3

The Daily Telegraph

THE TIMES

THE DAILY EXPRESS

The Sun

The Daily Mirror

The **Guardian**

Daily Mail

FINANCIAL TIMES

Daily Star

layout of your questionnaire should make it clear which boxes refer to which response category by placing them close to the appropriate text.

Ranking questions

A *ranking question* asks the respondent to place things in rank order. This means that you can discover their relative importance to the respondent. In question 9, taken from a postal questionnaire, the respondents are asked their beliefs about the relative importance of a series of features when choosing a new car. The catch-all feature of 'other' is included to allow respondents to add one other feature.

9 Please number each of the factors listed below in order of importance to you in your choice of a new car. Number the most important 1, the next 2 and so on. If a factor has no importance at all, please leave blank.

factor	importance
acceleration	[ ]
boot size	[ ]
depreciation	[ ]
safety features	[ ]
fuel economy	[ ]
price	[ ]
driving enjoyment	[ ]
other	[ ]
....	(⇦ please describe)

With such questions, you need to ensure that the instructions are clear and will be understood by the respondent. In general, respondents find that ranking more than seven or eight items takes too much effort, so you should keep your list to this length or shorter (Kervin, 1999). Respondents can rank accurately only when they can see or remember all items. This can be overcome with face-to-face questionnaires by using prompt cards on which you list all of the features to be ranked. However, telephone questionnaires should only ask respondents to rank a maximum of three or four items, as the respondent will need to rely on their memory (Kervin, 1999).

Rating or scale questions

Rating or scale questions are often used to collect opinion data. The most common approach is the *Likert-style rating scale* in which you ask the respondent how strongly they agree or disagree with a statement or series of statements, usually on a four-, five-, six- or seven-point rating scale. If you intend to use a series of statements, you should keep the same order of response categories to avoid confusing respondents (Dillman, 2000). You should, however, include both positive and negative statements so as to ensure that the respondent reads each one carefully and thinks about which box to tick.

10 For the following statement please tick ✓ the box that matches your view most closely.

	agree	tend to agree	tend to disagree	disagree
I feel that employees' views have influenced the decisions taken by management.	☐	☐	☐	☐

Question 10 has been taken from a delivery and collection questionnaire to employees in an organisation and is designed to collect opinion data. In this rating question, an even number of points (four) has been used to force the respondent to express their feelings towards an implicitly positive statement. By contrast question 11, also from a delivery and collection questionnaire, contains an odd number (five) of points on the rating scale. This rating scale allows the respondent to 'sit on the fence' by ticking the middle 'not sure' category when considering an implicitly negative statement. The phrase 'not sure' is used here as it is less threatening to the respondent than admitting they do not know. This question is designed to collect data on employees' opinions of the situation now.

11 For the following statement please tick ✓ the box that matches your view most closely.

	agree	tend to agree	tend to disagree	disagree
I believe there are 'them and us' barriers to communication in the company *now*.	☐	☐	☐	☐

You can expand this form of question further to record finer shades of opinion. However, respondents to telephone questionnaires find it difficult to distinguish between values on rating scales of more than five points plus 'don't know'. In addition, there is little point in collecting data for seven or nine response categories, if these are subsequently combined in your analysis (Chapter 11).

In question 12 the respondent's attitude is captured on a 10-point *numeric rating scale*. In such questions it is important that the numbers reflect the feeling of the respondent. Thus 1 reflects poor value for money and 10 good value for money. These end categories (and sometimes the middle) are labelled. As in this question, graphics may also be used to reflect the rating scale visually, thereby aiding the respondent's interpretation. An additional category of 'not sure' or don't know' can be added and should be separated slightly from the rating scale.

12 For the following statement please circle ◯ the number that matches your view most closely.

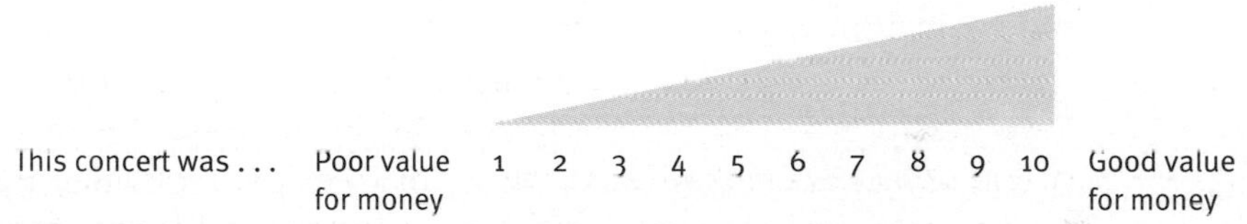

Another variation is the *semantic differential rating scale*. These are often used in consumer research to determine underlying attitudes. The respondent is asked to rate a single object or idea on a series of bipolar rating scales. Each *bipolar scale* is described by a pair of opposite adjectives (question 13) designed to capture respondents' attitudes towards service. For these rating scales, you should vary the position of positive and negative adjectives from left to right to reduce the tendency to read only the adjective on the left (Kervin, 1999).

13 On each of the lines below place a × to show how you feel about the service you received at our restaurant.

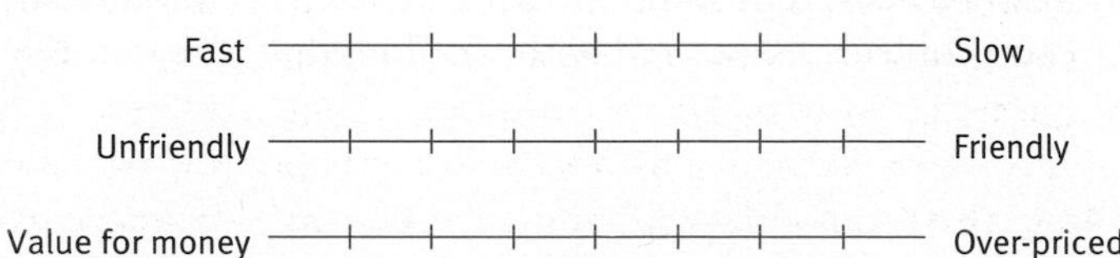

Rating questions have been combined to measure a wide variety of concepts such as customer loyalty, service quality and job satisfaction. For each concept the resultant measure or *scale* is represented by a scale score created by combining the scores for each of the rating questions. In the case of a simple Likert scale, for example, the scale score for each case would be calculated by adding together the scores of each of the questions selected (deVaus, 2002). A detailed discussion of creating scales, including those by Likert, Guttman and Thurstone, can be found in Foddy (1994). However, rather than developing your own scales, it often makes sense to use or adapt existing scales. Details of an individual scale can often be found by following up references in an article reporting research that uses that scale. In addition, there are a wide variety of handbooks that list these scales (for example: Miller and Salkind, 2002). However, you need to beware: they may be subject to copyright constraints. Even where there is no formal copyright, you should note where you obtained the scale and give credit to the author.

Quantity questions

The responses to a *quantity question* is a number, which gives the amount of a characteristic. For this reason, such questions tend to be used to collect behaviour or attribute data. A common quantity question, which collects attribute data, is:

14 What is your year of birth?	1	9			
(for example for 1980 write:)	1	9	*8*	*0*	

Because the data collected by this question could be entered into the computer without coding, the question can also be termed a *self-coded* question.

Grid

A *grid* or *matrix* enables you to record the responses to two or more similar questions at the same time. The 1991 UK census form was designed using a matrix format. Questions were listed down the left-hand side of the page, and each household member was listed across the top. The response to each question for each household member was then recorded in the cell where the row and column met. Although using a grid saves space, Dillman (2000) suggests that respondents have difficulties comprehending these designs and that they are a barrier to response.

Question wording

The wording of each question will need careful consideration to ensure that the responses are valid – that is, measure what you think they do. Your questions will need to be checked within the context for which they were written rather than in abstract. Given this, the checklist in Box 10.1 should help you to avoid the most obvious problems associated with wording that threaten the validity of responses.

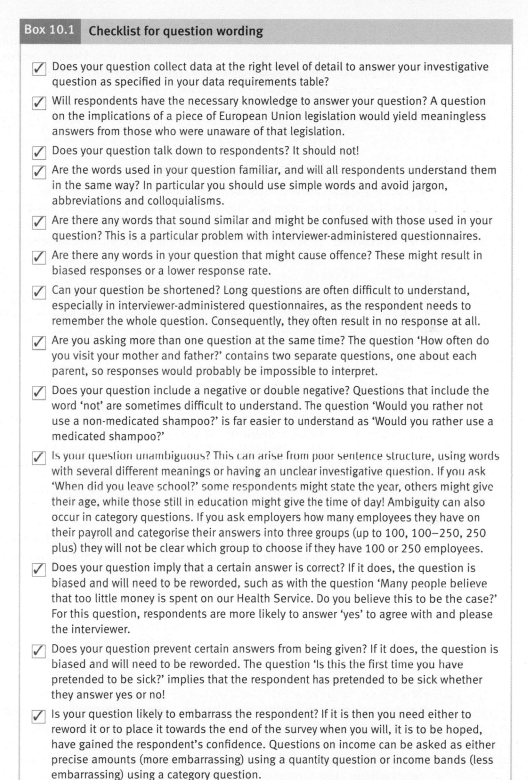

Box 10.1 Checklist for question wording

- ✓ Does your question collect data at the right level of detail to answer your investigative question as specified in your data requirements table?
- ✓ Will respondents have the necessary knowledge to answer your question? A question on the implications of a piece of European Union legislation would yield meaningless answers from those who were unaware of that legislation.
- ✓ Does your question talk down to respondents? It should not!
- ✓ Are the words used in your question familiar, and will all respondents understand them in the same way? In particular you should use simple words and avoid jargon, abbreviations and colloquialisms.
- ✓ Are there any words that sound similar and might be confused with those used in your question? This is a particular problem with interviewer-administered questionnaires.
- ✓ Are there any words in your question that might cause offence? These might result in biased responses or a lower response rate.
- ✓ Can your question be shortened? Long questions are often difficult to understand, especially in interviewer-administered questionnaires, as the respondent needs to remember the whole question. Consequently, they often result in no response at all.
- ✓ Are you asking more than one question at the same time? The question 'How often do you visit your mother and father?' contains two separate questions, one about each parent, so responses would probably be impossible to interpret.
- ✓ Does your question include a negative or double negative? Questions that include the word 'not' are sometimes difficult to understand. The question 'Would you rather not use a non-medicated shampoo?' is far easier to understand as 'Would you rather use a medicated shampoo?'
- ✓ Is your question unambiguous? This can arise from poor sentence structure, using words with several different meanings or having an unclear investigative question. If you ask 'When did you leave school?' some respondents might state the year, others might give their age, while those still in education might give the time of day! Ambiguity can also occur in category questions. If you ask employers how many employees they have on their payroll and categorise their answers into three groups (up to 100, 100–250, 250 plus) they will not be clear which group to choose if they have 100 or 250 employees.
- ✓ Does your question imply that a certain answer is correct? If it does, the question is biased and will need to be reworded, such as with the question 'Many people believe that too little money is spent on our Health Service. Do you believe this to be the case?' For this question, respondents are more likely to answer 'yes' to agree with and please the interviewer.
- ✓ Does your question prevent certain answers from being given? If it does, the question is biased and will need to be reworded. The question 'Is this the first time you have pretended to be sick?' implies that the respondent has pretended to be sick whether they answer yes or no!
- ✓ Is your question likely to embarrass the respondent? If it is then you need either to reword it or to place it towards the end of the survey when you will, it is to be hoped, have gained the respondent's confidence. Questions on income can be asked as either precise amounts (more embarrassing) using a quantity question or income bands (less embarrassing) using a category question.

▶

- ✓ Have you incorporated advice appropriate for your type of questionnaire (such as the maximum number of categories) outlined in the earlier discussion of question types?
- ✓ Are answers to closed questions written so that at least one will apply to every respondent?
- ✓ Are the instructions on how to record each answer clear?

Translating questions into other languages

Translating questions and associated instructions into another language requires care if your translated or target questionnaire is to be decoded and answered by respondents in the way you intended. For international research this is extremely important if the questionnaires are to have the same meaning to all respondents. For this reason Usunier (1998) suggests that when translating the source questionnaire attention should be paid to:

- *lexical meaning* – the precise meaning of individual words (for example, the French word *chaud* can be translated into two concepts in English and German, 'warm' and 'hot');
- *idiomatic meaning* – the meanings of a group of words that are natural to a native speaker and not deducible from those of the individual words (for example, the English expression for informal communication, 'grapevine', has a similar idiomatic meaning as the French expression *téléphone arabe*, meaning literally 'arab telephone');
- *grammar and syntax* – the correct use of language, including the ordering of words and phrases to create well-formed sentences (for example, in Japanese the ordering is quite different from English or Dutch, as verbs are at the end of sentences);
- *experiential meaning* – the equivalence of meanings of words and sentences for people in their everyday experiences (for example, terms that are familiar in the source questionnaire's context such as 'dual career household' may be unfamiliar in the target questionnaire's context).

Usunier (1998) outlines a number of techniques for translating your source questionnaire. These, along with their advantages and disadvantages, are summarised in Table 10.3. In this table, the *source questionnaire* is the questionnaire that is to be translated, and the *target questionnaire* is the translated questionnaire. When writing your final project report remember to include a copy of both the source and the target questionnaire as appendices. This will allow readers familiar with both languages to check that equivalent questions in both questionnaires have the same meaning.

Question coding

If you are planning to analyse your data by computer, they will need to be coded prior to entry. For quantity questions, actual numbers can be used as codes. For other questions, you will need to design a coding scheme. Whenever possible you should establish the coding scheme prior to collecting data and incorporate it into your questionnaire. This should take account of relevant existing coding schemes to enable comparisons with other data sets (Section 11.2).

Table 10.3 Translation techniques for questionnaires

	Direct translation	*Back-translation*	*Parallel translation*	*Mixed techniques*
Approach	Source questionnaire to target questionnaire	Source questionnaire to target questionnaire to source questionnaire; comparison of two new source questionnaires; creation of final version	Source questionnaire to target questionnaire by two or more independent translators; comparison of two target questionnaires; creation of final version	Back-translation undertaken by two or more independent translators; comparison of two new source questionnaires; creation of final version
Advantages	Easy to implement, relatively inexpensive	Likely to discover most problems	Leads to good wording of target questionnaire	Ensures best match between source and target questionnaires
Disadvantages	Can lead to many discrepancies (including those relating to meaning) between source and target questionnaire	Requires two translators, one a native speaker of the source language, the other a native speaker of the target language	Cannot ensure that lexical, idiomatic and experiential meanings are kept in target questionnaire	Costly, requires two or more independent translators. Implies that the source questionnaire can also be changed

Source: Developed from Usunier (1998)

For most closed questions you should be able to add codes to response categories. These can be printed on the questionnaire, thereby *pre-coding* the question and removing the need to code after data collection. Two ways of doing this are illustrated by questions 15 and 16, which collect data on the respondents' opinions.

15 Is the service you receive?

	Excellent	Good	Reasonable	Poor	Awful
(please circle ○ the number)	5	4	3	2	1

16 Is the service you receive?

	Excellent	Good	Reasonable	Poor	Awful
(please tick ✓ the box)	☐ 5	☐ 1	☐ 3	☐ 2	☐ 4

The codes allocated to response categories will affect your analyses. In question 15 an ordered scale of numbers has been allocated to adjacent responses. This will make it far easier to aggregate responses using a computer (Section 11.2) to 'satisfactory' (5, 4 or 3) and 'unsatisfactory' (2 or 1) compared with the codes in question 16. We therefore recommend that you do not allocate codes as in question 16.

In contrast, if you are considering administering your questionnaire on line you can create an *on-line form* (questionnaire) containing text boxes where the respondent enters information, check boxes that list the choices available to the respondent allowing them to 'check' or 'tick' one or more of them, and drop-down list boxes that restrict the respondent to selecting only one of the answers you specify. On-line forms are often included as part of word-processing software such as Microsoft Word. They allow you to create a professional questionnaire and the respondent to complete the questionnaire on-line and return the data electronically, usually as a comma-delimited file.

17 Which team do you work for? *double click to select your answer*

East Team ▼
North Team
South Team
West Team

For open questions you will need to reserve space on your data collection form to code responses after data collection. Question 18 has been designed to collect attribute data in a sample survey of 5000 people. Theoretically there could be hundreds of possible responses, and so sufficient spaces are left in the 'for Office use only' box.

18 In what country were you born? ....

for Office use only
☐ ☐ ☐

Open questions, which generate lists of responses, are likely to require more complex coding using either the multiple-response or the multiple-dichotomy method. These are discussed in Section 11.2, and we recommend that you read this prior to designing your questions.

Designing the survey form

The order and flow of questions

When constructing your questionnaire it is a good idea to spend time considering the order and flow of your questions. These should be logical to the respondent (and interviewer) rather than follow the order in your data requirements table (Table 10.2). To assist the flow of the survey it may be necessary to include *filter questions*. These identify those respondents for whom the following question or questions are not applicable, so they can skip those questions. You should beware of using more than two or three filter questions in self-administered questionnaires, as respondents tend to find having to skip questions annoying. More complex filter questions can be programmed into on-line questionnaires and CAPI and CATI software so that skipped questions are never displayed on the screen and as a consequence never asked (Dillman, 2000). In such situations the respondent is unlikely to be aware of the questions that have been skipped. The following example uses the answer to question 19 to determine whether questions 20 to 24 will be answered. (Questions 19 and 20 both collect data on attributes.)

19 Are you currently registered as unemployed? Yes ☐ 1
No ☐ 2

If 'no' go to question 25

20 How long have you been registered as unemployed? |_|_| years |_|_| months

(for example for no years and six months write:) |_|0| years |_|6| months

Where you need to introduce new topics, phrases such as 'the following questions refer to . . .' or 'I am now going to ask you about . . .' are useful. And when wording your questions, you should remember the particular population for whom your questionnaire is designed. For interviewer-administered questionnaires, you will have to include instructions for the interviewer. The checklist in Box 10.2 should help you to avoid the most obvious problems associated with question order and flow. For some questionnaires the advice contained may be contradictory. Where this is the case, you need to decide what is most important for your particular population.

Box 10.2 Checklist for question order

- ✓ Are questions at the beginning of your questionnaire more straightforward and ones the respondent will enjoy answering? Questions about attributes and behaviours are usually more straightforward to answer than those collecting data on opinions.
- ✓ Are questions at the beginning of your questionnaire obviously relevant to the stated purpose of your questionnaire? For example, questions requesting contextual information may appear irrelevant.
- ✓ Are questions and topics that are more complex placed towards the middle of your questionnaire? By this stage most respondents should be completing the survey with confidence but should not yet be bored or tired.
- ✓ Are personal and sensitive questions towards the end of your questionnaire, and is their purpose clearly explained? On being asked these a respondent may refuse to answer; however, if they are at the end of an interviewer-administered questionnaire you will still have the rest of the data!
- ✓ Are filter questions and routeing instructions easy to follow so that there is a clear route through the questionnaire?
- ✓ (For interviewer-administered questionnaires) Are instructions to the interviewer easy to follow?
- ✓ Are questions grouped into obvious sections that will make sense to the respondent?
- ✓ Have you re-examined the wording of each question and ensured it is consistent with the position in the questionnaire as well as with the data you require?

worked example

Introducing a series of rating questions in a telephone questionnaire

As part of a telephone questionnaire, you need to collect data on respondents' attitudes to motorway service stations. To do this you ask respondents to rate a series of statements on a Likert-type rating scale. Because the survey will be conducted by telephone the rating scale has been restricted to four categories: strongly agree, agree, disagree, strongly disagree.

In order to make the questionnaire easy for the interviewer to follow, instructions are in italics and the words that need to be read to the respondent are in bold. An extract is given below:

Now I'm going to read you several statements. Please tell me whether you strongly agree, agree, disagree or strongly disagree with each.

Interviewer: read out statements 21 to 30 one at a time and after each ask . . .

▶

Do you strongly agree, agree, disagree or strongly disagree?

Record respondent's response with a tick ✓

	strongly agree	agree	disagree	strongly disagree
21 **I wish there were a greater number of service stations on motorways**	☐ 4	☐ 3	☐ 2	☐ 1

The layout of the questionnaire

Layout is important for both self-administered and interviewer-administered questionnaires. Interviewer-administered questionnaires should be designed to make reading questions and filling in responses easy. The layout of self-administered questionnaires should, in addition, be attractive to encourage the respondent to fill it in and to return it, while not appearing too long. However, where the choice is between an extra page and a cramped questionnaire the former is likely to be more acceptable to respondents (Dillman, 2000). Survey design and analysis software such as Snap and SphinxSurvey contain a series of style templates for typefaces, colours and page layout, which are helpful in producing a professional-looking questionnaire more quickly (Mercator, 2002; Scolari Sage, 2002). For paper-based surveys, the use of colour will increase the printing costs. However, it is worth noting that the best way of obtaining valid responses to questions is to keep both the visual appearance of the questionnaire and the wording of each question simple (Dillman, 2000).

Research findings on the extent to which the length of your questionnaire will affect your response rate are mixed (deVaus, 2002). There is a widespread view that longer questionnaires should be avoided as this reduces response rates. However, it has been difficult to separate the effect that questionnaire length has on response rates from other factors such as topic, type of respondents and the way in which it is administered. A very short questionnaire may suggest that your research is insignificant and hence not worth bothering with. Conversely a questionnaire that takes over two hours to complete might just be thrown away by the intended respondent. In general, we have found that a length of between four and eight A4 pages has been acceptable for within-organisation self-administered questionnaires. Telephone questionnaires of up to half an hour have caused few problems, whereas the acceptable length for structured interviews can vary from only a few minutes in the street to over two hours in a more comfortable environment (Section 9.6). Based on these experiences we recommend you follows deVaus' (2002) advice:

- Do not make the questionnaire longer than is really necessary to meet your research questions and objectives.
- Do not be too obsessed with the length of your questionnaire.

One way you can reduce apparent length without reducing legibility is to record answers to questions with the same set of possible responses as a table. Usually you place questions in the rows and responses in the columns. Instructions on how to answer the question and column headings are given prior to the table and on each subsequent page as illustrated by questions 23 and 24. These were designed to collect data on respondents' behaviour using a delivery and collection questionnaire.

For each of the following statements please tick the box that most closely matches your experience . . .

	monthly	every 3 months	every 6 months	less often	never
23 I receive a company site newsletter . . .	☐ 1	☐ 2	☐ 3	☐ 4	☐ 5
24 I receive other company publications . . .	☐ 1	☐ 2	☐ 3	☐ 4	☐ 5

Box 10.3 summarises the most important layout issues as a checklist.

Box 10.3 Checklist for questionnaire layout

☑ (For self-administered questionnaires) Do questions appear squashed on the page? This will put the respondent off reading it and reduce the response rate. Unfortunately, a thick questionnaire is equally off-putting!

☑ (For self-administered questionnaires) Is the questionnaire going to be printed on good-quality paper? This will imply that the survey is important.

☑ (For self-administered questionnaires) Is the questionnaire going to be printed on warm-pastel-coloured paper? Warm pastel shades such as yellow and pink generate more responses than cool colours such as green or blue. White is a good neutral colour but bright or fluorescent colours should be avoided.

☑ (For structured interviews) Will the questions and instructions be printed on one side of the paper only? You will find it difficult to read the questions on back pages if you are using a questionnaire attached to a clipboard!

☑ Is your questionnaire easy to read? Questionnaires should be typed in 12 point or 10 point using a plain font. Excessively long and excessively short lines reduce legibility. Similarly, respondents find CAPITALS, *italics* and shaded backgrounds more difficult to read. However, if used consistently, they can make completing the questionnaire easier.

☑ Have you ensured that the use of shading, colour, font sizes, spacing and the formatting of questions is consistent throughout the questionnaire?

☑ Is your questionnaire laid out in a format that respondents are accustomed to reading? Research has shown that many people skim-read questionnaires (Dillman, 2000). Instructions that can be read one line at a time from left to right moving down the page are therefore more likely to be followed correctly.

Explaining the purpose of the questionnaire

The covering letter

Most self-administered questionnaires are accompanied by a *covering letter*, which explains the purpose of the survey. This is the first part of the questionnaire that a respondent should look at. Unfortunately some of your sample will ignore it, while others use it to decide whether to answer the accompanying questionnaire.

Research by Dillman (2000) and others has shown that the messages contained in a self-administered questionnaire's covering letter will affect the response rate. The results of this research are summarised in Box 10.4.

Box 10.4 Structure of a covering letter

Type of paper:	good quality, official letterhead, including address, telephone number and email address (if possible)
Maximum length of letter:	one side (12 point font size if possible)
Date:	in full e.g. 6 April 2002
Recipient's name	title, forename, surname (absence suggests impersonality)
Recipient's address	in full (absence suggests impersonality)
Salutation:	use recipient's title and name (if possible)
First set of messages:	what research is about, why it is useful
Second set of messages:	why recipient's response is important, how long it will take to complete
Third set of messages:	promises of confidentiality or anonymity
Fourth set of messages:	how results will be used; token reward or charity donation for participation (if any)
Final set of messages:	whom to contact if have any queries, who to return completed questionnaire to and date by which should be returned
Closing remarks:	thank recipient for their help
Signature:	yours, by hand, in blue
Name and title:	yours including forename and surname
Postscript:	express thanks or other appropriate message (optional, but postscript is often the most visible aspect of letter)

Source: Developed from Dillman (2000)

For some research projects you may also send a letter prior to administering your questionnaire. This will be used by the respondent to decide whether to grant you access. Consequently, it is often the only opportunity you have to convince the respondent to participate in your research. Ways of ensuring this are discussed in Section 5.4.

Introducing the questionnaire

At the start of your questionnaire you need to explain clearly and concisely why you want the respondent to complete the survey. Dillman (2000) argues that, to achieve as high a response rate as possible, this should be done on the first page of the questionnaire in addition to the covering letter. He suggests that in addition to a summary of the main messages in the covering letter (Box 10.4) you include a:

- clear unbiased title, which conveys the topic of the questionnaire and makes it sound interesting;
- subtitle, which conveys the research nature of the topic (optional);
- neutral graphic illustration or logo to add interest and to set the questionnaire apart (self-administered questionnaires).

Interviewer-administered questionnaires will require this information to be phrased as a short introduction, which the interviewer can read to each respondent. A template for this (developed from deVaus, 2002) is given in the next paragraph:

Good morning / afternoon / evening. My name is (your name) from (your organisation). We are doing a research project to find out (brief description of purpose of the research). Your telephone number was drawn from a random sample of (brief description of the total population). The questions I should like to ask will take about (number) minutes. If you have any queries, I shall be happy to answer them. (Pause). Before I continue please can you confirm that this is (read out the telephone number) and that I am talking to (read out name/occupation/position in organisation to check that you have the right person). Please can I ask you the questions now?

worked example

Introducing a self-administered questionnaire

Mark is often asked by students to comment on their questionnaires. One student, Liz, who was working for a National Health Service Trust, showed him what she hoped was the final draft of her questionnaire, which included the following introduction:

Anytown NHS Trust Inproving Working Lives Staff Survey

All your responses will be treated in the strictest of confidence and only aggregated data will be available to the Trust. All questionnaires will be shredded once the data have been extracted. The Trust will publish a summary of the results.

Not surprisingly, Mark suggested that Liz redraft her introduction. Her revised introduction follows:

Improving Working Lives: Staff Survey 2003

This survey is being carried out to find out how well the Trust's policies to improve the working lives of people like you are operating. Please answer the questions freely. You cannot be identified from the information you provide, and no information about individuals will be given to the Trust.

ALL THE INFORMATION YOU PROVIDE WILL BE TREATED IN THE STRICTEST CONFIDENCE

The questionnaire should take you about five minutes to complete. Please answer the questions in the space provided. Try to complete the questions at a time when you are unlikely to be disturbed. Also, do not spend too long on any one question. Your first thoughts are usually your best!

Even if you feel the items covered may not apply directly to your working life please do not ignore them. Your answers are essential in building an accurate picture of the issues that are important to improving the working lives of people working for this Trust.

WHEN YOU HAVE COMPLETED THE QUESTIONNAIRE PLEASE RETURN IT TO US IN THE ENCLOSED FREEPOST ENVELOPE

I hope you find completing the questionnaire enjoyable, and thank you for taking the time to help us. If you have any queries or would like further information about this project, please call me on 01234-5678910.

Thank you for your help.

Elizabeth Petrie
Human Resources Department
Anytown Memorial Hospital
Anytown National Health Service Trust

You will also need to have prepared answers to the more obvious questions that the respondent might ask you. These include the purpose of the survey, how you obtained the respondent's telephone number, who is conducting or sponsoring the survey, and why someone else cannot answer the questions instead (Lavrakas, 1993).

Closing the questionnaire

At the end of your questionnaire you need to explain clearly what you want the respondent to do with their completed questionnaire. It is usual to start this section by thanking her or him for completing the questionnaire, and by providing a contact name and telephone number for any queries she or he may have. You should then give details of the date by which you would like the questionnaire returned and how and where to return it. A template for this is given in the next paragraph:

> **Thank you for taking the time to complete this questionnaire. If you have any queries please do not hesitate to contact (your name) by telephoning (contact telephone number with answer machine/voice mail).**
>
> **Please return the completed questionnaire by (date) in the envelope provided to:**
>
> **(your name)**
>
> **(your address)**

Pilot testing and assessing validity

Prior to using your questionnaire to collect data it should be pilot tested. The purpose of the *pilot test* is to refine the questionnaire so that respondents will have no problems in answering the questions and there will be no problems in recording the data. In addition, it will enable you to obtain some assessment of the questions' validity and the likely reliability of the data that will be collected. Preliminary analysis using the pilot test data can be undertaken to ensure that the data collected will enable your investigative questions to be answered.

Initially you should ask an expert or group of experts to comment on the representativeness and suitability of your questions. As well as allowing suggestions to be made on the structure of your questionnaire, this will help establish *content validity* (Mitchell, 1996) and enable you to make necessary amendments prior to pilot testing with a group as similar as possible to the final population in your sample. For any research project there is a temptation to skip the pilot testing. We would endorse Bell's (1999:128) advice, 'however pressed for time you are, do your best to give the questionnaire a trial run', as, without a trial run, you have no way of knowing your questionnaire will succeed.

The number of people on whom you pilot your questionnaire and the number of pilot tests you conduct are dependent on your research question(s), your objectives, the size of your research project, the time and money resources you have available, and how well you have initially designed your questionnaire. Very large questionnaire surveys such as national censuses will have numerous field trials starting with individual questions and working up to larger and more rigorous pilots of later drafts.

For smaller-scale questionnaires you are unlikely to have sufficient financial or time resources for such testing. However, it is still important that you pilot test your questionnaire. The number of people you choose should be sufficient to include any major variations in your population that you feel are likely to affect responses. For most student questionnaires this means that the minimum number for a pilot is 10 (Fink, 1995b), although for large surveys between 100 and 200 responses is usual (Dillman, 2000). Occasionally you may be extremely pushed for time. In such instances it is better to pilot test the questionnaire using friends or family than not at all! This will provide you with at least some idea of your questionnaire's *face validity*: that is, whether the questionnaire appears to make sense.

As part of your pilot you should check each completed pilot questionnaire to ensure that respondents have had no problems understanding or answering questions and have followed all instructions correctly (Fink, 1995b). Their responses will provide you with an idea of the reliability and suitability of the questions. For self-administered questionnaires additional information about problems can be obtained by giving respondents a further short questionnaire. Bell (1999) suggests you should use this to find out:

- how long the questionnaire took to complete;
- the clarity of instructions;
- which, if any, questions were unclear or ambiguous;
- which, if any, questions the respondent felt uneasy about answering;
- whether in their opinion there were any major topic omissions;
- whether the layout was clear and attractive;
- any other comments.

Interviewer-administered questionnaires need to be tested with the respondents for all these points other than layout. One way of doing this is to form an assessment as each questionnaire progresses. Another is to interview any interviewers you are employing. However, you can also check by asking the respondent additional questions at the end of their interview. In addition, you will need to pilot test the questionnaire with interviewers to discover whether:

- there are any questions for which visual aids should have been provided;
- they have difficulty in finding their way through the questionnaire;
- they are recording answers correctly.

Once you have completed pilot testing you should write to your respondents thanking them for their help.

Testing for reliability

As outlined at the start of this section, the reliability of your questionnaire is concerned with the consistency of responses to your questions. Mitchell (1996) outlines three common approaches to assessing reliability, in addition to comparing the data collected with other data from a variety of sources. Although the analysis for each of these is undertaken after data collection, they need to be considered at the questionnaire design stage. They are:

- test re-test;
- internal consistency;
- alternative form.

Test re-test estimates of reliability are obtained by correlating data collected with those from the same questionnaire collected under as near equivalent conditions as possible. The questionnaire therefore needs to be administered twice to respondents.

This may result in difficulties, as it is often difficult to persuade respondents to answer the same questionnaire twice. In addition, the longer the time interval between the two questionnaires, the lower the likelihood that respondents will answer the same way. We therefore recommend that you use this method only as a supplement to other methods.

Internal consistency involves correlating the responses to each question in the questionnaire with those to other questions in the questionnaire. It therefore measures the consistency of responses across either all the questions or a subgroup of the questions from your questionnaire. There are a variety of methods for calculating internal consistency, of which one of the most frequently used is Cronbach's alpha. Further details of this and other approaches can be found in Mitchell (1996) and in books on more advanced statistical analysis software such as Pallant (2001).

The final approach to testing for reliability outlined by Mitchell (1996) is *alternative form*. This offers some sense of the reliability within your questionnaire through comparing responses to alternative forms of the same question or groups of questions. Where questions are included for this purpose, usually in longer questionnaires, they are often called *check questions*. However, it is often difficult to ensure that these questions are substantially equivalent. Respondents may suffer from fatigue owing to the need to increase the length of the questionnaire, and they may spot the similar question and just refer back to their previous answer! It is therefore advisable to use check questions sparingly.

10.5 Administering the questionnaire

Once your questionnaire is designed, pilot tested and amended and your sample selected, the questionnaire can be used to collect data. This final stage is called *administering* the questionnaire. As part of this you will need to gain access to your sample (Sections 5.2 and 5.3) and to attempt to maximise the response rate. Jobber and O'Reilly (1996) review six techniques used in postal surveys that can raise response rates at this stage, provided that your questionnaire is clearly worded and well laid out. These are summarised in Table 10.4 and although what happened in these experiments is no guarantee of similar success, the table does at least provide some indication of what you can do and the likely impact.

Which of these techniques you use to help to maximise responses will inevitably be dependent on the way in which your questionnaire is administered. It is the processes associated with administering each of the five types of questionnaire that we now consider.

On-line questionnaires

For on-line questionnaires it is also important to have a clear timetable that identifies the tasks that need to be done and the resources that will be needed. A good response is dependent on the recipient being motivated to answer the questionnaire and to send it back. Although the covering letter (Section 10.4) and good design will help to ensure a high level of response it must be remembered that, unlike paper questionnaires, the designer and respondent may see different images. Alternative computer operating systems, Internet browsers and display screens can all result in the image

Table 10.4 **Techniques for raising questionnaire response rates**

Technique	*Average impact*	*Comment*
Prior notification, if possible by telephone	+19%	Personal contact raises the perceived importance of the study
Pre-paid monetary incentives	+15% to +26% depending on amount	People feel more obliged to respond if they have received something; the incentive differentiates the questionnaire from others
Non-monetary incentives	+12% to +15% depending on incentive	Work for similar reasons to monetary incentives although some evidence suggests that they are not as effective
Stamps on return envelopes	+7%	Stamps raise the importance relative to Freepost as the researcher has gone to the trouble of using a stamp
Anonymity	+20% (in company), +10% (external)	Worthwhile along with confidentiality, especially where sensitive information is sought
Follow-up questionnaires	+12%	This may be due to better timing than the first questionnaire, and the fact that it raises the perceived importance of the study

Source: Developed from Jobber and O'Reilly (1996)

being displayed differently, emphasising the need to ensure the questionnaire design is clear (Dillman, 2000).

On-line questionnaires are usually administered in one of two ways: via email or via a web site. The first of these uses email to 'post' and receive questionnaires and is dependent on having a list of addresses. Although it is possible to obtain such lists from an Internet-based employment directory or via a search engine (Section 3.5), we would not recommend this approach. If you are considering using the Internet for research, you should abide by the general operating guidelines or *netiquette*. This includes not sending junk emails, often known as *spam*. Failure to do this is likely to result in 'few responses and a barrage of mail informing the researcher of their non-compliance' (Coomber, 1997:10). Despite this, questionnaires can be successfully administered by email within organisations provided that all of the sample have access to and use it. However, unless an anonymous server or mailbox that removes email addresses is used for returning questionnaires, respondents will be identifiable by their email addresses (Witmer *et al.*, 1999). If you choose to use email, we suggest that you:

1 contact recipients by email and advise them to expect a questionnaire – a *pre-survey contact* (Section 5.3);

2 email the questionnaire with a covering letter. Where possible, the letter and questionnaire should be part of the email message rather than an attached file. You should make sure that this will arrive when recipients are likely to be receptive. For most organisations Fridays and days surrounding major public holidays have been shown to be a poor time;

3 email the *first follow-up* one week after emailing out the questionnaire to all recipients. This should thank early respondents and remind non-respondents to answer (a copy of the questionnaire should be included);
4 email the *second follow-up* to people who have not responded after three weeks. This should include another covering letter and a copy of the questionnaire. The covering letter should be reworded to further emphasise the importance of completing the questionnaire;
5 also use a *third follow-up* if time allows or your response rate is low.

Alternatively, the questionnaire can be advertised by email or on the Internet and respondents invited to access a web site and to fill in an on-line questionnaire. Adopting this approach observes netiquette and means that respondents can remain anonymous and, of equal importance, are unable to modify the questionnaire (Witmer *et al.*, 1999). The stages involved are:

1 Ensure that a web site has been set up that explains the purpose of the research and how to complete the questionnaire (this takes the place of the covering letter).
2 Ensure that the questionnaire has been set up on line and has a direct link (*hyperlink*) from the web site.
3 Advertise the web site widely using a range of media (for example an email pre-survey contact or a banner advertisement on a page that is likely to be looked at by the target population).
4 When the respondent completes the questionnaire, ensure that the data file it generates is sent automatically to your designated email address.

Response rates from such an approach are likely to be very low, and there are considerable problems of non-response bias as the respondent has to take extra steps to locate and complete the questionnaire (Coomber, 1997). Consequently it is likely to be very difficult to obtain a representative sample from which you might generalise. This is not to say that this approach should not be used as it can, for example, enable you to contact difficult-to-access groups. It all depends, as you would expect us to say, on your research question and objectives!

Postal questionnaires

For postal questionnaires, it is also important to have a well-written covering letter and good design to help to ensure a high level of response. As with on-line questionnaires a clear timetable and well-executed administration process are important.

Our advice for postal questionnaires (developed from deVaus, 2002) can be split into six stages:

1 Ensure that questionnaires and letters are printed, and envelopes addressed.
2 Contact recipients by post, telephone or email and advise them to expect a questionnaire – a *pre-survey contact* (Section 5.3). This stage is often omitted for cost reasons.
3 Post the survey with a covering letter and a return envelope (and fax cover sheet). You should make sure that this will arrive when recipients are likely to be receptive. For most organisations Fridays and days surrounding major public holidays have been shown to be a poor time.

4 Post (or email) the *first follow-up* one week after posting out the survey to all recipients. For posted questionnaires this should take the form of a postcard designed to thank early respondents and to remind rather than to persuade non-respondents.
5 Post the *second follow-up* to people who have not responded after three weeks. This should contain another copy of the questionnaire, a new return envelope and a new covering letter. The covering letter should be reworded to emphasise further the importance of completing the questionnaire. For anonymous questionnaires a second follow-up will not be possible, as you should not be able to tell who has responded!
6 Also use a *third follow-up* if time allows or your response rate is low. For this it may be possible to use recorded delivery (post), telephone calls or even call in person to emphasise the importance of responding.

deVaus (2002) also advises placing a unique *identification number* on each questionnaire, which is recorded on your list of recipients. This makes it easy to check and follow-up non-respondents and, according to Dillman (2000) has little, if any, effect on response rates. However, identification numbers should not be used if you have assured respondents that their replies will be anonymous!

worked example

Questionnaire administration

Mark and Adrian undertook an attitude survey of parents of pupils at a school using a questionnaire. Prior to the survey, a pre-survey contact letter was sent to all parents, using their

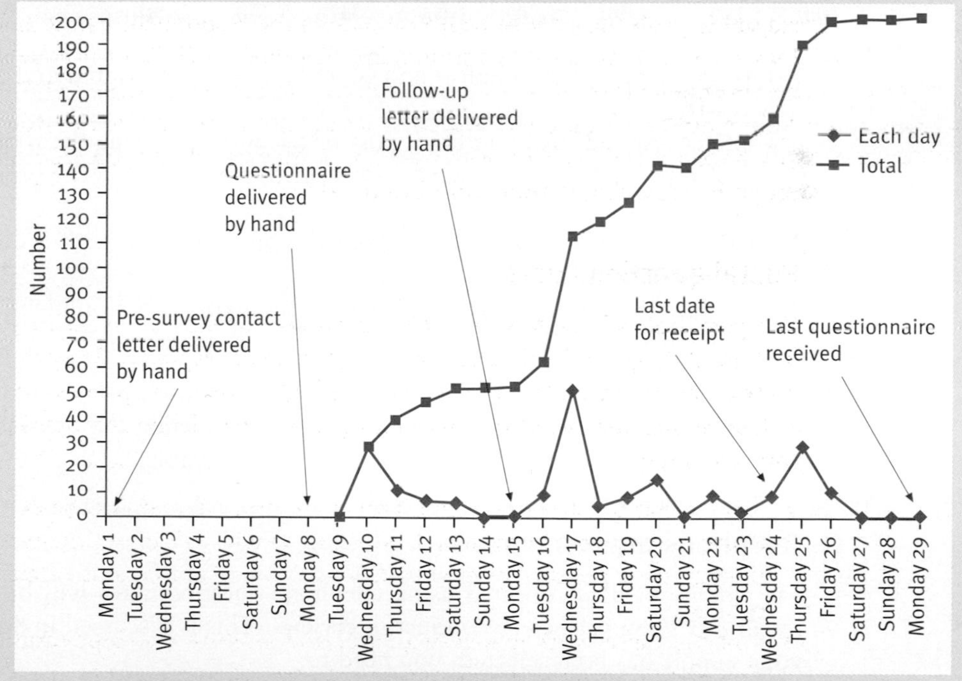

Daily and total number of questionnaires returned

Source: Survey of school parents, 2002.

children to deliver the letter. The questionnaire, covering letter and postage-paid reply envelope were delivered in the same manner a week later. By the end of the first week after the questionnaire had been delivered, 52 questionnaires had been returned. This represented 16 per cent of families whose children attended the school. At the start of the next week a follow-up letter was delivered by hand to all parents. This thanked those who had already responded and encouraged those parents who had yet to return their completed questionnaire to do so. After this, the rate at which questionnaires were returned increased. By the end of the second week 126 questionnaires had been returned, representing a 38 per cent response rate. By the last day for receipt of questionnaires specified in the covering letter, 161 had been returned, increasing the response rate to 48 per cent. However, an additional 41 questionnaires were received after this deadline, resulting in an overall response rate of 60 per cent. The administration of the questionnaire had taken over four weeks from the pre-survey contact letter to the receipt of the last completed questionnaire.

Delivery and collection questionnaires

The administration of delivery and collection questionnaires is very similar to that of postal questionnaires. However, you or field staff will deliver and call to collect the questionnaire. It is therefore important that your covering letter states when the questionnaire is likely to be collected. As with postal questionnaires follow-ups can be used, calling at a variety of times of day and on different days to try to catch the respondent.

A variation on this process that we have used widely in organisations allows for delivery and collection of questionnaires the same day and eliminates the need for a follow-up. The stages are:

1 Ensure that all questionnaires and covering letters are printed and a collection box is ready.
2 Contact respondents by internal post or telephone advising them to attend a meeting or one of a series of meetings to be held (preferably) in the organisation's time (Section 5.3).
3 At the meeting or meetings hand out the questionnaire with a covering letter to each respondent.
4 Introduce the questionnaire and stress its anonymous or confidential nature.
5 Ensure that respondents place their completed questionnaires in a collection box before they leave the meeting.

Although this adds to costs, as employees are completing the questionnaire in work time, response rates as high as 98 per cent are achievable!

Telephone questionnaires

The quality of data collected using telephone questionnaires will be affected by the researcher's competence to conduct interviews. This is discussed in Section 9.5. Once your sample has been selected, you need to:

1 ensure that all questionnaires are printed or, for CATI, that the software has been programmed and tested;

2 where possible and resources allow, contact respondents by post, email or telephone advising them to expect a telephone call (Section 5.3);
3 telephone each respondent, recording the date and time of call and whether or not the questionnaire was completed. You should note any specific times that have been arranged for callbacks. For calls that were not successful you should note the reason, such as no reply or telephone disconnected;
4 for unsuccessful calls where there was no reply, try three more times, each at a different time and on a different day, and note the same information;
5 make callback calls at the time arranged.

Structured interviews

Conducting structured interviews uses many of the skills required for in-depth and semi-structured interviews (Section 9.5). Issues such as interviewer appearance and preparedness are important and will affect the response rate (Section 9.4). However, once your sample has been selected you need to:

1 ensure that all questionnaires are printed or, for CAPI, that the software has been programmed and tested;
2 (for probability samples – Section 6.2) contact respondents by post, email or telephone advising them to expect an interviewer to call within the next week (Section 5.3). This stage is often omitted for cost reasons;
3 (for large-scale surveys) divide the sample into groups that are of a manageable size (50–100) for one interviewer;
4 contact each respondent or potential respondent in person, recording the date and time of contact and whether or not the interview was completed. You should note down any specific times that have been arranged for return visits. For contacts that were not successful, you should note down the reason;
5 (for probability samples) try unsuccessful contacts at least twice more, each at a different time and on a different day, and note down the same information;
6 visit respondents at the times arranged for return visits.

10.6 Summary

- Questionnaires collect data by asking people to respond to exactly the same set of questions. They are often used as part of a survey strategy to collect descriptive and explanatory data about opinions, behaviours and attributes. Data collected are normally coded and analysed by computer.
- Your choice of questionnaire will be influenced by your research question(s) and objectives and the resources that you have available. The five main types are on-line, postal, delivery and collection, telephone, and interview schedule.
- Prior to designing a questionnaire, you must know precisely what data you need to collect to answer your research question(s) and to meet your objectives. One way of helping to ensure that you collect these data is to use a data requirements table.

- The validity and reliability of the data you collect and the response rate you achieve depend largely on the design of your questions, the structure of your questionnaire, and the rigour of your pilot testing.
- When designing your questionnaire you should consider the wording of individual questions prior to the order in which they appear. Questions can be divided into open and closed. The six types of closed questions are list, category, ranking, rating (scale), quantity and grid.
- Wherever possible closed questions should be pre-coded on your questionnaire to facilitate analysis.
- The order and flow of questions in the questionnaire should be logical to the respondent. This can be assisted by filter questions and linking phrases.
- The questionnaire should be laid out so that it is easy to read and the responses are easy to fill in.
- Questionnaires must be introduced carefully to the respondent to ensure a high response rate. For self-administered questionnaires this should take the form of a covering letter; for interviewer-administered questions it will be done by the interviewer.
- All questionnaires should be pilot tested prior to collecting data to assess the validity and likely reliability of the questions.
- Administration of questionnaires needs to be appropriate to the type of questionnaire.

self-check Questions

10.1 In what circumstances would you choose to use a delivery and collection questionnaire rather than a postal questionnaire? Give reasons for your answer.

10.2 The following questions have been taken from a questionnaire about flexibility of labour.

i Do you agree or disagree with the use of nil hours contracts by employers?
(please tick appropriate box)

strongly agree ☐ 4
agree ☐ 3
disagree ☐ 2
strongly disagree ☐ 1

ii Have you ever been employed on a nil hours contract?
(please tick appropriate box)

yes ☐ 1
no ☐ 2
not sure ☐ 3

iii What is your marital status?
(please tick appropriate box)

single ☐ 1
married or living in long-term relationship ☐ 2
widowed ☐ 3
divorced ☐ 4
other ☐ 5

.... (⇦ please describe)

iv Please describe what you think would be the main impact on employees of a nil hours contract.

For each question identify:
a the sort of data that are being collected;
b the type of question.
You should give reasons for your answers.

10.3 You are undertaking research on the use of children's book clubs by householders within mainland Europe. As part of this you have already undertaken in-depth interviews with households who belong and do not belong to children's book clubs. This, along with a literature review, has suggested a number of investigative questions from which you start to construct a table of data requirements.

Research question/objective: *To establish mainland Europe's householders' opinions about children's book clubs*

Type of research: *Predominantly descriptive, although wish to explain differences between householders*

Investigative questions	Variable(s) required	Detail in which data measured	Check included in questionnaire ✓
a. Do householders think that children's book clubs are a good or a bad idea?			
b. What things do householders like most about children's book clubs?			
c. Would householders be interested in an all-ages book club?			
d. How much do households spend on children's books a year?			
e. Do households' responses differ depending on: i number of children? ii whether already members of a children's book club?			

a For each investigative question listed, decide whether you will need to collect data on opinions, behaviours or attributes.
b Complete the table of data requirements for each of the investigative questions already listed. (You may embellish the scenario to help in your choice of variables required and how the data will be measured as you feel necessary.)

10.4 Design pre-coded or self-coded questions to collect data for each of the investigative questions in self-check question 10.3. Note that you will need to answer self-check question 10.3 first (or use the answer at the end of this chapter).

10.5 What issues will you need to consider when translating your questionnaire?

10.6 You work for a major consumer research bureau that has been commissioned by 11 major UK companies to design and administer a telephone questionnaire. The purpose of this questionnaire is to describe and explain relationships between adult consumers' lifestyles, opinions and purchasing intentions. Write the introduction to this telephone questionnaire, to be read by an interviewer to each respondent. You may embellish the scenario and include any other relevant information you wish.

10.7 You have been asked by a well-known national charity 'Work for All' to carry out research into the effects of long-term unemployment throughout the UK. The charity intends to use the findings of this research as part of a major campaign to highlight public awareness about the effects of long-term unemployment. The charity has drawn up a list of names and addresses of people who are or were long-term unemployed with whom they have had contact over the past six months. Write a covering letter to accompany the postal questionnaire. You may embellish the scenario and include any other relevant information you wish.

10.8 You have been asked to give a presentation to a group of managers at an oil exploration company to gain access to undertake your research. As part of the presentation you outline your methodology, which includes piloting the questionnaire. In the ensuing question and answer session one of the managers asks you to justify the need for a pilot study, arguing that 'given the time constraints the pilot can be left out'. List the arguments that you would use to convince him that pilot testing is essential to your methodology.

progressing your research project

Using questionnaires in your research

- ☐ Return to your research question(s) and objectives. Decide on how appropriate it would be to use questionnaires as part of your research strategy. If you do decide that this is appropriate note down the reasons why you think it will be sensible to collect at least some of your data in this way. If you decide that using a questionnaire is not appropriate, justify your decision.
- ☐ If you decide that using a questionnaire is appropriate re-read Chapter 6 on sampling and, in conjunction with this chapter, decide which of the five types of questionnaire will be most appropriate. Note down your choice of questionnaire and the reasons for this choice.
- ☐ Construct a data requirements table and work out precisely what data you need to answer your investigative questions. Remember that you will need to relate your investigative questions and data requirements back to the literature you have reviewed and any preliminary research you have already undertaken.
- ☐ Design the separate questions to collect the data specified in your data requirements table. Wherever possible try to use closed questions and to adhere to the suggestions in the question wording checklist. If you are intending to analyse your questionnaire by computer read Section 11.2 and pre-code questions on the questionnaire whenever possible.
- ☐ Order your questions to make reading the questions and filling in the responses as logical as possible to the respondent. Wherever possible, try to adhere to the checklist for layout. Remember that interviewer-administered questionnaires will need instructions for the interviewer.
- ☐ Write the introduction to your questionnaire and, where appropriate, a covering letter.

- ☐ Pilot test your questionnaire with as similar a group as possible to the final group in your sample. Pay special attention to issues of validity and reliability.
- ☐ Administer your questionnaire and remember to send out a follow-up survey to non-respondents whenever possible.

References

Bell, J. (1999) *Doing Your Research Project* (3rd edn), Buckingham, Open University Press.

Bourque, L.B. and Clark, V.A. (1994) 'Processing data: the survey example', *in* Lewis-Beck, M.S., *Research Practice*, London, Sage, pp. 1–88.

Coomber, R. (1997) 'Using the Internet for survey research', *Sociological Research Online*, 2:2 (online) (cited 10 February 2002). Available from <URL:http://www.socresonline.org.uk/socresonline/2/2/2.html>

Cooper, D.R. and Schindler, D.A. (2001) *Business Research Methods* (7th edn), London, McGraw-Hill.

Dillman, D.A. (2000) *Mail and Internet Surveys: The Tailored Design Method* (2nd edn), New York, Wiley.

Fink, A. (1995a) *How to Ask Survey Questions*, Thousand Oaks, CA, Sage.

Fink, A. (1995b) *The Survey Handbook*, Thousand Oaks, CA, Sage.

Foddy, W. (1994) *Constructing Questions for Interviews and Questionnaires*, Cambridge, Cambridge University Press.

Ghauri, P. and Grønhaugh, K. (2002) *Research Methods in Business Studies: A Practical Guide* (2nd edn), Harlow, Financial Times Prentice Hall.

Gill, J. and Johnson, P. (1997) *Research Methods for Managers* (2nd edn), London, Paul Chapman.

Jankowicz, A.D. (2000) *Business Research Projects* (3rd edn), London, Chapman & Hall.

Jobber, D. and O'Reilly, D. (1996) 'Industrial mail surveys: techniques for inducing response', *Marketing & Intelligence Planning*, 14:1, 29–34.

Kervin, J.B. (1999) *Methods for Business Research* (2nd edn), Reading, MA, Addison-Wesley.

Lavrakas, P.J. (1993) *Telephone Survey Methods: Sampling, Selection and Supervision*, Newbury Park, CA, Sage.

Mercator (2002) 'Mercator home page' (online) (cited 10 February 2002). Available from <URL:http://www.mercator.co.uk>

Miller, D.C. and Salkind, N.J. (2002) (eds) *Handbook of Research Design and Social Measurement* (6th edn), Thousand Oaks, CA, Sage.

Mitchell, V. (1996) 'Assessing the reliability and validity of questionnaires: an empirical example', *Journal of Applied Management Studies*, 5:2, 199–207.

Oppenheim, A.N. (2000) *Questionnaire Design, Interviewing and Attitude Measurement* (new edn), London, Continuum International.

Pallant, J. (2001) *SPSS Survival Manual*, Buckingham, Open University Press.

Robson, C. (2002) *Real World Research* (2nd edn), Oxford, Blackwell.

Scolari Sage (2002) Methodologist's Toolchest (online) (cited 10 February 2002). Available from <URL:http://www.scolari.co.uk>

Usunier, J.-C. (1998) *International and Cross-Cultural Management Research*, London, Sage.

deVaus, D.A. (2002) *Surveys in Social Research* (5th edn), London, Routledge.

Witmer, D.F., Colman, R.W. and Katzman, S.L. (1999) 'From paper and pen to screen and keyboard: towards a methodology for survey research on the Internet', *in* Jones, S., *Doing Internet Research*, Thousand Oaks, CA, Sage, pp. 145–62.

Youngman, M.B. (1986) *Analysing Questionnaires*, Nottingham, University of Nottingham School of Education.

Further reading

Dillman, D.A. (2000) *Mail and Internet Surveys: The Tailored Design Method* (2nd edn), New York, Wiley. The second edition of this classic text contains an extremely detailed and well-researched discussion of how to design postal and Internet-based questionnaires to maximise response rates.

Foddy, W. (1994) *Constructing Questions for Interviews and Questionnaires*, Cambridge, Cambridge University Press. This contains a wealth of information on framing questions, including the use of scaling techniques.

deVaus, D.A. (2002) *Surveys in Social Research* (5th edn), London, Routledge. Chapters 7 and 8 provide a detailed guide to constructing and administering questionnaires respectively.

Wass, V.J. (1994) 'Minimizing and managing bias in a mail survey: a study of redundant miners', *in* Wass, V.J. and Wells, P.E. (eds), *Principles and Practice in Business and Management Research*, Aldershot, Dartmouth, pp. 91–121. This offers an excellent discussion and provides a good case study of the issues of controlling for bias when using a postal questionnaire.

Witmer, D.F., Colman, R.W. and Katzman, S.L. (1999) 'From paper and pen to screen and keyboard: towards a methodology for survey research on the Internet', *in* Jones, S., *Doing Internet Research*, Thousand Oaks, CA, Sage, pp. 145–62. This gives a clear insight into the issues concerning on-line survey methodology.

CASE 10 Job satisfaction in an Australian organisation

Centrelink, the one-stop shop for access to Australian government benefits and services, believes that employee satisfaction will influence employees' attitudes to customers, work and the organisation. Employee satisfaction is seen as crucial to the success of the organisation. Within its Western Australia (WA) area, Centrelink employs approximately 1500 people. Managers in this area were interested not only in the level of employee satisfaction at Centrelink, but also in finding out what factors were likely to influence it. They therefore commissioned a research project to discover how Centrelink employees' attitudes and perceptions were related to their job satisfaction and performance.

The research commisioned used external researchers, and consisted of an exploratory phase followed by a main data collection phase. Both of these used questionnaires administered using Centrelink's intranet and the Internet. The researchers felt that this offered three distinct advantages over other methods of administration:

- accuracy of data: employees' responses were captured directly, so that data entry errors were avoided;
- economy: although there were costs involved in setting up the research instruments, data entry costs were eliminated, with a resultant significant saving;
- universality: all employees had good access to the organisation's intranet facilities.

Exploratory data collection consisted of an introductory email to all employees introducing the research and asking them to complete a short survey posted on Centrelink's intranet. The questions were:

1 What aspects of your work make you satisfied?

2 What are the issues that prevent you from doing your job to the best of your ability?

3 What could be done by management and staff to make your work more satisfying?

Sixty questionnaires were returned to the academic researchers, representing a 4% response rate. Although this was a disappointing figure, the responses elicited were fairly consistent across the sample. Content analysis of these data revealed 23 key attitudes and perceptions. These were consistent with anecdotes and comments that had been related to Centrelink managers by employees. It seemed reasonable to think that the qualitative questionnaire had captured the major issues of concern to Centrelink staff.

Based upon these data a detailed questionnaire was developed to measure these attitudes and perceptions. In developing the questionnaire, published scales were used wherever possible to help ensure that valid and reliable measurements were obtained. The 23 attitudes and perceptions fell into four broad categories.

The team labelled the first category 'organisational environment'. This included scales measuring perceived organisational support, perceived fairness, team leader support, career development and workload. These areas were all felt to a greater or lesser extent able to be directly influenced by managers. The second category was job characteristics. The scales used were a modified version of Hackman and Oldham's (1975) job diagnostic survey. Although the research design did not allow for inferences of causality, published research suggested that a number of attitudes were likely to be influenced by the organisational environment and job characteristics. The researchers labelled this category 'attitudinal outcomes'. This included scales that measured:

- trust in management;
- commitment;
- satisfaction with extrinsic and intrinsic rewards;
- job satisfaction.

There were also a number of behaviours likely to be influenced by the organisational environment, job characteristics and attitudes included in the survey. The research team labelled these 'behavioural outcomes'. This included scales that measured citizenship behaviour, job-related effort, turnover intention, and self-reported measures of sick leave taken.

After pilot testing, the final questionnaire contained 178 questions. Of these, 144 questions came from established scales and questionnaires, and over 20 collected personal and work history details. Several different types of scale question were used to measure the attitudes and perceptions that the survey targeted.

▶

	Not at all likely				Extremely likely
How likely is it that you will actively look for a new job in the next year?	☐ 1	☐ 2	☐ 3	☐ 4	☐ 5

	Strongly disagree				Strongly agree
My job requires that I work very hard	☐ 1	☐ 2	☐ 3	☐ 4	☐ 5

	None				A very large amount
How much effort do you put into your job beyond what is required?	☐ 1	☐ 2	☐ 3	☐ 4	☐ 5

Scales with three and four points were used in the satisfaction measures, and a variety of different scales with both five and seven points were used to measure job characteristics.

The quantitative survey instrument was posted on Centrelink's intranet site, and an email request to complete the survey was sent to all employees. The database into which responses were directly entered resided on a server that was not part of Centrelink's network, protecting the confidentiality of employee responses. Employees were able to complete part of the form, save it and return later. Many respondents took several sessions to complete the survey. After eliminating partially completed questionnaires, there were 371 usable responses, a response rate of 25%.

The data indicated that employee satisfaction was linked to aspects of the organisational environment, as well as to characteristics of the work itself. This assisted managers and staff to determine how they might be able to make changes that would enhance staff satisfaction. The study also established that there were relationships between employee satisfaction, other attitudinal outcomes and each of the behavioural outcomes measured. Other research had indicated that these behavioural outcomes were likely to be linked to employee performance. The results of this study therefore supported the contention that staff satisfaction affects organisational performance. They tended to validate Centrelink's inclusion of staff satisfaction as one of the critical areas in its balanced scorecard.

Reference

Hackman, J.R. and Oldham, G.R. (1975) 'Development of the Job Diagnostic Survey', *Journal of Applied Psychology*, 60, 159–70.

Questions

1 The research design considered only how employees' attitudes and perceptions were related to job satisfaction and performance. It could also have explored what caused changes in job satisfaction and performance. What do you think were the reasons for this?

2 a Under what circumstances might it be appropriate to use web-based instruments for data collection?
b When might it be inappropriate to do so?

3 a How confident could the researchers be that the exploratory phase of the research had actually uncovered relevant issues?
b How might this phase have been more effectively carried out?

4 a Do you think the researchers were right to make such high use of already existing scales in their main questionnaire?
b Give reasons for your answer.

self-check Answers

10.1 When you:

- wanted to check that the person whom you wished to answer the questions had actually answered the questions;
- have sufficient resources to devote to delivery and collection and the geographical area over which the questionnaire is administered is small;
- can use field workers to enhance response rates. Delivery and collection questionnaires have a moderately high response rate of between 30 and 50 per cent compared with 30 per cent offered on average by a postal questionnaire;
- are administering a questionnaire to an organisation's employees and require a very high response rate. By administering the questionnaire to groups of employees in work time and collecting it on completion, response rates of up to 98 per cent can be achieved.

10.2 a i Opinion data: the question is asking how the respondent *feels* about the use of nil hours contracts by employees.
ii Behaviour data: the question is asking about the *concrete experience* of being employed on a nil hours contract.
iii Attribute data: the question is asking about the respondent's *characteristics*.
iv Opinion data: the question is asking the respondent what they *think* or *believe* would be the impact on employees.

b i Rating question using a Likert-type scale in which the respondent is asked how strongly she or he agrees or disagrees with the statement.
ii Category question in which the respondent's answer can fit only one answer.
iii Category question as before.
iv Open question in which the respondent can give her or his own answer in her or his own way.

10.3 Although your answer is unlikely to be precisely the same, the completed table of data requirements below should enable you to check you are on the right lines.

Research question/objective: *To establish householders' opinions about children's book clubs*			
Type of research: *Predominantly descriptive, although wish to explain differences between householders*			
Investigative questions	**Variable(s) required**	**Detail in which data measured**	**Check included in questionnaire ✓**
Do householders think that children's book clubs are a good or a bad idea? (opinion – this is because you are really asking how householders feel)	Opinion about children's book clubs	very good idea, good idea, neither a good nor a bad idea, bad idea, very bad idea	
What things do householders like most about children's book clubs? (opinion)	What householders like about children's book clubs	get them to rank the following things (generated from earlier in-depth interviews): monthly magazine, lower prices, credit, choice, special offers, shopping at home	
Would householders be interested in an all-ages book club? (behaviour)	Interest in a book club which was for both adults and children	interested, not interested, may be interested	
How much do households spend on children's books a year? (behaviour)	Amount spent on children's books by adults and children per year by household	(answers to the nearest €) €0 to €10, €11 to €20, €21 to €30, €31 to €50, €51 to €100, over €100	
Do households' responses differ depending on:			
■ *number of children?* (attribute)	Number of aged under 16	actual number	
■ *whether already members of a children's book club?* (behaviour)	Children's book club member	yes, no	

10.4 a Please complete the following statement by ticking the phrase that matches your feelings most closely . . .

I feel children's book clubs are . . .

. . . a very good idea	☐	5
. . . a good idea	☐	4
. . . neither a good nor a bad idea	☐	3
. . . a bad idea	☐	2
. . . a very bad idea	☐	1

b Please number each of the features of children's book clubs listed below in order of how much you like them. Number the most important 1, the next 2 and so on. The feature you like the least should be given the highest number.

feature	**how much liked**
monthly magazine	|__|
lower prices	|__|
credit	|__|
choice	|__|
special offers	|__|
shopping at home	|__|

c Would you be interested in a book club that was for both adults and children?

(please tick the appropriate box) yes ☐ 1
no ☐ 2
not sure ☐ 3

d How much money is spent in total each year on children's books by all the adults and children living in your household?

(please tick the appropriate box) €0 to €10 ☐ 1
€11 to €20 ☐ 2
€21 to €30 ☐ 3
€31 to €50 ☐ 4
€51 to €100 ☐ 5
over €100 ☐ 6

e i How many children aged under 16 are there living in your household?

|__| children

(for example for 3 write:) |3| children

ii Is any person living in your household a member of a children's book club?
(please tick the appropriate box) yes ☐ 1
no ☐ 2

10.5 When translating your questionnaire you will need to ensure that:

- the precise meaning of individual words is kept (lexical equivalence)
- the meanings of groups of words and phrases that are natural to a native speaker but cannot be translated literally are kept (idiomatic equivalence)
- the correct grammar and syntax are used.

In addition you should, if possible, use back translation, parallel translation or mixed translation techniques to ensure that there are no differences between the source and the target questionnaire.

10.6 Although the precise wording of your answer is likely to differ, it would probably be something like this:

Good morning/afternoon/evening. My name is __________ from JJ Consumer Research. We are doing an important national survey covering lifestyles, opinions and likely future purchases of adult consumers. Your telephone number has been selected at random. The questions I need to ask you will take about 15 minutes. If you have any queries I shall be happy to answer them (*pause*). Before I continue please can you confirm that this is (*read out telephone number including dialing code*) and that I am talking to a person aged 18 or over. Please can I ask you the first question now?

10.7 Although the precise wording of your answer is likely to differ it would probably be something like this:

Work for All

Registered Charity No: 123456789

B&J Market Research Ltd
St Richard's House
Malvern
Worcestershire WR14 12Z

Phone **01684–56789101**
Fax **01684–56789102**
Email **mark@b&jmarketresearch.co.uk**

Respondent's name

Respondent's address

Today's date

Dear *title name*

Work for All is conducting research into the effects of long-term unemployment. This is an issue of great importance within the UK and yet little is currently known about the consequences.

You are one of a small number of people who are being asked to give your opinion on this issue. You were selected at random from Work for All's list of contacts. In order that the results will truly represent people who have experienced long-term unemployment, it is important that your questionnaire is completed and returned.

All the information you give us will be totally confidential. You will notice that your name and address do not appear on the questionnaire and that there is no identification number.

The results of this research will be passed to Work for All, who will be mounting a major campaign in the New Year to highlight public awareness about the effects of long-term unemployment.

If you have any questions you wish to ask or there is anything you wish to discuss please do not hesitate to telephone me, or my assistant Benjamin Marks, on 01684–56789101 during the day. You can call me at home on 01234–123456789 evenings and weekends.

Thank you for your help.

Yours sincerely

Mark NK Saunders

Dr Mark NK Saunders
Project Manager

10.8 Despite the time constraints, pilot testing is essential to your methodology for the following reasons:

- to find out how long the questionnaire takes to complete;
- to check that respondents understand and can follow the instructions on the questionnaire (including filter questions);
- to ensure that all respondents understand the wording of individual questions in the same way and that there are no unclear or ambiguous questions;
- to ensure that you have the same understanding of the wording of individual questions as the respondents;
- to check that respondents have no problems in answering questions; for example:
  - all possible answers are covered in list questions,
  - whether there are any questions that respondents feel uneasy about answering;
- to discover whether there are any major topic omissions;
- to provide an idea of the validity of the questions that are being asked;
- to provide an idea of the reliability of the questions by checking responses from individual respondents to similar questions;
- to check that the layout appears clear and attractive;
- to provide limited test data so you can check that the proposed analyses will work.

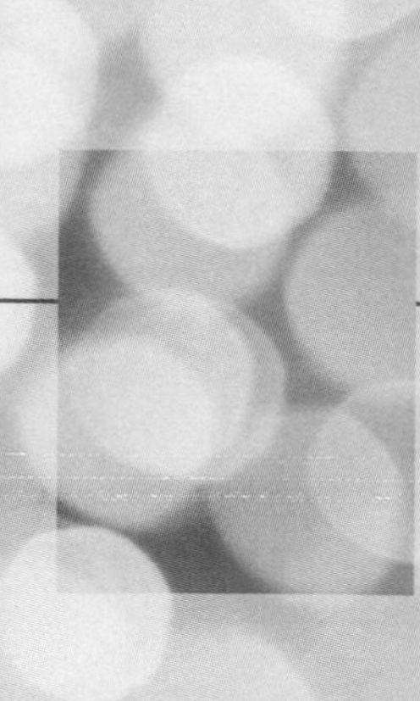

Chapter 11

Analysing quantitative data

By the end of this chapter, you should be able:

- to identify the main issues that you need to consider when preparing quantitative data for analysis and when analysing these data by computer;
- to recognise different types of data and understand the implications of data type for subsequent analyses;
- to create a data matrix and to code data for analysis by computer;
- to select the most appropriate tables and diagrams to explore and illustrate different aspects of your data;
- to select the most appropriate statistics to describe individual variables and to examine relationships between variables and trends in your data;
- to interpret the tables, diagrams and statistics that you use correctly.

11.1 Introduction

Virtually all research will involve some numerical data or contain data that could usefully be quantified to help you answer your research question(s) and to meet your objectives. *Quantitative data* refers to all such data and can be a product of all research strategies (Section 4.2). It can range from simple counts such as the frequency of occurrences to more complex data such as test scores or prices. To be useful these data need to be analysed and interpreted. Quantitative analysis techniques assist this process. These range from creating simple tables or diagrams that show the frequency of occurrence through establishing statistical relationships between variables to complex statistical modelling.

Until the advent of powerful personal computers, data were analysed either by hand or by using mainframe computers. The former of these was extremely time consuming and prone to error, the latter expensive. Fortunately, the by-hand or calculator 'number-crunching' and 'charting' elements of quantitative analysis have been incorporated into relatively inexpensive personal-computer-based analysis software. These range from spreadsheets such as Excel and Lotus 1–2–3 to more advanced data management and statistical analysis software packages such as Minitab, SAS, SPSS for Windows and Statview. They also include more specialised survey design and analysis packages such as Snap and SphinxSurvey. Consequently, it is no longer necessary for you to be able to draw presentation-quality diagrams or to calculate statistics by hand as these can be done by computer. However, if your analyses are to be straightforward and of any value you need:

- to have prepared your data with quantitative analyses in mind;
- to be aware of and to know when to use different charting and statistical techniques.

Robson (2002:393) summarises this, arguing that quantitative data analysis is:

> . . . a field where it is not at all difficult to carry out an analysis which is simply wrong, or inappropriate for your purposes. And the negative side of readily available analysis software is that it becomes that much easier to generate elegantly presented rubbish.

He also emphasises the need to seek advice regarding statistical analyses, a sentiment that we support strongly.

This chapter builds on the ideas outlined in earlier chapters about data collection. It assumes that you will use a personal computer (with at least a spreadsheet) to analyse all but the most simple quantitative data. It does not focus on one particular piece of analysis software as there are numerous books already published that concentrate on specific software packages (for example Kinnear and Gray, 2000; Morris, 1999; Pallant, 2001; Robson, 2002). Likewise it does not attempt to provide an in-depth discussion of the wide range of graphical and statistical techniques available or to cover more complex statistical modelling, as these are already covered elsewhere (for example Hays, 1994; Henry, 1995). Rather it discusses issues that need to be considered at the planning and analysis stages of your research project, and outlines analytical techniques that our students have found to be of most use. In particular the chapter is concerned with the process of:

- preparing your data for analysis by computer (Section 11.2);
- choosing the most appropriate tables and diagrams to explore and present your data (Section 11.3);
- choosing the most appropriate statistics to describe your data (Section 11.4);
- choosing the most appropriate statistics to examine relationships and trends in your data (Section 11.5).

11.2 Preparing data for analysis

If you intend to undertake quantitative analysis we recommend that you consider the:

- type of data (level of numerical measurement);
- format in which your data will be input to the analysis software;
- impact of data coding on subsequent analyses (for different data types);
- need to weight cases;
- methods you intend to use to check data for errors.

Ideally, all of these should be considered before obtaining your data. This is equally important for both primary and secondary data analysis, although you obviously have far greater control over the type, format and coding of primary data. We shall now consider each of these.

Data types

Many business statistics textbooks classify quantitative data into *data types* using a hierarchy of measurement, often in ascending order of numerical precision (Diamantopoulos and Schlegelmilch, 1997; Morris, 1999). These different *levels of numerical measurement* dictate the range of techniques available to you for the presentation, summary and analysis of your data. They are discussed in more detail in subsequent sections of this chapter.

Quantitative data can be divided into two distinct groups: categorical and quantifiable (Figure 11.1). *Categorical data* refer to data whose values cannot be measured numerically but can be either classified into sets (categories) according to the characteristics in which you are interested or placed in rank order. They can be further subdivided into descriptive and ranked. A car manufacturer might categorise the cars it produces as hatchback, saloon and estate. These are known as *descriptive* (or *nominal*) *data* as it is impossible to measure the category numerically or to rank it. For virtually all analyses the categories should be unambiguous and not overlap. This will prevent questions arising as to which category an individual case belongs to. Although these data are purely descriptive, you can count them to establish which category has the most and whether cases are spread evenly between categories (Morris, 1999). *Ranked* (or *ordinal*) *data* are more precise. In such instances you know the definite position of each case within your data set, although the actual numerical measures (such as scores) on which the position is based are not recorded.

Quantifiable data are those whose values you actually measure numerically as quantities. This means that quantifiable data are more precise than categorical as you can assign each data value a position on a numerical scale.* Within this group there is, again, a subdivision: continuous and discrete (Figure 11.1). *Continuous data* are those whose values can theoretically take any value (sometimes within a restricted range) provided that you can measure them accurately enough (Morris, 1999). Data such as furnace temperature, delivery distance and length of service are therefore continuous data. *Discrete data* can, by contrast, be measured precisely. Each case takes one of a finite number of values from a scale that measures changes in discrete units. These data are often whole numbers (*integers*) such as number of mobile phones manufactured or customers served. However, in some instances (for example UK shoe size) discrete data will include non-integer values.

Definitions of discrete and continuous data are, in reality, dependent on how your data values are measured. The number of customers served by a large organisation is strictly a discrete datum as you are unlikely to get a part customer! However, for a

---

* Some textbooks (for example Diamantopoulos and Schlegelmilch, 1997) use an alternative hierarchy of measurement: nominal, ordinal, interval and ratio. Nominal equates to descriptive and ordinal to ranked data. If you have interval data you can, in addition to ranking, state the difference between any two data values. For ratio data, you can also calculate the relative difference between any two data values – that is, the ratio.

large organisation with many customers you might treat this as a continuous datum; the discrete measuring units are exceedingly small compared with the total number being measured.

The more precise the level of measurement the greater the range of analytical techniques available to you. Data that have been collected and coded using precise numerical measurements can also be regrouped to a less precise level where they can also be analysed. For example, a student's score in a test could be recorded as the actual mark (discrete data) or as the position in their class (ranked data). By contrast, less precise data cannot be made more precise. Therefore, if you are not sure about the level of precision you require, it is usually better to collect data at the highest level possible and to regroup them if necessary.

worked example

Levels of numerical measurement

As part of a marketing survey, individual customers were asked to rank up to five features of a new product in order of importance to them. Data collected were therefore categorical and ranked. Initial analyses made use of the ranked data. Unfortunately a substantial minority of customers had ticked, rather than ranked, those features of importance to them.

All responses that had originally been ranked were therefore recoded to 'of some importance'. This reduced the precision of measurement from ranked to descriptive but enabled all responses to be used in subsequent analyses.

Data layout

Some primary data collection methods, such as computer-aided personal interviewing (CAPI), computer-aided telephone interviewing (CATI) and on-line questionnaires, can automatically enter and save data to a computer file at the time of collection. Survey design and analysis software such as Snap and SphinxSurvey goes one stage further and integrates the analysis software in the same package as the questionnaire design/data input software (Mercator, 2002; Scolari Sage, 2002). Alternatively secondary data (Section 7.3) accessed from CD-ROMs or via the Internet can be saved to a file, removing the need for re-entering. For such data, it is often possible to specify a data layout compatible with your analysis software. For other data collection

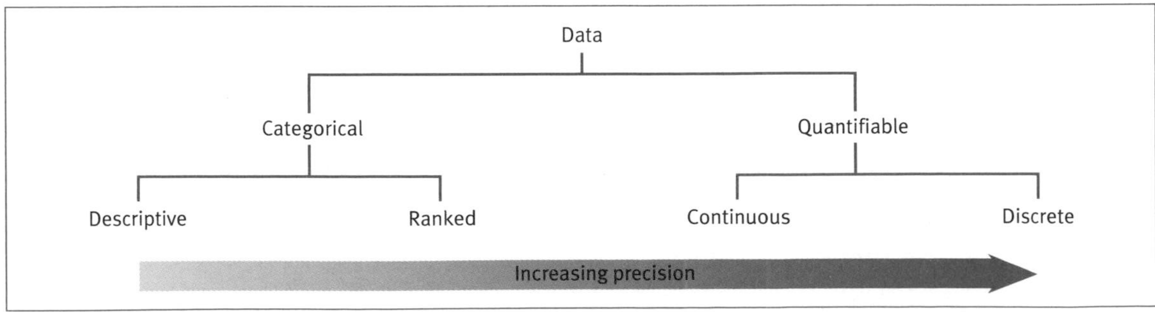

Figure 11.1 Types of data and levels of numerical measurement

methods, you will have to prepare and enter your data for computer analysis. You therefore need to be clear about the precise data layout requirements of your analysis software.

Virtually all analysis software will accept your data if they are entered in table format. This table is called a *data matrix* (Table 11.1). Once data have been entered into your analysis software, it is usually possible to save them in a format that can be read by other software. Within a data matrix, each column usually represents a single *variable* for which you have obtained data. Each matrix row contains the variables for an individual *case,* that is an individual unit for which data have been obtained. If your data have been collected using a survey, each row will contain the data from one survey form. Alternatively, for longitudinal data such as a company's share price over time, each row (case) might be a different time period. Secondary data that have already been stored in computer-readable form will almost always be held as a large data matrix. For such data sets you usually select the subset of variables and cases you require and save these on a disk as a separate matrix. If you are entering your own data, they are typed directly into your chosen analysis software one case (row) at a time. We recommend that you save your data regularly as you are entering it, to minimise the chances of deleting it all by accident! In addition, you should keep a back-up or security copy on a separate disk.

In Table 11.1 the first variable (id) is the *survey form identifier*. This means that you can link data for each case in your matrix to the survey form when error checking (discussed later). The second variable (age) contains quantifiable data, the age of each respondent (case) at the time of the survey. Subsequent variables contain the remaining data: the third (gender) records this descriptive data using code 1 for male and 2 for female; the fourth (service) records each case's length of service to the nearest year with their most recent employer. The final variable (employed) records whether each case is (code 1) or is not (code 2) currently in employment. Codes can therefore have different meanings for different variables. Larger data sets with more data variables and cases are recorded using larger data matrices. Although data matrices store data using one column for each variable, this may not be the same as one column for each question for data collected using surveys.

If you intend to enter data into a spreadsheet, the first variable is in column A, the second in column B and so on. Each cell in the first row (1) should contain a short variable name to enable you to identify each variable. Subsequent rows (2 onwards) will each contain the data for one case. Statistical analysis software follows the same logic, although the variable names are usually displayed 'above' the first row, as in Table 11.1.

Table 11.1 A simple data matrix

	id	*age*	*gender*	*service*	*employed*
case 1	1	27	1	2	1
case 2	2	19	2	1	2
case 3	3	24	2	3	1

worked example

Data input

As part of a market research interview survey you need to discover which of four products (tomato ketchup, brown sauce, soy sauce, vinegar) have been purchased within the last month by consumers. You therefore need to collect four data items from each respondent:

- tomato ketchup purchased within the last month? Yes/No
- brown sauce purchased within the last month? Yes/No
- soy sauce purchased within the last month? Yes/No
- vinegar purchased within the last month? Yes/No

Each of these data items is a separate variable. However, the data are collected using one question:

1 Which of the following items have you purchased within the last month?

item	purchased	not purchased	not sure
tomato ketchup	☐ 1	☐ 2	☐ 3
brown sauce	☐ 1	☐ 2	☐ 3
soy sauce	☐ 1	☐ 2	☐ 3
vinegar	☐ 1	☐ 2	☐ 3

The data collected from each respondent will form four separate variables in the data matrix using numerical codes (1 = purchased, 2 = not purchased, 3 = not sure). This is known as multiple-dichotomy coding:

	tomato	brown	soy	vinegar
respondent	1	1	1	2

Question 2 (below) could theoretically have millions of possible responses for each of the 'things'. The number that each respondent mentions may also vary. Our experience suggests that virtually all respondents will select five or less. Space therefore has to be left to code up to five responses after data have been collected.

2 List up to five things you like about your current job

....

....

....

....

....

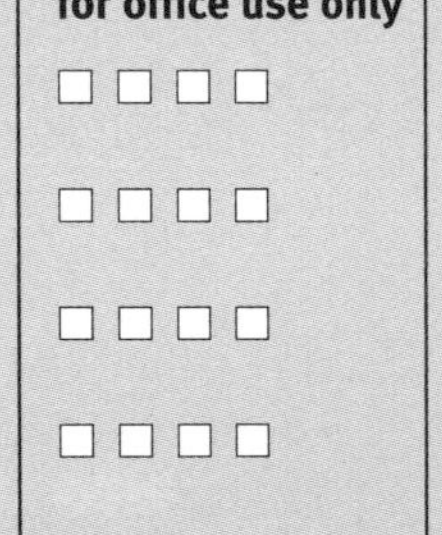
for office use only

The *multiple-dichotomy method* uses a separate variable for each different answer. For question 2 a separate variable could be used for each 'thing' listed: for example, salary, location, colleagues, hours, holidays, car and so on. You would subsequently code each variable as 'listed' or 'not listed' for each case. This makes it easy to calculate the number of responses for each 'thing' (deVaus, 2002). The alternative, the *multiple-response method*, uses the same number of variables as the maximum number of different responses from any one case. For question 2 these might be named 'like1', 'like2', 'like3', 'like4' and 'like5'. Each of these variables would use the same codes and could include any of the responses as a category. Statistical analysis software often contains special multiple-response procedures to analyse such data.

Coding

All data types should, with few exceptions, be recorded using numerical codes. This enables you to enter the data quickly and with fewer errors. It also makes subsequent analyses, in particular those that require re-coding of data to create new variables, more straightforward. Unfortunately, analyses of limited meaning are also easier, such as calculating a mean (average) gender from codes 1 and 2! A common exception to using a numerical code for categorical data is where a postcode is used as the code for a geographical reference. If you are using a spreadsheet, you will need to keep a list of codes for each variable. Statistical analysis software can store these so that each code is automatically labelled.

Coding quantifiable data

Actual numbers are often used as codes for quantifiable data, even though this level of precision may not be required. Once you have entered your data as a matrix, you can use analysis software to group or combine data to form additional variables with less detailed categories. This process is referred to as *re-coding*. A UK employee's salary could be coded to the nearest pound and entered into the matrix as 23543 (discrete data). Later, re-coding could be used to place it in a group of similar salaries, from £20 000 to £24 999 (categorical data).

Coding categorical data

Codes are often applied to categorical data with little thought, although you can design a coding scheme that will make subsequent analyses far simpler. For many secondary data sources (such as government surveys), a suitable coding scheme will have already been devised when the data were first collected. However, for some secondary and all primary data you will need to decide on a coding scheme. Prior to this, you need to establish the highest level of precision required by your analyses.

Existing coding schemes can be used for many variables. These include industrial classification (Great Britain Office for National Statistics, 1997), occupation (Great Britain Office for National Statistics, 2000a, 2000b), socioeconomic classification (National Statistics, 2002a) and ethnic group (National Statistics, 2002b) as well as social attitude variables (Jowell *et al.*, 2000). Wherever possible we recommend you use these as they:

- save time;
- are normally well tested;
- allow comparisons of your results with other (often larger) surveys.

These codes should be included on your data collection form as *pre-set codes* provided that there are a limited number of categories (Section 10.4), which will be understood by the person filling in the form. Even if you decide not to use an existing coding scheme, perhaps because of a lack of detail, you should ensure that your codes are still compatible. This means that you will be able to compare your data with those already collected.

Coding at data collection occurs when there is a limited range of well-established categories into which the data can be placed. These are included on your data collection form, and the person filling in the form selects the correct category.

Coding after data collection is necessary when you are unclear of the likely responses or there are a large number of possible responses in the coding scheme. To ensure that the coding scheme captures the variety in responses (and will work!) it is better to wait until data from the first 50 to 100 cases are available and then develop the coding scheme. This is called the *codebook*. As when designing your data collection method(s) (Chapters 7, 8, 9 and 10) it is essential to be clear about the intended analyses, in particular the:

- level of precision required;
- coding schemes used by surveys with which comparisons are to be made.

To create your codebook for each variable you:

1 examine the data and establish broad groupings;
2 subdivide the broad groupings into increasingly specific subgroups dependent on your intended analyses;
3 allocate codes to all categories at the most precise level of detail required;
4 note the actual responses that are allocated to each category and produce a codebook;
5 ensure that those categories that may need to be aggregated together are given adjacent codes to facilitate re-coding.

Coding missing data

Each variable for each case in your data set should have a code, even if no data have been collected. The choice of code is up to you, although some statistical analysis software have a code that is used by default. A *missing data* code is used to indicate why data are missing. deVaus (2002) identifies four main reasons for missing data:

- The data were not required from the respondent, perhaps because of a skip generated by a filter question in a survey.
- The respondent refused to answer the question (a *non-response*).
- The respondent did not know the answer or did not have an opinion. Sometimes this is treated as implying an answer; on other occasions it is treated as missing data.
- The respondent may have missed a question by mistake, or the respondent's answer may be unclear.

In addition, it may be that:

- leaving part of a question in a survey blank implies an answer; in such cases the data are not classified as missing (Section 10.4).

Statistical analysis software often reserves a special code for missing data. Cases with missing data can then be excluded from subsequent analyses when necessary. For some analyses it may be necessary to distinguish between reasons for missing data using different codes.

worked example

Creating a codebook and coding multiple responses

As part of research on vacancy notification procedures Mark collected data from personnel files about how vacancies were notified by the employer. These data specified the precise notification outlets used, and can be thought of as the answer to the question: 'Which outlets did you use to notify this vacancy?' The data included over 100 different outlets for over 1500 vacancies, although the maximum number of outlets used for any one vacancy was eight.

Once data had been collected, Mark devised a hierarchical coding scheme based on the type and geographical circulation of each notification outlet. Codes were allocated to each outlet as shown in the extract below.

Notification codes for each vacancy were entered into eight (the maximum number of notification outlets used) variables in the data matrix using the multiple-response method for coding. This meant that any notification outlet could appear in any of the eight variables. When fewer than eight outlets were used the code 0 was entered in the remaining outlet variables. The first vacancy in the extract below was notified through outlets 1, 90, 91 and 61, the next through outlets 90, 91, 63, 41, 1, 7 and 8, and so on. No significance was attached to the order of variables to which outlets were coded.

outlet 1	*outlet 2*	*outlet 3*	*outlet 4*	*outlet 5*	*outlet 6*	*outlet 7*	*outlet 8*
1	90	91	61	0	0	0	0
90	91	63	41	1	7	8	0
6	23	22	1	11	0	0	0

Extract from coding scheme used to classify notification outlets

Code	*Outlet*	*Subgrouping*	*Grouping*
1	Internal vacancy sheet		Internal
6	Job centre		Employment agencies
7	Careers office		
8	Professional executive register		
9	Private sector employment agency		
11	Oxford Mail	Daily	Local newspapers
12	Swindon Evening Advertiser		
13	Wantage Evening Advertiser		
20	Herald Series	Weekly	
21	Wiltshire Gazette		
22	Oxford Times		
26	Oxford Journal	Free	
27	Oxford Star		

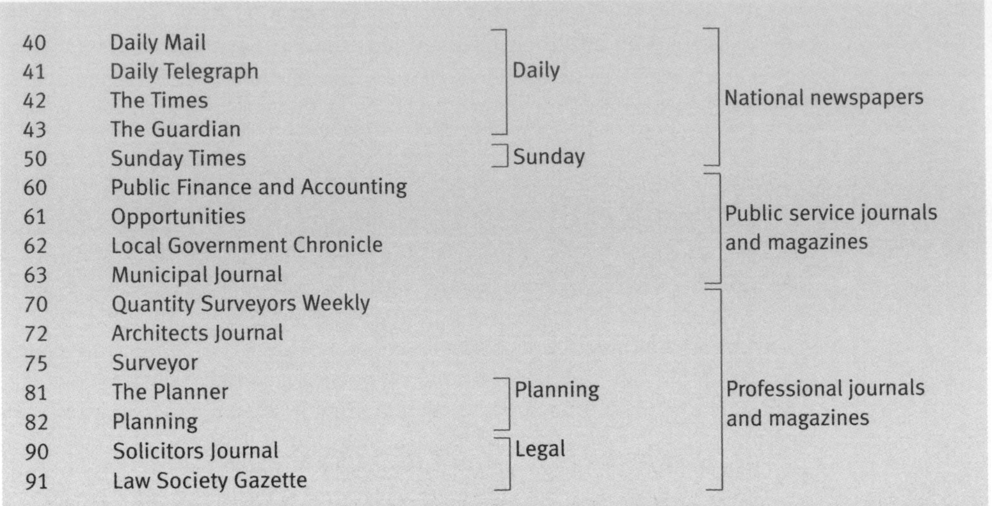

Code	Outlet		
40	Daily Mail	Daily	National newspapers
41	Daily Telegraph		
42	The Times		
43	The Guardian		
50	Sunday Times	Sunday	
60	Public Finance and Accounting		Public service journals and magazines
61	Opportunities		
62	Local Government Chronicle		
63	Municipal Journal		
70	Quantity Surveyors Weekly		Professional journals and magazines
72	Architects Journal		
75	Surveyor		
81	The Planner	Planning	
82	Planning		
90	Solicitors Journal	Legal	
91	Law Society Gazette		

The hierarchical coding scheme meant that notification outlets could subsequently be recoded into groupings such as those indicated above as well as local, regional or national to facilitate a range of different analyses. These were undertaken using statistical analysis software.

Weighting cases

Most data you use will be a sample. For some forms of probability sampling, such as stratified random sampling (Section 6.2), you may have used a different sampling fraction for each stratum. Alternatively, you may have obtained a different response rate for each of the strata. To obtain an accurate overall picture you will need to take account of these differences in response rates between strata. A common method of achieving this is to use cases from those strata that have lower proportions of responses to represent more than one case in your analysis. Most statistical analysis software allows you to do this by *weighting cases*. To *weight* the cases you:

1 calculate the percentage of the population responding for each stratum;

2 establish which stratum had the highest percentage of the population responding;

3 calculate the weight for each stratum using the formula

$$\text{weight} = \frac{\text{highest proportion of population responding for any stratum}}{\text{proportion of population responding in stratum for which calculating weight}}$$

(Note: if your calculations are correct this will always result in the weight for the stratum with the highest proportion of the population responding being 1.)

4 apply the appropriate weight to each case.

Beware: many authors (for example Hays, 1994) question the validity of using statistics to make inferences from your sample if you have weighted cases.

worked example

Weighting cases

To select your sample for a survey you have used stratified random sampling. The percentage of each stratum's population that responded is given below:

upper stratum: 90%
lower stratum: 65%

To account for the differences in the response rates between strata you decide to weight the cases prior to analysis.

The weight for the upper stratum is: $\frac{90}{90} = 1$

This means that each case in the upper stratum will count as 1 case in your analysis.

The weight for the lower stratum is: $\frac{90}{65} = 1.38$

This means that each case in the lower stratum will count for 1.38 cases in your analysis.

You enter these as a separate variable in your data set and use the statistical analysis software to apply the weights.

Checking for errors

No matter how carefully you code and subsequently enter data there will always be some errors. The main methods to check data for errors are as follows:

- Look for illegitimate codes. In any coding scheme, only certain numbers are allocated. Other numbers are therefore errors. Common errors are the inclusion of letters O and o instead of zero, letters l or I instead of 1, and number 7 instead of 1.
- Look for illogical relationships. For example, if a person is coded to the professional socioeconomic group and their social class is unskilled manual an error has occurred.
- Check that rules in filter questions are followed. Certain responses to filter questions (Section 10.4) mean that other variables should be coded as missing values. If this has not happened there has been an error.

For each possible error you need to discover whether it occurred at coding or data entry and then correct it. By giving each case a unique identifier (normally a number) it is possible to link the matrix to the original data. You must remember to write the identifier on the data collection form and enter it along with the other data into the matrix.

Data checking is very time consuming and so is often not undertaken. Beware: not doing it is very dangerous and can result in incorrect results from which false conclusions are drawn!

11.3 Exploring and presenting data

Once your data have been entered and checked for errors, you are ready to start your analysis. We have found Tukey's (1977) *exploratory data analysis* approach useful in these initial stages. This approach emphasises the use of diagrams to explore and understand your data. As you would expect, we believe that it is important to keep your research question(s) and objectives in mind when exploring your data. However, the exploratory data analysis approach also formalises the common practice of looking for other relationships in data, which your research was not initially designed to test. This should not be discounted, as it may suggest other fruitful avenues for analysis. In addition, computers make this relatively easy and quick.

Even at this stage it is important that you structure and label clearly each diagram and table to avoid possible misinterpretation. Box 11.1 provides a summary checklist of the points to remember when designing a diagram or table.

We have found it best to begin exploratory analysis by looking at individual variables and their components. The key aspects you may need to consider will be guided by your research question(s) and objectives, and are likely to include (Sparrow, 1989):

- specific values;
- highest and lowest values;
- trends over time;
- proportions;
- distributions.

Box 11.1 Checklist for diagrams and tables

For both diagrams and tables

✓ Does it have a brief but clear and descriptive title?

✓ Are the units of measurement used clearly stated?

✓ Are the sources of data used clearly stated?

✓ Are there notes to explain abbreviations and unusual terminology?

✓ Does it state the size of the sample on which the values in the table are based?

For diagrams

✓ Does it have clear axis labels?

✓ Are bars and their components in the same logical sequence?

✓ Is more dense shading used for smaller areas?

✓ Is a key or legend included (where necessary)?

For tables

✓ Does it have clear column and row headings?

✓ Are columns and rows in a logical sequence?

Once you have explored these you can then begin to compare and look for relationships between variables, considering in addition (Sparrow, 1989):

- conjunctions (the point where values for two or more variables intersect);
- totals;
- interdependence and relationships.

These are summarised in Table 11.2. Most analysis software contains procedures to create tables and diagrams. Your choice will depend on those aspects of the data that you wish to emphasise and the level of measurement at which the data were recorded. This section is concerned only with tables and two-dimensional diagrams available on most spreadsheets (Table 11.2). Pictograms and three-dimensional diagrams are not discussed, as these can hinder interpretation. Those tables and diagrams most pertinent to your research question(s) and objectives will eventually appear in your research report to support your arguments. You should therefore save a disk copy of all tables and diagrams you create.

Exploring and presenting individual variables

To show specific values

The simplest way of summarising data for individual variables so that specific values can be read is to use a *table (frequency distribution)*. For descriptive data, the table summarises the number of cases (frequency) in each category. For variables where there are likely to be a large number of categories (or values for quantifiable data), you will need to group the data into categories that reflect your research question(s) and objectives.

To show highest and lowest values

Tables attach no visual significance to highest or lowest values unless emphasised by alternative fonts. Diagrams can provide visual clues, although both categorical and quantifiable data may need grouping (Henry, 1995). For categorical and discrete data, bar charts and pictograms are both suitable. However, bar charts provide a more accurate representation and are used for most research reports. In a *bar chart*, sometimes called a *column chart*, the heights of the bars represent the frequency of occurrence (Figure 11.2). Bars are separated by gaps, usually half the width of the bars.

Most researchers use a histogram for continuous data. Prior to being drawn, data will need to be grouped into class intervals. In a *histogram*, the area of each bar represents the frequency of occurrence, and the continuous nature of the data is emphasised by the absence of gaps between the bars. For equal-width class intervals, the height of your bar still represents the frequency of occurrences (Figure 11.3) and so the highest and lowest values are easy to distinguish. For histograms with unequal class interval widths, this is not the case.

Analysis software treats histograms for data of equal width class intervals as a variation of a bar chart. Unfortunately, few spreadsheets will cope automatically with the calculations required to draw histograms for unequal class intervals. Consequently, you may have to use a bar chart owing to the limitations of your analysis software.

Table 11.2 Data presentation by data type: a summary

	Categorical		*Quantifiable*	
	Descriptive	*Ranked*	*Continuous*	*Discrete*
To show one variable so that any *specific* value can be read easily	Table/frequency distribution (data often grouped)			
To show the frequency of occurrences of categories or values for one variable so that *highest* and *lowest* are clear	Bar chart (data may need grouping)		Histogram or frequency polygon (data must be grouped)	Bar chart or pictogram (data may need grouping)
To show the *trend* for a variable		Line graph or bar chart	Line graph or histogram	Line graph or bar chart
To show the *proportion* of occurrences of categories or values for one variable	Pie chart or bar chart (data may need grouping)		Histogram or pie chart (data must be grouped)	Pie chart or bar chart (data may need grouping)
To show the *distribution* of values for one variable			Frequency polygon, histogram (data must be grouped) or box plot	Frequency polygon, bar chart (data may need grouping) or box plot
To show the *interdependence* between two or more variables so that any *specific* value can be read easily	Contingency table/cross-tabulation (data often grouped)			
To compare the frequency of occurrences of categories or values for two or more variables so that *highest* and *lowest* are clear	Multiple bar chart (continuous data must be grouped, other data may need grouping)			
To compare the *trends* for two or more variables so that *conjunctions* are clear		Multiple line graph or multiple bar chart		
To compare the *proportions* of occurrences of categories or values for two or more variables	Comparative pie charts or percentage component bar chart (continuous data must be grouped, other data may need grouping)			
To compare the *distribution* of values for two or more variables			Multiple box plot	
To compare the frequency of occurrences of categories or values for two or more variables so that *totals* are clear	Stacked bar chart (continuous data must be grouped, other data may need grouping)			
To compare the *proportions* and *totals* of occurrences of categories or values for two or more variables	Comparative proportional pie charts (continuous data must be grouped, other data may need grouping)			
To show the *relationship* between cases for two variables		Scatter graph/scatter plot		

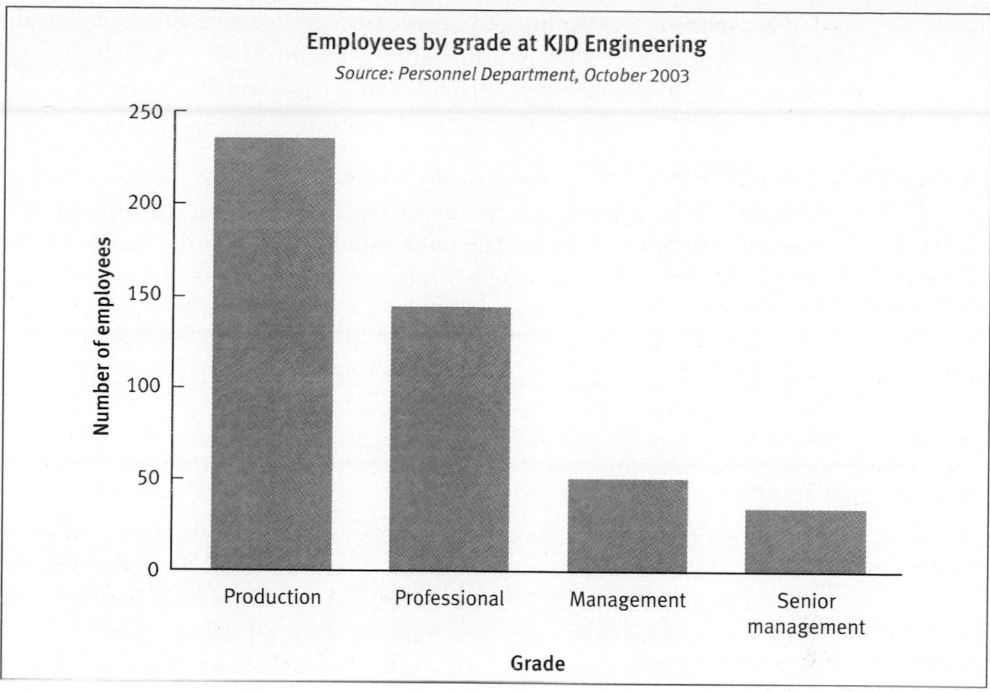

Figure 11.2 Bar chart

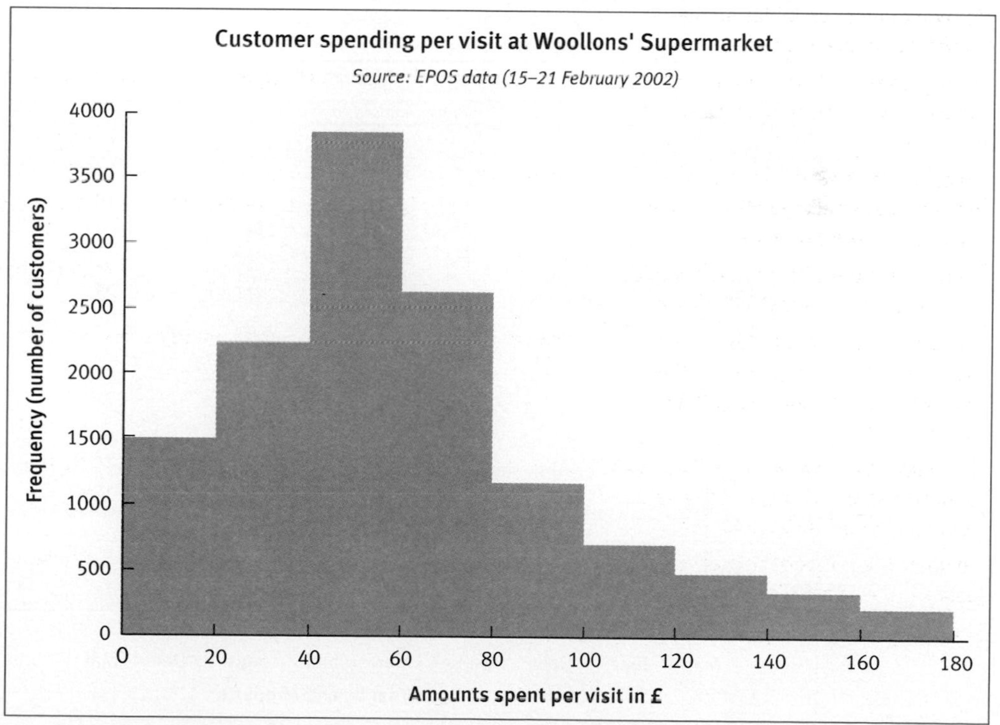

Figure 11.3 Histogram

Frequency polygons are used less often to illustrate limits. Most analysis software treats them as a version of a line graph (Figure 11.4) in which the lines are extended to meet the horizontal axis, provided that class widths are equal.

To show the trend

Trends can be presented only for variables containing quantifiable (and occasionally ranked) longitudinal data. The most suitable diagram for exploring the trend is a *line graph* (Henry, 1995) in which your data values for each time period are joined with a line to represent the trend (Figure 11.4). You can also use bar charts (Figure 11.2) to show trends between discrete time periods and histograms (Figure 11.3) for continuous time periods. The trend can also be calculated using time series analysis (Section 11.5).

To show proportions

Research has shown that the most frequently used diagram to emphasise the proportion or share of occurrences is the pie chart, although bar charts have been shown to give equally good results (Henry, 1995). A *pie chart* is divided into proportional segments according to the share each has of the total value (Figure 11.5). For continuous and some discrete and categorical data you will need to group data prior to drawing the pie chart, as it is difficult to interpret pie charts with more than six segments (Morris, 1999).

Figure 11.4 **Line graph**

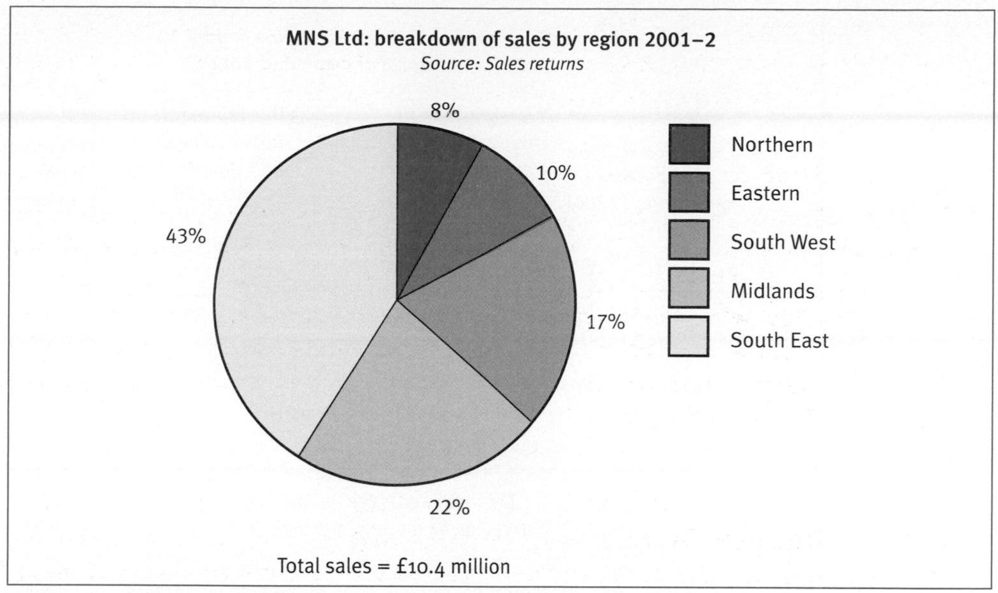

Figure 11.5 Pie chart

To show the distribution of values

Prior to using many statistical tests it is necessary to establish the distribution of values for variables containing quantifiable data (Sections 11.4, 11.5). This can be seen by plotting either a frequency polygon or a histogram (Figure 11.3) for continuous data or a frequency polygon or bar chart for discrete data (Figure 11.2). If your diagram shows a bunching to the left and a long tail to the right as in Figure 11.3 the data are *positively skewed*. If the converse is true, the data are *negatively skewed*. If your data are equally distributed either side of the highest frequency then they are *symmetrically distributed*. A special form of the symmetric distribution, in which the data can be plotted as a bell-shaped curve, is known as the *normal distribution*.

An alternative often included in more advanced statistical analysis software is the *box plot* (Figure 11.6). This diagram provides you with a pictorial representation of the distribution of the data for a variable. The plot shows where the middle value or median is, how this relates to the middle 50 per cent of the data or inter-quartile range, and highest and lowest values or *extremes* (Section 11.4). In this example we can see that the data values for the variable are positively skewed as there is a long tail to the right.

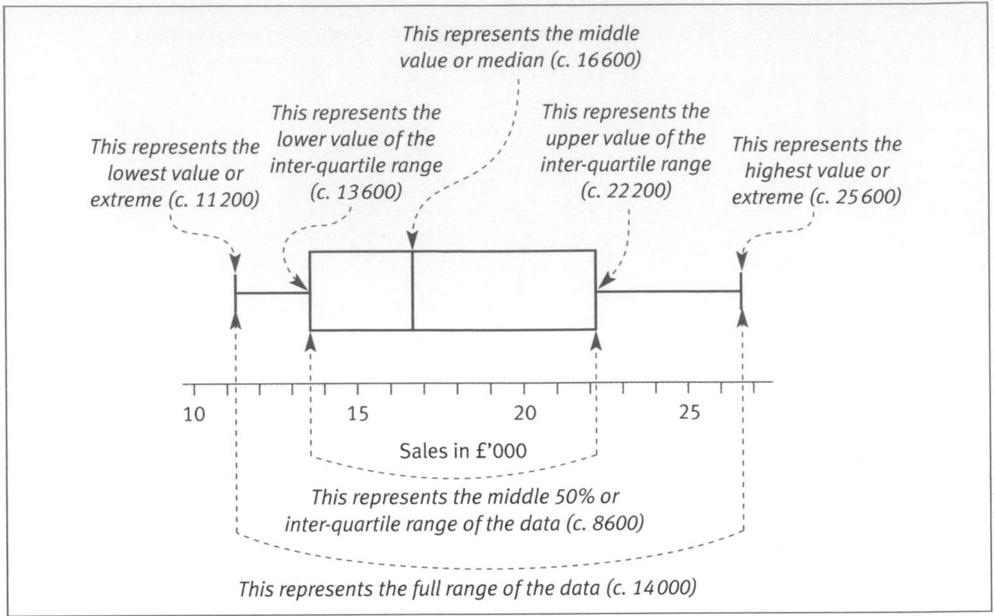

Figure 11.6 Annotated sketch of a box plot

worked example

Exploring and presenting data for individual variables

As part of audience research, people attending a play at a provincial theatre were asked to complete a short questionnaire. This collected responses to 25 questions including:

3 How many plays (including this one) have you seen at this theatre in the past year?

____ ____

11 This play is good value for money

strongly disagree	disagree	agree	strongly agree
☐ 1	☐ 2	☐ 3	☐ 4

24 How old are you?

Under 18	☐ 1	35 to 64	☐ 3
18 to 34	☐ 2	Over 65	☐ 4

Exploratory analyses were undertaken using analysis software and diagrams were generated. For question 3, which collected discrete data, the aspects that were most important were the distribution of values and the highest and lowest numbers of plays seen. A bar chart was therefore drawn:

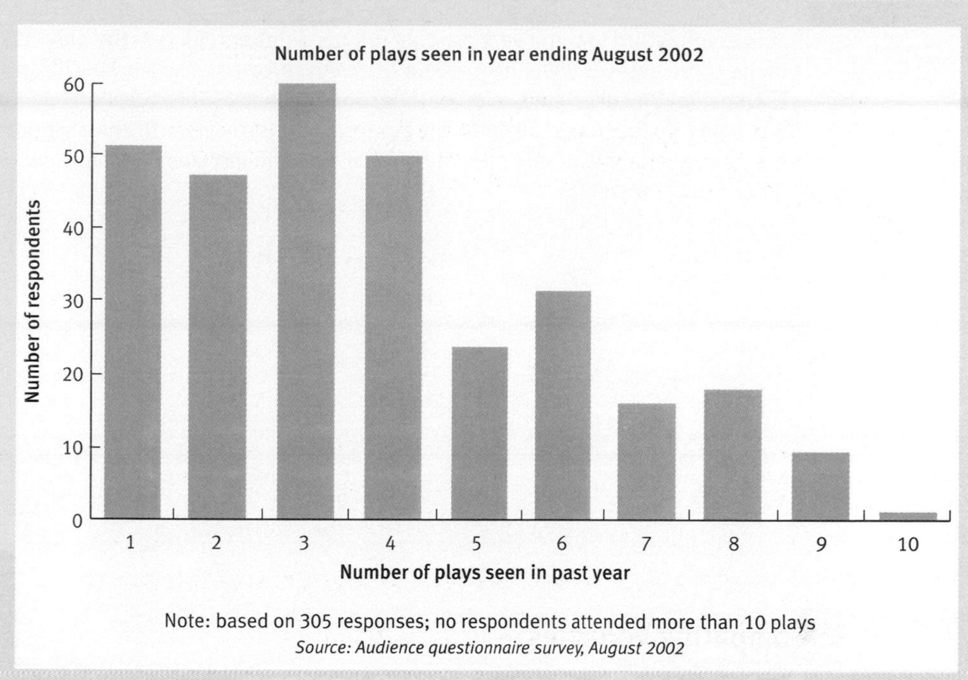

Note: based on 305 responses; no respondents attended more than 10 plays
Source: Audience questionnaire survey, August 2002

This emphasised that the most frequent number of plays seen by respondents was three and the least frequent 10. It also showed that the distribution was positively skewed towards lower numbers of plays seen.

For question 11 (categorical data), the most important aspect was the proportions of people agreeing and disagreeing with the statement. A pie chart was therefore drawn using similar shadings for the two agree categories and for the two disagree categories:

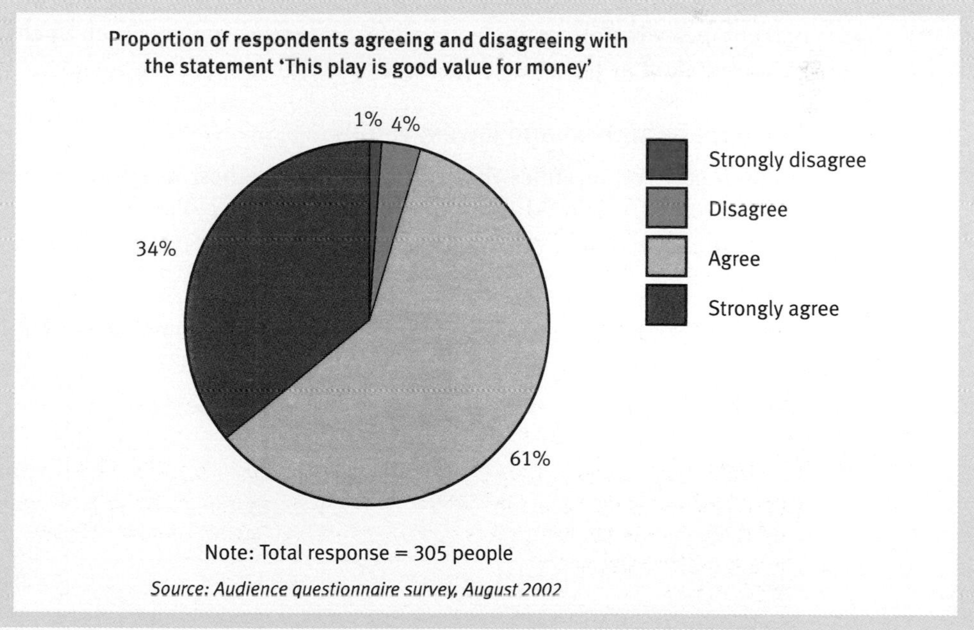

Note: Total response = 305 people
Source: Audience questionnaire survey, August 2002

This emphasised that the vast majority (95 per cent) agreed that the play was good value for money. Percentages were included on the chart to emphasise the specific proportions.

Question 24 collected data on each respondent's age. This question had grouped continuous data into four unequal-width age groups. For this analysis, the most important aspect was the specific number of respondents in each age category and so a table was constructed:

Age of respondents

Age group	Number
Less than 18	13
18 to 34	63
35 to 64	160
65 plus	64
Total	300

Note: 5 people did not respond

Source: Audience questionnaire survey, August 2002

Comparing variables

To show specific values and interdependence

As with individual variables the best method of finding specific data values is a table. This is known as a *contingency table* or *cross-tabulation* (Table 11.3), and it also enables you to examine interdependence between the variables. For variables where there are likely to be a large number of categories (or values for quantifiable data), you may need to group the data to prevent the table from becoming too large.

Most statistical analysis software allows you to add totals, and row and column percentages when designing your table. Statistical analyses such as chi square can also be undertaken at the same time (Section 11.5).

To compare highest and lowest values

Comparisons of variables that emphasise the highest and lowest rather than precise values are best explored using a *multiple bar chart* (Henry, 1995), also known as a *compound bar chart*. As with a bar chart, continuous data – or data where there are

Table 11.3 Contingency table: number of insurance claims by gender, 2002

*Number of claims**	*Male*	*Female*	*Total*
0	10 032	13 478	23 510
1	2 156	1 430	3 586
2	120	25	145
3	13	4	17
Total	12 321	14 937	27 258

*No clients had more than 3 claims
Source: PJ Insurance Services

many values or categories – need to be grouped. Within any multiple bar chart you are likely to find it easiest to compare between adjacent bars. Thus Figure 11.7 has been drawn to emphasise comparisons between years rather than between companies.

To compare proportions

Comparison of proportions between variables uses either a *percentage component bar chart* or two or more pie charts. Either type of diagram can be used for all data types provided that continuous data, and data where there are more than six values or categories, are grouped. Percentage component bar charts are more straightforward to draw than comparative pie charts using most spreadsheets. Within your percentage component bar chart, comparisons will be easiest between adjacent bars. The chart in Figure 11.8 has been drawn to compare proportions of each type of response between products. Consumers' responses for each product therefore form a single bar.

To compare trends and conjunctions

The most suitable diagram to compare trends for two or more quantifiable (or occasionally ranked) variables is a *multiple line graph* where one line represents each variable (Henry, 1995). You can also use multiple bar charts (Figure 11.7) in which bars for the same time period are placed adjacent.

If you need to look for conjunctions in the trends – that is, where values for two or more variables intersect – this is where the lines on a multiple line graph cross.

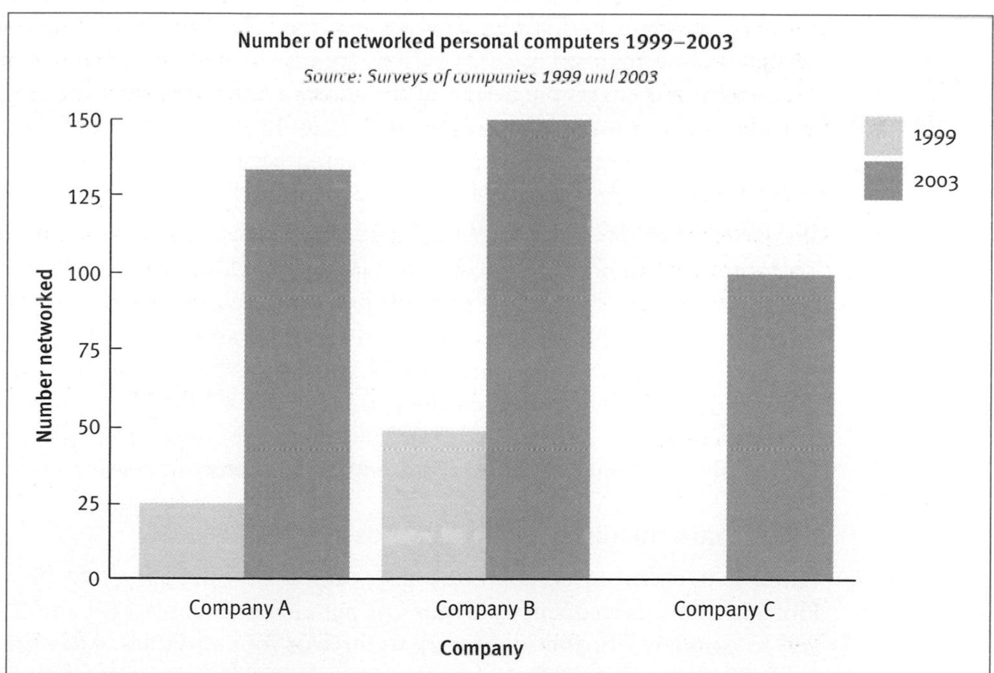

Figure 11.7 Multiple bar chart

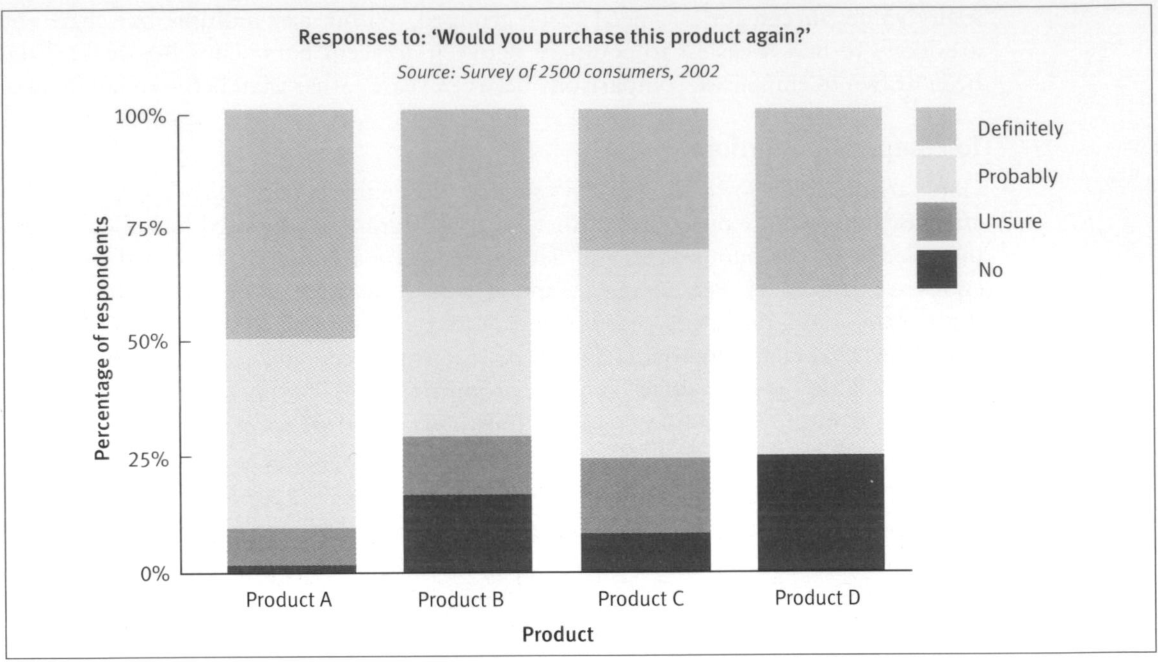

Figure 11.8 Percentage component bar chart

To compare totals

Comparison of totals between variables uses a variation of the bar chart. A *stacked bar chart* can be used for all data types provided that continuous data and data where there are more than six possible values or categories are grouped. As with percentage component bar charts the design of the stacked bar chart is dictated by the totals you want to compare. For this reason, in Figure 11.9 sales for each quarter have been stacked to give totals which can be compared between companies.

To compare proportions and totals

To compare both proportions of each category or value and the totals for two or more variables it is best to use *comparative proportional pie charts* for all data types. For each comparative proportional pie chart the total area of the pie chart represents the total for that variable. By contrast, the angle of each segment represents the relative proportion of a category within the variable (Figure 11.5). Because of the complexity of drawing comparative proportional pie charts, they are rarely used for exploratory data analysis although they can be used to good effect in research reports.

To compare the distribution of values

Often it is useful to compare the distribution of values for two or more variables. Plotting multiple frequency polygons or bar charts (Figures 11.4 and 11.7) will enable you to compare distributions for up to three or four variables. After this your diagram is likely just to look a mess! An alternative is to use a diagram of multiple box plots, similar to the one in Figure 11.6. This provides a pictorial representation of the dis-

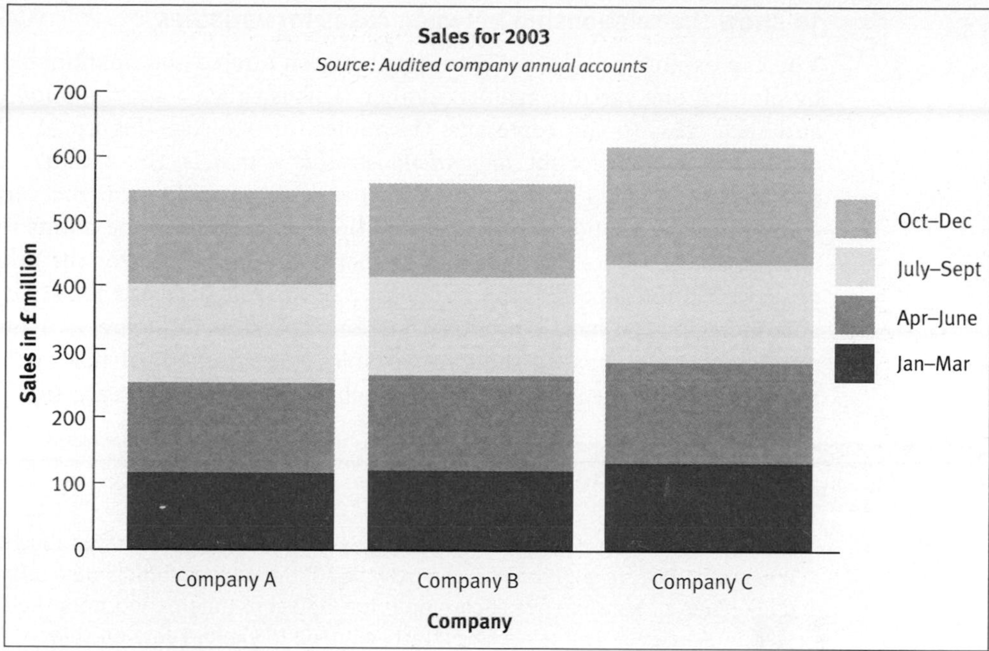

Figure 11.9 Stacked bar chart

tribution of the data for the variables in which you are interested. These plots can be compared and are interpreted in the same way as the single box plot.

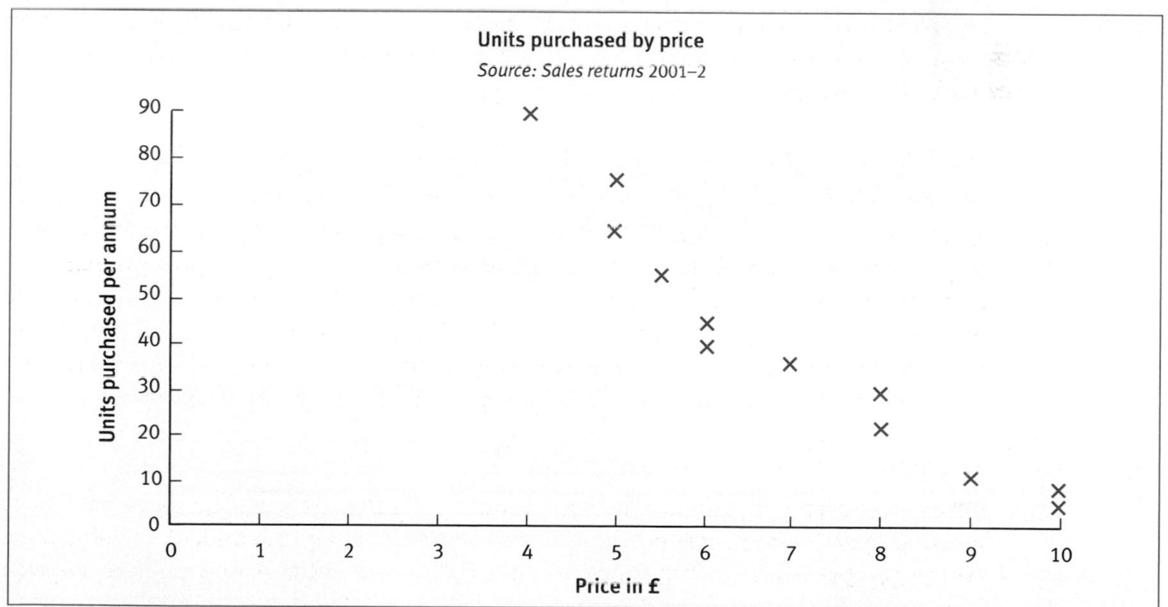

Figure 11.10 Scatter graph

To show the relationship between cases for variables

You can explore possible relationships between ranked and quantifiable data variables by plotting one variable against another. This is called a *scatter graph* or *scatter plot*, and each cross (point) represents the values for one case (Figure 11.10). Convention dictates that you plot the *dependent variable* – that is, the variable that changes in response to changes in the other (*independent*) variable – on the vertical axis. The strength of the relationship is indicated by the closeness of the points to an imaginary line. If, as the values for one variable increase, so do those for the other, you have a positive relationship. If, as the values for one variable decrease, those for the other variable increase, you have a negative relationship. Thus in Figure 11.10 there is a negative relationship between the two variables. The strength of this relationship can be assessed statistically using techniques such as correlation or regression (Section 11.5).

worked example

Comparing variables

An independent ice cream manufacturer has kept records of monthly sales of ice cream for 2001 and 2002. In addition, the company has obtained longitudinal data on average (mean) daily hours of sunshine for each month for the same time period from their local weather station. As part of your research project you need to explore data on sales of the three best-selling flavours (vanilla, strawberry and chocolate), paying particular attention to:

- comparative trends in sales;
- the relationship between sales and amount of sunshine.

To compare trends in sales between the three flavours you plot a multiple line graph:

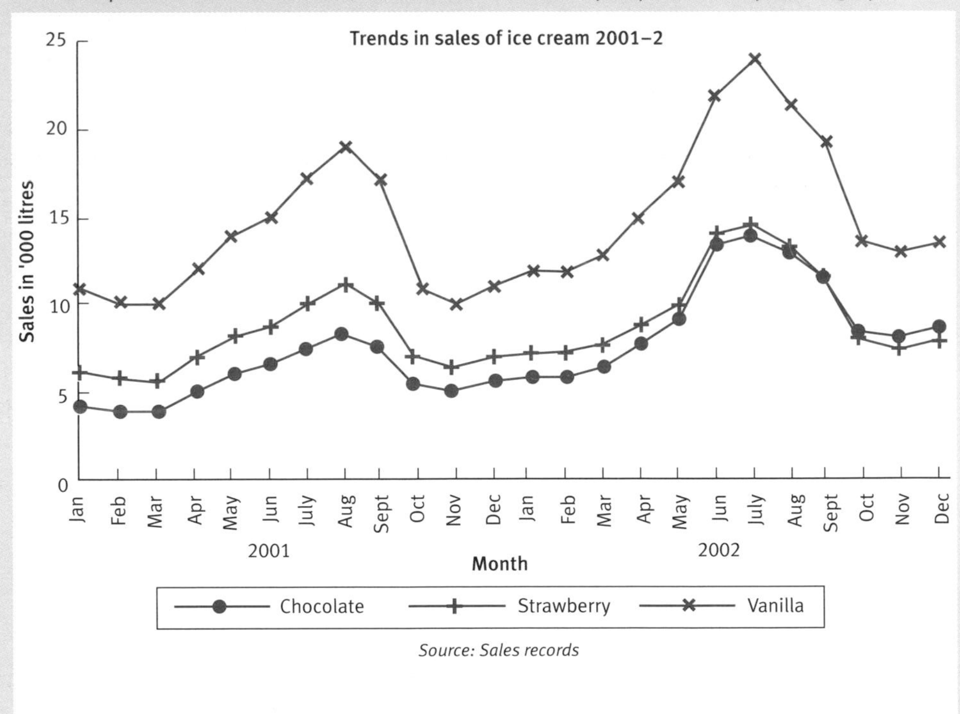

Source: Sales records

This indicates that sales for all flavours of ice cream are following a seasonal pattern but with an overall upward trend. It also shows that sales of vanilla ice cream are highest, and that those of chocolate have overtaken strawberry. The multiple line graph highlights the conjunction when sales of chocolate first exceeded strawberry, September 2002.

To show relationships between sales and amount of sunshine you plot scatter graphs for sales of each ice cream flavour against average (mean) daily hours of sunshine for each month. You plot sales on the vertical axis, as you presume that these are dependent on the amount of sunshine, for example:

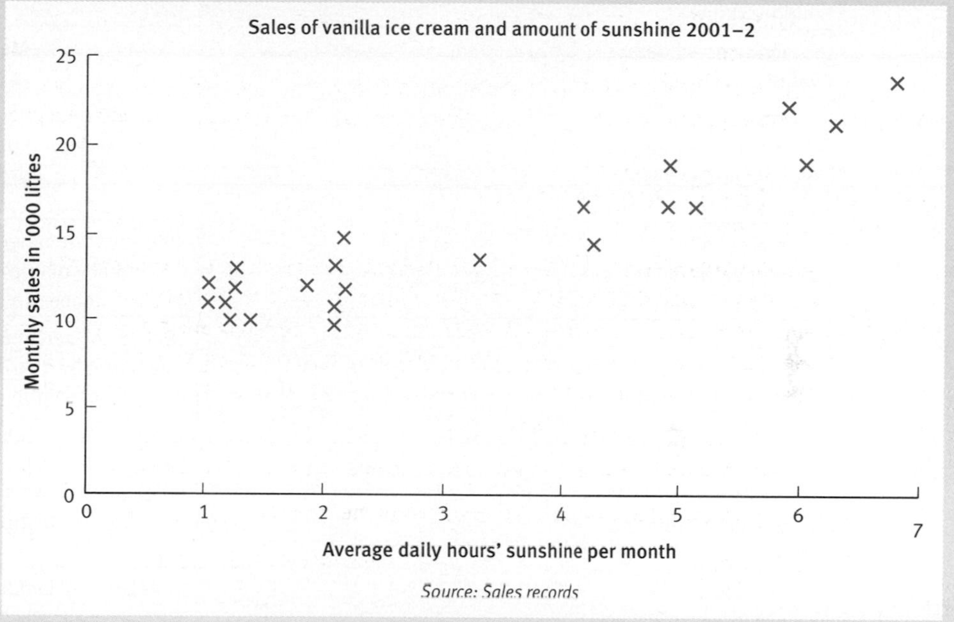

The scatter graph shows that there is a positive relationship between the amount of sunshine and sales of vanilla flavour ice cream. Subsequent scatter plots reveal similar relationships for strawberry and chocolate flavours.

11.4 Describing data using statistics

The exploratory data analysis approach (Section 11.3) emphasised the use of diagrams to understand your data. *Descriptive statistics* enable you to describe (and compare) variables numerically. Your research question(s) and objectives, although limited by the type of data (Table 11.4), should guide your choice of statistics. Statistics to describe a variable focus on two aspects:

- the central tendency;
- the dispersion.

These are summarised in Table 11.4. Those most pertinent to your research question(s) and objectives will eventually be quoted in your research report as support for your arguments.

Table 11.4 Descriptive statistics by data type: a summary

To calculate a measure of:		*Categorical*		*Quantifiable*	
		Descriptive	*Ranked*	*Continuous*	*Discrete*
Central tendency that ...	... represents the value that occurs most frequently	Mode			
	... represents the middle value			Median	
	... includes all data values (average)			Mean	
Dispersion that ...	... states the difference between the highest and lowest values			Range (data need not be normally distributed but must be placed in rank order)	
	... states the difference within the middle 50% of values			Inter-quartile range (data need not be normally distributed but must be placed in rank order)	
	... states the difference within another fraction of the values			Deciles or percentiles (data need not be normally distributed but must be placed in rank order)	
	... describes the extent to which data values differ from the mean			Variance, or more usually, the standard deviation (data should be normally distributed)	
	... compares the extent to which data values differ from the mean between variables			Coefficient of variation (data should be normally distributed)	

Describing the central tendency

When describing data for both samples and populations quantitatively it is usual to provide some general impression of values that could be seen as common, middling or average. These are termed measures of *central tendency* and are discussed in virtually all statistics textbooks. The three ways of measuring the central tendency most used in business research are the:

- value that occurs most frequently (mode);
- middle value or mid-point after the data have been ranked (median);
- value, often known as the average, that includes all data values in its calculation (mean).

However, beware: if you have used numerical codes most analysis software can calculate all three measures whether or not they are appropriate!

To represent the value that occurs most frequently

The *mode* is the value that occurs most frequently. For descriptive data, the mode is the only measure of central tendency that can be sensibly interpreted. You might read in a report that the most common (*modal*) colour of motor cars sold last year was red, or that the two most common makes were Ford and Vauxhall (it is possible to have more than one mode). The mode can be calculated for variables where there is likely to be a large number of categories (or values for quantifiable data) although it may be less useful. One solution is to group the data into suitable categories and to quote the most frequently occurring or *modal group*.

To represent the middle value

If you have quantitative data it is also possible to calculate the middle or *median* value by ranking all the values in ascending order and finding the mid-point (or *50th percentile*) in the distribution. For variables that have an even number of data values the median will occur halfway between the two middle data values. The median has the advantage that it is not affected by extreme values in the distribution.

To include all data values

The most frequently used measure of central tendency is the *mean* or *average*, which includes all data values in its calculation. However, it is usually only possible to calculate a meaningful mean using quantifiable data.

The value of your mean is unduly influenced by extreme data values in skewed distributions (Section 11.3). In such distributions the mean tends to get drawn towards the long tail of extreme data values and may be less representative of the central tendency. For this and other reasons Hays (1994) suggests that the median may be a more useful descriptive statistic. However, because the mean is the building block for many of the statistical tests used to explore relationships (Section 11.5), it is usual to include it as at least one of the measures of central tendency for quantifiable data in your report. This is, of course, provided that it makes sense!

worked example

Measuring the central tendency

As part of your research project, you have obtained secondary data from the service department of your organisation on the length of time for which customers have held service contracts:

Length of time held contract	*Number of customers*
< 3 months	50
3 to < 6 months	44
6 months to < 1 year	71
1 to < 2 years	105
2 to < 3 years	74
3 to < 4 years	35
4 to < 5 years	27
5+ years	11

▶

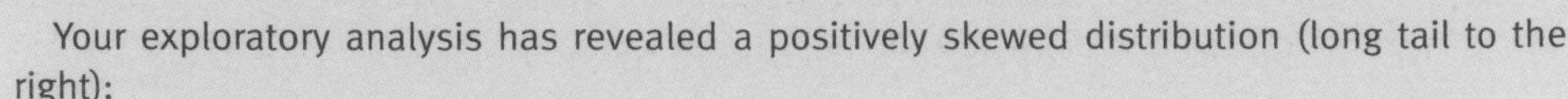

Your exploratory analysis has revealed a positively skewed distribution (long tail to the right):

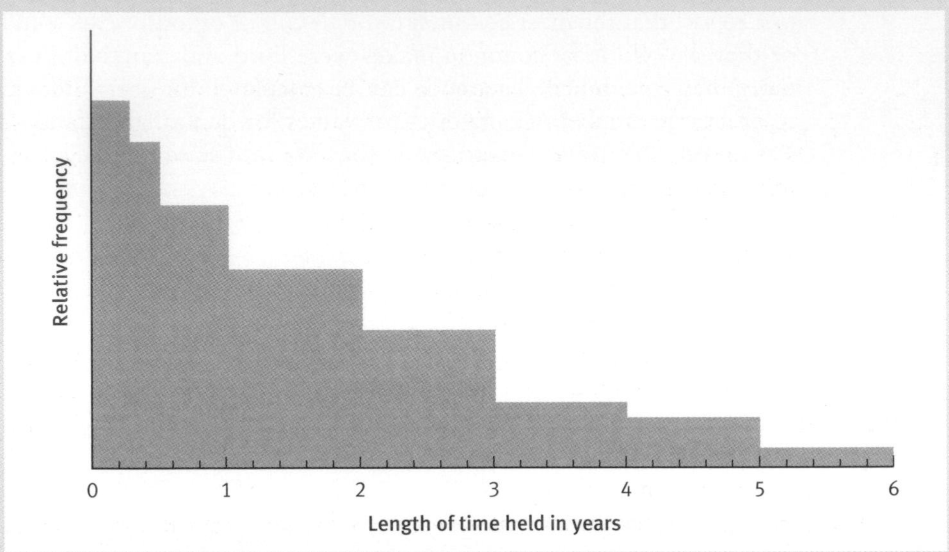

From the table the largest single group of customers is those who have held contracts for 1 to < 2 years. This is the modal time period (most commonly occurring). However, the usefulness of this statistic is limited owing to the variety of class widths. By definition, half the customers will have held contracts below the median time period (approximately 1 year 5 months) and half above it. However, there are 11 customers who have held service contracts for over 5 years. As a consequence, the mean time period (approximately 1 year 9 months) is pulled towards longer times. This is represented by the skewed shape of the distribution.

You need to decide which of these measures of central tendency to include in your research report. As the mode makes little sense you quote the median and mean when interpreting the data:

> The length of time for which customers have held service contracts is positively skewed. Although mean length of time is approximately 1 year 9 months, half of customers have held service contracts for less than 1 year 5 months (median). Grouping of these data means that it is not possible to calculate a meaningful mode.

Describing the dispersion

As well as describing the central tendency for a variable, it is important to describe how the data values are dispersed around the central tendency. As you can see from Table 11.4 this is only possible for quantifiable data. Two of the most frequently used ways of describing the dispersion are the:

- difference within the middle 50 per cent of values (inter-quartile range);
- extent to which values differ from the mean (standard deviation).

Although these *measures of dispersion* are suitable only for quantifiable data most statistical analysis software will also calculate them for categorical data if you have used numerical codes!

To state the difference between values

In order to get a quick impression of the distribution of data values for a variable you could simply calculate the difference between the lowest and the highest values – that is, the *range*. However, this statistic is rarely used in research reports as it represents only the extreme values.

A more frequently used statistic is the *inter-quartile range*. As we discussed earlier, the median divides the range into two. The range can be further divided into four equal sections called *quartiles*. The lower quartile is the value below which a quarter of your data values will fall; the upper quartile is the value above which a quarter of your data values will fall. As you would expect, the remaining half of your data values will fall between the lower and upper quartiles. The difference between the upper and lower quartiles is the inter-quartile range (Diamantopoulos and Schlegelmilch, 1997). As a consequence it is concerned only with the middle 50 per cent of data values and ignores extreme values.

You can also calculate the range for other fractions of a variable's distribution. One alternative is to divide your distribution using *percentiles*. These split your distribution into 100 equal parts. Obviously the lower quartile is the 25th percentile and the upper quartile the 75th percentile. However, you could calculate a range between the 10th and 90th percentiles so as to include 80 per cent of your data values. Another alternative is to divide the range into 10 equal parts called *deciles*.

To describe and compare the extent by which values differ from the mean

Conceptually and statistically in research it is important to look at the extent to which the data values for a variable are *spread* around their mean, as this is what you need to know to assess its usefulness as a typical value for the distribution. If your data values are all close to the mean, then the mean is more typical than if they vary widely. To describe the extent of spread of quantifiable data you use the *standard deviation*. If your data are a sample (Section 6.1) this is calculated using a slightly different formula than if your data are a population, although if your sample is larger than about 30 cases there is little difference in the two statistics (Morris, 1999).

You may need to compare the relative spread of data between distributions of different magnitudes (for example, one may be measured in hundreds of tonnes, the other in billions of tonnes). To make a meaningful comparison you will need to take account of these different magnitudes. A common way of doing this is:

1 to divide the standard deviation by the mean;
2 then to multiply your answer by 100.

This results in a statistic called the *coefficient of variation* (Diamantopoulos and Schlegelmilch, 1997). The values of this statistic can then be compared. The distribution with the largest coefficient of variation has the largest relative spread of data.

worked example

Describing variables and comparing their dispersion

A bank collects data on the total value of transactions at each of its main and sub-branches. The mean value of total transactions at the main branches is five times as high as that for the sub-branches. This makes it difficult to compare the relative spread in total value of transactions between the two types of branches. Calculating the coefficients of variation reveals that there is relatively more variation in the total value of transactions at the main branches than the sub-branches:

Branch type	Mean total transaction value	Standard deviation	Coefficient of variation
Main	£6 000 000	£1 417 000	23.62
Sub	£1 200 000	£217 000	18.08

This is because the coefficient of variation for the main branches is larger (23.62) than the coefficient for the sub-branches (18.08).

11.5 Examining relationships, differences and trends using statistics

One of the questions you are most likely to ask in your analysis is: 'How does a variable relate to another variable?' In statistical analysis you answer this question by testing the likelihood of the relationship (or one more extreme) occurring by chance alone, if there really was no difference in the population from which the sample was drawn (Robson, 2002). This is known as the *statistical significance* and can be thought of as helping to rule out the possibility that your result could be due to random variation in your sample. The way in which this significance is tested can be thought of as answering one from a series of questions, dependent on the data type:

- Is the association statistically significant?
- Are the differences statistically significant?
- What is the strength of the relationship, and is it statistically significant?
- Are the predicted values statistically significant?

These are summarised in Table 11.5 along with statistics used to help examine trends.

Testing for significant relationships and differences

Testing the probability of a relationship between variables occurring by chance alone if there really was no difference in the population from which that sample was drawn is known as *significance testing*. As part of your research project, you might have collected sample data to examine the relationship between two variables. Once you have entered data into the analysis software, chosen the statistic and run the program, an answer will appear as if by magic! With most statistical analysis software this will consist of a test statistic, the degrees of freedom and, based on these, the probability (*p-value*) of your test result or one more extreme occurring by chance alone. If the

Table 11.5 Statistics to examine relationships, differences and trends by data type: a summary

	Categorical		***Quantifiable***	
	Descriptive	*Ranked*	*Continuous*	*Discrete*
To test whether two variables are associated	Chi square (data may need grouping)		Chi square if variables grouped into discrete classes	
To test whether two groups (categories) are different	Kolmogorov–Smirnov (data may need grouping)		Independent *t*-test or paired *t*-test (often used to test for changes over time)	
To test whether three or more groups (categories) are different			Analysis of variance (ANOVA)	
To assess the strength of relationship between two variables		Spearman's rank correlation coefficient	Pearson's product moment correlation coefficient (PMCC)	
To assess the strength of a relationship between one dependent and one or more independent variables			Regression coefficient	
To predict the value of a dependent variable from one or more independent variables			Regression equation	
To compare relative changes over time			Index numbers	
To determine the trend over time of a series of data			Time series: moving averages Regression equation	

probability of your test statistic or one more extreme having occurred by chance alone is very low (usually $p = 0.05$ or lower*), then you have a statistically significant relationship. If the probability of obtaining the test statistic or one more extreme by chance alone is higher than 0.05, then you conclude that the relationship is not statistically significant. There may still be a relationship between the variables under such circumstances, but you cannot make the conclusion with any certainty.

The statistical significance of the relationship indicated by the test statistic is determined in part by your sample size (Section 6.2). One consequence of this is that it is very difficult to obtain a significant test statistic with a small sample. Conversely, because the impact of sample size declines rapidly for samples over about 30 cases, if you have an extremely large sample it is relatively easy to obtain a significant test statistic for a relationship that is in reality not that obvious!

Type I and Type II errors

Inevitably, errors can occur when making inferences from samples. Statisticians refer to these as Type I and Type II errors. An error made by wrongly coming to a decision

* A probability of 0.05 means that the probability of your test result or one more extreme occurring by chance alone, if there really was no difference in the population from which the sample was drawn, is 5 in 100, that is 1 in 20.

that something is true when in reality it is not, is known as a *Type I error*. Type I errors might involve your concluding that two variables are related when they are not, or incorrectly concluding that a sample statistic exceeds the value that would be expected by chance alone. This means that the term 'statistical significance' discussed earlier refers to the probability of making a Type I error. A *Type II error* involves the opposite occurring. In other words you conclude that something is not true, when in reality it is. This means that Type II errors might involve you in concluding that two variables are not related when they are, or that a sample statistic does not exceed the value that would be expected by chance alone.

Given that a Type II error is the inverse of a Type I error, it follows that if we reduce our chances of making a Type I error by setting the significance level to 0.001 rather than 0.01, we increase our chances of making a Type II error by a corresponding amount. This is not an insurmountable problem, as researchers usually consider Type I errors more serious and prefer to take a small chance of saying something is true when it is not. It is therefore generally more important to minimise Type I than Type II errors.

To test whether two variables are associated

Often descriptive or quantifiable data will be summarised as a two-way contingency table (such as Table 11.3). The *chi square test* enables you to find out how likely it is that the two variables are associated. It is based on a comparison of the observed values in the table with what might be expected if the two distributions were entirely independent. Therefore you are assessing the likelihood of the data in your table, or data more extreme, occurring by chance alone by comparing it with what you would expect if the two variables were independent of each other.

The test relies on:

- the categories used in the contingency table being mutually exclusive, so that each observation falls into only one category or class interval;
- no more than 20 per cent of the cells in the table having expected values of less than 5. For contingency tables of two rows and two columns no expected values of less than 10 are preferable (Hays, 1994).

If the latter assumption is not met, the accepted solution is to combine rows and columns.

The chi square test calculates the probability that the data in your table, or data more extreme, could occur by chance alone. Most statistical analysis software does this automatically. However, if you are using a spreadsheet you will usually need to look up the probability in a 'critical values of chi square' table using your calculated chi square value and the degrees of freedom.* This table is included in most statistics textbooks. A probability of 0.05 means that there is only a 5 per cent chance of the data in your table occurring by chance alone, and is termed statistically significant. Therefore a probability of 0.05 or smaller means you can be at least 95 per cent certain that the relationship between your two variables could not have occurred by

* Degrees of freedom are the number of values free to vary when computing a statistic. The number of degrees of freedom for a contingency table of at least 2 rows and 2 columns of data is calculated from (number of rows in the table − 1) × (number of columns in the table − 1).

chance factors alone. When interpreting probabilities from software packages beware: owing to statistical rounding of numbers a probability of 0.000 does not mean zero, but that it is less than 0.0005.

worked example

Testing whether two variables are associated

As part of your research you wish to discover whether there is a significant association between grade of the respondent and gender. Earlier analysis has indicated that there are 760 respondents in your sample with no missing data for either variable. However, it has also highlighted the small numbers of respondents in the lowest grade and very small numbers in the three highest-grade categories:

Gender	*Grade 1*	*Grade 2*	*Grade 3*	*Grade 4*	*Grade 5*	*Grade 6*	*Grade 7*
Male	13	52	100	45	15	3	1
Female	27	233	209	49	12	0	1

Bearing in mind the assumptions of the chi square test you decide to combine categories to give three new grades: lower (grades 1 and 2), middle (grade 3) and higher (grades 4, 5, 6 and 7). The statistical analysis software creates a new data table and provides the following output:

	lower grade	middle grade	higher grade	row totals
male	65	100	64	229 (30.1%)
female	260	209	62	531 (69.9%)
column totals	325 (42.8%)	309 (40.7%)	126 (16.6%)	760 (100%)

Chi square = 42.13, degrees of freedom = 2, probability <.001.

As can be seen there is an overall chi square value of 42.13 with 2 degrees of freedom. This means that the probability of the values in your table occurring by chance alone is less than 0.001. You therefore conclude that the relationship between gender and grade is extremely unlikely to be explained by chance factors alone and quote the statistics in your project report:

[$\chi = 42.13, p = <.001$]*

To explore this association further, you examine the cell values in relation to the row and column totals. Of males, 27.9 per cent are in higher grades. This is high compared with the column totals, which indicate that only 16.6 per cent of the total sample were in higher grades. The row totals indicate that males in the sample represent 30.1 per cent of the total. Yet column frequencies show that males represented just over half (50.8 per cent) of the higher grades. Thus males are over-represented (and females under-represented) in higher grades.

* You will have noticed that the computer printout in this worked example does not have a zero before the decimal point. This is because most software packages follow the North American convention, in contrast to the UK convention of placing a zero before the decimal point.

To test whether two groups are different

Categorical data

Sometimes it is necessary to see whether the distribution of an observed set of values for each category of a variable differs from a specified distribution, for example whether your sample differs from the population from which it was selected. The *Kolmogorov–Smirnov test* enables you to establish this (Kanji, 1998). It is based on a comparison of the cumulative proportions of the observed values in each category with the cumulative proportions in the same categories for the specified population. Therefore you are testing the likelihood of the distribution of your observed data differing from that of the specified population by chance alone.

The Kolmogorov–Smirnov test calculates a *D* statistic that is then used to work out the probability of the two distributions differing by chance alone. Although the test and statistic are not often found in analysis software, they are relatively straightforward to calculate using a spreadsheet. A reasonably clear description of this can be found in Cohen and Holliday (1996). Once calculated you will need to look up the significance of your *D* value in a 'critical values of *D* for the Kolmogorov–Smirnov test' table. A probability of 0.05 means that there is only a 5 per cent chance that the two distributions differ by chance alone, and is termed statistically significant. Therefore a probability of 0.05 or smaller means you can be at least 95 per cent certain that the difference between your two distributions cannot be explained by chance factors alone.

worked example

Testing the representativeness of a sample

Benson's research question was 'To what extent do the espoused values of an organisation match the underlying cultural assumptions?' As part of his research he sent a questionnaire to the 155 employees in the organisation where he worked. Ninety-nine of these responded. The responses from each department were as follows:

		Administration	*Consultants*	*Systems*	*Trainers*	*Directorate*	*Total*
Respondents	**Number**	15	49	8	6	21	99
	Cumulative proportion	0.152	0.647	0.728	0.788	1.000	
Total employees	**Number**	31	73	17	10	24	155
	Cumulative proportion	0.200	0.671	0.781	0.846	1.000	
Difference		*0.048*	*0.024*	*0.053*	*0.058*	*0*	

The maximum difference between his observed cumulative proportion (that for respondents) and his specified cumulative proportion (that for total employees) was 0.058. This was the value of his *D* statistic. Consulting a 'critical values of *D* for the Kolmogorov–Smirnov test' table for a sample size of 99 revealed the probability that the two distributions differed by chance alone was less than 0.01: in other words less than 1 per cent. He concluded that those employees who responded did not differ significantly from the total population in terms of the department in which they were located. This was stated in his research report:

> Statistical analysis showed the sample selected did not differ significantly from all employees in terms of departmental representation [$D = .058, p<.01$].

Quantifiable data

If a quantifiable variable can be divided into two distinct groups using a descriptive variable you can assess the likelihood of these groups being different using an *independent groups t-test.* This compares the difference in the means of the two groups using a measure of the spread of the scores. If the likelihood of any difference between these two groups occurring by chance alone is low this will be represented by a large *t* statistic with a probability less than 0.05. This is termed statistically significant.

Alternatively you might have quantifiable data for two variables that measure the same feature but under different conditions. Your research could focus on the effects of an intervention such as employee counselling. As a consequence you would have pairs of data that measure work performance before and after counselling for each case. To assess the likelihood of any difference between your two variables (each half of the pair) occurring by chance alone you would use a *paired t-test.* Although the calculation of this is slightly different your interpretation would be the same as for the independent groups *t*-test.

Although the *t*-test assumes that the data are normally distributed (Section 11.3) this can be ignored without too many problems even with sample sizes of less than 30 (Hays, 1994). The assumption that the data for the two groups have the same variance (standard deviation squared) can also be ignored provided that the two samples are of similar size (Hays, 1994).

worked example

Testing whether two groups are different

As part of your research project you need to compare the performance of two international companies to see whether there is a difference in average (mean) share yield. You decide to use the following secondary data from the financial pages of a national newspaper:

Xofen	*Yield*	*Yffer*	*Yield*
Belgium	5.7	France	6.2
Denmark	6.0	Germany	6.2
Eire	5.7	Italy	5.9
Luxembourg	4.8	Portugal	4.5
Netherlands	6.0	Spain	4.8
Norway	7.2	United Kingdom	5.8
Sweden	5.1		
Switzerland	5.4		

Source: National Newspaper, *2002: 22*

After defining the two groups (Xofen and Yffer) using the descriptive variable you use a *t*-test to find out the likelihood of the difference between average yields for the two sectors occurring by chance alone.

Your statistical analysis software provides you with the means and standard deviations for the two groups as well as the *t* value, degrees of freedom and probability:

```
                      Xofen     Yffer
Mean                  5.74      5.57
Standard deviation    0.73      0.73

t value = 0.43, degrees of freedom = 12, probability = 0.672
```

▶

As the standard deviations for both sectors are the same the assumption that the two variables have the same variance is satisfied. The *t* value is only 0.43 with 12 degrees of freedom. A probability of 0.672 (much greater than 0.05) indicates that the likelihood of any difference between the two groups occurring by chance alone is high. You conclude that there is no statistically significant difference in average (mean) yields between Xofen and Yffer. This is stated in your research report:

There is no statistically significant difference [$t = .43, p = .672$] in mean yields between Xofen and Yffer

To test whether three or more groups are different

If a quantifiable variable is divided into three or more distinct groups using a descriptive variable, you can assess the likelihood of these groups being different occurring by chance alone by using *one-way analysis of variance* or *one-way ANOVA* (Table 11.5). As you can gather from its name, ANOVA analyses the variations within and between groups of data by comparing means. The *F* ratio or *F* statistic represents these differences. If the likelihood of any difference between groups occurring by chance alone is low, this will be represented by a large *F* ratio with a probability of less than 0.05. This is termed statistically significant.

Hays (1994) lists the following assumptions that need to be met before using one-way ANOVA:

- Each data value is independent and does not relate to any of the other data values. This means that you should not use one-way ANOVA where data values are related in some way, such as the same person being tested repeatedly.
- The data for each group are normally distributed (Section 11.3). This assumption is not particularly important provided that the number of cases in each group is large (30 or more).
- The data for each group have the same variance (standard deviation squared). However, provided that the number of cases in the largest group is not more than 1.5 times that of the smallest group, this appears to have very little effect on the test results.

worked example

Testing whether three groups are different

Andy and a colleague were interested to discover whether there were differences in job satisfaction across three groups of employees (managers, administrators, shop floor workers) within a manufacturing organisation. They decided to measure job satisfaction using a tried-and-tested scale based on five questions that resulted in a job satisfaction score (quantifiable data) for each employee.

After ensuring that the assumptions of one-way ANOVA were satisfied they analysed their data using statistical analysis software. The output included the following:

```
ANALYSIS OF VARIANCE
Source   D.F.        Sum of     Mean        F Ratio     F Prob.
                     Squares    Squares     Squares
Between  2           455.7512   227.8756    24.3952     <.0001
Groups
```

```
Within   614          5735.3834    9.3410
Groups
Total    616          6191.1345
```

This output shows that the *F* ratio value of 24.3952 with 2 and 614 degrees of freedom (D.F.) has a probability of occurrence by chance alone of less than 0.0001 if there was no significant difference between the three groups. In their report Andy and his colleague concluded that there was a:

> statistically significant [$F = 24.39$, $p < .0001$] difference in job satisfaction between managers, administrators, shop floor workers.

Assessing the strength of relationship

As part of your exploratory data analysis you will already have plotted the relationship between cases for two ranked or quantifiable variables using a scatter graph (Figure 11.10). Such relationships might include those between weekly sales of a new product and those of a similar established product, or age of employees and their length of service with the company. These examples emphasise the fact that your data can contain two sorts of relationship:

- those where a change in one variable is accompanied by a change in another variable but it is not clear which variable caused the other to change, a *correlation*;
- those where a change in one or more (independent) variables causes a change in another (dependent) variable, a *cause-and-effect* relationship.

To assess the strength of relationship between pairs of variables

A *correlation coefficient* enables you to quantify the strength of the relationship between two ranked or quantifiable variables. This coefficient (represented by the letter r) can take on any value between -1 and $+1$ (Figure 11.11). A value of $+1$ represents a perfect *positive correlation*. This means that the two variables are precisely related and that, as values of one variable increase, values of the other variable will increase. By contrast a value of -1 represents a perfect *negative correlation*. Again this means that the two variables are precisely related; however, as the values of one variable increase those of the other decrease. Correlation coefficients between $+1$ and -1 represent weaker positive and negative correlations, a value of 0 meaning the variables are perfectly independent. Within business research it is extremely unusual to obtain perfect correlations.

For data collected from a sample you will need to know the probability of your correlation coefficient having occurred by chance alone. Most statistical analysis software calculates this probability automatically. As outlined earlier, if this probability is very

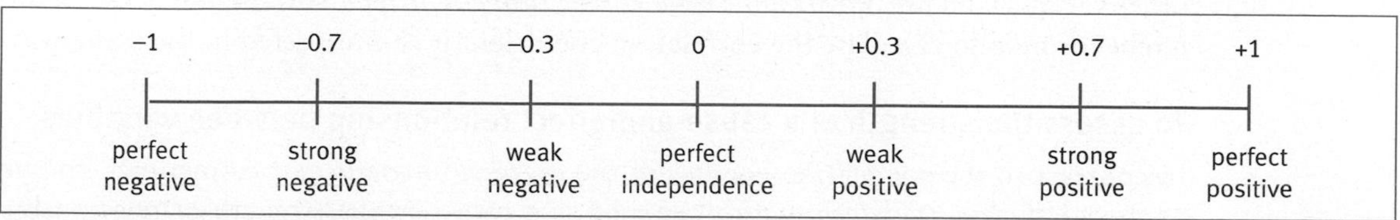

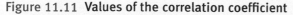

Figure 11.11 Values of the correlation coefficient

worked example

Assessing the strength of relationship between pairs of variables

As part of their market research a company has collected data on the number of newspaper advertisements, number of enquiries and number of sales for a product. These data have been entered into their statistical analysis software. They wish to discover whether there are any relationships between the following pairs of these variables:

- number of newspaper advertisements and number of enquiries;
- number of newspaper advertisements and number of sales;
- number of enquiries and number of sales.

As the data are quantifiable they program the statistical analysis software to calculate Pearson's product moment correlation coefficients for all pairs of variables. The output is provided in the form of a correlation matrix:

```
Correlation Coefficients
                 advert              enquiry             sales
advert           1.0000              0.3441*             0.2030
enquiry          0.3441*             1.0000              0.7002**
sales            0.2030              0.7002**            1.0000
*significance < .05,  **significance < .01
```

The matrix is symmetrical because correlation implies only a relationship rather than a cause-and-effect relationship. The value in each cell of the matrix is the correlation coefficient. Thus the correlation between the variable 'advert' and the variable 'enquiry' is 0.3441. This coefficient shows that there is a fairly weak but positive relationship between the number of newspaper advertisements and the number of enquiries. The * indicates that the probability of this correlation coefficient occurring by chance alone is less than 0.05 (5 per cent). This correlation coefficient is therefore statistically significant.

Using the data in this matrix the company concludes that there is:

a statistically significant strong positive relationship between the number of enquiries and the number of sales ($r = .700$, $p < .01$) and a statistically significant but weaker relationship between the number of newspaper advertisements and the number of enquiries ($r = 0.344$, $p < .05$). However, there is no statistically significant relationship between the number of newspaper advertisements and the number of sales ($r = 0.203$, $p > .05$).

low (usually less than 0.05) then it is considered statistically significant. If the probability is greater than 0.05 then your relationship is not statistically significant.

If both your variables contain quantifiable data you should use *Pearson's product moment correlation coefficient* (PMCC) to assess the strength of relationship (Table 11.5). However, if one of your variables contains rank data you will need to rank the other variable and use *Spearman's rank correlation coefficient*. Although this uses a different formula to calculate the correlation coefficient it is interpreted in the same way.

To assess the strength of a cause-and-effect relationship between variables

In contrast to the correlation coefficient the *regression coefficient* (sometimes known as the *coefficient of determination*) enables you to assess the strength of relationship between a quantifiable dependent variable and one or more quantifiable independent variables. For a dependent variable and one (or perhaps two) independent variables you will have probably already plotted this relationship on a scatter graph. If you have more than two independent variables this is unlikely as it is very difficult to represent four or more scatter graph axes visually!

The regression coefficient (represented by r^2) can take on any value between 0 and +1. It measures the proportion of the variation in a dependent variable (amount of sales) that can be explained statistically by the independent variable (marketing expenditure) or variables (marketing expenditure, number of sales staff etc.). This means that if all the variation in amount of sales can be explained by the marketing expenditure and the number of sales staff the regression coefficient will be 1. If 50 per cent of the variation can be explained the regression coefficient will be 0.5, and if none of the variation can be explained the coefficient will be 0. Within our research we have rarely obtained a regression coefficient above 0.8.

The process of calculating a regression coefficient and regression equation using one independent variable is normally termed *regression analysis*. Calculating the regression coefficient and regression equation using two or more independent variables is termed *multiple regression analysis*. The calculations and interpretation required by multiple regression are relatively complicated, and we advise you to use statistical analysis software and consult a detailed statistics textbook or computer manual such as Norusis (2000). Most statistical analysis software will calculate the significance of the regression coefficient for sample data automatically. A very low significance value (usually 0.05) means that your coefficient is unlikely to have occurred by chance alone. A value greater than 0.05 means you can conclude that your regression coefficient could have occurred by chance alone.

worked example

Assessing a cause-and-effect relationship

As part of your research you wish to assess the relationship between all the employees' annual salary and the number of years they have been employed by the organisation. You believe that annual salary will be dependent on the number of years for which they have been employed (the independent variable).

You enter the data into your analysis software and calculate a regression coefficient (r^2) of 0.37.

As you are using data from the population rather than a sample the probability of the coefficient occurring by chance alone is 0. You therefore conclude that 37 per cent of the variation in employees' salary can be explained by the number of years they have been employed by the organisation.

To predict the value of a variable from one or more other variables

Regression analysis can also be used to predict the values of a dependent variable given the values of one or more independent variables by calculating a *regression equation*. You may wish to predict the amount of sales for a specified marketing expenditure and number of sales staff. You would represent this as a regression equation:

$$\text{amount of sales} = a + (b_1 \times \text{marketing expenditure}) + (b_2 \times \text{number of sales staff})$$

Using regression analysis you would calculate the values of a, b_1 and b_2 from data you had already collected on amount of sales, marketing expenditure and number of sales staff. A specified marketing expenditure and number of sales staff could then be substituted into the regression equation to predict the amount of sales that would be generated.

The regression coefficient (discussed earlier) can be used as a measure of how good a predictor your regression equation is likely to be. If your equation is a perfect predictor then the regression coefficient will be 1. If the equation can predict only 50 per cent of the variation then the regression coefficient will be 0.5, and if the equation predicts none of the variation the coefficient will be 0.

worked example

Forecasting journey time

A mini-cab firm needs to establish the relationship between the time a journey takes (dependent variable) and the distance travelled in towns and the country (independent variables) in order to be able to provide their customers with an estimate of journey time. To do this they have collected data for a sample of 250 journeys on the miles travelled in towns, the miles travelled in the country and the time taken in minutes. The data are entered into statistical analysis software and a multiple regression performed. The output includes the following statistics:

```
R Square = .60459           F = 24.14    Signif F = .0012
Variables in the Equation
Variable                    B
town                        2.7651
country                     1.3453
constant (a)                4.7452
```

The 'variables in the equation' are substituted into the regression equation (after rounding the values of a and b):

$$\text{journey time} = 4.7 + (2.8 \times \text{town miles}) + (1.3 \times \text{country miles})$$

The time for any journey, such as one of 2 town miles and 3 country miles, can now be estimated:

$$4.7 + (2.8 \times 2) + (1.3 \times 3)$$
$$= 12.9 \text{ minutes}$$

However, care should be taken with these estimates as, although the values in the equation are unlikely to have occurred by chance alone (significance of $F = 0.0012$), they explain only just over 60 per cent ($r^2 = 0.60459$) of the variation in the journey time.

Examining trends

When examining longitudinal data the first thing we recommend you do is to draw a line graph to obtain a visual representation of the trend (Figure 11.4). Subsequent to this, statistical analyses can be undertaken. Two of the more common uses of such analyses are:

- to compare trends for variables measured in different units or of different magnitudes;
- to determine the long-term trend and forecast future values for a variable.

These are summarised in Table 11.5.

To compare trends

To answer some research question(s) and to meet some objectives you may need to compare trends between two or more variables measured in different units or at different magnitudes. To compare changes in prices of fuel oil and coal over time is difficult as the prices are recorded for different units (litres and tonnes). One way of overcoming this is to use *index numbers* and compare the relative changes in prices rather than actual figures. Index numbers are also widely used in business publications and by organisations. The *Financial Times* share indices and the Retail Price Index are well-known examples.

Although such indices can involve quite complex calculations they all compare change over time against a base period. The *base period* is normally given the value of 100 (or 1000 in the case of many share indices), and change is calculated relative to this. Thus a value greater than 100 would represent an increase relative to the base period, and a value less than 100 a decrease.

To calculate simple index numbers for each case of a longitudinal variable you use the following formula:

$$\text{index number for case} = \frac{\text{data value for case}}{\text{data value for base period}} \times 100$$

Thus if a company's sales were 125 000 units in 1999 (base period) and 150 000 units in 2000 the index number for 1999 would be 100 and for 2000 it would be 120.

To determine the trend and forecasting

The trend can be estimated by drawing a freehand line through the data on a line graph. However, these data are often subject to variations such as seasonal variations (Figure 11.4), and so this method is not very accurate. A straightforward way of overcoming this is to calculate a moving average for the *time series* of data values. Calculating a *moving average* involves replacing each value in the time series with the mean of that value and those values directly preceding and following it (Morris, 1999). This smooths out the variation in the data so that you can see the trend more clearly. The calculation of a moving average is relatively straightforward using either a spreadsheet or statistical analysis software.

Once the trend has been established it is possible to forecast future values by continuing the trend forward for time periods for which data have not been collected. This involves calculating the *long-term trend* – that is, the amount by which values are changing each time period after variations have been smoothed out. Once again this is relatively straightforward to calculate using analysis software. Forecasting can also be undertaken using other statistical methods including regression.

11.6 Summary

- Data for quantitative analysis can be collected and subsequently coded at different levels of numerical measurement. The data type (precision of measurement) will constrain the data presentation, summary and analysis techniques you can use.
- Data are entered for computer analysis as a data matrix in which each column usually represents a variable and each row a case. Your first variable should be a unique identifier to facilitate error checking.
- All data should, with few exceptions, be recorded using numerical codes to facilitate analyses.
- Where possible you should use existing coding schemes to enable comparisons.
- For primary data you should include pre-set codes on the data collection form to minimise coding after collection. For variables where responses are not known you will need to develop a codebook after data have been collected for the first 50 to 100 cases.
- You should enter codes for all data values including missing data.
- The data matrix must be checked for errors.
- Your initial analysis should explore data using both tables and diagrams. Your choice of table or diagram will be influenced by your research question(s) and objectives, the aspects of the data you wish to emphasise, and the level of measurement at which the data were recorded. This may involve using:
  - tables to show specific values;
  - bar charts, multiple bar charts and histograms to show highest and lowest values;
  - line graphs to show trends;
  - pie charts and percentage component bar charts to show proportions;
  - box plots to show distributions;
  - scatter graphs to show relationships between variables.
- Subsequent analyses will involve describing your data and exploring relationships using statistics. As before, your choice of statistics will be influenced by your research question(s) and objectives and the level of measurement at which the data were recorded. Your analysis may involve using statistics such as:
  - the mean, median and mode to describe the central tendency;
  - the inter-quartile range and the standard deviation to describe the dispersion;
  - chi square to test whether two variables are significantly associated;
  - Kolmogorov–Smirnov to test whether the values differ significantly from a specified population;
  - *t*-tests and ANOVA to test whether groups are significantly different;
  - correlation and regression to assess the strength of relationships between variables;
  - regression analysis to predict values.
- Longitudinal data may necessitate selecting different statistical techniques such as:
  - index numbers to compare trends between two or more variables measured in different units or at different magnitudes;
  - moving averages and regression analysis to determine the trend and forecast.

self-check Questions

11.1 The following secondary data have been obtained from the Park Trading Company's audited annual accounts:

Year	*Income (£)*	*Expenditure (£)*
1994	11 000 000	9 500 000
1995	15 200 000	12 900 000
1996	17 050 000	14 000 000
1997	17 900 000	14 900 000
1998	19 000 000	16 100 000
1999	18 700 000	17 200 000
2000	17 100 000	18 100 000
2001	17 700 000	19 500 000
2002	19 900 000	20 000 000

a Which are the variables and which are the cases?
b Sketch a possible data matrix for these data for entering into a spreadsheet.

11.2 a How many variables will be generated from the following request?

Please tell me up to five things you like about the Home Care Service.

for office use

.... ☐☐☐

.... ☐☐☐

.... ☐☐☐

.... ☐☐☐

.... ☐☐☐

b How would you go about devising a coding scheme for these variables from a survey of 500 Home Care Service clients?

11.3 a Illustrate the data from the Park Trading Company's audited annual accounts (self-check question 11.1) to show trends in income and expenditure.
b What does your diagram emphasise?
c What diagram would you use to emphasise the years with the lowest and highest income?

11.4 As part of research into the impact of television advertising on donations by credit card to a major disaster appeal, data have been collected on the number of viewers reached and the number of donations each day for the past two weeks.
a Which diagram or diagrams would you use to explore these data?
b Give reasons for your choice.

11.5 a What measures of central tendency and dispersion would you choose to describe the Park Trading Company's income (self-check question 11.1) over the period 1994–2002?
b Give reasons for your choice.

11.6 A colleague has collected data from a sample of 103 students. He presents you with the following output from the statistical analysis software:

```
Information technology facilities at this University are....
                     good         reasonable        poor         row
                                                                 totals
undergraduate        63           18                5            86
                                                                 (83.5%)
postgraduate         6            4                 7            17
                                                                 (16.5%)
column totals        69           22                12           103
                     (67.0%)      (21.4%)           (11.6%)      103
Chi square = 18.33, degrees of freedom = 2, probability <.01.
```

Explain what this tells you about undergraduate and postgraduate students' opinion of the information technology facilities.

11.7 Briefly describe when you would use regression analysis and correlation analysis, using examples to illustrate your answer.

11.8 **a** Use an appropriate technique to compare the following data on share prices for two financial service companies over the past six months, using the period six months ago as the base period:

	EJ Investment Holdings	*AE Financial Services*
Price 6 months ago	€10	€587
Price 4 months ago	€12	€613
Price 2 months ago	€13	€658
Current price	€14	€690

b Which company's share prices have increased most in the last six months? (Note: you should quote relevant statistics to justify your answer.)

progressing your research project

Analysing your data quantitatively

- ☐ Examine the technique(s) you are proposing to use to collect data to answer your research question. You need to decide whether you are collecting any data that could usefully be analysed quantitatively.
- ☐ If you decide that your data should be analysed quantitatively you must ensure that the data collection methods you intend to use have been designed to make analysis by computer as straightforward as possible. In particular you need to pay attention to the coding scheme for each variable and the layout of your data matrix.

- ☐ Once your data have been entered into a computer, you will need to explore and present them. Bearing your research question in mind you should select the most appropriate diagrams and tables after considering the suitability of all possible techniques. Remember to label your diagrams clearly and to keep a copy, as they may form part of your research report.
- ☐ Once you are familiar with your data, describe and explore relationships using those statistical techniques that best help you to answer your research questions and are suitable for the data type. Remember to keep an annotated copy of your analyses, as you will need to quote statistics to justify statements you make in the findings section of your research report.

References

Cohen, L. and Holliday, M. (1996) *Practical Statistics for Students*, London, Paul Chapman Publishing.

Diamantopoulos, A. and Schlegelmilch, B.B. (1997) *Taking the Fear Out of Data Analysis*, London, Dryden Press.

Great Britain Office for National Statistics (1997) *Index to the UK Standard Industrial Classification of Economic Activities 1992, UK SIC(92)*, London, The Stationery Office.

Great Britain Office for National Statistics (2000a) *Standard Occupation Classification Volume 1: Structure and Description of Unit Groups*, London, The Stationery Office

Great Britain Office for National Statistics (2000b) *Standard Occupation Classification Volume 2: The Coding Index*, London, The Stationery Office

Hays, W.L. (1994) *Statistics* (4th edn), London, Holt-Saunders.

Henry, G.T. (1995) *Graphing Data: Techniques for Display and Analysis*, Thousand Oaks, CA, Sage.

Jowell, R., Curtice, J., Park, A., Thomson, K., Jarvis, L., Bromley, C. and Stratford, N. (2000) *British Social Attitudes – the 17th Report: focusing on diversity*, Aldershot, Ashgate.

Kanji, G.K. (1998) *100 Statistical Tests* (2nd edn), London, Sage.

Kinnear, P.R. and Gray, C.D. (2000) *SPSS for Windows Made Simple, Release 10*, Hove, Psychology Press.

Mercator (2002) 'Mercator home page' (online) (cited 10 February 2002). Available from <URL:http://www.mercator.co.uk>

Morris, C. (1999) *Quantitative Approaches in Business Studies* (5th edn), Harlow, Financial Times Prentice Hall.

National Statistics (2002a) 'The NS-SEC self coded method' (online) (cited 15 February 2002). Available from <URL:http://www.statistics.gov.uk/methods_quality/ns_sec/nssec_self_coded_method.asp>

National Statistics (2002b) 'The classification of ethnic groups' (online) (cited 15 February 2002). Available from <URL:http://www.statistics.gov.uk/themes/compe…nce/ns_ethnic_classification.asp>

Norusis, M.J. (2000) *SPSS 10.0 Guide to Data Analysis*, London, Prentice Hall.

Pallant, J. (2001) *SPSS Survival Manual*, Buckingham, Open University Press.

Robson, C. (2002) *Real World Research*, (2nd edn), Oxford, Blackwell.

Scolari Sage (2002) 'Methodologist's Toolchest' (online) (cited 10 February 2002). Available from <URL:http://www.scolari.co.uk>

Sparrow, J. (1989) 'Graphic displays in information systems: some data properties influencing the effectiveness of alternate forms', *Behaviour and Information Technology*, 8:1, 43–56.

Tukey, J.W. (1977) *Exploratory Data Analysis*, Reading, MA, Addison-Wesley.

deVaus, D.A. (2002) *Surveys in Social Research* (5th edn), London, Routledge.

Further reading

Diamantopoulos, A. and Schlegelmilch, B.B. (1997) *Taking the Fear out of Data Analysis*, London, Dryden Press. This is a statistics book that is both humorous and informative. It assumes very little in the way of statistical knowledge, and is written for people who do not like data analysis and do not think they can understand numbers!

Hays, W.L. (1994) *Statistics* (4th edn), London, Holt-Saunders. This book provides a detailed discussion of statistics, emphasising both the theoretical and applied aspects. It is aimed at the first-year postgraduate student who will probably have already taken an undergraduate statistics module.

Morris, C. (1999) *Quantitative Approaches in Business Studies* (5th edn), Harlow, Financial Times Prentice Hall. This gives a clear introduction to the use of mathematical and statistical techniques and diagrams in business. Guidance is given on using the Excel spreadsheet.

Pallant, J. (2001) *SPSS Survival Manual*, Buckingham, Open University Press. This book offers a non-technical approach to using SPSS for Windows version 10. It assumes no familiarity with the data analysis software, and covers both inputting data and how to generate and interpret a wide range of tables, diagrams and statistics. If you are using an earlier version of SPSS, be sure to use a book written specifically for that version as there are a number of changes between versions.

Robson, C. (2002) *Real World Research* (2nd edn), Oxford, Blackwell. Chapter 13 provides an introduction to quantitative data analysis and guidance on using the SPSS statistical analysis software. The discussion of statistical significance is particularly clear.

deVaus, D.A. (2002) *Surveys in Social Research* (5th edn), London, Routledge. Chapters 9 and 10 contain an excellent discussion about coding data and preparing data for analysis. Part IV (Chapters 12–18) provides a detailed discussion of how to analyse survey data.

CASE 11 Marketing a golf course

Jane's year-long industrial placement was with a company that developed and managed golf courses. The company was concerned that over the last two years the number of golfers using its courses was declining, despite an overall growth in popularity of the sport. The company had undertaken a survey of users of its courses to establish who used them and reasons for this decline in usage. The data from the responses to the survey had been entered into a spreadsheet, and Jane had been asked to analyse it and write a report based on her analysis.

Looking at the data, Jane wondered whether she would be able to write a report that could establish why the numbers using the company's golf courses were declining despite an overall growth in popularity of the sport.

A copy of a completed questionnaire is shown below:

The Green Golf Group

Customer Questionnaire

22 September

Dear Customer,

We are always seeking ways to improve our courses for our customers. Please help us to do so by taking a few minutes to complete this form and tell us what you think. Completed questionnaires returned by **29 September** will be entered in a free prize draw for a year's membership for one of our courses.

Please return your completed questionnaire by placing it in the box in the club house entrance.

Please fill in the following details:

Name: Mr Geoffrey Thomas

Address: 29 St Aidans Drive, Huntsville, READING

Postcode: RG3 3BG

1 Are you male? ☑ 1 female? ☐ 2

2 Which age group do you fall into?

Under 18 ☐ 1 19–25 ☐ 2 26–30 ☐ 3 31–35 ☐ 4
36–40 ☑ 5 41–45 ☐ 6 46–50 ☐ 7 51–55 ☐ 8
56–60 ☐ 9 61–65 ☐ 10 66–70 ☐ 11 Over 71 ☐ 12

3 Which Green Golf Group golf course do you use most regularly?

Bircheley ☑ 1 Greenacres ☐ 2 The Oaks ☑ 3 Sandy Lane ☐ 4

4 Do you use any of these other golf courses?

The Common ☐ 1 Lochgreen ☑ 2 Fullerton ☑ 3 Other ☑ 4

5 In what band is your current golf handicap?

1–6 ☐ 1 7–12 ☐ 2 13–18 ☐ 3 25–30 ☑ 4 30–36 ☐ 5

6 Which category of user best describes you?

Full member ☑ 1 Casual user ☐ 2 Occasional visitor ☐ 3

7 How frequently do you play golf?

1–3 rounds per week ☐ 1 1–4 rounds per month ☑ 3
4–7 rounds per week ☐ 2 Occasionally ☐ 4
Rarely ☐ 5

8 Please rate the quality of the following elements of the golf course you use most regularly:

Very good	*Good*	*Fair*	*Poor*	*Very poor*	
Greens			✓		
Tees			✓		
Bunkers		✓			
Fairways			✓	✓	
Semi-rough		✓			
Rough			✓		
Locker room		✓			
Clubhouse and catering			✓		
Golf marshalling		✓			
Booking procedures		✓			

▶

9 How would you rate the overall quality and value for money of our golf courses?

Poor ☐ 1 ☐ 2 ☑ 3 ☐ 4 ☐ 5 ☐ 6 Excellent

10 Please add any other general comments . . . The Car Park at The Oaks gets very muddy. It could do with being resurfaced.

Thank you for spending time telling us your views.

Please place your completed questionnaire in the box in the clubhouse entrance

Questions

1 a To what extent does the questionnaire sent to customers enable the company to establish why the number of golfers using its courses is declining?
  b How would you suggest improving the questionnaire?

2 a Which questions are likely to be most useful to Jane in writing a report about the relative qualities of the Green Golf Group's courses?
  b For each of these questions or groups of questions list the tables, diagrams or statistical approaches that you would advise Jane to use in her analysis.

self-check Answers

11.1 a The variables are 'income', 'expenditure' and 'year'. There is no real need for a separate case identifier as the variable 'year' can also fulfil this function. Each case (year) is represented by one row of data.

b When the data are entered into a spreadsheet the first column will be the case identifier, for these data the year. Income and expenditure should not be entered with the £ sign as this can be formatted subsequently using the spreadsheet.

	A	*B*	*C*
1	year (id)	income	expenditure
2	1994	11 000 000	9 500 000
3	1995	15 200 000	12 900 000
4	1996	17 100 000	14 000 000
4	1997	17 900 000	14 900 000
6	1998	19 000 000	16 100 000
7	1999	18 700 000	17 200 000
8	2000	17 100 000	18 100 000
9	2001	17 700 000	19 500 000
10	2002	19 900 000	20 000 000

11.2 a There is no one correct answer to this question as the number of variables will depend on the method used to code these descriptive data. If you choose the multiple response method five variables will be generated. If the multiple dichotomy method is used the number of variables will depend on the number of different responses.

b Your first priority is to decide on the level of detail of your intended analyses. Your coding scheme should, if possible, be based on an existing coding scheme. If this is of insufficient detail then it should be designed to be compatible to allow comparisons. To design the coding scheme you need to take the responses from the first 50–100 cases and establish broad groupings. These can be subdivided into increasingly specific subgroups until the detail is sufficient for the intended analysis. Codes can then be allocated to these subgroups. If you ensure that similar responses receive adjacent codes, this will make any subsequent grouping easier. The actual responses that correspond to each code should be noted in a codebook. Codes should be allocated to data on the data collection form in the 'for Office use' box. These codes need to include missing data, such as when four or less 'things' have been mentioned.

11.3 a Park Trading Company – Income and Expenditure 1994–2002

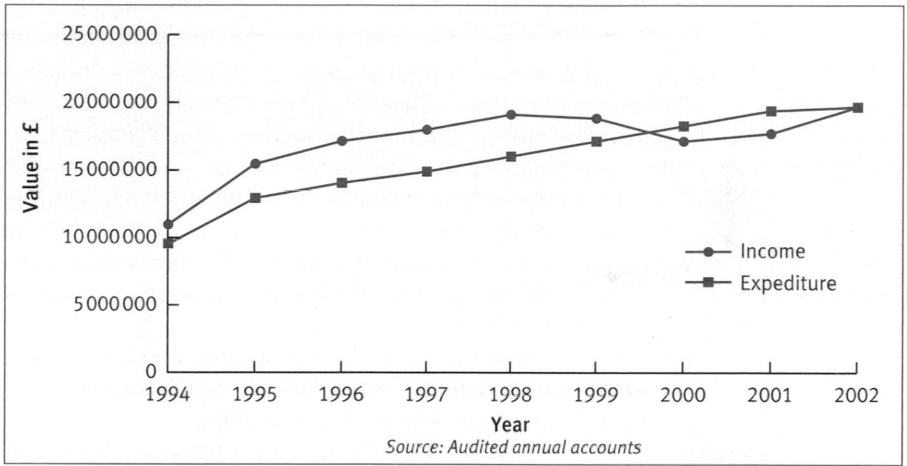

Source: Audited annual accounts

b Your diagram (it is hoped) emphasises the upward trends of expenditure and (to a lesser extent) income. It also highlights the conjunction where income falls below expenditure in 2000.

c To emphasise the years with the lowest and highest income you would probably use a histogram because the data are continuous. A frequency polygon would also be suitable.

11.4 a You would probably use a scatter graph in which number of donations would be the dependent variable and number of viewers reached by the advertisement the independent variable.

b This would enable you to see whether there was any relationship between number of viewers reached and number of donations.

11.5 a The first thing you need to do is to establish the data type. As it is quantifiable, you could theoretically use all three measures of central tendency and both the standard deviation and inter-quartile range. However, you would probably calculate the mean and perhaps the median as measures of central tendency and the standard deviation and perhaps the inter-quartile range as measures of dispersion.

b The mean would be chosen because it includes all data values. The median might be chosen to represent the middle income over the 1994–2002 period. The mode would be of little use for these data as each year has different income values.

If you had chosen the mean you would probably choose the standard deviation, as this describes the dispersion of data values around the mean. The inter-quartile range is normally chosen where there are extreme data values that need to be ignored. This is not the case for these data.

11.6 The probability of a chi square value of 18.33 with 2 degrees of freedom occurring by chance alone for these data is less than 0.01. This means that statistically the association between type of student and their opinion of the information technology facilities is extremely unlikely to be explained by chance alone.

To explore this association further, you examine the cell values in relation to the row and column totals. Of the postgraduates, 41.1 per cent thought the information technology facilities were poor. This is high compared with the column totals, which indicate that only 11.6 per cent of total students thought the information technology facilities were poor. The column frequencies indicate that undergraduates represent 91.3 per cent of those students who thought information technology facilities were good. Yet only 83.5 per cent of the total students thought information technology facilities were good. Thus postgraduate students have a poorer opinion of information technology facilities than undergraduate students do.

11.7 Your answer needs to emphasise that correlation analysis is used to establish whether a change in one variable is accompanied by a change in another. In contrast, regression analysis is used to establish whether a change in a dependent variable is caused by changes in one or more independent variables – in other words a cause-and-effect relationship.

Although it is impossible to list all the examples you might use to illustrate your answer, you should make sure that your examples for regression illustrate a dependent and one or more independent variables.

11.8 **a** These quantitative data are of different magnitudes. Therefore, the most appropriate technique to compare these data is index numbers. The index numbers for the two companies are:

	EJ Investment Holdings	*AE Financial Services*
Price 6 months ago	100	100.0
Price 4 months ago	120	104.4
Price 2 months ago	130	112.1
Current price	140	117.5

b The price of AE Financial Services' shares has increased by €103 compared with an increase of €4 for EJ Investment Holdings' share price. However, the proportional increase in prices has been greatest for EJ Investment Holdings. Using six months ago as the base period (with a base index number of 100) the index for EJ Investment Holdings' share price is now 140 while the index for AE Financial Services' share price is 117.5.

Chapter 12

Analysing qualitative data

By the end of this chapter you should be:

- able to evaluate the nature and value of qualitative data;
- aware of a range of approaches to and processes for analysing qualitative data;
- aware of the use of deductively based and inductively based analytical strategies and procedures to analyse qualitative data;
- able to consider the limitations of quantifying qualitative data as a means of analysis;
- aware of computer-assisted qualitative data analysis software.

12.1 Introduction

This chapter is designed to help you to analyse the qualitative data that you collect. However, the chapter commences by considering the nature of this type of data so that you can recognise the issues associated with attempting to analyse them systematically and rigorously (Section 12.2). Section 12.3 provides an overview of the process of qualitative analysis. In reading this overview you will recognise the interrelated and interactive nature of qualitative data collection and analysis. The stages of the process of qualitative analysis outlined in this overview demonstrate that you will need to undertake your data collection and analysis in a systematic and well-planned manner, in order to be able to analyse your data rigorously and to draw verifiable conclusions from them.

It is possible to approach qualitative data collection and analysis from either a deductive or an inductive perspective (Section 12.4). We therefore consider analytical strategies and procedures that commence with theoretical propositions that can be tested against the data collected (Section 12.5). We also discuss a range of inductively based analytical strategies and procedures, some of which are likely to combine deductive and inductive elements (Section 12.6). We also refer very briefly to the issue of quantifying some of your qualitative data in order to analyse it (Section 12.7).

Personal computers have made a significant impact on the way in which qualitative data can be processed and analysed, and the use of software to facilitate this is also discussed (Section 12.8).

12.2 Understanding qualitative data

Many authors draw a distinction between qualitative and quantitative research (for example, Bryman, 1988; Easterby-Smith *et al.*, 2002). However, attempts to define the distinctiveness of qualitative research, and therefore the way in which it can be distinguished from quantitative research, can be problematic (Silverman, 1993). Nevertheless, when we look at the data produced by qualitative research we are able to draw some significant distinctions from those that result from quantitative work. These are helpful in terms of understanding what is necessary in order to be able to analyse these data meaningfully. Table 12.1 highlights three distinct differences between quantitative and qualitative data.

While 'number depends on meaning' (Dey, 1993:28), it is not always the case that meaning is dependent on number. Dey (1993:28) points out that 'The more ambiguous and elastic our concepts, the less possible it is to quantify our data in a meaningful way'. Qualitative data are associated with such concepts and are characterised by their richness and fullness based on your opportunity to explore a subject in as real a manner as is possible (Robson, 2002). A contrast can thus be drawn between the 'thin' abstraction or description that results from quantitative data collection and the 'thick' or 'thorough' abstraction or description associated with qualitative data (Dey, 1993; Robson, 2002).

The nature of qualitative data therefore has implications for both its collection and its analysis. To be able to capture the richness and fullness associated with qualitative data they cannot be collected in a standardised way, like that of quantitative data. During analysis, however, the non-standardised and complex nature of the data that you have collected will probably need to be classified into categories before they can be meaningfully analysed (discussed later), otherwise the most that may result may be an impressionistic view of what they mean. While it may be possible to make some use of diagrams and statistics at this stage, such as the frequency of occurrence of certain categories of data (Sections 11.3 and 11.4), the way in which you are likely to analyse the qualitative data that you collect is through the creation of a conceptual framework. This may be formulated before or during your data collection (discussed later).

Table 12.1 Distinctions between quantitative and qualitative data

Quantitative data	*Qualitative data*
■ Based on meanings derived from numbers	■ Based on meanings expressed through words
■ Collection results in numerical and standardised data	■ Collection results in non-standardised data requiring classification into categories
■ Analysis conducted through the use of diagrams and statistics	■ Analysis conducted through the use of conceptualisation

Sources: Developed from Dey (1993); Healey and Rawlinson (1994); authors' experience

The analysis of qualitative data involves a demanding process and should not be seen as an 'easy option'. Yin (1994) refers to those who leave the data that they have collected unanalysed for periods of time because of their uncertainty about the analytical process required.

Where you have been through the various stages of formulating and clarifying your research topic (Chapter 2), reviewing appropriate literature (Chapter 3), deciding on a research strategy (Chapter 4), considering access and ethical issues and negotiating the former (Chapter 5) and collecting your data (Chapters 6–10), you clearly will not wish to be halted by an inability to analyse this type of data. Equally you will not wish to be 'marked down' because the analysis of the data collected is perceived to be a weak aspect of your work and one that casts doubt on the thoroughness and validity of the conclusions that you draw from the data.

Indeed, two further aspects spring from this cautionary note. First, you should take the advice of Marshall and Rossman (1999), who include data analysis as one of the issues that you should consider at the time you are formulating a proposal to undertake qualitative research. Second, the act of analysing qualitative data is very likely to occur at the same time as you collect these data as well as afterwards, and this is a matter that we discuss in detail below. This leads us to the next section, which provides an overview of qualitative analysis as a process.

12.3 An overview of qualitative analysis

The features of qualitative data outlined above indicate the diverse nature of qualitative analysis. To add to this, or because of it, there is not a standardised approach to the analysis of qualitative data. There are many qualitative research traditions or approaches, with the result that there are also different strategies to deal with the data collected (e.g. Coffey and Atkinson, 1996; Dey, 1993; Miles and Huberman, 1994; Tesch, 1990). Tesch (1990) groups these strategies into four main categories:

- understanding the characteristics of language;
- discovering regularities;
- comprehending the meaning of text or action;
- reflection.

These categories indicate a number of broad ways of differentiating approaches to qualitative analysis. In this way, some approaches to analyse qualitative data may be highly structured, whereas other approaches adopt a much lower level of structure. Related to this, some approaches to analyse qualitative data may be highly formalised and proceduralised, whereas other approaches rely much more on the researcher's interpretation. In broad terms, the first two categories listed above are associated with analytic strategies that require greater structure and set procedures to follow, in comparison with the second two. As a further way of differentiating between approaches to qualitative analysis, some approaches begin deductively, whereas others begin inductively. Again, in broad terms, the first two categories in the list above are associated with some analytic strategies that commence deductively, where data categories and codes to analyse data are derived from theory and your predetermined analytical framework. In contrast, other analytic strategies associated with this list commence

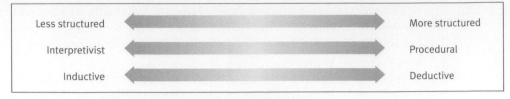

Figure 12.1 Dimensions of qualitative analysis

inductively, without predetermined, or a priori, categories and codes to direct your analysis. This distinction is discussed further in Section 12.4. These means of differentiating approaches to qualitative analysis, while not comprehensive, are shown as three dimensions in Figure 12.1.

These means to differentiate approaches to qualitative analysis may themselves be problematic when used to map some analytic strategies or methods. For example, variants of grounded theory (discussed in Section 12.6) may be more or less structured and proceduralised. However, in general terms the use of these dimensions should allow you to compare different approaches to qualitative analysis more easily. Care also needs to be taken in relation to any action that results from a consideration of these dimensions. For example, the adoption of a more 'interpretivist' approach should not be seen as implying less analytical rigour (Coffey and Atkinson 1996; Tesch, 1990). These three dimensions are not therefore used to indicate higher quality at one end of a continuum.

While different approaches to qualitative analysis share several features, as we outline below, they nevertheless allow us to outline a number of analytic strategies that you may consider using to analyse your qualitative data. We resume this discussion in Section 12.4.

Before commencing the task of outlining a number of reasonably distinct strategies to analyse qualitative data, we seek to identify a number of features of the process involved that are common to several of these approaches – or at least to those that are highly or fairly highly structured and proceduralised. One particular feature that is common to these types of strategy involves you in disaggregating the mass of qualitative data that you collect, as you collect them, into meaningful and related parts or *categories*. This allows you to rearrange and analyse these data systematically and rigorously. Adopting this approach essentially means transforming the nature of the data that you collect in order to allow you to:

1 comprehend and manage them;
2 integrate related data drawn from different transcripts and notes;
3 identify key themes or patterns from them for further exploration;
4 develop and/or test hypotheses based on these apparent patterns or relationships;
5 draw and verify conclusions (e.g. Dey, 1993; Miles and Huberman, 1994).

The general set of processes discussed below elaborates on these aspects of qualitative analysis, and involves the following activities:

- categorisation;
- 'unitising' data;

- recognising relationships and developing the categories you are using to facilitate this;
- developing and testing hypotheses to reach conclusions.

Categorisation

The first activity involves classifying your data into meaningful *categories*, which may be derived from these data or from your theoretical framework (see Sections 12.5 and 12.6 for a discussion of this aspect) and which should in any case 'fit' what you have revealed. These categories are in effect codes or labels that you will use to rearrange your data. They provide you with an emergent structure that is relevant to your research project to organise and analyse your data further.

The identification of these categories will be guided by the purpose of your research as expressed through your research question and objectives. Another analyst, for example, with a different purpose, may be able to derive different categories from the same data depending on their research objectives (Dey, 1993). Strauss and Corbin (1998) suggest that there are three main sources to derive names for these categories:

- you utilise terms that emerge from your data;
- they are based on the actual terms used by your participants ('*in vivo*' codes);
- or they come from terms used in existing theory and the literature.

However, the categories that you devise need to be part of a coherent set so that they provide you with a well-structured, analytical framework to pursue your analysis. Dey (1993:96–7) states that 'categories must have two aspects, an internal aspect – they must be meaningful in relation to the data – and an external aspect – they must be meaningful in relation to the other categories'. The categories you develop initially, especially where you use an inductive, grounded approach, are likely to be essentially descriptive. As your analysis develops you will develop a more hierarchical approach to the categorisation of your data, whereby some category codes or labels will be developed and used to indicate analytical linkages between, and interpretation of, the data emerging (e.g. King, 1998; Strauss and Corbin, 1998).

'Unitising' data

The next activity of the analytical process will be to attach relevant 'bits' or 'chunks' of your data, which we will refer to as *units* of data, to the appropriate category or categories that you have devised. A unit of data may be a number of words, a sentence, a number of sentences, a complete paragraph, or some other chunk of textual data that fits the category.

You may use a computer to help you to process your data (Section 12.8) or you may use a manual approach. Where you use the second approach, you can label a unit of data with the appropriate category (or categories) in the margin of the transcript or set of notes. This may then be copied, cut up and stuck onto a data card, or otherwise transferred, and filed so that you end up with piles of related units of data. An alternative is to index categories by recording where they occur in your transcripts or notes on cards headed with particular category labels (Easterby-Smith *et al.*, 2002). Undertaking this stage of the analytic process means that you are engaging in a selective process, guided by the purpose of your research, which has the effect of reducing and rearranging your data into a more manageable and comprehensible form.

worked example

Extract of an interview with analytical categories

The categories listed below were initially used to label the following interview extract.

Some initial categories

RED	Redundancy
RED/STR	Redundancy strategy
RED/STR/ISS	Redundancy strategy issues
RED/STR/VOL	Voluntary redundancy strategy
RED/STR/COM	Compulsory redundancy strategy
RED/CONS	Redundancy consultation
RED/MGT	Redundancy management
RED/MGT/ROLE	Redundancy management roles
SUR	Survivors
SUR/REAC	Survivors' reactions
SUR/REAC/PSY	Psychological reactions
SUR/REAC/BEH	Behavioural reactions
SUR/STR/LINK	This category was created to denote a link or relationship between two other categories: survivors' reactions and the choice of redundancy strategy

Extract showing use of analytical categories to commence analysis of this data

RED/CONS	The first stage is to find out what particular employees want for themselves and how they want this to happen.
RED/CONS	Staff are seen by their line manager and/or a member of personnel. An
RED/MGT/ROLE	employee might want to talk to someone from personnel rather than talk with their line manager – well, you know, for obvious reasons, at least as they see it – and this would be acceptable to the organisation.
RED/STR/VOL	This meeting provides them with the opportunity to opt for voluntary redundancy.
RED/STR/ISS	We do not categorise employees into anything like core or non-core,
RED/CONS	although we will tell a group of employees something like 'there are four of you in this particular function and we only need two of you, so you think about what should happen'.
RED/CONS	Sometimes when we attempt to give employees a choice about who might
RED/STR/COM	leave, they actually ask us to make the choice. This is one such situation where a compulsory selection will occur.
SUR/STR/LINK	We prefer to avoid this compulsory selection because of the impact on
SUR/REAC/PSY	those who survive – negative feelings, guilt and so on.

One way of achieving this reduction and rearrangement of your data, depending on the suitability of the data, is to use one or more of the analytical techniques described by Miles and Huberman (1994). These include a range of different matrices, charts, graphs and networks to use as a means to arrange and display your data. Use of these may allow you to recognise emergent patterns in your data that will provide you with an indication about how to further your data collection. The approach of Miles and Huberman (1994) is considered in more detail in Section 12.6.

Recognising relationships and developing categories

Generating categories and reorganising your data according to them, or designing a suitable matrix and placing the data gathered within its cells, means that you are engaging in the process of analysing your data (Dey, 1993; Miles and Huberman, 1994; Yin, 1994). This analysis will continue as you search for key themes and patterns or relationships in your rearranged data. This may lead you to alter your categories and continue to rearrange your data as you search for meaning in your data set. You may decide to 'subdivide or integrate categories as ways of refining or focusing [your] analysis' (Dey, 1993:95).

There may be practical reasons for seeking to divide or join your initial categories. Some categories, for example, may attract large numbers of units of data and prove to be too broad for further analysis without being subdivided. You may also gain new insights within existing categories that suggest new ones. A related piece of advice is to keep an up-to-date definition of each of the categories you are using, so that you can maintain consistency when assigning these to units of data as you continue to undertake interviews or observations (Miles and Huberman, 1994). According to several approaches to qualitative analysis, you will continue to generate a more hierarchical approach to the categorisation and coding of your data as you move towards the generation of an explanation for the research question and objectives that form the focus of your research.

worked example

Assigning data to and developing categories

'After each interview, I transcribed the interview verbatim and filed its material according to the categorisation then in use. The material was typically in the form of paragraphs [that] were cross-classified to several categories. As I filed each statement, I compared it with previous statements in that category and kept running notes on the content of the category. The categories changed over time; some disappeared and were merged under more general titles. Some emerged out of previous categories that became too heterogeneous. Some categories became parts of matched pairs or triads in which any given comment would typically be filed in each constituent category. For example, comments [that] described instances of lax work or bad workmanship also typically mentioned abusive management. Similarly, statements that described devising one's own procedures also typically included statements of satisfaction with the autonomy that provided. This helped to reveal connections between categories.'

Source: Hodson (1991), cited in Erlandson *et al.* (1993: 119). *Journal of Contemporary Ethnography*.

Developing and testing hypotheses

As you seek to reveal patterns within your data and to recognise relationships between categories you will be able to develop hypotheses in order to test these. Silverman (1993:1) defines a *hypothesis* as 'a testable proposition'. The appearance of an *apparent* relationship or connection between categories will need to be tested if you are to be able to conclude that there is an actual relationship.

worked example

Research hypotheses

During the process of qualitative data analysis a researcher evaluating the effectiveness of employee communication within a particular organisation formulated the following hypothesis:

The credibility of employee communication depends on managerial action in the organisation.

A research student exploring mortgage borrowers' decision-making drew up this hypothesis:

Potential mortgage borrowers' choice of lending institution is strongly affected by the level of customer service that they receive during the initial inquiry stage.

Another researcher investigating cause-related marketing formulated the following hypothesis:

Companies engaging in cause-related marketing are motivated principally by altruism.

A relationship is evident in each of these hypotheses. Each hypothesis was used to test the relationship within it through the data that had been collected or that were to be collected.

It is important to test the hypotheses that inductively emerge from the data by seeking alternative explanations and negative examples that do not conform to the pattern or relationship being tested. Alternative explanations frequently exist, and only by testing the propositions that you identify will you be able to move towards formulating valid conclusions and an explanatory theory, even a simple one (Dey, 1993; Miles and Huberman, 1994). Dey (1993:48) points out that 'the association of one variable with another is not sufficient ground for inferring a causal or any other connection between them'. The existence of an intervening variable may offer a more valid explanation of an association that is apparent in your data.

worked example

The impact of an intervening variable

A research project was established to look at legal issues arising from redundancies in organisations in a number of industries. A relationship appeared to emerge between organisations in a particular industry and the frequency of industrial tribunal applications. This could have led the researchers to conclude that managerial competence in relation to this process was lower in this industry than in the other industries in the study.

In reality, the firms included in the study from this particular industry had a much higher incidence of using a compulsory approach to declaring redundancies than those organisations in the other industries in the study. These organisations tended to use a voluntary approach to secure redundancies. The use of this compulsory strategy turned out to be highly associated with applications to industrial tribunals, especially when compared with a voluntary approach. The variable of redundancy strategy proved to be a much more valid way of explaining the apparent association that initially emerged, rather than any explanation linked to managerial competence or any other variable.

By rigorously testing your propositions and hypotheses against your data, looking for alternative explanations and seeking to explain why negative cases occur, you will be able to move towards the development of valid and well-grounded conclusions. Thus the validity of your conclusions will be verified by their ability to withstand alternative explanations and the nature of negative cases. This important aspect of your analysis is considered further in Sections 12.5 and 12.6.

The interactive nature of the process

The course of events outlined above demonstrates that data collection, data analysis and the development and verification of relationships and conclusions are very much an interrelated and interactive set of processes. Analysis occurs during the collection of data as well as after it. This analysis helps to shape the direction of data collection, especially where you are following a more inductive, grounded approach (Section 12.6). As hypotheses or propositions emerge from your data, or if you commence your data collection with a theoretical framework or propositions already worked out (Section 12.5), you will seek to test these as you compare them against the cases in your study (Erlandson *et al.*, 1993; Glaser and Strauss, 1967). The key point here is the relative flexibility that this type of process permits you.

The interactive nature of data collection and analysis allows you to recognise important themes, patterns and relationships as you collect data: in other words, to allow these to emerge from the process of data collection and analysis. As a result you will be able to recategorise your existing data to see whether these themes, patterns and relationships are present in the cases where you have already collected data. You will also be able to adjust your future data collection approach to see whether they exist in cases where you intend to conduct your research (Strauss and Corbin, 1998). In comparison, the collection of data before their analysis during a quantitative research study may prevent this course of action.

The concurrent process of data collection and analysis also has implications for the way in which you will need to manage your time and organise your data and related documentation. It will be necessary to arrange interviews or observations with enough time between them to allow yourself sufficient time to write up or type a transcript, or set of notes, and to analyse this before proceeding to your next data collection session (Easterby-Smith *et al.*, 2002; Erlandson *et al.*, 1993). Where you conduct a small number of interviews in one day you will need time during the evening to undertake some initial analysis on these before carrying out further interviews. You may also be able to find a little time between interviews to carry out a cursory level of analysis. However, there is a clear limit to the value of continuing to undertake interviews or observations without properly analysing these in the manner described above.

Analytical aids

In addition to writing or typing up the recording or notes made of a research session and assigning units of data to appropriate categories, it will also help your analysis if you make a record of additional information. This will help you to recall the context and content of the interview or observation. You may also consider other techniques aimed at helping you to analyse your qualitative data, such as those outlined by Riley (1996). Various researchers have advanced methods to help you to record information that will usefully supplement your written-up notes or transcripts and your categorised data (for example, Glaser, 1978; Miles and Huberman, 1994; Riley, 1996; Strauss and Corbin, 1998). We consider the following suggestions:

- summaries, including those for interviews, observations and documents, and also interim ones;
- self-memos;
- a researcher's diary.

Summaries

After you have written up your notes, or produced a transcript, of an interview or observation session, you can produce a *summary* of the key points that emerge from undertaking this activity. At this point you will be conversant with the principal themes that have emerged from the interview or observation and how you would like to explore these further in forthcoming data collection sessions. You may be able to identify apparent relationships between themes that you wish to note down so that you can return to these to seek to establish their validity. It will also be useful to make some comments about the person(s) you interviewed or observed, the setting in which this occurred and whether anything occurred during the interview or observation that might have affected the nature of the data that you collected.

worked example

The importance of noting an event that affected the nature of data collection

Adrian recalls an interview where the first part was conducted with two participants before their manager joined them. It was noticeable that after this person had joined the interview process the first two deferred and said very little. The interview was considered highly valuable, and all the questions asked were answered fully. However, he recorded this incident in a post-transcript summary in case any divergence was apparent between the nature of the data in the two parts of the interview.

Once you have produced a summary of the key points that emerge from the interview or observation and its context you should attach a copy to the set of your written-up notes or transcript for further reference (Miles and Huberman, 1994; Riley, 1996; Robson, 2002).

Qualitative research may also involve the use of organisational documentation. This may be an important source of data in its own right (for example, using minutes of meetings, internal reports, briefings, planning documents and schedules), or you may use such documentation as a means of triangulating other data that you collect (Section 7.2). Where you use any sort of documentation you can also produce a summary that describes the purpose of the document, how it relates to your work and why it is significant, as well as providing a list of the key points that it contains. This type of summary may be useful when you undertake further analysis if you want to refer to sources of data (that is, the document) as well as the way in which your categorical data have been categorised into their component parts.

An *interim summary* is an attempt by you to take stock of your progress to date through the production of a written paper that looks at the following aspects:

- what you have found out so far;
- what level of confidence you have in your findings and conclusions to date;
- what you need to do in order to improve the quality of your data and/or to seek to substantiate your apparent conclusions, or to seek alternative explanations;
- how you will seek to achieve the needs identified by the above interim analysis.

This can become a working document to which you make continued reference as your research project continues to make progress (Miles and Huberman, 1994; Riley, 1996; Robson, 2002).

Self-memos

Self-memos allow you to make a record of the ideas that occur to you about any aspect of your research, as you think of them. Where you omit to record any idea as it occurs to you it may well be lost. The occasions when you are likely to want to write a memo include:

- when you are writing up interview or observation notes, or producing a transcript of this event;
- when you are categorising these data;
- as you continue to categorise and analyse these data;
- when you engage in the process of writing.

Ideas may also occur as you engage in an interview or observation session. In this case you may record the idea very briefly as a margin note and write it as a memo to yourself after the event. Similarly, ideas may occur as you work through a documentary source.

It may be useful to carry a reporter's notebook in order to be able to record your ideas, whenever and wherever they occur. When you are undertaking the production of notes, or a transcript, or any aspect of qualitative analysis, a notebook can be ready to hand to record your ideas.

These memos may vary in length from a few words to one or more pages. They can be written as simple notes – they do not need to be set out formally. Miles and Huberman (1994) suggest, however, that it will be useful to date them and to provide cross-references to appropriate places in your written-up notes or transcripts, where appropriate. Alternatively, an idea that is not grounded in any data (which may nevertheless prove to be useful) should be recorded as such. Memos should be filed together, not with notes or transcripts, and may themselves be categorised where this will help you to undertake later stages of your qualitative analysis. Memos may also be updated as your research progresses, so that your bank of ideas continues to have currency and relevance (Glaser, 1978).

Researcher's diary

An alternative approach to recording your ideas about your research is to maintain a *researcher's diary*. You may of course maintain such a diary alongside the creation of self-memos. Its purpose will be similar to the creation of self-memos: to record your ideas and your reflections on these, and to act as an *aide-mémoire* to your intentions about the direction of your research. However, its chronological format may help you to identify the development of certain ideas (such as data categories or hypotheses) and the way in which your research methodology developed, as well as providing an approach that suits the way in which you like to think (Riley, 1996).

12.4 Strategies for qualitative analysis

In providing an overview of qualitative analysis, it is apparent that there are different approaches to the process of analysing qualitative data. These relate to the level of structure and the procedural requirements that are specified in the approach adopted and whether you start from a deductive or an inductive perspective. Where you commence your research project from a *deductive* position you will seek to use existing theory to shape the approach that you adopt to the qualitative research process and to aspects of data analysis. Where you commence your research project from an *inductive* position you will seek to build up a theory that is adequately grounded in a number of relevant cases. We have chosen to use this relationship between research and theory as the principal means to present our discussion of a range of different approaches to qualitative analysis. In the remainder of this section we shall therefore discuss the difference between using theory at the commencement of your research to analyse qualitative data and commencing your research by collecting and exploring your data without a predetermined theoretical or descriptive framework (Yin, 1994). The design of qualitative research requires you to recognise this choice and to devise an appropriate strategy to guide your research project.

Using a theoretical or descriptive framework

Yin (1994) suggests that, where you have made use of existing theory to formulate your research question and objectives, you may also use the theoretical propositions that helped you do this as a means to devise a framework to help you to organise and direct your data analysis. This approach demonstrates a preference for commencing with and utilising theory in qualitative research, rather than allowing it to develop from the work.

There is a debate about this approach as applied to qualitative analysis (Bryman, 1988). Bryman (1988:81) sums up the argument against it as follows:

> The prior specification of a theory tends to be disfavoured because of the possibility of introducing a premature closure on the issues to be investigated, as well as the

possibility of the theoretical constructs departing excessively from the views of participants in a social setting.

If this occurs when you use a theoretical framework to design and analyse your research you will clearly need to adapt your approach (Section 12.5).

worked example

Incorporating an inductive approach

Phil commenced a research project by adopting a deductive approach, but found that the theoretical framework he adopted did not yield a sufficiently convincing answer to his research questions and objectives. He therefore decided to reanalyse his data inductively. This revealed themes that had not figured prominently in the deductive analysis. A combination of the two approaches generated a more convincing answer to Phil's research questions and objectives.

Even though you may incorporate an inductive approach, commencing your work from a theoretical perspective may have certain advantages. It will link your research into the existing body of knowledge in your subject area, help you to get started and provide you with an initial analytical framework.

To devise a theoretical or descriptive framework you need to identify the main variables, components, themes and issues in your research project and the predicted or presumed relationships between them (Miles and Huberman, 1994; Robson, 2002; Yin, 1994). A descriptive framework will rely more on your prior experience and what you expect to occur, although it is of course possible to develop an explanatory framework based on a mixture of theory and your own expectations. You will use this framework as the means to start and direct the analysis of your data. A more detailed discussion regarding how to develop a theoretical or descriptive framework is given by Miles and Huberman (1994).

Exploring without a predetermined theoretical or descriptive framework

The alternative to the deductive approach is to start to collect data and then explore them to see which themes or issues to follow up and concentrate on (e.g. Glaser and Strauss, 1967; Schatzman and Strauss, 1973; Strauss and Corbin, 1998; Yin, 1994). Yin (1994) believes that this inductive approach may be a difficult strategy to follow and may not lead to success for someone who is an inexperienced researcher. This is likely to be the case where you simply go ahead and collect data without examining them to assess which themes are emerging from the data being gathered. Where you commence your data collection with this type of approach – related initially to an exploratory purpose – you will need to analyse the data as you collect them (Section 12.3) and develop a conceptual framework to guide your subsequent work. This is referred to as a *grounded* approach because of the nature of the theory or explanation that emerges as a result of the research process. In this way:

- theory emerges from the process of data collection and analysis;
- therefore you do not commence such a study with a defined theoretical framework;

- instead you identify relationships between your data and develop questions and hypotheses or propositions to test these.

You will, however, need to commence this type of approach with a clear research purpose. To use an inductive approach successfully may involve a lengthy period of time and prove to be resource intensive. It is also likely that this approach will combine some element of a deductive approach as you seek to develop a theoretical position and then test its applicability through subsequent data collection and analysis. This suggests that, while you may commence with either an inductive or a deductive approach, in practice your research may combine elements of both.

In the next two sections we describe and discuss specific analytic strategies and procedures related to a deductive approach and to an inductive approach to research. We also consider how these differing approaches are likely to affect the process for analysing qualitative data outlined in Section 12.3.

12.5 Deductively based analytical strategies and procedures

Yin's (1994) preference for devising theoretical propositions prior to data collection as a means to analyse data leads to a number of specific analytical procedures to achieve this. This section will first outline the specific analytical procedures described by Yin (1994) that are particularly applicable to qualitative analysis. These are briefly described and discussed in turn, although more detail is provided by Yin (1994). This section will then examine how the deductive perspective that underpins these specific analytical procedures affects the process for analysing qualitative data (Section 12.3).

Pattern matching

The first analytic procedure is termed *pattern matching*, and essentially involves predicting a pattern of outcomes based on theoretical propositions to explain what you expect to find. Using this approach, you will first need to establish a conceptual or analytical framework, utilising existing theory, and then test the adequacy of the framework as a means to explain your findings. If the pattern of your data matches that which has been predicted through the conceptual framework you will have found an explanation, where possible threats to the validity of your conclusions can be discounted. Examples are provided in relation to two variations of this procedure that we now describe.

These variations depend on the nature of the variables being considered. The first of these is associated with a set of *dependent* variables where you suggest the likely outcomes arising from another, *independent* variable. For example, based on theoretical propositions drawn from appropriate literature you specify a number of related outcomes (dependent variables) that you expect to find as a result of the implementation of a particular change management programme (independent variable) in an organisation where you intend to undertake research. Having specified these expected outcomes, you then engage in the process of data collection and analysis. Where your predicted outcomes are found then it is likely that your theoretically based explanation is appropriate to explain your findings. If, however, you reveal one or more outcomes that have not been predicted by your explanation then you will need to seek an alternative one (Yin, 1994).

The second explanatory variation is associated with variables that are independent of each other. In this case you would identify a number of *alternative* explanations to explain the pattern of outcomes that you expect to find. As a consequence only one of these predicted explanations may be valid. In other words, if one explanation is found to explain your findings then the others may be discarded. Where you find a match between one of these predicted explanations and the pattern of your outcomes you will have evidence to suggest that this is indeed an explanation for your findings. Further evidence that this is a correct explanation will flow from finding the same pattern of outcomes related to other similar cases (Yin, 1994).

worked example

Alternative predicted explanations

The objective of your research project is to explain why productivity has increased in a case study organisation even though a number of factors have been held constant (technology, numbers of staff employed, pay rates and bonuses, and the order book) during the period of the increase in productivity. You suggest two alternative explanations based on different theoretical propositions to explain why this increase in productivity has occurred in the organisation. Your explanations are related to the following propositions:

- first, that the increase is due to better management, which has been able to generate greater employee commitment, where this proposition is based on theory related to strategic and human resource management;
- second, that the increase is due to fears about change and uncertainty in the future, where this proposition is, in addition, based on theory related to organisational behaviour and change management.

These propositions offer you two possible and exclusive reasons why the described phenomenon has occurred, so that where evidence can be found to support one of these the other that does not match your outcomes can be discounted.

Explanation building

Another approach to pattern matching, which Yin (1994) refers to as a special type, involves an attempt to build an explanation while collecting data and analysing them, rather than testing a predicted explanation as set out above. Yin (1994) recognises that this procedure, which he labels *explanation building*, appears to be similar to the grounded theory (or analytic induction) approach, which we discuss later (Section 12.6). However, he differentiates between these since the explanation-building approach is still designed to test a theoretical proposition, albeit in an iterative manner, rather than to generate 'grounded' theory (Section 12.6). Yin states that his hypothesis-testing approach is related to *explanatory* case studies, while the hypothesis-generating approach developed by Glaser and Strauss (1967) is relevant for *exploratory studies*. This explanation building procedure is designed to go through the following stages (Yin, 1994):

1 devising a theoretically based hypothesis or proposition, which you will then seek to test;
2 undertaking data collection through an initial case study in order to be able to compare the findings from this in relation to this theoretically based proposition;
3 where necessary, amending this theoretically based proposition in the light of the findings from the initial case study;
4 undertaking a further round of data collection in order to compare the findings from this in relation to the revised proposition;
5 where necessary, further amending this revised proposition in the light of the findings from this second case study;
6 undertaking further iterations of this process until a satisfactory explanation is derived.

Impact of a deductive approach on the analysis process

In relation to pattern matching and explanation building, you will still be able to follow the general process outlined earlier for analysing qualitative data (Section 12.3), with some modification. First, you will be in a position to commence your data collection with a well-defined research question and objectives, and a clear framework and propositions, derived from the theory that you will have used. Second, with regard to sampling (Section 6.3), you will be in a position to identify the number and type of organisations to which you wish to gain access in order to undertake data collection. However, this strategy should not be used as a means to adopt a less than rigorous approach to selecting sufficient cases to test the propositions that have been advanced and to answer your research question and meet your objectives. Third, the literature that you used and the theory within it will shape the data collection questions that you wish to ask those who participate in your research project (Section 3.2). It is also to be expected that categories for analysis will emerge from the nature of these interview questions. Therefore you will be able to commence data collection with an initial set of categories derived from your theoretical propositions/hypotheses and conceptual framework, linked to your research question and objectives (e.g. Miles and Huberman, 1994).

Of course, these categories may be subject to change, depending on their appropriateness for the data that your participants provide (Dey, 1993). However, where your predicted theoretical explanations appear to fit the data being revealed, your predetermined categories may prove to be useful, subject to some revision and development (Miles and Huberman, 1994).

Your use of this analytic strategy will of course also provide you with key themes and patterns to search for in your data. Therefore as you carry out your research and conduct analysis through attaching units of data to categories, and examine these for emergent patterns, your analysis will be guided by the theoretical propositions and explanations with which you commenced. Your hypotheses will still need to be tested with rigour – associated with the thoroughness with which you carry out this analytical process and by seeking negative examples and alternative explanations that do not conform to the pattern or association being tested for.

However, the use of predicted explanations should mean that the pathway to an answer to your research question and objectives is a more defined one. This will of course depend on two factors: first, your level of thoroughness in using existing theory to define clearly the theoretical propositions and conceptual framework that will guide your research project; second, the appropriateness of these theoretical propositions and the conceptual framework for the data that you reveal.

In summary, this section has briefly discussed two of the analytic procedures suggested by Yin (1994) that are particularly relevant to the analysis of qualitative data. The use of these procedures is underpinned by the need to specify theoretical propositions before the commencement of data collection and its analysis. Even in explanation building a theoretically based proposition is suggested initially even though this may be revised through the iterative stages of the process involved. It has also been shown that the general process outlined earlier for analysing qualitative data will be useful to you in carrying out these deductive analytical procedures. However, the stages of this process related to devising categories and identifying patterns are likely to be more apparent, at least initially, because this approach is based on existing theory.

12.6 Inductively based analytical strategies and procedures

This section of the chapter outlines and briefly discusses a number of inductively based analytic strategies to analyse qualitative data. These strategies are:

- data display and analysis;
- template analysis;
- analytic induction;
- grounded theory;
- narrative analysis.

In practice, however, a number of these analytic strategies combine inductive and deductive approaches to analyse qualitative data, as we discuss below.

There may be a number of good reasons for adopting an inductive approach to your research project and the analysis of the data that are produced. First, as we discussed in Section 12.4, you may commence on an exploratory project seeking to generate a direction for further work. Second, the scope of your research may be constrained by adopting restrictive theoretical propositions that do not reflect your participants' views and experience (e.g. Bryman, 1988). In this case, the use of a theoretically based approach to qualitative analysis would prove to be inadequate, as we noted above. The use of an inductive approach in such a case should allow a good 'fit' to develop between the social reality of the research participants and the theory that emerges – it will be 'grounded' in that reality. This relationship should also mean that those who participated in the research process would understand any theory that emerges. Third, the theory may be used to suggest subsequent, appropriate action to be taken because it is specifically derived from the events and circumstances of the setting in which the research was conducted. Finally, the theory's generalisability may also be tested in other contexts (e.g. Glaser and Strauss, 1967; Strauss and Corbin, 1990, 1998).

However, you should not draw the conclusion that you may use an inductive approach as a means of avoiding a proper level of preparation before commencing on your research project. Qualitative analysts who use such an approach do not 'jump' into a subject area without a competent level of knowledge about that area. Their research will commence with a clearly defined purpose, even though this may be altered by the nature of the data that they collect. For example, Hodson (1991, cited in Erlandson *et al.*, 1993) reported that his initial purpose was focused on organisational sabotage, although the research process led him to develop and seek to verify an hypothesis related to more subtle forms of non-cooperation with an employer. The avoidance of a predetermined theoretical basis in this type of approach is related to the desire to search for and recognise meanings in the data and to understand the social context and perceptions of your research participants. It is not to avoid the burden of producing this before the process of data collection! You should seek to compare your explanations with existing theory once these have emerged. The use of an inductive approach may also involve you in a lengthy period of data collection and concurrent analysis in order to analyse a theme adequately or to derive a well-grounded theory. Strauss and Corbin (1990) suggest that this type of approach may take months to complete.

Data display and analysis

This approach is based on the work of Miles and Huberman (1994). Their book focuses on the process of 'doing analysis'. For Miles and Huberman the process of analysis is composed of three concurrent subprocesses, which are data reduction, data display and drawing and verifying conclusions. As part of the process of analysis, *data reduction* includes summarising and simplifying the data collected and/or selectively focusing on some parts of this data. As with the process of qualitative analysis outlined in Section 12.3, the aim of this process is to transform the data and to condense it. Miles and Huberman outline a number of methods for reducing data, some of which we have already referred to above. These include the production of interview or observation summaries, document summaries, interim summaries, coding and categorising data, and writing memos.

Data display involves organising and assembling your reduced or selected data into diagrammatic or visual displays. Miles and Huberman describe a number of ways of displaying data, and refer to two main families of data display: matrices and networks. Matrices are generally tabular in form, with defined columns and rows, where data are selectively entered into the appropriate cells of such a matrix. A network is a collection of nodes or boxes that are joined or linked by lines, perhaps with arrows to indicate relationships. The boxes or nodes contain brief descriptions or labels to indicate variables or key points from the data.

Miles and Huberman believe that there are a number of advantages associated with using these forms of data display. Data collection tends to produce extensive piles of notes, once these have been written up, that are generally referred to as 'extended text'. They refer to extended text as an unreduced form of display that is difficult to analyse because it is both extensive and poorly ordered. Based on the logic that 'you know what you display', they believe that the analysis of data and the drawing of conclusions from these will be helped by using matrices, networks or other visual forms to display reduced or selected data drawn from your extended text. Miles and Huberman also believe that these forms of display are relatively easy to generate, can be developed to fit your data specifically, and will help you develop your analytical thinking as you work through several iterations to develop a visual form that represents your data well.

They also believe that recognising relationships and patterns in the data, as well as drawing conclusions and verifying these, will be helped by the use of data displays. The use of a display will allow you to make comparisons between the elements of the data that are included in it and to identify any relationships, key themes, patterns and trends that may be evident. These will be worthy of further exploration and analysis. In this way, the use of data displays will help you to interpret your data and to draw meaning from it. Miles and Huberman describe and discuss a number of techniques to develop conclusions as well as to verify these (also see Section 12.3 for a discussion of some similar techniques).

Use of this analytic strategy may provide you with an appropriate approach to analyse your qualitative data, or alternatively one or more of the techniques that Miles and Huberman outline may be useful as part of your approach to analysing this type of data. They describe the analysis of qualitative data as an interactive process, and in this sense their approach includes many aspects of analysis that complement the general process outlined in Section 12.3. Indeed, there are a number of references to the work of Miles and Huberman in Section 12.3. Their approach is a systematic and structured one, and they recognise that the techniques or methods that they outline are often associated with a fairly high level of formalisation. However, unlike the approach outlined below for grounded theory, the exact procedures to be followed within their framework of data reduction, display and conclusion drawing and verification are not specified. Miles and Huberman refer to their work as a 'sourcebook', and as such they offer a number of possible techniques that may be appropriate within their overall approach. If you intend to use this book we suggest you take care in identifying what is useful for you in the context of your own research project.

The approach of Miles and Huberman is suited to an inductive strategy to analyse qualitative data, although it is also compatible with a more deductive strategy through use of many of the techniques that they outline. Their book is useful both for its overall discussion of the analysis of qualitative data and in relation to the many suggestions relating to particular aspects of and techniques for the successful conduct of this process.

Template analysis

This subsection is based on the work of King (1998). He describes and discusses an approach to analyse qualitative data known as template analysis. A *template* is essentially a list of the codes or categories that represent the themes revealed from the data that have been collected. Like the data display approach just discussed, template analysis combines a deductive and an inductive approach to qualitative analysis in the sense that codes will be predetermined and then amended or added to as data are collected and analysed. In the worked example in this subsection we provide part of a predetermined template of codes that was derived deductively by considering existing literature and theory before proceeding to collect and analyse data.

King provides a number of ways of differentiating template analysis from a grounded theory approach, which he says it resembles. Grounded theory, as we discuss later in this section, does not permit the prior specification of any codes to analyse data, holding as it does to a more purely inductive analytical approach as far as is practically possible. Grounded theory is also more structured than template analysis, with a set of procedures that must be used, according to Strauss and Corbin (1990). In this sense King comments that grounded theory is much more prescriptive. In contrast, template analysis is similar to the data display and analysis approach in that it offers a more flexible route to analysis, which would allow you to amend its use to the needs of your own research project (King, 1998).

Like the general approach to analysing qualitative data outlined earlier in Section 12.3, template analysis involves categorising and unitising data. Data are coded and analysed to identify and explore themes, patterns and relationships. The template approach allows codes and categories to be shown hierarchically to help this analytical process. In the worked example a hierarchical relationship is shown between the codes listed. In this example three levels of codes are listed, with greater depth of analysis indicated by those lower-order codes shown towards the right-hand side of the template. Codes are also grouped together in levels 2 and 3 to show how higher-order codes are constituted.

worked example

Part of an initial template to analyse a managing change research project

1 Contextual factors
- 1 Reasons for change
- 2 Environmental climate
- 3 Nature of the organisation
  - *1 Organisational objectives*
  - *2 Culture*
  - *3 Ownership*
- 4 Organisational size and structure
- 5 Employee relations history to date

2 Nature of the change
- 1 Internally driven
- 2 Externally driven

3 Perceptions of those affected
- 1 Directly affected
  - *1 Contract unaffected*
  - *2 Contract altered*
  - *3 Contract terminated*
- 2 Indirectly affected

As data collection proceeds, the template will be subject to revision as part of the process of qualitative analysis. The process of analysing interview transcripts or observation notes will lead to the revision of some of the codes being used and even changes to their place or level in the template hierarchy. This process will also involve unitising data according to the list of codes currently in use. Where you consider introducing a new code or altering the level of an existing code in the template, you will need to verify this action and explore its implications in relation to your previous coding activity.

King outlines four ways in which a template may be modified. The first of these is the insertion of a new code, as the result of a relevant issue being identified through data collection for which there isn't an existing code. Codes may be inserted at different levels in the template hierarchy. Alternatively, a code included in the original template may not be needed and so it may be deleted. The third way in which a template may be modified is through changing the level of a code. The issue or theme indicated by a lower-order code may assume a greater importance than expected once data collection and analysis occurs. For example, in the worked example above, 'culture' as a third-level code may prove to be of greater importance in relation to the research project and therefore require to be reclassified as a level 1 code or category. Equally, the analytical relevance of some higher-order codes may be restricted in practice so that they are reclassified at a lower level as a subset of another higher-order code. The fourth way of modifying a template involves recognising that a code originally included as a subcategory of one higher-order code should be reclassified as a subcategory of another. For example, in the worked example above, the third-order code 'contract unaffected' may be disconnected from the second-order code 'directly affected' and moved to 'indirectly affected' during the process of data collection and analysis.

The template may continue to be revised until all of the data collected have been coded and analysed carefully. It will therefore serve as an analytical technique through which to devise an initial conceptual framework that will be subsequently revised and then finalised as a means to represent and explore key themes and relationships in your data. The template approach will also help you to select key themes to explore and to identify emergent issues that arise through the process of data collection and analysis that you may not have intended to focus on as you commenced your research project (King, 1998).

Analytic induction

Analytic induction is an inductive version of the explanation-building procedure outlined earlier in Section 12.5 (Yin, 1994). Johnson (1998: 28) defines *analytic induction* as 'the intensive examination of a strategically selected number of cases so as to empirically establish the causes of a specific phenomenon'. As an inductively led approach to analyse qualitative data, it therefore commences with a less defined explanation of the phenomenon to be explored, which is not derived from existing theory. This explanation is then tested through a case study that is selected purposively (Section 6.3) to allow the phenomenon to be explored. Given the loosely defined nature of the explanation it is likely either that the explanation will need to be redefined or that the scope of the phenomenon to be explained will need to be narrowed. Adopting one of these courses of action leads to a redefinition (of the phenomenon or its explanation) and the need to explore a second case study that will also be selected purposively. Where the explanation appears to be confirmed, you may either cease data collection on the basis that you believe that you have found a valid explanation or seek to test the explanation in other purposively selected cases to see whether it does indeed stand as a valid explanation. Where the explanation is not adequate, it will again be necessary to revise it and to test this in the context of another purposively selected case. This process may continue until a refined explanation is generated that reasonably explains the phenomenon in relevant cases where you collected and analysed data.

As an inductive and incremental approach to the collection and analysis of qualitative data, this strategy has the capability of leading to the development of well-grounded explanations. In this way, analytic induction encourages the collection of data that are thorough and rich, based on the explored actions and meanings of those who participate in this process, whether through in-depth interviews or observation, or some combination of these methods. However, this approach has been evaluated in different ways in relation to the nature of the explanations that its use is likely to produce. On the one hand, it has been claimed that thorough and rigorous use of this approach may lead to unassailable explanations where all negative cases are either accounted for by the final revised explanation or excluded by redefining the phenomenon being studied (Johnson, 1998; Kidder, 1981). On the other hand, analytic induction has been criticised because it seeks to find an explanation for the necessary conditions that exist in cases where a phenomenon occurs, whereas there may well be other cases where the same conditions exist but the phenomenon does not occur. For example, an explanation may be developed to explain the conditions that exist in cases where organisational theft occurs, whereas there are likely to be other cases where the same conditions apply but where such theft may or may not occur. In this way, it would also be necessary to study a range of cases where such conditions apply, having identified these, to find out whether the phenomenon (theft) also exists in all or only some of these cases (Johnson, 1998). However, such an approach is likely to be highly time consuming and resource intensive and perhaps suitable only for major research projects. A detailed discussion of this analytic strategy is given by Johnson (1998).

Grounded theory

Grounded theory procedures are designed to build an explanation or to generate a theory around the core or central theme that emerges from your data. Some prominent advocates of grounded theory lay down fairly precise procedures to be followed in relation to each of the stages of the qualitative analysis process that was outlined in general terms in Section 12.3. In this way, the grounded theory approach of Strauss and Corbin (1998) is structured and systematic, with set procedures to follow at each stage of analysis. Where you do not pay particular attention to the nature of the procedures outlined for grounded theory, you may not produce a research report that is sufficiently rigorous to substantiate the explanation or theory that you are seeking to advance. However, grounded theory may be approached as a strategy as much as a set of procedures. Such an approach may therefore result in the process of analysis being conducted in a less formalised and proceduralised way while still maintaining a systematic and rigorous approach to arrive at a grounded explanation or theory (Section 12.3).

In the grounded theory approach of Strauss and Corbin (1998) the disaggregation of data into units is called *open coding*, the process of recognising relationships between categories is referred to as *axial coding*, and the integration of categories to produce a theory is labelled *selective coding*. We shall briefly outline each of these in turn, drawing on the work of Strauss and Corbin (1990, 1998). Within grounded theory, choice of cases through which to gather data and refine concepts is termed *theoretical sampling* (Glaser and Strauss, 1967; Strauss and Corbin, 1998). In this way, sampling is purposive (Chapter 6.3), where critical cases are chosen to further the development of concepts and categories and to explore relationships between these to develop a theory. Underpinning this is the procedure of *constantly comparing* the data being collected with the concepts and categories being used, so as to aid the process of developing an emerging theory that will be thoroughly grounded in that data. Theoretical sampling continues until a situation of *theoretical saturation* is reached. This situation is reached when data collection ceases to reveal new data that are relevant to a category, where categories have become well developed and understood and relationships between categories have been verified (Strauss and Corbin, 1990, 1998).

Open coding

Open coding is essentially the first stage of the process of qualitative analysis outlined in Section 12.3. The data that you collect will be disaggregated into conceptual units and provided with a label. The same label or name will be given to similar units of data. However, because this research process commences without an explicit basis in existing theory, the result may be the creation of a multitude of conceptual labels related to the lower level of focus and structure with which you commence your research. The emphasis in this grounded theory approach will be to derive meaning from the subjects and settings being studied. In Section 12.3 we stated that a unit of data might relate to a few words, a sentence or number of sentences, or a paragraph. The need to understand meanings and to generate categories to encompass these in a grounded theory approach will therefore probably lead you to conduct your early analysis by looking at smaller rather than larger units of data. The resulting multitude of code labels will therefore need to be compared and placed into broader, related groupings or categories. This will allow you to produce a more manageable and focused research project and to develop the analytical process.

Strauss and Corbin (1998) suggest that there are three main sources to derive names for these categories: you utilise terms that emerge from your data; they are based on actual terms used by your participants ('*in vivo*' codes); or they come from terms used in existing theory and the literature. However, Strauss and Corbin counsel against names being derived from existing theory and literature in a grounded approach. This is because their use in the written account of your research may lead readers to interpret these according to their prior understanding of such theoretical concepts rather than the particular meaning now being placed on such terms.

The categorisation that you derive from your data will indicate significant themes and issues and help you to consider where data collection should be focused in the future. In conjunction with this, it will also help you to develop a sharper focus in relation to your research question. The nature of this research approach will inevitably mean that your initial research question will be broadly focused, although still within manageable exploratory confines. As you develop a narrower focus through this process you will be able to refine and limit the scope of your research question (Strauss and Corbin, 1998).

Axial coding

This stage refers to the process of looking for relationships between the categories of data that have emerged from open coding. It indicates a process of theoretical development. As relationships between categories are recognised, they are rearranged into a hierarchical form, with the emergence of subcategories. The essence of this approach is to explore and explain a phenomenon (the subject of your research project, or one of them) by identifying what is happening and why, the environmental factors that affect this (such as economic, technological, political, legal, social and cultural ones), how it is being managed within the context being examined, and what the outcomes are of the action that has been taken. Clearly there will be a relationship between these aspects, or categories, and the purpose of your analysis will be to explain this.

Once these relationships have been recognised, you will then seek to verify them against actual data that you have collected. Strauss and Corbin (1990, 1998) recommend that you undertake this by formulating questions or statements, which can then be phrased as hypotheses, to test these apparent relationships. As you undertake this process you will be looking for evidence that supports these questions and for negative cases that will demonstrate variations from these relationships.

Selective coding

Strauss and Corbin (1990) suggest that after a lengthy period of data collection, which may take several months, you will have developed a number of principal categories and related subcategories. The stage that follows is called *selective coding*. This is intended to identify one of these principal categories, which becomes known as the central or core category, in order to relate the other categories to this with the intention of integrating the research and developing a grounded theory (Strauss and Corbin, 1998). In the previous stage the emphasis was placed on recognising the relationships between categories and their subcategories. In this stage the emphasis is placed on recognising and developing the relationships between the principal categories that have emerged from this grounded approach in order to develop an explanatory theory. A detailed discussion of this approach, outlining the procedural steps, is given by Strauss and Corbin (1990, 1998).

Summary implications of using a grounded theory approach

A number of implications have emerged from this brief outline of the main procedures involved in the use of a grounded theory approach. These may be summed up by saying that the use of a grounded theory approach will involve you in a process that will be time consuming, intensive and reflective. Before you commit yourself to this particular approach, you will need to consider the time that you have to conduct your research, the level of competence you will need for this approach, your access to data, and the logistical implications of immersing yourself in such an intensive approach to research. There may also be a concern that little of significance will emerge at the end of the research process, and this will be an important aspect for you to consider when determining the focus of your research if you use this approach.

Narrative analysis

Grounded theory involves the fragmentation of qualitative data to further the process of analysis. However, some approaches to qualitative research consider the fragmentation of data to be inappropriate. More interpretative approaches advocate that researchers should retain the integrity of the data that they collect and commence analysis from the basis of the verbatim transcripts or complete sets of notes that are produced. Examples of this include phenomenological research (e.g. Moustakas, 1994) and the life history approach (e.g. Musson, 1998). These approaches to qualitative research are based on individuals' accounts of their experiences and the ways in which they explain these through their subjective interpretations and relate them to constructions of the social world in which they live. This type of strategy commences inductively, and needs to remain sensitive to the social constructions and meanings of those who participate in the research.

The primary method to collect data during these approaches will be in-depth interviews. As part of this process, it is likely that participants will provide accounts that take the form of narratives, or stories. Researchers may also deliberately seek to encourage this by asking participants to provide responses in this form. A *narrative* is broadly defined as an account of an experience that is told in a sequenced way, indicating a flow of related events that, taken together, are significant for the narrator and which convey meaning to the researcher (e.g. Coffey and Atkinson, 1996). It follows that understanding and meaning are likely to be promoted through analysing narrative accounts in their originally told form rather than by seeking to fragment them through a process of coding and categorisation. This is not to say that such accounts cannot also be subjected to this type of analysis (that is, categorisation). However, a narrative account that clearly explains, for example, the social and organisational context within which a research participant operates, the nature of their engagement, the actions that they took, the consequences of these and events that followed may be analysed most effectively in its original form. This will retain the narrative flow of the account and avoid losing the significance of the social context within which these events occurred, or decontextualising the data.

A narrative, as a story with a beginning, middle and an end, will broadly follow a perceptible structure. Coffey and Atkinson (1996) draw on previous research to outline the structural elements that are often present in narratives. These broadly take the following form:

- What is the story about?
- What happened, to whom, whereabouts, and why?
- What consequences arose from this?
- What is the significance of these events?
- What was the final outcome?

Coffey and Atkinson point out that these elements may not occur in the order listed and may also recur in a given narrative. Nevertheless, as they point out, the presence of structural elements in narratives may also be helpful in analysing this type of account.

Depending on the nature of your research question and objectives, the data collection methods used and the data that are produced, this type of analytical approach may be suitable for you to use. It may be used either as the principal means to analyse your qualitative data, or as a complementary means by which some of your data are produced in the form of narrative accounts. In this way, narrative analysis may be used as a means to explore linkages, relationships and socially constructed explanations that naturally occur within narrative accounts, where fragmentation of these into categories and themes would therefore be rendered unnecessary. Second, the structural elements that are present in narratives may also help you to analyse each narrative account and perhaps to compare the course of events in different narratives where there is likely to be some analytical benefit in comparing these.

12.7 A note on quantifying your qualitative data

There may be occasions when you decide to quantify some of your qualitative data. This is likely to be the case when you wish to count the frequency of certain events, or of particular reasons that have been given, or in relation to specific references to a phenomenon. These frequencies can then be shown using a table or diagram (Section 11.3). This form of representation will provide you with the capacity to display a large amount of data that you will be able to discuss through the use of text.

This approach to describing and presenting your data will provide you with a very useful supplement to the principal means of analysing your qualitative data discussed above. It may also enable you to undertake other quantitative analyses, such as those discussed in Sections 11.4–11.6. However, it is indeed a supplementary means of achieving this, and there is clearly only limited purpose in collecting qualitative data if you intend to ignore the nature and value of these data by reducing most of them to a simplified form.

12.8 Using a computer for qualitative analysis

The use of computer-assisted qualitative data analysis software (CAQDAS) (Fielding and Lee, 1995) potentially offers a number of advantages in relation to the analytical approaches we have been discussing. However, the use of this type of software may be problematic. We briefly summarise some of the current issues related to CAQDAS, before outlining its principal functions. We then highlight Internet addresses of some of the CAQDAS available to which you may connect to explore the latest versions of these packages and the features that they offer.

Current issues related to CAQDAS

The literature that evaluates CAQDAS has raised a number of issues associated with its use. While there are a number of different CAQDAS programs available for purchase, these vary in relation to the type of facilities that they offer and therefore potentially in their usefulness for different analytic situations. This points to the need to develop some familiarity with a range of programs to be able to evaluate their applicability for the particular nature of the data that you will collect for analysis. However, many of these programs may not be available for you to explore and evaluate in your institution. Even where different programs are accessible, your ability to experiment with different software is likely to be impeded by incompatibility. Fisher (1997:9) summarises this: 'Few researchers are likely to "play" with coding facilities in different programs if each requires the re-entry of original codes.'

One danger is that you will end up using a program that is unsuitable for the analytical procedures that you wish to perform and will abandon the attempt for this reason (Fielding and Lee, 1995). Fielding and Lee (1995) also recognise that many researchers collect data before considering the need for a program to analyse it, rather than first evaluating the nature of their research project and exploring suitable software for its analysis. Where you are commencing as a qualitative analyst you will be confronted by a need to learn how to analyse qualitative data as well as by the need to choose and use appropriate software for this purpose (Fielding and Lee, 1995). This is a far from easy combination given the nature of the resulting data and the purpose of qualitative analysis to explore meaning.

The use of CAQDAS may lead some researchers, perhaps, to overlook this purpose, at least in part. Siedel (1991, cited in Fisher, 1997:26) raises the concern that 'we will be lured into analytical practices and conceptual problems more conducive to breadth analysis than depth analysis'. This is referred to as 'word crunching', where the analyst becomes more concerned with analysis based on quantification than with the exploration of meaning (Fisher, 1997).

The use of some CAQDAS may also encourage analytical procedures that lead to the fragmentation of the data that you collect where it would be more appropriate to analyse this using an approach that preserves the narrative flow and qualities of this data. In this way, you will need to remain sensitive to the nature of the data that you wish to analyse (see Section 12.6).

While the use of CAQDAS may be problematic, it also offers a number of advantages to those who undertake qualitative analysis. Box 12.1 outlines several key functions that will help you in your role as a qualitative analyst. These advantages are clearly related to the suitability of the software that you use for your analysis. Fisher (1997) offers very useful advice to allow qualitative researchers to evaluate the suitability of such software. His criteria for assessing choice of software include consideration of the following aspects:

- Will a particular program allow you to work between different analytical tasks as you seek to develop your analysis?
- Will it allow you to maintain a close relationship with your data?
- Will it allow you to make revisions to your codes and analytical frameworks as your analysis develops?

A detailed discussion of the use of CAQDAS is given by Fisher (1997).

Principal functions

CAQDAS may potentially help you in your role as a qualitative analyst by acting as an aid to:

- project management;
- coding and retrieval;
- data management;
- hypothesis building and theorising.

Box 12.1 summarises these different functions.

Box 12.1 Functions of CAQDAS

Project management

Your data need to be organised in such a way that access to them is both quick and accurate. In achieving this, a good qualitative analysis program will display an index of documents, with facilities to select and retrieve individual documents. Computer-readable text-based documents can be displayed in full, so that units of text can be selected for operations such as editing, indexing (coding or categorising) or note making (memos), simply by highlighting and without affecting the primary document. One of the most powerful tools in CAQDAS is the ability to search swiftly any number of documents for specified units of data or codes. The software's ability to cluster units of text containing the words you select, and to display the cluster in a window together with reference to the *source document*, replaces the tedious process of multiple photocopying, slicing copies into paper slips and annotating each one before sticking them onto data cards and filing them in piles, or sticking them in appropriate places on a vast 'clipboard'. This process can be undertaken without any damage to your primary data, which are still held in the original primary documents.

Coding and retrieval

If all your data are word processed, or in some other computer-readable form, it will be possible for your primary documents to be accessed directly by the software. The software can search the text itself and allocate codes to specified units of text. More powerful software will display the documents on screen in your chosen format. Identification of text units may be by line number, although more powerful software offers you the facility of choosing the most appropriate size of text unit for your type of data (see Section 12.3) by highlighting the appropriate section of text in the document window. Data are coded by selecting a unit of text and directing it either to a new or to an existing code 'address'. A text unit may be directed to any number of code addresses. Some software offers a facility for coding non-computer-readable data such as videotapes, audiotapes, maps, photographs or archival texts.

Data management

As your research project progresses, you will quickly gather more and more data. These need to be managed in such a way that they can be accessed and reviewed readily. You will have primary data, index codes and memos. The qualitative analysis software will retrieve and display all or any of these individually, in specified groups or clusters, and will indicate cross-references or links between them. Some more powerful software incorporates a *linked window system* whereby the selection of a unit of text from the primary document results in the automatic display of its code, any memos associated with it, and the text of cross-references from other primary documents. *System closure* is often also available, whereby your notes and memos are themselves open to the same search and retrieve procedures as the primary documents.

Hypothesis building and testing

The foundation of *hypothesis building* lies in discovering links between elements of your data. CAQDAS can help you to discover these links and, with graphic facilities, display them for you. Two basic ways of organising and linking your data are available. The first of these involves a *hierarchical organisation*. This is where your data may be classified in a few broad themes, then each theme classified into a number of subcategories, each of these into sub-subcategories, and so on. This is similar to the coding used for quantitative data analysis (Section 11.2). For example, in Figure 12.2 you may classify your data under the broad themes of 'Values', 'Concepts' and 'Strategies'. On reviewing all the data under 'Strategies', you may wish to divide them into 'Mature' and 'Immature', or 'Long term' and 'Short term'. Your 'Values' theme may fall naturally into, say, 'Internal' and 'External', and then you may identify several subcategories such as 'Duty', 'Trust' and 'Liking'.

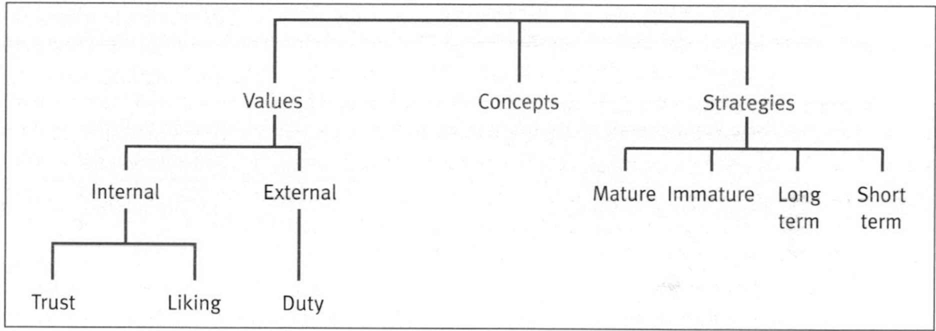

Figure 12.2 Hierarchical organisation and linking of data

An alternative approach is to code each section of data as you work through it, and later on to discover ways of gathering together like categories that can be grouped together under common headings, which can in turn be grouped together in broad themes, and so on. For example, in the case above you might identify the concepts of 'Duty', 'Trust' and 'Liking' from your reading of the data and then decide to group all these under a common heading of 'Values'. Later you may wish to have distinct subheadings under 'Values', which you call 'Internal' and 'External', allocating to them your original categories accordingly.

The second way of organising and linking your data involves a *network organisation*. This is where your categories are more flexibly linked to one another, without the rigidity implicit in the hierarchical structure discussed above. The ability to represent your data graphically can be a very powerful aid to theory building. Networks can be rearranged in whatever way suits your developing research project. Some software offers the opportunity to work with both networks and hierarchies, with tools for moving between them.

Source: Summarised from Mark Saunders, Philip Lewis, Adrian Thornhill and John Wilkin in Saunders *et al.* (1997:358–60).

Exploring the latest versions of CAQDAS

Published materials about computing and particular programs are likely to become out of date fairly quickly. We would therefore advise you to explore the Internet sites of CAQDAS providers to locate details of the latest versions of these packages and the features that they offer. This search may provide you with the opportunity to download demonstration versions of some of these programs. The Internet addresses for a number of established programs are listed in Table 12.2.

Table 12.2 **Internet addresses for some CAQDAS**

Name	*Internet address*	*Comment*
ATLAS.ti	http:www.scolari.co.uk/atlasti/atlasti.htm http:www..atlasti.de/	Scolari website includes program description, list of key features, user profile, platforms supported, system requirements, facility to download demonstration version and short manual, ordering information
The Ethnograph	http:www.scolari.co.uk/ethnograph/ethnograph.htm http:www.qualisresearch.com/banner.htm	Scolari website includes program description, list of key features, user profile, platforms supported, system requirements, facility to download demonstration version and pdf files providing package overview etc., ordering information
NUD*IST	http:www.scolari.co.uk/qsr/qsr_n6.htm	Scolari website includes program description, list of key features, user
QSR N6	http:www.qsr.com.au	profile, related publications, platforms supported, system requirements, facility to download demonstration version, ordering information
QSR NVivo 1.3	http:www.scolari.co.uk/qsr/qsr_nvivo.htm http:www.qsr.com.au	Scolari website includes program description, list of key features, user profile, related publications, platforms supported, system requirements, facility to download demonstration version and workbook, ordering information

12.9 Summary

- Qualitative data are based on meanings expressed through words. They result in the collection of non-standardised data that require classification and are analysed through the use of conceptualisation.
- The process of qualitative analysis generally involves the development of data categories, allocating units of your original data to appropriate categories, recognising relationships within and between categories of data, and developing and testing hypotheses to produce well-grounded conclusions.
- The process of data analysis and data collection is necessarily an interactive one.
- There are a number of aids that you might use to help you through the process of qualitative analysis, including interview, observation, document and interim summaries, self-memos and maintaining a researcher's diary.
- Different qualitative analytical strategies can be identified, related to using either a deductively based or an inductively based approach to research. The use of these different strategies has implications for the procedures involved in the analysis of qualitative data.

- Quantifying some categories of qualitative data may help you to analyse this.
- The use of computer-assisted qualitative data analysis software can help you to perform four basic and useful functions during qualitative analysis, related to project management, coding and retrieval, data management, and hypothesis building and theorising.

self-check Questions

12.1 Why do we describe qualitative analysis as an 'interactive process'?

12.2 What types of data will you need to retain and file while you are undertaking qualitative research?

12.3 How would you differentiate between a deductive and an inductive analytical strategy?

12.4 What are the main implications of using a deductive analytical strategy for the way in which you conduct the process of qualitative analysis?

12.5 What are the main implications of using an inductive analytical strategy for the way in which you conduct the process of qualitative analysis?

progressing your research project

Analysing your data qualitatively

- ☐ Undertake an initial semi-structured or in-depth interview related to your research project, transcribe this interview, and make a few copies of your transcript.
- ☐ Where your research project is based on a deductive strategy, develop a provisional set of categories from your research question and objectives, conceptual framework, research themes and initial propositions. Produce a description of each of these categories. Evaluate these categories to see whether they appear to form a coherent set in relation to the aim of your research.
- ☐ Using one of the transcript copies attempt to allocate units of data to appropriate categories by writing their code labels alongside the text in the left-hand margin. Again evaluate this provisional set of categories and modify any that appear to be inappropriate.
- ☐ Where your research project is based on an inductive strategy, work through one of the transcript copies and seek to identify categories related to your research purpose. Write appropriate code labels for these categories alongside the text in the left-hand margin. List these categories and their labels and produce a description for each of the categories that you have devised.
- ☐ Once you have allocated units of data to the set of categories in use cut these out and transfer them to an appropriately labelled index card (reference to the interview, location of the text in the transcript and the date and so forth). Read through the units of data within each category.

▶

- ☐ Commence your analysis of this categorised data by asking questions of it, such as those that follow. What are the points of interest that emerge within each category? How will you seek to follow these up during your next data collection session? How does the material that has been revealed through this interview relate to any theoretical explanation or initial propositions that you commenced your data collection with? Are any connections evident between the categories?
- ☐ Produce a summary of the interview and attach it to a copy of the transcript. Memo any ideas that you have and file these.
- ☐ Repeat the procedure for the remaining qualitative data and revise your ideas as necessary.

References

Bryman, A. (1988) *Quantity and Quality in Social Research*, London, Unwin Hyman.

Coffey, A. and Atkinson, P. (1996) *Making Sense of Qualitative Data*, Thousand Oaks, CA, Sage.

Dey, I. (1993) *Qualitative Data Analysis*, London, Routledge.

Easterby-Smith, M., Thorpe, R. and Lowe, A. (2002) *Management Research: An Introduction* (2nd edn), London, Sage.

Erlandson, D.A., Harris, E.L., Skipper, B.L. and Allen, S.D. (1993) *Doing Naturalistic Inquiry*, Newbury Park, CA, Sage.

Fielding, N.G. and Lee, R.M. (1995) 'Confronting CAQDAS: choice and contingency', *in* Burgess, R.G. (ed.), *Studies in Qualitative Methodology Computing and Qualitative Research*, Greenwich, CT, JAI Press, pp. 1–23.

Fisher, M. (1997) *Qualitative Computing: Using Software for Qualitative Data Analysis*, Aldershot, Ashgate.

Glaser, B. (1978) *Theoretical Sensitivity: Advances in the Methodology of Grounded Theory*, Mill Valley, CA, Sociology Press.

Glaser, B. and Strauss, A. (1967) *The Discovery of Grounded Theory*, Chicago, IL, Aldine.

Healey, M.J. and Rawlinson, M.B. (1994) 'Interviewing techniques in business and management research', *in* Wass, V.J. and Wells, P.E., *Principles and Practice in Business and Management Research*, Aldershot, Dartmouth, pp. 123–45.

Hodson, R. (1991) 'The active worker: compliance and autonomy at the workplace', *Journal of Contemporary Ethnography*, 20:1, 47–8.

Johnson, P. (1998) 'Analytic induction', *in* Symon, G. and Cassell, C. (eds), *Qualitative Methods and Analysis in Organizational Research*, London, Sage, pp. 28–50.

Kidder, L.H. (1981) 'Qualitative research and quasi-experimental frameworks', *in* Brewer, M.B. and Collins, B.E. (eds), *Scientific Enquiry and the Social Sciences*, San Francisco, Jossey Bass, pp. 226–56.

King, N. (1998) 'Template Analysis', *in* Symon, G. and Cassell, C. (eds), *Qualitative Methods and Analysis in Organizational Research*, London, Sage, pp. 118–34.

Marshall, C. and Rossman, G.B. (1999) *Designing Qualitative Research* (3rd edn), Thousand Oaks, CA, Sage.

Miles, M.B. and Huberman, A.M. (1994) *Qualitative Data Analysis* (2nd edn), Thousand Oaks, CA, Sage.

Moustakas, C. (1994) *Phenomenological Research Methods*, Thousand Oaks, CA, Sage.

Musson, G. (1998) 'Life Histories', *in* Symon, G. and Cassell, C. (eds), *Qualitative Methods and Analysis in Organizational Research*, London, Sage, pp. 10–27.

Riley, J. (1996) *Getting the Most from your Data: A Handbook of Practical Ideas on How to Analyse Qualitative Data* (2nd edn), Bristol, Technical and Educational Services Ltd.

Robson, C. (2002) *Real World Research* (2nd edn), Oxford, Blackwell.

Saunders, M., Lewis, P. and Thornhill, A. (1997) *Research Methods for Business Students*, London, Pitman Publishing.

Schatzman, L. and Strauss, A. (1973) *Field Research: Strategies for a Natural Sociology*, Englewood Cliffs, NJ, Prentice-Hall.

Siedel, J. (1991) 'Method and madness in the application of computer technology to qualitative data analysis', *in* Fielding, N.G. and Lee, R.M. (eds), *Using Computers in Qualitative Research*, London, Sage, pp. 107–16.

Silverman, D. (1993) *Interpreting Qualitative Data*, London, Sage.

Strauss, A. and Corbin, J. (1990) *Basics of Qualitative Research*, Newbury Park, CA, Sage.

Strauss, A. and Corbin, J. (1998) *Basics of Qualitative Research* (2nd edn), Thousand Oaks, CA, Sage.

Tesch, R. (1990) *Qualitative Research: Analysis Types and Software Tools*, New York, Falmer.

Yin, R.K. (1994) *Case Study Research: Design and Methods* (2nd edn), Thousand Oaks, CA, Sage.

Further reading

Dey, I. (1993) *Qualitative Data Analysis*, London, Routledge. Provides a very thorough discussion of the stages of qualitative analysis without being bound to any of the approaches referred to in the sources below.

Fisher, M. (1997) *Qualitative Computing: Using Software for Qualitative Data Analysis*, Aldershot, Ashgate. Provides a very useful review of this subject area.

Miles, M.B. and Huberman, A.M. (1994) *Qualitative Data Analysis* (2nd edn), Thousand Oaks, CA, Sage. Provides an excellent source of reference to the elements involved in qualitative research as well as offering a number of particular techniques that may help you to analyse your data.

Strauss, A. and Corbin, J. (1998) *Basics of Qualitative Research* (2nd edn), Newbury Park, CA, Sage. Provides a very thorough introduction to the grounded theory approach

Symon, G. and Cassell, C. (eds) (1998) *Qualitative Methods and Analysis in Organizational Research*, London, Sage. This edited work contains an excellent range of chapters related to analytical strategies.

Yin, R.K. (1994) *Case Study Research: Design and Methods* (2nd edn), Thousand Oaks, CA, Sage. Chapter 5 very usefully examines analytical strategies and procedures based on a deductive approach.

CASE 12 Paying for competence at Investco?

Heleen undertook an interview in an organisation that had been changing its reward system. The grading system in the organisation had been changed, and the factors that affected employees' pay levels had also been altered. The organisation wanted to reflect market rates so as to affect new staff and to retain existing employees. It had also introduced an increased emphasis on paying for performance and for the acquisition of competences that were relevant to the work of its employees. Heleen's research questions included: 'What factors are used in the design of organisational pay systems?' and 'What are the implications of introducing competence-related pay?' The following extract is part of an in-depth interview that relates to these research questions.

▶

Is there a link between pay and the acquisition of competence at Investco?

We have now removed the link between pay and the development of people's competence. The problem became one where people were saying: 'If I do such and such that will definitely give me so much extra money.' We could have looked again at how we rewarded people for increasing their competence in the job, but we decided not to do that at this point in time. We thought it was better just to end this.

Can you tell me more about why you decided to do this?

Well I think that there were a number of reasons for this. Some of these were related to what individuals were seeking from developing their competence; some were related to what we – the organisation – wanted from this; and others were related to, well, you know, the practical possibilities of trying to make this work, especially in our area of the business. People were targeting competences. They were acquiring competences that weren't really needed in their jobs here in this part of the organisation. We had a number of staff go on the training course to become better presenters. But in this part of the organisation we don't really need lots of people with those skills. In the customer-facing parts of the organisation those skills are probably very important, but here we don't have that much call for making presentations. That sort of thing made it increasingly difficult to compare different people's level of competence and say, well, who has the most useful to us in relation to what they're being paid.

The organisation hadn't really looked at it in this sort of way. The idea of paying people to develop their competence is really great, in theory that is. We want people to develop themselves. We want them to make an extra contribution. We also want them to progress in the organisation, grow into bigger jobs and stay with us. For these reasons this seemed like a great idea. In practice it's just a bit more difficult. In our part of the organisation this made us ask, well, what is it that we really want, what do we really need from our staff to do the job really well? This made us think. We decided that we needed a break from what was happening. We needed to gently say, yeah, these competences look great but let's just think about what we really need. It's also a question of focus. When I'm on that two-day course improving my presentation skills, who's answering my 'phone? Who's dealing with that system breakdown? We want to get our people well trained but to do certain things that we really need.

But when we sat down and looked at this again we found that it wasn't easy. It may be easier to define and measure competences in some parts of the organisation because of the greater degree of standardisation. But in our area we need to really think hard about defining and measuring the competences that we really need. This is a really big job in our area, so we're still thinking about this. In the meantime we decided to cut the link.

So is there any link now between pay and competence – say, any sort of indirect link that remains?

Yes there is. We don't pay for the acquisition of competence, as I said, but there is still a link through performance appraisal – an indirect link. We set staff performance targets, and some of these involve level of competence. In this sense there is still a link, but it's more in the background. We won't pay someone directly for achieving a particular competence or skill. But they will be rewarded for achieving a particular target that means that they have to go away over the period of the performance review and work away at something in order to be able to meet that target that was set for them.

Do you see this approach as being better that the directly linked one between pay and competence?

Oh yes, I definitely think so.

Can you say why?

Sure! I think that there are a number of reasons. By developing competences through performance targets this has the effect of making sure that these are relevant to the job. The system that was introduced, of paying for certain competences when they were obtained, was too general. It wasn't defined enough. They weren't related to the job enough. Using performance targets means that you can get more focus, encourage staff to work on those things that will be really important in the way that their job needs to develop.

I also think that, because of this point, this approach gives the manager more discretion. It's the manager who gets to work out with their staff what needs to be developed to produce more effectiveness. The previous system was just too general, and it took away too much discretion in this way. It set up some conflict between what was needed and what people ended up doing. That wasn't good.

Questions

Given the focus of the research questions above conduct the following process to commence the analysis of this qualitative data.

1 Devise categories to label these data and 'unitise' or code these data using these categories.

2 Do any relationships or patterns begin to emerge in the data and, if so, what are they?

3 What are the important themes that you feel stand out in your categorisation that you would seek to explore in subsequent interviews?

self-check Answers

12.1 There are a number of reasons why we may describe qualitative analysis as an 'interactive process'. Analysis needs to occur during the collection of data as well as after it. This helps to shape the direction of data collection, especially where you are following a grounded theory approach. The interactive nature of data collection and analysis allows you to recognise important themes, patterns and relationships as you collect data. As a result you will be able to re-categorise your existing data to see whether these themes, patterns and relationships are present in the cases where you have already collected data. In addition, you will be able to adjust your future data collection approach to see whether they exist in cases where you intend to conduct your research.

12.2 You will generate three broad types of data that you will need to retain and file as the result of undertaking qualitative research.

The first of these may be referred to as raw data files. These are your original notes and tapes made during the conduct of interviews or observations, or from consulting documentation. In addition, you will also retain transcripts and written-up notes of interviews and observations, although these may also be contained in a computer file.

The second of these is analytical files containing your categorised data. These may of course also be contained in a computer file.

The third of these may be referred to as a supporting file, or indeed it may be different files, containing working papers, self-memos, interim reports and so forth. Again, these may also be contained in a computer file. You are well advised to keep all of this until the end of your research project.

Eventually you will create a fourth file – containing your finished work!

12.3 A *deductive* analytical strategy is one where you will seek to use existing theory to shape the approach that you adopt to the qualitative research process and to aspects of data analysis. An *inductive* analytical strategy is one where you will seek to build up a theory that is adequately grounded in a number of relevant cases. The design of qualitative research requires you to recognise this choice and to devise an appropriate strategy to guide your research project.

12.4 There are a number of implications of using a deductive analytical strategy for the way in which you conduct the process of qualitative analysis:

- You will be in a position to commence your data collection with a well-defined research question and objectives and a clear framework and propositions, derived from the theory that you will have used.
- With regard to sampling, you will be in a position to identify the number and type of organisations to which you wish to gain access in order to undertake data collection to answer your research question and meet your objectives.
- The use of literature and the theory within it will shape the data collection questions that you wish to ask those who participate in your research project.
- You will be able to commence data collection with an initial set of categories derived from your theoretical propositions/hypotheses and conceptual framework linked to your research question and objectives.
- This strategy will provide you with key themes and patterns to search for in your data, and your analysis will be guided by the theoretical propositions and explanations with which you commenced.

12.5 The main implications of using an inductive analytical strategy for the process of qualitative analysis are likely to be related to:

- managing and categorising a large number of code labels, which are likely to emerge from the data that you collect;
- working with smaller rather than larger units of data;

- recognising significant themes and issues during early analysis to help you to consider where data collection should be focused in the future;
- recognising the relationships between categories and rearranging these into a hierarchical form, with the emergence of subcategories;
- seeking to verify apparent relationships against the actual data that you have collected;
- understanding how negative cases broaden (or threaten) your emerging explanation;
- recognising the relationships between the principal categories that have emerged from this grounded approach in order to develop an explanatory theory;
- being rigorous in your use of the procedures that are advocated in order to be able to produce a research report that contains findings that are sufficiently 'grounded' to substantiate the analysis or theory that you are seeking to advance.

Chapter 13

Writing and presenting your project report

By the end of this chapter you should be able to:

- view the writing of the final project report as an exciting prospect;
- write in such a way that you can reflect on all you have learned while conducting the research;
- write a final project report that presents an authoritative account of your research;
- adopt an appropriate format, structure and style for the final project report;
- ensure that your report meets the necessary assessment criteria;
- plan and design an oral presentation of your report.

13.1 Introduction

Some of you may view the process of writing your project report and presenting it orally as an exciting prospect. However, it is more likely that you will approach this stage of your research with a mixture of resignation and trepidation. This is a great pity. We believe that writing about your work is the most effective way of clarifying your thoughts. This suggests that writing should not be seen as the last stage of your research. It should be thought of as something that is continuous throughout the research process.

Writing is a powerful way of learning (Griffiths, 1993). Most teachers will tell you that the best way to learn is to teach. This is because of the necessity to understand something thoroughly yourself before you can begin to explain it to others. This is the position you are in as the writer of your project report. You have to explain a highly complex set of ideas and facts to an audience that you must assume has little or no knowledge of your subject. There is another problem here, which has a parallel with teaching. Often, the more familiar you are with a subject, the more difficult it is to explain it to others with no knowledge of that subject. You will be so familiar with your subject that, like the teacher, you will find it difficult to put yourself in the place of the reader. The result of this is that you may fail to explain something that you assume the reader will know. Even worse, you may leave out important material that should be included.

However, why do most of us view writing with such concern? Veroff (2001) argues that much of this is rooted in the experience we have of writing. Many of us are afraid of exposing our efforts to an audience that we feel will be more likely to criticise than encourage. In our education much of our writing has been little more than rehashing the ideas of others. This has taught us to think of writing as a boring, repetitive process. Some of us are impatient. We are unwilling to devote the time and energy (and inevitable frustration) that are needed for writing.

This fear of criticism is captured perfectly by Richards (1986), who recites the story of being asked by the distinguished sociologist Howard Becker to adopt his method of sitting down and writing what came into her head about the research she had done without even consulting her notes. Her fears of producing poor-quality material, which would be derided by colleagues who saw her work, are described vividly. It is a fear most of us experience.

We agree with Phillips and Pugh (2000), who note that writing is the only time when we really think. This suggests that writing your project report is something that should not be left until every other part of your research has been completed. However, there will be more on that in the next section.

For many of us the fear of making an oral presentation is even more daunting. As we note in the final part of this chapter, some of this apprehension can be overcome by thorough preparation. But at least you have the consolation of knowing that you will be an expert in your topic.

13.2 Getting started with writing

If writing is synonymous with thinking, it follows that writing is something you should do throughout the whole research process. Chapter 2 emphasises the need for clear ideas in writing about research questions and objectives. If you have done this already you will know the difficulty of committing your vague ideas to paper and amending them continually until they express your ideas with brevity, clarity and accuracy. However, there is no reason why your research proposal and plan should be the last writing you do before you finally write up your research in the project report. We encourage you to write as a continual process throughout the research.

Many researchers find it helpful to write the literature review early on in their research. This has clear benefits. It gets you writing on a part of the research process that necessarily comes early in that process. Also, it focuses your thinking on the way in which the literature will inform the research strategy you adopt. You will be pleased you wrote this part of the report when the time pressure is on as the submission deadline for your report approaches. Do not worry that early writing of the literature review means that later relevant publications are ignored in your review. They can always be incorporated at a later date. This is one of the advantages of using a word processor, a topic that we shall cover later in this section.

Having discouraged you from thinking of writing as a process you leave until the end of your research, this section goes on to consider a number of practical hints to assist you to get started.

Create time for your writing

Writing is not an activity that can be allocated an odd half-hour whenever it is convenient. It requires sustained concentration. The amount of time needed to make real progress in your writing is dependent on the way in which you prefer to work. Most people find that it takes a day to write about 2000 words, but we all work in different ways. Once some people have started, they prefer to continue until they drop from exhaustion! Others like to set a strict timetable where three or four hours a day are devoted to writing. Whichever category you are in, make sure that you have time for writing allocated in your diary. We have found that it is helpful to have blocks of time where writing can take place on successive days. This ensures a degree of continuity of ideas, which is not as easy if you keep having to 'think your way back' into your research.

Write when your mind is fresh

We have emphasised so far in this chapter that writing should be a highly creative process. It is important, therefore, that you write at the time of day when your mind is at its freshest. All of us have jobs to do during the day that require little or no creativity. Arrange your day so the uncreative jobs are done in the time when you are at your least mentally alert.

Find a regular writing place

Most of us have one place where we do our writing. It is so important that we often cannot write in unfamiliar surroundings. If this is the case with you it is essential that you combine this psychological comfort with a few practical features of your writing place that will enhance your productivity. One of the most important of these is to ensure that you are not interrupted. A simple 'do not disturb' sign on the door usually works wonders. You may, like Phil, find a telephone-answering machine a useful investment. Remove all distractions, such as television, magazines and computer games, from the room. It may be that you need background noise, even your personal stereo, to help you concentrate. One person's distractions are another person's necessities. What is important is to know what distracts you and to remove those distractions.

Set goals and achieve them

This is the height of self-discipline. Most writers set themselves targets for the period of writing. Usually this is a set number of words. It is better to be realistic about these goals. If you are too ambitious the quality of your work may suffer as you rush to meet the goal. You may be as self-disciplined as Mark, who sets himself subgoals during the day and rewards the achievement of these goals with coffee breaks. What is important is that you see this as entering into a contract with yourself. If you break this contract by not meeting your goal you are the one who should feel guilty. You may like to enter into a similar arrangement with a close friend on the understanding that each of you will insist on the other meeting your goals.

Use a word processor

The word processor has revolutionised writing. There are still some who prefer to write longhand before word-processing the final report. However, for those of us who 'think onto the screen' the main advantage of the word processor is that it enables us to keep amending copy without having to fill the waste paper basket with numerous unsatisfactory attempts. In addition, the word processor enables you to keep updating your project report as you develop new ideas or become dissatisfied with old ones. There is, however, a potential problem here. The ease with which you can keep inserting and deleting text means that relevant '*flagging*' material will need to be changed. At its simplest this may be the contents page or the announcement at the beginning of a chapter that the chapter will cover certain ground. However, it is just as likely to be an obscure reference buried in the text to a table that you have deleted, thus making the reference redundant.

worked example

Using the word processor to transcribe field notes to the final project report

Phil made interview notes in longhand during the interviews that he conducted with managers about the pay system in their organisations. He was particularly careful to note verbatim especially relevant comments from the managers.

Phil ensured that he word-processed these notes, either on the return train journey at the end of the day or at home in the evening.

When writing the project report Phil found the word-processed notes invaluable. He wanted to use some of the verbatim quotes to illustrate key arguments that he was developing from the data. He was able to insert many of these into the report, thus saving time and ensuring accuracy of transcription.

One other advantage of the word processor may have occurred to you. Most packages have a word count facility. You can use this to check your progress towards the word goal you have set yourself for the writing session.

The necessity of keeping back-up copies of your work should go without saying. However, do learn from the experience of one of our students, who lost all his research material as a consequence of not keeping adequate back-up copies. This led to him having to abandon his research project completely.

Generate a plan

Few of us can sit down and write without a lot of thought and planning. We all have our own systems for doing this. However, most people find it essential to construct a plan before they start writing. Veroff (2001) describes the 'clustering' method. This may be familiar to you. The method's stages are:

1 Write the main topic in the middle of a sheet of paper.
2 Jot down the other ideas that occur to you at other points on the page.

3 As the page begins to fill, relationships between the ideas suggest themselves and lines between the ideas may be drawn.
4 This allows you to group the ideas into discrete but related 'chunks', which enables you to devise an outline structure for a section, or chapter.

This chapter started out as just such a pencilled plan written on four pieces of A4 held together with sticky tape. It is essential to get your ideas into some form of order at the outset. This will give you encouragement to start writing.

Finish the writing session on a high point

Many writers prefer to finish their writing session while they are in the middle of a section to which they will look forward to returning. This eases the way in next time. The worse thing you can do is to leave a complex section half completed. It will be difficult to pick up the threads.

Get friends to read your work

Writing is creative and exciting, but checking our work is not. The importance of getting someone else to read through your material cannot be overemphasised. Your project tutor should not be the first person who reads your report, even in its draft form.

Ask your friend to be constructively critical. Your friend must be prepared to tell you about things in the text that are not easy to understand – to point out omissions, spelling, punctuation and grammatical errors. Overall, your friend must tell you whether the piece of writing makes sense and achieves its purpose.

This is not an easy process for you or your critical friend. Most of us are sensitive to criticism, particularly when the consequence of it is the necessity to do a lot more work. Many of us are also hesitant about giving criticism. However, if your project report does not communicate to the reader in the way it should you will get it back for revision work in the long run. It is much better to try and to ensure that this does not happen.

13.3 Structuring your project report

Suggested structure

Most writers agree with Robson (2002) on the general structure to adopt for a project report that is the end product of your research. This is:

- **Abstract**
- **Introduction**
- **Literature review**
- **Method**
- **Results**
- **Conclusions**
- **References**
- **Appendices**

However, this suggested structure should not inhibit you from adopting something different. The structure outlined above fits the deductive approach particularly closely. It assumes that the literature was reviewed to establish the current state of knowledge on the topic and this informed the method adopted. Reporting the findings in a factual manner gives rise to a detailed consideration of what these findings mean to the specific piece of research that has been conducted and to the current state of knowledge on the topic. However, if your research is essentially inductive, it may be that you prefer to structure the report in a different way. You may prefer to tell your story (that is, to explain your conclusions) in the early part of the report. This may include a clear explanation of how this story relates to the existing literature on the topic. This could be followed by a detailed explanation of how you arrived at these conclusions (a combination of an explanation of method adopted and findings established). The precise structure you adopt is less important than the necessity for your reader to be absolutely clear what you are saying and for you to meet the assessment criteria.

Phillips and Pugh (2000) note that these general sections can be subdivided into one or more relevant chapters depending on the topic and the way in which you want to present your particular *storyline*. This is a vital point. Your structure should have a logical flow. Your readers should know the journey on which they are being taken, and should know at all times the point in the journey that has been reached. Above all, the structure you adopt should enable your reader, having read the report, to identify the storyline clearly.

We shall now explain how to distinguish between these broad sections by outlining their purpose and content.

The abstract

The *abstract* is probably the most important part of your report because it may be the only part that some will read. It is a short summary of the complete content of the project report. This enables those who are not sure whether they wish to read the complete report to make an informed decision. For those who intend to read the whole report the abstract prepares them for what is to come. It should contain four short paragraphs with the answers to the following questions:

1 What were my research questions, and why were these important?
2 How did I go about answering the research questions?
3 What did I find out in response to my research questions?
4 What conclusions do I draw regarding my research questions?

Smith (1991) lists five principles for the writing of a good abstract. He argues that:

1 It should be short. Try to keep it to a maximum of two sides of A4. (Some universities stipulate a maximum length, often 300–500 words.)
2 It must be self-contained. Since it may be the only part of your report that some people see it follows that it must summarise the complete content of your report.
3 It must satisfy your reader's needs. Your reader must be told about the problem, or central issue, that the research addressed and the method adopted to pursue the issue. It must also contain a brief statement of the main results and conclusions.

4 It must convey the same emphasis as the report, with the consequence that the reader should get an accurate impression of the report's contents from the abstract.
5 It should be objective, precise and easy to read. The project report contents page should give you the outline structure for the abstract. Summarising each section should give you an accurate résumé of the content of the report. Do ensure that you stick to what you have written in the report. The abstract is not the place for elaborating any of your main themes. Be objective. You will need to write several drafts before you eliminate every word that is not absolutely necessary. The purpose is to convey the content of your report in as clear and brief a way as possible.

Writing a good abstract is difficult. The obvious thing to do is to write it after you have finished the report. We suggest that you draft it at the start of your writing so that you have got your storyline abundantly clear in your mind. You can then amend the draft when you have finished the report so that it conforms to the five principles above.

The introductory chapter

The *introduction* should give the reader a clear idea about the central issue of concern in your research and why you thought that this was worth studying. It should also include a full statement of your research question(s) and research objectives. If your research is based in an organisation, we think that it is a good idea to include in this chapter some details of the organisation, such as its history, size, product and services. This may be a general background to the more specific detail on the research setting you include in the method chapter. It is also important to include in this chapter a 'route map' to guide the reader through the rest of the report. This will give brief details of the content of each chapter and present an overview of how your storyline unfolds.

This will usually be a fairly brief chapter, but it is vitally important.

The literature review

Chapter 3 deals in detail with the writing of a literature review. All that it is necessary to comment on here is the position of this chapter in the project report. We suggest that this is placed before the methodology chapter.

The main purposes of your literature review are to set your study within its wider context and to show the reader how your study supplements the work that has already been done on your topic. The literature review, therefore, may inform directly any specific hypotheses that your research was designed to test. These hypotheses will also suggest a particular research approach, strategy and data collection methods. If, on the other hand, you are working inductively (that is, from data to theory) your literature review may serve the purpose of illuminating and enriching your conclusions.

The title of your literature review chapter should reflect the content of the chapter. It may draw on one of the main themes in the review. We recommend that you do not call it simply 'literature review'. It may be that your literature is reviewed in more than one chapter. This would be the case, for example, where you were using more than one body of literature in your research.

worked example

Using the literature review to inform the research questions

Guiyan was a Chinese student studying for an MA in a UK university. In her research dissertation she was interested to know whether Chinese managers would be able to conduct performance appraisal schemes effectively in China with Chinese employees. She was aware that there were certain aspects of Chinese culture that would make this difficult. Guiyan studied two bodies of literature: that relating to the managerial skills of performance appraisal, and a second concerned with the effects of Chinese culture on the ways in which Chinese managers manage their employees. She presented both in a literature review chapter. She structured her chapter around three questions:

1. What are the key skills needed by managers to conduct performance appraisal effectively?
2. What are the most important aspects of Chinese culture which impact upon on the ways in which Chinese managers manage their employees?
3. To what extent will the aspects of Chinese culture, explained in the answer to question 2, affect the ability of Chinese managers to conduct performance appraisal effectively?

From this Guiyan developed a theoretical proposition that supported her initial idea that certain aspects of Chinese culture would make the conduct of performance appraisal by Chinese managers with Chinese employees difficult. She was then ready to move on to her method chapter, which was an explanation of the way in which she would test her theoretical proposition.

The method chapter

This should be a detailed chapter giving the reader sufficient information to make an estimate of the reliability and validity of your methods. Box 13.1 is a useful list of the points that you should include in the method chapter.

Box 13.1 Points for inclusion in the method chapter

Setting

- ✓ What was the research setting?
- ✓ Why did you choose that particular setting?
- ✓ What ethical issues were raised by the study, and how were these addressed?

Participants

- ✓ How many?
- ✓ How were they selected?
- ✓ What were their characteristics?
- ✓ How were refusals/non-returns handled?

Materials

- ✓ What tests/scales/interview or observation schedules/questionnaires were used?
- ✓ How were purpose-made instruments developed?
- ✓ How were the resulting data analysed?

▶

Procedures

- ✓ What were the characteristics of the interviewers and observers, and how were they trained?
- ✓ How valid and reliable do you think the procedures were?
- ✓ What instructions were given to participants?
- ✓ How many interviews/observations/questionnaires were there; how long did they last; where did they take place?
- ✓ When was the research carried out?

Source: Developed from Robson (2002).

The results chapter(s)

It may well be that your report will contain more than one results chapter. The question you should ask yourself is: 'Is more than one results chapter necessary to communicate my findings clearly?'

The results chapter or chapters are probably the most straightforward to write. It is your opportunity to report the facts that your research discovered. This is where you will include such tables and graphs that will illustrate your findings (do not put these in the appendices). The chapter may also contain verbatim quotes from interviewees, or sections of narrative account that illustrate periods of unstructured observation. This is a particularly powerful way in which you can convey the richness of your data. It is the qualitative equivalent of tables and graphs. Often, a short verbatim quote can convey with penetrating simplicity a particularly difficult concept that you are trying to explain. Do not be afraid to capture precisely what the interviewee said. Slang and swear words are often the most revealing, and provide amusement for the reader!

There are two important points to bear in mind when writing your results. The first is to stress that the purpose is to present facts. It is normally not appropriate in this chapter to begin to offer opinions on the facts. This is for the following chapter. Many of us become confused about the difference between findings and conclusions. One way of overcoming the confusion is to draw up a table with two columns. The first should be headed 'what I found out' and the second 'what judgements I have formed as a result of what I found out'. The first list is entirely factual (for example, 66 per cent of respondents indicated they preferred to receive email messages rather than paper memos) and therefore the content of your findings chapter. The second list will be your judgements based on what you found out (for example, it appears that electronic forms of communication are preferred to traditional) and therefore the content of your conclusions section.

The second point links to the first. Drawing up a table will lead you to a consideration of the way in which you present your findings. The purpose of your project report is to communicate the answer to your research question to your audience in as clear a manner as possible. Therefore you should structure your findings in a clear, logical and easily understood manner. There are many ways of doing this. One of the simplest is to return to the research objectives and let these dictate the order in which you present your findings. Alternatively, you may prefer to report your findings thematically. You could present the themes in descending order of importance.

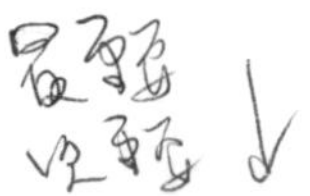

Whichever method you choose should be obvious to the reader. As with the literature review, the chapter(s) devoted to research should be titled in an interesting way that reflects the content of findings.

The conclusions chapter(s)

Logically, for each finding there should be at least one conclusion. This suggests that the *conclusions* chapter(s) should be at least as long as the findings chapter(s). This is certainly the case. Findings presented without reflective thought run the risk of your reader asking 'so what?'

The conclusions chapter (which, again, should have a more interesting title than 'conclusions') is where you have the opportunity to shine. It is your conclusions that will demonstrate whether you have answered the research question and show the degree of insight that you exhibit in reaching your conclusions. However, it is the part of the report that most of us find difficult. It is the second major opportunity in the research process to demonstrate real originality of thought (the first time being at the stage where you choose the research topic). Because of that, we urge you to pay due attention to the conclusions chapter. In the conclusions you are making judgements rather than reporting facts, so this is where your maturity of understanding can shine through. The key questions to ask of each of the findings are: 'So what?' and, importantly, 'To what extent have I answered my research question(s) and met my research objective(s)?' Often students do little more than write a conclusions section that is a rehash of their findings. It is essential that you give the content of this chapter careful thought over a long period of time.

You may find that the clearest way to present your conclusions is to follow a similar structure to the one used in your findings section. If that structure reflects the research objectives then it should make certain that your conclusions would address the research question(s). Drawing up a matrix similar to that in Figure 13.1 may help you in structuring your findings and conclusions.

You may also have a final section in your conclusion chapter(s) called *'discussion'*. Alternatively you may make this a separate chapter with this general heading. Here you would turn to your conclusions and ask such questions as: 'What does this mean?' 'What are the implications for organisations?' 'What are the implications for the current state of knowledge of the topic?' 'How does it add to the literature?' 'What are the implications for future research?' The conclusions chapter should not include new material but the discussion may do so, as long as it is germane to the point you are making about your conclusions.

An alternative approach to the matrix is to draw a 'mind map' (see Section 2.3), which places the findings randomly on a blank page and links conclusions to these findings by way of lines and arrows. For some of you this may be a more creative approach, which enables you to associate groups of findings with conclusions and vice versa.

Answering the research question(s), meeting the objectives and, if appropriate, supporting or otherwise the research hypotheses is the main purpose of the conclusions chapter. This is where you will consider the findings presented in the previous chapter. You should also return to your literature review and ask yourself 'What do my conclusions add to the understanding of the topic displayed in the literature?'

Research questions	Results (what factual information did I discover in relation to the specific research questions?)	Conclusions (what judgements can I make about the results in relation to the specific research questions?)
What are the operational differences between different shifts in the production plant?	Cases of indiscipline in the last six months have been twice as frequent on the night shift as on the day shift	The night shift indiscipline problems may be due to the reluctance of operators to work on this shift

Figure 13.1 Using a matrix in the planning of the content for the results and conclusions chapters

It may be that there are practical implications of your findings. In a management report this would normally form the content of a chapter specifically devoted to recommendations. We suggest that you check with your project tutor whether this is expected. In the reports that students are required to prepare on some professional courses this is an important requirement. For academic degree programmes it is often unnecessary.

Even if you do not specify any practical implications of your research you may comment in the conclusions chapter on what your research implies for any future research. This is a logical extension of a section in the conclusions chapter that should be devoted to the limitations of your research. These limitations may be the size of sample, the snapshot nature of the research, or the restriction to one geographical area of an organisation. Virtually all research has its limitations. This section should not be seen as a confession of your weaknesses, but as a mature reflection on the degree to which your findings and conclusions can be said to be the 'truth'.

References

A range of conventions are used to reference the material of other writers' material that you have cited in your text. Appendix 2 illustrates three of the most popular of these, the Harvard, footnotes and American Psychological Association (APA) systems. However, we suggest that you consult your project tutor about the system that is appropriate for your project report, as many universities require their own variation of these systems.

It is a good idea to start your references section at the beginning of the writing process and add to it as you go along. It will be a tedious and time-consuming task if left until you have completed the main body of the text. If you do leave it until the end, the time spent on compiling the reference section is time that will be better spent on checking and amending your report.

Appendices

In general, *appendices* should be kept to the minimum. If they are so important that your reader's understanding of the points you are making in the text makes their inclusion in the report necessary, then they should be in the main body of the text. If, on the other hand, the material is 'interesting to know' rather than 'essential to know' then it should be in the appendices. Often we feel tempted to include appendices to 'pad out' a project report. Resist this temptation. Your readers will not be reading your report for leisure reading. They will be pressed for time and will probably not look at your appendices. Your project report will stand or fall on the quality of the main text. However, your appendices should include a blank copy of your questionnaire, interview or observation schedule. Where these have been conducted in a language different from that in which you write your submitted project report you will need to submit both this version and the translation.

The management report

You may have wondered why we made no reference to recommendations in the report structure. In the typical *management report* this may be the most important section. The hard-pressed executive reading your report may turn to your recommendations first to see what action needs to be taken to tackle the issue.

Whether you include a recommendation section depends on the objectives of your research. If you are doing exploratory research you may well write recommendations, among which will be suggestions for the pursuit of further research. However, if your research is designed to explain or describe, recommendations are less likely. For example, the research question 'Why do small engineering companies in the UK reinvest less of their profits in their businesses than their German counterparts?' may imply clear points for action. However, strictly speaking, recommendations are outside the scope of the research question, which is to discover 'Why?' not 'What can be done about it?' The message is clear. If you want your research to change the situation that you are researching, then include the need to develop recommendations in your research objectives.

Length of the project report

You will probably have guidelines on the amount of words your project report should contain. Do stick to these. However interesting your report, your tutors will have others to read, so they will not thank you for exceeding the limit. Indeed, if you can meet your research objectives fully in a clear and absorbing report that is significantly shorter than the word limit, the good mood in which you put your tutors may be reflected in a higher grade. Reports that exceed the word limit are usually excessively verbose. It is more difficult to be succinct. Do not fall into the trap of writing a long report because you did not have the time to write a shorter one.

13.4 Organising the project report's content

Choosing a title

This is the part of the project report on which most of us spend the least time. Yet it is the only knowledge that many people have of the project. Day (1995:15) describes a good *title* as one that has 'the fewest possible words that adequately describe the content of the paper'. Try choosing a title and then ask a colleague who knows your subject what she or he thinks the title describes. If her or his description matches your content then stick with your title.

Tell a clear story

Be prepared for your project tutor to ask you 'What's your main *storyline*?' Your storyline (your central argument or thesis) should be clear, simple and straightforward. It should be so clear that you can stop the next person you see walking towards you and tell that person what your project report's storyline is and he or she will say 'Yes, I understand that'. This is where writing the abstract helps. It forces you to think clearly about the storyline because you have to summarise it in so few words.

A simple format for developing the storyline is shown in Figure 13.2.

Another way of checking to see whether your storyline is clear is to 'reason backwards'. An example of this may be a report that ends in clear recommendations for action. Start by explaining your recommendations to the manager who, for example, may have to spend money on their implementation. This invites the question from that manager: 'What makes you recommend this action?' Your answer should be: 'I came to the conclusion in my report that they are necessary.' The follow-up question from the manager here could be: 'On what basis do you draw these conclusions?' Here your answer is, of course, on the findings that you established. The next question asked by the manager is: 'How did you arrive at these findings?', in response to which you explain your method. The manager may counter by asking you why she should take any notice of your findings. The response to this is that you took care to design a research strategy that would lead to valid and reliable findings. Moreover, that research strategy is based on clear research objectives and a detailed review of the relevant literature.

Such 'reasoning backwards' is a useful check to see not only whether your storyline is clear but also that it stands up to logical analysis.

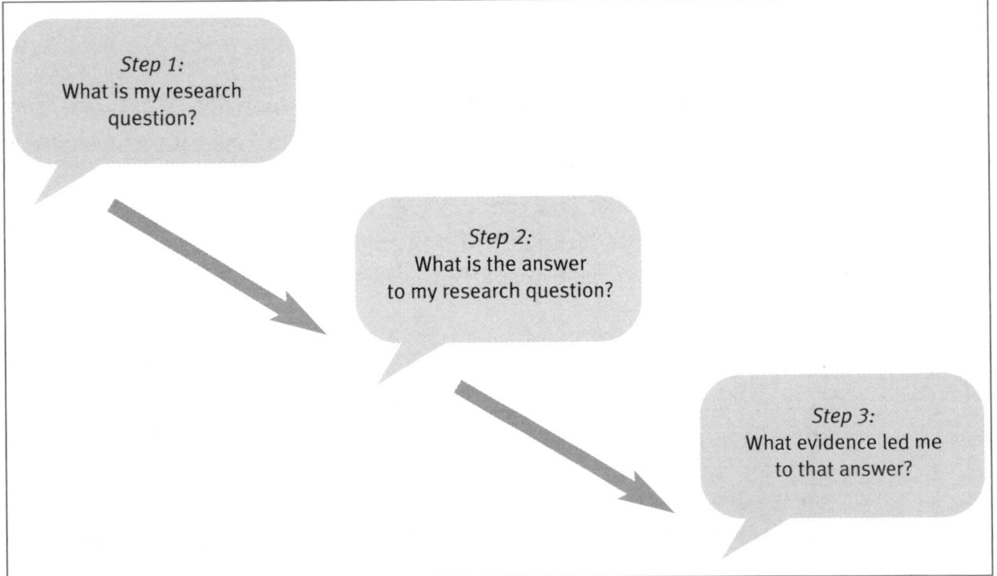

Figure 13.2 A format for developing the storyline

Source: Developed from Raimond (1993:175)

Helping the reader to get all the information out

Dividing your work

One of us once received the first draft of a 20 000-word project report that had virtually no divisions except the chapters. It was like looking at a road map of Britain that did not illustrate any road numbers or towns. It was just as difficult to find your way around that report as it would be to journey from Southampton to Harrogate using a townless road map. The content of the project report seemed fine. However, it was hard to be sure about this because it was so difficult to spot any gaps in the ground it covered. What was needed were some signposts and some town names. Do not think about how you can put in all your information. Instead, concentrate on helping the reader to get all the information out.

worked example

Developing a storyline

Step 1

I wanted to know whether, as the literature suggested, organisational structures are determined by their strategies.

Step 2

The answer is that organisation structures are in part determined by strategies and in part by ad hoc factors that owe little to strategy considerations.

Step 3

I based this answer on interviews with senior managers in three large UK organisations and examination of the minutes of meetings at which structural issues were discussed. The particular focus was on the removal of management positions.

The message is simple. Divide your work in such a way that it is easy for readers to find their way round it and for them always to be clear where they are, where they have come from, and where they are going.

To do this you may find it helpful to return to the matrix idea in Figure 13.1. You will see that each column of the matrix represents the broad content of a chapter. The cells indicate the way in which the chapters may be divided. Each division may have a subdivision.

We hope that you have noticed that we have employed a similar system in this book. However, this is two-colour. The equivalent would be that each chapter section is identified by bold upper-case letters. The subheadings are bold lower-case, and further divisions of the subsection content are denoted by bold, lower-case italics. Smith (1991) explains various ways of organising and signposting text. It is not important which way you do this as long as your approach is consistent and it helps the reader around the report and matches the ways specified by your examining institution.

Previewing and summarising chapters

A further way in which you can signpost your work is to 'top and tail' each chapter.

This is to include a few words at the beginning of the chapter (Smith, 1991) that provide a description of how the chapter is to contribute to answering the research question, the methods used in this part of the study, and the points that are covered. At the end of each chapter it is useful if the reader has a brief summary of the content of the chapter and a very brief indication of how this content links to the following chapter. This may seem like repetition. However, it helps the reader on her or his journey through your report and ensures that you, the writer, are on the correct road.

Tables and graphics

Your reader will find your project report more accessible and easier to read if you present some of your data and ideas in *tables* and *graphics*. It is not only numerical data that can be presented in tables. You can also present ideas that can be easily compared. Table 12.1 is an example of this.

Do not be tempted to put your numerical tables in the appendices. They will probably be some of your most important data. Include them and comment on them in the text. Your commentary should note the significance of the data in the tables. It should not simply describe the table's contents.

Section 11.3 has detail on the presentation of tables and graphics.

A final note of caution should be sounded. To avoid confusing your reader, do make sure that wherever possible you have introduced the table or graphic before it appears in the text.

One report or two?

Many researchers of management topics face the dilemma of having to write for two audiences: the academic audience, who possibly will mark and grade the report for a degree or a diploma, and the organisation's managers, who will be interested in the practical benefit that the report promises. This raises the thorny question, 'For whom should the report be written?'

Many people have resolved this dilemma by writing two reports: one for each audience. The academic report will usually be much longer and contain contextual description that the organisational audience does not require. Similarly, those managers reading the report will probably be less interested in the literature review and the development of theory than the academic audience. If the research question did not imply the necessity for recommendations for future action, these may need to be written for the organisational version.

Fortunately, the advent of word processors makes this job easy. Some careful cutting and pasting will be necessary. However, what should always be kept in mind is the audience that each specific report is addressing. Take care not to fall between two stools. Write each report for its audience in style and content.

As well as presenting two written reports you may have to present your report orally. In the next two sections we address the writing of reports, and in the final section, Section 13.7, we turn our attention to their oral presentation.

13.5 Developing an appropriate writing style

Much of your concern in writing your project report will be about what you write. In this section of the chapter we ask you to think about the way you write. Your writing style is just as important as the content, structure and layout of your report. 'Good writing cannot cure bad thought' (Phillips and Pugh, 2000:67). In fact, the clearer the writing the more bad thought is exposed. However, bad writing can spoil the effect of good thought.

Clarity and simplicity

> The ... lack of ready intelligibility [in scholarly writing], I believe, usually has little or nothing to do with the complexity of the subject matter, and nothing at all to do with profundity of thought. It has to do almost entirely with certain confusions of the academic writer about his own status ... To overcome the academic prose you first of all have to overcome the academic pose ...
>
> Wright Mills (1970:239–40)

Each Christmas Mark accompanies his Christmas cards with a family newsletter. It is written in a simple, direct and friendly manner that is easy and enjoyable to read. Few of the project reports we read are written in such a simple, direct manner. They are more elaborate in their explanation: they use difficult words where Mark's family newsletter would use simple ones. They adopt the academic pose.

Phil tells a story that reinforces the point made by Wright Mills in the above quotation. He was asked by a student to comment on her thesis in progress, which was about the impact of a particular job advertising strategy. He thought that it was written in an over-elaborate and academic way. After many suggestions for amendments Phil came across a sentence that explained that the strategy his student was studying 'was characterised by factors congruent with the results of a lifestyle analysis of the target market'. Phil thought that this was too wordy and academic. He suggested making it simpler. His student examined the sentence at length and declared she could see no way of improving it. Phil thought that it could say 'it was a strategy that matched the lifestyles of those at whom it was aimed'. His student protested. She agreed it was shorter and clearer but protested that it was less 'academic'. We think that clarity and simplicity are more important than wishing to appear academic. Your project report is a piece of communication in the same way as Mark's Christmas newsletter.

Phillips and Pugh (2000) advise that you should aim to provide the reader with a report that she or he cannot put down until 2.00 a.m. or later for fear of spoiling the flow. (If you are reading this chapter at 2.30 a.m. we have succeeded!)

Write simple sentences

A common source of lack of clarity is the confusing sentence. This is often because it is too long. A simple rule to adopt is: one idea – one sentence. Mark reads his work out loud. If the sentences are too long he runs out of breath! This is another useful guide to sentence length.

worked example

Writing clearer sentences

> While it is true to say that researchers have illusions of academic grandeur when they sit down to write their project report, and who can blame them because they have had to demonstrate skill and resilience to get to this point in their studies, they nonetheless must consider that writing a project report is an exercise in communication, and nobody likes reading a lot of ideas that are expressed in such a confusing and pretentious way that nobody can understand them, let alone the poor tutor who has to plough through it all to try and make some sense of it.

There appear to be at least six separate ideas in this sentence. It contains 101 words (when marking, we sometimes come across sentences with over 150!). In addition, it contains a common way of introducing multiple ideas into a sentence: the embedded clause. In the sentence above the embedded clause is '. . . and who can blame them because they have had to demonstrate skill and resilience to get to this point in their studies, . . .' The give-away is the first word in the sentence: 'While'. This invites an embedded clause. The point here is that potentially rich ideas get buried away in the literary undergrowth. Dig them up and replant them. Let them breathe in a sentence of their own.

The sentence needs to be clearer and simpler. However, it should not lose any of its meaning. Halving the amount of words and dividing up the sentence into smaller clearer sentences results in the following:

> Researchers have illusions of academic grandeur when they write their project report. This is understandable. They have demonstrated skill and resilience to reach this point in their studies. However, writing a project report is an exercise in communication. Nobody likes confusing and pretentious writing that is difficult to understand. Pity the tutor who has to make sense of it.

Avoid jargon

Jargon should not be confused with technical terminology. Some technical terms are unavoidable. To assist your reader, it is best to put a glossary of such terms in the appendices. However, do not assume that your reader will have such a full knowledge as you of the subject and, in particular, the context. Here, and in all cases, try to put yourself in the position of the reader. Phil makes this point to MBA students who use their organisations as vehicles to write assignments. He asks them to 'mark' past (anonymous) assignments. They are usually horrified at the assumptions that their fellow students make about the tutor's prior knowledge.

What can be avoided is the sort of jargon that the Oxford dictionary defines as 'gibberish' and 'debased language'. You will know the sort of phrases: 'ongoing situation'; 'going down the route of'; 'at the end of the day'; 'the bottom line'; 'at this moment in time'. It is not just that they are ugly but they are not clear and simple. For example, 'now' is much clearer and simpler than 'at this moment in time'.

Beware of using large numbers of quotations from the literature

We believe that quotations from the literature should be used infrequently in your project report. Occasionally we receive draft projects that consist of little more than a series of quotations from books and journal articles that a student has linked together with a few sentences of her or his own. This tells us very little about the student's understanding of the concepts within the quotations. All it shows is that he or she has looked at the book or journal article and, it is hoped, can acknowledge sources correctly! In addition, by using quotations in this way the student's line of argument tends to become disjointed and less easy to follow. It is therefore usually better to explain other people's ideas in your own words.

That is not to say that you should never use quotations. As you have seen, we have used direct quotations from other people's work in this book. Rather we would advise you to use them sparingly to create maximum impact in supporting your storyline.

Check your spelling and grammar

Spelling is still a problem for many of us, in spite of the word processor's spelling check. It will not correct your 'moral' when you wished to say 'morale' or sort out when you should write 'practise' rather than 'practice'. This is where the friend who is reading your draft can help, provided that friend is a competent speller. Tutors tend to be more patient with errors of this kind than those that reflect carelessness. However, the point remains that spelling errors detract from the quality of your presentation and the authority of your ideas.

The ten commandments of good writing

Day (1995:160) provides a useful checklist for those of us who make the sort of *grammatical errors* that threaten the credibility of our writing. He demonstrates cleverly the error in each of the points listed in Table 13.1.

It is not our intention here to conduct an English grammar lesson. Some of the common errors in Table 13.1 are self-explanatory.

Table 13.1 Common grammatical errors

Often we write	The correct way is
1 Each pronoun should agree with **their** antecedent	Each pronoun should agree with **its** antecedent.
2 Just between you and **I**, case is important	Just between you and **me**, case is important.
3 A preposition is a poor word to end a sentence **with.**	A preposition is a poor word **with which** to end a sentence.
4 Verbs **has** to agree with their subject.	Verbs **have** to agree with their subject.
5 Do not use **no** double negatives	Do not use double negatives.
6 Remember **to never split** an infinitive.	Remember **never to split** an infinitive.
7 When dangling, do not use participles.	Do not use dangling participles.
8 Avoid clichés like the plague.	To avoid clichés like the plague!
9 Do not write a run-on sentence it is difficult when you got to punctuate it so it makes sense when the reader reads what you wrote.	Do not write a run-on sentence. It is difficult to punctuate it so that it makes sense to the reader.
10 About sentence fragments.	What about sentence fragments? (!)
11 The data **is** included in this section.	The data **are** included in this section.

Source: Developed from Day, 1995:160

You may argue that the *split infinitive* is not often thought of as an error these days. However, 'to boldly go' ahead with your project report ignoring this rule risks irritating your reader – something you can ill afford to do. You want the reader to concentrate on your ideas.

Day's '*dangling participle*' warning is amusingly illustrated by the draft questionnaire shown to us by a student. This asked for 'the amount of people you employ in your organisation, broken down by sex'. We wrote on our copy: 'We haven't got people in that category: they've not got the energy when they work here!' (Remember that when writing your questionnaire!)

Some of the more obvious grammatical errors you can spot by reading your text aloud to yourself. You need not know the grammatical rules; they often just sound wrong.

Person, tense and gender

Traditionally, academic writing has been dry and unexciting. This is partly because the convention has been to write impersonally, in the past *tense* and in the *passive voice* (for example, 'interviews were conducted following the administration of questionnaires').

The writer was expected to be distanced from the text. This convention is no longer as strong. It is a matter of preferred style rather than rules. The research approach that dominates your methods may dictate your choice of *personal pronoun*. Section 4.1 lists 'the observer is independent of what is being observed' as one feature of positivism. It follows from this that an impersonal style is more appropriate. By contrast, Section 8.2 notes that the participant observer 'participates in the daily life of people under study'. The researcher is an intrinsic part of the research process. Use of the first person seems more logical here. However, style is important. Use of the term 'the author' sounds too impersonal and stilted. In contrast, excessive use of 'I' and 'we' may raise questions in your readers' minds about your ability to stand outside your data and to be objective.

Day (1995:160) identifies rules for the use correct use of tense. He suggests that 'you should normally use the present tense when referring to previously published work (e.g. Day identifies) and you should use the past tense when referring to your present results (e.g. I found that . . .)'. Although he notes exceptions to this rule, it serves as a useful guide.

Day (1995) and Becker (1986) both stridently attack the passive voice (it was found that) and champion the use of the *active voice* (I found that). Certainly it is clearer, shorter and unambiguous. It is a good idea to check with your project tutor here which is most likely to be acceptable.

Finally, a note about the use of language that assumes the *gender* of a classification of people. The most obvious example of these is the constant reference to managers as 'he'. Not only is this inaccurate in many organisations, it also gives offence to many people of both sexes. Those offended will probably include your readers! It is simple enough to avoid (for example, 'I propose to interview each executive unless he refuses' becomes 'I propose to interview each executive unless I receive a refusal') but often less easy to spot. The further reading section in the first draft of this chapter referred to Becker as a 'master craftsman'. These notes on language and gender prompted us to change it to 'an expert in the field'. Appendix 5 gives more detailed guidance on the use of non-discriminatory language.

Preserving anonymity

You may have given the participants (and the organisations) from whom you collected data an undertaking that you would not disclose their identity in anything you write. In this case you will need to conceal their identity in your project report. The usual way of doing this is to invent pseudonyms for organisations and not to name individual participants. This should not detract from the impact of your report.

Similarly, your sponsoring organisation(s) may have requested sight of your report before it is submitted. Should there be misgivings about the content of the report you should be able to alleviate these by the use of pseudonyms. This is usually a better option than significant text changes.

The need for continual revision

Adrian recently asked a group of undergraduate students how many of them did more than one draft of their assignment papers. He did not expect that many would reply that they did. What he did not predict was that many of them had not even thought that this was necessary.

Submitting the first attempt is due partly to the heavy assessment loads on many courses, which means that students are constantly having to 'keep up with the clock'. On part-time courses, students these days have so many demands in their daily work that writing an assignment just once is all that is possible. Becker (1986) argues that this is the way most of us learned to write at school. The paper is usually seen only by the teacher. The arrangement is a private one.

However, project reports are different. They will be seen by an audience much wider than one tutor. They will usually be lodged in the library to be read by succeeding students. You will be judged on the quality of your work. For that reason we urge you most strongly to polish your work with successive drafts until you are happy that you can do no better.

The final version of this chapter (which, incidentally, even for the first edition of this book, was read by five people and is the last of seven or eight drafts) contains guidelines that you can use to evaluate your first draft. These are summarised in the checklist in Box 13.2.

Box 13.2 Checklist for evaluating your first draft

- ✓ Is there a clear structure?
- ✓ Is there a clear storyline?
- ✓ Does your abstract reflect accurately the whole content of the report?
- ✓ Does your introduction state clearly the research question(s) and objectives?
- ✓ Does your literature review inform the later content of the report?
- ✓ Are your methods clearly explained?

▶

- ✓ Have you made a clear distinction between findings and conclusions in the two relevant chapters?
- ✓ Have you checked all your references and presented these in the required manner?
- ✓ Is there any text material that should be in the appendices or vice versa?
- ✓ Does your title reflect accurately your content?
- ✓ Have you divided up your text throughout with suitable headings?
- ✓ Does each chapter have a preview and a summary?
- ✓ Are you happy that your writing is clear, simple and direct?
- ✓ Have you eliminated all jargon?
- ✓ Have you eliminated all unnecessary quotations?
- ✓ Have you checked spelling and grammar?
- ✓ Have you checked for assumptions about gender?
- ✓ Is your report in a format that will be acceptable to the assessing body?

Having been through this checklist you may decide to make minor alterations to your text. On the other hand you may rewrite sections or move sections within chapters to other chapters. Keep asking yourself 'How easy can I make the reader's task?'

After each successive draft do leave a space of time for your thoughts to mature. It is amazing how something you wrote a few days before will now make no sense to you. However, you will also be impressed with the clarity and insight of some passages.

Having completed a second draft you may now feel confident enough to give it to your colleague or friend to read. Ask your reader to use the checklist above, to which you can add specific points that you feel are important (for example, are my arguments well reasoned?).

13.6 Meeting the assessment criteria

Your readers will be assessing your work against the assessment criteria that apply to your research programme. Therefore it is essential that you familiarise yourself with these criteria. Easterby-Smith *et al.* (2002) cite Bloom's (1971) well-known taxonomy of educational objectives to illustrate the level that project reports should meet. At the lower levels project reports should show *knowledge* and *comprehension* of the topic covered. At the intermediate levels they should contain evidence of *application* and *analysis*. Application is thought of as the ability to apply certain principles and rules in particular situations. Your method section should be the principal vehicle for demonstrating application. Analysis may be illustrated by your ability to break down your data and to clarify the nature of the component parts and the relationship between them. Whatever your assessment criteria, it is certain that you will be expected to demonstrate your ability at these lower and intermediate levels.

The higher levels are *synthesis* and *evaluation*. Rowntree (1987:103) defines synthesis as 'the ability to arrange and assemble various elements so as to make a new statement or plan or conclusion – a unique communication'. The emphasis put on conclusions and, in particular, on the development of a storyline in your project report suggests that we feel that you should be showing evidence of synthesis. Evaluation refers to 'the ability to judge materials or methods in terms of internal accuracy and consistency or by comparison with external criteria' (Rowntree, 1987:103). You have the chance to show this ability in the literature review and in the awareness of the limitations of your own research (see Section 13.3).

In summary, we think that each of the levels of educational objectives should be demonstrated in your project report.

13.7 Oral presentation of the report

Many students, particularly on professional courses, have to present their project report orally as part of the assessment process. The skills required here are quite different from those involved with writing. We discuss them here under three headings: planning and preparation; the use of visual aids; and presenting.

Planning and preparing

We make no apology for starting this section with the old trainer's adage 'Failing to prepare is preparing to fail'. Your assessors will forgive any inadequacies that stem from inexperience, but they will be much less forgiving of students who have paid little attention to preparation. You can be sure of one thing about insufficient preparation: it shows, particularly to the experienced tutor.

All presentations should have clear aims and objectives. This is not the place to analyse the difference between these. Suffice to say that your aim to should be to give the audience members an overview of your report in such a way that it will capture their interest. Keep it clear and simple. By doing so you will meet the most basic assessment criterion: that some time later the tutor in the audience can remember clearly your main project storyline. Your objectives are more specific. They should start you thinking about the interests of your audience. These should be phrased in terms of what it is you want your audience members to be able to do after your presentation. Since your presentation will usually be confined to the imparting of knowledge it is sufficient to phrase your objectives in terms of the audience members being able, for example, to define, describe, explain or clarify. It is a good idea to share the objectives with your audience members so they know about the journey on which they are being taken.

worked example Objectives for a project presentation

Phil created the following slide as part of a lecture on project presentation. To help give a professional appearance to his slide he used Microsoft PowerPoint's design template 'Notebook'. The slide offers a framework to help you think about the objectives of your project presentation.

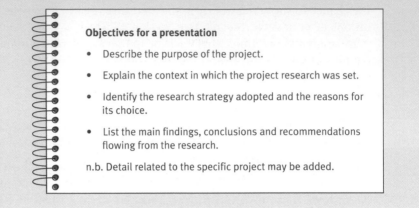

Objectives for a presentation

- Describe the purpose of the project.
- Explain the context in which the project research was set.
- Identify the research strategy adopted and the reasons for its choice.
- List the main findings, conclusions and recommendations flowing from the research.

n.b. Detail related to the specific project may be added.

Setting clear objectives for your presentation leads you neatly to deciding the content. This should be straightforward because your abstract should serve as your guide to the content. After all, the purpose of the abstract is to give the reader a brief overview of the report, which is precisely the same purpose as the presentation. How much detail you go into on each point will be determined largely by the time at your disposal. But the audience member who wants more detail can always ask you to elaborate, or read it in the report.

The final point to note here is to think about the general approach you will adopt in delivering your presentation. It is a good idea to involve the audience members rather than simply tell them what it is you want them to know. Thirty minutes of you talking at the audience members can seem like an age, for you and sometimes for them! Asking them to ask questions throughout the presentation is a good way of ensuring that the talk is not all in one direction. Rarely will tutors miss the opportunity of asking you to 'dig a little deeper' to test your understanding, so don't worry that no questions will arise. However, you must be careful to ensure that you do not let questions and answers run away with time. The more you open up your presentation to debate, the less control you have of time. In general we do not think it is a good idea to attempt to emulate tutors and turn your presentation into a teaching session. We have seen students set the audience mini-exercises to get them involved, but often these tend to fall flat. Play to your strengths and enjoy the opportunity to share your detailed knowledge with an interested audience.

Using visual aids

Now another old adage: 'I hear and I forget, I see and I remember' (Rawlins, 1993: 37). The use of *visual aids* will do more than enhance the understanding of your audience. It will help you to look better prepared and therefore more professional. It is unlikely that you will have the time to use elaborate media such as video or photographic slides, and often your subject matter will not lend itself to their use. So we shall confine our discussion here to the use of more prosaic media such as the overhead projector and the whiteboard.

A simple set of *overhead slides* will perform the same function as a set of notes, in that it will ensure that you do not forget key points, and will help you to keep your presentation on track. You will know the material so well that a key point noted on the overhead will be enough to trigger your thought process and focus the attention of the audience. Key points will also ensure that you are not tempted to read a script for your presentation, something that will not sustain the attention of your audience for very long.

The use of Microsoft *PowerPoint* has revolutionised the preparation of overhead projector transparencies. It is now easy to produce a highly professional presentation, which can include simple illustrations to reinforce a point or add a little humour. You may have the facility to project the slides direct to a screen using a computer, which clearly adds to the degree of professionalism. This allows you electronically to reveal each point as you talk about it while concealing forthcoming points. Alternatively, you may need to print the slides from PowerPoint and copy these to acetates and show them using an overhead projector. The latter method means that you must ensure that your slides are numbered and kept in a neat pile when shown, otherwise you will be searching for the correct slide to show at a particular time. PowerPoint also allows you to print miniature versions of your slides as handouts, which is a very useful *aide-mémoire* for the audience.

You may want to supplement your pre-prepared slides with the use of the whiteboard. This may be useful for explaining points in relation to questions you receive. A word of warning here: ensure that you use dry markers that can be wiped from the board. A vain attempt to erase the results of a permanent pen in front of your audience will do nothing to enhance your confidence. Ensuring you have dry wipe markers (use only black and blue pens – red and green are too feint), and checking computers and overhead projectors before the presentation, serves to emphasise the need for careful preparation.

Making the presentation

The first thing to say here is: don't worry about nerves. As Janner (1984:15) says: 'Confidence comes with preparation, practice and training'. Your audience will expect you to be a little nervous. Indeed, without some nervous tension before your presentation it is unlikely you will do yourself justice. Be positive about your presentation and your report. Trial your presentation on a friend to ensure that it flows logically and smoothly and that you can deliver it in the allotted time. In our experience most students put too much material in their presentations although they worry beforehand that they have not got enough.

It is important that your presentation has a clear structure. We can do no better than repeat the words of a famous evangelist: when asked how he held the attention of his audience, he replied 'First I tell them what I'm going to say, then I say it, then I tell them what I've said' (Parry, 1991:17). Parry calls this 'the three-step rule'.

Audiences like to know where they are going, they like to know how they are progressing on the journey, and they like to know when they have arrived.

Finally some practical points that will help.

- Think about whether you would prefer to sit or stand at the presentation. The former may be better to foster debate, the latter is likely to give you a sense of 'control' (Rawlins, 1993). Which you choose may depend upon the circumstances of the presentation, including the approach you wish to adopt, the room layout, the equipment you are using and your preferred style.
- Consider how you will deal with difficult questions. Rehearse these and your answers in your mind so that you can deal with them confidently during the presentation.
- Avoid jargon.
- Check the room before the presentation to ensure you have everything you need, you are happy and familiar with the layout, and all your equipment is working.

13.8 Summary

- Writing is a powerful way of clarifying your thinking.
- Writing is a creative process, which needs the right conditions if it is to produce successful results.
- Your project report should have a clear structure that enables you to develop a clear storyline.
- Your report should be laid out in such a way that your reader finds all the information readily accessible.
- You should try to develop a clear, simple writing style that will make reading the report an easy and enjoyable experience.
- Spelling and grammatical errors should be avoided.
- Do not think of your first draft as your last. Be prepared to rewrite your report several times until you think it is the best you can do.
- Failing to prepare for your presentation is preparing to fail.
- Visual aids will enhance the understanding of your audience and lend your presentation professionalism.
- Remember the three-step rule: tell them what you going to say, say it, then tell them what you've said.

self-check Questions

13.1 Your project tutor has returned your draft project report with the suggestion that you make a clearer distinction between your results and your findings. How will you go about this?

13.2 Why is it considered good practice to acknowledge the limitations of your research in the project report?

13.3 Look again at the quote from Wright Mills cited early in Section 13.5. Rewrite this so that his idea is communicated to the reader in the clearest way possible.

13.4 There are other problems that must be avoided when repositioning sections of your report in the redrafting processes. What are they?

13.5 Look at the PowerPoint slide below and comment on any weaknesses.

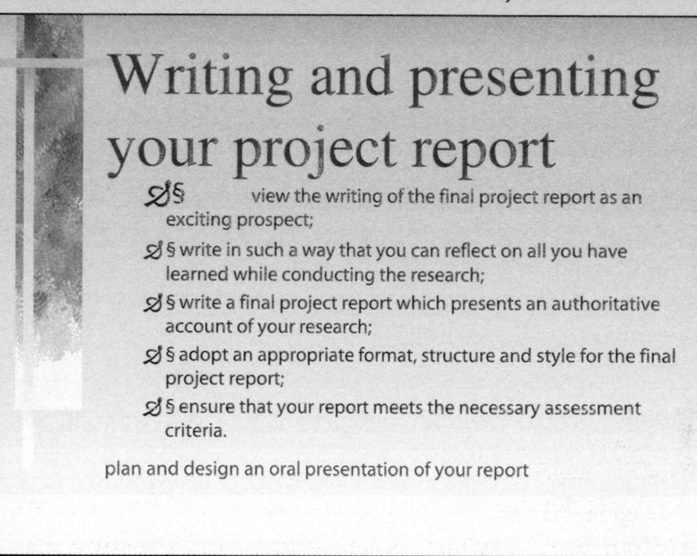

progressing your research project

Writing your project report

- ☐ Design a clear structure for your report that broadly fits the structure suggested in Section 13.3. Ensure that the structure you design accommodates a clear storyline.
- ☐ Write the report's abstract. Remember that you will need to rewrite this when you have finished your first draft.
- ☐ Compile the main body of the report. How will you ensure that the literature review relates to the following chapters? What method will you adopt to make the distinction between result and conclusions?
- ☐ Give your report the 'reader-friendly' test to ensure that the style is easy to read and free from avoidable errors.

References

Becker, H. (1986) *Writing for Social Scientists*, Chicago, IL, University of Chicago Press.

Bloom, B. (ed.) (1971) *Taxonomy of Educational Objectives: Cognitive Domain*, New York, McKay.

Day, R. (1995) *How to Write and Publish a Scientific Paper* (4th edn), Cambridge, Cambridge University Press.

Easterby-Smith, M., Thorpe, R. and Lowe, A. (2002) *Management Research: An Introduction* (2nd edn), London, Sage.

Griffiths, M. (1993) 'Productive writing', *The New Academic*, Autumn, pp. 29–31.

Janner, G. (1984) *Janner on Presentations*, London, Business Books Ltd.

Parry, H. (1991) *Successful Business Presentations*, Kingston upon Thames, Croner Publications Ltd.

Phillips, E. and Pugh, D. (2000) *How to Get a PhD* (3rd edn), Buckingham, Open University Press.

Raimond, P. (1993) *Management Projects: Design, Research and Presentation*, London, Chapman & Hall.

Rawlins, K. (1993) *Presentation and Communication Skills: A Handbook for Practitioners*, London, Emap Healthcare Ltd.

Richards, P. (1986) 'Risk', *in* Becker, H., *Writing for Social Scientists*, Chicago, IL, University of Chicago Press, pp. 108–20.

Robson, C. (2002) *Real World Research* (2nd edn), Oxford, Blackwell.

Rowntree, D. (1987) *Assessing Students: How Shall We Know Them?* (revised edn), London, Harper & Row.

Smith, C.B. (1991) *A Guide to Business Research*, Chicago, IL, Nelson-Hall.

Veroff, J. (2001) 'Writing', *in* Rudestam, K. and Newton, R. *Surviving your Dissertation* (2nd edn), Newbury Park, CA, Sage.

Wright Mills, C. (1970) 'On intellectual craftsmanship', *in The Sociological Imagination*, London, Pelican.

Further reading

Becker, H. (1986) *Writing for Social Scientists*, Chicago, IL, University of Chicago Press. This is a highly readable book, full of anecdotes, from an expert in the field. It is rich in ideas about how writing may be improved. Most of these have been developed by Becker from his own writing and teaching. Such is the emphasis that Becker puts on rewriting that the title would more accurately be 'Rewriting for Social Scientists'.

Day, R. (1995) *How to Write and Publish a Scientific Paper* (4th edn), Cambridge, Cambridge University Press. This takes the reader through the whole process, with a host of useful advice. It is funny and irreverent but nonetheless valuable for that!

Rawlins, K. (1993) *Presentation and Communication Skills: A Handbook for Practitioners*, London, Emap Healthcare Ltd. A very useful and practical guide for the inexperienced.

Smith, C.B. (1991) *A Guide to Business Research*, Chicago, IL, Nelson-Hall. Chapters 7–10 provide an excellent introduction to writing for business and management researchers.

CASE 13 Amina's story

Amina was a diligent student who had worked very hard on her MBA. Her research had been on the marketing strategies of UK main car dealerships in the wake of the trend for UK new car buyers to import their vehicles from continental Europe. She had submitted her draft project report, and was awaiting the comments of her supervisor with quiet confidence. She anticipated that there would be some more work to do on the report, but she thought that this would be minor amendments. She was sure that the main thrust of the report was fine. However, when Amina went to see Dr Wang, her project advisor, she was disappointed to learn that he was not impressed with what she had written. In fact Dr Wang told Amina that as it stood her report was some way from MBA standard, and that if she wanted to obtain the degree she had a lot of work to do to improve it.

Amina was taken aback to hear this news, but she listened carefully to Dr Wang's explanation and made notes. His main criticism was that the report was too 'rambling' and insufficiently succinct. The context of the research was explained clearly. Indeed Dr Wang thought that Amina had spent far too much time on her description of the UK retail motor market. Her statement of the problem facing UK retail dealers was also clear. However, he was critical of the way in which Amina had used the literature. He thought that there was far too much on the car industry and too little on marketing theory. Dr Wang had emphasised to Amina in all their meetings that her project was about how organisations develop their marketing strategies in the light of unexpected competition. In that sense Amina's project could be about any organisation in any market. However, Amina's interest in cars had dominated her consideration of the theory of marketing strategy.

Amina had conducted interviews with senior sales managers in a sample of dealerships representing the main manufacturers. She had explained how she did this, but there was little about any alternative data collection methods that could have been pursued. Dr Wang was critical of this, but his main criticism concerned the final third of Amina's report. In this she had described the results of the interviews in great detail. But after this detailed presentation of the findings were a mere two pages of conclusions. Even these were little more than a summary of the findings.

Dr Wang thought Amina's report was well written and very interesting, but not what was needed for a successful MBA project report. His overall comment was that 'it tells a very interesting story, Amina, but your job as a management Master's degree student is to use theory to help to explain and even solve management problems. Leave the storytelling to the business journalists.'

At first Amina was bitterly disappointed, and she complained incessantly to the friends with whom she shared an apartment about Dr Wang's unfairness. However, as the days passed she became more reflective – so much so that this was what she admitted to her friend Gisela:

'I suppose I am to blame. The tutors told us that we should start the writing process early and write separate sections on each aspect of the research, keeping in mind the purpose of each aspect and ensuring that there was a logical flow to the report and it fitted together as a coherent whole. But I got so involved in the research interviews, and all the other course assignments, that there never seemed to be time to write. Then when the deadline approached I panicked and wrote the whole thing in less than a week, using days and nights. I can see now that I should have built it up, read it and reread it and amended it, but I never had time.

'I can also see what Dr Wang means about telling the story like a business journalist. That's much easier than academic work. It's less rigorous. As long as it reads ok I suppose that's all there is to it.'

Oh well, back to it!

▶

Questions

1 What did Dr Wang mean by 'your job as a management Master's degree student is to use theory to help to explain and even solve management problems'?

2 How might Amina improve her findings section?

3 What do you think Amina has to do to get Dr Wang's full approval for submission of her MBA project for assessment?

4 How would you suggest Amina now approaches the rewriting of her report?

self-check Answers

13.1 This is easier said than done. Start by going through your results chapter continually asking yourself 'Did I find this out?' You will probably weed out a lot of things that you have thought about that are related to points you found out. These belong in the conclusions (or discussion) chapter.

Now turn to the conclusions chapter asking yourself the same question. You will probably find fewer results in the conclusions chapter than vice versa.

13.2 It shows that you have thought about your research design. It demonstrates that you have insight into the various ways of pursuing research. Remember that there is no perfect research design. Look again at Section 4.4. This asked the question 'How do you know that the answer to the research question(s) is the correct one?' The answer, of course, is that in the literal sense of the question you cannot know. All you can do is reduce the possibility of getting the answer wrong.

13.3 Academic writing is often difficult to understand. This is not usually because the subject matter is complex or the thoughts profound. It is because the writer thinks it necessary to write in an 'academic' way.

13.4 The 'road map' you announced in the introduction may not now be correct. The previews and summaries at the beginning and end of the relevant chapters may need changing. A more serious potential problem is that the storyline may be altered. This should not be the case. Nonetheless, it is important to reread the whole report to ensure that the repositioning does not alter its sense of coherence.

13.5 Well, it looks a bit of a mess! The title is too big: it is out of proportion to the rest of the text. Not all the points are 'bulleted', and the spaces between the bullet and text are not consistent. There are three different types of font and, most importantly, there is too much text on the slide. All of these faults are easily rectifiable. It is worth playing around with it and making a few mistakes – it's a good way of learning!

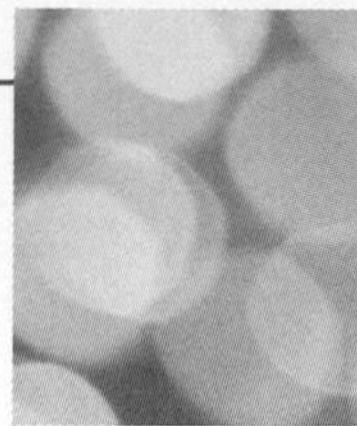

Bibliography

Ackroyd, S. and Hughes, J. (1992) *Data Collection in Context* (2nd edn), London, Longman.

Adams, G. and Schvaneveldt, J. (1991) *Understanding Research Methods* (2nd edn), New York, Longman.

American Psychological Association (2001) *Publication Manual of the American Psychological Association* (5th edn), Washington, American Psychological Association.

Anderson, J. and Poole, M. (2001) *Assignment and Thesis Writing* (4th edn), Brisbane, John Wiley and Sons.

Barnett, V. (1991) *Sample Survey Principles and Method*, London, Edward Arnold.

Becker, H. (1986) *Writing for Social Scientists*, Chicago, IL, University of Chicago Press.

Bell, J. (1999) *Doing Your Research Project* (3rd edn), Buckingham, Open University Press.

Bennett, R. (1991) 'What is management research?', *in* Smith, N.C. and Dainty, P. (eds), *The Management Research Handbook*, London, Routledge, pp. 67–77.

Bloom, B. (ed.) (1971) *Taxonomy of Educational Objectives: Cognitive Domain*, New York, McKay.

Bouma, G. and Atkinson, G. (1995) *A Handbook of Social Science Research: A Comprehensive and Practical Guide for Students* (2nd edn), Oxford, Oxford University Press.

Bourque, L.B. and Clark, V.A. (1994) 'Processing data: the survey example', *in* Lewis-Beck, M.S., *Research Practice*, London, Sage, pp. 1–88.

Branscomb, H.E. (1998) *Casting Your Net: A Student's Guide to Research on the Internet*, Boston, MA, Allyn and Bacon.

British Psychological Society (1988) 'Guidelines for the use of non-sexist language', *The Psychologist*, 1:2, 53–4.

Bryman, A. (1988) *Quantity and Quality in Social Research*, London, Unwin Hyman.

Bryman, A. (1989) *Research Methods and Organisation Studies*, London, Unwin Hyman.

Bryson, B. (1995) *Made in America*, London, Minerva.

Buchanan, D., Boddy, D. and McCalman, J. (1988) 'Getting in, getting on, getting out and getting back', *in* Bryman, A. (ed.), *Doing Research in Organisations*, London, Routledge, pp. 53–67.

Buzan, T. with Buzan, B. (2000) *The Mind Map Book* (Millennium edn), London, BBC Worldwide.

Carroll, L. (1989) *Alice's Adventures in Wonderland*, London, Hutchinson.

Clausen, H. (1996) 'Web information quality as seen from libraries', *New Library World* 97: 1130, 4–8.

Coffey, A. and Atkinson, P. (1996) *Making Sense of Qualitative Data*, Thousand Oaks, CA, Sage.

Coghlan, D. and Brannick, T. (2001), *Doing Action Research in Your Own Organisation*, London, Sage.

Cohen, L. and Holliday, M. (1996) *Practical Statistics for Students*, London, Paul Chapman Publishing.

Coomber, R. (1997) 'Using the Internet for survey research', *Sociological Research Online*, 2:2 (online) (cited 10 February 2002). Available from <URL:http://www.socresonline.org.uk/socresonline/2/2/2.html>

Cooper, D.R. and Schindler, D.A. (2001) *Business Research Methods* (7th edn), London, McGraw-Hill.

Cowton, C.J. (1998) 'The use of secondary data in business ethics research', *Journal of Business Ethics*, 17:4, 423–34.

Creswell, J. (1994) *Research Design: Quantitative and Qualitative Approaches*, Thousand Oaks, CA, Sage.

Cully, M., O'Reilly, A., Millward, N., Forth, J., Woodlands, S., Dix, G. and Bryson, A. (1999) *The 1998 Workplace Employment Relations Survey: First Findings* [Online] [cited 28 July 2002], available from <url:http://www.dti.gov.uk/emar>.

Cunningham, J.B. (1995) 'Strategic considerations in using action research for improving personnel practices', *Public Personnel Management*, 24:2, 515–29.

Dale, A., Arber, S. and Procter, M. (1988) *Doing Secondary Research*, London, Unwin Hyman.

Dale, P. (1993) *Guide to Libraries in Key UK Companies*, London, British Library.

Dale, P. (1998) *Guide to Libraries and Information Units in Government Departments and Other Organisations*, London, British Library.

Davies, J. (2001) 'International comparisons of labour disputes in 1999', *Labour Market Trends*, 109:4, 195–201.

Davis, S.M. and Saunders, M.N.K. (1997) 'Freedom of movement for professionals: an assessment of the European Union policy and the barriers that remain', *Journal of Applied Management Studies*, 6:2, 199–218.

Day, R. (1995) *How to Write and Publish a Scientific Paper* (4th edn), Cambridge, Cambridge University Press.

Deci, E.L. (1972) 'The effects of contingent and non-contingent rewards and controls on intrinsic motivation', *Organisational Behaviour and Human Performance*, 8, 217–19.

Dees, R. (2000) *Writing the Modern Research Paper* (3rd edn), Boston, MA, Allyn and Bacon.

Delbridge, R. and Kirkpatrick, I. (1994) 'Theory and practice of participant observation', *in* Wass, V. and Wells, P. (eds), *Principles and Practice in Business and Management Research*, Aldershot, Dartmouth, pp. 35–62.

Dennis, D. (ed.) (2000) *Family Spending: A Report on the 1999–2000 Family Expenditure Survey*, London, Stationery Office.

Denscombe, M. (1998) *The Good Research Guide*, Buckingham, Open University Press.

Denzin, N. (1989) *The Research Act: A Theoretical Introduction to Sociological Methods* (3rd edn), Englewood Cliffs, NJ, Prentice-Hall.

Dey, I. (1993) *Qualitative Data Analysis*, London, Routledge.

Diamantopoulos, A. and Schlegelmilch, B.B. (1997) *Taking the Fear Out of Data Analysis*, London, Dryden Press.

Dillman, D.A. (2000) *Mail and Internet Surveys: The Tailored Design Method* (2nd edn), New York, Wiley.

Ditton, J. (1977) *Part-Time Crime: An Ethnography of Fiddling and Pilferage*, London, Macmillan.

Dochartaigh, N.O. (2002) *The Internet Research Handbook: A Practical Guide for Students and Researchers in the Social Sciences*, London, Sage.

Dunkerley, D. (1988) 'Historical methods and organizational analysis', *in* Bryman A (ed.), *Doing Research in Organisations*, London, Routledge, pp. 82–95.

Easterby-Smith, M., Thorpe, R. and Lowe, A. (1991) *Management Research: An Introduction*, London, Sage.

Easterby-Smith, M., Thorpe, R. and Lowe, A. (2002) *Management Research: An Introduction* (2nd edn), London, Sage.

Economist, The (1997) *The Economist Numbers Guide: The Essentials of Business Numeracy* (3rd edn), London, Profile Books.

Eden, C. and Huxham, C. (1996) 'Action research for management research', *British Journal of Management*, 7:1, 75–86.

ELC International (2001) *Europe's 15,000 Largest Companies* (27th edition), Oxford, ELC International.

Erlandson, D.A., Harris, E.L., Skipper, B.L. and Allen, S.D. (1993) *Doing Naturalistic Inquiry*, Newbury Park, CA, Sage.

Fielding, N.G. and Lee, R.M. (1995) 'Confronting CAQDAS: choice and contingency', *in* Burgess, R.G. (ed.), *Studies in Qualitative Methodology Computing and Qualitative Research*, Greenwich, CT, JAI Press, pp. 1–23.

Fink, A. (1995a) *How to Ask Survey Questions*, Thousand Oaks, CA, Sage.

Fink, A. (1995b) *The Survey Handbook*, Thousand Oaks, CA, Sage.

Fisher, M. (1997) *Qualitative Computing: Using Software for Qualitative Data Analysis*, Aldershot, Ashgate.

Foddy, W. (1994) *Constructing Questions for Interviews and Questionnaires*, Cambridge, Cambridge University Press.

Gall, M.D., Borg, W.R. and Gall, J.P. (1996) *Educational Research: An Introduction* (6th edn), New York, Longman.

Ghauri, P. and Grønhaugh, K. (2002) *Research Methods in Business Studies: A Practical Guide* (2nd edn), Harlow, Financial Times Prentice Hall.

Gibb, F. (1995) 'Consumer group accuses lawyers of shoddy service', *The Times*, 5 October.

Gibbons, M.L., Limoges, H., Nowotny, S., Schwartman, P., Scott, P. and Trow, M. (1994) *The New Production of Knowledge: The Dynamics of Science and Research in Contemporary Societies*, London, Sage.

Gill, J. and Johnson, P. (1997) *Research Methods for Managers* (2nd edn), London, Paul Chapman.

Glaser, B. (1978) *Theoretical Sensitivity: Advances in the Methodology of Grounded Theory*, Mill Valley, CA, Sociology Press.

Glaser, B. and Strauss, A. (1967) *The Discovery of Grounded Theory*, Chicago, IL, Aldine.

Great Britain Office for National Statistics (1997) *Index to the UK Standard Industrial Classification of Economic Activities 1992, UK SIC(92)*, London, The Stationery Office.

Great Britain Office for National Statistics (2000a) *Standard Occupation Classification Volume 1: Structure and Description of Unit Groups*, London, The Stationery Office.

Great Britain Office for National Statistics (2000b) *Standard Occupation Classification Volume 2: The Coding Index*, London, The Stationery Office.

Griffiths, M. (1993) 'Productive writing', *The New Academic*, Autumn, 29–31.

Grummitt, J. (1980) *Interviewing Skills*, London, Industrial Society.

Gummesson, E. (2000) *Qualitative Methods in Management Research* (2nd edn), Thousand Oaks, CA, Sage.

Hahn, H. (2002) *Harley Hahn's Internet Yellow Pages*, New York, McGraw-Hill.

Hakim, C. (1982) *Secondary Analysis in Social Research*, London, Allen & Unwin.

Hakim, C. (1987) *Research Design: Strategies and Choices in the Design of Social Research*, London, Allen & Unwin.

Hakim, C. (2000) *Research Design: Successful Designs for Social and Economic Research*, London, Routledge.

Hart, C. (1998) *Doing a Literature Review*, London, Sage.

Hays, W.L. (1994) *Statistics* (4th edn), London, Holt-Saunders.

Haywood, P. and Wragg, E.C. (1982) *Evaluating the Literature: Rediguide 2*, Nottingham, University of Nottingham School of Education.

Healey, M.J. (1991) 'Obtaining information from businesses', *in* Healey, M.J. (ed.), *Economic Activity and Land Use*, Harlow, Longman, pp. 193–251.

Healey, M.J. and Rawlinson, M.B. (1993) 'Interviewing business owners and managers: a review of methods and techniques', *Geoforum*, 24:3, 339–55.

Healey, M.J. and Rawlinson, M.B. (1994) 'Interviewing techniques in business and management research', *in* Wass, V.J. and Wells, P.E., *Principles and Practice in Business and Management Research*, Aldershot, Dartmouth, pp. 123–45.

Hedrick, T.E., Bickmann, L. and Rog, D.J. (1993) *Applied Research Design*, Newbury Park, CA, Sage.

Henry, G.T. (1990) *Practical Sampling*, Newbury Park, CA, Sage.

Henry, G.T. (1995) *Graphing Data: Techniques for Display and Analysis*, Thousand Oaks, CA, Sage.

Higgins, R. (1996) *Approaches to Research: A Handbook for Those Writing a Dissertation*, London, Jessica Kingsley.

Hodgkinson, G.P., Herriot, P. and Anderson, N. (2001) 'Re-aligning the stakeholders in management research: lessons from industrial, work and organizational psychology', *British Journal of Management*, 12, Special Edition, 41–8.

Hodson, R. (1991) 'The active worker: compliance and autonomy at the workplace', *Journal of Contemporary Ethnography*, 20:1, 47–8.

Hofstede, G. (2001) *Culture's Consequences: Comparing Values, Behaviours, Institutions and Organisations across Nations*, London, Sage.

Hussey, J. and Hussey, R. (1997) *Business Research: A Practical Guide for Undergraduate and Postgraduate Students*, Basingstoke, Macmillan Business.

Jacob, H. (1994) 'Using published data: errors and remedies', *in* Lewis-Beck, M.S., *Research Practice*, London, Sage and Toppan Publishing, pp. 339–89.

Jankowicz, A.D. (2000) *Business Research Projects* (3rd edn), London, Business Press Thomson Learning.

Janner, G. (1984) *Janner on Presentations*, London, Business Books Ltd.

Jenkins, J. and Bird, D. (2001) 'Patterns of pay: results of the New Earnings Survey', *Labour Market Trends*, 109:3, 145–57.

Jobber, D. and O'Reilly, D. (1996) 'Industrial mail surveys: techniques for inducing response', *Marketing & Intelligence Planning*, 14:1, 29–34.

Johnson, J.M. (1975) *Doing Field Research*, New York, Free Press, pp. 28–50.

Johnson, P. (1998) 'Analytic induction', *in* Symon, G. and Cassell, C. (eds), *Qualitative Methods and Analysis in Organizational Research*, London, Sage.

Jones, A. and Smith, A. (eds) (2001) 'What exactly is the Labour Force Survey?' [online](cited 20 December 2001). Available from: <URL:http://www.statistics.gov.uk/nsbase/downloads.theme_labour/what_exactly_is_LFS1.pdf>

Jowell, R., Curtice, J., Park, A., Thomson, K., Jarvis, L., Bromley, C. and Stratford, N. (2000) *British Social Attitudes – The 17th Report: Focusing on Diversity*, Aldershot, Ashgate.

Kahn, R. and Cannell, C. (1957) *The Dynamics of Interviewing*, New York and Chichester, Wiley.

Kanji, G.K. (1998) *100 Statistical Tests* (2nd edn), London, Sage.

Kerlinger, F. and Lee, H. (2000) *Foundations of Behavioral Research* (4th edn), Fort Worth, Harcourt College Publishers.

Kervin, J.B. (1992) *Methods for Business Research*, New York, HarperCollins.

Kervin, J.B. (1999) *Methods for Business Research* (2nd edn), New York, HarperCollins.

Kidder, L.H. (1981) 'Qualitative research and quasi-experimental frameworks', *in* Brewer, M.B. and Collins, B.E. (eds), *Scientific Enquiry and the Social Sciences*, San Francisco, Jossey Bass.

King, N. (1998) 'Template analysis', *in* Symon, G. and Cassell, C. (eds), *Qualitative Methods and Analysis in Organizational Research*, London, Sage, pp. 118–34.

Kingsbury, P. (1997) *IT Answers to HR Questions*, London, Institute of Personnel and Development.

Kinnear, P.R. and Gray, C.D. (2000) *SPSS for Windows Made Simple, Release 10*, Hove, Psychology Press.

Lavrakas, P.J. (1993) *Telephone Survey Methods: Sampling, Selection and Supervision* (2nd edn), Newbury Park, CA, Sage.

Lewin, P. (1997) *Economic Trends Annual Supplement* (1997 edn), London, Stationery Office.

Library Association (1997) *Libraries in the United Kingdom and Republic of Ireland*, London, Library Association.

Mackintosh, N. (ed.) (1995) *Cyril Burt: Fraud or Framed?*, Oxford, Oxford University Press.

Marshall, C. and Rossman, G.B. (1999) *Designing Qualitative Research* (3rd edn), Thousand Oaks, CA, Sage.

Marsick, V.J. and Watkins, K.E. (1997) 'Case study research methods', *in* Swanson, R.A. and Holton, E.F. (eds), *Human Resource Development Research Handbook*, San Francisco, CA, Berrett-Koehler, pp. 138–57.

McGinty, J. and Williams, T. (eds) (2001) *Regional Trends 36* (2001 edn), London, Stationery Office.

McGuinness, K. and Short, T. (1998) *Research on the Net*, London, Old Bailey Press.

McNeill, P. (1990) *Research Methods* (2nd edn), London, Routledge.

Mercator (2002) 'Mercator home page' (online) (cited 10 February 2002). Available from <URL:http://www.mercator.co.uk>

Meyer, H., Kay, E. and French, J. (1965) 'Split roles in performance appraisal', *Harvard Business Review*, 43:1, 123–9.

Miles, M.B. and Huberman, A.M. (1994) *Qualitative Data Analysis* (2nd edn), Thousand Oaks, CA, Sage.

Miller, D.C. and Salkind, N.J. (eds) (2002) *Handbook of Research Design and Social Measurement* (6th edn), Thousand Oaks, CA: Sage.

Millward, N., Stevens, M., Smart, D. and Hawes, W.R. (1992) *Workplace Industrial Relations in Transition*, Aldershot, Dartmouth.

Mintzberg, H. (1973) *The Nature of Managerial Work*, New York, Harper & Row.

Mintzberg, H. and Waters, J. (1989) 'Of strategies, deliberate and emergent', *in* Asch, D. and Bowman, C. (eds), *Readings in Strategic Management*, Basingstoke, Macmillan Education, pp. 4–19.

Mitchell, V. (1996) 'Assessing the reliability and validity of questionnaires: an empirical example', *Journal of Applied Management Studies*, 5:2, 199–207.

Moody, P.E. (1983) *Decision Making: Proven Methods for Better Decisions*, Maidenhead, McGraw-Hill.

Morgan, M. (1995) 'The case of the dubious data', *The Guardian*, 4 August, second section, pp. 10–11.

Morris, C. (1999) *Quantitative Approaches in Business Studies* (5th edn), Harlow, Financial Times Prentice Hall.

Morris, T. and Wood, S. (1991) 'Testing the survey method: continuity and change in British industrial relations', *Work Employment and Society*, 5:2, 259–82.

Moustakas, C. (1994) *Phenomenological Research Methods*, Thousand Oaks, CA, Sage.

Mullins, L. (2002) *Management and Organisational Behaviour* (6th edn), Harlow, Financial Times Prentice Hall.

Musson, G. (1998) 'Life histories', *in* Symon, G. and Cassell, C. (eds), *Qualitative Methods and Analysis in Organizational Research*, London, Sage, pp. 10–27.

Naipaul, V.S. (1989) *A Turn in the South*, London, Penguin.

National Statistics (2002a) 'The NS-SEC self coded method' (online) (cited 15 February 2002). Available from <URL:http://www.statistics.gov.uk/methods_quality/ns_sec/nssec_self_coded_method.asp>

National Statistics (2002b) 'The classification of ethnic groups' (online) (cited 15 February 2002). Available from <URL:http://www.statistics.gov.uk/themes/compe...nce/ns_ethnic_classification.asp>

Neuman, W.L. (2000) *Social Research Methods* (2nd edn), London, Allyn and Bacon.

North, D.J., Leigh, R. and Gough, J. (1983) 'Monitoring industrial change at the local level: some comments on methods and data sources', *in* Healey, M.J. (ed.) *Urban and Regional Industrial Research: The Changing UK Data Base*, Norwich, Geo Books, pp. 111–29.

Norusis, M.J. (2000) *SPSS 10.0 Guide to Data Analysis*, London, Prentice Hall.

Office for National Statistics (1996) *30 Years of Regional Trends*, London, Stationery Office.

Office for National Statistics (2000) 'Dataset: average earning index and retail prices index, 1991–1999: Social Trends'. [online] (cited 19 December 2001). Available from: <URL:http://www.statistics.gov.uk/statbase/xsdataset.asp?vlnk=202&More=Y>.

Office for National Statistics (2001) 'Retail Price Index: price indicators used in 2000'. [online] (cited 19 December 2001). Available from: <URL:http://www.statistics.gov.uk/themes/economy/articles/pricesandinflation/rpiitart.pdf>.

Oja, S.N. and Smulyan, L. (1989) *Collaborative Action Research: A Developmental Approach*, London, Falmer Press.

Oppenheim, A.N. (2000) *Questionnaire Design, Interviewing and Attitude Measurement* (new edn), London, Continuum International.

Owen, F. and Jones, R. (1994) *Statistics* (4th edn), London, Pitman Publishing.

Pallant, J. (2001) *SPSS Survival Manual,* Buckingham, Open University Press.

Parry, H. (1991) *Successful Business Presentations*, Kingston upon Thames, Croner Publications Ltd.

Patton, M.Q. (2002) *Qualitative Research and Evaluation Methods* (3rd edn), Thousand Oaks, CA, Sage.

Patzer, G.L. (1996) *Using Secondary Data in Market Research: United States and World-wide*, Westport, CT, Quorum Books.

Peters, T. and Waterman, R. (1982) *In Search of Excellence*, New York, Harper & Row.

Phillips, E.M. and Pugh, D.S. (2000) *How to get a PhD* (3rd edn), Buckingham, Open University Press.

Pointon, G. (no date) *Disability and Television: Guidelines on Representation for Producers*, London, Channel 4.

Powney, J. and Watts, M. (1987) *Interviewing in Educational Research*, London, Routledge and Kegan Paul.

Punch, M. (1993) 'Observation and the police: the research experience', *in* Hammersley, M., *Social Research Philosophy Politics and Practice*, London, Sage, pp. 181–99.

Raimond, P. (1993) *Management Projects: Design, Research and Presentation*, London, Chapman & Hall.

Rawlins, K. (1993) *Presentation and Communication Skills: A Handbook for Practitioners*, London, Emap Healthcare Ltd.

Reichman, C.S. (1962) *Use and Abuse of Statistics*, New York, Oxford University Press.

Remenyi, D., Williams, B., Money, A. and Swartz, E. (1998) *Doing Research in Business and Management: An Introduction to Process and Method*, London, Sage.

Richards, P. (1986) 'Risk', *in* Becker, H., *Writing for Social Scientists*, Chicago, IL, University of Chicago Press, pp. 108–20.

Riley, J. (1996) *Getting the Most from your Data: A Handbook of Practical Ideas on How to Analyse Qualitative Data* (2nd edn), Bristol, Technical and Educational Services Ltd.

Robson, C. (1993) *Real World Research: A Resource for Social Scientists and Practitioner–researchers,* Oxford, Blackwell.

Robson, C. (2002) *Real World Research* (2nd edn), Oxford, Blackwell.

Rogers, C.R. (1961) *On Becoming a Person*, Constable, London.

Rosen, M. (1991) 'Breakfast at Spiro's dramaturgy and dominance', *in* Frost, P., Moore, L., Louis, M., Lundberg, C. and Martin, J. (eds), *Reframing Organisational Culture*, Newbury Park, CA, Sage, pp. 77–89.

Rowntree, D. (1987) *Assessing Students: How Shall We Know Them?* (rev. edn), London, Harper & Row.

Roy, D. (1952) 'Quota restriction and goldbricking in a machine shop', *American Journal of Sociology*, 57, 427–42.

Saunders, M.N.K. and Lewis, P. (1997) 'Great ideas and blind alleys? A review of the literature on starting research', *Management Learning*, 28:3, 283–99.

Saunders, M.N.K. and Williams C.S. (2000) Towards a new approach to understanding service encounters: establishing, learning about and reconciling different views, *Journal of European Industrial Training*, 24:2/3/4, 220–7.

Saunders, M.N.K., Lewis, P. and Thornhill, A. (1997) *Research Methods for Business Students*, London, Pitman Publishing.

Schatzman, L. and Strauss, A. (1973) *Field Research: Strategies for a Natural Sociology*, Englewood Cliffs, NJ, Prentice-Hall.

Schein, E. (1992) 'Coming to a new awareness of organisational culture', *in* Salaman, G., *Human Resource Strategies*, London, Sage, pp. 237–9.

Schein, E. (1995) 'Process consultation, action research and clinical enquiry: are they the same?', *Journal of Managerial Psychology*, 10:6, 14–19.

Schein, E. (1999) *Process Consultation Revisited: Building the Helping Relationship*, Reading, MA, Addison-Wesley.

Schmitz, R. (2002) 'Searching the World Wide Web: a basic tutorial' [online] (cited 18 February 2002). Available from <URL:http://www.tilbrguniversity.nl/services/library/instruction/www/onlinecourse/>.

Scolari Sage (2002) 'Methodologist's Toolchest' (online) (cited 10 February 2002). Available from <URL:http://www.scolari.co.uk>

Sekaran, U. (2000) *Research Methods for Business: A Skill-Building Approach* (3rd edn), New York, Wiley.

Sharp, J. and Howard, K. (1996) *The Management of a Student Research Project* (2nd edn), Aldershot, Gower.

Siedel, J. (1991) 'Method and madness in the application of computer technology to qualitative data analysis', *in* Fielding, N.G. and Lee, R.M. (eds), *Using Computers in Qualitative Research*, London, Sage, pp. 107–16.

Silverman, D. (1993) *Interpreting Qualitative Data*, London, Sage.

Smith, C.B. (1991) *A Guide to Business Research*, Chicago, IL, Nelson-Hall.

Smith, H. (1975) *Strategies of Social Research: The Methodological Imagination*, Englewood Cliffs, NJ, Prentice-Hall.

Smith, N.C. and Dainty, P. (1991) *The Management Research Handbook*, London, Routledge.

Sparrow, J. (1989) 'Graphic displays in information systems: some data properties influencing the effectiveness of alternate forms', *Behaviour and Information Technology*, 8:1, 43–56.

Starkey, K. and Madan, P. (2001) 'Bridging the relevance gap: aligning stakeholders in the future of management research', *British Journal of Management*, 12, Special Issue, 3–26.

Stewart, D.W. and Kamins, M.A. (1993) *Secondary Research: Information Sources and Methods* (2nd edn), Newbury Park, CA, Sage.

Strauss, A. and Corbin, J. (1990) *Basics of Qualitative Research*, Newbury Park, CA, Sage.

Strauss, A. and Corbin, J. (1998) *Basics of Qualitative Research* (2nd edn), Thousand Oaks, CA, Sage.

Sykes, W. (1991) 'Taking stock: issues from the literature in validity and reliability in qualitative research', *Journal of Market Research Society* 33:3–12.

Teague, A. (2001) 'New methodologies for the 2001 Census in England and Wales'. [online] (cited 11 February 2002). Available from: <URL:http://www.statistics.gov.uk/nsbase/census2001/pdfs/NewMethodologies.pdf>.

Tesch, R. (1990) *Qualitative Research: Analysis Types and Software Tools*, New York, Falmer.

Thornhill, A., Lewis, P., Millmore, M. and Saunders M.N.K. (2000) *Managing Change: A Human Resource Strategy Approach*, Harlow, Financial Times Prentice Hall.

Torrington, D. (1991) *Management Face to Face*, London, Prentice Hall.

Tranfield, D. and Starkey, K. (1998) 'The nature, social organization and promotion of management research: towards policy', *British Journal of Management*, 9, 341–53.

Tukey, J.W. (1977) *Exploratory Data Analysis*, Reading, MA, Addison-Wesley.

Tyrrell, K. (ed.) (2001) *Annual Abstract of Statistics 2001*, London, Stationery Office.

UK Data Archive (2002) 'UK Data Archive' [online] [cited 3 January] available from <URL: http://www.data-archive.ac.uk>.

Usunier, J.-C. (1998) *International and Cross-Cultural Management Research*, London, Sage.

deVaus, D.A. (2002) *Surveys in Social Research* (5th edn), London, Routledge.

Veroff, J. (2001) 'Writing', *in* Rudestam, K. and Newton, R. *Surviving your Dissertation* (2nd edn), Newbury Park, CA, Sage.

Walker, A. (2002) *Living in Britain: Results from the 2000 General Household Survey*, London, Stationery Office.

Walker, R. (1985) *Doing Research: A Handbook for Teachers*, London, Methuen.

Walliman, N. (2001) *Your Research Project: A Step by Step Guide for the First-Time Researcher*, London, Sage

Wass, V. and Wells, P. (1994) 'Research methods in action: an introduction', *in* Wass, V.J. and Wells, P.E. (eds), *Principles and Practice in Business and Management Research*, Aldershot, Dartmouth, pp. 1–34.

Wells, P. (1994) 'Ethics in business and management research', *in* Wass, V.J. and Wells, P.E. (eds), *Principles and Practice in Business and Management Research*, Aldershot, Dartmouth, pp. 277–97.

Whyte, W. (1955) *Street Corner Society* (2nd edn), Chicago, IL, University of Chicago Press.

Willimack, D.K., Nichols, E. and Sudman, S. (2002) 'Understanding unit and item nonresponse in business surveys', *in* Dillman, D.A., Eltringe, J.L., Groves, J.L. and Little, R.J.A. (eds) (2002) *Survey Nonresponse*, New York, Wiley Interscience, pp. 213–27.

Witmer, D.F., Colman, R.W. and Katzman, S.L. (1999) 'From paper and pen to screen and keyboard: towards a methodology for survey research on the Internet', *in* Jones, S., *Doing Internet Research*, Thousand Oaks, CA, Sage, pp. 145–62.

Wright Mills, C. (1970) 'On intellectual craftsmanship', *in The Sociological Imagination*, London, Pelican, pp. 239–40.

Yin, R.K. (1994) *Case Study Research: Design and Methods* (2nd edn), Beverly Hills, CA, Sage.

Youngman, M.B. (1986) *Analysing Questionnaires*, Nottingham, University of Nottingham School of Education.

Zikmund, W.G. (2000) *Business Research Methods* (6th edn), Fort Worth, TX, Dryden Press.

Zuber-Skerritt, O. (1996) 'Emancipatory action research for organisational change and management development, *in* Zuber-Skerritt, O. (ed.), *New Directions in Action Research*, London, Falmer, pp. 83–105.

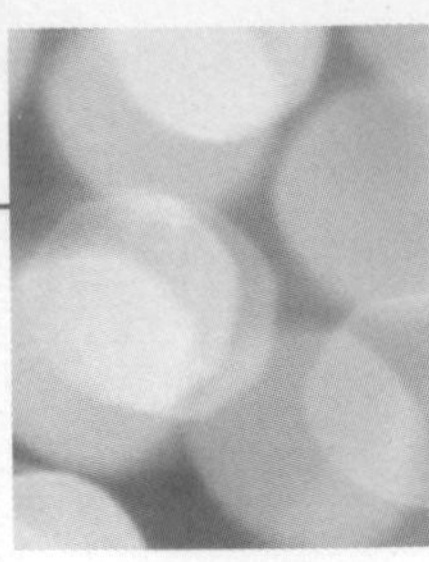

Appendix 1

Example research project titles

The following titles are included to help stimulate possible research ideas. You should not take the inclusion of a title as an indication of the quality of the title or any associated research project.

Accountability of accountants

Competitor strategies in the mortgage market

Do the new direct methods of selling financial services pose a major threat to existing providers and, if so, what impact will this have in the future?

Does activity-based costing give companies a competitive edge?

FRSI: are cash flow statements a useful vehicle for conveying relevant and clear information about a business's liquidity and financial viability?

Has the introduction of the self-regulatory organisation (PIA) brought about better advice for the public?

How do financial services market to the 'youth' market?

In 1995 England had a total of 80 building societies. In 20 years' time, how many will still exist?

Insider dealing: the development of the criminal law and an evaluation of alternative approaches

Is the demand for pension products increasing from the female sector, and if so how are life assurance companies reacting to this change?

An assessment of the potential of a major domestic and industrial food manufacturer within the children's confectionery market

The acquisition of mortgage books – managing change

The cashless society – imminent reality or impossible dream?

The change of banks and building societies to public companies

The changing face/future of banks and building societies with regard to products and services

The impact of developments in IT on financial services

The impact on the financial management of NHS hospitals with the granting of 'trust' status: case study

The implementation of principles of sound corporate governance within organisations

The implications of introducing compulsory competitive tendering to white collar services within local government: a critical evaluation

The importance of group personal pensions to individual employees at an organisation compared with company pension schemes

The use and application of purchasing within the organisation

With ever-increasing improvements in modern technology, will a career in accountancy become a thing of the past?

Commercial organisations and the green consumer phenomenon

Has the National Lottery had a detrimental impact on the fund-raising of charitable bodies?

Global warming: what does it mean for commercial insurers?

Green revolution in the consumer goods market – a consumer-led phenomenon or the marketing industry's profit-making creation?

The impact of ozone depletion and the greenhouse warming effect on the marketing policies of the domestic refrigeration industry in recent years

The relationship between tobacco advertising and sport on television – can it be justified?

Why is there a need for a standard definition of 'cruelty free', and to what extent does the cosmetic and toiletry industry's definition correspond to the consumer's preferred interpretation?

A comparison of recruitment and selection procedures used in the UK and elsewhere in Europe

A study of the role of human resources today and its effectiveness – is there a real future for it?

Age discrimination in the workplace

An investigation into how skills are acquired on an outdoor management development course and transferred to the workplace

Corporate strategy and planning: the role of the personnel department in its formulation

Disability awareness training within leisure organisations: a case study

Equal opportunities: a marketing and recruitment concept or a reality?

From job interview to promoting a business – how effective is marketing yourself?

Graduates' job attribute preferences: to what extent can they be explained by Maslow's hierarchy of needs?

Internal communications – what role does it have within the organisation of the future?

Investors in people – an investigation into how IIP is introduced in organisations in order to gain staff support for IIP

Is personality testing a valid tool in the recruitment and selection process?

Honesty and integrity testing and the security industry

How important is employee communication today?

Performance appraisal: a review of the benefits

Psychometric testing – an effective way for selection?

Racial discrimination in recruitment and selection

Recruitment on the Internet – is this a step forward in the recruitment process or just the new fad?

Stress – the cost to employers

The armed forces, equal opportunities and equality

The changing role of HRM

The effectiveness of middle management on a culture change

The extended interview technique and its validity as a method of selection

To what extent can 'teleworking' benefit the relocating organisation?

Human resource management and outsourcing

Workplace harassment and bullying: causes and effects and the need for organisations to protect their employees from behavioural excesses

A critical review of the prospects for interactive services to the home and the implications for marketing strategy

A study of the influence of information technology on management development – implementation of IT policy

Has modern technology destroyed customer services within the financial services sector?

How can information technology aid marketing communications?

Preparing for the worst – an investigation into the need for and methods of backing up business computer files

RSI in the workplace: a study of causation and management

The development and relationship of office automation, information technology strategies and their impact on the use of information technology: a case study

A woman's place – an investigation of the factors that facilitate the achievement of equal opportunities

Great British culture versus women in manufacturing

Women in management – the glass ceiling

Opportunity 2000 addressing the barriers to women's progress in organisations: a critical evaluation of current theories and practice

The rise in the number of female entrepreneurs: why is it happening and what problems are they facing?

A comparative study of marketing techniques adopted by body-building supplement manufacturers

A consideration of the promotional strategies and tools used in achieving greater sales in retail organisations

A critical evaluation of strategic planning and marketing techniques used in the public sector recreation provision

A study of global brands: what makes them and what can break them?

A study on the evolution of the use of target marketing in the media, entertainment and show business

Airline marketing – is there a difference between what business travellers want and what is promoted to them?

An analysis into the marketing methods employed by a professional football club

An investigation into branding within the new premium bottled lager market

An investigation into marketing activity aimed at children

An investigation into market segmentation. Has social group E developed from previous ideas?

An investigation into the marketing techniques employed by the motor industry in the UK

Marketing in the NHS – is it an alien concept?

Marketing is an essential aspect of successful tourism. How can competitive analysis of similar companies improve one's product and maximise sales?

Marketing of non-profit-making organisations

Marketing the changing face of licensed premises

Marketing tourism in urban areas – a comparison of Gloucester and Bradford

The role of loyalty schemes in grocery retailing and their effectiveness as part of a relationship marketing strategy

Benefits and disbenefits of press and radio advertising to small businesses

Brands marketing, positioning – launching of new brands

Can a leading retailer rely on their name to sell pensions?

Do marketers exploit customers through manipulative marketing?

Measurement of results within the marketing mix. Can public relations be accurately compared with the other marketing disciplines?

Employee rights in the event of transfers of undertakings: an examination of local government

Global advertising: a review?

How can small businesses produce an effective marketing plan given the limited resources available?

How effective is billboard advertising within the UK?

How have Eurotunnel advertised, and has this been successful in affecting people's perceptions of cross-Channel travel?

How marketers use sex to sell advertising

Justification for marketing in the food industry

Niche marketing in the service industry – when a niche market ceases to become a niche market!

The effectiveness of marketing and PR in the manufacturing industry and the place of PR in the marketing mix

What are the problems of marketing a 'services' product such as insurance, compared with that of a tangible product?

Why do businesses sponsor sport?

Are quality assurance and total quality management a cost or a benefit for professional service firms?

Benchmarking: a critical evaluation

Is it possible to achieve total quality management and a high level of customer service within a commercial vehicle supplier?

Is there a link between benchmarking and total quality management (TQM)?

Quality initiatives within the insurance industry

Quality management and BS5750 in small to medium manufacturing enterprises

The digital revolution – a case study examining the Xerox Corporation in the light of the digital explosion

A study of the industrial branch, examining its past, its present and its future

An evaluation of the extent to which language training equips managers to better understand foreign business cultures

An investigation into how the management of technical and cultural change can have an effect on the organisation

An investigation into management buy-outs/buy-ins within the UK economy

A comparative analysis of offshore companies in Cyprus and the Isle of Man

Can JIT be successfully implemented within service organisations?

Compulsory competitive tendering in local government

Could UK export capabilities in the Asian region be improved by gaining an understanding of their national cultures?

Competition in the parcel delivery industry

Funding of NHS and private health care

How beneficial is management consultancy to the manufacturing industry?

How have the theories of the quality gurus developed into the standards employed by a pharmaceutical printing firm?

Britain's future within the EU: is full economic and monetary union in the national interest?

Is the British film industry beyond recovery?

Japanese investment and economic regeneration in South Wales

Quality systems in the insurance industry

Selling to the Japanese: a critical evaluation of current theories and practice for successful market entry

The brewing industry – why did the investigation by the Monopolies and Mergers Commission have such a big impact on the industry?

The development of mail order/home shopping: a case study

The flexible organisation. Is it a myth or reality?

The impact of charging for sport for 'fun'

Strategy for shareholder value

Survival of the fittest: a comparison between local independent and national/ international music outlets

What are the consequences of the trade war in the yellow fat market?

Will a single European currency benefit British business?

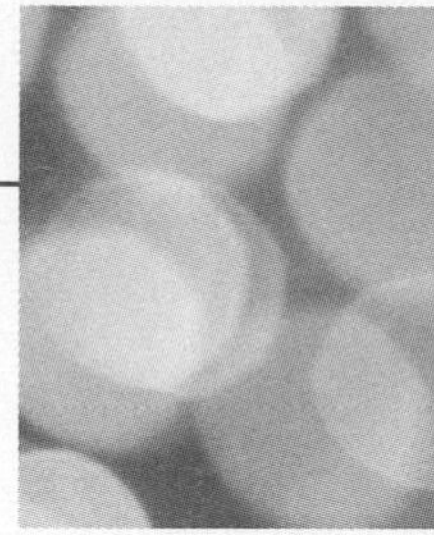

Appendix 2

Systems of referencing

Four points are important when referencing:

- Credit must be given when quoting or citing other work.
- Adequate information must be provided to enable a reader to locate each reference.
- References must be consistent and complete.
- References must be recorded in the precise format required by your university.

The Harvard system

Referencing in the text

The *Harvard system* is an *author–date system*, a variation of which we use in this book. It was developed at Harvard University in the 1930s (Anderson and Poole, 2001) and usually uses the author's name and year of publication to identify cited documents within the text. The system for referencing work in the text is outlined in Table A2.1.

Referencing in the references or bibliography

In the references or bibliography the publications are listed alphabetically by author's name, and all authors' surnames and initials are listed in full. If there is more than one work by the same author, these are listed chronologically. The system for referencing work in the references or bibliography is outlined in Table A2.2. While it would be impossible for us to include an example of every type of reference you might need to include, the information contained in this table should enable you to work out the required format for all your references.

For copies of journal articles from printed journals that you have obtained electronically via the Internet it is usually acceptable to reference these using exactly the same format as printed journal articles (Table A2.2), provided you have obtained and read a facsimile (exact) copy of the article. Exact copies of journal articles have precisely the same format as the printed version, including page numbering, tables and diagrams. They are usually obtained by downloading the article via the Internet as a file that can be read on the screen and printed using Adobe Acrobat Reader.

Finally, remember to include a, b, c etc. immediately after the date when you are referencing different publications by the same author from the same year. Do not forget to ensure that these are consistent with the letters used for the references in the main text.

Table A2.1 Using the Harvard system to reference in the text

To refer to	*Use the general format*	*For example*
A single author	(Surname date)	(Saunders 1993)
Dual authors	(Surname and Surname date)	(Saunders and Cooper 1993)
More than two authors	(Surname *et al.* date)	(Slack *et al.* 1996)
Work by different authors generally	(Surname date; Surname date) in alphabetical order	(Baker 1996; Lewis 1998; Thornhill 1997)
Different authors with the same surname	(Surname, Initial date)	(Smith, J 1998)
Different publications by the same author	(Surname date; date) in ascending date order	(Lewis 1991; 1998)
Different publications by the same author from the same year	(Surname date letter), make sure the letter is consistent throughout	(Forster 1991a)
An author referred to by another author where the original has not been read (*secondary reference*)	(Surname date; cited by Surname date)	(Granovetter 1974; cited by Saunders 1993)
A corporate author	(Corporate name date)	(Hanson Trust plc 1990)
A newspaper article with no obvious author	(Newspaper name date)	(*The Guardian* 2002)
Another type of publication with no obvious author	(Publication title date)	(*Labour Market Trends* 2001)
An Internet site	(Site title date)	(Advertising Association 1999)
A publication for which the year of publication cannot be identified	(Surname or Corporate name nd), where 'nd' means no date (Surname or Corporate name, c. date) where 'c.' means circa	(Woollons nd) (Hattersley c. 1977)
A direct quotation	(Surname or Corporate name date, p. number) where 'p.' means 'page' and number is the page in the original publication on which the quotation appears	'The Harvard method, which I use in this book, has a number of advantages over other methods' (Bell 1999, p. 51)

The American Psychological Association (APA) system

The *American Psychological Association system* or *APA system* is a variation on the author–date system. Like the Harvard system it dates from the 1930s and 1940s, and has been updated subsequently. The latest updates are outlined in the latest edition of the American Psychological Association's (2001) *Publication Manual of the American*

Table A2.2 Using the Harvard system to reference in the references or bibliography

To reference		*Use the general format*	*For example*
Books and chapters in books	Book (first edition)	Surname, Initials and Surname, Initials (date) *Title*, Publisher, Place of publication	Saunders, MNK and Cooper, SA (1993) *Understanding Business Statistics*, DP Publications Ltd, London
	Book (other than first edition)	Surname, Initials and Surname, Initials (date) *Title* (? edn), Publisher, Place of publication	Morris, C (1999) *Quantitative Approaches to Business Studies* (5th edn), Financial Times Pitman Publishing, London.
	Book (no obvious author)	Corporate name or Publication name (date) *Title*, Publisher, Place of publication	Mintel Marketing Intelligence (1998) *Designerwear: Mintel Marketing Intelligence Report,* Mintel International Group Ltd., London
	Chapter in a book	Surname, Initials and Surname, Initials (date) *Title*, Publisher, Place of publication, Chapter ?	Robson, C (2002) *Real World Research* (2nd edn), Blackwell, Oxford, Chapter 3.
	Chapter in an edited book	Surname, Initials (date) 'Chapter title', *in* Surname, Initials and Surname, Initials (eds), *Title*, Publisher, Place of publication, page numbers	Craig, PB (1991) 'Designing and using mail questionnaires' *in* Smith, NC and Dainty, P (eds), *The Management Research Handbook*, Routledge, London, pp. 181–9
Journal articles	Journal article	Surname, Initials and Surname, Initials (date) 'Title of article', *Journal name*, volume number, part number, pages	Storey, J, Cressey, P, Morris, T and Wilkinson, A (1997) 'Changing employment practices in UK banking: case studies', *Personnel Review*, 26:1, 24–42
	Journal article (no obvious author)	Corporate name or Publication name (date) 'Title of article', *Journal name*, volume number, part number, pages	Local Government Chronicle (1993) 'Westminster poised for return to AMA fold', *Local Government Chronicle*, 5 November, p. 5
Government publications	Parliamentary papers including acts and bills	Country of origin (date) *Title*, Publisher, Place of publication	Great Britain (1994) *Criminal Justice and Public Order Act 1994*, HMSO, London
	Others (with authors)	As for books	As for books
	Others (no obvious authors)	Department name or Committee name (date) *Title*, Publisher, Place of publication	Department of Trade and Industry (1992) *The Single Market: Europe Open for Professions, UK Implementation*, HMSO, London
Newspapers, including CD-ROM databases	Newspaper article	Surname, Initials and Surname, Initials (date) 'Title of article', *Newspaper name*, place of printing, day, month, pages	Roberts, D (1998) 'BAe sells property wing for £301m', *The Daily Telegraph*, London, 10 October, p. 31

►

Table A2.2 (continued)

To reference		*Use the general format*	*For example*
Newspapers including CD-Rom databases continued	Newspaper article (no obvious author)	Newspaper name (date) 'Title of article', *Newspaper name*, place of printing, day, month, pages	Guardian (1992) 'Fraud trial at Britannia Theme Park', *The Guardian*, Manchester, 5 February, p. 4
	Newspaper article (from CD-ROM database)	Newspaper name or Surname, Initials (date) 'Title of article', *Newspaper name* (CD-ROM), day, month, pages	Financial Times (1998) 'Recruitment: lessons in leadership: moral issues are increasingly pertinent to the military and top corporate ranks', *Financial Times* (CD-ROM), London, 11 March, p. 32
Other CD-ROM publications		Title of CD-ROM or Surname, Initials (date) (CD-ROM), Publisher, Place of publication	Encarta 98 Encyclopaedia (1997) (CD-ROM), Microsoft, Redmond, WA
Unpublished conference papers		Surname, Initials and Surname, Initials (date) 'Title of paper', *paper presented at the Conference name*, days, month, location of conference	Saunders, MNK, Thornhill, A and Lewis P (2001)'Employees' reactions to the management of change: an exploration from an organisational justice framework', *paper presented at the Eighth Annual International Conference on Advances in Management*, 11–14 July, Athens
Letters, personal emails and electronic conferences/ bulletin boards	Letter	Surname, Initials and Surname, Initials (date) 'Unpublished letter: Subject matter'	MacClelland, S (1998) 'Unpublished letter: Reviewer's feedback'
	Personal email	Surname, Initials (date) 'Subject matter' (email to the author) (online)	MacClelland, S (1998) 'Reviewer's feedback' (email to the author) (online)
	Electronic conference/ Bulletin Boards	Surname, Initials (date) Subject matter, *name of electronic conference/bulletin board* [online]	Jones, K (1999), 101 reasons why we need the pound, Britain and European Monetary Union [online]
Internet items excluding emails	Journal published on the Internet	‹URL:http://www. remainder of full Internet electronic conference/bulletin board›	‹URL:http://www.stingray.ivision. co.uk/groups/emu/frindex.htm›
	Journal article published on the Internet	Surname, Initials and Surname, Initials (date) 'Title of article', *journal name*, volume number, part number [online] (cited day month year) Available from ‹URL:http://www. remainder of full Internet address›.	Illingworth, N (2001) 'The Internet matters: exploring the use of the Internet as a research tool', *Sociological Research Online* 6:2, [online] (cited 20 March 2002) Available from ‹URL:http://www. socresonline.org.uk/6/2/ illingworth.html›

Table A2.2 (continued)

To reference		*Use the general format*	*For example*
Internet items excluding emails continued	Internet site/specific site pages	Site title (date) 'Title of page within site where applicable' [online] (cited day month year) Available from ‹URL:http://www. remainder of full Internet address›	Chartered Institute of Personnel and Development [online] (cited 7 January 2002) Available from ‹URL:http://www.cipd.co.uk›
	Internet article	Surname, Initials and Surname Initials (date) 'Title of article' [online] (cited day month year) Available from ‹URL:http://www. remainder of full internet address›	Jones A and Smith A (eds) (2001) 'What exactly is the Labour Force Survey? [online] (cited 20 December 2001) Available from ‹URL:http//www.statistics.gov.uk/nsbase/downloads.theme_labour/what_exactly_is_LFS1.pdf›

Psychological Association, which is likely to be available for reference in your university's library.

Relatively small but significant differences exist between the Harvard and APA systems, and many authors adopt a combination of the two systems. The key differences are outlined in Table A2.3.

Table A2.3 Key differences between Harvard and APA systems of referencing

Harvard system	*APA system*	*Comment*
Referencing in the text		
(Lewis 2001)	(Lewis, 2001)	Note punctuation
(Saunders and Williams 2001)	(Saunders & Williams, 2001)	'&' not 'and'
(Williams *et al.* 1999)	(Williams, Saunders & Staughton, 1999)	For 1st occurrence
(Williams *et al.* 1999)	(Williams *et. al.*, 1999)	For subsequent occurrences; note punctuation
Referencing in the references or bibliography		
Thornhill A, Lewis P, Millmore M and Saunders MNK (2000) *Managing Change: A Human Resource Strategy Approach*, FT Prentice Hall, Harlow	Thornhill, A., Lewis, P., Millmore, M. & Saunders, M.N.K. (2000) *Managing change: A human resource strategy approach.* Harlow: FT Prentice Hall.	Note full stops and commas; Note use of 'and', '&' Note use of capitals in title Note order, use of colon, comma and full stop

Footnotes

Referencing in the text

When using *footnotes*, sometimes referred to as the *Vancouver system*, references within the research report are shown by a number. This number refers directly to the references, and it means it is not necessary for you to include the authors' names or date of publication:

'Recent research[1] indicates that . . .'

Referencing in the references

These list sequentially the referenced works in the order they are referred to in your research report. This can be useful as it enables you to include comments and footnotes as well as the references (Jankowicz, 2000). It does, however, mean that the references are unlikely to be in alphabetical order. When using the footnotes system you need to ensure that:

- the layout of individual references is the same as that for the Harvard system (Table A2.2), other than that they are preceded by a number, for example:

  1 Ritzer, G (1996) *The McDonaldization of Society* (revised edn), Thousand Oaks, CA, Pine Forge Press

- the publications referred to include only those you have cited in your report. They should therefore be headed 'References' rather than 'Bibliography';
- you refer to the same item more than once using standard bibliographic abbreviations to save repeating the reference in full (Table A2.4).

Table A2.4 **Bibliographic abbreviations**

Abbreviation	*Explanation*	*For example*
op. cit. ***(opere citato)***	Meaning 'in the work cited'. This refers to a work previously referenced, and so you must give the author and date and, if necessary, the page number.	Robson (1993) *op. cit.* pp. 23–4
loc. cit. ***(loco citato)***	Meaning 'in the place cited'. This refers to the same page of a work previously referenced, and so you must give the author and date.	Robson (1993) *loc. cit.*
ibid. ***(ibidem)***	Meaning 'the same work given immediately before'. This refers to the work referenced immediately before, and replaces all details of the previous reference other than a page number if necessary.	*ibid.*

References

American Psychological Association (2001) *Publication Manual of the American Psychological Association* (5th edn), Washington, American Psychological Association.

Anderson, J. and Poole, M. (2001) *Assignment and Thesis Writing* (4th edn), Brisbane, John Wiley and Sons.

Further reading

American Psychological Association (2001) *Publication Manual of the American Psychological Association* (5th edn), Washington, American Psychological Association. The most recent version of this manual contains full details of how to use this form of the author–date system of referencing as well as how to lay out tables, figures, equations and other statistical data. It also provides guidance on grammar and writing.

Anderson, J. and Poole, M. (2001) *Assignment and Thesis Writing*, (4th edn), Brisbane, John Wiley and Sons. Chapter 13 provides a thorough, up-to-date discussion of the layout required for a wide range of information sources using the Harvard, American Psychological Association and footnotes referencing systems.

Branscomb, H.E. (1998) *Casting Your Net: A Student's Guide to Research on the Internet*, Boston, MA, Allyn and Bacon. Appendix 2 provides a detailed discussion of documenting a wide range of sources from the Internet.

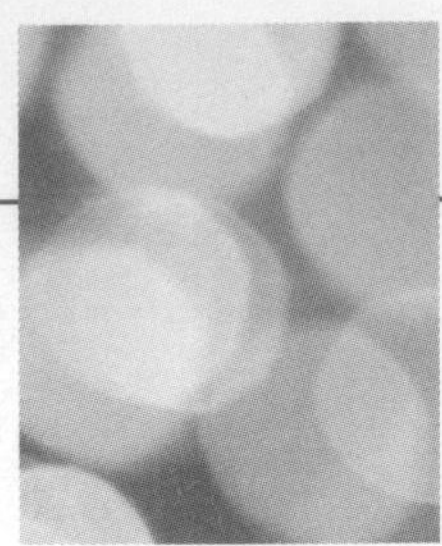

Appendix 3

Calculating the minimum sample size

In some situations, such as experimental research, it is necessary for you to calculate the precise *minimum sample size* you require. This calculation assumes that data will be collected from all cases in the sample and is based on:

- how confident you need to be that the estimate is accurate (the *level of confidence* in the estimate);
- how accurate the estimate needs to be (the *margin of error* that can be tolerated);
- the proportion of responses you expect to have some particular attribute.

Provided that you know the level of confidence and the margin of error it is relatively easy to estimate the proportion of responses you expect to have a particular attribute. To do this, ideally you need to collect a pilot sample of about 30 observations and from this to infer the likely proportion for your main survey. It is therefore important that the pilot sample uses the same methods as your main survey. Alternatively you might have undertaken a very similar survey and so already have a reasonable idea of the likely proportion. If you do not, then you need either to make an informed guess or to assume that 50 per cent of the sample will have the specified attribute – the worst scenario. Most surveys will involve collecting data on more than one attribute. deVaus (2002) argues that for such multi-purpose surveys you should determine the sample size on the basis of those variables in the sample that are likely to have the greatest variability.

Once you have all the information you substitute it into the formula

$$n = p\% \times q\% \times \left[\frac{z}{e\%}\right]^2$$

where n is the minimum sample size required
$p\%$ is the proportion belonging to the specified category
$q\%$ is the proportion not belonging to the specified category
z is the z value corresponding to the level of confidence required (see Table A3.1)
$e\%$ is the margin of error required.

Table A3.1 Levels of confidence and associated *z* values

Level of confidence	*z value*
90% certain	1.65
95% certain	1.96
99% certain	2.57

Where your population is less than 10 000 a smaller sample size can be used without affecting the accuracy. This is called the *adjusted minimum sample size*. It is calculated using the following formula:

$$n' = \frac{n}{1 + \left(\frac{n}{N}\right)}$$

where n' is the adjusted minimum sample size
n is the minimum sample size (as calculated above)
N is the total population.

worked example

Calculating the minimum sample size

To answer a research question you need to estimate the proportion of a total population of 4000 home care clients who receive a visit from their home care assistant at least once a week. You have been told that you need to be 95 per cent certain that the 'estimate' is accurate (the level of confidence in the estimate); this corresponds to a z score of 1.96 (Table A3.1). You have also been told that your 'estimate' needs to be accurate to within plus or minus 5 per cent of the true percentage (the margin of error that can be tolerated).

You still need to estimate the proportion of responses who receive a visit from their home care assistant at least once a week. From your pilot survey you discover that 12 out of the 30 clients receive a visit at least once a week – in other words, that 40 per cent belong to the specified category. This means that 60 per cent do not.

These figures can then be substituted into the formula:

$$\begin{aligned} n &= 40 \times 60 \times \left(\frac{1.96}{5}\right)^2 \\ &= 2400 \times (0.392)^2 \\ &= 2400 \times 0.154 \\ &= 369.6 \end{aligned}$$

Your minimum sample size is therefore 370 returns.

As the total population of home care clients is 4000 the adjusted minimum sample size can now be calculated:

$$\begin{aligned} n' &= \frac{369.6}{1 + \left(\frac{369.6}{4000}\right)} \\ &= \frac{369.6}{1 + 0.092} \\ &= \frac{369.6}{1.092} \\ &= 338.46 \end{aligned}$$

Because of the small total population you need a minimum sample size of only 339. However, this assumes a response rate of 100 per cent.

Reference

deVaus, D.A. (2002) *Surveys in Social Research* (5th edn), London, Routledge.

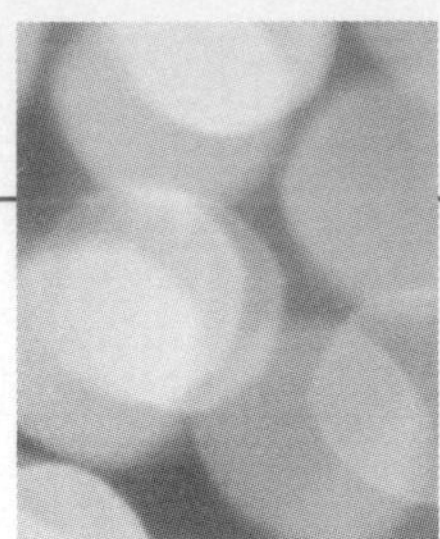

Appendix 4

Random sampling numbers

78 41	11 62	72 18	66 69	58 71	31 90	51 36	78 09	41 00
70 50	58 19	68 26	75 69	04 00	25 29	16 72	35 73	55 85
32 78	14 47	01 55	10 91	83 21	13 32	59 53	03 38	79 32
71 60	20 53	86 78	50 57	42 30	73 48	68 09	16 35	21 87
35 30	15 57	99 96	33 25	56 43	65 67	51 45	37 99	54 89
09 08	05 41	66 54	01 49	97 34	38 85	85 23	34 62	60 58
02 59	34 51	98 71	31 54	28 85	23 84	49 07	33 71	17 88
20 13	44 15	22 95	98 97	60 02	85 07	17 57	20 51	01 67
36 26	70 11	63 81	27 31	79 71	08 11	87 74	85 53	86 78
00 30	62 19	81 68	86 10	65 61	62 22	17 22	96 83	56 37
38 41	14 59	53 03	52 86	21 88	55 87	85 59	14 90	74 87
18 89	40 84	71 04	09 82	54 44	94 23	83 89	04 59	38 29
34 38	85 56	80 74	22 31	26 39	65 63	12 38	45 75	30 35
55 90	21 71	17 88	20 08	57 64	17 93	22 34	00 55	09 78
81 43	53 96	96 88	36 86	04 33	31 40	18 71	06 00	51 45
59 69	13 03	38 31	77 08	71 20	23 28	92 43	92 63	21 74
60 24	47 44	73 93	64 37	64 97	19 82	27 59	24 20	00 04
17 04	93 46	05 70	20 95	42 25	33 95	78 80	07 57	86 58
09 55	42 30	27 05	27 93	78 10	69 11	29 56	29 79	28 66
46 69	28 64	81 02	41 89	12 03	31 20	25 16	79 93	28 22
28 94	00 91	16 15	35 12	68 93	23 71	11 55	64 56	76 95
59 10	06 29	83 84	03 68	97 65	59 21	58 54	61 59	30 54
41 04	70 71	05 56	76 66	57 86	29 30	11 31	56 76	24 13
09 81	81 80	73 10	10 23	26 29	61 15	50 00	76 37	60 16
91 55	76 68	06 82	05 33	06 75	92 35	82 21	78 15	19 43
82 69	36 73	58 69	10 92	31 14	21 08	13 78	56 53	97 77
03 59	65 34	32 06	63 43	38 04	65 30	32 82	57 05	33 95
03 96	30 87	81 54	69 39	95 69	95 69	89 33	78 90	30 07
39 91	27 38	20 90	41 10	10 80	59 68	93 10	85 25	59 25
89 93	92 10	59 40	26 14	27 47	39 51	46 70	86 85	76 02
99 16	73 21	39 05	03 36	87 58	18 52	61 61	02 92	07 24
93 13	20 70	42 59	77 69	35 59	71 80	61 95	82 96	48 84
47 32	87 68	97 86	28 51	61 21	33 02	79 65	59 49	89 93
09 75	58 00	72 49	36 58	19 45	30 61	87 74	43 01	93 91
63 24	15 65	02 05	32 92	45 61	35 43	67 64	94 45	95 66
33 58	69 42	25 71	74 31	88 80	04 50	22 60	72 01	27 88
23 25	22 78	24 88	68 48	83 60	53 59	73 73	82 43	82 66
07 17	77 20	79 37	50 08	29 79	55 13	51 90	36 77	68 69
16 07	31 84	57 22	29 54	35 14	22 22	22 60	72 15	40 90
67 90	79 28	62 83	44 96	87 70	40 64	27 22	60 19	52 54
79 52	74 68	69 74	31 75	80 59	29 28	21 69	15 97	35 88
69 44	31 09	16 38	92 82	12 25	10 57	81 32	76 71	31 61
09 47	57 04	54 00	78 75	91 99	26 20	36 19	53 29	11 55
74 78	09 25	95 80	25 72	88 85	76 02	29 89	70 78	93 84

Source: Morris (1999), reproduced by permission

Appendix 5

Guidelines for non-discriminatory language

Writing in a non-discriminatory manner is important in all areas of business and management. For example, in Section 13.5 we noted how the use of language that assumes the gender of a group of people, such as referring to a clerical assistant as 'she', not only is inaccurate but also gives offence to people of both sexes. Similar care needs to be exercised when using other gender-based terms, referring to people from different ethnic groups, and writing about people with disabilities. Without this, the language used may be prejudiced, oppressive, offensive, unfair or even incorrect. The impact of this is summarised clearly by Bill Bryson (1995: 425) in his book *Made in America* when he observes: '. . . at the root of the bias-free language movement lies a commendable sentiment: to make language less wounding or demeaning to those whose sex, race, physical condition or circumstances leave them vulnerable to the raw power of words.'

Therefore, although the task of changing the language you use may seem difficult at first, it is important that you do so in order that your communication is accurate, and unbiased, and does not cause offence.

Guidelines for gender

When referring to both sexes it is inappropriate to use the terms 'men' or 'women' and their gender-based equivalents. Some of the more common alternatives are listed in Table A5.1.

Table A5.1 Gender-specific terms and gender-neutral alternatives

Gender-specific term	*Gender-neutral alternative*
Chairman	Chair, chairperson
Forefathers	Ancestors
Foreman	Supervisor
Layman	Lay person
Man	Person
Mankind	Humanity, people
Man-made	Manufactured, synthetic
Manning	Resourcing, staffing
Manpower	Human resources, labour, staff, workforce
Master copy	Original, top copy
Policeman	Police officer
Policewoman	Police officer
Women	People

Source: Developed from British Psychological Society (1988)

Guidelines for ethnicity

Attention needs to be paid when referring to different ethnic groups. This is especially important where the term used refers to a number of ethnic groups. For example, the term 'Asian' includes a number of diverse ethnic groups that can be recognised with the terms 'Asian peoples' or Asian communities'. Similarly, the diversity of people represented by the term 'Black' can be recognised by referring to 'Black peoples' or 'Black communities'. Where possible the individual groups within these communities should be identified separately.

'Black' as a term used to be regarded as offensive. More recently it has acquired connotations of unity against racism and has been reclaimed as a source of pride and identity. 'Afro-Caribbean' is a term that is also associated with a commitment to anti-racism and is used to describe black people from the Caribbean islands.

Other terms that are regarded as offensive include 'coloured', 'half-caste', 'mixed race', 'Negress', 'Negro' and 'West Indian'.

If you are unsure of the term to use then ask someone from the appropriate community for the most acceptable current term. In addition, you need to try to ensure that the language you are using is not inadvertently reinforcing racism or xenophobia.

Table A5.2 Disability language: what to avoid and preferences

Avoid	*Preference*	*Comment*
The disabled	Disabled people, people with disabilities	Individuals often have strong preferences, so ask
The blind	Blind people, people who are blind, people with a visual impairment	'Blind' on its own is dehumanising and distancing
The deaf	Deaf people, people who have a hearing impairment, the deaf community	'Deaf' and other collective names on their own are dehumanising and distancing
The handicapped	People with impairments, disabled students, employees with disabilities	'Handicapped' is regarded as outdated by many
Mentally handicapped	Person with learning difficulties	'Mentally handicapped' is regarded as offensive and inaccurate
An epileptic, epileptics	Person who has epilepsy	'Epileptic' implies a medical condition rather than a person
Spastic	Person who has cerebral palsy	'Spastic' is both inaccurate and offensive
Dumb/mute	Unable to speak, having a speech impairment	'Dumb' implies stupid
Wheelchair-bound	Wheelchair user	Conveys helplessness when wheelchair aids mobility
Victim of, afflicted by, suffering from	Person who has	Makes assumption of tragedy, reinforces ideas of dependence or frailty

Source: Developed from Pointon, G. (no date)

Guidelines for disability

Disability is an area where terminology is constantly changing as people voice their own preferences. Despite this, guidelines can be offered for the more common terms. These are summarised in Table A5.2. However, if you are unsure of the term to use, ask someone from the appropriate group for the most acceptable current term.

References

British Psychological Society (1988) 'Guidelines for the use of non-sexist language', *The Psychologist*, 1:2, 53–4. This offers useful advice about the use of non-sexist language.

Bryson, B. (1995) *Made in America*, London, Minerva.

Pointon, G. (no date) *Disability and Television: Guidelines on Representation for Producers*, London, Channel 4.

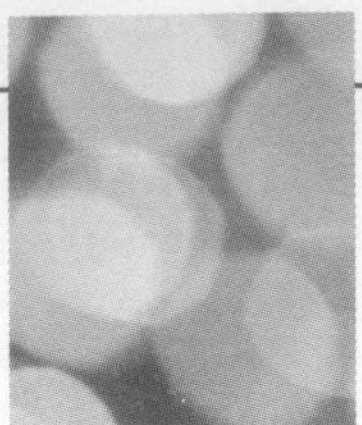

Glossary

abstract (1) Summary, usually of an article or book, also containing sufficient information for the original to be located. (2) Summary of the complete content of the project report.

access (1) The process involved in gaining entry into an organisation to undertake research. (2) The situation where a research participant is willing to share data with a researcher. *See also* cognitive access, continuing access, physical access.

action research Research strategy concerned with the management of a change and involving close collaboration between practitioners and researchers. The results flowing from action research should also inform other contexts.

active response rate The total number of responses divided by the total number in the sample after ineligible and unreachable respondents have been excluded. *See* ineligible respondent, unreachable respondent.

active voice The voice in which the action of the verb is attributed to the person. For example, 'I conducted interviews'.

analysis The ability to break down data and to clarify the nature of the component parts and the relationship between them.

analysis of variance Statistical test to determine the probability (likelihood) that the values of a quantifiable data variable for three or more independent samples or groups are different. The test assesses the likelihood of any difference between these groups occurring by chance alone.

analytic induction Analysis of qualitative data that involves the iterative examination of a number of strategically selected cases to identify the cause of a particular phenomenon.

analytic reflection The process of enquiry often used in the participant as observer role whereby key informants are encouraged to reflect analytically on the processes in which they are involved. This stems from the fact that research subjects know the identity of the researcher and, consequently, the researcher asks questions of those subjects promoting in the research subjects the process of analytic reflection. *See also* participant as observer.

ANOVA *See* analysis of variance.

appendix A supplement to the project report. It should not normally include material that is essential for the understanding of the report itself, but additional relevant material in which the reader may be interested.

application The ability to apply certain principles and rules in particular situations.

applied research Research of direct and immediate relevance to practitioners that addresses issues they see as important and is presented in ways they can understand and act upon.

attribute variable Variable that records data about respondents' characteristics, in other words things they possess.

bar chart Diagram for showing frequency distributions for a categorical or grouped discrete data variable, which highlights the highest and lowest values.

base period The period against which index numbers are calculated to facilitate comparisons of trends or changes over time. *See also* index number.

basic research Research undertaken purely to understand processes and their outcomes, predominantly in universities as a result of an academic agenda, for which the key consumer is the academic community.

behaviour variable Variable that records what respondents actually do.

bibliographic details The information needed to enable readers to find original items consulted or used for a research project. These normally include the author, date of publication, title of article, title of book or journal. Full details are given in Table 3.6.

bibliography Alphabetical list of the bibliographic details for all relevant items consulted and used, including those items not referred to directly in the text. The university will specify the format of these.

Boolean logic System by which the variety of items found in a search based on logical propositions that can be either true or false can be combined, limited or widened.

box plot Diagram that provides a pictorial representation of the distribution of the data for a variable and statistics such as median, inter-quartile range, and the highest and lowest values.

brainstorming Technique that can be used to generate and refine research ideas. It is best undertaken with a group of people.

broker *See* gatekeeper.

case (1) Individual element or group member within a sample or population such as an employee. (2) Individual unit for which data have been collected.

case study Research strategy that involves the empirical investigation of a particular contemporary phenomenon within its real-life context, using multiple sources of evidence.

categorical data Data whose values cannot be measured numerically but can either be classified into sets (categories) or placed in rank order.

category question Closed question in which the respondent is offered a set of mutually exclusive categories and instructed to select one.

causal relationship Relationship between two or more variables in which the change (effect) in one variable is caused by the other variable(s).

census The collection and analysis of data from every possible case or group member in a population.

central tendency measure The generic term for statistics that can be used to provide an impression of those values for a variable that are common, middling or average.

chi square test Statistical test to determine the probability (likelihood) that two categorical data variables are associated. A common use is to discover whether there are statistically significant differences between the observed frequencies and the expected frequencies of two variables presented in a cross-tabulation.

closed question Question that provides a number of alternative answers from which the respondent is instructed to choose.

cluster sampling Probability sampling procedure in which the population is divided into discrete groups or clusters prior to sampling. A random sample (systematic or simple) of these clusters is then drawn.

codebook Complete list of all the codes used to code data variables.

code of ethics Statement of principles and procedures for the design and conduct of research. *See also* privacy, research ethics, research ethics committee.

coefficient of determination *See* regression coefficient.

coefficient of variation Statistic that compares the extent of spread of data values around the mean between two or more variables containing quantifiable data.

cognitive access The process of gaining access to data from intended participants. This involves participants agreeing to be interviewed or observed, within agreed limits. *See also* informed consent.

cohort study Study that collects data from the same cases over time using a series of 'snapshots'.

comparative proportional pie chart Diagram for comparing both proportions and totals for all types of data variables.

compiled data Data that have been processed, such as through some form of selection or summarising.

complete observer Observational role in which the researcher does not reveal the purpose of the research activity to those being observed. However, unlike the complete participant role, the researcher does not take part in the activities of the group being studied.

complete participant Observational role in which the researcher attempts to become a member of the group in which research is being conducted. The true purpose of the research is not revealed to the group members.

computer-aided personal interviewing (CAPI) Type of interviewing in which the interviewer reads questions from a computer screen and enters the respondent's answers directly into the computer.

computer-aided telephone interviewing (CATI) Type of telephone interviewing in which the interviewer reads questions from a computer screen and enters the respondent's answers directly into the computer.

computer-assisted qualitative data analysis software (CAQDAS) Analytical software that may be used in one or more of the following processes when analysing qualitative data: project management, coding and retrieval, data management, and hypothesis building and theorising.

conclusion The section of the project report in which judgements are made rather than just facts reported. New material is not normally introduced in the conclusion.

consent *See* informed consent.

content validity *See* face validity.

contingency table Technique for summarising data from two or more variables so that specific values can be read.

continuing access Gaining agreed research access to an organisation on an incremental basis.

continuous data Data whose values can theoretically take any value (sometimes within a restricted range) provided they can be measured with sufficient accuracy.

controlled index language The terms and phrases used by databases to index items within the database. If search terms do not match the controlled index language, the search is likely to be unsuccessful.

controls to allow the testing of hypotheses Ways of being sure that the outcome being measured (the dependent variable) is caused by the predicted phenomena alone (the independent variable) rather than extraneous unpredicted variables.

convenience sampling Non-probability sampling procedure in which cases are selected haphazardly on the basis that they are easiest to obtain.

correlation The extent to which two variables are related to each other. *See also* correlation coefficient, negative correlation, positive correlation.

correlation coefficient Number between +1 and −1 representing the strength of the relationship between two ranked or quantifiable variables. A value of +1 represents a perfect positive correlation. A value of −1 represents a perfect negative correlation. Correlation coefficients between +1 and −1 represent weaker positive and negative correlations, a value of 0 meaning the variables are perfectly independent. *See also* negative correlation, Pearson's product moment correlation coefficient, positive correlation, Spearman's rank correlation coefficient.

coverage The extent to which a data set covers the population it is intended to cover.

covering letter Letter accompanying a questionnaire, which explains the purpose of the survey. *See also* introductory letter.

covert research Research undertaken where those being researched are not aware of this fact.

creative thinking technique One of a number of techniques for generating and refining research ideas based on non-rational criteria. These may be, for example, biased heavily in favour of the individual's preferences or the spontaneous ideas of the individual or others. *See also* brainstorming, Delphi technique, relevance tree.

critical literature review Detailed and justified analysis and commentary of the merits and faults of the literature within a chosen area, which demonstrates familiarity with what is already known about your research topic.

cross-sectional research The study of a particular phenomenon (or phenomena) at a particular time, i.e. a 'snapshot'.

cross-tabulation *See* contingency table.

data Facts, opinions and statistics that have been collected together and recorded for reference or for analysis.

data display and analysis A process for the collection and analysis of qualitative data that involves three concurrent subprocesses of data reduction, data display, and drawing and verifying conclusions.

data matrix The table format in which data are usually entered into analysis software consisting of rows (cases) and columns (variables).

data requirements table A table designed to ensure that, when completed, the data collected will enable the research question(s) to be answered and the objectives achieved.

debriefing Providing research participants with a retrospective explanation about a research project and its purpose where covert observation has occurred.

deception Deceiving participants about the nature, purpose or use of research by the researcher(s). *See also* informed consent, research ethics.

deductive approach Research approach involving the testing of a theoretical proposition by the employment of a research strategy specifically designed for the purpose of its testing.

deliberate distortion Form of bias that occurs when data are recorded inaccurately on purpose. It is most common for secondary data sources such as organisational records.

delivery and collection questionnaire Data collection technique in which the questionnaire is delivered to each respondent. She or he then reads and answers the same set of questions in a predetermined order without an interviewer being present before the completed questionnaire is collected.

Delphi technique Technique using a group of people who are either involved or interested in the research topic to generate and select a more specific research idea.

dependent variable Variable that changes in response to changes in other variables.

descriptive data Data whose values cannot be measured numerically but can be distinguished by classifying into sets (categories).

descriptive observation Observation where the researcher concentrates on observing the physical setting, the key participants and their activities, particular events and their sequence and the attendant processes and emotions involved.

descriptive research Research for which the purpose is to produce an accurate representation of persons, events or situations.

descriptive statistics Generic term for statistics that can be used to describe variables.

discrete data Data whose values are measured in discrete units and therefore can take only one of a finite number of values from a scale that measures changes in this way.

discussion The section of the project report in which the wider implications of the findings (and conclusions) are considered.

dispersion measures Generic term for statistics that can be used to provide an impression of how the values for a variable are dispersed around the central tendency.

dissertation The usual name for research projects undertaken as part of undergraduate and taught masters degrees. Dissertations are usually written for an academic audience.

documentary secondary data Written documents such as notices, minutes of meetings, diaries, administrative and public records and reports to shareholders as well as non-written documents such as tape and video recordings, pictures, films and television programmes.

ecological validity A kind of external validity referring to the extent to which findings can be generalised from one group to another. *See also* external validity.

ethics *See* research ethics, research ethics committees, code of ethics.

ethnography Research strategy that focuses upon describing and interpreting the social world through first-hand field study.

evaluation The process of judging materials or methods in terms of internal accuracy and consistency or by comparison with external criteria.

experiential data Data about the researcher's perceptions and feelings as the process the research develops.

experiential meaning The equivalence of meaning of a word or sentence for different people in their everyday experiences.

experiment Research strategy that involves the definition of a theoretical hypothesis; the selection of samples of individuals from known populations; the allocation of samples to different experimental conditions; the introduction of planned change on one or more of the variables; and measurement on a small number of variables and control of other variables.

expert system Computer-based system that contains much of the knowledge used by experts in a specific field and is designed to assist non-experts in problem solving.

explanation building Deductive process for analysing qualitative data that involves the iterative examination of a number of strategically selected cases to test a theoretical proposition.

explanatory study Research that focuses on studying a situation or a problem in order to explain the relationships between variables.

exploratory data analysis (EDA) Approach to data analysis that emphasises the use of diagrams to explore and understand the data.

exploratory study Research that aims to seek new insights into phenomena, to ask questions, and to assess the phenomena in a new light.

external researcher Researcher who wishes to gain access to an organisation for which she or he does not work. *See also* access, internal researcher.

external validity The extent to which the research results from a particular study are generalisable to all relevant contexts.

face validity Agreement that a question, scale, or measure appears logically to reflect accurately what it was intended to measure.

filter question Closed question that identifies those respondents for whom the following question or questions are not applicable, enabling them to skip these questions.

focus group Group interview, composed of a small number of participants, facilitated by a 'moderator', in which discussion is focused on aspects of a given theme or topic.

follow-up Contact made with respondents to thank them for completing and returning a survey and to remind non-respondents to complete and return their surveys.

forced-choice question *See* closed question.

free text searching Feature that allows searching of an entire database rather than just those terms included in the controlled index language.

frequency distribution Table for summarising data from one variable so that specific values can be read.

fundamental research *See* basic research.

Gantt chart Chart that provides a simple visual representation of the tasks or activities that make up a project, each being plotted against a time line.

gatekeeper The person, often in an organisation, who controls research access.

general focus research question Question that flows from the research idea and may lead to several more detailed questions or the definition of research objectives.

generalisability The applicability of the results of a research study to other settings.

generalisation The making of more widely applicable propositions based upon the process of deduction from specific cases.

grammatical error Error of grammar that detracts from the authority of the project report.

grey literature *See* primary literature.

grid question Series of two or more closed questions in which each respondent's answers are recorded using the same matrix.

grounded theory Research strategy in which theory is developed from data generated by a series of observations or interviews principally involving an inductive approach. *See also* deductive approach, inductive approach.

group interview Interview facilitated by a 'moderator', in which a small number of participants engage in a fairly free-flowing discussion, where the identification of jointly constructed meanings, explanations and/or themes for subsequent research may be important.

habituation Situation where, in observation studies, the subjects being observed become familiar with the process of observation so that they take it for granted. This is an attempt to overcome 'observer effect' or reactivity.

histogram Diagram for showing frequency distributions for a grouped continuous data variable in which the area of each bar represents the frequency of occurrence.

hypothesis Testable proposition about the relationship between two or more events or concepts.

idiomatic meaning The meaning ascribed to a group of words that are natural to a native speaker, but which is not deducible from the individual words.

independent groups *t*-test Statistical test to determine the probability (likelihood) that the values of a quantifiable data variable for two independent samples or groups are different. The test assesses the likelihood of any difference between these two groups occurring by chance alone.

independent variable Variable that causes changes to a dependent variable or variables.

in-depth interview *See* unstructured interview.

index number Summary data value calculated from a base period for quantifiable variables, to facilitate comparisons of trends or changes over time. *See also* base period.

inductive approach Research approach involving the development of a theory as a result of the observation of empirical data.

ineligible respondent Respondent selected for a sample who does not meet the requirements of the research.

informant interview Interview guided by the perceptions of the interviewee.

informant verification Form of triangulation in which the researcher presents written accounts of, for example, interview notes to informants for them to verify the content. *See also* triangulation.

informed consent Position achieved when intended participants are fully informed about the nature, purpose and use of research to be undertaken and their role within it, and where their consent to participate, if provided, is freely given. *See also* deception.

integer A whole number.

intelligence gathering The gathering of facts or descriptive research.

inter-library loan System for borrowing a book or obtaining a copy of a journal article from another library.

internal researcher Person who conducts research within an organisation for which they work. *See also* cognitive access, external researcher.

interpretivism Research philosophy that requires the researcher to seek to understand the subjective reality and meanings of participants.

inter-quartile range The difference between the upper and lower quartiles, representing the middle 50% of the data when the data values for a variable have been ranked.

interviewee bias Attempt by an interviewee to construct an account that hides some data or when she or he presents herself or himself in a socially desirable role or situation.

interviewer bias Attempt by an interviewer to introduce bias during the conduct of an interview, or where the appearance or behaviour of the interviewer has the effect of introducing bias in the interviewee's responses.

interviewer-administered questionnaire Data collection technique in which an interviewer reads the same set of questions to the respondent in a predetermined order and records his or her responses. *See also* structured interview, telephone questionnaire.

introduction The opening to the project report, which gives the reader a clear idea of the central issue of concern of the research, states the research question(s) and research objectives, and explains the research context and the structure of the project report.

introductory letter Request for research access, addressed to an intended participant or organisational broker/gatekeeper, stating the purpose of the research, the nature of the help being sought, and the requirements of agreeing to participate. *See also* covering letter, gatekeeper.

intrusive research methods Methods that involve direct access to participants, including qualitative interviewing, observation, longitudinal research based on these methods and phenomenologically based approaches to research. *See also* access, cognitive access.

investigative question One of a number of questions that need to be answered in order to address satisfactorily each research question and meet each objective.

journal *See* professional journal, refereed academic journal.

judgemental sampling *See* non-probability sampling.

key word Basic term that describes the research question(s) and objectives, which can be used in combination to search the tertiary literature.

Kolmogorov–Smirnov test Statistical test to determine the probability (likelihood) that an observed set of values for each category of a variable differs from a specified distribution. A common use is to discover whether a sample differs significantly from the population from which it was selected.

lexical meaning The precise meaning of an individual word.

Likert-style rating scale Scale that allows the respondent to indicate how strongly she or he agrees or disagrees with a statement.

line graph Diagram for showing trends in longitudinal data for a variable.

list question Closed question, in which the respondent is offered a list of items and instructed to select those that are appropriate.

literature review *See* critical literature review.

long-term trend The overall direction of movement of quantifiable data values for a single variable after variations have been smoothed out. *See also* moving average.

longitudinal study The study of a particular phenomenon (or phenomena) over an extended period of time.

lower quartile The value below which a quarter of the data values lie when the data values for a variable have been ranked.

management report Abbreviated version of the project report, usually written for a practitioner audience. Normally includes a brief account of objectives, method, findings, conclusions and recommendations.

mean The average value calculated by adding up the values of each case for a variable and dividing by the total number of cases.

measurement validity The extent to which a scale or measuring instrument measures what it is intended to measure.

median The middle value when all the values of a variable are arranged in rank order; sometimes known as the 50th percentile.

method The tools and techniques used to obtain and analyse research data, including for example questionnaires, observation, interviews, and statistical and non-statistical techniques.

methodology The theory of how research should be undertaken, including the theoretical and philosophical assumptions upon which research is based and the implications of these for the method or methods adopted.

minimal interaction Process in which the observer tries as much as possible to 'melt into the background', having as little interaction as possible with the subjects of the observation. This is an attempt to overcome observer effect. *See also* observer effect.

mode The value of a variable that occurs most frequently.

Mode I knowledge creation Research of a fundamental rather than applied nature, in which the questions are set and solved by academic interests with little, if any, focus on exploitation of research by practitioners.

Mode II knowledge creation Research of an applied nature, governed by the world of practice and highlighting the importance of collaboration both with and between practitioners.

moderator Facilitator of group interviews. *See also* focus group, group interview.

moving average Statistical method of smoothing out variations in quantifiable data recorded for a single variable over time to enable the long-term trend to be seen more clearly. *See also* long-term trend.

multi-methods The combination of a number of data collection methods in one piece of research.

multiple bar chart Diagram for comparing frequency distributions for categorical or grouped discrete or continuous data variables, which highlights the highest and lowest values.

multiple dichotomy method Method of data coding using a separate variable for each possible response to an open question or an item in a list question. *See also* list question, open question.

multiple line graph Diagram for comparing trends over time between quantifiable data variables.

multiple regression analysis The process of calculating a regression coefficient and regression equation using two or more independent variables and one dependent variable. For data collected from a sample, there is also a need to calculate the probability of the regression coefficient having occurred by chance alone. *See also* regression analysis, regression coefficient, regression equation.

multiple response method Method of data coding using the same number of variables as the maximum number of different responses to an open question or a list question by any one case. *See also* list question, open question.

multiple source secondary data Secondary data created by combining two or more different data sets prior to the data being accessed for the research. These data sets can be based entirely on documentary or on survey data, or can be an amalgam of the two.

multi-stage sampling Probability sampling procedure that is a development of cluster sampling. It involves taking a series of cluster samples, each of which uses random sampling (systematic or simple).

narrative account The researcher's detailed account of the research process, written in much the same style as that used by an investigative journalist.

narrative analysis The collection and analysis of qualitative data that preserves the integrity and narrative value of data collected, thereby avoiding their fragmentation.

negative correlation Relationship between two variables for which, as the values of one variable increase, the values of the other variable decrease. *See also* correlation coefficient.

negative skew Distribution of quantifiable data for a variable in which the majority of the data are found bunched to the right, with a long tail to the left.

netiquette General operating guidelines for using the Internet, including not sending junk emails.

nominal data *See* descriptive data.

non-probability sampling Selection of sampling techniques in which the chance or probability of each case being selected is not known.

non-random sampling *See* non-probability sampling.

non-standardised interview *See* semi-structured interview, unstructured interview.

normal distribution Special form of the symmetric distribution in which the quantifiable data for a variable can be plotted as a bell-shaped curve.

notebook of ideas Technique for noting down any interesting research ideas as you think of them.

numeric rating scale Rating scale that uses numbers as response options to identify and record the respondent's response. The end response options, and sometimes the middle, are labelled.

objectivity Avoidance of (conscious) bias and subjective selection during the conduct and reporting of research. In some research philosophies the researcher will recognise that interpretation is likely to be related to a set of values and therefore will attempt to recognise and explore this.

observation The systematic observation, recording, description, analysis and interpretation of people's behaviour.

observer as participant Observational role in which the researcher observes activities without taking part in those activities in the same way as the 'real' research subjects. The researcher's identity as a researcher and research purpose is clear to all concerned. *See also* participant as observer.

observer bias This may occur when observers give inaccurate responses in order to distort the results of the research.

observer effect The impact of being observed on how people act. *See also* habituation, reactivity.

observer error Systematic errors made by observers, as a result of tiredness, for example.

one-way analysis of variance *See* analysis of variance.

on-line questionnaire Data collection technique in which the questionnaire is delivered via the Internet or an intranet to each respondent. She or he then reads and answers the same set of questions in a predetermined order without an interviewer being present before returning it electronically.

open question Question allowing respondents to give answers in their own way.

operationalisation The translation of concepts into tangible indicators of their existence.

opinion variable Variable that records what respondents feel about something or what they think or believe is true or false.

optical mark reader Data input device that recognises and converts marks on a data collection form such as a questionnaire into data that can be stored on a computer.

ordinal data *See* ranked data.

paired *t*-test Statistical test to determine the probability (likelihood) that the values of two (a pair of) quantifiable data variables collected for same cases are different. The test assesses the likelihood of any difference between two variables (each half of the pair) occurring by chance alone.

participant as observer Observational role in which the researcher takes part in and observes activities in the same way as the 'real' research subjects. The researcher's identity as a researcher and research purpose is clear to all concerned. *See also* observer as participant.

participant observation Observation in which the researcher attempts to participate fully in the lives and activities of the research subjects and thus becomes a member of the subjects' group(s), organisation(s) or community. *See also* complete observer, complete participant, observer as participant, participant as observer.

participant researcher See internal researcher.

passive voice The voice in which the subject of the sentence undergoes the action of the verb: for example, 'interviews were conducted'.

pattern matching Analysis of qualitative data involving the prediction of a pattern of outcomes based on theoretical propositions to seek to explain a set of findings.

Pearson's product moment correlation coefficient Statistical test that assesses the strength of the relationship between two quantifiable data variables. For data collected from a sample there is also a need to calculate the probability of the correlation coefficient having occurred by chance alone.

percentage component bar chart Diagram for comparing proportions for all types of data variables.

personal data Category of data, defined in law, relating to identified or identifiable persons.

personal entry Situation where the researcher needs to conduct research within an organisation, rather than rely on the use and completion of self-administered, postal questionnaires or the use of publicly available secondary data. *See* access.

personal pronoun One of the pronouns used to refer to people: I, me, you, he, she, we, us, they, him, her, them.

phenomenology Research philosophy that sees social phenomena as socially constructured, and is particularly concerned with generating meanings and gaining insights into those phenomena.

physical access The initial level of gaining access to an organisation to conduct research. *See also* cognitive access, continuing access, gatekeeper.

pie chart Diagram frequently used for showing proportions for a categorical data or a grouped continuous or discrete data variable.

pilot test Small-scale study to test a questionnaire or interview checklist, to minimise the likelihood of respondents having problems in answering the questions and of data recording problems as well as to allow some assessment of the questions' validity and the reliability of the data that will be collected.

population The complete set of cases or group members.

positive correlation Relationship between two variables for which, as the value of one variable increases, the values of the other variable also increase. *See also* correlation coefficient.

positive skew Distribution of quantifiable data for a variable in which the majority of the data are found bunched to the left, with a long tail to the right.

positivism Research philosophy that involves working with an observable social reality. The emphasis is on highly structured methodology to facilitate replication, and the end product can be law-like generalisations similar to those produced by the physical and natural scientists.

postal questionnaire Data collection technique in which the questionnaire is delivered by post to each respondent. She or he then reads and answers the same set of questions in a predetermined order without an interviewer being present before returning it by post.

PowerPoint Microsoft computer package that allows the presenter to design overhead slides using text, pictures, photographs etc., which lend a professional appearance.

practitioner–researcher Role occupied by a researcher when she or he is conducting research in an organisation, often her or his own, while fulfilling her or his normal working role.

pragmatism Research philosophy that employs the thinking of both the positivist and the phenomenologist. It applies a practical approach, integrating different perspectives to help collect and interpret data. *See also* phenomenology, positivism.

pre-coding The process of incorporating coding schemes in questions prior to a questionnaire's administration.

preliminary search This way of searching the literature may be a useful way of generating research ideas. It may be based, for example, on lecture notes or course textbooks.

preliminary study The process by which a research idea is refined in order to turn it into a research project. This may be simply a review of the relevant literature.

pre-set codes Codes established prior to data collection and often included as part of the data collection form.

pre-survey contact Contact made with a respondent to advise them of a forthcoming survey in which she or he will be asked to take part.

primary data Data collected specifically for the research project being undertaken.

primary literature The first occurrence of a piece of work, including published sources such as government white papers and planning documents and unpublished manuscript sources such as letters, memos and committee minutes.

primary observation Observation where the researcher notes what happened or what was said at the time. This is often done by keeping a research diary.

privacy Primary ethical concern relating to the rights of individuals not to participate in research and to their treatment where they agree to participate. *See also* research ethics, informed consent.

probability sampling Selection of sampling techniques in which the chance, or probability, of each case being selected from the population is known and is not zero.

probing questions Questions used to further explore responses that are of significance to the research topic.

professional journal Journals produced by a professional organisation for its members, often containing articles of a practical nature related to professional needs. Articles in professional journals are usually not refereed.

project report The term used in this book to refer generally to dissertations, theses and management reports. *See also* dissertation, management report, thesis.

pure research *See* basic research.

purposive sampling Non-probability sampling procedure in which the judgement of the researcher is used to select the cases that make up the sample. This can be done on the basis of extreme cases, heterogeneity (maximum variation), homogeneity (maximum similarity), critical cases, or typical cases.

qualitative data Non-numerical data or data that have not been quantified.

qualitative interview Collective term for semi-structured and unstructured interviews aimed at generating qualitative data.

quantifiable data Data whose values can be measured numerically as quantities.

quantitative data Numerical data or data that have been quantified.

quantity question Closed question in which the respondent's answer is recorded as a number giving the amount.

questionnaire General term including all data collection techniques in which each person is asked to respond to the same set of questions in a predetermined order. *See also* delivery and collection questionnaire, interviewer-administered questionnaire, on-line questionnaire, postal questionnaire, self-administered questionnaire.

quota sampling Non-probability sampling procedure that ensures that the sample represents certain characteristics of the population chosen by the researcher.

random sampling *See* simple random sampling.

range The difference between the highest and the lowest values for a variable.

ranked data Data whose values cannot be measured numerically but which can be placed in a definite order (rank).

ranking question Closed question in which the respondent is offered a list of items and instructed to place them in rank order.

rating question Closed question in which a scaling device is used to record the respondent's response. *See also* Likert-type rating scale, numeric rating scale, semantic differential rating scale.

rational thinking technique One of a number of techniques for generating and refining research ideas based on a systematic approach such as searching the literature or examining past projects.

raw data Data for which little, if any, data processing has taken place.

reactivity Reaction by research participants to any research intervention that affects data reliability. *See also* habituation, observer effect.

realism Research philosophy that believes in, and seeks to understand, the existence of an external and objective reality that influences people's social interpretations and behaviours but which may not be perceptible to them. It recognises that people themselves are not objects to be studied in the style of natural science.

re-coding The process of grouping or combining a variable's codes to form a new variable, usually with less detailed categories.

reductionism The idea that problems as a whole are better understood if they are reduced to the simplest possible elements.

refereed academic journal Journal in which the articles have been evaluated by academic peers prior to publication to assess their quality and suitability. Not all academic journals are refereed.

references, list of Bibliographic details of all items referred to directly in the text. The university will specify the format required.

regression analysis The process of calculating a regression coefficient and regression equation using one independent variable and one dependent variable. For data collected from a sample, there is also a need to calculate the probability of the regression coefficient having occurred by chance alone. *See also* multiple regression analysis, regression coefficient, regression equation.

regression coefficient Number between 0 and +1 that enables the strength of the relationship between a quantifiable dependent variable and one or more quantifiable independent variables to be assessed. The coefficient represents the proportion of the variation in the dependent variable that can be explained statistically by the independent variable or variables. A value of 1 means that all the variation in the dependent variable can be explained statistically by the independent variable(s). A value of 0 means that none of the variation in the dependent variable can be explained by the independent variable(s). *See also* multiple regression analysis, regression analysis.

regression equation Equation used to predict the values of a dependent variable given the values of one or more independent variables. The associated regression coefficient provides an indication of how good a predictor the regression equation is likely to be. *See* regression coefficient.

relevance tree Technique for generating research topics that starts with a broad concept from which further (usually more specific) topics are generated. Each of these topics forms a separate branch, from which further sub-branches that are more detailed can be generated.

reliability The degree to which data collection method or methods will yield consistent findings, similar observations would be made or conclusions reached by other researchers or there is transparency in how sense was made from the raw data.

representative sample Sample that represents exactly the population from which it is drawn.

representative sampling *See* probability sampling.

research The systematic collection and interpretation of information with a clear purpose, to find things out. *See also* applied research, basic research.

research ethics The appropriateness of the researcher's behaviour in relation to the rights of those who become the subject of a research project, or who are affected by it. *See also* code of ethics, privacy, research ethics committee.

research ethics committee Learned committee established to produce a code of research ethics, examine and approve or veto research proposals and advise in relation to the ethical dilemmas facing researchers during the conduct and reporting of research projects. *See also* code of ethics.

research idea Initial idea that may be worked up into a research project.

research objectives Clear, specific statements that identify what the researcher wishes to accomplish as a result of doing the research.

research question One of a number of key questions that the research process will address. These are often the precursor of research objectives.

research strategy General plan of how the researcher will go about answering the research question(s).

respondent interview Interview directed by the questions posed by the interviewer, to which the interviewee responds.

respondent The person who answers the questions usually either in an interview or on a questionnaire.

response bias *See* interviewee bias.

response rate *See* active response rate.

review article Article, normally published in a refereed academic journal, that contains both a considered review of the state of knowledge in a given topic area and pointers towards areas where further research needs to be undertaken. *See also* refereed academic journal.

sample Subgroup or part of a larger population.

sampling fraction The proportion of the total population selected for a probability sample.

sampling frame The complete list of all the cases in the population, from which a probability sample is drawn.

scale question See rating question.

scale Measure of a concept, such as customer loyalty or organisational commitment, created by combining scores to a number of rating questions.

scatter graph Diagram for showing the relationship between two quantifiable or ranked data variables.

scientific research Research that involves the systematic observation of and experiment with phenomena.

search engine Automated software that searches an index of documents on the Internet using key words and Boolean logic.

secondary data Data used for a research project that were originally collected for some other purpose. *See also* documentary secondary data, multiple source secondary data, survey-based secondary data.

secondary literature Subsequent publication of primary literature such as books and journals.

secondary observation Statement made by an observer of what happened or was said. By necessity this involves that observer's interpretations.

self-administered questionnaire Data collection technique in which each respondent reads and answers the same set of questions in a predetermined order without an interviewer being present.

self-selection sampling Non-probability sampling procedure in which the case, usually an individual, is allowed to identify their desire to be part of the sample.

semantic differential rating scale Rating scale that allows the respondent to indicate his or her attitude to a concept defined by two opposite adjectives or phrases.

semi-structured interview Wide-ranging category of interview in which the interviewer commences with a set of interview themes but is prepared to vary the order in which questions are asked and to ask new questions in the context of the research situation.

sensitive personal data Category of data, defined in law, that refers to certain specified characteristics or beliefs relating to identified or identifiable persons.

shadowing Process that the researcher would follow in order to gain a better understanding of the research context. This might involve following employees who are likely to be important in the research.

simple random sampling Probability sampling procedure that ensures that each case in the population has an equal chance of being included in the sample.

snowball sampling Non-probability sampling procedure in which subsequent respondents are obtained from information provided by initial respondents.

social constructionism Research philosophy that views the social world as being socially constructed.

social norm The type of behaviour that a person ought to adopt in a particular situation.

socially desirable response Answer given by a respondent due to her or his desire, either conscious or unconscious, to gain prestige or appear in a different social role.

source questionnaire The questionnaire that is to be translated from when translating a questionnaire.

Spearman's rank correlation coefficient Statistical test that assesses the strength of the relationship between two ranked data variables. For data collected from a sample, there is also a need to calculate the probability of the correlation coefficient having occurred by chance alone.

split infinitive Phrase consisting of an infinitive with an adverb inserted between 'to' and the verb: for example, 'to readily agree'.

stacked bar chart Diagram for comparing totals and subtotals for all types of data variable.

standard deviation Statistic that describes the extent of spread of data values around the mean for a variable containing quantifiable data.

statistical significance The likelihood of the pattern that is observed (or one more extreme) occurring by chance alone, if there really was no difference in the population from that which the sample was drawn.

storyline The way in which the reader is led through the research project to the main conclusion or the answer to the research question. The storyline is, in effect, a clear theme that runs through the whole of the project report to convey a coherent and consistent message.

stratified random sampling Probability sampling procedure in which the population is divided into two or more relevant strata and a random sample (systematic or simple) is drawn from each of the strata.

structured interview Data collection technique in which an interviewer physically meets the respondent, reads them the same set of questions in a predetermined order, and records his or her response to each.

structured methodology Data collection methods that are easily replicated (such as the use of an observation schedule or questionnaire) to ensure high reliability.

subject directory Hierarchically organised index categorised into broad topics, which, as it has been compiled by people, is likely to have its content partly censored and evaluated.

subject or participant bias Bias that may occur when research subjects are giving inaccurate responses in order to distort the results of the research.

subject or participant error Errors that may occur when research subjects are studied in situations that are inconsistent with their normal behaviour patterns, leading to atypical responses.

survey Research strategy that involves the structured collection of data from a sizeable population. Although the term 'survey' is often used to describe the collection of data using questionnaires, it includes other techniques such as structured observation and structured interviews.

survey-based secondary data Data collected by surveys, such as by questionnaire, which have already been analysed for their original purpose.

symbolic interactionism Social process through which the individual derives a sense of identity from interaction and communication with others. Through this process of interaction and communication the individual responds to others and adjusts his or her understandings and behaviour as a shared sense of order and reality is 'negotiated' with others.

symmetric distribution Description of the distribution of data for a variable in which the data are distributed equally either side of the highest frequency.

symmetry of potential outcomes Situation in which the results of the research will be of similar value whatever they are.

synthesis Process of arranging and assembling various elements so as to make a new statement, or conclusion.

systematic sampling Probability sampling procedure in which the initial sampling point is selected at random, and then the cases are selected at regular intervals.

table Technique for summarising data from one or more variables so that specific values can be read. *See also* contingency table, frequency distribution.

tailored design method Approach to designing questionnaires specifying precisely how to construct and use them; previously referred to as the 'total design method'.

target questionnaire The translated questionnaire when translating from a source questionnaire.

telephone questionnaire Data collection technique in which an interviewer contacts the respondent and administers the questionnaire using a telephone. The interviewer reads the same set of questions to the respondent in a predetermined order and records his or her responses.

template analysis Analysis of qualitative data that involves creating and developing a hierarchical template of data codes or categories representing themes revealed in the data collected and the relationships between these.

tense The form taken by the verb to indicate the time of the action (i.e. past, present or future).

tertiary literature source Source designed to help locate primary and secondary literature, such as an index, abstract, encyclopaedia or bibliography.

theory Formulation regarding the cause and effect relationships between two or more variables, which may or may not have been tested.

theory dependent If we accept that every purposive decision we take is based on the assumption that certain consequences will flow from the decision, then these decisions are theory dependent.

thesis The usual name for research projects undertaken for Master of Philosophy (MPhil) and Doctor of Philosophy (PhD) degrees, written for an academic audience.

time error Error, usually associated with structured observations, where the time at which the observation is being conducted provides data that are untypical of the time period in which the event(s) being studied would normally occur.

time series Set of quantifiable data values recorded for a single variable over time usually at regular intervals. *See also* moving average.

triangulation The use of two or more independent sources of data or data collection methods within one study in order to help ensure that the data are telling you what you think they are telling you.

***t*-test** *See* independent groups *t*-test, paired *t*-test.

Type I error Error made by wrongly coming to the decision that something is true when in reality it is not.

Type II error Error made by wrongly coming to the decision that something is not true when in reality it is.

unreachable respondent Respondent selected for a sample who cannot be located or who cannot be contacted.

unstructured interview Loosely structured and informally conducted interview that may commence with one or more themes to explore with participants but without a predetermined list of questions to work through. *See also* informant interview.

upper quartile The value above which a quarter of the data values lie when the data values for a variable have been ranked.

validity (**1**) The extent to which data collection method or methods accurately measure what they were intended to measure. (**2**) The extent to which research findings are really about what they profess to be about.

variable Individual element or attribute upon which data have been collected.

visual aid Item such as an overhead projector slide, whiteboard, video recording or handout that is designed to enhance professional presentation and the learning of the audience.

weighting The process by which data values are adjusted to reflect differences in the proportion of the population that each case represents.

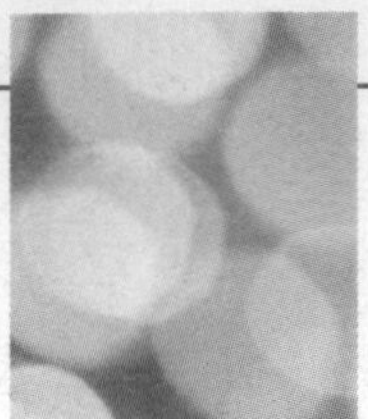

Index